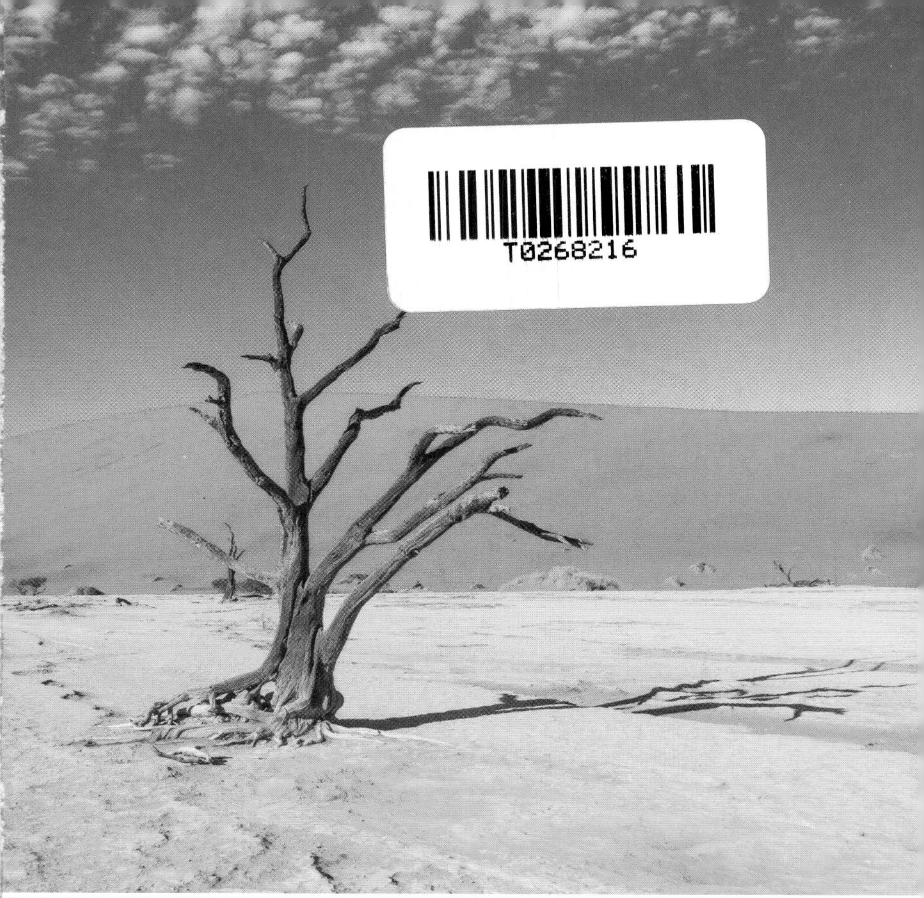

THE ROUGH GUIDE TO

NAMIBIA

WITH VICTORIA FALLS

Written and researched by
Sara Humphreys

With additional contributions by
Rob Humphreys

Contents

A LEOPARD ON WATCH

Introduction to **Namibia**

Namibia promises adventure, a vast land of mesmerising landscapes, abundant wildlife and an astonishing array of natural wonders. Its defining feature is the Namib, an ancient desert that runs 1,500km (932 miles) of the country's wind-lashed coastline. Encompassing towering dunes, dramatic mountains and lichen-encrusted gravel plains, it's populated by desert-adapted beasts, with flamingos and colonial German architecture bringing splashes of colour to the waterfront. Parts of the capital, Windhoek, have a distinctly European feel – a legacy of colonialism – but you probably won't want to linger too long; from here, tempting arterial roads reach out to geological wonders in the south and the beguiling Kalahari to the east, inhabited by some of Africa's oldest peoples. To the north lie wildlife-rich reserves and most of Namibia's elusive population, from where the country's lush panhandle lures you to within touching distance of Victoria Falls.

The Fish River Canyon in the far south, which affords breathtaking views across a deep serpentine chasm in the Earth's crust, is arguably Namibia's most impressive **natural wonder**. While in the northeast, the imposing sandstone Waterberg Plateau stands sentinel over the surrounding bushveld. At the very north of Namibia, the species-rich wetlands of the Zambezi Region, a 450km (279.6-mile) arm of luxuriant subtropical forest that stretches out above Botswana towards Zimbabwe and Victoria Falls, provide a wholly different landscape.

Traditionally, tourists have been drawn to Namibia for its wilderness terrains; however, the country is now also attracting attention for its **wildlife**, specifically, the increasing numbers of rare large mammals that thrive in the semi-arid areas. Beyond the game-heavy confines of Etosha – Namibia's premier national park – the world's largest concentrations of free-roaming cheetahs stalk the plains while desert-adapted

SOSSUSVLEI

elephants and black rhinos lumber along the valleys and riverbeds of northwest Namibia. In many cases, these beasts are protected by conservationists working hand in hand with local communities – communities that are also beginning to open up so visitors can learn more about these cultures and lifestyles.

The Namib also hosts many extraordinary succulent plants and dune-dwelling endemics – especially lizards – that have adapted to the harsh conditions and have featured in dozens of nature documentaries. In contrast, the lush, subtropical Zambezi Region holds almost three-quarters of the country's bird species and many large mammals not seen elsewhere.

As with most other African countries, Namibia's socio-political landscape has been indelibly shaped by **colonialism**, specifically the regimes of Germany and later South Africa, which resulted in the imposition of **apartheid** and the Namibian **War of Independence** that lasted over twenty years. While the adverse effects were considerable – and many still endure – it's true to say that Namibia's **cuisine** has benefited from its colonial past, from cream-laden German cakes, tasty filled *brötchen* and good coffee, to the dried, cured meats favoured by South Africans. Namibia was one of the last countries in Africa to gain **independence** – in 1990 – and it has taken time for the government to realise the country's tourism potential, just as foreign tourists have been slow to appreciate Namibia's haunting scenery, fascinating wildlife and rich cultural diversity. Now, Namibia is becoming established on the tourist

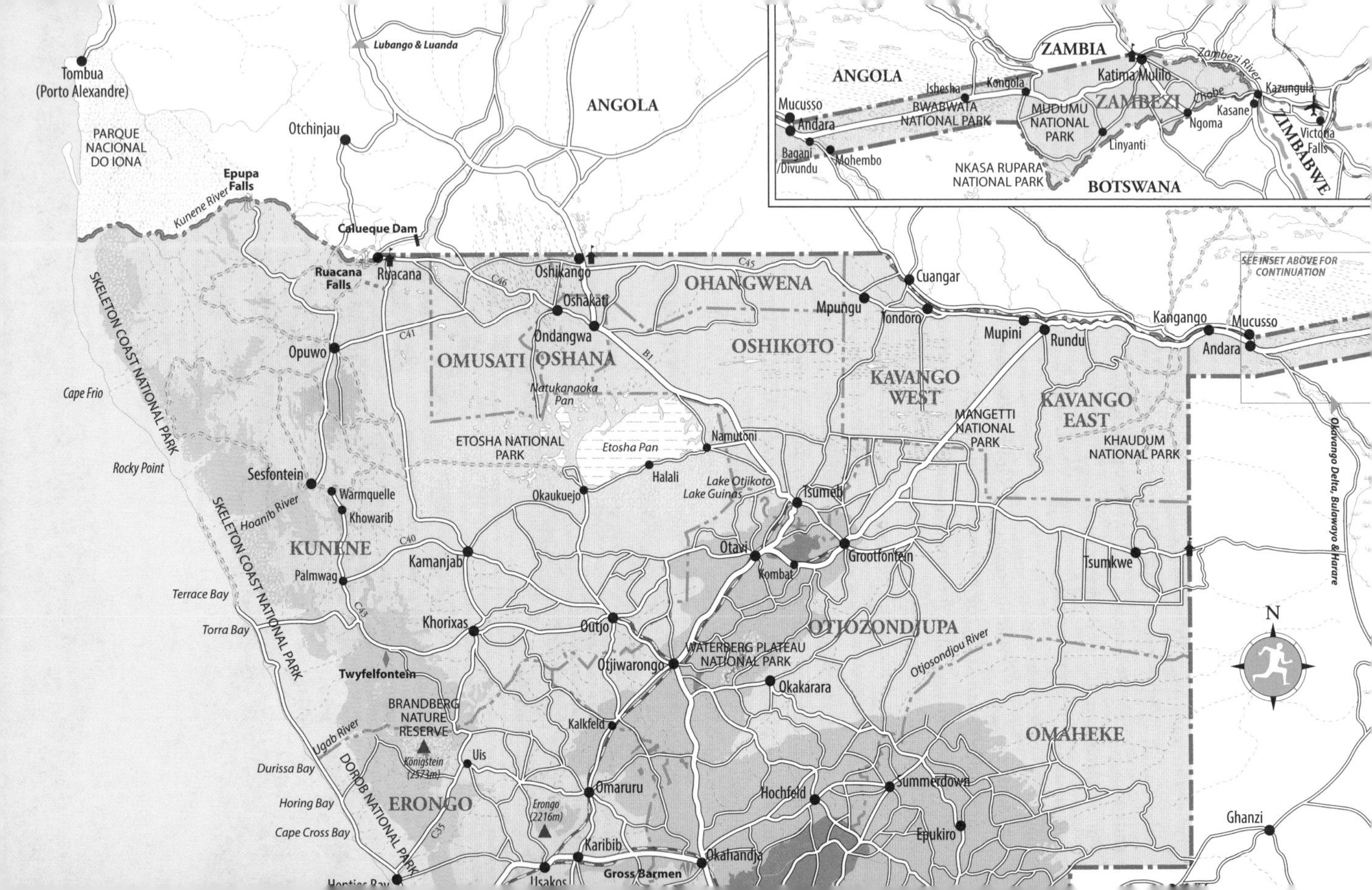

Tombua
(Porto Alexandre)
PARQUE NACIONAL DO IONA
Lubango & Luanda
ANGOLA
Otchinjau
Epupa Falls
Kunene River
Calueque Dam
Ruacana Falls
Ruacana
Oshikango
Oshakati
Ondangwa
C46
C45
C41
B1
OHANGWENA
OSHIKOTO
OMUSATI
OSHANA
Natukanaoka Pan
ETOSHA NATIONAL PARK
Etosha Pan
Namutoni
Halali
Okaukuejo
Lake Otjikoto
Lake Guinas
Cuangar
Mpungu
Tondoro
Mupini
Rundu
Kangango
Mucusso
Andara
KAVANGO WEST
KAVANGO EAST
MANGETTI NATIONAL PARK
KHAUDUM NATIONAL PARK
SEE INSET ABOVE FOR CONTINUATION
Okavango Delta, Bulawayo & Harare
Opuwo
Cape Frio
SKELETON COAST NATIONAL PARK
Rocky Point
Sesfontein
Warmquelle
Khowarib
Hoanib River
KUNENE
C40
Kamanjab
Palmwag
Terrace Bay
Torra Bay
C43
Khorixas
Twyfelfontein
BRANDBERG NATURE RESERVE
Königstein (2573m)
Uis
Ugab River
Durissa Bay
Horing Bay
Cape Cross Bay
DOROB NATIONAL PARK
ERONGO
C35
Erongo (2216m)
Omaruru
Karibib
Usakos
Gross Barmen
Okahandja
Kalkfeld
Otjiwarongo
Outjo
WATERBERG PLATEAU NATIONAL PARK
Okakarara
Otavi
Kombat
Tsumeb
Grootfontein
Tsumkwe
OTJOZONDJUPA
Otjosondjou River
OMAHEKE
Hochfeld
Summerdown
Epukiro
Ghanzi
N
ZAMBIA
ANGOLA
Mucusso
Andara
Bagani /Divundu
Mohembo
Ishesha
Kongola
BWABWATA NATIONAL PARK
MUDUMU NATIONAL PARK
NKASA RUPARA NATIONAL PARK
Katima Mulilo
ZAMBEZI
Linyanti
Chobe
Ngoma
Kasane
Kazungula
Zambezi River
Victoria Falls
ZIMBABWE
BOTSWANA

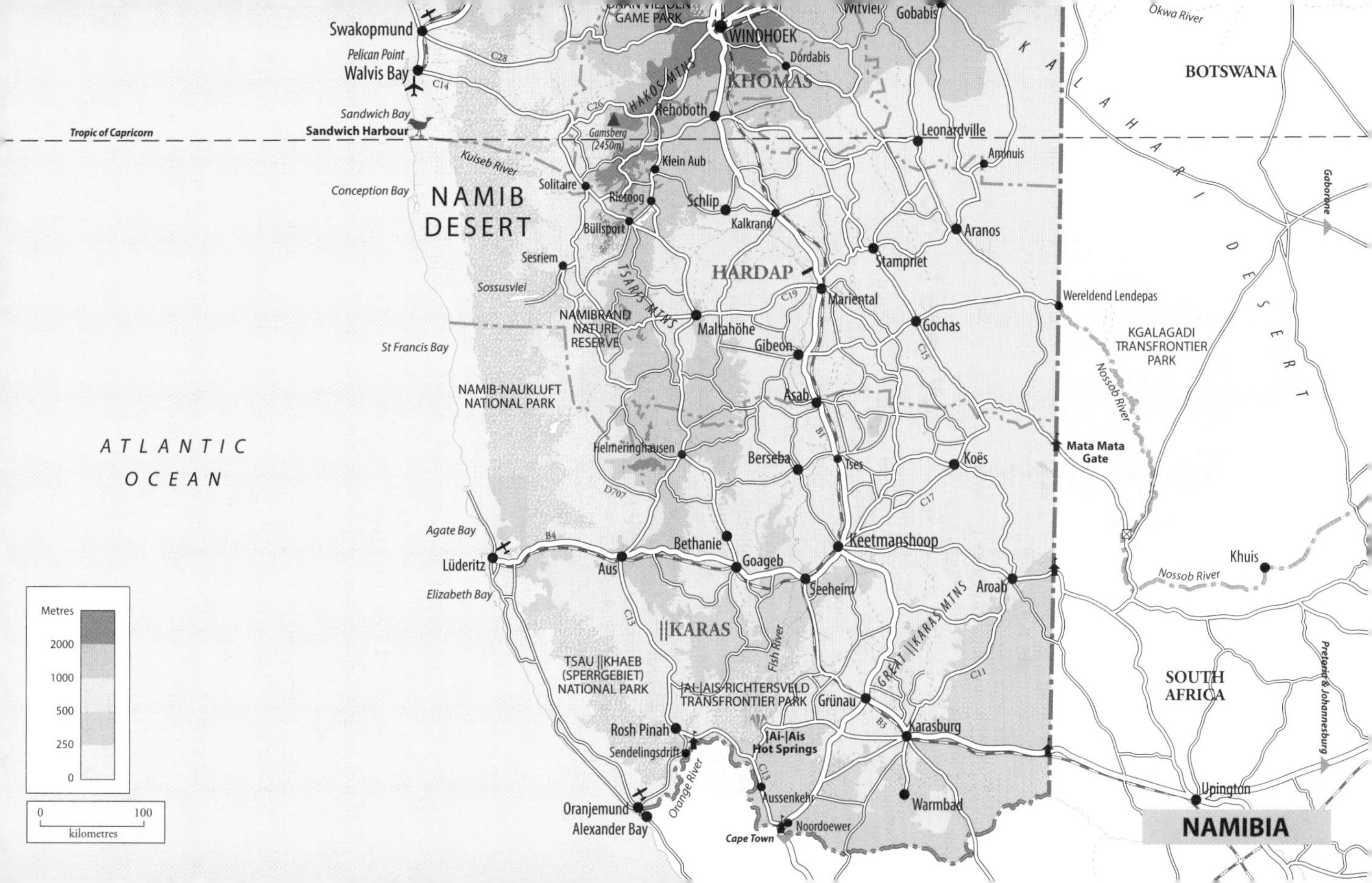
NAMIBIA
BOTSWANA
SOUTH AFRICA
ATLANTIC OCEAN
KALAHARI DESERT
NAMIB DESERT
Tropic of Capricorn
Swakopmund
Pelican Point
Walvis Bay
Sandwich Bay
Sandwich Harbour
Conception Bay
Kuiseb River
St Francis Bay
Agate Bay
Lüderitz
Elizabeth Bay
Oranjemund
Alexander Bay
Orange River
Cape Town
WINDHOEK
Witvlei
Gobabis
Dordabis
KHOMAS
HAKOS MTNS
Rehoboth
Gamsberg (2450m)
Klein Aub
Solitaire
Rietoog
Schlip
Kalkrand
Büllsport
Sesriem
Sossusvlei
TSARIS MTNS
HARDAP
Mariental
Maltahöhe
NAMIBRAND NATURE RESERVE
NAMIB-NAUKLUFT NATIONAL PARK
Gibeon
Asab
Helmeringhausen
Berseba
Tses
Leonardville
Aminuis
Aranos
Stampriet
Gochas
Koës
Wereldend Lendepas
KGALAGADI TRANSFRONTIER PARK
Nossob River
Mata Mata Gate
Khuis
Okwa River
Gaborone
Pretoria & Johannesburg
Upington
Keetmanshoop
Bethanie
Goageb
Aus
Seeheim
Aroab
GREAT ||KARAS MTNS
||KARAS
Fish River
TSAU ||KHAEB (SPERRGEBIET) NATIONAL PARK
|AI-|AIS/RICHTERSVELD TRANSFRONTIER PARK
Grünau
Karasburg
Warmbad
Rosh Pinah
Sendelingsdrift
|Ai-|Ais Hot Springs
Aussenkehr
Noordoewer
C28
C14
C26
C19
C15
C17
C13
C11
B1
B3
B4
D707
Metres
2000
1000
500
250
0
100
kilometres

FACT FILE

- Namibia is the second **least densely populated** country after Mongolia, with only three **inhabitants** per sq km.
- **Rugby union** has been played in Namibia since 1916, and the national team has qualified for the last seven Rugby World Cups.
- Because of low population density and low light pollution, the country's glittering **night sky** is one of the world's top **stargazing** destinations.
- Though **social inequalities** are slowly improving, the wealthiest 10 percent of the population – including the 6 percent white minority – receive over half the national income.
- The Kunene Region has the world's greatest concentration of free-roaming **black rhinos**.
- Over a tenth of the Namibian population – from the Nama, Damara and San peoples – speak a **click language**.
- **Etosha Pan** is Africa's largest **saline pan**, a vast white sheet visible from space.
- Namibia's all-time greatest athlete, **Frankie Fredericks**, held the indoor world 200m record for eighteen years before Usain Bolt broke it in 2014.

map: high-quality, affordable **lodges and campgrounds** are sprouting up, often in conjunction with local conservancies; rural communities are inviting visitors to learn about their cultures, traditions and modern-day challenges; and new ways of experiencing Namibia are constantly being devised, from skydiving or hot-air ballooning over the desert to tracking rhino or kayaking with crocs.

Where to go

International flights arrive at **Windhoek**, the country's capital and transport hub, conveniently located in the centre of Namibia. A small city, more like a provincial town, it's a pleasant spot to wander around for a couple of days, taking in the few modest sights, browsing the shops and sampling the local cuisine. From here, you need to plot your route carefully; although the tarred and gravel roads are maintained to high standards in Namibia, the distances are vast, so you can easily spend most of your time just getting to places. That said, much of Namibia's appeal lies in its immense, uninhabited landscapes, which are best appreciated by driving through them.

Most first-time visitors, and those short of time, travel a circuit around central and northern Namibia, but with a quick detour – by Namibian standards – southwest to the **Sossusvlei** area of the **Namib-Naukluft National Park**, where the towering apricot dunes that change colour with the light are truly spectacular. From here, many visitors head northwest to enjoy the milder climate and colonial architecture of the country's top coastal resort, **Swakopmund**, which lies almost due west of Windhoek. Though no beach hangout – it's too cold to swim most of the year – it's a fascinating place, surrounded by dunes that you can explore on foot, on horseback or even by bike; it's also rapidly emerging as a centre for **adventure sports**, such as skydiving and sand-boarding. A short excursion south takes you to **Walvis Bay**, the country's principal port, where you can consort with seals, dolphins and pelicans on the lagoon.

Moving north, organised tours and self-drive travellers often take in the **Cape Cross seal colony** before cutting inland via the desolate, mist-shrouded **Skeleton Coast**

National Park to **Damaraland**, where some of the country's most evocative scenery lies. At the southerly limit of this region, the domed **Erongo Mountains** and the pointed **Spitzkoppe** – composed of giant burnished granite slabs – provide fantastic hiking and birdwatching opportunities and some examples of San rock paintings. Far better-preserved images are to be found at the **Brandberg**, Namibia's largest massif, further north, while the continent's oldest rock engravings at **Twyfelfontein** give fascinating insights into the spiritual world of some of Africa's oldest inhabitants. The wonderful lodges in the area make the most of the picturesque scenery and offer the chance to spot desert-adapted elephants and rhinos (see box below).

THE GIANT DESERT SURVIVORS

Roaming the weathered mountains, gravel plains and broad, mopane-shaded sandy riverbeds of Namibia's arid Kunene Region, some of the planet's most hunted animals are fighting for survival. This inhospitable environment is home to the world's largest numbers of free-ranging, yet critically endangered, **black rhinos** – distinguishable from the white rhino on account of its hook-shaped upper lip – as well as swelling numbers of desert-adapted **elephants, lions and even giraffes**. While the elephants and rhinos roam inland, the lions more often prowl the dunes of the Skeleton Coast. All three majestic species share the ability to **go without water** for several days – or weeks, in the case of lions – provided they manage a gemsbok, ostrich, or even a seal kill.

They have also all been brought back from the brink of extinction through the combined efforts of dedicated professional conservationists, committed local communities, government support, and – more surprisingly – **tourism**. However, the war against poaching is far from being won. Volunteer programmes and sensitive rhino and elephant tracking, often on foot, are being promoted by various foundations, often in collaboration with private lodges and community conservancies. Community involvement, above all, is critical to conservation success since they are bearing the brunt of this increase in elephant and lion populations as they compete for scarce food and water resources.

For further **information,** contact the Save the Rhino Trust (SRT; Ⓦ savetherhinotrust.org), Elephant-Human Relations Aid (EHRA; Ⓦ ehranamibia.org), Desert Lion Conservation (Ⓦ desertlion.info) and the Giraffe Conservation Foundation (Ⓦ giraffeconservation.org). Wilderness Safaris (Ⓦ wilderness-safaris.com), a pioneer in this type of tourism conservation, offers some of the best tracking experiences in their Desert Rhino, Hoanib Skeleton Coast and Damaraland camps (See page 200) – the last one being almost wholly community-owned and managed.

AVERAGE MONTHLY TEMPERATURES AND RAINFALL

	Jan	Feb	March	April	May	June	July	Aug	Sept	Oct	Nov	Dec
WINDHOEK												
Max temp (°C)	30	28	27	26	23	20	20	23	29	29	30	30
Min temp (°C)	17	16	15	13	9	7	6	9	11	15	15	16
Rainfall (mm)	77	73	81	38	6	1	1	0	1	12	33	47
WALVIS BAY												
Max temp (°C)	23	23	23	24	23	23	21	20	19	19	22	22
Min temp (°C)	15	16	15	13	11	9	8	8	9	11	11	14
Rainfall (mm)	0	5	8	2	2	1	1	3	1	0	0	0
KEETMANSHOOP												
Max temp (°C)	35	34	32	28	24	21	21	24	27	30	33	35
Min temp (°C)	19	19	17	14	10	7	6	8	11	13	16	17
Rainfall (mm)	18	30	34	16	6	2	1	1	1	6	11	13
RUNDU												
Max temp (°C)	31	30	31	30	29	27	27	30	33	35	33	32
Min temp (°C)	19	18	18	15	10	6	6	9	14	17	19	19
Rainfall (mm)	128	147	96	37	2	0	1	1	1	15	67	83
VICTORIA FALLS												
Max temp (°C)	30	29	30	29	27	25	25	28	32	33	20	30
Min temp (°C)	18	18	17	14	10	6	6	8	13	17	18	18
Rainfall (mm)	168	126	70	24	3	1	0	0	2	27	64	174

It's a bit of a detour to the mountainous northwest, where the rocky, reddish-brown land and the frontier town of Opuwo are home to the semi-nomadic **Himba**; a further two-hour drive north takes you up to the scenic **Epupa Falls** on the Kunene River, which marks the border with Angola. Many miss out on this area and head straight to **Etosha National Park** – indisputably the top wildlife-watching spot – where they spend a few days before returning to Windhoek, sometimes via the scenic **Waterberg Plateau**. With more time, a journey northeast to the verdant **Zambezi Region** in the panhandle reaps many rewards: lush, broad-leaved forests, gliding rivers and plentiful wildlife roaming in unfenced reserves. The less-visited far south is also worth the trek for its remarkable geological fault, the **Fish River Canyon**, from where it's a few hours' drive to the isolated historical German town of **Lüderitz** on the coast and the famous diamond-mining ghost town of Kolmanskop. A trip to the sinuous **Orange River**, which marks the border with South Africa, provides a welcome respite from the relentless heat of the interior: an opportunity to paddle through beautiful scenery and indulge in some gentle birdwatching.

Visitors with more time should consider heading southeast to gaze at the rippling red dunes of the **Kalahari**, even popping over the South African border into the **Kgalagadi Transfrontier Park**, where vast herds of large mammals follow ancient migration

TWYFELFONTEIN, HUAB VALLEY

routes. Alternatively, around **Tsumkwe**, in the northern reaches of this semi-desert, an increasing number of San communities are opening up to visitors, keen to share their ancient traditions and survival skills.

When to go

A semi-arid country possessing a climate generally characterised by **low rainfall** and **low humidity**, Namibia is a year-round destination, though the searing summer temperatures (Oct–Feb), which can exceed 40°C in some areas, deter many European visitors from holidaying at this time.

The **peak tourist season** in Namibia is in winter – **June to September** – which coincides with the **dry season**: there is virtually no rain and no clouds, so you'll witness stunning night skies. It's also easier to spot **wildlife** during these months as vegetation is sparse and animals are forced to congregate at established waterholes. Days are sunny, but average maximum daytime temperatures are more tolerable – 20–30°C, depending where you are – though they plummet at night: at the height of winter (June–Aug), they can drop to between 5°C and 10°C, even dropping below 0°C in the desert and more mountainous areas. The downside of visiting in the Namibian summer is that lodge prices and visitor numbers are often higher. However, since the country is so vast, only Etosha, Swakopmund and Sossusvlei get crowded.

Although climate change is making weather patterns less predictable – and indeed, droughts have been a feature of recent years – the **rains** usually start in earnest in late November or early December, transforming the landscape into a pale green carpet – where sufficient rain falls – and tail off in March or April. Rainfall is highly localised and generally occurs in the late afternoon as intense thundery showers, so it is unlikely to spoil your trip. The countryside is more scenic at this time; animals are breeding, and the birdlife is at its best, with many migratory species present. On the other hand, wildlife spotting is much more difficult as the vegetation is denser. With food more readily available, animal movements are less predictable since they are not restricted to waterholes. After heavy rain, gravel roads can become impassable.

Generally, Namibia is hotter and drier in the **south** and wetter in the far **north** and across the Zambezi Region. Indeed, the far northeast and the Zambezi Region possess a **subtropical climate**, receiving, on average, close to 500mm (19.7in) of rain between December and February. In September and October, before the main rains arrive, the humidity and temperatures build, and it can be very uncomfortable. In contrast, much of the country receives very little precipitation, even in the rainy season. The nearer the coast you get, the less rainfall there is – under 15mm (0.6in) annually in some places – though a thick morning **fog** hangs in the air for much of the year on the coast itself, making it feel unpleasantly cold.

Author picks

Our author has driven, hiked and paddled the length and breadth of Namibia, across deserts, over mountains, down rivers and through the bush. These are some of her favourite travel experiences.

Close encounters with wildlife While Etosha deservedly ranks as one of Africa's finest national parks, the Kwando Core Area of the Bwabwata National Park in the Zambezi Region (see page 283), can offer more unexpected encounters with nature and more abundant birdlife – without the crowds.

Desert panoramas You don't need to scale great heights to be rewarded with mesmerising desert vistas that stretch to the horizon: clamber up a simple kopje, take on the Spitzkoppe (see page 191) or drive up the Spreetshoogte Pass (see page 115).

Kayaking down the Orange River Spend four days paddling through idyllic scenery, enjoy campfire dinners and sleep on the riverbank (see page 160).

Scale the Brandberg The slog to the top is not easy, but the rewards are enormous: phenomenal views and pristine ancient rock art that few people have seen in modern times (see page 193).

A braai in the bush The wilderness campsites of the northern Namib-Naukluft (see page 106) and Spitzkoppe (see page 191) provide perfect locations to enjoy some of the country's game meat – cooked to perfection over a campfire.

Meet the Ju|'hoansi San It's worth spending several days with a San community (see page 272), learning from the ancestors of one of the continent's most ancient peoples, and experiencing the stillness of the desert.

Sleep out under the stars Namibia's clear night skies sparkle and amaze in equal measure. Do it in style in one of the lodges around Sossusvlei (see page 112) or be adventurous and camp out on top of the Brandberg (see page 193).

Our author recommendations don't end here. We've flagged up our favourite places – a perfectly sited hotel, an atmospheric café, a special restaurant – throughout the Guide, highlighted with the ★ symbol.

JU|'HOANSI SAN

SOUTHERN MILKY WAY

20

things not to miss

It's impossible to see everything Namibia offers in one trip – and we don't suggest you try. What follows is a selective and subjective taste of the country's highlights, including cultural encounters, spectacular wildlife, unforgettable activities and extraordinary desert landscapes. Each highlight has a page reference to take you straight into the guide, where you can learn more.

1 SOSSUSVLEI

See page 112

The Namib Desert at its most spectacular: the vibrantly-coloured, giant dunes, alongside eerie mineral-encrusted vleis, are an awe-inspiring sight.

2 FISH RIVER CANYON

See page 153

Marvel at this breathtaking serpentine chasm – one of the world's largest canyons – as it carves its way through the desert.

3 WALVIS BAY LAGOON

See page 222

A chance to gaze across a pink carpet of flamingos and kayak among playful seal pups.

4 STARGAZING

See page 69

Namibia's unpolluted atmosphere makes for a genuinely glittering night sky and a chance to explore the Milky Way through a telescope.

5 VICTORIA FALLS

See page 309

An absolute must-see, the world's largest falls straddling Zimbabwe and Zambia are awe-inspiring and a short hop from Namibia.

6 HIGH-OCTANE ACTIVITIES

See page 331

Whether rafting down the Zambezi, bungee jumping off the bridge or peering over the precipice in the Devil's Pool, Vic Falls, as the adrenaline capital of Southern Africa, does not disappoint.

7 ETOSHA NATIONAL PARK

See page 238

The country's premier national park is chock-full of large mammals and colourful birds and has a vast, shimmering saline pan.

8 CRAFT SHOPPING

See page 73

Though Vic Falls Town takes the prize for souvenirs, from soapstone and wood carvings to textiles, woven dolls and basketry, Windhoek and Swakopmund offer plenty of choices.

9 SWAKOPMUND

See page 206

It's not your average seaside resort, with palm-lined boulevards fronting freezing seas and surrounded by desert.

10 SAN ROCK ART

See page 197

Namibia boasts an abundance of ancient rock art tucked away in caves and among boulders or spread across bare rock faces.

11 DESERT-ADAPTED WILDLIFE

See page 26

Namibia's least hospitable landscape is home to desert-adapted lions, black rhinos and elephants.

12 ANCIENT LIFESTYLES

See page 60

Learn about the ancient traditions and modern-day challenges of the San or the Himba by spending time in a rural settlement.

13 HOT-AIR BALLOONING

See page 113

An unforgettable way to appreciate the vastness and beauty of the desert is to catch the sunrise as you float above the dunes.

14 WILDERNESS LODGES

See page 113

An array of desert lodges, like *Little Kulala* near Sesriem, lets you get close to nature without sacrificing creature comforts.

15 A SUNSET CRUISE

See page 302

There's no better way to end the day than with a magical sunset cruise along the Zambezi.

12

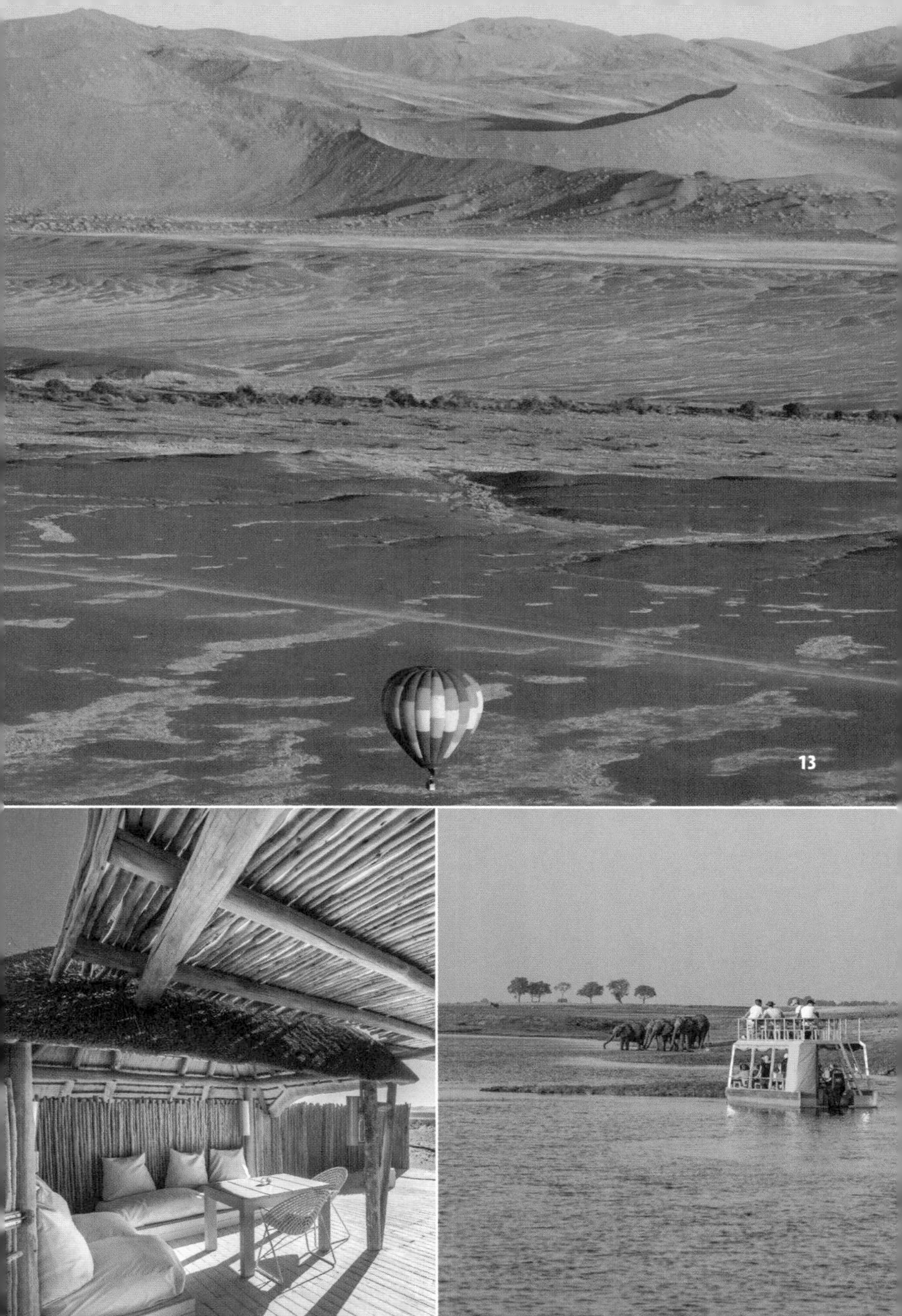
13
14
15

16 QUIVER TREES
See page 147
Southern Namibia's most emblematic and distinctive plant makes a splendid photo – whatever the angle.

17 WINDHOEK
See page 78
Namibia's scenically situated capital offers a chance to unwind in one of its many homely guesthouses, restaurants and vibrant bars.

18 WATERBERG
See page 174
Towering above the surrounding plains, this impressive sandstone plateau offers varied, lush vegetation, excellent birdwatching and superlative views from the top.

19 LÜDERITZ AND KOLMANSKOP
See pages 124 and 131
Namibia's best-preserved colonial town is relatively tourist-free thanks to its isolated coastal location. Don't miss the abandoned mining town of Kolmanskop, partly submerged in sand.

20 CAMPING IN THE BUSH
See page 59
Whether in a roof tent on a self-drive holiday or a well-equipped safari tent when glamping, a night under canvas in Namibia's otherworldly landscapes is an unmissable experience.

18
19
20

Itineraries

THE GRAND TOUR

The distances are too vast to cover all the country's highlights in one tour, but starting in the capital and finishing in Victoria Falls, you could manage the most well-known sights by road in three weeks – longer if you want to linger.

❶ **Windhoek** Namibia's quaint capital, tucked away in the Central Highlands, is a good place to get your bearings, browse for crafts and sample the local cuisine. See page 78

❷ **Fish River Canyon** Peer over the canyon rim, hike along the valley floor or relax in the hot springs of this jaw-dropping geological wonder. See page 153

❸ **Lüderitz** Admire the colonial architecture here; then visit the abandoned mining town of Kolmanskop, whose buildings are gradually being swallowed by sand. See page 124

❹ **Sossusvlei** A photographer's paradise; catch sunrise or sunset across the dunes and hike over the sand to the ghostly vleis, spotted with skeletal trees. See page 112

❺ **Swakopmund** Namibia's main seaside resort offers desert tours, adrenaline sports and the chance to wine, dine and relax. See page 206

❻ **Twyfelfontein** This UNESCO World Heritage Site has many San rock engravings, and curious geological formations nearby. See page 195

❼ **Etosha** Set aside several days to explore Etosha National Park, where a day- or night-time stakeout of a waterhole will get you up close to a host of wildlife. See page 238

❽ **Zambezi Region** The lush riverine vegetation makes the perfect backdrop to a sunset river cruise and a chance to see some stunning birdlife and large animals not present in the rest of the country. See page 283

❾ **Victoria Falls** Cross the border into Zimbabwe or Zambia to marvel at these iconic falls, where you can partake in everything from canoeing with crocs to high tea. See page 309

THE ACTIVITY CIRCUIT

You'd need close to three action-packed weeks to fit in all these activities, longer if you want to make the whole five-day canoe trip down the Orange River.

❶ **Orange River** Float for a day or paddle for five down the scenic Orange River, camping on sandbanks under the stars and cooking on campfires. See page 160

❷ **Fish River Canyon** Hike this brutal five-day trail in the bowels of the canyon, scrambling over boulders and cooling off in rock pools before collapsing in the hot springs of |Ai-|Ais. See page 153

❸ **Aus Mountains** Rent a bike and hit the trails in the scenic, underexplored Aus Mountains. See page 122

❹ **Naukluft Mountains** For an exhilarating bird's-eye view of the desert, balloon over the

Namib at dawn, soaring above the rippling dune sea with the brooding Naukluft Mountains in the distance. See page 117

❺ **Swakopmund** Get your blood pumping in Namibia's adventure capital: sand-boarding the dunes, skydiving into the desert or surfing the Atlantic waves. See page 206

❻ **The Brandberg** A strenuous climb up this imposing massif is rewarded with stunning ancient rock art, peerless vistas and the chance to sleep under the stars. See page 193

❼ **Victoria Falls** The adrenaline hub of Africa offers any number of ways to set your pulse racing: whitewater rafting down the Zambezi, ziplining across the Batoka Gorge or peering over the Falls themselves. See page 309

WILDLIFE AND CONSERVATION

Bank on three weeks to get around all these sites; if you're short of time, you could omit the Zambezi reserves – and save yourself an extra 1,000km (621.4 miles) driving.

❶ **Kgalagadi Transfrontier Park** drive into this vast South African–Botswana park for a couple of days to catch large herds of migrating wildebeest, hartebeest and eland. See page 150

❷ **Namib-Naukluft** The dunes of the Namib are home to some extraordinary desert creatures, while the spring-fed kloofs of the Naukluft Mountains nourish some surprisingly lush vegetation and plenty of birdlife. See page 106

❸ **Walvis Bay and Sandwich Harbour** Spend a glorious morning kayaking on the lagoon, before an exhilarating drive over the dunes to the wetlands of Sandwich Harbour. See pages 220 and 224

❹ **Rhino tracking and desert-adapted elephants** Some Damaraland lodges offer unique opportunities to get close to elephants and black rhinos. See page 200

❺ **Etosha** Namibia's premier national park is the place to spot large mammals; it also boasts fabulous birds and reptiles. See page 238

❻ **Zambezi reserves** The small reserves of Bwabwata, Mudumu and Nkasa Rupara boast prolific birdlife and large mammals that you won't see elsewhere in Namibia. See pages 282, 285 and 286

❼ **Waterberg** This striking sandstone table mountain protects rare roan antelope and rhinos and is within reach of the educational Cheetah Conservation Fund sanctuary. See page 174

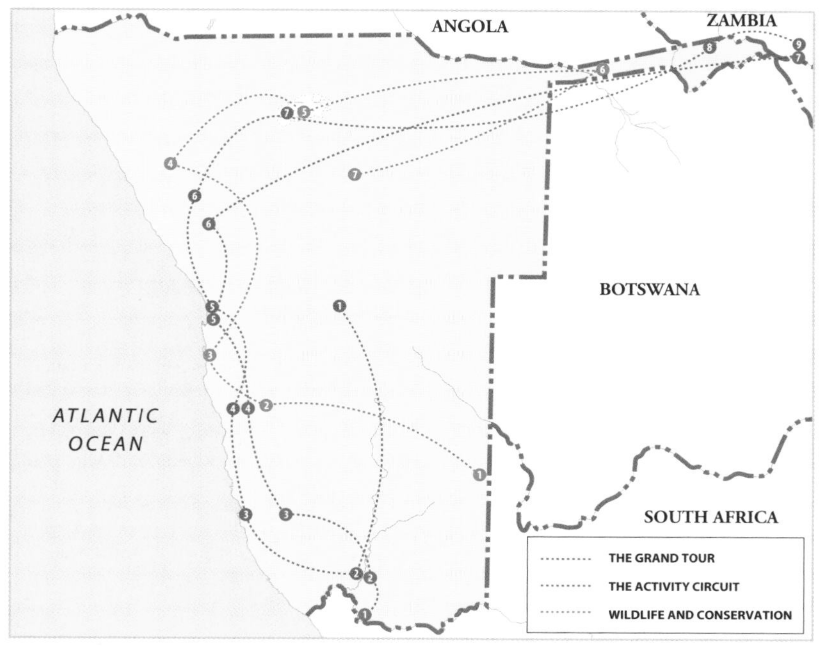

Sustainable Travel

Most travellers are aware of the importance of low-impact travel. There are various ways when visiting Namibia that you can help minimise your impact on the environment and have a positive effect on the country's many rural communities, which are often left at the fringes of development.

Namibia extends for 824,292sqkm and is more than three times the size of the United Kingdom. Its vast arid landscapes support multiple fragile ecosystems and dispersed rural populations, many of whom rely on subsistence agriculture. As such, water is a precious resource for both, even without taking into account the impact of climate change.

SUPPORTING COMMUNITY-BASED TOURISM

Namibia's pioneering conservancy system (see box, page 360) has been instrumental in developing community-based tourism, producing joint ventures between communities and private companies in establishing lodges, camps, and campgrounds. Income from tourism can support rural communities in diversifying their economies, which, in turn, can help them survive extreme climatic events, such as droughts and floods, as well as support wildlife conservation, including human-wildlife conflicts.

BUYING SOUVENIRS FROM THE ARTISANS

Buying crafts from the women and men who make them, rather than in Windhoek's souvenir shops, ensures that the artisans themselves are the primary beneficiaries from the sale – in some of the cooperative craft centres in the Zambezi Region (see box, page 286) or the Living Museums, for example, (see box, page 60), you can meet the artisans. Not only can you learn about the skills involved, but you may also get to have a go at making something that you can take home as a lovely souvenir.

CHECK YOUR LODGE'S GREEN CREDENTIALS

Namibia has an eco-certification system for lodges, campsites, tour operators and even schools (ⓦ ecoawards-namibia.org), where up to five green flowers can be awarded. Although the assessment criteria are by no means comprehensive, they indicate the establishment's attitude towards environmental sustainability, staff welfare and social responsibility towards the community. Several lodges support community development projects – check the lodge websites when planning where to stay.

THE CONUNDRUM OF AIR-CONDITIONING

Namibia can be baking hot in summer, especially before the rains, and the temptation can be to rush for the a/c. But lower impact fan-ventilated accommodation is often sufficient in camps and lodges that have been thoughtfully designed to keep their clients cool through the choice of building materials and their location and orientation in relation to the sun and cooling breezes. What's more, by eschewing a/c, you get to fully experience the magical stillness of the desert or the alluring sounds of the African bush.

THE 5 FLOWER AWARDED ONGAVA TENTED CAMP

BUYING HIMBA CRAFTS

TRAVELLING LESS, STAYING LONGER

Self-drive holidays are among the best ways to experience Namibia's dramatic wildernesses and varied cultures. But rather than trying to race around as much of the country as possible, consider focusing on a few areas and lingering longer in each place. Not only will this reduce your carbon footprint, but you will be able to learn more about the places you visit and enjoy more meaningful interaction with the local populace. Staying at community-run campsites is a great way to support local communities and minimise your environmental impact since facilities may lack flush toilets and electricity.

USING WATER SPARINGLY

If you're planning a lodge-based stay, spending longer in one place also helps conserve water – an imperative in a desert land – as bedding is washed less frequently. You can also help reduce water use by sticking to one towel, folding away the rest, and informing housekeeping. And then, of course, there's the toilet, when on occasions, you might consider the adage, 'when it's brown, flush it down; when it's yellow, let it mellow'.

WHAT ABOUT DRINKING WATER?

Keeping well hydrated is essential in such a dry and frequently hot climate, but bottled water does not necessarily have to be the solution. Many places do not have the means to dispose of or recycle the plastic – although check out the Sijwa Project in the Zambezi Region (Ⓦ africanmonarchlodges.com/sijwa-project). While Namibia's making strides in recycling its plastic – rather than transporting it to South Africa – it's still very much limited to the Windhoek area. Besides, much of Namibia's tap water is safe to drink – though you should enquire beforehand. If you need purified water, consider buying a large water container, refilling it where possible (some lodges provide refill stations), and adding water purification tablets where necessary. You can easily pick these up at most outdoor adventure shops before you travel.

FRAGILE ECOSYSTEMS

Namibia's landscapes have taken millennia to form – from the lichen-topped gravel plains of the central Namib Desert to the sparsely vegetated, rippling red dunes of the Kalahari. Driving off-road can cause untold damage to these scarcely visible ecosystems and leave unsightly tyre tracks that may take decades to disappear.

Wildlife

While Namibia cannot compete with the vast quantities of megafauna that roam the plains of East Africa, a surprising range of animals manages to survive in the country's harsh, arid landscapes, including some extraordinary desert-adapted creatures, both large and small. Namibia boasts around two hundred species of terrestrial mammal – 114 of which can be found in Etosha National Park – as well as over seven hundred birds, and it tops the continent for lizard diversity with over 160 varieties.

The photos and accompanying notes in this field guide provide a quick reference to help you identify some of Namibia's most common, sought-after and intriguing land mammals, alongside a few other desert creatures and a handful of the country's most emblematic birds. The notes give pointers as to where and when you might find these animals.

PRIMATES

Not counting humans, there are three main primates you are likely to encounter in Namibia: the Chacma baboon and the vervet monkey are both highly visible both inside and outside the reserves. Far less visible but highly engaging is the nocturnal lesser bushbaby, a relative of the lemurs of Madagascar.

1 CHACMA BABOON *(PAPIO URSINUS)*

These unmistakable large primates live in large troops – usually between fifty and a hundred – led by a dominant male and are governed by a complex social hierarchy in which gender, precedence, physical strength and kinship determine status. While the female hierarchy is established matrilineally, male dominance is often in flux, and there are often mixed-sex friendships within the chacma baboon troop. Grooming forms part of the social glue and you'll commonly see baboons lolling about while performing this activity. At night, they take refuge from predators on kopjes, clifftops, among rocks or up a large tree. Though they prefer fruit, baboons are highly opportunistic omnivores and will just as readily tuck into a scorpion or a newborn antelope. Males can be intimidating and are bold enough to raid vehicles or accommodation in search of food, undeterred by the presence of people. They are ubiquitous in central Namibia and notorious in Naukluft.

2 VERVET MONKEY *(CHLOROCEBUS PYGERYTHRUS)*

Vervet monkeys need to be near water and prefer savannah woodlands, so they are mainly located in the Zambezi Region in the north of Namibia and round the Orange River in the south. However, some populations inhabit the rocky terrain near Tsumeb and Grootfontein. Like baboons, these smaller primates also live in complex social groups, where grooming each other's silvery-grey coats is a core activity. The female hierarchy is inherited and male dominance fluctuates depending on a range of factors, including age, physical stature and allies within the troop. Mature males are notable for their bright sky-blue testicles. Both females and males possess cheek pouches to store food. Roosting in trees at night, vervets forage for food during the day; their mainly vegetarian diet is supplemented with small invertebrates, birds and rodents, and like their larger relatives, they too are not afraid to raid campground food stores.

3 LESSER BUSHBABY *(GALAGO SENEGALENSIS)*

The lesser bushbaby is more often heard than seen, being a vocal, nocturnal creature. Arboreal and highly agile, they can jump great distances between branches. Preferring acacia woodland and riverine forests, their distribution is limited to northern Namibia, from northern Kunene eastwards to Etosha, Waterberg – where they are frequent visitors to the rest camp – and the Zambezi Region. Their diet is mixed as they lick the sap of trees and eat fruit, but they also feed on moths, grasshoppers, beetles and the like. They are attractive creatures with soft fur, bushy tails, large saucer-like eyes and highly mobile and sensitive outsized ears. Living in small family groups (usually between two and seven), they gained their name because of their frequent baby-like nocturnal wailings, used to mark territory or communicate within the group. Females usually give birth to twins, sometimes twice a year.

1
2
3

CATS

Besides lions, the only genuinely sociable examples, and cheetahs, which often hunt in pairs or small groups, cats are solitary carnivores that generally prefer to move around at night. However, they can also be seen at twilight. During the day, they escape the sun's heat by resting up or under a tree.

1 LION *(PANTHERA LEO)*

Given that lions tend to top most visitors' wildlife-spotting wish lists, it's fortunate that they're relatively easy to spot, being large – the shaggy-maned male usually weighs in at 250kg (39.4st) – and lazy, prone to lolling about in the shade of a large tree for much of the day. The only genuinely gregarious cats, lions can live in prides of up to thirty, though more typically are found in groups of eleven to thirteen comprising a handful of related females, their offspring and one or two males. The females do almost all the hunting, generally at night, and are notoriously inefficient, with only around a 30 percent success rate, and only if operating as a group. Males don't hunt if they can help it but look after the cubs during the pursuit and then tuck in when the prey's been killed, though a large percentage of the lion's diet is scavenged. There are between six hundred to eight hundred lions in Namibia, mainly in the north; the largest concentration is in Etosha, with smaller populations in Kunene – including desert-adapted lions (see page 9) – Khaudum and the Zambezi Region.

2 LEOPARD *(PANTHERA PARDUS)*

The elusive leopard is the most numerous and arguably beautiful of Namibia's cats. Usually on the prowl at night, its excellent camouflage – typically a beige, tawny or golden coat dappled with square or round 'rosettes' – allows it to creep to within a couple of metres of its prey before lunging and gripping the animal in its vice-like jaw. To safeguard the kill from other predators, the leopard often uses its powerful muscles to drag its meal – which can be well over its body weight – up a large tree, where it also rests during the day, perfectly hidden among the foliage. Though rarely sighted due to their camouflage and secretiveness, leopards are widespread across Namibia. They can live in a range of habitats, from mountainous areas to low-lying plains, though they prefer plenty of tree cover. Leopards are particularly numerous on farms in central and northern areas, where they are frequently hunted because of their penchant for tucking into livestock. Your best chance of seeing one is in the private reserve of Okonjima, near Otjiwarongo (see page 173), where leopards wear radio collars and can be tracked.

3 CHEETAH *(ACINONYX JUBATUS)*

With a light streamlined body, long legs and a small head, cheetahs are built for speed and capable of topping 70km/h (43.5mph) for short bursts. Its lean, spotted form and the characteristic tear-like marks down its face distinguish it from the more muscular leopard, with which it is sometimes confused. Unlike leopards, cheetahs don't climb trees; they range across open land, hiding in tall grass where possible and relying on pace to catch their prey, hoping to knock it off balance since they lack the strength of lions and leopards to bring it down by force. Generally, hunting alone or in small social groups during the cooler parts of the day, they usually succeed with every second hunt. Namibia is said to host the world's largest cheetah population – an estimated 3,500, the vast majority inhabiting commercial and communal farmland – and the world's leading cheetah research centre near Otjiwarongo (see page 178). In addition to here and Etosha, cheetahs are most easily sighted in one of the small private reserves, like *Hobatere Lodge* (see page 244).

4 CARACAL *(CARACAL CARACAL)*

Resembling a small Eurasian lynx with pointed, black-tufted ears and long canines, the agile, beige-coloured caracal is rarely seen. A supreme nocturnal and solitary hunter, it preys on small antelope – often much heavier than itself – rodents and birds, sometimes snatching them out of the air as they attempt to take flight. It prefers dry savannah and scrubland, though it is occasionally arboreal and occurs everywhere in Namibia except the western coastal desert strip.

5 SERVAL *(FELIS SERVAL)*

Long-legged, small-headed and mainly spotted, the elegant serval bears some resemblance to a cheetah, though it is more diminutive, with some streaking near the head. It also has acute hearing, thanks to its large upright ears with distinctive white marks on the back, which help show the way to young kittens through long grass or reeds. A primarily nocturnal yet also crepuscular hunter, it inhabits the moister savannah regions of northeast Namibia, needing water within reach. Its diet is varied; though specialising in rodents, it also feasts on small mammals, frogs and fish, and, like a caracal, it can leap into the air to kill birds in flight.

1
2
3
4
5

DOGS AND HYENAS

Namibian members of the canid family include the elusive wild dog, two kinds of fox and two jackal species. The hyena family, including the aardwolf, is more closely related to dogs than cats.

1 AFRICAN WILD DOG *(LYCAON PICTUS)*

Brought to the verge of extinction primarily through hunting, disease, and their need for a vast territory, the African wild dog remains one of the continent's most threatened predators. However, it is making a cautious comeback: Africa's estimated population is around six thousand. Since one of their last strongholds is in northern Botswana, African wild dogs occasionally cross the border into the Zambezi Region and Khaudum and Tsumkwe areas; attempts to introduce them into Etosha have so far failed, though a pack exists in Erindi (see page 173). Also known as painted hunting dogs for their colourful, blotchy markings, they prefer relatively open areas where they can use their speed to catch antelope. Wild dogs are the most successful of the world's large predators as they hunt intelligently in substantial packs and can maintain speeds of around 50km/h (31mph) for some distance. Sociable animals, they live in groups of up to twenty, and the entire pack shares the kill as well as parenting duties, regurgitating the food to give to the pups. If you're lucky enough to spot them, it will likely be during the cooler temperatures of early morning or late afternoon.

2 BLACK-BACKED JACKAL *(CANIS MESOMELAS)*

Commonly sighted sloping off at dusk and dawn, alone or in pairs, the black-backed jackal is a versatile, opportunistic omnivore that relies heavily on scavenging – look out for them around the rubbish bins in Etosha. The black-backed jackal is widespread throughout Namibia, except for the Zambezi Region, because it prefers more arid terrain, including the desert. It is distinguishable from the less common side-striped jackal, which inhabits the lusher parts of the Zambezi Region by its black saddle flecked with white, to which it owes its name.

3 BAT-EARED FOX *(OTOCYON MEGALOTIS)*

The bat-eared fox can easily be distinguished from jackals or the Cape fox (*Vulpes chama*) by its outsized ears, Zorro-like mask and diminutive size. Like other dog relatives, it is an omnivore, eating small rodents, lizards, fruit and insects. However, it favours harvester termites. Its radar dish-like ears help triangulate the position of invertebrates underground before digging them up with its paws. Though relatively widespread in open scrub and savannah, they are most commonly seen foraging in a monogamous pair – sometimes accompanied by offspring – in the southern Kalahari. Mainly nocturnal, they are also active during the day during the cooler months.

4 SPOTTED HYENA *(CROCUTA CROCUTA)*

Often dismissed as mere scavengers – they can smell a carcass from several kilometres away – spotted hyenas are formidable hunters, alone or in small groups. They are often seen where zebra and medium-sized antelope – their favourite meals – are to be found. The spotted hyena's hunched appearance belies that it is the second-largest predator after the lion and is similarly sociable, living in loose clans led by the larger females. Numbers range from three to five in desert areas to over twenty, where food is more plentiful. Possessing powerful teeth and jaws, spotted hyenas are the most efficient consumers, eating almost every part of their prey, including bones and hide. They are most active at night when their distinctive whooping call counts as one of the eeriest sounds of the bush. Once widely distributed, they are now more common in northern areas, including the Skeleton Coast, though they also inhabit central Namib.

5 BROWN HYENA *(HYAENA BRUNNEA)*

The more elusive brown hyena is the dominant predator along the northern coast and drier parts of the Namib, but its range extends to the dry savannah areas inland. Smaller than the spotted hyena, with a shaggy dark brown coat and a beige mantle, the brown hyena also differs in that it scavenges the vast majority of its food and is a typical visitor to the Cape Cross seal colony at dusk. It also lives in generally smaller clans, ranging from a female and her offspring to groups of up to twelve, though brown hyenas typically look for food alone.

6 AARDWOLF *(PROTELES CRISTATA)*

Resembling and related to the striped hyena (not found in Namibia), the otherwise sandy-coloured aardwolf, with a similarly sloping back, bushy tail and dorsal mane, is much smaller. The aardwolf is further distinguished from other hyenas by its insectivorous diet and particular preference for termites, using its broad sticky tongue to lap them up en masse – over two hundred thousand in one night. Active at night, they rest up during the day in burrows, often abandoned by aardvarks. Fairly widely, if thinly distributed, aardwolves are absent from the coastal desert strip and the forests of the Zambezi Region. Their timidity means they are rarely sighted.

SMALL CARNIVORES

1 SMALL-SPOTTED OR COMMON GENET (GENETTA GENETTA)

Once encountered, never forgotten, the sinuous small-spotted genet has beautiful markings: a spotted body with a long black spine and a soft, striped tail with a white tip. This distinguishes it from the less prevalent large-spotted genet (*Genetta tigrina*), which flaunts a black-tipped tail. Genets prefer drier woodlands but can be found in riverine habitats. The small-spotted genet is found throughout Namibia, barring the western desert areas, whereas the larger relation is restricted to the Zambezi Region. An accomplished climber, the small-spotted genet sometimes rests up in a tree during the day but prefers to unwind in a burrow or rocky crevice, just as it inclines towards hunting on the ground. Though technically a carnivore whose diet encompasses amphibians, insects, rodents, reptiles and birds, it also takes eggs and fruit and can sometimes be spotted scavenging around game lodges; Okaukuejo Camp in Etosha boasts frequent sightings. It is almost exclusively a solitary nocturnal animal, pairing up only for mating.

2 AFRICAN CIVET (CIVETTICTIS CIVETTA)

Formerly, African civets were famously hunted and later kept in captivity for their anal gland secretions (musk) used in perfumes, which they rub onto trees to mark territory. Almost raccoon-like in appearance, this stubby-legged nocturnal predator boasts coarse fur covered in blotches and stripes and an impressive erectile dorsal crest that rises to intimidating effect when it's threatened. Mainly carnivorous, the civet feeds on fruit and carrion and can digest poisonous invertebrates such as millipedes that many other animals avoid. A versatile climber, swimmer and terrestrial hunter, it is rarely observed in the dense savannah, woodland and riverine areas of the Zambezi Region that it inhabits.

3 HONEY BADGER (MELLIVORA CAPENSIS)

Sounding like a character out of *Winnie the Pooh*, the low-slung honey badger gains its name from the eponymous liquid that it steals from bees' nests with the help of its symbiotic partner in crime, the equally aptly named honey guide. This small bird leads the badger to the nest, which the badger then rips open for the two to share the spoils. Despite having a sweet tooth, the honey badger is predominantly a carnivorous forager. It uses its ferocious claws to dig out food, often shadowed by pale chanting goshawks or black-backed jackals looking for scraps. Mainly nocturnal, it is also nomadic, ranging over a large territory and digging a new den in the ground or a hollow log or tree stump most nights. It is also highly aggressive: when threatened, it emits a foul smell through its anal glands to deter would-be predators and has been known to attack much larger mammals. Widely, if sparsely, distributed across diverse habitats in Namibia – though absent from the Namib – it is a known visitor to the rubbish bins of Halali Camp in Etosha.

4 BANDED MONGOOSE (MUNGOS MUNGO)

There are mongooses aplenty in southern Africa in terms of numbers and diversity, and Namibia is no exception, harbouring over a quarter of the world's 34 species – some solitary, some very sociable. The stocky, dark-brown, banded mongoose is the most frequently observed, living in highly gregarious, chattering groups (generally between ten and thirty). They build warrens in gullies, thickets and rock shelters, but most commonly in abandoned termite mounds in the dry open scrub and grassland across the country. In addition to termites and beetles, they'll feed opportunistically on small rodents, reptiles or amphibians, steal eggs or take fruit. Also quite widespread is the smaller, sociable, sandy-coloured yellow mongoose, with a whitish tip on its tail, which co-habits in colonies of up to twenty but generally forages alone. The dwarf mongoose, which, as the name suggests, is the smallest of Africa's mongooses, also favours old termite mounds for its den. It is a similar colour to its banded relative but without the stripes and only half its size and weight. All three species are diurnal.

5 MEERKAT OR SURICATE (SURICATA SURICATTA)

Popularised and anthropomorphised in television and film, the meerkat – a relative of the mongoose – is renowned for its complex social behaviour. Typically, they live in clans of ten to fifteen, though groups can be much larger; some will be scratching around foraging for food, noisily chattering and squabbling, while others babysit the young ones, groom each other, and, most characteristically, keep guard duty. For this, they stand tall on their hind legs on raised ground, looking out for predators; a sounding of the alarm prompts a mass scarper for cover into their underground den, if nearby. Although mainly insectivorous, they also eat small rodents, amphibians, reptiles, plants and even scorpions, as they are immune to their venom. Meerkats are distinguishable from the heavier banded mongoose by their silvery-greyish brown colouration and the dark rings around their eyes. Inhabiting Namibia's semi-arid scrubland and savannah and even the dry riverbeds of the western desert, they are notoriously skittish, which makes them difficult to observe. Your best chance is just after sunrise, when they often start the day by stretching up on their hind legs to warm themselves in the sun and at dusk. *Bagatelle Kalahari Game Ranch* (see page 143) has a clan semi-habituated to humans. They are also prominent in the Kgalagadi Transfrontier Park (see page 150).

1
2
3
4
5

LARGE ANTELOPE

While travelling through Namibia, antelope are the large mammals you'll most commonly come across. Around twenty types of antelope roam the various landscapes of Namibia, which is just over a quarter of all African antelope species.

1 ELAND *(TAUROTRAGUS ORYX)*

Africa's largest antelope, the beige-coloured eland, is built like an ox and moves with the slow deliberation of one, though it is also a superb jumper. Both males and females possess large dewlaps and shortish, spiralling horns. You'll see herds browsing, though they also graze when grass is available. Once reasonably widespread, populations are now restricted to Waterberg, Etosha and private reserves in north-central Namibia and over the border in South Africa (see page 150).

2 KUDU *(TRAGELAPHUS STREPSICEROS)*

The kudu – or, more accurately, the greater kudu – is the most commonly observed of the large antelope in Namibia. The male is a magnificent beast: sporting a greyish-brown or tawny coat with vertical white stripes, it possesses a shaggy mane, a white chevron across the nose, and is adorned with spiralling horns that reach 1.5m (4.9ft) in length at maturity. The more diminutive female, striped and with large ears, lacks horns. Known for athleticism, kudu can easily vault over a 2m (6.6ft) fence. Males are solitary or move around in small bachelor herds. Females co-exist in larger herds (six to twelve) with their young, which males join in the breeding season. Kudu prefer savannah woodland but can also manage more rocky mountainous terrain. They are widely distributed across Namibia, though absent from the Namib.

3 ORYX OR GEMSBOK *(ORYX GAZELLA)*

Featuring on Namibia's coat of arms, this archetypal desert antelope is unmistakable, with its pale greyish coat and tall, straight horns, combined with striking black and white facial markings and 'leggings'. Able to go for long periods without water, the oryx can also tolerate extremes of over 40°C; the brain is kept cool by a blood supply from the nose. When grass and leaves aren't available, they'll dig up roots or eat nara melons. They can be seen lying by the roadsides across the Namib and Kalahari, and they are also an incongruous feature of the centre of Oranjemund.

4 SABLE ANTELOPE *(HIPPOTRAGUS NIGER)*

The majestic jet-black male sable antelope has distinctive white facial markings and underbelly and fabulous curved horns. Young males start chestnut brown, like the smaller females, but turn black after three years when the bull expels them from the female herd. Predominantly diurnal browsers, they range in herds of ten to thirty over savannah woodlands and grasslands. In Namibia, they are present in pockets of the northeast, with populations in the Zambezi Region, notably in Mahango National Park and Waterberg and Khaudum.

5 ROAN ANTELOPE *(HIPPOTRAGUS EQUINUS)*

Sometimes confused with a juvenile or female sable antelope, the endangered roan antelope is of a slightly larger build, with smaller horns and a lighter greyish-brown colour. Grazing on medium and longish grasses, the roan antelope also likes to be near water. Harem herds typically comprise five to sixteen females accompanied by a dominant male, who defends them and his territory. In Namibia, the roan is rare, existing only in parts of the Zambezi Region, Khaudum, and where it has successfully been reintroduced in Waterberg and western Etosha.

6 WATERBUCK *(KOBUS ELLIPSIPRYMNUS)*

Instantly recognisable by the white target ring on its rump, the male waterbuck has a shaggy coat and U-shaped horns, which the female lacks. As the name suggests, it needs to be close to water, so in Namibia, it is an uncommon sighting, only found in the wetlands of the eastern Zambezi Region and on farmland in north-central Namibia. Predominantly grazers, they feed mainly in the cool daytime hours. They are sociable animals, gathering in herds of six to thirty; the males either lead a territorial herd of females or maintain a territory visited by wandering female herds.

7 RED HARTEBEEST *(ALCELAPHUS BUSELAPHUS)*

A rather awkward-looking creature, the red hartebeest can reach speeds up to 65km/h (40.4mph). Both males and females possess small horns and a smart, gleaming reddish-chestnut coat. You'll find them grazing during the day in semi-arid bush savannah and sometimes open woodland in northern and eastern Namibia. Like oryx, they cool the blood to the brain by taking it from their nasal membranes. The red hartebeest is easily confused with the darker and even faster tsessebe (*Damaliscus lunatus*), which can be distinguished by its fawn 'socks' and the fact that it only occurs occasionally in the Zambezi Region.

8 BLUE WILDEBEEST *(CONNOCHAETES TAURINUS)*

Famed for their migrations in vast herds across the plains of East Africa, blue wildebeest nevertheless congregate in relatively large herds by Namibian standards (twenty to forty). Also known less commonly as the brindled gnu, their heavy heads and shaggy manes are a common sight grazing the savannah plains. They are most active during the day but will also feed after dark. Keenly preyed on by lions and hyenas, wildebeest are understandably skittish. Prevalent in northern and eastern Namibia, including Etosha, they prefer to be near water.

1
2
3
4
5
6
7
8

SMALL ANTELOPE

1 IMPALA *(AEPECEROS MELAMPUS)*

Larger and heavier than the springbok, which it superficially resembles, the elegant and athletic impala is a prodigious jumper; it has been recorded leaping distances of 11m (36ft) and heights of 3m (9.8ft). Only the male carries the distinctive lyre-shaped horns. Though exceedingly common across southern Africa, its need for water close by and preference for mopane and acacia woodland mean its range is restricted to browsing and grazing the lusher forests of the eastern Zambezi and Etosha, where it is quite numerous. Far rarer is the threatened black-faced impala *(Aepeceros melampus petersi)*, an almost identical subspecies found only in southwestern Etosha and northern Kunene; its black facial stripes mark the only visible difference from its more common relative.

2 SPRINGBOK *(ANTIDORCAS MARSUPIALIS)*

Graceful and relatively diminutive, springbok are very common in certain parts of Namibia. In Etosha, in particular, you'll come across them in their thousands. You'll also encounter large, generally mixed herds in the Kalahari and even in the dunes around Sossusvlei, as they can go for a long time without drinking. Favouring dry open plains and savannah, they can reach up to 90km/h (55.9mph) at full throttle. They are also renowned for their extraordinary 'pronking'; when en masse, they arch their backs, straighten their legs, and make multiple leaps into the air as though on a pogo stick, scientists continue to puzzle over what it might mean. Predominantly browsers on succulents and shrubs, and at their most active at dawn and dusk, they can also graze on grass and feed at other times. They are recognisable by their distinctive white underbelly, accentuated by a horizontal dark patch above, and both sexes possess small, lyre-shaped horns.

3 COMMON OR GREY DUIKER *(SYLVICAPRA GRIMMIA)*

The common duiker derives its name from the Afrikaans word *duik*, meaning 'dive', a reference to the fact that, when threatened and after initially freezing, they plunge off into the bush in an erratic zigzagging fashion designed to throw pursuers off balance. Often confused with a steenbok of similar height, the duiker is heavier, especially the female, and has a greyish rather than brownish coat and a dark blaze down its forehead and nose. It can also be told apart from other antelope by the little black tuft between its small horns. The duiker has a varied diet: beyond herbivorous browsing, it eats small mammals, amphibians, birds and even carrion. Though both diurnal and nocturnal, it tends to feed more at night when close to human settlements, of which it is relatively tolerant. It is widely distributed throughout Namibia, except in true forests and very open areas, including the Namib.

4 STEENBOK *(RAPHICERUS CAMPESTRIS)*

One of the most commonly observed species, the golden-brown steenbok is widely encountered singly or in pairs, selectively grazing and browsing in open woodland and grassland across the country, generally during the day. It likes to take cover in bushes, where it crouches down to avoid detection from predators once its antenna-like ears have picked up the threat. However, it occasionally bolts and may take temporary refuge in other animals' burrows. The single young calf can be born at any time of year, and for the first few weeks, the mother takes extra precautions to keep her offspring safe from predation by eating its faeces and drinking its urine to reduce the telltale smell.

5 KLIPSPRINGER *(OREOTRAGUS OREOTRAGUS)*

This stocky yet surprisingly agile klipspringer, or dwarf antelope, lives up to its Afrikaans name (meaning 'rockhopper') as its raised hooves allow it to climb goat-like up near-sheer cliffs, making it at home on kopjes and in mountainous terrain. Being browsers and not dependent on pasture, they can often be seen far from water in remote, desolate districts, out and about in the heat of the day. Their thick, coarse hair, which ranges from a brownish to a greyish colour, depending on habitat, helps keep out the cold on winter nights. They are most likely to be seen in the central highlands and the western escarpment; look out for them in the Naukluft Mountains and the Fish River Canyon, for example. Males are horned (though occasionally females are too) and territorial, living with a mate or small family group in quite restricted, often long-term, territories.

6 DAMARA DIK-DIK *(MADOQUA KIRKII DAMARENSIS)*

Weighing no more than a small turkey and standing only 50cm (19.7in) tall on spindly legs, the tiny, fragile-looking Damara dik-dik is Namibia's smallest antelope and, therefore, unlikely to be confused with the larger steenbok, which it otherwise resembles. Despite its name, it is rarely found in Damaraland, more readily frequenting the dense scrub areas of Kunene, Etosha (close to Namutoni) and Waterberg. Dik-diks, which gained their name from their alarm call ('zik-zik'), mate for life; females are larger, whereas the males possess short, spiky horns. They are predominantly diurnal browsers, though they will feed at night, and they use their curious prehensile nose to sniff out the best parts of plants and to help regulate their body temperature.

1
2
3
4
5
6

ZEBRA

Two of Africa's three species of zebra, which are related to horses, live in Namibia. The key to telling them apart is the stripes, though they inhabit different terrains. Burchell's zebra has thick black stripes and fawn 'shadow stripes', both fading out on the legs. In contrast, the thinner, black stripes of Hartmann's mountain zebra continue down the legs. The mountain zebra also has more prominent ears and a small dewlap, which the Burchell's zebra lacks.

1 BURCHELL'S ZEBRA *(EQUUS BURCHELLI)*

Burchell's zebra is by far the more widespread species, numbering 15,000–21,000 in Etosha alone. They are similarly numerous in other reserves and farms across the country. Also dubbed the plains zebra, it ranges across savannah grasslands, often in large herds, grazing alongside wildebeest and other antelope. Diurnal and dependent on water, zebra also like to take dust baths.

2 HARTMANN'S MOUNTAIN ZEBRA *(EQUUS ZEBRA HARTMANNAE)*

Closely related to the Cape mountain zebra of South Africa, the Hartmann's mountain zebra is only found in isolated pockets along the western escarpment, including the western area of Etosha, around Dolomite Camp. They live in much smaller family groups of several mares and a stallion. Their slighter frame allows for greater agility in negotiating the rocky terrain.

RHINO

'Hook-lipped' and 'square-lipped' are technically more accurate terms distinguishing the two rhino species. 'Black' and 'white' are probably based on a linguistic misunderstanding; somewhere along the line, the Dutch word *wijd* or Afrikaans *wyd* –meaning 'wide' and referring to the square-lipped rhino's wide mouth – was misheard as 'white'. The hook-lipped rhino was named 'black' to distinguish it from 'white'. The truth is that both are a dull grey, though their appearance often depends on the colour of the dust or mud they've been wallowing in. Almost poached to extinction due to misplaced beliefs about the potency of their horns, the rhino's cause is not helped by the fact that populations grow very slowly, as the female only gives birth to a single calf every two to three years.

3 BLACK RHINO *(DICEROS BICORNIS)*

Thanks in no small part to the efforts of the Save the Rhino Trust (see page 9), the country now boasts the largest number of free-ranging black rhinos in the world, many of which are desert-adapted, able to go several days without water. Namibia's estimated 1,700-plus black rhinos can be found in the wild and on communal conservancies in the Kunene and Erongo regions, as well as on private reserves and in the national parks of Waterberg and Etosha, where your best chance of spotting them is at one of the floodlit waterholes at night. Unlike the white rhino, the smaller, more cantankerous black rhino is generally solitary, coming together only for mating. It also differs from its relative in being a browser, not a grazer, using its characteristic prehensile upper lip to grasp shoots and leaves.

4 WHITE RHINO *(CERATOTHERIUM SIMUM)*

Twice as heavy as its black counterpart, the southern white rhino is less aggressive. It is also more sociable, living in small family groups. Its large square muzzle is ideally shaped for grazing short grass on the plains. Often seen at the floodlit waterholes of Etosha – particularly Namutoni – white rhinos can also be found in Waterberg. Look out for the smooth 'rubbing posts', thin tree stumps that have been 'polished' by years of rhinos scratching themselves after a mud bath to eliminate parasites.

1
2
3
4

OTHER LARGE MAMMALS

1 AFRICAN ELEPHANT
(LOXODONTA AFRICANA)

The continent's most emblematic beast and the world's largest and heaviest land mammal – it can weigh up to 6,000kg (944.8st) – the African elephant is a sight to behold. In the flesh, elephants seem even bigger than you would imagine. You'll need little persuasion from the flapping, warning ears of the matriarch to back off if you're too close, but they are, at the same time, surprisingly graceful, silent animals on their padded, carefully placed feet. In moments, a large herd can merge into the trees and disappear, their presence betrayed only by the noisy cracking of branches as they strip trees and uproot saplings. Elephants are the most engaging animals to watch, perhaps because their interactions, behaviour patterns and personalities have many human parallels. Babies are born after a 22-month gestation, with other cows in close attendance. Calves will suckle for up to three years. The basic family unit is a group of ten to twenty related females, tightly protecting their babies and young and led by a venerable matriarch. Old elephants die in their seventies when their last set of teeth wears out and they can no longer feed. Grieving elephants pay much attention to the disposal of their dead relatives, often dispersing the bones and spending time near the remains. There are around 2,500 elephants in Etosha. Herds also roam freely in Khaudum and across the Zambezi, many drifting over the border from Botswana. Namibia's famous desert-adapted elephant – generally slightly smaller with broader feet – is to be found in the ephemeral riverbeds of the Kunene Region; the camps at Palmwag (see page 201) and the *White Lady Lodge* in Brandberg (see page 194) are well known for their sightings.

2 GIRAFFE *(GIRAFFA CAMELOPARDALIS)*

Giraffes are among the easiest animals to spot because their long necks make them visible above the low scrub. The tallest mammals on Earth – some males reaching over 5m (16.4ft) – with the longest necks. They have a distinctive lolloping gait, and in order to drink, they splay their front legs to lower their mouth to the water. Their unique circulatory system ensures that the blood, which is usually pumped at high pressure up to the head, doesn't cause brain damage once the head is lowered. Giraffe spend their daylight hours browsing on the leaves of acacia trees too high up for other species. Their highly flexible lips and prehensile tongues enable them to select the most nutritious leaves while avoiding deadly sharp thorns. At night, they lie down and spend the evening ruminating. If you encounter a bachelor herd, look out for young males testing their strength with neck wrestling, or 'necking', as it is known. Of Africa's nine subspecies of giraffes, two are found in Namibia, with most of the estimated twelve thousand being Angolan giraffes. Healthy populations occur in Etosha, but they also occur in Khaudum and the Zambezi Region and are common on private reserves, game farms and communal land elsewhere in northern Namibia.

3 AFRICAN OR CAPE BUFFALO
(SYNCERUS CAFFER)

A powerful ox-like beast with a rather lugubrious aspect – thanks to its droopy ears – the African or Cape buffalo must be near water and prefers lush savannah, wetlands or even forests. In Namibia, therefore, buffalo are mainly restricted to the Zambezi Region, though they have also been reintroduced to the Waterberg Plateau. The savannah buffalo tends to live in larger herds and is much bigger and heavier, with adult bulls weighing 500–900kg (78.7–141.7st). The bulls are distinguishable from the cows by their larger horns and more prominent 'boss', the part where the two horns fuse. Despite being such large beasts, lions prey on them, though when the herd works together, it can often repel the attack. Buffalo are prolific grazers that also sometimes browse, feeding both during the day and at night. Lone bulls, especially when wounded, are easily provoked and exceedingly dangerous.

4 HIPPOPOTAMUS
(HIPPOPOTAMUS AMPHIBIUS)

Though highly adaptable, hippopotamuses need rivers or lakes that are deep enough to submerge, with neighbouring areas of suitable grazing grass. Thus, in Namibia, you'll only see hippos in and around the major rivers of the Zambezi Region, although the private reserves of Mount Etjo and Erindi also have a few. They spend most of the day in water to protect their thin, hairless skin from dehydration, and males are highly territorial. After dark, they move onto land and spend the whole night grazing, often covering several kilometres in one session. Despite being herbivores, hippos are reckoned to be responsible for more human deaths in Africa than any other large animal (the diminutive mosquito is by far the most deadly). Deaths occur mainly on the water when boats accidentally steer into hippo pods (usually five to twenty). Still, they can be aggressive on land, too, charging and slashing with their fearsomely long incisors, especially if you get between them and water. Their barrel-like bodies and stubby legs belie that they can reach speeds of 30km/h (18.6mph) and have a small turning circle. Although uncertain on land (hence their aggression when cornered), they are supremely adapted to long periods in water. Their nostrils, eyes and ears are in the right places and their clumsy feet become supple paddles. A single calf is born every two to three years in water so it can swim before it can walk.

1
2
3
4

OTHER SMALL MAMMALS

1 AARDVARK *(ORYCTEROPUS AFER)*

One of Africa's – indeed the world's – strangest animals, a solitary mammal weighing up to 70kg (11st). Its name, Afrikaans for 'earth pig', is an apt description as it possesses a long tubular snout and holes up during the day in extensive burrows excavated with remarkable speed and energy, using its thick claws. It emerges at night to visit termite mounds within a radius of up to 5km (3.1 miles), digging for its main diet before licking the termites with its long, sticky tongue. It's most likely to be found in bush country, well scattered with tall termite mounds, so it is pretty widely distributed, though rare.

2 PANGOLIN *(MANIS TEMMINCKII)*

Sharing the aardvark's penchant for termites and ants, the pangolin – another extraordinary-looking nocturnal creature – has a distinctive 'armour plating' of overlapping keratin scales. This protection is used to good effect since, when threatened, it curls up into a tight ball, which gave rise to its name – in Malay, *peng-guling* means 'roller'. It is also known as the scaly anteater, and although it inhabits the central, northern and eastern areas of the country where termite mounds are in evidence, it is rarely observed.

3 ROCK HYRAX *(PROCAVIA CAPENSIS)*

A common sight in rocky terrain, the rock hyrax – also known as a dassie or rock rabbit – looks like an oversized hamster. Yet, despite being fluffy and small, its closest relative (admittedly from some way back) is the elephant. Like reptiles, hyraxes are poor at regulating body temperature and rely on shelter against cold and hot sunlight. They wake up sluggish and seek out rocks to catch the early morning sun – this is one of the best times to look out for them. Like meerkats, one or more adults stand sentry against predators and issue a low-pitched warning cry to the colony in response to a threat. They will browse or graze depending on what's available and are preyed upon by raptors and cats.

4 WARTHOG *(PHACOCHOERUS AETHIOPICUS)*

A ubiquitous and often comical sight, particularly across central and northern Namibia, the warthog is unmistakable with its trademark facial 'warts' – more abundant and prominent on the heavier male – upturned tusks and thin covering of dishevelled hair. Diurnal warthogs are commonly spotted grazing on the verges of the main roads before nonchalantly trotting into the bush, their antenna-like tails erect, to guide their offspring single-file through the undergrowth. They also frequently feed on bended front knees and enjoy wallowing in mud. At night, warthogs typically take refuge from predators by reversing into disused aardvark burrows to make a quick escape if necessary. The warthog is unlikely to be confused with its relative, the heavier, hairier and browner bushpig *(Potomochoerus larvatus)* – a rarely observed nocturnal presence in the dense thickets of the Zambezi Region.

5 CAPE PORCUPINE
(HYSTRIX AFRICAEAUSTRALIS)

The region's largest rodent, the Cape porcupine, occurs throughout the country, except in Namib's western coastal strip. Its emblematic banded black-and-white quills provide a prickly defence against predators; the ones at the back are hollow and rattle when shaken to intensify the effect, which is further augmented by erectile coarse hairs that extend from the back of the head to its shoulders. During the day, it lies low in one of an assortment of burrows – often made by others – rock crevices or caves, coming out to feed alone or with its monogamous mate at night. Farmers often brand it a pest since part of the porcupine's herbivorous diet of roots, bark, and tubers consists of crops.

1
2
3
4
5

BIRDS

Over seven hundred species of birds have been recorded in Namibia, and many are migratory, arriving when the rains are due (Sept–Nov) and leaving again in March or April. There are also around sixteen endemics or near-endemics. Here are just a handful of the more ubiquitous or striking birds that even non-birdwatchers can appreciate.

1 AFRICAN FISH EAGLE

(HALIAEETUS VOCIFER)

A handsome and unmistakable sight perched on a treetop, branch or post overlooking fresh water, the African fish eagle is the national bird of Namibia (as well as Zimbabwe and South Sudan) and is distinguishable from other large raptors by its white head. Its main diet is fish, though it occasionally eats small waterfowl, amphibians and reptiles; swooping down from a lookout post, the fish eagle grabs the prey in its large barbed talons, then returns to its perch to feast. Fish eagles tend to maintain and reuse several treetop nests, adding extra sticks each year. One to three chicks are usually reared during the dry season, when water levels are low, and fish therefore more concentrated. The larger female does most of the incubation and feeding, handing over care duties to the male when she flies off to hunt. The easily recognisable haunting cry of the fish eagle is known as the 'voice of Africa'.

2 OSTRICH *(STRUTHIO CAMELUS)*

The ostrich is the planet's biggest bird – reaching 2.7m (8.9ft) in height and weighing up to 145kg (22.8st) – and lays the biggest egg, twenty times larger than that of a hen. It's also fast, able to reach 70km/h (43.5mph), aided by its wings, which, though unable to help it fly, make useful stabilisers when running. The larger males have smart black feathers and a white tail, whereas the females and juveniles are greyish brown and white; both have long hairy necks. Their large fluffy feathers are well suited to regulating the bird's body temperature. Preferring open terrain, as their keen eyesight can spot predators from a great distance, they are a common sight around the gravel plains and even on the dunes of the Namib. Living in large nomadic groups of between ten and fifty, female ostriches lay their eggs collectively in a shallow pit in the ground, which may accommodate up to sixty eggs, incubated by both males and females.

3 HELMETED GUINEAFOWL

(NUMIDA MELEAGRIS)

Clucking, gregarious flocks of helmeted guineafowl are common in much of the Namibian savannah and scrubland, including on farms and near human habitation. The guineafowl's large body is attractively covered in spotted slate-grey feathers, whereas its tiny, red-and-blue, bald head, topped with a bony 'helmet', makes it look rather comical. These gallinaceous birds spend most of the day on the ground scratching around for seeds and insects, covering up to 10km (6.2 miles) a day, only taking flight with incredible difficulty.

4 LILAC-BREASTED ROLLER

(CORACIAS CAUDATUS)

It's dazzling when the kaleidoscopic lilac-breasted roller dives off its vantage point – often the top of a bare tree or post – to swoop down on an unsuspecting insect or small lizard. Its green crown, violet breast and patchwork of turquoise, royal- and sky-blue feathers become even more breathtaking when the bird is seen diving, twisting and rolling – hence its name – during its acrobatic aerial courtship display. Living in predominantly monogamous pairs, rollers lay their clutch of two to four eggs in a tree hollow, some distance from the ground. Though absent from the coastal strip, they are widespread throughout northern Namibia, including in Etosha, in woodland and savannah land with some tree cover.

5 GREATER AND LESSER FLAMINGO

(PHOENICOPTERUS RUBER AND PHOENICOPTERUS MINOR)

While it's hard to mistake a flamingo for any other bird – its distinctive pink feathers, long spindly legs and heavy bill being rather a giveaway – it's less easy to tell a greater from a lesser flamingo, both of which inhabit selected coastal areas of Namibia in vast numbers. The greater flamingo is taller, capable of reaching 1.5m (4.9ft) in height, and usually paler. However, the most notable difference lies in the bill: where the larger bird's is pale with a black tip, the lesser flamingo's is almost entirely black. Flamingos need shallow, saline water, where they filter feed algae, crustaceans and molluscs by holding their shovel-shaped bill upside down and swinging their head from side to side. Pink carpets of thousands of flamingos extend across Namibia's coastal mudflats, notably in Walvis Bay Lagoon – up to 85,000 have been recorded – and Sandwich Harbour, but they also occur in much smaller numbers in Oranjemund and Lüderitz. In seasons of exceptional rain, when Etosha Pan floods – usually March or April – they flock there to breed; otherwise, they migrate further afield.

6 MONTEIRO'S HORNBILL

(TOCKUS MONTEIRI)

Apart from a small corner of southwest Angola, Monteiro's hornbill is endemic to Namibia – one of the country's ten hornbill species. Inhabiting rugged terrain in the Erongo and Kunene regions, including western parts of Etosha, it is medium-sized with a white underbelly and outer tail feathers and sports a red bill. Its all-black neck can distinguish it from the red-billed hornbill (*Tockus rufirostris*). As with most hornbills, when the time comes to lay eggs, the female holes herself up in a natural tree cavity or rocky crevice and stays there throughout the incubation period, being fed by the male through the small hole that remains.

1
2
3
4
5
6

Animal tracks

Cats

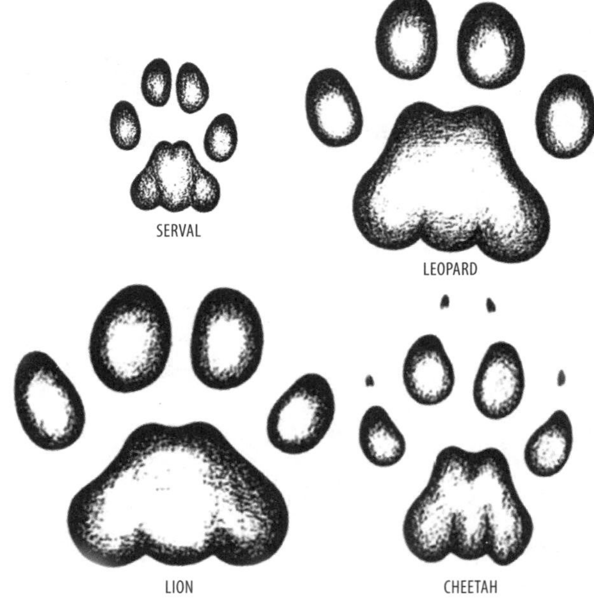

Dogs and hyenas

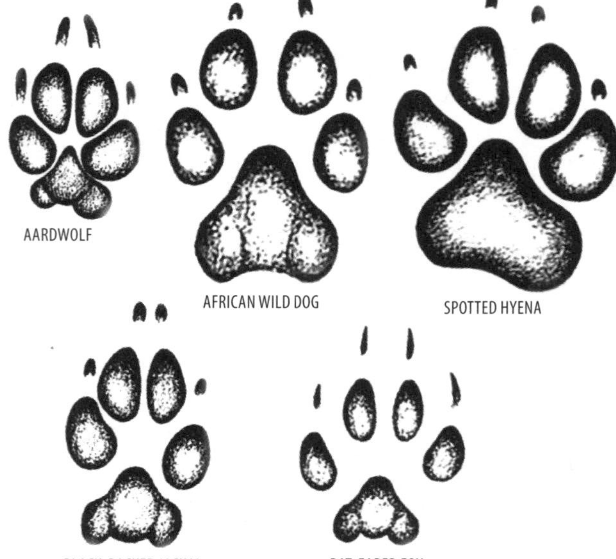

Large antelopes

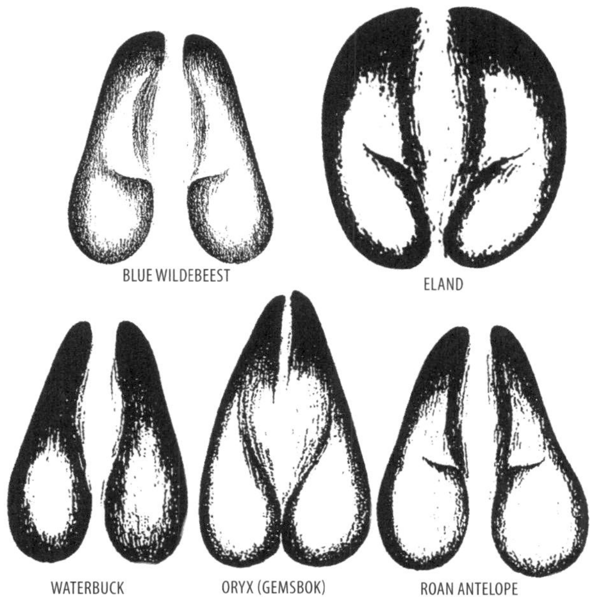

Small antelope

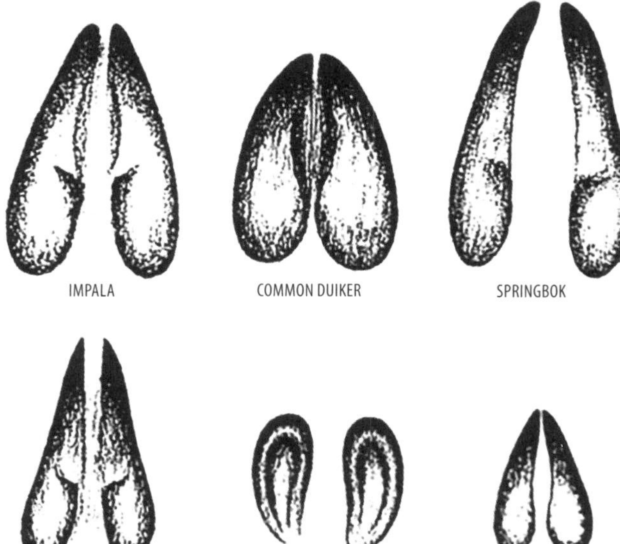

Primates

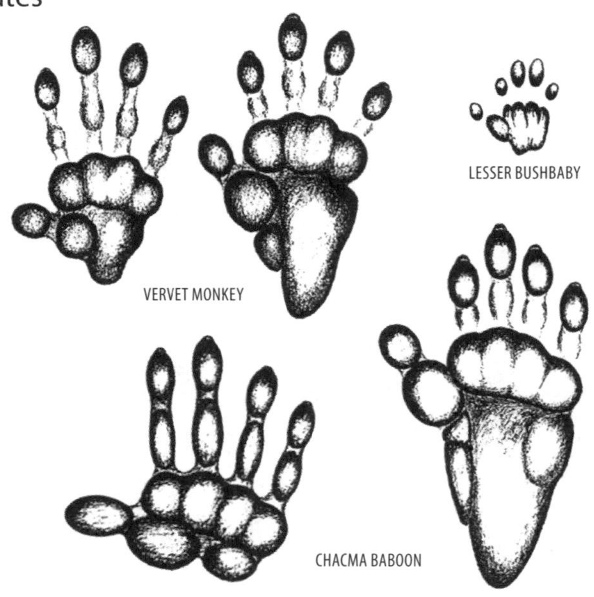

Small carnivores

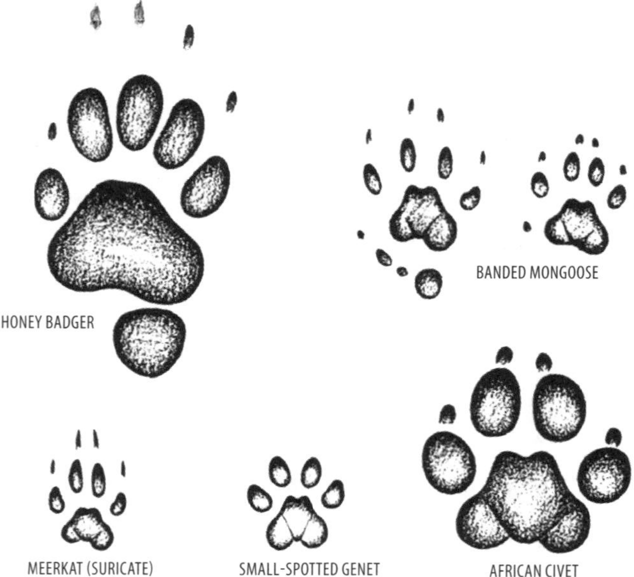

Other large mammals

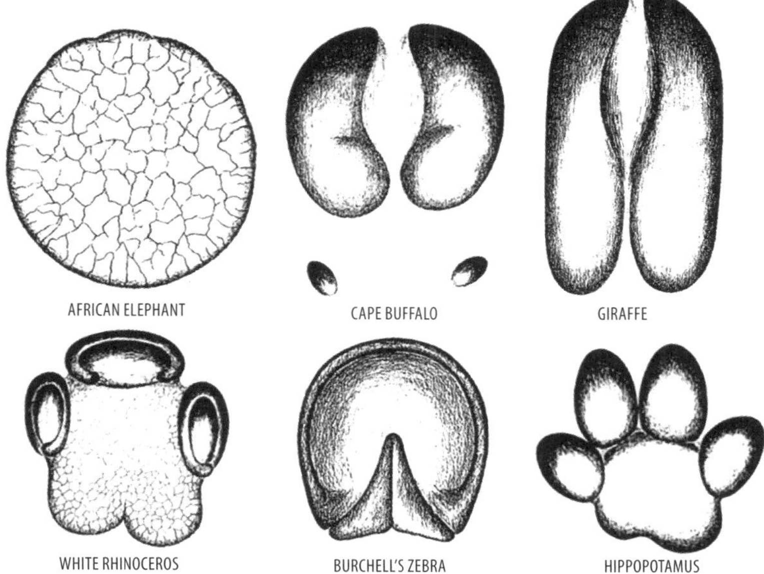

Other small mammals

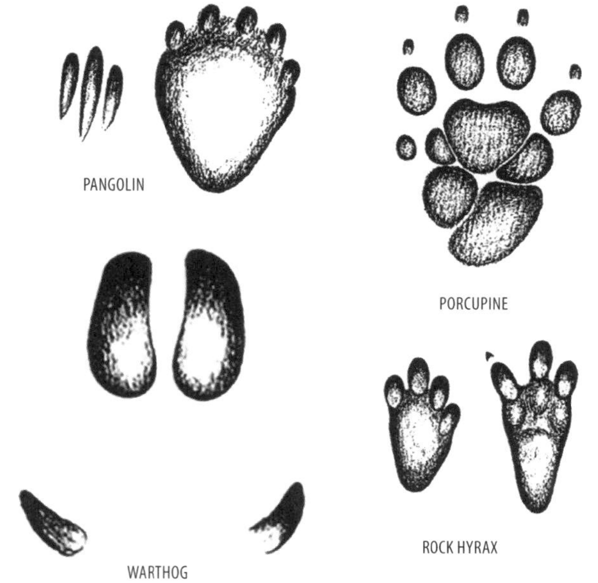

LIGHT AIRCRAFT ABOVE THE NAMIB DESERT

Basics

Getting there

Most visitors to Namibia arrive by air, the majority flying via Johannesburg in South Africa since the only direct flight to Namibia from Europe is from Frankfurt, Germany, and there are no direct flights from North America or Australasia.

International flights arrive at Windhoek's **Hosea Kutako International Airport** (see page 92), 42km (26 miles) east of the capital. The **Johannesburg route** to Namibia is more popular as you have a greater chance of getting a cheaper last-minute deal to Johannesburg, provided you're prepared to shop around online, scour newspaper ads and/or make more stops. What's more, there are numerous daily connections between Johannesburg and Windhoek. At the time of writing, the **Frankfurt–Namibia route** is operated by Eurowings Discover (ⓦeurowings-discover.com), part of the Lufthansa Group, which offers only one daily flight. Seats are generally more expensive and heavily subscribed during the high season (July–Oct) and over the Christmas and New Year holidays. That said, low-season prices are not particularly low. Generally, the further in advance you book, the cheaper the ticket – as with anywhere else in the world. However, you can cut costs by completing the last leg of the journey from South Africa by long-distance bus. It's also possible to reach Namibia by bus from other countries in Southern Africa (see page 52).

Flights from the UK and Ireland

There are no direct flights from either the UK or Ireland to Namibia. The easiest route is via Johannesburg by one of several carriers from the UK. Virgin (ⓦvirgin-atlantic.com) and British Airways (ⓦba.com) offer daily direct overnight flights to Johannesburg, with onward connections via local carriers, South African Airlines (ⓦflysaa.com) and Airlink (ⓦflyairlink.com). South African Airlines (ⓦflysaa.com) was set to resume long-haul flights from London by the end of 2023. Fares from the UK (generally Heathrow) are inevitably pricier in high season, starting from at least £1,000. Qatar Airways (ⓦqatarairways.com), via Doha, and Ethiopian Airlines (ⓦethiopianairlines.com), via Addis Ababa, also offer flights several times a week at competitive rates.

Travelling from Ireland, you can transfer in London or one of the other major European cities with carriers operating flights to Johannesburg, such as Air France (ⓦairfrance.com) in Paris or KLM (ⓦklm.com) in Amsterdam. Alternatively, cheap flights from Dublin to Frankfurt connect you with the Eurowings Discover flight to Windhoek.

Flights from the US and Canada

None of the US or Canadian carriers offer direct flights to Namibia. However, Delta Airlines (ⓦdelta.com) offers flights from Atlanta to both Johannesburg and Cape Town (just over 15hr), and United Airlines (ⓦunited.com) operates flights from New York to Johannesburg. Since Canada has no direct flights to South Africa, the best bet is to connect with a US carrier or fly via Europe. A return flight to Windhoek from Atlanta or New York costs around US$2,000 in the high season and US$1,600 in the low season.

Flights from Australia and New Zealand

The most direct way to reach Namibia from Australia is to take one of the daily Qantas (ⓦqantas.com) flights to Johannesburg from either Sydney (13hr) or Perth (around 11hr) and change there (AU$2,000–2,400). From New Zealand, the easiest route is via Sydney.

Flights within Southern Africa

There are several daily direct flights to Windhoek **from Johannesburg** with South African Airways (from around ZAR3,000 one-way). Airlink operates daily flights to Walvis Bay **from Cape Town** (also from around ZAR3,600 one-way) and via Johannesburg. Fly Namibia (ⓦflynam.com) also flies between Cape Town and Windhoek four times a week. After a

A BETTER KIND OF TRAVEL

At Rough Guides we are passionately committed to travel. We believe it helps us understand the world we live in and the people we share it with – and of course tourism is vital to many developing economies. But the scale of modern tourism has also damaged some places irreparably, and climate change is accelerated by most forms of transport, especially flying. We encourage all our authors to consider the carbon footprint of the journeys they make in the course of researching our guides.

BY BUS FROM SOUTH AFRICA AND BOTSWANA

Long-distance **bus travel** to/from Namibia and across Southern Africa is synonymous with Intercape (intercape.co.za), though there are other cheaper, if less reliable, providers. Since distances are vast, the journey times are long, though buses are modern, comfortable, selling hot and cold drinks and, crucially, have air conditioning. Note, however, that on-board entertainment comprises a selection of 'wholesome, family entertainment', much of which 'promotes the Christian faith'. If that is not your cup of tea, bring headphones.

The two main routes from South Africa to Namibia are **Johannesburg** to Windhoek (changing at Upington, South Africa; 24hr; from ZAR1,300 one way) and **Cape Town** to Windhoek (22hr; from ZAR1,100 one way). Both services operate several days a week and can drop off passengers in Keetmanshoop, Mariental and Rehoboth on the way. Tickets tend to be cheaper the further in advance that you book.

In addition, Tok Tokkie Shuttle (shuttlesnamibia.com) offers services across the Trans Kalahari Highway between **Gaborone**, Botswana, and Windhoek, provided sufficient demand exists. The latter also runs a shuttle service between Johannesburg and Windhoek.

stopover in Windhoek, the Eurowings Discover flight from Frankfurt flies on to Victoria Falls, **Zimbabwe** (three times a week, 2hr). At the time of writing, Air Namibia, the country's national carrier, was not operating, although there are plans for its revival.

Overland by car

The main **entry points** for vehicles **from South Africa** are on the B1 at Noordoewer (the Cape Town route) and Ariamsvlei on the B3 (the Johannesburg route); both borders are open 24 hours. From **southern Botswana**, the Trans Kalahari Highway enters Namibia at Buitepos (open 24hr), 315km (195.7 miles) east of Windhoek; travelling from **northern Botswana**, the main border posts are at Ngoma (6am–6pm) and Mohembo (6am–6pm), both in the Zambezi Region. The Wenela Bridge across the Zambezi at Katima Mulilo – usually shortened to Katima – hosts the main border post with **Zambia** (6am–6pm), whereas Oshikango (8am–6pm) is the main entry point from **Angola**. There are several other border crossings into Namibia, from South Africa and Botswana in particular, often at the end of a dusty road, with more limited opening times. Times and contact numbers for all border posts can be found on the Namibia Tourist Board website (visitnamibia.com.na/border-posts-point-of-entry).

If you're driving to Namibia from one of these neighbouring countries, **border procedures** are pretty straightforward, though if you are not driving a Namibian-registered vehicle, you will need to pay cross-border charges, which allow you to bring your vehicle into the country for a maximum of three months. If you come for business, you'll face additional charges. What's more, if you are driving a rental car, you'll need to arrange that with the company beforehand at extra cost and have the papers handy to prove you have their permission to take it across the border (see page 56).

AGENTS AND OPERATORS

In addition to Namibia-specific holidays, various tour operators offer wildlife-viewing safaris combining Namibia and Botswana, and various overlander trips between Cape Town and Victoria Falls feature Namibia on their itinerary. As well as the small selection of international tour operators listed below, several reliable local operators based in Windhoek (and a couple in Swakopmund) can organise your itinerary (see pages 94 and 214), often at less cost.

African Budget Safaris South Africa africanbudgetsafaris.com. Recommended budget operator based in Cape Town, specialising in overlander and other inexpensive trips across Southern Africa, including for families.

North South Travel UK northsouthtravel.co.uk. Friendly, competitive travel agency offering discounted fares worldwide. Profits support development projects in the global south, especially promoting sustainable tourism.

Responsible Travel UK responsibletravel.com. Leading ethical tourism company offering various tours of Namibia, from cycling to camping or self-drive (including wheelchair accessible), some focusing on conservation work. It has a sibling site in the US (responsiblevacation.com).

Safari Drive UK safaridrive.com. Specialists in fly-drive safaris to Africa for over 25 years; offers several itineraries in Namibia or can organise bespoke tours for couples, groups and families.

StudentUniverse US studentuniverse.com. Youth and student travel firm offering discount flights. It also operates in Canada, the UK and Australia.

Wilderness Safaris South Africa Ⓦ wilderness-safaris.com. This pioneering ecotourism company owns around a dozen exclusive lodges in Sossusvlei and northwest Namibia, often in partnership with local communities. It works through other tour operators rather than accepting direct bookings.

Entry requirements

If you are a visitor from Western Europe, including the UK and Ireland, or from the US, Canada, New Zealand, Australia or South Africa, you do not need a **visa** to enter Namibia. Otherwise, you should check with the Namibian diplomatic mission in your country. Even if a visa is not necessary, you do need a **passport** valid for six months after the entry date with at least two blank pages for stamps, and you should be able to show proof of onward travel (by air or bus), though this is unlikely to be requested. On arrival in Namibia, your passport will be stamped for up to ninety days; visa extensions (N$580) can be obtained from the Ministry of Home Affairs, Immigration, Safety and Security in Windhoek (Ⓦ mha.gov.na), on the corner of Hosea Kutako Drive and Harvey Street, Windhoek North.

FOREIGN EMBASSIES IN NAMIBIA

Australia Australian Honorary Consul, 56 Chalcedoon St Ⓣ 061 300194, Ⓔ australian.consulate.namibia@gmail.com.
Canada Contact Canadian High Commission in Pretoria, South Africa Ⓣ 027 12 4223000, Ⓔ pret-consul@international.gc.ca.
New Zealand New Zealand Consulate, 23 Bodin St, Pioneers Park, Windhoek Ⓣ 061 220346, Ⓔ ethomas@iway.na
Republic of Ireland Contact Embassy of Ireland in Pretoria, South Africa Ⓦ dfa.ie/south-africa
South Africa South African High Commission, Corner of Nelson Mandela Avenue and Jan Jonker Street Ⓣ 061 2057111, Ⓦ dirco1.azurewebsites.net/windhoek.
UK British High Commission, 116 Robert Mugabe Ave, Ⓣ 061 274800, Ⓔ general.windhoek@fcdo.gov.uk.
USA United States Embassy, 14 Lossen St, Ausspanplatz Ⓣ 061 2958500, Ⓦ na.usembassy.gov

Getting around

While getting around Namibia's relatively few population centres is possible by bus and even rail in some cases, to reach most of the parks, reserves and other places you are most likely to want to visit, you will need to book yourself on a tour or rent a vehicle. Hitchhiking is now banned on some roads in Namibia and national parks, but in other, more remote, parts of the country, it is almost the only way to get around if you are without your own wheels, but be prepared to pay the equivalent of a bus fare.

By bus

Even though most Namibians do not own cars, organised transport is relatively scarce outside the main population centres. Intercape (Ⓦ intercape.co.za) provides the most reliable **luxury buses** (see page 52), running daily services from Windhoek to South Africa, stopping off at Rehoboth, Mariental and Keetmanshoop, or Otjiwarongo, and north to Tsumeb, Oshakati and the Angolan border at Oshikango. They also operate a service from Windhoek to Livingstone, Zambia (and therefore access to Victoria Falls), several times a week via Rundu and Katima Mulilo. Other private operators also run **shuttles** to specific destinations: Town Hoppers (Ⓦ namibiashuttle.com) and Welwitschia Shuttle (Ⓦ welwitschiashuttle.com), both Swakopmund-based firms, operate daily air-conditioned shuttle services between the capital and the coast for around N$300. Details are given in the relevant sections. There is also a twice-weekly (Tues & Fri) inexpensive Orange Bus service – also known as the SWAPO bus – operated by Namib Contract Haulage (Ⓦ nch.com.na) that runs between Soweto Market, Katutura and various towns in the north, including Oshakati, Outapi and Ruacana, as well as from Swakopmund and Walvis Bay to the north. A couple of bus companies based in Katima Mulilo, at the far end of the country, run daily services bound for Windhoek, returning the next day. Most Namibians, however, get around on the less comfortable **minibuses** that don't have a fixed schedule; they leave when full and can be overloaded and more prone to accidents, but are faster. The 1,200km (745.6-mile) journey between Windhoek and Katima Mulilo costs under N$400.

By plane

Given the distances involved in Namibia, it's no surprise that **internal flights** are available, patronised mainly by government officers and business folk. In addition to the international airport at Walvis Bay, small airports are scattered across the country at Katima Mulilo, Lüderitz, Ondangwa, Oranjemund and Rundu. Although state-owned Air Namibia stopped operating in 2021 – at least for now – independent airline Fly Namibia (Ⓦ flynam.com) has stepped into the breach. It offers several weekly flights on the domestic routes from Eros Airport, Windhoek's domestic airport, 5km (3.1 miles) south of the capital, just off the B1 (see page 92). Domestic **fares** range from around N$1,500 for Windhoek–Walvis Bay one way to around N$3,000 for a one-way ticket to Katima Mulilo, at the eastern tip of the Zambezi Region, over 1,200km (745.6 miles) from the capital by road. Fly Namibia also offers 'safari flights' to various airstrips at the main tourist destinations, such as Sossusvlei, Swakopmund, Twyfelfontein and Etosha. These airstrips dotted around the country mainly serve charter flights; most isolated luxury lodges have landing strips. Several good charter flight operators regularly fly tourists between lodges. Still, it is best to ask the lodge(s) you're staying at to advise on flights since many have agreements with particular charter operators.

By train

Trains have been running in Namibia since 1895, and today, as then, they mainly transport freight, so they are exceedingly slow. Most routes on this small network also offer a **passenger service** (economy and business). Since most departures entail overnight travel, you can save a night's accommodation, which may interest budget travellers.

The **routes** of most interest to tourists are Windhoek–Walvis Bay via Swakopmund and Windhoek to Keetmanshoop (see page 93); the line from there to Lüderitz is still unusable due to sand from the dunes blowing onto the tracks. Designs to construct a 4.5km (2.8-mile) sand tunnel are said to have been finalised.

Fares are inexpensive, though it's worth paying extra for the fully reclining seats available in business class. Even then, however, the level of comfort is unremarkable – remember to take food with you and a blanket to ward off the desert chill. Prices are slightly higher at the end of the month and during the December/January holidays. The rail network is owned by the parastatal TransNamib (Ⓦ transnamib.com.na) and tickets can be booked at the various train stations in advance or on the day. You should turn up thirty minutes before departure. That said, at the time of writing, services were still to be resumed after the COVID-19 pandemic suspension.

At the other end of the scale is the luxurious *Desert Express* (see page 56), a travel experience in its own right rather than a means of getting from A to B. While the *Desert Express* has suspended operations, lovers of luxurious train journeys might consider the multiday train safaris to Namibia offered by Rovos Rail (Ⓦ rovos.com).

DISTANCES BASED ON THE BEST ROUTE BY ROAD BETWEEN TOWNS

	Etosha (Namutoni gate)	Katima Mulilo	Keetmanshoop	Lüderitz	Noordoewer	Opuwo
Etosha (Namutoni gate)	-	925	1015	1350	1320	615
Katima Mulilo	925	-	1870	2030	1996	1090
Keetmanshoop	1015	1870	-	335	304	1157
Lüderitz	1350	2030	335	-	609	1490
Noordoewer	1320	1996	304	609	-	1460
Opuwo	615	1090	1157	1490	1460	-
Oranjemund	1365	2052	483	394	233	1560
Oshakati	245	1100	1190	1524	1494	320
Otjiwarongo	288	970	727	1060	1030	430
Rundu	415	510	1185	1516	1486	810
Sesriem	852	1530	517	559	820	920
Swakopmund	660	1340	840	730	1144	624
Tsumeb	105	830	932	1118	1230	510
Tsumkwe	445	850	1235	1422	1532	843
Windhoek	533	1210	475	820	786	675

By car

The most convenient way to see the country is by having your own wheels; once you've made that decision, the main question is whether to go for a two- or four-wheel drive. Many of the main highways are high-quality tarred roads, and the gravel roads necessary for reaching most (though not all) of the main sights are generally navigable in a **two-wheel drive** outside the rainy season, though the higher the clearance, the more comfortable the ride. On the other hand, fuel consumption will be much more economical in the two-wheel drive. However, if you do a lot of gravel road driving, you must be prepared for the greater likelihood of punctures.

Most lodges that demand four-wheel drive access have a safe parking area for saloon cars and will transfer guests in their four-wheel drive vehicles, usually at no extra cost. They will similarly be able to take you out on game drives in their vehicles. That said, most self-drive visitors rent a four-wheel drive, though they rarely, if ever, actually use the lower gears.

High-clearance four-wheel drive is essential to reach more remote areas, but this needs to be accompanied by the knowledge of how to drive such a vehicle – for example, in sand, across riverbeds and over rocks. What's more, if you tackle challenging terrain off the proverbial beaten track, you will probably need to be in a **convoy** of at least two vehicles with all the necessary **equipment** (see page 65).

The Advance Driving Academy (ⓦ advancedriving-namibia.com) in Windhoek runs one-day **courses** on four-wheel drive and off-road training.

Car rental

Car rental is not prohibitively expensive in Namibia; still, it is not as cheap as in South Africa. You'll likely get a better deal with an advance online booking, though rates differ significantly according to the season. Moreover, four-wheel drive vehicles can be hard to come by during the peak holiday season. You certainly can't expect to turn up and rent a car on the spot. In high season, **rates** generally start from around £250/week for a small, manual two-wheel drive with a/c; after that, the rate decreases slightly. For a mid-size two-wheel drive, bank on paying over £350/week. Four-wheel drive vehicles cost from around £750/week and guzzle fuel, though they offer a more comfortable ride on dirt roads and afford you better views of the countryside; moreover, in some parts of the country, and especially during the rains, a high-clearance four-wheel drive is the only

Oranjemund	Oshakati	Otjiwarongo	Rundu	Sesriem	Swakopmund	Tsumeb	Tsumkwe	Windhoek
1365	245	288	415	852	660	105	445	533
2052	1100	970	510	1530	1340	830	850	1210
483	1190	727	1185	517	840	932	1235	482
394	1524	1060	1516	559	730	1118	1422	820
233	1494	1030	1486	820	1144	1230	1532	786
1560	320	430	810	920	624	510	843	675
-	1540	1078	1543	642	937	1260	1563	826
1540	-	463	590	992	834	286	618	708
1078	463	-	455	564	370	184	487	245
1543	590	455	-	1020	826	319	338	700
642	992	564	1020	-	297	735	1038	320
937	834	370	826	297	-	554	857	356
1260	286	184	319	735	554	-	340	432
1563	618	487	338	1038	857	340	-	735
826	708	245	700	320	356	432	735	-

THE NAMIBIA DESERT EXPRESS

Somewhat of a misnomer, the luxury **Namibia Desert Express** takes 22 hours to cover the 350km (217.5 miles) from Windhoek to Swakopmund, but that allows you plenty of time to appreciate the train's opulence and gaze at the desert landscape through vast windows while reclining in soft leather seats. The en-suite sleeping compartments are supremely comfortable; the three-course dinner and extensive breakfast included in the price are delicious, and there's video entertainment and a well-stocked bar to keep you occupied, leaving you little time to sleep. The tour includes a stopover at Okapuka Ranch, north of Windhoek, for some game-viewing activity.

When the train is operating, departures are once a week, leaving Windhoek station on Friday at noon in winter or 1pm in summer and departing from Swakopmund on Saturday at 3pm. Each sleeper compartment accommodates two adults and a child. In addition, if you want to go one way by train and drive back, vehicles can be loaded onto the train for an extra fee. At certain times of the year, you can also book a seven-day tour by train that goes up to Etosha, Swakopmund, and Walvis Bay.

PRACTICALITIES

Contact TransNamib at Windhoek Station for details (T 061 2982600, E desert.express@transnamib.com.na). Note that the *Desert Express* has had a stop-start history and at the time of writing, operations had been suspended again, but keep checking for developments.

form of transport to reach remote areas, especially in northwest Namibia. Local four-wheel drive rental specialists usually also offer rates that include camping equipment from an extra N$200 per day. Otherwise, several companies in Windhoek provide this service.

Some of the cheapest deals have a mileage limit, though most offer unlimited mileage, which is advisable in such a large country. However, rental rates can vary quite considerably for the same vehicle, depending on how many kilometres it's clocked up and on the conditions for the collision and theft damage waivers (CDW and TDW); you can often opt to pay a higher daily rental rate to reduce the excess payable in case of accident. Damage to tyres, windscreen and headlights (often from gravel on the road) is usually not included in the standard insurance, but you can take out extra cover. Including an **additional driver** is highly recommended given the long hours on the road you're likely to face and may not necessarily cost extra. **Dropping off at a different location** can be done, and again, charges depend upon the distance from the pick-up point; for example, you'll pay around N$10,000 to leave a car in Katima Mulilo that you have rented in Windhoek. Taking the vehicle **across the borders** in most of Southern Africa, especially South Africa and Botswana, is pretty straightforward. Still, advance notice is necessary to give the rental company time to sort out the relevant papers and insurance, for which you'll be charged extra. In addition, you'll have to pay cross-border charges at the border, generally in the relevant local currency.

As for **age restrictions**, drivers of two-wheel drive cars generally need to be over 21, and in some cases over 23, though younger drivers may be accepted for an additional charge; for four-wheel drive, you generally need to be over 25 and have held a licence for several years. Theoretically, an international driving permit (purchased before you leave home) is required for car rental – to be presented alongside your national driving licence. It is rarely requested if your licence is written in English or at least in Roman script. In addition, you should carry your driving licence when on the road to show up at police checkpoints.

As well as the usual international car rental companies (Avis, Budget, Hertz, etc), there are several good local operators, often specialising in four-wheel drive rental, based in Windhoek, and some of the local tour operators even have a fleet of vehicles. Gondwana, which owns the largest number of lodges across Namibia, also provides car rental.

CAR RENTAL AGENCIES

Aloe Car Hire W aloecarhire-namibia.com. Friendly, efficient, family-run outfit with competitive prices, especially in the low season (Jan–June).

Asco Car Hire W ascocarhire.com. Prices are higher than some competitors, but you're paying for a highly professional outfit specialising in four-wheel drive across Southern Africa, with a wide

range of vehicles in good condition and excellent briefings and backup service; it also rents out satellite phones and GPS gear.
Melbic Car Rentals Ⓦ melbic.com. This efficient, friendly, family-owned company rents out Toyota four-wheel drives with or without camping equipment, including several types of roof tents.
Namibia Car Rentals Ⓦ namibiacarrentals.com. This is a broker for the big agencies, with offices across Namibia and reasonable rates, especially for two-wheel drives.
Namibia2Go Ⓦ namibia2go.com. Gondwana's car rental arm offers a variety of vehicles, including a two-wheel drive compact hybrid SUV. Their rates include unlimited kilometres, unlimited additional drivers and zero excess payable unless negligence is proven.
Savanna Car Hire Ⓦ savannacarhire.com.na. A small, family-run business specialising in Toyota four-wheel drives.

TYRE PRESSURE

Views differ on the optimum tyre pressure for different surfaces; it also depends on various factors such as the type of vehicle, the kind of tyres on it and the load it's carrying. That said, a rule of thumb for the average four-wheel drive is 2–2.2 bar for **tarred roads**, 1.8 bar for **gravel roads** and 1 bar (15psi) for **sand**. For sand, it's essential to deflate the tyres to increase the surface area, which can improve the vehicle's traction. Ask your rental agency what they recommend.

Driving tips and regulations

As in most Southern Africa, cars are driven on the left in Namibia. Although the quality of the roads is high, so is the **accident rate**, especially on gravel roads and for foreign tourists who are unused to the conditions. Losing concentration at the wheel is also a hazard, given the vast distances involved and the monotony of some of the driving, so making regular stops is essential. The **speed limit** is 120km/h (74.6mph) on tarred roads out of town, 60km/h (37.3mph) in urban areas, 80km/h (49.7mph) on gravel roads, and 60km/h (37.3mph) in most reserves and parks. Note also that **seat belts** are compulsory. Many rental cars have devices that register the speed; companies will not pay the insurance if you have an accident when exceeding the speed limit. Along the coast roads during the morning mist, it's recommended to drive with **headlights** on; drivers also tend to keep them on when there is a lot of dust around. A substantial number of accidents also occur from vehicles hitting pedestrians or wildlife, more often at night, which is why you should not **drive in the dark** if at all possible, especially on gravel roads or in the north of the country, where there are plenty of domesticated animals loose on the roads to add to the hazards.

Whether you opt for a two- or four-wheel drive, there are certain basic provisions you should have with you and **precautions** you need to take since getting stranded in the desert is no joke and can be fatal (see page 65).

Petrol stations are located in all the main towns – usually 24 hours – and even in some more remote corners of the country (with more restricted hours). Most, though not all, take credit card payments (when the machine is working) and are not self-service, so you should be prepared to tip the very underpaid pump attendant (N$5) if they do a good job. On request, they will wash your windscreen and check your tyre pressure, which should be done at regular intervals, especially after a long period on gravel roads.

At the time of writing, unleaded petrol and diesel were around N$20/litre in Windhoek, more in more remote areas. Remember that using four-wheel drive gears and a/c will increase fuel consumption. Four-wheel drive vehicles often have reserve fuel-carrying capacity, but it's worth having spare fuel canisters even in a two-wheel drive so that if you take a wrong turn, which is easily done, you don't run out in the middle of nowhere. For the same reason, fill up whenever you pass a petrol station.

By organised tour

If you don't have your own vehicle or don't want to spend hours driving (or want to minimise your carbon footprint), the easiest way to visit places is to go on

BICYCLE EMPOWERMENT NETWORK

What grew from a project to supply second-hand bikes and mechanical support for outreach health workers has developed into a successful development enterprise in its own right: a network of over thirty self-supporting community-based **bicycle repair workshops** is now thriving. See the Bicycle Empowerment Network's (BEN) website for the location and contact details of the bike shops (Ⓦ bennamibia.org).

an **organised tour** or safari. These can be arranged via one of the specialist tour operators in your home country (see page 65) or through a Windhoek- or Swakopmund-based tour operator. These range from a budget three-day camping trip to Sossusvlei for N$8,500/person sharing to bespoke tours for as long and as far as you like to suit a range of budgets (see pages 94 and 214).

By bike

While you'd imagine the hot dusty roads and huge distances between sights would deter most people from pedalling around Namibia, there are a surprising number of **cycling holidays** on offer from specialist tour operators (such as Mountain Bike Namibia, Ⓦmountainbikenamibia.com; African Bikers, Ⓦafricanbikers.com; and Bike Tours, Ⓦbiketours.com), as well as more mainstream companies (such as Exodus, Ⓦexodus.co.uk, and Trailfinders, Ⓦtrailfinders.com); the latter will also organise your flights. The fact that many roads are deserted and the scenery can be spectacular makes Namibia, in some respects, ideal for cycling. However, the extreme heat, dust and isolation mean that **independent cyclists** must be experienced, fit and self-sufficient in case of breakdown, carrying plenty of water and food and adequately protecting the head and neck from the brutal sun. The BEN network of bike shops (see box, page 57) offers **bike repairs**.

Hitchhiking

Despite being forbidden in national parks and along some routes, such as the Swakopmund–Windhoek road, **hitchhiking** is a common way of getting about in less populated areas. However, you'd be wise not to do it alone. You should offer to contribute to fuel costs (generally the price of a bus fare), though if you're lucky, your ride may decline to take you up on the offer. On some roads, you could be waiting hours for a vehicle to pass, so it's essential to have enough food and water to sustain you and adequate protection from the sun. Shared rides are sometimes advertised in the backpacker hostels in Windhoek.

Accommodation

Although accommodation can seem expensive compared to many parts of Africa, standards are usually high, and the value for money is often excellent, especially if you're from a country with favourable exchange rates. Moreover, there's much variety to suit a range of budgets, from basic campgrounds to all-inclusive luxury lodges and tented camps or moderately priced B&Bs and guest farms on private reserves. Backpacker hostels outside Windhoek are pretty thin on the ground, but staying at community campgrounds is another budget alternative, which helps provide the community with much-needed income. Self-catering options are also widespread. Almost all lodges and guesthouses require you to check out by 10am and check in after 3pm.

Hotels, B&Bs and guesthouses

Hotels are generally confined to the major urban centres, and by law, **hotel** rooms must all be en suite (with a bath or shower and toilet) and have windows. More common – even in Windhoek – are family-run **guesthouses** and smaller **B&Bs**. You'll also find them sprinkled around the smaller towns in Namibia. They are usually owner-managed, offer more personalised hospitality and are generally cheaper than hotels. Some guesthouses also provide evening meals and/or packed lunches on request.

Many lodgings still follow the German tradition of preferring **twin beds** rather than doubles, though the two beds will often be arranged side by side. If having a double bed is essential, ascertain the bed configurations before booking.

Lodges and tented camps

Namibia's **lodge** scene has grown substantially over the last fifteen years, particularly at the luxury end of the market, where you can pay over N$14,000 per person sharing per night for an **all-inclusive package**. Lodges inside the national parks are run by the parastatal Namibia Wildlife Resorts (see page

ACCOMMODATION ALTERNATIVES

Useful websites that provide alternatives to standard hotel and hostel accommodation include:
CouchSurfing (Ⓦcouchsurfing.org) and **Airbnb** (Ⓦairbnb.com). Hosts for both are mainly located in Windhoek, with some in Swakopmund, Otjiwarongo, Lüderitz and Walvis Bay.

ACCOMMODATION PRICES

Price codes for hotels, guesthouses, lodges and B&Bs in this guide are for the most part given in Namibian dollars, except for places that deal in South African rand, US dollars or the Zambian Kwacha for the Victoria Falls chapter. We have used the exchange rate to convert all prices to match the codes below. Prices refer to the cheapest en-suite double or twin room in high season. Breakfast (**B&B**) is usually included. Many lodges, tented camps and guest farms only offer accommodation on a dinner, bed and breakfast basis (**DBB**), and a handful of the more luxury establishments prefer all-inclusive (**AI**) rates that also cover activities. In the accommodation listings, we have indicated what the price includes. Because we have used the same coding to cover urban accommodation and lodges, the most expensive five-star hotel accommodation will only fall under N$$$. In contrast, most lodges will fall into the more expensive price codes, even relatively modestly priced ones, because rates include much more than simply board and lodging. Indeed, some of the most exclusive lodges cost six times that of others in the top category. Campgrounds, where travellers use their own tent, tend to charge per person, though we have coded assuming two people share a tent.

N$	under 500
N$$	501–2,500
N$$$	2,501–6,000
N$$$$	over 6,000

67), with a few notable exceptions. Still, many private concessions border the parks, catering to a range of budgets. In addition to them is a handful of remote, luxury wilderness camps – often reached by a charter flight – whose isolation and spectacular desert scenery are generally the main attraction. Several tour operators manage a portfolio of lodgings within Namibia. The Gondwana Collection (Ⓦ gondwana-collection.com), for example, owns over twenty diverse and distinctive properties and campgrounds right across the country, characterised by efficient, friendly service; a strong emphasis on sustainability; excellent buffet food and good-quality but affordable accommodation, including upmarket campgrounds. South Africa-based Wilderness Safaris (Ⓦ wilderness-safaris.com), which has ecotourism operations in several African countries, owns half a dozen exclusive camps in Namibia, predominantly in the northwest, including the pioneering Damaraland Camp, which is jointly owned and managed mainly by the local community conservancy. Other collections of lodges and tented camps are owned, managed and/or marketed by umbrella companies, such as Ondili (Ⓦ ondili.com) or Ultimate Safaris (Ⓦ ultimatesafaris.na).

Guest farms

Guest farms are generally run by Namibians of German or white South African heritage; they are large working farms that look to supplement their income to a greater or lesser extent through tourism. They often combine the family-style hospitality of a guesthouse, which includes communal dining with the hosts, with the advantage of being surrounded by nature. Several guest farms offer hiking trails around their property, and some have reserves stocked with large mammals, offering good opportunities for **wildlife viewing**; they may also be involved in conservation work; others (though none listed in this guide) are hunting farms. Other activities provided by guest farms include farm tours, four-wheel drive trails, stargazing, sundowner excursions and horse riding.

Hostels and budget accommodation

The country's few **backpacker hostels** are concentrated in Windhoek (see page 95) and in the coastal resorts of Swakopmund (see page 215) and Lüderitz (see page 128), with a couple also in Tsumeb (see page 184), charging around N$300 for a bed in a dorm and from N$700 for a double or twin with shared or private bathroom. Camping is another option for budget travellers, especially at the cheaper community-run campgrounds. **Rest camps**, which by law have to offer at least four types of accommodation, also tend to be good value, usually providing inexpensive self-catering units and camping pitches, among other no-frills options.

Camping

Camping is the best way to experience Namibia's wilderness scenery, the sounds of the bush and the country's magical sunsets. Moreover, it doesn't have

NAMIBIA'S LIVING MUSEUMS

There are seven '**living museums**' across northern Namibia, which aim to preserve and transfer aspects of traditional culture, educate fellow Namibians and foreign tourists, provide opportunities for intercultural exchange and, importantly, create sources of income for rural communities.

The Ju |'Hoansi-San, Mafwe, Khwe, Damara, Mbunza and Himba are represented in the living museums. They are supported by the non-profit organisation, The Living Culture Foundation of Namibia (W lcfn.info). By visiting one of these sites, you can choose from a menu of **interactive programmes**, ranging from a couple of hours to a whole day, or even an **overnight stay** (which will afford you far greater insight), as you learn about and practise traditional skills, herbal remedies or dances, before sampling traditional food. Provided you avoid arriving when the village is being stage-managed to entertain large tour groups, engaging in genuine interaction with community members is possible, not only about traditional life but also about how the communities have adapted to modern life.

to be the unforgiving endurance activity of guide or scout camps. On the contrary, camping can be pretty luxurious and relatively inexpensive in Namibia. Bank on paying from around N$300 per person per night, though some campgrounds charge for the vehicle and/or have an additional site charge. Increasingly, campgrounds offer private washing facilities and even private food preparation areas and sinks, particularly in lodges that cater to campers. Hot-water showers are the norm, though in some cases, the water may be heated by a donkey (wood-fired water heater), and you may need to buy the wood and build the fire yourself. Electricity is usually available, except in community or wilderness campsites, as are power points to charge electrical equipment. You'll almost certainly have a private braai stand or pit, but not necessarily a grill, which you can rent. Larger places, such as the NWR camps (see page 67), will have communal ablution blocks and a camp shop that sells basic provisions, including 'braai packs', which usually comprise a couple of steaks, pork chops or kebabs and boerewors with which to kick-start your barbecue. These are also often available on guest farms, where the meat comes straight from their livestock.

Several places also rent out tents already set up and equipped with beds (or mattresses), bedding and electricity for little more than a campground fee.

Wild camping should not be undertaken unless there's no other option – such as a breakdown somewhere; usually, there's a community campground, however rudimentary, within reach in even the remotest areas.

Community-based tourism

Namibia's community-based tourism (CBT) has rightly been championed worldwide, especially through the country's progressive conservancy system. Though it's not without its share of challenges (see page 360), it offers travellers a way of engaging with rural populations while helping to support communities without threatening their lifestyles, which more conventional tourism does not (W conservationtourism.com.na). That said, it takes various forms: most notably, there are several excellent **community-run campgrounds** across the country, usually comprising only a handful of pitches, which sometimes lack electricity. The tourist board's CBT webpage (W visitnamibia.com.na/community-based-tourism) lists some activities. The outstanding success story in CBT is the international award-winning **Conservancy Safaris Namibia** (W kcs-namibia.com.na), almost entirely owned by the Himba and Herero communities. In existence in the Kunene Region for several years, it is starting to expand its operations into the Zambezi Region. Increasingly, conservancies are entering into joint ventures with more experienced lodge operators; there are now over thirty such ventures.

Another way some communities benefit from tourism, which is not without its critics, is through the 'living museum' experience (see page 60).

In urban areas, 'township tourism' is also taking off; run by local Black operators in the former townships of Windhoek (see page 94), Swakopmund (see page 214) and Walvis Bay (see page 222), it's an area where they can outdo the leading (almost exclusively white-owned) tour operators in Namibia. A couple of the more successful companies have now succeeded in branching out into offering more mainstream activities to tourists.

At its best, a township tour gives tourists insights into the various changing cultures, challenges and everyday lives of people in these areas and a chance for intercultural interaction. At its worst, it can be very voyeuristic – hence why it is often referred to as 'slum' or 'poverty' tourism.

It's not everyone's cup of tea, and much depends on the attitudes and actions of the people doing the tour, how the tour is managed, and the interactions that take place. Ambivalence exists among township residents, too; research in Katutura (Windhoek's former Black township) showed that, although some residents felt happy that visitors valued their lives and what they were doing, others thought they were coming to gawp at their poverty. The research also showed that the money from the tours did not spread widely into the community since tourists visit the same places and people each time (such as Penduka in Windhoek). To ensure that your tourist dollars are spread more widely, make enquiries beforehand and see where you might go that is off the beaten track.

Eating and drinking

Eating and drinking in Namibia can be an absolute pleasure, especially for carnivores, as the country has a reputation for excellent meat, particularly game meat. On the coast, too, the Benguela Current ensures an ample selection of fresh fish. Though locally grown vegetables and fruit are harder to come by, the supermarkets in the main towns stock plenty of imported fruit and vegetables from South Africa.

Traditional dishes

Most visitors will never get to taste the sort of food eaten by the vast majority of the population, which varies according to location, cultural traditions and season, but whose staple is usually sorghum or pearl millet made into a thick **porridge** – *oshifima*, *oshimbombo*, to give just two names. The Herero and Himba, in particular, often mix sour milk (*omaere*) with the porridge, which may be eaten with wild or dried spinach (*ombidi* or *ekaka*) or other vegetables, and sometimes meat or chicken. Head for Soweto market in Katutura, though, and you'll easily come across the popular street food **kapana** – bite-sized strips of red meat sizzled on the grill then dipped in a chilli, tomato and onion sauce; they go well with the ubiquitous **fat cakes** – deep-fried balls of dough, which are surprisingly tasty if eaten straight from the pan.

For most tourists, though Namibian cuisine is about **venison** or **game meat**, you're just as likely to see springbok, kudu and oryx laid out on your plate as you are to spot them bounding across the road. On the coast, **seafood** is abundant: kabeljou, kingklip, hake, sole and lobster are popular, while Namibian oysters have garnered an international reputation. If staying by the Zambezi and Kavango rivers, you can count on some tasty tigerfish, tilapia and bream. Being the most fertile regions of the country, they also produce more vegetables and fruit than elsewhere in Namibia: check out the market and roadside stalls for monkey orange (*maguni*), Kavango litchi (*makwevo*), bird plum (*eembe*) and *marula* – as used to make the cream liqueur Amarula.

German culinary traditions heavily influence what is commonly billed as 'Namibian cuisine'. Expect to spot wiener schnitzel and spaetzle (thick egg noodles) on menus, and rolls (*brötchen*) and calorific cakes laden with cream in coffee shops in Windhoek, Swakopmund and Lüderitz. Similarly, no camping trip to Namibia is complete without that Afrikaner institution, the braai (it rhymes with 'dry'), or barbecue, on which you need to toss a hefty coil of boerewors (farmer's sausage), large steaks and sosaties (lamb or mutton kebabs), to be washed down with gallons of beer. Potjies (stews cooked in a three-legged metal pot – traditionally over a few coals) are also popular.

Vegetarians and **vegans** will have a more challenging time. However, there are almost always a couple of vegetarian options on restaurant menus; they rarely stray beyond a plateful of roasted vegetables or mushroom risotto.

PRICING AND TAXES

Most advertised prices on restaurant menus and for accommodation include **government taxes**. In all cases, we have included them in the price codes given in this guide.

EATING PRICE CODES

The price codes for restaurants reflect the average price of a two-course meal plus a drink, such as a beer or a glass of wine, for one person. Cafés only offering breakfast, a snack or a slice of cake will inevitably fall into the lower two categories.

N$	under N$150
N$$	N$151–250
N$$$	N$251–400
N$$$$	over N$400

Drink

Tap water is generally very safe in Namibia, even though the taste varies. It is incredibly pure when it comes from lodge or farm boreholes. That said, bottled water is widely available. However, as an alternative, you might consider bringing water **purifying tablets** with you – these days sold with neutralising tablets to take away the aftertaste – to help alleviate the massive amount of plastic waste generated by getting through multiple bottles of water each day.

Fresh **fruit juice** is only available in the lusher Zambezi and Kavango regions – seek out, for example, the delicious *sabdariffa* juice made from wild hibiscus flowers. But cans and cartons of the South African brands of Ceres and Liqui-Fruit, which contain 100 percent fruit juice without additional sugar, are not harmful substitutes and are widely stocked in shops, supermarkets and petrol stations. Coke and all the usual fizzy beverages are widespread. However, you might try the popular, refreshing, near-enough non-alcoholic **rock shandy**, consisting of half lemonade, half soda water or sparkling water, a slice of lemon and a dash of Angostura bitters.

Namibia's Teutonic heritage has ensured that good **coffee** is widely available in towns and lodges; a cup of **tea** is equally easy to come by, including the popular herbal rooibos (or red bush) tea. You may need to specify cold milk with your tea, as hot milk is the default way to drink tea in Southern Africa.

Probably the most widely appreciated German colonial legacy, however, is Namibia's **beer**, made according to Bavarian purity laws, resulting in the excellent Windhoek Lager, Tafel Lager and the premium Windhoek Draught. Namibia Breweries also produces a winter bock beer, Urbock, and several other beers under licence. More recently, it's introduced a range of craft beers. Namibia's desert landscape is not ideal for viticulture, yet amazingly the country possesses a few small **wineries**: the Neuras Winery, now part of the N|a'ankusê Collection (Ⓦ naankusecollection.com; see page 117), 80km (49.7 miles) from Sesriem, which produces several reds; Kristall Kellerei (see page 188) outside Omaruru, which also makes the award-winning Nappa (Namibian grappa) and has a sibling distillery by Naute Dam near Keetmanshoop (see page 147); and Thonningii Wine Cellar (see page 182), in the northern Otavi Mountains, which produces several artisanal wines. Several craft gins are now made in Namibia. Cheaper and more established South African wines are widely available; you can pick up a drinkable bottle of wine for under N$120. Note that alcohol isn't sold after 1pm on Saturdays in either supermarkets or bottle stores (off-licences). Licensing hours are Monday to Friday 9am–5pm, Saturday 9am–1pm. Of course, there are plenty of shebeens selling their own, much cheaper and more potent tipple at any time of day and night: **oshikundu** (made from fermented millet and drunk the same day) or **mataku** (watermelon wine), for example.

Health

Provided you're up to date with vaccinations and take antimalarials if visiting malarial areas, your primary health risks are likely to be dehydration, heatstroke or sunburn due to the intensity of the desert sun. However, travellers' diarrhoea is always possible. These, however, are easily prevented by taking the simple precautions below.

SEASONAL DELICACIES

Namibia has a few standout seasonal delicacies you should take the opportunity to sample. **Kalahari truffles** – known as *|nabba* or *mafumpula* locally – are dug out of the desert sands of eastern Namibia after the rains in April/May and used to flavour sauces and soups. **Omajava** – tasty giant wild mushrooms – are plucked from the bases of termite mounds from late January to March, when they are occasionally available from roadside stalls. Swakopmund **asparagus** (Sept–May) is another favourite, possessing a distinctive flavour due to being grown in brackish water.

For many tourists, the culinary rite of passage is the chance to tuck into a bowl of **mopane worms** (*omagungu* in Oshiwambo), something you are only likely to want to do once. Harvested across northern Namibia (and indeed in other parts of Africa) from February to April, they are the caterpillars of emperor moths that gain their name from the fact they are found in mopane trees. Highly nutritious, they are dried and sold as crispy snacks or cooked in a variety of ways. Still, no amount of frying in onion and tomato can disguise their bulging heads and prickly legs, nor does the knowledge that they are packed with protein make them any easier for the unpractised to swallow.

Should you be unfortunate enough to fall ill or have an accident, you can take heart from the fact that Namibia generally enjoys high-quality private **medical facilities** – though they are only located in the main towns, which could be some distance away. For this reason, you should ensure your medical cover includes emergency evacuation; this is especially important if you intend to travel to any remote parts of the country.

Inoculations

Namibia has no mandatory inoculations, although **tetanus, typhoid and hepatitis A** are typically recommended. In addition to checking online medical resources (see page 64) for further advice, consult a **travel clinic** six to eight weeks before travel to give you time for any jabs or boosters. Clinics often suggest further injections for hepatitis B and maybe even rabies. Still, they are only likely to be of relevance if you intend to spend extended periods living among poor rural communities. In the case of rabies, even if you have the vaccinations, you will still need post-exposure treatment – a series of jabs – in the improbable event of being bitten by a dog or wild animal. Travellers from countries where yellow fever vaccinations are mandatory must be able to produce a yellow fever inoculation certificate. Similarly, if you have come from a yellow fever–prone country like Angola, you may be required to show proof of vaccination upon entry.

Sunstroke and sunburn

The danger of **sunstroke** or **heatstroke** posed by Namibia's intense desert sun cannot be overemphasised. Wherever possible, you should avoid any exertion during the heat of the day, walk in the shade, wear a wide-brimmed hat and cover yourself with sunblock. Shoulders, noses, bald heads and feet (especially if wearing sandals) are particularly prone to **sunburn**. Drink plenty of water and other non-alcoholic drinks to avoid dehydration and keep up your salt intake. It's wise to carry a few rehydration sachets with you on your travels; these are widely available in pharmacies.

Traveller's diarrhoea

That catch-all phrase **traveller's diarrhoea**, which usually results from drinking or eating contaminated food, is not commonly experienced in Namibia, in part because the water most visitors get to drink is of good quality and the amount of street food available in Namibia – usually confined to open markets – is limited. If in doubt, however, follow the tried and tested maxim – if a tad clichéd: peel it, boil it, cook it or forget it. If you do happen to get the runs, dehydration is a more likely risk, so you should ensure you drink plenty of water afterwards, with some of it preferably mixed with rehydration salts, which are readily available at pharmacies.

Malaria

Malaria – transmitted by a parasite in the saliva of an infected female anopheles mosquito – can be fatal if left untreated. **Symptoms** – fever, chills, headaches and muscle pains – are easily confused with flu. Thankfully, only the northern strip of Namibia along the perennial rivers is a year-round high-risk area; other areas, broadly covering the northern third of the country, hold some risk during the rains (Nov/Dec–April/May), when periodically there are areas of stagnant water where mosquitoes can breed.

Malaria is most effectively combated through **prevention** – wearing long loose sleeves and trousers for protection at dawn and dusk, when the mosquitoes are at their most active, dousing yourself in repellent, and sleeping under a mosquito net or in screened rooms. A course of appropriate **prophylactics** – consult a travel clinic – is also strongly advised.

Bites, stings and parasites

Snakes and scorpions may feature heavily in films set in deserts, but in reality, there's very little chance of your seeing one, let alone getting bitten by one, as most scarper at the mere approach of a human. Moreover, the vast majority of snakes in Namibia are not dangerous. Still, it's wise to take precautions: where there are places for snakes to hide, wear long trousers and closed shoes to minimise the risk of getting bitten; carry a torch when walking at night; and if camping, shake your shoes out before putting them on in the morning. If someone is bitten, ensure they don't panic – but don't try to suck or cut out the venom or apply a tourniquet in true Hollywood style; all these measures will do more harm than good. Remember what the snake looked like: keep the infected area immobile, tie a bandage (not too tight) a few centimetres above the area, and seek immediate medical attention.

In the sluggish or slow-moving water areas in the Kavango and Zambezi regions, there's a very low risk of **bilharzia** (schistosomiasis). However, you're unlikely to swim in the rivers due to the greater risk of providing a crocodile with a good meal.

MEDICAL RESOURCES

UK AND IRELAND

Fitfortravel ⓦ fitfortravel.nhs.uk. Excellent NHS (Scotland) public access site with country-specific advice, the latest health bulletins and immunisation information.

Hospital for Tropical Diseases Travel Clinic ⓣ 020 7388 9600 (Travel Clinic), ⓣ 020 7950 7799 (24hr Travellers Healthline Advisory Service). See the website for additional country-specific information (ⓦ thehtd.org).

MASTA (Medical Advisory Service for Travellers Abroad) ⓣ 0870 606 2782, ⓦ masta-travel-health.com. List affiliated travel clinics where you can get vaccinations and detailed country-specific health briefs.

National Travel Health Network and Centre ⓦ nathnac.org. This is an excellent website for health professionals and the travelling public, providing fact sheets on various travel health risks and a free database of country-specific health info.

Tropical Medical Bureau ⓣ 1850 487 674, ⓦ tmb.ie. List of travel clinics in Ireland.

US AND CANADA

Centers for Disease Control and Prevention (CDC) ⓣ 800 232 4636 (24hr health helpline), ⓦ nc.cdc.gov/travel. Official US government travel health site that's laden with info.

Public Health Agency of Canada ⓦ phac-aspc.gc.ca. Distributes free pamphlets on travel health and provides a comprehensive list of travel clinics nationwide.

AUSTRALIA, NEW ZEALAND AND SOUTH AFRICA

Travellers' Medical and Vaccination Centre ⓦ traveldoctor.com.au. User-friendly site listing travel clinics in Australia, New Zealand and South Africa, accessible fact sheets on travel health and postings of health alerts worldwide.

Festivals

Namibia hosts a handful of national and regional festivals.

A FESTIVAL CALENDAR

Bank Windhoek Arts Festival Feb–Sept. Windhoek. The annual visual and performing arts festival in venues across the capital climaxes in September. Includes the national Triennial Visual Arts competition, in which prize-winning works are exhibited.

Enjando Street Festival March. Central Windhoek. Also known as Mbapira, this festival sees a two-day extravaganza of music, dance and colourful costumes, attracting groups from all over Namibia.

|Ae||Gams Cultural Festival April. Zoo Park, Central Windhoek. Focusing on cultural diversity, the festival combines traditional and modern cultural events, involving plenty of music, dance, food and celebration.

Herero Day Sunday closest to 23 Aug. Okahandja. Colourful Herero costumes, poetry and military parades remember those who died in the resistance against the German army.

Küske Karneval Aug. Swakopmund. Annual German street carnival involving parades, food stalls and plenty of partying for adults and kids.

Lusata Festival Last week of Sept. Chinchimani Village, 6km (3.7 miles) from Katima Mulilo. The annual traditional cultural celebration of the Mafwe people takes place in the village of the tribal chief, Chinchimani Village, and attracts Mafwe from outside Namibia, too.

Oruuano of Namibia Arts Festival Sept & Nov. Soweto Market, Katutura. Organised by the Oruuano Namibian Artists' Union, it involves lots of dance and music.

Windhoek Show First week of Oct. Windhoek. The country's leading agricultural and industrial trade fair, accompanied by funfair entertainment, live music and food stalls.

Oktoberfest Last week of Oct. Windhoek. A German import, the Oktoberfest draws an international crowd with beer-swilling, games, lederhosen, dirndl dresses and oompah bands.

Going on safari

Although Namibia isn't a conventional safari destination – Etosha aside – in terms of gazing at herds of wildebeest migrating across the plains, there are several good reasons why it is a top place to head out on safari, especially a self-drive adventure. Roads are generally in good condition and most are suitable for first-time safari-goers; even in high season, there are few crowds – unlike in some of Africa's more renowned wildlife-viewing hotspots; and it's very safe. What's more, it's a great deal of fun. The main drawback is the distances you'll likely cover, the fuel costs involved, and your contribution to CO2 emissions.

Planning your trip

There are various decisions to be made before embarking on a safari adventure regarding whether you drive yourself or travel as part of a group. Should you book accommodation through a travel agent in your home country or Namibia? If money's not a concern, but time is, will you fly in and out of some or all of your destinations? It's also possible to arrange a combination tour, with some organised activities and other self-drive elements, which you can sort out yourself or pay a tour operator to do everything for you.

Three issues you need to be clear on before planning can begin relate to your budget, the time available, and the destinations you want to cover within Namibia. This last issue is particularly relevant if you're going to be driving or be driven everywhere, which in turn has a bearing on the time it will take. Given that lodges and camps have to be vacated by 10am, and check-in is usually not before 3pm, it makes sense to plan for at least two nights, preferably three per destination – providing you with at least one full day – to allow you to make the most of your surroundings and the activities on offer. Otherwise, you may feel you're constantly on the road.

Organised tours

Organised tours take any spontaneity out of the equation but can help reduce the time and stress of planning everything yourself. Larger companies tend to offer set itineraries, generally on specific dates. However, they may also arrange bespoke tours, which many smaller operators specialise in and inevitably cost more. Price primarily relates to the type of accommodation (camping or luxury lodge?), the associated degree of pampering, and the group size. However, the number and quality of the guides is also an important factor. Group tours can be organised through specialist tour operators in your home country, or ones in Namibia, or even South Africa.

If you book through a **company in your own country**, the trip can be more expensive since agencies are covering overheads and wages higher than those in Namibia (unless you're coming from South Africa); moreover, they usually work in tandem with a local operator. On the other hand, a home-based operator may also sort your flights, include better insurance deals in case of cancellation, and you may be able to pay using a credit card or PayPal. Increasingly, lodges are using online booking systems in Namibia, but many operators still do not accept credit cards and demand bank transfers before you arrive in Namibia. This is fine if you're transferring from South Africa (within the Common Monetary Area). No big deal if you're only paying one tour operator – and indeed, it is a good reason for working through an operator rather than planning your itinerary yourself; otherwise, you'll find yourself having to pay for international bank transfers for every night's accommodation or activity that you book, which can be costly. Some lodgings may accommodate you if you write and explain and will hold your credit card details (though they often ask you to email them!) as insurance until you reach the country and can pay cash (from an ATM or bank withdrawal) directly into a bank account or turn up on their doorstep with the required sum.

Self-drive

Bespoke tour operators can also organise self-drive safaris for you; they'll make all the bookings for lodgings and sort your transport and any extras you may want (such as renting camping gear), and, if they are in Namibia, they can meet and greet you at the airport. Self-organised self-drive safaris, on the other hand, offer the greatest flexibility, especially if you decide to equip yourself with a tent. However, you'll still need to make some reservations should you visit during the high season, even if camping. Should remote areas like Kaokoland be on your itinerary, but you are unsure of your self-drive skills and/or travelling alone, you might consider a guided self-drive safari, which some companies offer.

If you decide to drive yourself for at least some of the trip, the next decision concerns whether to rent a two- or a four-wheel drive. Both have pros and

STAYING SAFE ON THE ROAD

Though all rental agencies should give you a full briefing about the vehicle and check that all equipment is present and in working order, some don't, especially the international rental agencies, when handing over a two-wheel drive in high season and staff are stretched. Ensure that you get fully briefed; stories abound of tourists being given vehicles with no **functioning jack** or without being advised not to **travel in the dark**. Make sure you're not one of them.

Check that the car has a jack and one, or preferably two (which you can pre-book at extra cost), **spare wheels** in good condition before you start. Most four-wheel drive rentals should also include a **first-aid kit**, a **shovel** to dig yourself out of sand or mud, and a **tow rope** in case the digging fails. A **tyre pressure gauge and pump** are also essential if you're going to remote areas such as the Kaokoveld or need to deflate (and then reinflate) your tyres after driving through deep sand.

Also, make sure you always travel with plenty of **water and snacks** in case of a long wait for the cavalry to arrive should your vehicle break down.

cons, but your likely itinerary and budget (see page 69) will be determining factors. Also, if you intend to do some camping, you'll need to decide whether you want a roof tent or one you can leave in a campground while driving around.

For novice safari self-drivers, Namibia can provide the easiest initiation as long as you stick to the main roads and sights; even so, there are a few basic rules to follow to ensure you stay safe (see page 65).

Wildlife viewing

Namibia's most famous reserve and the best location for spotting big mammals, including four of the 'Big Five' – which is what many visitors obsess over – is **Etosha National Park**. Here, you stand a good chance of seeing large numbers of animals, especially in the dry season (July–Oct). However, herds of elephants and buffalo are beginning to return to the newer reserves in the Zambezi Region. Namibia also hosts the world's largest cheetah population, and there are several **cheetah conservation projects** that you can visit if you want a near-guaranteed sighting (see page 178). More intriguing, perhaps, and unique to Namibia are the guided excursions into the Namib Desert from Swakopmund that focus on Namibia's 'Small Five' – some of the extraordinary tiny creatures that have adapted to this harsh environment (see page 358).

While seeking out wildlife is likely to be one of your main motivations for visiting Namibia, there may well be times when you need to steer clear or beat a hasty retreat.

Birdwatching

Over 680 species of birds have been recorded in Namibia, including numerous near-endemics, which means the country offers plenty of birdwatching opportunities. Peak times for avian activity are during the **rainy season** (Nov–April) when food is more plentiful and nesting occurs. Migrants from Europe and other parts of Africa generally arrive in October and leave around April. While most of the country is home to desert bird species, **Walvis Bay** hosts Southern Africa's most important coastal wetlands, enjoyed by around 250,000 birds during the migration season (see page 220). Though Walvis Bay is synonymous with flamingos, which constitute the bulk of the population and are visible all year, other waders and seabirds draw birders and casual visitors alike. The freshwater wetlands and rivers of the **Zambezi Region** also provide a wealth of tropical birdlife, from the iconic fish eagle to rainbow-coloured bee-eaters and the extraordinary-looking spoonbill and hammerhead (also hammerkop). Several river lodges here offer birdwatching river trips. Two specialist birding tour operators are based in Swakopmund: Batis Birding Safaris – now part of the Naturalist Collection (W thenaturalistcollection.com) – and Safariwise (W safariwisetours.com); both offer day tours as well as multiday birding trips all around Namibia and further afield.

National parks

National parks and other reserves comprise almost a fifth of Namibia's vast terrain, managed predominantly by the Ministry of the Environment, Forestry and Tourism (MEFT).

While only **Etosha National Park** in the north can claim to host vast quantities of 'big game', Namibia's parks and reserves are famous for their extraordinary **wilderness landscapes**, such as the spectacular dunes around Sossusvlei in what is currently the country's largest protected area, the **Namib-Naukluft National Park** (see page 106), and the inaccessible, eerie coastline of the Skeleton Coast National Park (see page 228), in the northwest. One of the more recent national parks, created in 2009, is the Tsau ||Khaeb – known for many years as the Sperrgebiet; located in the southwest of the country, it was formerly an out-of-bounds diamond-mining area and can currently only be visited on a guided tour from Lüderitz (see page 124). These three major parks are now linked by the Dorob National Park, a relatively open park that includes areas around Swakopmund and Walvis Bay, for which there is no fee. Collectively, these four parks form the **Namib-Skeleton Coast National Park**, extending the entire 1,500km (932-mile) length of Namibia's coastline.

Other major reserves include the dramatic sandstone cliffs of the **Waterberg Plateau Park**, on the road north from Windhoek, and the **|Ai-|Ais/Richtersveld Transfrontier Park**, which extends into South Africa on Namibia's southern border and includes the awe-inspiring Fish River Canyon. We have a full summary of each park's major features and attractions and the types of accommodation available. Downloadable e-brochures on all the flora, fauna and geography of Namibia's main national parks and government-owned reserves are available from the tourist board website (see W namibia-tourism.com.na/page/national-parks).

In addition to the state-managed national parks and reserves, Namibia boasts a wealth of **private reserves** – often called guest farms (see page 59) – and **community-managed conservancies** aimed at combining nature conservation with poverty alleviation initiatives, including many associated with tourism (see pages 60 and 360).

Accommodation and permits

Almost all national park accommodation must be booked through **Namibia Wildlife Resorts** (Ⓦnwr.com.na), either online or in person at one of their offices located in Windhoek (see box, page 94), Swakopmund (see page 213) or in Cape Town, South Africa. Lodgings range from campgrounds (N$100–610/person) to chalets that vary in levels of comfort, sophistication and location, with **prices** to match: from around NS$1,600–12,180 for a double room/chalet, including breakfast. The camp/resort restaurants usually serve à la carte during the day and a fixed-price buffet in the evening (N$150–300), though it depends on visitor numbers. The newer, smaller exclusive camps may provide a limited à-la-carte or set menu.

Chalet prices are significantly lower in the low season (Nov–June), though camping rates remain the same. Children aged 6–12 sharing chalet accommodation with a full fee-paying adult get a 50 percent discount, and children under 6 stay free. There are reductions for Namibians and residents of countries from the Southern African Development Community (SADC). These prices do not include the park/reserve **entry fees**, which go to the MEFT and are usually payable on entry and valid for 24 hours. They currently stand at N$100 per person per day for the more popular parks of Etosha, the |Ai-|Ais/Richtersveld Transfrontier Park, the Skeleton Coast, the Sesriem (Sossusvlei) entrance to Namib-Naukluft and Waterberg, and N$60 per person per day for other reserves, plus N$50 per day for each vehicle. To visit some places, such as parts of the Skeleton Coast and the restricted areas of Namib-Naukluft, you will also need to obtain in advance a special **permit** from the MEFT permit office in Windhoek, Swakopmund or Walvis Bay (see pages 94, 213 and 222). If you are going as part of an organised tour, the tour operator will arrange the permit, which is usually included in the price. Plastic bags have recently been banned in the parks; theoretically, you are liable for a fine of N$500 if you are found to have one in your possession. In practice, vehicles are rarely searched.

Park **activities** such as wildlife-viewing drives, fishing trips, guided walks or boat trips can also be booked through the NWR office. Wildlife drives in Etosha and round the dunes in Namib-Naukluft cost N$650–750 per person, but rates are cheaper in the smaller or less visited parks. Activities, like the accommodation, fill up early in high season, so book in advance for these too.

Sports and outdoor activities

Namibia's dramatic landscapes provide the perfect backdrop to a wealth of outdoor activities, from ballooning across the spectacular dunes of Sossusvlei to hiking down the Fish River Canyon or gazing up at the stars from the darkness of the desert. There's also plenty of scope for extreme sports, such as skydiving, kitesurfing or hauling your body through the desert in an ultramarathon.

Hiking

While the harsh desert terrain does not make for ideal hiking conditions, Namibia offers a few classic **multiday trails**, for which you'll need to be in good physical condition. You will usually need to carry your camping gear, food and water. In addition, several private reserves and guest farms have developed a range of **one-day trails**, some for tourists of more moderate fitness levels.

The most popular hike is the hardcore, five-day, 85km (52.8-mile) hike along the spectacular **Fish River Canyon** (see page 153), which needs a minimum of three people for safety reasons and cannot be done in the extreme heat of summer. Because of the trail's popularity, bookings must be made many months in advance. The rocky terrain of **Naukluft** in central Namibia is also favoured by hikers, offering a variety of trails, some of which can be walked in a day, though others need several days (see page 116).

Though only established in 2015, the six-day Khomas Hochland hiking trail, which covers 91km (56.5 miles) across five guest farms (with a shorter 53km/32.9-mile route over four days), is becoming increasingly popular. It offers fine views of the highlands; what's more, there are ways of easing the endurance pain by slackpacking – having your food, bedding and any other luggage transported from camp to camp for you (Ⓦhikenamibia.com; see page 103). Many of the lodges and guest farms have self-guided trails on their property.

Other favourite places to explore on foot include the private **NamibRand Reserve**, which abuts the Namib-Naukluft National Park, where you can undertake the interpretive three-day guided Tok Tokkie Trail, which offers a desert experience that includes fine dining and camping out under the stars (see page 118). Alternatively, consider ascending Namibia's **Brandberg massif**, which towers 2km (1.2 miles) out of the gravel plains of former Damaraland (see page

193); three- to five-day hikes are available, taking in some of the best-preserved San rock art on the continent, and offering spectacular panoramic views.

Adventure sports

Swakopmund is the country's centre for adventure sports, with several operators offering an increasingly diverse array of activities (see page 214). On land, the action centres on the **dunes**: sand-surfing or sand-boarding are possible, along with more established diversions such as quad biking (see page 214). Skydiving and paragliding are airborne diversions, while the truly fit and masochistic might consider one of Namibia's ultramarathons and other desert challenges that take place in the Namib and elsewhere (see Ⓦ racingtheplanet.com/namibrace and Ⓦ ahotu.com/calendar/running/marathon/namibia).

Watersports

Given Namibia's general lack of water, **watersports** are inevitably restricted to the perennial rivers at the north and south ends of the country and to the coast. **Surfing** and **kitesurfing** are available in Swakopmund and Walvis Bay, though Lüderitz, further south down the coast, has a reputation for **windsurfing** and **kite-boarding** world speed records.

A limited range of **kayaking** opportunities exists. You can paddle about on the Walvis Bay lagoon, where the aim is to get close to the wildlife, particularly the Cape fur seals and the prolific birdlife (see page 222). On the other hand, you can enjoy day and multiday kayaking trips through stunning scenery along the Orange River on the South African border (see page 160). The camps and lodges on the Kunene at Epupa offer seasonal half-day **rafting** trips (see page 260).

Horse riding

Travelling by horseback is a great way to get off the beaten track in the desert without the hum of a four-wheel drive. The experienced international outfit Hidden Trails (Ⓦ hiddentrails.com), which specialises in multiday high-end **horse safaris** worldwide, offers several all-inclusive itineraries in Namibia for experi-

DESERT ECOLOGY AND RESPONSIBLE TRAVEL

Namibia's desert landscape is fragile; it's easy to inflict lasting damage through careless actions. Careering across seemingly desolate dunes on a quad bike can be exhilarating fun, as can charging down the side of a dune, but both actions threaten some of the **desert micro-fauna**, most of which live less than 10cm (3.9in) below the dune surface. The eggs, larvae and young beetles, spiders and reptiles are especially vulnerable on the dune slip face (the steeper incline on the lee side), where these animals concentrate. In particular, you should keep clear of patches of stabilising vegetation. Generally, the least damage is caused by walking up and down the dune's crest.

In Swakopmund and Walvis Bay, most tour operators are responsible and operate within designated areas, aimed at **minimising the impact on the dunes** and employing guides who ensure that sand-boarding is carried out only on specific slopes and that on quad bike tours, everyone follows in the same tracks, on set routes, behind the guide – generally, individuals with bikes and vehicles driving 'off-piste' cause the most damage.

Several companies (notably in Lüderitz) offer off-road wilderness camping adventures through the Namib. Still, before embarking on one, you must satisfy yourself that they are trying to minimise their environmental impact. It is worth asking: what is the maximum number of vehicles they travel in; whether they always follow the same tracks; what they do with their camping waste; and whether they use stoves rather than making fires. A machismo culture among some off-road drivers – evident even in some of the Sandwich Harbour tour drivers – can lead to a more significant environmental footprint than is necessary.

Similarly, when corrugations on some gravel roads become uncomfortable, driving onto the adjacent, often harder, desert crust and making new parallel tracks is very tempting. As well as leaving unsightly marks that can stain the landscape for years, this poses a **threat to birds' nests**, such as those of the endangered Damara tern, and may also destroy **barely discernible lichen** and other plants that have taken hundreds of years to grow, and which provide vital nutrients or shelter for other wildlife. Penetrating the desert crust by off-road driving exposes softer sand and soil to wind erosion.

BALLOONING

There are few more magical experiences than **ballooning across the dunes of the Namib** at dawn, topped off by a champagne breakfast in the desert (N$8,200/person). Although you'll only be in the air for around an hour, you'll need to set aside a large chunk of the morning once pick-ups and preparation time have been factored in. Ballooning is available at Sossusvlei and Swakopmund (see page 113).

enced, fit riders. The Namibia Horse Safari Company (Ⓦ namibiahorsesafari.com) in Aus, southern Namibia, also organises all-inclusive ten- to eleven-day horse safaris for fit intermediate and experienced riders through the Namib along the Fish River Canyon and in Damaraland.

Catering for riders of all abilities and those who wish to spend less time in the saddle, several Namib-Naukluft National Park and adjacent NamibRand Reserve lodges offer popular **sunrise and sunset rides**. For example, check out the *Desert Homestead Lodge* (Ⓦ ondili.com). In the Eros Mountains, and accessible from Windhoek, Namibia-based Equitrails (Ⓦ equitrails.org; see box, page 102) caters to riders of all abilities offering a range of less pricey **tours**, from a couple of hours to a couple of days in the saddle, overnighting on a guest farm. Okakambe Trails (Ⓦ okakambe.iway.na; see page 214) in Swakopmund also has a varied equestrian menu, from short rides into the Swakop riverbed and the moon landscape to overnight horse safaris of one or two nights, covering 20–30km (12.4–18.6 miles) per day and sleeping in tented camps.

Stargazing

Thanks to a low population density, low air pollution and virtually non-existent light pollution, the pitch-black sky above Namibia's desert landscape is one of the top places in the world for stargazing, especially in the dry winter months. Though almost anywhere away from the few urban areas can provide you with a glittering night sky and opportunities to marvel at the Milky Way, for prime viewing, head for the **Gamsberg Mountains** around 100km (62.1 miles) southwest of Windhoek, where the Hakos Guest Farm (Ⓦ hakos-astrofarm.com; see page 234) specialises in astrotourism. Kiripotib Guest Farm (Ⓦ kiripotib.com; see page 163) is another magnet for astronomers or would-be astronomers, while top of the pile sits the **NamibRand Reserve** – Africa's first **International Dark Sky Reserve**. The most luxurious accommodation here, *Sossusvlei Desert Lodge*, has its own telescope and resident astronomer for guests (see page 118).

Travel essentials

Costs

Given the favourable exchange rates, if you're travelling from Europe or North America, costs in Namibia may not seem that high. On the other hand, expenses can add up with limited public transport, vast distances between sights, and only a small number of budget lodgings available. With a combination of hitchhiking and public transport, staying only in budget hostels campgrounds and cooking your meals, you can probably get by on N$1,200 per person per day; add an extra N$700–1,000 per person for an excursion or activity. Staying in mid-range lodge accommodation in a shared room on a dinner, bed and breakfast basis, which is the norm, can mean a daily food and lodging budget from around N$1,500–2,500 per person sharing, with park fees, car rental costs and fuel on top. Four-wheel drive rental will cost double, and if you fancy the exclusive, high-end accommodation near Sossusvlei or the Skeleton Coast, where you're not necessarily paying for traditional hotel luxury – marble bathrooms, infinity pools and high thread counts – but for remote wilderness and/or incredible wildlife experiences, you can be paying from around N$10,000 to 24,000 per person per day for full board, activities and park fees in high season.

Crime and personal safety

Namibia is an extremely **safe** country to travel around, even on your own, though **petty crime** is increasing in Windhoek and some of the larger towns. That said, being street-savvy goes a long way towards avoiding problems: not wearing expensive jewellery or watches, not opening your bag or wallet to get cash out in a public place, and always making sure your **car** is locked, the windows are closed, and your belongings are out of sight when you stop in towns or at petrol stations. If you have to leave your car for a time, and there is no guarded, secure car park available, it pays to park in front of a shop or bank, where there will be a security guard whom you can ask (and tip on your return) to keep an eye on your vehicle. Remember, if you get robbed, you will need a police report to complete an insurance claim once you get home.

Culture and etiquette

Greetings are key to ensuring good social relations in Namibia, as in many parts of Africa. Before you ask a question or a favour, you should always greet the person and enquire about their health. If you can manage that in the relevant local language (see page 365), then so much the better. Handshakes are the most common greeting, especially among men, and always with the right hand. Men will often use the three-part African handshake when greeting other men. Women are more likely to greet each other and men with words, though they may shake hands. If in a more traditional rural setting, the junior may give a slight nod, bow or curtsy to acknowledge seniority.

Modest **dress** is also important, especially when visiting rural areas – often dominated by Christian conservatism. In the extreme heat, you may be tempted to strip down to the bare essentials, but bear in mind that while short, skimpy attire is acceptable for the beach, it can offend in villages. Generally, men wear long trousers and shirts while women wear something covering their shoulders and knees.

While on the subject of village life, if offered something to **drink or eat**, you should always accept the offer. When eating with your hands, often in rural communities, you should eat with your right hand, even if left-handed, as the left hand is considered unclean.

Photography is a thorny area that has been poorly handled by many tourists over the years, especially regarding the Himba, Herero and the San, where taking photos tends to dominate interactions to a worrying extent. The crass behaviour of some tourists who snap away without permission of the individuals concerned and with minimal interaction with them has led to difficult relations between some Namibian communities and tourists. Some Himba and Herero women, in particular, are now demanding payment for having their photos taken. Always ask permission to take a picture only after interacting meaningfully with the person or people concerned.

Electricity

Electricity is **220 volts** in Namibia, and large three-pin round plugs are used, as in South Africa. You're advised to bring an adaptor for sale in Johannesburg airport and Windhoek, but it's hard to come by elsewhere in Namibia.

Insurance

Full insurance for flights, medical emergencies and personal possessions is highly recommended. Make sure it covers any adventure sports you might want to do. If you intend to rent a car, consider taking out a standalone car rental excess insurance policy since this can work out cheaper than the additional fees charged by car rental firms to reduce the excess payable in case of an accident.

Internet

Finding somewhere to access the internet will seldom be a problem in Namibia, even in remote areas. However, connections are often slow in many parts of the country, and the service is unreliable. A few **internet cafés** exist in Windhoek and Swakopmund – expect to pay around N$30/hour – and many hotels and hostels nationwide have a PC or two available for guest use. However, in most accommodations, as well as in shopping malls and cafés, **wi-fi** is a more common means of getting online. In lodges, wi-fi is usually confined to the main building, and – understandably, given their remoteness – the signal strength is generally relatively weak.

Laundry

You'll find launderettes and dry cleaners in Windhoek and the larger towns. In addition, most hotels, lodges and guesthouses offer a laundry service, though this is more expensive. Water is an incredibly precious resource in Namibia, so try to minimise your laundry.

LGBTQ+ Travellers

Sexual relations between men are illegal in Namibia, and its attitude towards LBGTQ+ rights is generally one of intolerance. LGBTQ+ travellers can enjoy a hassle-free holiday in Namibia, provided they are discreet about their sexuality. Consult JJ Tours in Kamanjab (W namibiajjtours.com) for advice, or Out2Africa (W out2africa.com), which specialises in luxury tours for LGBTQ+ travellers across Africa, including to Namibia.

Maps

A range of **maps**, updated every few years, is widely available in specialist map shops and online in Europe and the US. The bookshops in Windhoek and Swakopmund also stock a selection. The Namibian Tourist Board and most tour operators can supply you with the annually updated Roads Authority

ROUGH GUIDES TRAVEL INSURANCE

Looking for travel insurance? Rough Guides partners with top providers worldwide to offer you the best coverage. Policies are available to residents of anywhere in the world, with a range of options whether you are looking for single-trip, multi-country or long-stay insurance. There's coverage for a wide range of adventure sports, 24-hour emergency assistance, high levels of medical and evacuation cover and a stream of travel safety information. Even better, roughguides.com users can take advantage of these policies online 24/7, from anywhere in the world – even if you're already travelling. To make the most of your travels and ensure a smoother experience, it's always good to be prepared for when things don't go according to plan. For more information go to Ⓦ roughguides.com/bookings/insurance.

Map of Namibia, which also has details of many campgrounds but is not very useful. Better quality, however, is the **Reise Know-How map**, which is easy to read and includes almost all lodges, guest farms and registered campgrounds, community or private, as well as marking petrol stations. This map alone is adequate for most self-drive visitors. If you're intending to go off the beaten track, on the other hand, then the downloadable **Tracks4Africa GPS map** – which only works for Garmin GPS – and their new paper map should be high on your shopping list (Ⓦ tracks4africa.com). You can download it in advance or purchase the software in Namibia somewhere, like Radio Electronic (Ⓦ re.com.na).

Media

There is generally a high level of press freedom in Namibia, particularly in the print media. The country's top **newspaper**, both in quality and circulation, is the mainly English-language (with some content in Oshiwambo) daily *The Namibian* (Ⓦ namibian.com.na). *The New Era* is the state-owned daily paper. Several other dailies exist, including ones in Afrikaans and German, as well as several weekly papers and monthly magazines. There are over twenty private and community-owned **radio stations** and ten channels in different languages, operated by the government-owned Namibian Broadcasting Corporation (NBC). Many guesthouses, hotels and lodges pay for the DStv satellite package, which is based in South Africa and predominantly offers a diet of South African and US channels.

Money

The **Namibian dollar** (N$), often abbreviated to 'Nam dollar' in common parlance, has been the official currency since 1993. Coins are produced for 5, 10 and 50 cents, and 1, 5 and 10 Namibian dollars. Notes are available in N$10, 20, 50, 100 and 200 denominations. Until 2012, the notes exclusively featured Hendrik Witbooi (see page 340). Then, in 2012, a series of more fraud-secure notes was introduced, featuring the post-independence president, Sam Nujoma, on the ten- and twenty-dollar bills.

To add to the currency confusion, the South African rand was the official currency before independence. Since the Namibian dollar is still pegged to the rand (1:1), it is still accepted as legal tender in the country. If you're withdrawing money near the end of your trip or travelling elsewhere, it's better to ask for South African rands rather than Namibian dollars, as they're easier to exchange in other countries.

Changing money at a bank is relatively quick and painless, except at the end of the month, when queues can be substantial. The main **banks** in Namibia are South African Nedbank, Standard Bank, First National Bank (FNB) and Bank Windhoek, which has 53 branches countrywide. Banking hours are usually Monday to Friday, 8.30am to 3.30pm and Saturday, 8.30am to noon. At the time of writing, the **exchange rates** were approximately N$24 to £1, N$19 to US$1 and N$21 to €1.

Credit and debit cards are widely used to pay for goods and services in Windhoek and the major towns, especially Visa and MasterCard – American Express is less readily accepted. Credit cards are also generally accepted for mid- and high-end accommodation payments. Although paying by credit card is becoming more widespread, several petrol stations only accept cash. Thankfully, petrol stations often have an ATM on the premises.

Though widespread in more remote areas, **ATMs** are sometimes out of order or run out of cash, especially at the end of the month or before public holidays. The

EMERGENCY NUMBERS

Police emergency Ⓣ 10111
Namibian Tourist Protection Unit Ⓣ 061 2094345

daily withdrawal limit varies widely between N$3,000–5,000. You will need cash in the more rural areas; make sure you carry some smaller denominations.

10 December International Human Rights Day
25 December Christmas Day
26 December Family Day

Opening hours and public holidays

Shops usually open at 9am, closing around 5.30pm. They also often close for lunch and shut down for the weekend at 1pm on Saturdays. Supermarkets tend to open earlier (7–8am) and remain open until 7–8pm Monday to Friday; they may operate reduced trading hours on Saturday and Sunday, though some remain closed on Sunday. **Government offices** are open Monday to Friday, 8am–5pm, often taking a lunch hour at 1pm.

Namibia doesn't have many **public holidays**; if the date falls on a Sunday, the holiday is usually held on the following Monday. During these days, most government offices, businesses and shops close. Many businesses and government departments also effectively close from mid-December to mid-January for the summer holidays.

PUBLIC HOLIDAYS

1 January New Year's Day
21 March Independence Day
March/April Good Friday and Easter Monday
1 May Workers Day
4 May Cassinga Day. Commemorates the attack on a SWAPO base in Angola by the SADF in 1978, which killed six hundred.
May/June Ascension Day
26 May Africa Day. Remembers the foundation of the Organisation of African Unity (OAU) in 1963.
26 August Heroes' Day. The UN recognised Namibia Day, commemorating the official start of the War of Independence in 1966.

Phones

Since **mobile phones** are increasingly more popular than landlines – and indeed the only form of communication in many rural areas – you may want to bring your mobile phone and purchase a Namibian SIM card (N$10) on arrival. These are available at the international airport and various Independence Avenue locations in Windhoek, and you can buy credit with pay-as-you-go cards. Old unlocked mobile phones work best if you just want a phone rather than internet connectivity. If your phone is locked, you will need to pay a standard charge of around N$250 to have it unlocked, a process that usually takes 24 hours. The mobile provider with the greatest coverage is MTC; see their website (Ⓦ mtc.com.na) for the various smartphone packages. However, since in many remote areas, there is no coverage at all, you might want to rent a satellite phone (from around NS$80/day or N$500/week plus call charges), which can be done at Radio Electronic (Ⓦ re.com.na) or through your car-rental agency, with advance notice.

To **call Namibia from abroad**, dial the international access code for the country you're in, followed by the country code 264. Note that mobile phone numbers in Namibia are ten digits, beginning with 081.

Post

Across the country, there are over 130 **post offices** run by NamPost. Their smart, modern exteriors belie a somewhat less than efficient service: while fairly

HERERO DAY

On the weekend closest to 23 August, **Herero Day** or **Red Flag Heroes' Day** (not to be confused with the national Heroes' Day), Herero gather in their thousands in Okahandja to commemorate their deceased chiefs and, in particular, **Chief Samuel Maharero**, who led the revolt against the German colonial army. The chosen date coincides with the reburial of his remains here, following his death in 1923 in South Africa, where he'd been living in exile (see page 341). Since then, Herero has congregated annually for a three-day gathering, culminating in a **procession** around various grave sites of Herero chiefs, followed by a church service. This homage to the dead, which has since become a symbol of resistance against colonialism, is an impressive sight, with the Herero women decked out in their voluminous crimson missionary-era dresses and 'cow-horn' headgear, and the men marching in their military-style uniforms according to their paramilitary regiments. Followers of other flags meet at other times of the year in different locations; for example, the White Flag Herero gather in Omaruru in August (see page 188). The Green Flag Mbanderu (see page 352) meet in Okahandja on the weekend nearest 11 June.

reliable for non-valuable objects, the system is pretty slow, although they also operate a courier service. Hours are generally Monday to Friday, 8am–4.30pm, Saturday 8am–noon. FedEx (Ⓦfedex.com/na) and DHL (Ⓦdhl.com.en/na) have offices in Windhoek, Swakopmund, Walvis Bay and Lüderitz.

Shopping

Shopping for most visitors to Namibia revolves around **crafts and curios**. The main area of production is in the north, so if you are travelling to the Kunene, Kavango and Zambezi regions, you might want to wait until then to buy (see pages 286 and 324), especially since more of the money is likely to go to the artisan. Note that several shops sell crafts imported from South Africa and elsewhere; the ubiquitous Namcrafts, for example, with several outlets in the capital, has 'Namcraft' labels on all its products, though they are not necessarily from Namibia. So, if the origin is important to you, make thorough enquiries before purchasing.

There is no shortage of places to look for crafts, both in the street, where you can bargain and in shops where you can't. The main craft shops are in Windhoek and Swakopmund, and there are two large craft markets in Okahandja (see page 171). The selections, however, are often quite samey: soapstone figures and wooden carvings, particularly of animals; jewellery made from seeds, beads and shells; and batik cloth and cushion covers, again with animal designs aplenty. Namibia is also renowned for its semi-precious **stones and crystals**, but you'll not find many bargains. Still, the Kristall Galerie in Swakopmund (Ⓦnamibiangemstones.com; see page 211) is a good place to garner information, or, if you want to make sure the money is benefiting the local community, try one of the Spitzkoppe roadside stalls, selling uncut gemstones.

Time

Namibia is usually GMT+2hr, but from the first Sunday in September to the first Sunday in April, Namibia is GMT+1, known as Daylight Saving Time (DST).

Tipping

Tipping is always tricky, and the best advice is to ask locally. There is no culture of automatic tipping in **restaurants**, although, for formal establishments, 10 percent of the total bill is the norm if the service is decent. For **porters** at airports or hotels, expect to pay N$5 per bag. Similarly, N$5–10 would suffice for the **petrol pump attendant** who fills your vehicle if they clean your windows, check oil, tyres, etc, and for anyone you ask to watch over your car for a few hours while you're parked in town.

If staying in a **lodge** for several days, only tip at the end – seek advice about what constitutes a fair tip; it will depend to an extent on whether the camp/lodge is budget or high-end and how many people are attached to one guide. Generally, it should not be more than US$10/day per person in a small group. Enquire whether there are communal tip boxes for the behind-the-scenes staff, many of whom get paid far less than the more high-profile guide. Many lodges pay meagre wages and presume that tips make up the shortfall. The only way to exert pressure and change this behaviour is to complain to the management and/or give feedback online. Many tourists tip their guide if they have been accommodating and informative.

Remember that **overtipping** is not helpful: it sets a precedent that other travellers may not be able to live up to; it can create professional jealousy among workers and upset the micro-economy, especially in poor, rural communities.

CALLING HOME FROM NAMIBIA

To make an international call, dial the international access code (in Namibia, it's 00), then the destination's country code before the rest of the number. The initial zero is omitted from the area code when dialling the UK, Ireland, Australia and New Zealand from abroad.

UK international access code + 44
Ireland international access code + 353
US and Canada international access code + 1
Australia international access code + 61
New Zealand international access code + 64
South Africa international access code + 27

Tourist information

The **Windhoek tourist office** is located on the ground floor of the city's municipal building on the corner of Independence Avenue and Sam Nujoma Drive. It can provide you with basic information about Windhoek and a map and tourist maps for other parts of the country. The National Tourist Board also operates a useful, up-to-date website (Ⓦvisitnam-

USEFUL WEBSITES

Useful websites to help you plan your trip include the following:

Communal Conservancies Ⓦ conservationtourism.com.na. Comprehensive info on conservancies' involvement in tourism with useful maps and listings of community campgrounds and activities.

Ⓦ **namibian.org**. Gondwana owns the website, so the emphasis is on its services. However, other accommodation options do feature, and it's helpful when planning your safari. It also links with Gondwana's other info platform, Ⓦ safari2go.travel.

Namibia Tourist Board Ⓦ visitnamibia.com.na. Updated in 2023, this excellent website offers a wealth of information on various topics, from national parks to activities, museums to border opening hours, and a helpful page on some community-based tourism ventures.

Open Africa Ⓦ openafrica.org. Useful site promoting locally owned accommodation, restaurants, shops, attractions and other businesses in nine Southern African countries.

Safari Bookings Ⓦ safaribookings.com/namibia. This site is dedicated to safaris in Africa, giving user reviews and the opinions of an expert panel of writers on tours, tour operators and national parks.

Travel News Namibia Ⓦ venture.com.na/travel-news-namibia1.com. Glossy online magazine produced quarterly, consisting of short articles and many impressive photos covering most of the main sights and some more intriguing, less publicised, activities and places.

ibia.com.na). In other towns, tourist information is provided privately, often by tour operators. Many hostels and guesthouses can also help with information and make bookings.

Travellers with disabilities

Travellers with **visual, hearing or mobility impairments**, including wheelchair users and 'senior travellers', are well catered for by Endeavour Safaris (Ⓦ endeavour-safaris.com), a company based in Botswana, offering a range of safaris in Namibia, Botswana and South Africa. UK company Responsible Travel (Ⓦ responsibletravel.com) offers accessible holidays to Namibia. Independent wheelchair travellers should note that many hotels and lodges, including NWR properties in the national parks, have wheelchair-adapted rooms and bathrooms. A list of wheelchair-accessible accommodation in Namibia's major towns can be found on the website of Disabled Holidays (Ⓦ disabledholidays.com), which also offers a Namibia holiday package.

Travelling with children

Travelling with children is relatively straightforward in Namibia, provided they can cope with many hours of travel between sights. Many **lodgings** offer discounts for children under 12, usually giving a 50 percent reduction for youngsters aged 6–12, with children under 6 staying for free. Some smaller, more exclusive lodges that build their reputation on offering peace and tranquillity do not accept children under 12. **Restaurants** often have kids' menus. When it comes to **activities**, there's plenty to entertain kids, especially on the coast, from kayaking to sandboarding. Children under a certain age (or height when it comes to ballooning) are often discouraged from participating in some activities. Still, with parental consent and supervision, this can also be waived.

If you're travelling with a baby, it makes sense to carry it around in a baby sling rather than a pushchair, given the lack of pavements or even paved roads outside the main streets of the principal towns, never mind the countryside. Baby care products, such as bottled baby food and disposable nappies, are available in the main towns, but bear in mind that when you're camping in the bush, you'll need to transport the used ones with you until you reach a place where they can be disposed of properly. Breastfeeding in public is socially acceptable in Namibia, though the prevalence of breastfeeding babies in Namibia has decreased in recent years due to fears of mother-to-child HIV transmission.

Volunteering

Voluntourism is a growing industry and is becoming a preferred way of travelling for those who want to 'make a difference'. Be aware that this can be fraught with pitfalls for the volunteer and – in the case of social development projects – the people being 'helped'. A good place to start is Ⓦ ifrevolunteering.org, which has a useful webpage on ethical volunteering. Getting feedback from former volunteers is also helpful.

In Namibia, the focus is often on **conservation**, with volunteer programmes concerning cheetah, desert-adapted elephant or rhino conservation – sometimes involving scientific research – and at animal welfare sanctuaries. There is stiff competition for high-profile organisations like the Cheetah Conservation Fund (Ⓦ cheetah.org; see page 178).

Generally, you have to pay for your flight to Namibia, transport to and from the location and board and lodging once there; conversely, if volunteering on a guest farm or a private reserve, you might have your board and accommodation paid for in return for services. In this case, you need to be assured that you will not be exploited in terms of working hours and time off, nor that you are taking the job a paid local Namibian could be doing if the owner were only willing to spend the money.

Almost invariably, the volunteer gets more out of the experience than the people they are there to support. If you are contemplating becoming involved in community development, consider whether you have the appropriate skills for the job; what Namibia – like other African countries – does not need is unskilled labour constructing buildings or untrained teachers in schools. Also, if you want to make a difference working with people, then you should think about committing to several months, at least, rather than several weeks, especially if the job involves interacting with vulnerable people, such as young children, for whom a constant relay of changing volunteers can be very disruptive. Several websites list volunteer projects in Namibia, which you should submit to scrutiny. They include Go Overseas (Ⓦ gooverseas.com/volunteer-abroad/Namibia) and Go Abroad (Ⓦ goabroad.com), including reviews from former volunteers.

Windhoek and around

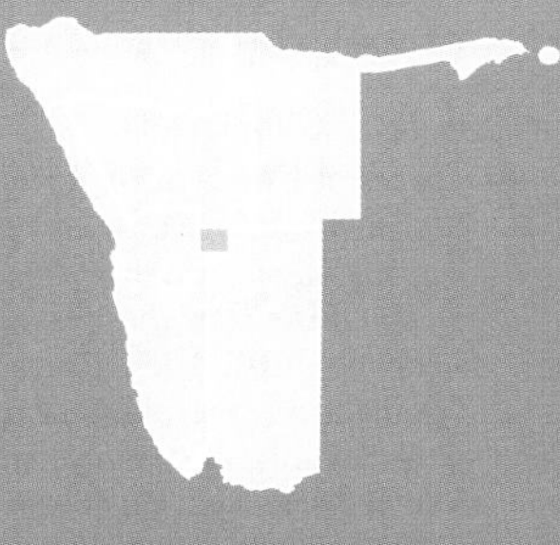

THE TINTENPALAST

1

Windhoek and around

Nestled among rolling hills in a valley created by the sloping Khomas Hochland Plateau to the west and the Auas Mountains to the east, Namibia's capital, Windhoek, is scenically situated. At an altitude of almost 1,700m (5,577ft), the city avoids the excessive heat experienced in much of the country, with daytime temperatures rarely topping 30°C in summer or dipping under 10°C in winter. Moreover, whether due to meticulous German planning or luck, Windhoek lies almost in the centre of the country, making it the perfect starting point for any tour of Namibia.

Strolling down Independence Avenue, Windhoek **city centre**'s orderly tree-lined main boulevard, it's easy to forget you're in Africa. Its tidy, clean pavements, dotted with German colonial architecture, lack the frenetic and chaotic pace and horn-honking mayhem more readily associated with African capital cities. This is a city striving for modernity, keen to shrug off its small-town image and colonial past: new high-rise buildings now pierce the CBD skyline, and brash multimillion-dollar post-independence constructions, such as the new State House and Heroes' Acre, dominate the surrounding hillsides.

Windhoek is somewhat short on sights beyond a few modest museums; however, a wander around the National Botanical Gardens in the **suburbs** and a day's outing **beyond Windhoek** to the attractive surroundings of Daan Viljoen Game Park – Namibia's smallest reserve – will whet your appetite for some of the extraordinary landscapes and wildlife that await. Windhoek's comfortable guesthouses and handful of pleasant alfresco dining options make it an agreeable environment to spend a couple of days getting your bearings at the start of a trip – as well as stocking up on supplies – or unwinding at the end of a hectic safari.

Brief history

The 5,000-year-old archaeological remains of elephants and hunting implements found in central Windhoek prove that the city's hot springs played host to hunter-gatherers. However, the first recorded settlement – established by **Kaptein Jonker Afrikaner** of the Oorlam (see page 339) – dates to 1840. At that time, Windhoek was known as |Ae||Gams – 'fire water' in Nama – and Otjomuise – 'place of steam' in Otjiherero; both names highlight the importance of the springs to the future capital's location and development. The origin of the name Windhoek is more of a mystery, either recalling the Winterhoek Mountains in South Africa, home to Jonker's ancestors, or a corruption of the Afrikaans for 'windy corner'. Either way, the name stuck, whereas the settlement did not – at least not initially, as the ongoing conflict between the Nama, whom Jonker was leading, and the Herero more or less destroyed the place.

German colonial rule

The establishment of colonial rule in Windhoek came in 1890, six years after German South-West Africa had been claimed as a protectorate, when **Major Curt von François**, leading the German Imperial army, laid the cornerstone of the Alte Feste (Old Fort), establishing it as the headquarters for the Schutztruppe (German colonial troops; see page 340). The chosen location served as a strategic buffer between the warring Nama and Herero and was ideal for agriculture because of the natural springs.
After an initially slow start, the influx of German colonists from both Europe and South Africa was given greater impetus when the Swakopmund–Windhoek railway track was completed in 1902, and some of the colony's main buildings, such as the

JOE'S BEERHOUSE

Highlights

❶ **Old Breweries Complex** This all-in-one destination boasts the Warehouse Theatre, the city's best arts venue, and the Namibia Craft Centre, the top spot for souvenir shopping and an excellent place for a light lunch. See page 84

❷ **Parliament Gardens** Take a lunchtime stroll in this leafy spot, which offers shady lawns, landscaped gardens and even a manicured bowling green. See page 87

❸ **National Earth Science Museum** Fascinating fossils and glistening semi-precious minerals are well displayed in this small but informative museum. See page 92

❹ **Sundowner with a view** Sip a cocktail on a terrace bar as you soak up the sweeping cityscape and surroundings; try the hotels *Heinitzburg* and *Thule* or *Nimms* restaurant. See pages 96 and 99

❺ **Joe's Beerhouse** Offering good vibes, good food and plenty to drink, this Windhoek institution draws tourists and Namibians alike. See page 98

❻ **Daan Viljoen Game Park** Only a twenty-minute drive from the city centre, amid rolling hills, this peaceful spot is ideal for a gentle hike, birdwatching or a picnic. See page 101

HIGHLIGHTS ARE MARKED ON THE MAPS ON PAGES 80 AND 82

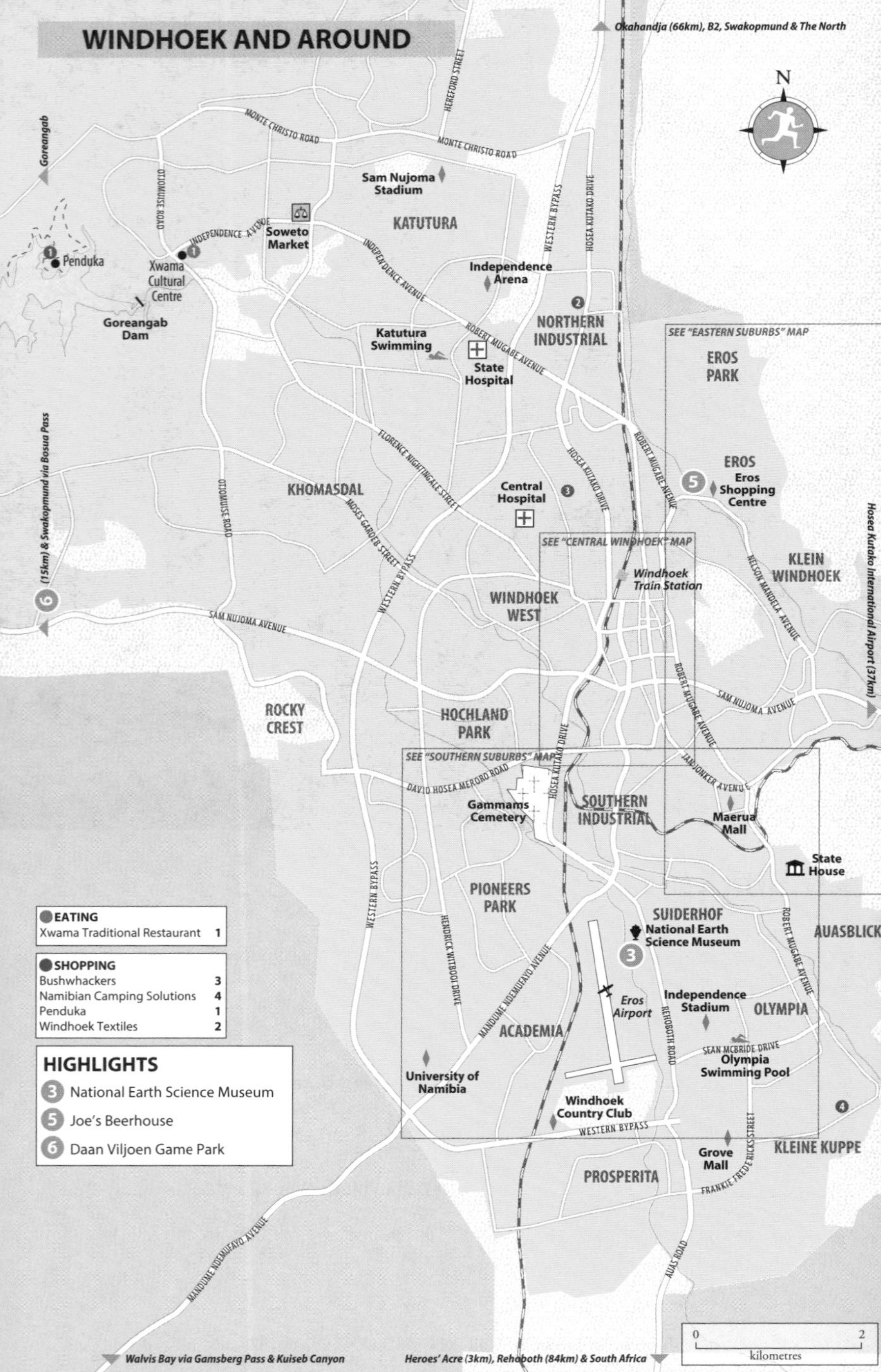
WINDHOEK AND AROUND
Okahandja (66km), B2, Swakopmund & The North
N
Goreangab
Penduka
Xwama Cultural Centre
Goreangab Dam
Soweto Market
Sam Nujoma Stadium
KATUTURA
Independence Arena
NORTHERN INDUSTRIAL
Katutura Swimming
State Hospital
SEE "EASTERN SUBURBS" MAP
EROS PARK
EROS
Eros Shopping Centre
KHOMASDAL
Central Hospital
SEE "CENTRAL WINDHOEK" MAP
Windhoek Train Station
KLEIN WINDHOEK
Hosea Kutako International Airport (37km)
(15km) & Swakopmund via Bosua Pass
WINDHOEK WEST
ROCKY CREST
HOCHLAND PARK
SEE "SOUTHERN SUBURBS" MAP
Gammams Cemetery
SOUTHERN INDUSTRIAL
Maerua Mall
State House
PIONEERS PARK
SUIDERHOF
National Earth Science Museum
AUASBLICK
Eros Airport
Independence Stadium
OLYMPIA
ACADEMIA
Olympia Swimming Pool
University of Namibia
Windhoek Country Club
Grove Mall
KLEINE KUPPE
PROSPERITA
MONTE CHRISTO ROAD
HEREFORD STREET
OTJOMUISE ROAD
INDEPENDENCE AVENUE
WESTERN BYPASS
HOSEA KUTAKO DRIVE
ROBERT MUGABE AVENUE
FLORENCE NIGHTINGALE STREET
MOSES GAROEB STREET
NELSON MANDELA AVENUE
SAM NUJOMA AVENUE
JAN JONKER AVENUE
DAVID HOSEA MERORO ROAD
HENDRICK WITBOOI DRIVE
MANDUME NDEMUFAYO AVENUE
REHOBOTH ROAD
SEAN MCBRIDE DRIVE
FRANKIE FREDERICKS STREET
AUAS ROAD
Walvis Bay via Gamsberg Pass & Kuiseb Canyon
Heroes' Acre (3km), Rehoboth (84km) & South Africa
0
2
kilometres
EATING
Xwama Traditional Restaurant 1
SHOPPING
Bushwhackers 3
Namibian Camping Solutions 4
Penduka 1
Windhoek Textiles 2
HIGHLIGHTS
3 National Earth Science Museum
5 Joe's Beerhouse
6 Daan Viljoen Game Park

Christuskirche and the Tintenpalast, were erected. Businesses were established and small-scale farming took root. By 1909, when Windhoek finally became a municipality, the population topped 2,700. Indigenous peoples were gradually pushed to the margins to serve the colonists' interests or were driven away altogether.

South African rule

German rule ended abruptly with defeat in World War I. Black populations were forced to exchange one colonial power for another as the South African military moved in to rule on behalf of Britain. Periods of growth followed, especially after World War II. The next seismic shift in Windhoek's development occurred in the late 1950s and 1960s as South Africa began to impose **apartheid** policies of segregation and surveillance, forcibly removing large swathes of non-white residents to townships (see page 342).

Post-independence

Despite the post-independence dismantlement of the apartheid state in 1990 and the reclassification of the former townships as 'suburbs', the capital's racial and socio-economic divisions persist. In the years since independence, **migration** to the capital has intensified, with bulging informal settlements or 'shanty towns' proliferating on the periphery, especially around Katutura. These are stark reminders to the municipality and the central government of the ongoing challenge of addressing the city's swelling population – currently estimated to be approaching half a million – and its continuing inequalities.

GETTING ORIENTED IN WINDHOEK

Given its diminutive size, Windhoek is more confusing to drive around than it should be. This is mainly due to its rolling hills and dispersed residential areas – largely a hangover from successive colonial governments' urban planning. On the plus side, however, streets are well signposted; although most have been renamed since independence, some residents occasionally refer to the old names. The city's main arteries run broadly parallel from north to south: Namibia's principal highway, the **B1** – which stretches 1,500km (932 miles) between the South African and Angolan borders – becomes **Auas Road** as it approaches from the south, passing Eros Airport (the small domestic airport), and then Hosea Kutako Drive as it enters the city. Peeling off to the west, just south of the airport, the aptly named **Western Bypass** circumvents the city, continuing the apartheid-era separation of the former non-white townships of Khomasdal and Katutura from the rest of the city, before the two main roads rejoin, north of Windhoek. Two other major north/south roads to get a handle on are **Robert Mugabe Avenue**, which undulates along the eastern flank of the city, and **Mandume Ndemufayo Avenue**, which starts in the town centre and heads southwest, through the Southern Industrial Area (where several vehicle rental companies are located), to emerge as the **C26**, the back road to Walvis Bay. The main highway on the east-west axis is **Sam Nujoma Drive**: eastwards it heads out through the Klein Windhoek Valley and on to Hosea Kutako International Airport – where all international flights arrive – Gobabis and the Botswana border, as the **B6**; to the west it skirts Khomasdal and becomes the **C28**, the back road to Swakopmund, passing the Dan Viljoen Game Park.

The **city centre**, however, consists of little more than a kilometre of **Independence Avenue** and a block or two on either side, which can easily be explored on foot. Independence Avenue continues northwards to the former Black township of **Katutura**, crossing Hosea Kutako Drive and the Western Bypass en route. Most accommodation and restaurants lie in Klein Windhoek – along or just off Sam Nujoma Drive and Nelson Mandela Avenue – and the other eastern suburbs, with a sprinkling of restaurants in the city centre. Some cheaper lodgings are to be found in Windhoek West and Pioneers Park (also Pionierspark), to the south, beyond Eros Airport.

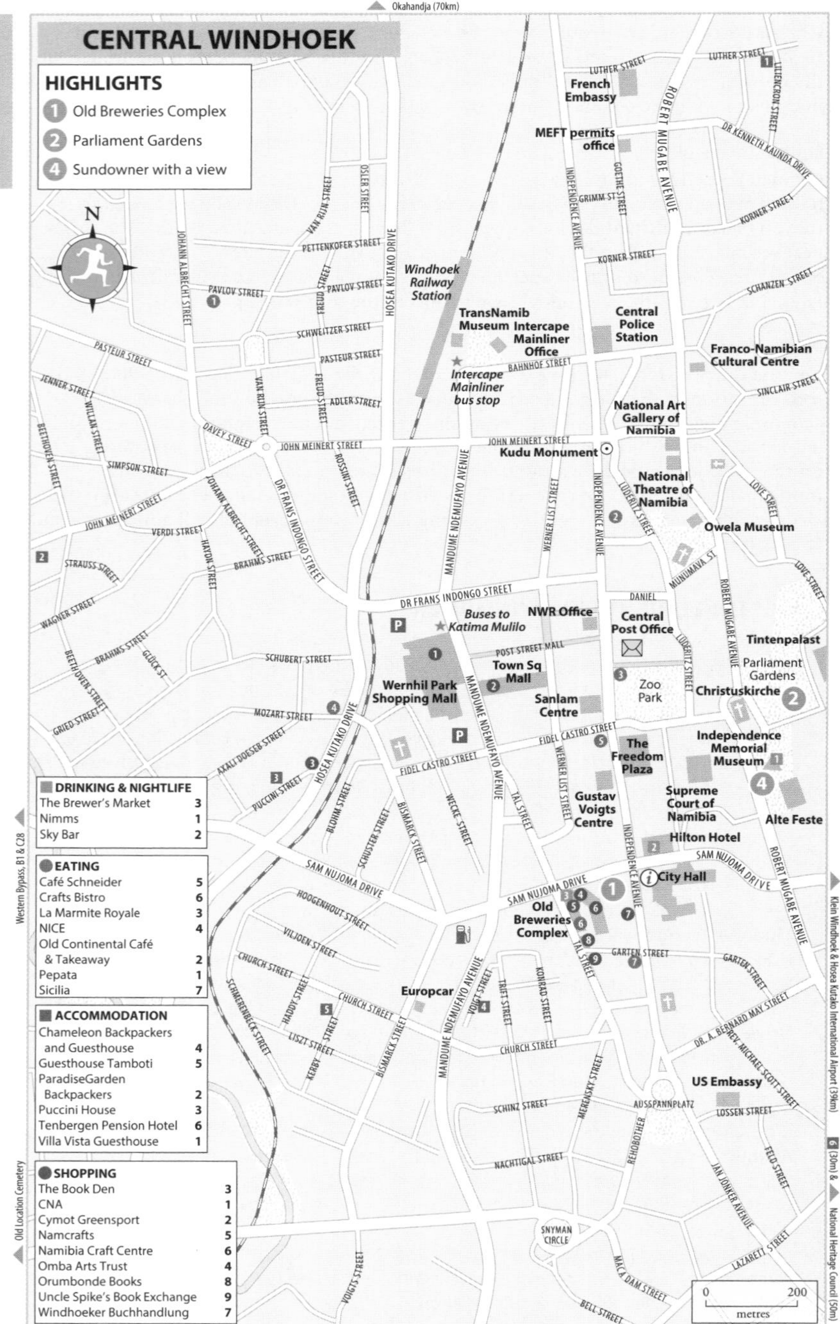

CENTRAL WINDHOEK
HIGHLIGHTS
1 Old Breweries Complex
2 Parliament Gardens
4 Sundowner with a view
DRINKING & NIGHTLIFE
The Brewer's Market 3
Nimms 1
Sky Bar 2
EATING
Café Schneider 5
Crafts Bistro 6
La Marmite Royale 3
NICE 4
Old Continental Café & Takeaway 2
Pepata 1
Sicilia 7
ACCOMMODATION
Chameleon Backpackers and Guesthouse 4
Guesthouse Tamboti 5
ParadiseGarden Backpackers 2
Puccini House 3
Tenbergen Pension Hotel 6
Villa Vista Guesthouse 1
SHOPPING
The Book Den 3
CNA 1
Cymot Greensport 2
Namcrafts 5
Namibia Craft Centre 6
Omba Arts Trust 4
Orumbonde Books 8
Uncle Spike's Book Exchange 9
Windhoeker Buchhandlung 7
Okahandja (70km)
Eros Airport (3km)
Western Bypass, B1 & C28
Old Location Cemetery
Klein Windhoek & Hosea Kutako International Airport (39km)
6 (30m) & National Heritage Council (50m)
French Embassy
MEFT permits office
Windhoek Railway Station
TransNamib Museum
Intercape Mainliner Office
Intercape Mainliner bus stop
Central Police Station
Franco-Namibian Cultural Centre
National Art Gallery of Namibia
Kudu Monument
National Theatre of Namibia
Owela Museum
Buses to Katima Mulilo
NWR Office
Central Post Office
Tintenpalast
Parliament Gardens
Christuskirche
Zoo Park
Wernhil Park Shopping Mall
Town Sq Mall
Sanlam Centre
The Freedom Plaza
Independence Memorial Museum
Gustav Voigts Centre
Supreme Court of Namibia
Alte Feste
Hilton Hotel
City Hall
Old Breweries Complex
Europcar
US Embassy
LUTHER STREET
LILIENCRON STREET
ROBERT MUGABE AVENUE
DR KENNETH KAUNDA DRIVE
KORNER STREET
GOETHE STREET
GRIMM ST
INDEPENDENCE AVENUE
SCHANZEN STREET
OSLER STREET
VAN RIJN STREET
PETTENKOFER STREET
JOHANN ALBRECHT STREET
PAVLOV STREET
FREUD STREET
HOSEA KUTAKO DRIVE
SCHWEITZER STREET
PASTEUR STREET
BAHNHOF STREET
SINCLAIR STREET
JENNER STREET
WILLAN STREET
ADLER STREET
BEETHOVEN STREET
DAVEY STREET
JOHN MEINERT STREET
SIMPSON STREET
ROSSINI STREET
MANDUME NDEMUFAYO AVENUE
WERNER LIST STREET
LUDERITZ STREET
LOVE STREET
VERDI STREET
DR FRANS INDONGO STREET
HAYDN STREET
BRAHMS STREET
STRAUSS STREET
MUNUMAVA ST
DANIEL
WAGNER STREET
POST STREET MALL
GLÜCK ST
SCHUBERT STREET
GRIED STREET
MOZART STREET
AXALI DOESEB STREET
FIDEL CASTRO STREET
PUCCINI STREET
BLOHM STREET
SCHUSTER STREET
BISMARCK STREET
WECKE STREET
TAL STREET
SAM NUJOMA DRIVE
HOOGENHOUT STREET
VILJOEN STREET
CHURCH STREET
GARTEN STREET
SCHMERENBECK STREET
HADDY STREET
LISZT STREET
KERBY STREET
VOIGT STREET
TRIFT STREET
KONRAD STREET
DR. A. BERNARD MAY STREET
REV. MICHAEL SCOTT STREET
MERENSKY STREET
SCHINZ STREET
AUSSPANNPLATZ
LOSSEN STREET
REHOBOTHER
NACHTIGAL STREET
JAN JONKER AVENUE
FELD STREET
SNYMAN CIRCLE
LAZARETT STREET
MACA DAM STREET
BELL STREET
VOIGTS STREET
0 200 metres

The city centre

Windhoek's modest sights and tourist attractions are predominantly located in a compact 1km (0.6-mile) area along or between Independence Avenue, the city's main drag, and Robert Mugabe Avenue, which runs parallel along a ridge to the east. Most can be covered on foot in a day – or two if you want to take your time and trawl all the disparate sections of the national museum (some areas were closed to the public at the time of writing).

Independence Avenue and around

Though not a spectacular street, **Independence Avenue** is pleasant enough, containing a few interesting examples of colonial architecture, an eclectic collection of monuments, and a handful of chic shops – some selling souvenirs – and small arcades. The best place to start a walking tour is on the corner of Independence Avenue and John Meinert Street, at the splendid life-size, bronze **kudu monument**, designed by a visiting German sculptor and erected in 1960 to celebrate the kudu's – and other wildlife's – survival of the 1896 rinderpest epidemic (see page 341), which all but wiped them out. Halfway along the west side of the busiest section, you'll come across Independence Avenue's most distinctive landmark, the domed **clock tower**, a replica of one that originally fronted the Deutsche-Afrika Bank. The tower marks the entrance to **Post Street Mall**, a bustling pedestrianised area.

Further south on Independence Avenue, somewhat obscured by the trees and best appreciated from across the road, stand a few **German colonial facades** designed in the early twentieth century. The most striking is the Erkrath Building – housing the NWR office – with a steeply sloping roof to prevent snow from accumulating.

It's worth climbing the steps on the south side of the FNB building, which leads up to the imposing **Supreme Court of Namibia**. It is said to have been inspired by North African architecture, utilising a hierarchy of space moving from the public to the private domains. Take a peek at the light, airy foyer and colonnaded courtyard containing a memorial garden.

Back on Independence Avenue, you pass a **curio market**, where Himba traders garner the greatest interest. A little further on, at the corner of Sam Nujoma Drive, stands an empty plinth, which, until November 2022, supported a bronze **statue of Curt von François**, the cartographer and leader of the German imperial forces often credited – from a colonial perspective – with founding modern-day Windhoek. The statue was an unwelcome reminder of German colonial rule for many; 1,600-plus signatories demanded its removal. It is currently locked away alongside the Reiterdenkmal (see box, page 86) in the Alte Feste.

Post Street Mall

A short raised pedestrianised walkway, **Post Street Mall** is probably the city centre's liveliest street, connecting Independence Avenue with Wernhil Park, which harbours the capital's central shopping mall and supermarket. Thronging with activity on weekday lunchtimes, it is somewhat overwhelmed by the sprawling displays of street vendors' wares: ornate walking sticks, soapstone sculptures, acres of colourful cloth, jewellery, basketry, leatherwork and carvings of every animal you're ever likely to see on safari. Amid this dizzying cornucopia of crafts, it's easy to miss the street's impressive centrepiece, the **Gibeon Meteorite Fountain** (see page 84).

Zoo Park

On the east side of Independence Avenue, **Zoo Park** provides a welcome shady retreat and contains a couple of contrasting monuments. The more unusual is the **elephant column**, which marks the spot where 5,000-year-old elephant bones and tools were found; precious

1

THE GIBEON METEORITE

No artistic representation, the Gibeon Meteorite Fountain sculpture is comprised of genuine lumps of iron-rich meteorite from what is thought to have been the **largest meteor shower** ever to have hit the planet, some 600 million years ago. It was named after the place in southern Namibia where the meteors fell, covering an area of around 13,000 sq km (5,019.3 sq miles). Although Nama had been fashioning tools and weapons out of the extra-terrestrial rocks for many years, it took the 'discovery' by a British explorer, **James Alexander**, in the 1830s and subsequent tests in London to determine the meteoric origin of the samples. In the early 1900s, 33 fragments were collected by Dr Paul Range, the chief geologist of the colonial administration, and sent to Windhoek. These were displayed in Zoo Park for many years before being installed in Post Street Mall. Two lumps went missing during the move when in temporary storage in the Alte Feste in 1975, while a third was swiped from the sculpture once in place – their three empty plinths still stand forlornly alongside the other thirty specimens on display. Further meteorite pieces are displayed in the **National Earth Science Museum** (see page 92).

Despite the Namibian government's 2004 ban on removing any meteorite material from its site and the threat of a hefty fine, pieces continue to make their way out of the country. Some end up in museums, others in private hands, which is no great surprise as meteorite smuggling is big business. Large chunks of Gibeon meteorite can fetch thousands, which a quick look at eBay can confirm. The notion of wearing a bit of outer space on the finger or around the neck has also made Gibeon meteorite jewellery very popular, especially since an attractive lattice-like patterning – known as Widmanstätten – stands out once the stone has been cut, polished and acid etched.

evidence of early human settlement in the area is now on display in the National Earth Science Museum (see page 92). The column is an intriguing bas-relief of an elephant hunt topped with a sculpted elephant skull. More contentious is the century-old **German war memorial**, crowned by a gilt imperial eagle, commemorating the fallen German soldiers who died in the Nama uprising against colonial rule. Conspicuously, there is no sibling monument to honour the Nama who died. The park also hosts the annual **|Ae||Gams Cultural Festival** in April, with plenty of singing, dancing, craft and food stalls.

Old Breweries Complex

While in the city centre, don't forget to check out the **Old Breweries Complex**, one block west of Independence Avenue on Tal Street; the former production site for Windhoek Lager, it is now a vibrant, multifaceted arts, crafts and nightlife venue, notably home to the Brewer's Market (see page 99) and its various components, and the Namibia Craft Centre, which also hosts a great café (see page 100).

National Museum of Namibia

As part of the re-visioning of Namibia's history and construction of post-independence identity, the country's **National Museum** collections (W museums.com.na/museums/windhoek) are now dispersed across several sites after being hosted predominantly in the Alte Feste. All are located in the central area, except for the National Earth Science Museum, which shares a building with the Ministry of Mines and Energy, to the south, by Eros Airport.

Owela Museum

4 Robert Mugabe Ave • Closed for renovations • Free • T 061 276800

The **Owela Museum** takes its name from the Oshiwambo name for the popular wooden board-and-bean game you see played under trees across Africa. Primarily concerned with ecology and the **ethnography** of Namibia's Indigenous peoples, the museum depicts the traditional lives of the Nama, Damara, Herero, Himba, Kavango and San. This is achieved through dioramas, artefacts and photos, giving insights into their varied cultural practices – from methods of hunting and agriculture to music and puberty rituals – some of which exist in mutated form even today. Highlights include Nama cosmetic powder boxes made of tortoiseshell and embellished with beads and an oryx-horn trumpet used by the Himba to herd cattle. While most displays adhere to the 'pickled-in-aspic' approach to preserving cultural traditions, more recent displays on the San and the Zambezi Region cultures show greater critical engagement with the complexities of cultures undergoing modernisation.

The smaller **ecology** section inevitably involves overdosing on taxidermy. However, there are attempts to bring the hapless animals to life by locating them in dioramas of their natural habitat, some in striking action poses: vultures tuck into a zebra carcass, while a caracal snatches at a fleeing guineafowl.

Independence Memorial Museum

Robert Mugabe Avenue & Fidel Castro Street • Mon–Fri 8am–5pm • Free • Ⓦ museums.com.na/museums/windhoek/independence-museum

The gleaming gold spaceship that dwarfs the Christuskirche and the Alte Feste on either side is the **Independence Memorial Museum**, whose aim is to pay homage to those who fought to establish the Namibian state – don't expect too much critical commentary. Fronted by a larger-than-life statue of Namibia's founding father, Sam Nujoma (see page 344), brandishing the constitution, this predominantly **photographic documentation** of the struggle for independence is still lacking background contextual information, which would greatly help visitors unfamiliar with Namibian history. Sadly, the video screens designed to do just that have not been operational since the museum opened in 2014 when some early visitors made off with the relevant touch-screen hardware. Other exhibits have also been stolen.

The narrative sets off at a gallop on the first floor with a brief idealised portrayal of pre-colonial life as 'peaceful coexistence' before speeding through the Scramble for Africa, early resistance against colonialism, Namibia under apartheid and the formation of the People's Liberation Army of Namibia (PLAN), primarily told through labelled photographs but also including some graphic slavery-themed friezes. The second floor documents guerrilla operations from neighbouring states with more photos supplemented with a couple of tanks and some weaponry, while the final floor illustrates some of South-West Africa People's Organisation's (SWAPO) activities in exile (see page 344) and celebrates the resettlement and repatriation of exiles and the final achievement of independence. Don't miss the opportunity to soak up the capital's best view from the museum's fifth-floor bar and restaurant (see page 99).

The Alte Feste

Robert Mugabe Avenue near Fidel Castro Street • Closed for renovation

Resembling a toy-town fort with its corner turrets and neat crenellations, the **Alte Feste** (Old Fort) is Windhoek's oldest surviving building. As it has been closed for renovations since 2014, the most you can do is admire its exterior and peer through the locked gate. Designed as a headquarters for the Schutztruppe, its cornerstone was laid in 1890, though it wasn't completed in its present design until some 25 years later. Since then, the fort has had a varied history: as well as housing German and, later, South African Union troops, it has also been a hostel for the adjacent Windhoek High School, and up until 2014, it played host to most of the national museum collection. However, beyond a few historical ox-carts by the entrance and the Genocide Memorial by its steps, there's now little to see inside while the government debates how best to utilise the space. The controversial Reiterdenkmal, a bronze equestrian monument erected to commemorate some of the German soldiers and civilians who died during

1

THE REITERDENKMAL

The controversy surrounding the siting and status of the **Reiterdenkmal** – an equestrian memorial monument depicting a German soldier (Schutztruppe; see page 340) – is symptomatic of the tensions within post-independence Namibia as it comes to terms with its colonial history. Designed in Berlin and erected in Windhoek next to the Christuskirche in 1912 on the birthday of German Emperor Kaiser Wilhelm II, the monument commemorates the German soldiers and civilians who lost their lives during the Herero and Nama uprisings against colonial rule and the Kalahari Expedition of 1908. However, the bronze, armed cavalryman that presided over the city centre for almost a hundred years is, understandably, viewed by Black Namibians as a symbol of **colonial oppression** and a blatant reminder of the genocide of thousands of Nama and Herero by German troops (see page 342). As a result, the Reiterdenkmal has long been on SWAPO's list for removal – it has already been axed from the country's list of historical monuments. But with opposition from the powerful German-speaking minority – because, for better or worse, it is part of Namibia's heritage and its removal would be a breach of their minority rights – it has been a protracted affair. First, in 2009, the monument was shunted sideways from its hillside vantage point – to make way for the new Independence Memorial Museum – to sit outside the Alte Feste. Then, under cover of darkness on Christmas Eve 2013, it was taken inside the old fort to avoid confrontation. Many Black Namibians hope this is a prelude to the monument being shipped back to Germany, while some members of the German-Namibian community have threatened to sue the government if such a move is made. It remains locked inside the old fort, which has been closed for renovations for several years. To stir matters further, a miniature replica was erected outside the *Aldstadt Restaurant* in Swakopmund in 2019.

the colonial era (see page 86), is conveniently locked inside, out of sight, and in 2022 was joined by the statue of Curt von François. When (or even whether) the fort will re-open is open to speculation.

The TransNamib Museum

First floor of Windhoek train station, Bahnhof Street • Temporarily closed • Free, donations welcome • ⓣ 061 2982186

While the specialist **TransNamib Museum** will have railway enthusiasts in raptures, the average visitor will probably be satisfied with having a peer around Windhoek's quaint historical train station. Built in 1913, the museum is fronted by *Poor Old Joe*, a narrow-gauge steam locomotive that used to chug between Swakopmund and Windhoek.

The handful of small rooms are packed with railway memorabilia. Still, it is like poking around someone's attic as potentially interesting finds are often unexplained and lie cheek-by-jowl with pieces that would not be out of place in a car boot or garage sale. However, the train-buff curator will be happy to help you understand it all. There are even a couple of tiny rooms dedicated to Namibia's aviation and maritime history. Of more general appeal is the re-creation of a first-class train compartment, complete with an original sink tucked beneath the stow-away table.

National Art Gallery of Namibia

John Meinert Street & Robert Mugabe Avenue • Mon 2–5pm, Tue–Fri 8am–5pm, Sat 9am–2pm • Free • ⓦ nagn.org.na

The **National Art Gallery of Namibia** possesses a collection of around 270 pieces of contemporary art – an array of paintings, drawings, sculptures, work in mixed and new media and crafts by Namibian artists, including a substantial number of original linocuts by the internationally acclaimed John Muafangejo. The gallery currently lacks the space to display the whole collection, so it rotates the works in a string of temporary exhibitions, sometimes alongside art by other regional and international artists.

The gallery also provides the central exhibition space to display the winning entries in the **Bank Windhoek Triennial**.

The Christuskirche

Robert Mugabe Avenue & Fidel Castro Street • Mon–Fri 9am–6pm, Sat & Sun 10am–5pm • Free

Though still a must-see sight on any tour of Windhoek, it is hard to imagine how the pretty gingerbread **Christuskirche** dominated Windhoek's skyline for over a hundred years as one of Namibia's most distinctive landmarks. It's probably no coincidence that these days, it's encircled by a busy roundabout and physically overshadowed by the adjacent brash Independence Memorial Museum.

A predominantly neo-Romanesque confection, topped with a steeple and neo-Gothic spire, it was designed by German architect and engineer Gottlieb Redecker – who was also responsible for the Tintenpalast, Namibia's parliament building. Locally quarried quartz sandstone was used to construct the main building, but most other elements were imported from Germany: parts of the roof, the three bells, the clock, the organ and the stained-glass windows, which were a gift from Kaiser Wilhelm II. Marble for the altar and portal was procured from Italy. Since the church was conceived by the German colonisers as a symbol of peace in the wake of the Herero and Nama uprisings and subsequent massacres, it is a sad irony that the vast plaque inside that commemorates the fallen German soldiers and settlers is not matched by any such remembrance of the far greater numbers of the Indigenous population who lost their lives.

The Tintenpalast

Robert Mugabe Avenue, behind the Christuskirche • Gardens only open to the public • Free • ⓣ 061 2885111

Built to house the administration of German South-West Africa in 1912–13, the **Tintenpalast** (Ink Palace) gained its enduring sobriquet through reference to the copious amounts of ink used in bureaucratic paperwork. Successive governments have occupied the two-storey structure, accommodating the National Assembly (lower chamber) and the National Council (upper chamber) comprising **Namibia's parliament**.

The restrained, elegant design was the work of Gottlieb Redecker, the same architect-engineer who had earlier planned the Christuskirche. Still, the parliament building stands out because it was constructed almost entirely from locally sourced materials. Given its diminutive stature, a new, larger parliament building has been under discussion for a number of years. However, this controversial multimillion-dollar project has been shelved for some years as the country's economy struggles.

Parliament Gardens

Open access • Free

Surrounding the Tintenpalast are the delightful, shady, landscaped **Parliament Gardens**, which merit a stroll. They are particularly popular at lunchtimes and weekends when students laze on the lawns, poring over their books or each other. Don't miss the bougainvillea-lined bowling green and thatched clubhouse to the north of parliament, which are kept in immaculate condition. Post-independence additions to the grounds include the three bronze **statues** of liberation heroes that flank the steps up to parliament's main entrance: Kaptein Hendrik Witbooi – not to be confused with the better-known Hendrik Witbooi (see page 340), who graces Namibian currency notes – an opponent of Bantu education; Hosea Kutako, the Herero chief who was instrumental in petitioning the UN for Namibian independence (see page 346); and the less frequently championed – and not so easily pronounced – Reverend Theophilus Hamutumbangela, a priest and vociferous independence activist, who was arrested on various occasions and was allegedly poisoned by the South African authorities under apartheid.

The suburbs

Outside the Central Business District (also known as Windhoek Central), the capital melts outwards in all directions in a collection of suburbs, which include the former townships of Katutura and Khomasdal (see page 90) to the northwest. These, in turn, have spawned an even greater number of informal settlements, which house an estimated third of the city's population, predominantly in collections of aluminium shacks, which lack adequate access to basic services such as clean water, sanitation, medical care and schooling. Although the Namibian government is committed to building affordable, low-cost housing, the serried ranks of boxlike structures in the newer suburbs are still beyond the incomes of many Black Namibians.

The eastern suburbs

The old, eastern suburbs are synonymous with affluence and include the former white residential areas of **Klein Windhoek** and **Ludwigsdorf**, which are also home to many of the city's boutique hotels and guesthouses, upmarket restaurants and embassies. Characterised by slick four-wheel drives and empty roads that weave their way through high-walled, gated properties and leafy gardens, these areas have changed little in terms of their racial make-up since pre-independence days.

Klein Windhoek, the oldest district, is where Jonker Afrikaner first settled in 1840. It was also the first area to be developed as a residential zone outside the garrison area of Gross Windhoek when the Germans established themselves half a century later. Notable landmarks, standing sentinel along the ridge that announces the entrance to the Klein Windhoek Valley, are the three whimsical **castles** of Sanderburg, Heinitzburg and Schwerinsburg. Built in the early 1900s by German architect Wilhelm Sander, Schwerinsburg is the largest of the three and incorporates a nineteenth-century military watchtower into its design. Only Heinitzburg, however, is open to visitors as it now houses a luxury hotel, though even non-residents can enjoy its splendid terrace views by lingering over a sundowner or a meal there.

National Botanical Gardens

Oban Street, signposted off Sam Nujoma Drive • Mon–Fri 8am–5pm, every second Sat of the month 8–11am • Free; charge for guided walks • Ⓦ www.nbri.org.na/sections/botanic-garden

Despite only covering a small area, the patch of arid land that comprises the **National Botanical Gardens** provides welcome relief from the surrounding concrete. As long as you limit your expectations, you can easily spend a happy hour or two here. Although not landscaped – partly to save water – the 'gardens' claim over six hundred indigenous plant species, many labelled, and around 75 bird species. The small desert house gives a taster of what to expect once you get out to the Namib itself, including many protected species that can otherwise only be seen in remote and inaccessible areas, while elsewhere, you can find some splendid examples of *Euphorbia candelabra*. Tucked away near the picnic area lies the grave of a Damara chief who was allegedly captured and beheaded by the German authorities after opposing colonial rule.

The reception desk also has maps with plant listings for the **Aloe Trail**, a short, circular walking trail (2km/1.2 miles), which affords views over the Klein Windhoek valley. The trail begins close to the entrance, but do it only if you are in a group, as muggings have been known to occur. A map, as well as bird and plant lists, can be downloaded from the website.

Northwestern suburbs

The former townships of Katutura and Khomasdal dominate the northwestern suburbs, surrounded by an ever-increasing sprawl of makeshift shacks, as more and more people

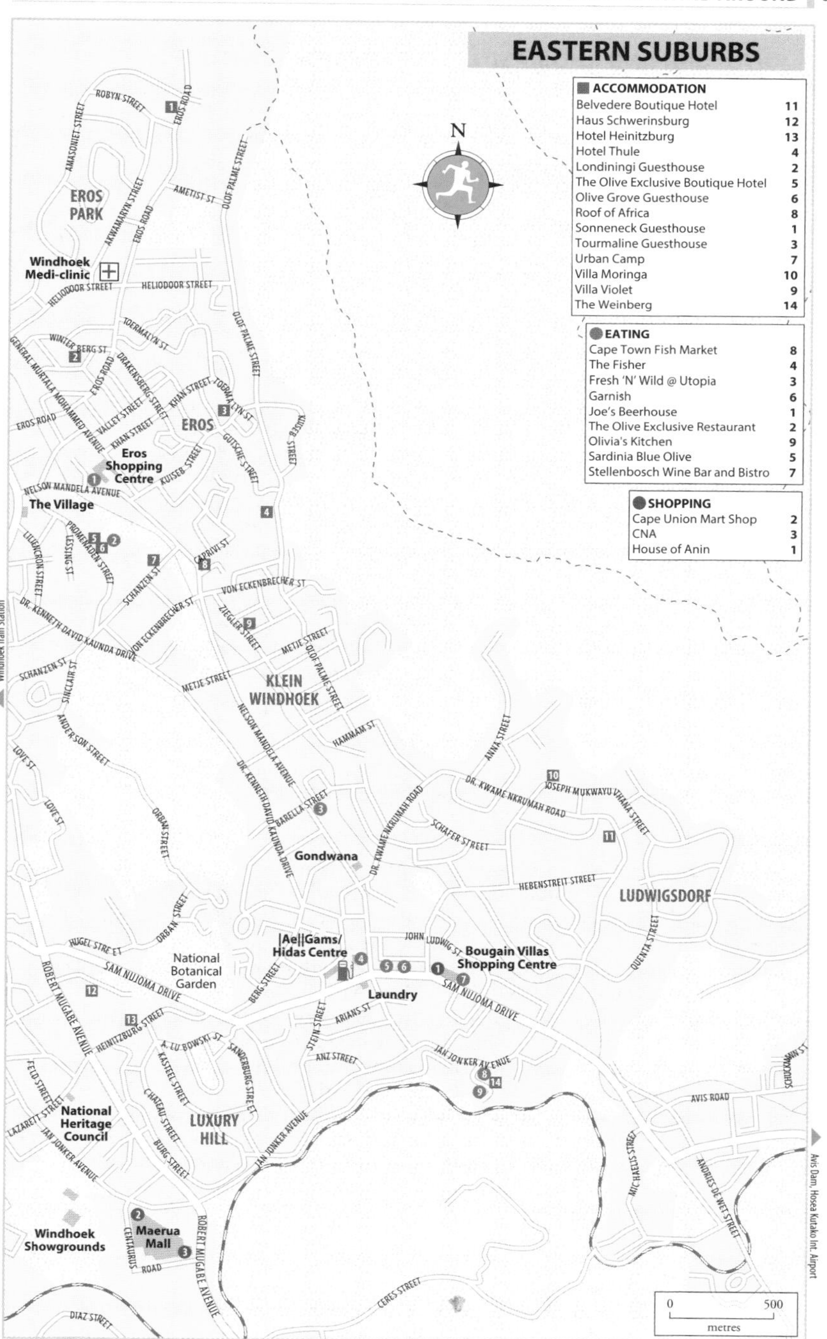
EASTERN SUBURBS
ACCOMMODATION
Belvedere Boutique Hotel 11
Haus Schwerinsburg 12
Hotel Heinitzburg 13
Hotel Thule 4
Londiningi Guesthouse 2
The Olive Exclusive Boutique Hotel 5
Olive Grove Guesthouse 6
Roof of Africa 8
Sonneneck Guesthouse 1
Tourmaline Guesthouse 3
Urban Camp 7
Villa Moringa 10
Villa Violet 9
The Weinberg 14
EATING
Cape Town Fish Market 8
The Fisher 4
Fresh 'N' Wild @ Utopia 3
Garnish 6
Joe's Beerhouse 1
The Olive Exclusive Restaurant 2
Olivia's Kitchen 9
Sardinia Blue Olive 5
Stellenbosch Wine Bar and Bistro 7
SHOPPING
Cape Union Mart Shop 2
CNA 3
House of Anin 1
N
EROS PARK
Windhoek Medi-clinic
EROS
Eros Shopping Centre
The Village
KLEIN WINDHOEK
Gondwana
LUDWIGSDORF
|Ae||Gams/ Hidas Centre
Bougain Villas Shopping Centre
National Botanical Garden
Laundry
National Heritage Council
LUXURY HILL
Windhoek Showgrounds
Maerua Mall
Windhoek Train Station
Avis Dam, Hosea Kutako Int. Airport
ROBYN STREET
EROS ROAD
AMASONIET STREET
AMETIST ST
OLOF PALME STREET
AKWAMARYN STREET
HELIODOOR STREET
TOERMALYN ST
WINTERBERG ST
GENERAL MURTALA MOHAMMED AVENUE
DRAKENSBERG STREET
VALLEY STREET
KHAN STREET
GUTSCHE STREET
KAISER STREET
KUISEB STREET
NELSON MANDELA AVENUE
PROMENADEN STREET
LESSING ST
LILIENCRON STREET
SCHANZEN ST
CAPRIVI ST
VON ECKENBRECHER ST
ZIEGLER STREET
DR. KENNETH DAVID KAUNDA DRIVE
METJE STREET
SINCLAIR ST
ANDERSON STREET
LOVE ST
HAMMAM ST
ANNA STREET
DR. KWAME NKRUMAH ROAD
JOSEPH MUKWAYU VHANA STREET
BARELLA STREET
SCHAFER STREET
ORBAN STREET
HEBENSTREIT STREET
QUENTA STREET
HUGEL STREET
JOHN LUDWIG ST
SAM NUJOMA DRIVE
ROBERT MUGABE AVENUE
BERG STREET
ARIANS ST
STEIN STREET
HEINITZBURG STREET
A. LU BOWSKI ST
SANDERBURG STREET
KASTEEL STREET
ANZ STREET
JAN JONKER AVENUE
FELD STREET
LAZARETT STREET
CHATEAU STREET
BURG STREET
AVIS ROAD
MIC HAELIS STREET
ANDRIES DE WET STREET
CENTAURUS ROAD
CERES STREET
DIAZ STREET
0 500
metres

1

KATUTURA AND KHOMASDAL: THE FORMER TOWNSHIPS

Although Namibia's Black and mixed-heritage populations had experienced racial segregation and resettlement well before the apartheid era, it was the mass protests of 1959 at the forced removal of the capital's 'Black' population to the township of **Katutura** – meaning 'place where we will not stay/settle' in Otjiherero – that were subsequently identified as the landmark rallying call for independence (see page 344). By 1912, non-whites had been forced to live in two areas of the capital: a segregated area within Klein Windhoek and the Main Location (now called the Old Location), between present-day Hochland Park and Pioneers Park, to the south of the city – in areas that were further subdivided according to ethnicity. In 1959, the South African regime declared that all Black people had to move to a new township 8km (5 miles) northwest of central Windhoek, and those who were considered to be of mixed heritage, dubbed 'coloured', had to move to one called Khomasdal, 5km (3.1 miles) away, there was a huge outcry. Residents of Katutura would have fewer rights, smaller plots and a longer walk to the city centre. **Protests** followed as tensions escalated, police brutality increased, and matters came to a head when a march by a group of Herero women and a subsequent boycott of municipal services resulted in clashes with police in what is now known as the **Old Location Uprising**. It resulted in at least eleven dead and 44 injured, while several thousand residents fled from the city for fear of further state reprisals. The dead are buried in the Old Location Cemetery, off Hochland Road, which is the focus for the annual national commemoration of Human Rights Day on 10 December.

Though Katutura and Khomasdal have been reclassified as 'suburbs', and the apartheid-era stadium-like surveillance lights that deprived residents of a decent night's sleep for many years were torn down long ago, many of the residents in Katutura and the surrounding informal settlements, in particular, are still very poor. Black people who can afford to move out often prefer to live in **Khomasdal**, where there is a similar sense of community, rather than in the eastern suburbs – where houses hide behind high walls, barbed-wire fences and electronic gates – or in other newer developments, which are designed to fit European planning models premised on separate nuclear family units.

migrate from rural areas searching for a better life in Windhoek. That said, tourists are beginning to venture into Katutura, searching for the 'real Africa'.

Katutura

Travelling 8km (5 miles) northwest of downtown Windhoek, along Independence Avenue, brings you to **Katutura**, the former apartheid-era Black township, arguably the city's heartbeat. With an official population of around 43,000 but unofficially housing over four times more if you include the surrounding informal settlements – many in makeshift shanty huts – Katutura is everything that central Windhoek is not: thronging with people, bustling with activity, full of markets, bicycles, running kids and load-carrying guys weaving their way across traffic. To get a greater appreciation of this city within a city, take one of the local operators' 'township tours' (see page 94), which will allow you to visit the small business ventures of Soweto Market, the sizzling *kapana* grills cooking spiced strips of meat, or the Singles' Quarters meat market – not for the faint-hearted. Then, there's throbbing Eveline Street, 'the street that never sleeps', a packed parade of shebeens, hairdressers, mobile phone kiosks and car washers. Tours also sometimes take in the Xwama Cultural Village (see page 98) or Penduka, a successful craft-making women's development project at Goreangab Dam.

Penduka

Goreangab Dam • Daily 8am–5pm • Ⓦ penduka.com

The main reason to venture this far, beyond Katutura and through the informal settlement of Goreangab, is to visit **Penduka**, a long-standing women's self-help craft-making development project scenically situated by **Goreangab Dam**. Penduka has expanded in recent years to include food and accommodation: the restaurant has a pleasant aspect across the water and the thatched rondavels are inexpensive and cheery, if somewhat incongruous. If you want to do more than visit their well-stocked craft shop, consider booking a morning workshop to learn about basketry and embroidery or try drumming or cooking a *potjiekos* (stew in a three-legged metal pot). Penduka can also organise informative visits to nearby Katutura or a daycare centre in the informal settlement of Otjomuise. Their tours tend to lack the voyeurism that characterises some of these excursions.

Southern and western suburbs

South of the centre is a mixed bag of neighbourhoods separated by the Southern Industrial Area and Eros Airport, on whose access road the National Earth Science Museum is located. Before the airport, just south of Hochland Park, lies the Old Location Cemetery (see page 90) – signposted off Hosea Kutako Drive. Beyond, to the southwest, Pioneers Park and Academia – appropriately located next to the University of Namibia campus – comprise pleasant middle-class residential areas that are not as wealthy as the eastern suburbs and where some of Windhoek's less expensive tourist accommodation is situated. More affluent areas lie to the east, including the garden suburbs of Suiderhof, Olympia, which hosts an Olympic-sized swimming pool, well worth a plunge in summer (see page 101), the Independence Stadium, as well

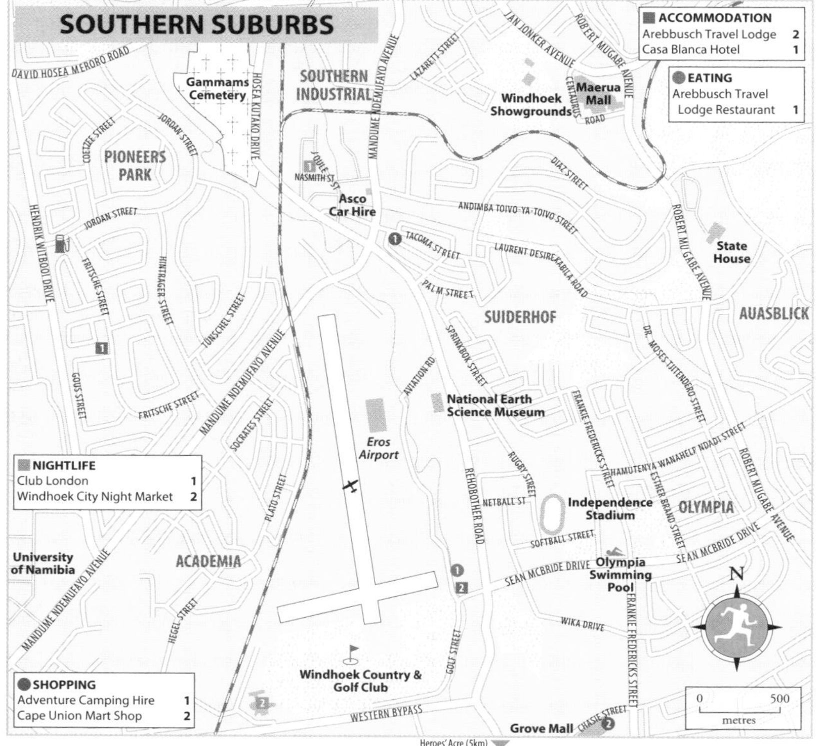

as Windhoek's glitziest mall (thegrovemallofnamibia.com), which contains a state-of-the-art cinema. The Olympic theme continues in the renaming of one of its main roads, Frankie Fredericks Street, in honour of Namibia's all-time great, multi-Olympic medal-winning track athlete. Presiding over the area from the hillside of Auasblick sprawls the unmissable architectural monstrosity that is the new State House. Designed and predominantly built by North Koreans and costing some unspecified sum between N$400–600 million, it was completed in 2008. The far more modest old State House, on Robert Mugabe Avenue, a stone's throw from the parliament buildings, is now home to the prime minister.

The National Earth Science Museum

The ground floor of the Ministry of Mines and Energy, 1 Aviation Rd, opposite the *Safari Court Hotel* • Mon–Fri 8am–1pm, 2–5pm • Free • museums.com.na/museums/windhoek/earth-sciences

It is worth trekking to Namibia's **National Earth Science Museum**, which boasts small but impressive displays on Namibian palaeontology, minerals and mining. Well-labelled glass cabinets show **fossil collections** from diverse eras, some remarkably preserved, such as the eggs of an ostrich ancestor, the carapace of a giant 19-million-year-old tortoise, and the almost-complete fossilised impression of a *Mesosaurus* found on a farm near Keetmanshoop, in southern Namibia (see page 145). Fear not if you're struggling to picture such beasts since they come alive in the wonderful accompanying illustrations by the late Christine Marais, a South African artist renowned for her portrayals of the Namibian environment.

The museum's **geological section** is a more mixed bag: though the detailed, specialist displays may fail to grip the casual visitor, the collection of sparkling gemstones holds more general appeal – don't miss the cabinet showing UV radiation and fluorescence in minerals and the exhibits illustrating their household uses in such mundane products as toothpaste and make-up. Namibia's mining industry has sponsored the displays on the country's various mines, so although informative, they are inevitably laden with PR-speak.

ARRIVAL AND DEPARTURE — WINDHOEK

BY PLANE

INTERNATIONAL

Hosea Kutako International Airport All international flights, including connections with other southern African destinations (see page 51) and some domestic flights, arrive at and depart from Hosea Kutako International Airport, 42km (26 miles) east of the capital. It has a bureau de change, post office, ATM and a small mobile phone shop, where you can buy a Namibian SIM card and credit. There is no fixed public transport to or from the airport. However, many hotels and guesthouses run shuttle services, which you can prebook online. Reliable, independent shuttle services you can prebook include Windhoek Airport Shuttle (windhoekairportshuttle.com) and Tok Tokkie Shuttle (shuttlesnamibia.com). Otherwise, the official taxi/shuttle fare, if you engage a driver on the spot outside the terminal, is currently N$380 for one passenger and N$280 per person for two or three people. If no transport is available on your arrival, which is often the case in high season, ask the airport information desk to call a taxi, but you'll have to wait until they arrive from Windhoek.

DOMESTIC

Eros Airport Only 5km (3.1 miles) south of the city centre, just off the B1, the main road south, this tiny domestic airport only services a handful of scheduled flights a day, though more charter plane traffic passes through. FlyNamibia (flynam.com) operates services to the following domestic airports: Katima Mulilo (3 weekly; 1hr 40min); Lüderitz (4 weekly; 1hr); Andimba Toivo ya Toivo (formerly Ondangwa; daily, except Sat; 1hr); Oranjemund (weekdays; 1hr 15min); Rundu (3 weekly; 1hr 5min); Walvis Bay (3 weekly; 40min).

There are a few car-rental desks (Avis, Budget, Europcar and Hertz), but these are frequently unstaffed. A taxi to/from the airport from/to the city centre costs around N$100.

AIRLINE OFFICES

Air Namibia Operations are suspended at the time of writing. airnamibia.com

Ethiopian Airlines Corner of Independence Avenue and Garten Street. ethiopianairlines.com

FlyNamibia No physical office. flynam.com

Qatar Airways 7 Luther St. qatarairways.com

South African Airways Corner of List and Bismarck streets. ⓦ flysaa.com
TAAG Angola Airlines Corner of Schinz and Trift streets. ⓦ taag.com

BY BUS

LUXURY BUS SERVICES

Intercape Off Bahnhof Street, opposite the train station ⓦ intercape.co.za. The comfortable Intercape service offers long-distance services and shorter trips within Namibia (see page 52). The ticket office is open Mon–Thurs 6am–5/6pm, Fri 6am–8pm, Sat 6am–noon, Sun 9.30am–5.30pm. Prices start at N$280 for the three-hour hop to Otjiwarongo and N$1,100 for the 21-hour haul to Cape Town.
Destinations Cape Town, South Africa (via Keetmanshoop and Noordoewer; 4 weekly; 22hr); Johannesburg, South Africa (via Upington, 26hr) – though the route via Botswana is faster (see below); Keetmanshoop and Noordoewer (3 weekly; 5hr 35min & 9hr 10min); Livingstone, Zambia (4 weekly; 12hr), via Grootfontein (6hr30min), Rundu (9hr) and Katima Mulilo (16hr); Ondangwa and Oshakati (daily; 10hr 10min & 11hr).
Oasis ⓦ oasis-bus-services.business.site. Based in Katima Mulilo, Oasis offers daily afternoon departures to the capital (18hr), stopping off en route in Rundu and Grootfontein. The return buses leave Windhoek from outside Wernhil Park shopping centre around 3pm for the trip north. You can buy a ticket on the bus.
Silas Ndapuka ⓦ safaribay.net/silas-ndapuka-transport-windhoek. Silas Ndapuka provides bi-weekly transport from Windhoek (Katutura) to the north – Oshakati and Tsumeb – and south to Oranjemund via Keetmanshoop.

SHUTTLE SERVICES

Tok Tokkie Shuttle 149C, 4th Floor, Maerua Mall South ⓦ shuttlesnamibia.com. In addition to airport shuttle services, Tok Tokkie Shuttle runs services (minimum six passengers) to Johannesburg, South Africa (19hr), via Gaborone in Botswana (12hr) – where you have to overnight – in comfortable minibuses with a/c and free wi-fi.

COASTAL AND AIRPORT SHUTTLE SERVICES

Established shuttle services based in Swakopmund include Town Hoppers and Welwitschia Shuttle, which run daily services in air-conditioned minibuses from Walvis Bay and Swakopmund to Windhoek (5hr & 4hr 30min; N$280), offering home pick-ups in the early morning, and return pick-ups early afternoon. Both can organise a private transfer to/from Hosea Kutako International Airport at extra cost.
Town Hoppers Ane Court, Shop No. 2, Otavi Street, Swakopmund ⓦ namibiashuttle.com. In Windhoek, the shuttle does doorstep pick-ups and collects passengers outside the train station.
Welwitschia Shuttle 32 Sam Nujoma Drive, Swakopmund ⓦ welwitschiashuttle.com. Welwitschia Shuttle offers a weekday service similar to Town Hoppers at the same rates, with pick-up from your lodgings or the Christuskirche car park in Windhoek.

MINIBUSES

Most of the Namibians travel on minibuses (also known as combis) that often have no fixed schedule but depart when full, usually lack a/c, and can be prone to accidents. There are two main departure points in the city. Buses that head north to Oshakati, Rundu (8hr) and Katima (11–12hr) depart from the Monte Christo service station just outside Katutura. Transport heading south (to Keetmanshoop (5hr) and Lüderitz (8hr) and west (to Swakopmund (4hr) leaves from the Engen service station in Rhino Park, north of the city centre. It's best to get a taxi out to the stop early in the morning if you want to be sure of a ride, especially during holiday periods, and also to ensure you are not arriving at your final destination in the dark when traffic accidents are more likely. Fares for the above destinations range from about N$150 to N$400.

BY TRAIN

The delightful railway station in Windhoek is the centre of Namibia's railway network, TransNamib (ticket office Mon–Fri 7am–7.30pm, Sat 7–10am, Sun 3–8pm; ⓦ transnamib.com.na), which is primarily concerned with transporting goods around the country very slowly. However, it is possible to travel as a passenger on these snail trains, though not in much comfort, even in business class; it's very inexpensive and a good way to meet people and have an adventure of sorts. Since trains take three times as long as cars to reach their destination, few people bother with them. Departures for Swakopmund and Walvis Bay ordinarily leave Tuesday, Thursday, Friday and Sunday at 7.15pm and are due to arrive at Swakopmund at 5.30am, though they frequently arrive late. A similar schedule on the same days operates for Keetmanshoop, leaving at 7.40pm and arriving at 7am. In either case, you'll need to take food to eat on the way, and for much of the year, you'll need a blanket for when the temperature drops at night. Suspended due to the COVID-19 pandemic, at the time of writing, passenger services had yet to resume but are likely to restart at some stage during the lifetime of the guide.

GETTING AROUND

On foot Windhoek's city centre is small and most places you will likely want to visit are within walking distance. Though it's safe to wander around the city during the day, you should take a taxi at night since muggings are becoming more commonplace.
By taxi Taxis abound on Independence Avenue and are

plentiful outside supermarkets, the Intercape bus stop and hotels – where they tend to be more expensive – though it is safer to phone for a taxi at night; most accommodation has its own recommended companies, so take a number before you head out if you're anxious about stopping one in the street or phone Dial-A-Cab (T 081 1270557, W dialacab.com.na). A short trip anywhere in the town centre will likely cost around N$100; for places further afield, such as Klein Windhoek or Katutura, a fare of N$120 is more usual. Prices are higher at night. Dial-A-Cab advertises the standard rates on its website. Much cheaper shared taxis broadly follow a set route, from which they will deviate slightly. They are easily flagged down outside the Gustav Voigts building on Independence Avenue. The driver will tell you whether your destination is on their route. Namibia's answer to Uber is Lefa (W Lefa.com.na), which functions reliably in and around Windhoek.

INFORMATION AND TOURS

TOURIST INFORMATION

Windhoek tourist information office (Mon–Fri 7.30am–4.30pm, T 061 2902093) is on the ground floor of the municipal building at the corner of Independence Avenue with Sam Nujoma. Staff are helpful and able to answer most questions about Windhoek but are less equipped to deal with questions about places further afield (see W namibiatourism.com.na). They can, however, furnish you with city and regional maps, brochures and fliers. You'll also find a wealth of knowledge at the two main backpacker hostels, *Chameleon* and *ParadiseGarden Backpackers*. Most guesthouses are also pretty knowledgeable and there's plenty of good, up-to-date information online (see page 74).

TOUR OPERATORS

There is an increasing number of tour operators in Namibia, most of whom work out of Windhoek but do business without an office. The quality of service given by the majority is very high; what follows is only a small selection of recommended companies.

ATI Holidays W ati-holidays.com. This well-established, professional owner-operated company offers a range of set and bespoke tours – fly-in, fly-drive, camping, the lot – across Southern Africa, catering for all purses.

Blue Crane Safaris 136 Sesriem St, Kleine Kuppe W bluecranesafaris.com. This highly respected local company runs bespoke and set tours, from day excursions around Windhoek through budget camping and glamping (for four to eight people) to pricier accommodation or fly-in safaris (for two to eight people) around the country.

Blue Sky Namibia Tours W blueskynamibia.com. This acclaimed family-run business organises bespoke self-drive or guided tours for small groups of people who already know each other to suit their budget. The owner/qualified guide has many years of experience in wildlife management.

Chameleon Safaris Namibia 5–7 Voigt St North W chameleonsafaris.com. Located at the backpackers of the same name (see page 95), this friendly, professional outfit specialises in short, budget to mid-range tours for individuals or small groups, including several popular day tours.

Gondwana 42 Nelson Mandela Ave W gondwana-collection.com. In addition to their extensive accommodation portfolio, Gondwana now offers a guided Namibia 'highlights' safari and bi-weekly departures for a three-day trip to Sossusvlei as well as several self-drive itineraries, including vehicle rental and accommodation at a selection of their properties across the country.

Mabaruli African Safaris W mabaruli.com. This experienced owner-managed operation can organise camping or lodge-based tours, family-friendly trips and even

VISITING THE NATIONAL PARKS

All bookings for **National Park accommodation** can be made in person at the **Namibia Wildlife Resorts (NWR)** office in the Erkrath Building, 189 Independence Ave (Mon–Fri 8am–5pm; W nwr.com.na), though you'll need to have made the reservation in advance of your trip if you're hoping to stay at the popular resorts of Etosha and Sossusvlei, and even for the less well-patronised places in high season. Even if you've booked online, it's worth popping in to reconfirm your reservation. The office staff can also provide limited information about the parks. In addition to any accommodation booking, you must pay daily park entry fees to the Ministry of the Environment, Forestry and Tourism (MEFT).

The **MEFT** permit office, where you can pay park fees or acquire permits, is on Robert Mugabe Avenue at Kenneth Kaunda Street (Mon–Fri 8am–4pm; T 061 2842046). You can buy your **park entry permits** in advance here, though they can usually also be purchased at the gate of the respective park. If you're contemplating climbing the Brandberg (see page 193), you must acquire a permit at the **National Heritage Council**, 52 Robert Mugabe Ave (Mon–Fri 8am–5pm; W nhc–nam.org), which is no easy process.

cycling safaris.

Namibia JJ Tours Kamanjab, Kunene Region namibiajjtours.com. Small owner-operated company based in northern Namibia that can organise personalised tours in Namibia and South Africa and caters to the LGBTQ+ community.

Nature Travel Namibia naturetravelnamibia.com. A highly acclaimed outfit that guides and plans safaris in Namibia, often in conjunction with other countries in Southern Africa, though it is based in Namibia. It focuses on cultural tours and wildlife viewing, especially birdwatching, and offers budget versions of some itineraries.

Ultimate Safaris 5 & 7 Brandberg St, Eros Park ultimatesafaris.na. Acclaimed, family-run business operating personalised, small-group tours, often in conjunction with source-country tour operators. Committed to conservation, sustainability and community development, their selection of small, low-impact but exclusive tented lodges can also be booked independently.

CITY TOUR GUIDES

Contact numbers are often changed, so if you get no joy, call in at the tourist office and they'll help you get in touch.

Japa Tours 081 2501148. This operator runs three- to four-hour city tours that cover the city centre, then takes you to Katutura to experience the markets, visit Penduka and try some *kapana*.

Katutours Penduka, Goreangab Dam and 105 Eveline St, Katutura katutours.com. This small enterprise offers informative guided half-day bicycle tours around Katutura for groups of two to fifteen. Tours leave from Soweto Market – ring to reserve the day before.

ACCOMMODATION

There is plenty of comfortable accommodation in Windhoek, from inexpensive **backpacker hostels** to family-run **guesthouses**, **self-catering chalets** and modern **hotels**. Guesthouses form the bulk of the properties, with many places only having a handful of rooms, so it pays to book well in advance. Most of the smarter guesthouses, smaller hotels and restaurants are in the leafy eastern suburbs of **Klein Windhoek**, **Ludwigsdorf** and **Eros Park**. However, they're little more than a ten-minute drive into the town centre. Other areas offering generally less expensive lodgings include **Windhoek West**, just west of the city centre and within walking distance of Independence Avenue, and **Pioneers Park**, a fifteen-minute drive on the main road south, next to the University of Namibia and close to a shopping centre – good for self-catering options. Within a thirty-minute drive of downtown, accommodation at **Daan Viljoen Game Park** (see page 101) offers a viable alternative. Many owner-managed places close from mid-December to mid-January as people migrate to the coast for the main annual holidays.

CENTRAL WINDHOEK, SEE MAP PAGE 82

★ Chameleon Backpackers and Guesthouse 5–7 Voigt St chameleonbackpackers.com. Head and shoulders above the competition, this superior hostel and adjoining guesthouse boast clean rooms, friendly and efficient staff, plus a pleasant bar and common area set around a splash pool in a shady enclosed garden. The cheaper rooms share facilities, whereas the pricier, brighter, more cheerfully decorated guesthouse ones are en suite. Other pluses include the DIY continental breakfast, a well-equipped kitchen, a bar area and secure off-road parking. B&B. Camping N$, dorms N$, doubles N$$

Guesthouse Tamboti 9 Kerby St guesthouse-tamboti.com. A stalwart of the B&B scene, used by several budget tour operators, this welcoming, central place offers fifteen simple but clean en-suite rooms (single, twin, triple and family). It has a pleasant terrace with city and mountain views and an open thatch bar-dining area where you can enjoy a cold buffet breakfast. B&B N$$

Tenbergen Pension Hotel Corner of Lazarett Street and Robert Mugabe Avenue tenbergenpensionhotel.com-namibia.com/en. Offering exceptional value, this central hotel comprises immaculate, spacious modern suites aimed at business executives – hence the desks, high-speed wi-fi and business centre. Some rooms also have kitchenettes. Though the hotel is by a busy road, the rooms are well sound-proofed. Breakfast is a quick hop next door. B&B N$$

★ Villa Vista Guesthouse 5 Luther St (entrance on Liliencron Street) villavista.com.na. Rather goldfish-bowl-like in design – you can peer into your opposite neighbour's room – this two-level guesthouse is super-stylish, laden with original art, and delivers on the vista from a fabulous rooftop terrace, where you can linger over an excellent buffet breakfast. B&B N$$

WINDHOEK WEST, SEE MAP PAGE 82

ParadiseGarden Backpackers 5 Roentgen St windhoekhostel.com. Popular with long-term residents, this suburban house in a relaxed neighbourhood has been converted into a small, homely backpackers, where you can lounge in a hammock by the large pool or curl up with a book on the terrace. Camping is also an option; there is even a tree tent! Camping N$, dorms N$, doubles N$$

Puccini House 6 Puccini St 081 1272273. This is a solid budget bet with a handful of fan-cooled basic rooms with en suites or shared bathrooms in a converted house. There are shared kitchen facilities and the tree-filled yard has a pleasant patio area, barbecue facilities, bird feeders and a small pool to cool off in summer. Doubles N$$

1

EASTERN SUBURBS, SEE MAP PAGE 89

★ **Belvedere Boutique Hotel** 76–78 Dr Kwame Nkrumah Rd, Ludwigsdorf ⓦ belvedere-boutiquehotel.com. Attracting business and holiday clientele, this delightful boutique hotel has a personal touch. It comprises standard, family and four superb luxury rooms, where you can enjoy scented candles while soaking in the bath, pillows galore on the bed, and a balcony overlooking leafy grounds. The place stands out for its numerous stylishly and comfortably furnished quiet areas: a cosy TV lounge and a spacious open-plan kitchen-lounge with a fireplace. Other pluses include the jacuzzi, tennis court, spa, superb breakfasts, high-speed wi-fi, and efficient, friendly service. B&B N$$$

★ **Haus Schwerinsburg** 5 Schwerinsburg St ⓦ hausschwerinsburg.com. Elegant boutique guesthouse comprising a clutch of sumptuous suites blending modern comforts (a/c, fridge, microwave, Smart TV, tea and coffee-making facilities) with antique furniture. When not watching the sunset on your private balcony, you can sink into the sofas overflowing with cushions in the lounge. Breakfast spreads are top-notch. B&B N$$–$$$

Hotel Heinitzburg 22 Heinitzburg St ⓦ heinitzburg.com. With unmistakable Disneyland-like turrets, this former hilltop German fort offers a mix of colonial-style elegance and modern comfort. The sixteen generous rooms have been individually refurbished with plenty of modern glitz and a fondness for bed canopies and mirrors. Service is courteous and fairly formal, especially at the fine-dining hotel restaurant, but the gardens and pool are relaxing and the delightful terrace affords stellar views across the city. B&B N$$$

Hotel Thule 1 Gorges St, Klein Windhoek ⓦ hotelthule.com. Illuminated at night on the Windhoek skyline, you'd think the mother ship had landed. The place is more down-to-earth in the daylight, with undistinguished carpeted rooms aimed firmly at the business market – workspace, minibar, safe, etc. The fabulous views from the terrace make the place perfect for a cocktail while watching the sun's last rays on the Auas Mountains. B&B N$$$

Londiningi Guesthouse 11 Winterberg St, Eros Park ⓦ londiningi.com. Set in a lovely tropical garden with a small pool, this place offers a variety of rooms, from doubles to a family room for five, with sophisticated African-themed decor and modern amenities. Light lunches and dinners can also be prepared. The French–Namibian cuisine reflects the ownership. B&B N$$

★ **The Olive Exclusive Boutique Hotel** 22 Promenaden St, Klein Windhoek ⓦ theolive-namibia.com. The seven sumptuous suites here are in a class of their own in Windhoek regarding style, comfort and price. The three junior suites and four stunning premier suites – the latter with vast windows and a private deck with a plunge pool – have each been themed on a different region of Namibia. Laden with antique books and objets d'art and decorated with paintings and photographic murals, they also contain all modern comforts: sofas you can sink into, vast beds, a laptop, a Nespresso machine, a fireplace and fluffy bathrobes. A swimming pool is set in the olive grove, and dining is top-notch (see page 98). B&B N$$$$

Olive Grove Guesthouse 22 Promenaden St, Klein Windhoek ⓦ quiverandco.com/olive-grove-guesthouse. The gloomy contemporary decor (floor-to-ceiling cement, including the bedroom and bathroom) of this popular guesthouse – a more economical sibling to the adjacent *Olive Exclusive Boutique Hotel* – is partially offset by supremely comfortable beds and superior bed linen. Standard rooms downstairs are noisier, opening onto the kitchen-dining area and car park, whereas the upstairs luxury rooms open onto a shared terrace. The staff is helpful, the breakfasts are excellent, and there is the option of fine dining at the exclusive *Olive Restaurant* (see page 98) next door. B&B N$$$

Roof of Africa 124–126 Nelson Mandela Ave, Klein Windhoek ⓦ roofofafrica.com. Popular mid-priced business hotel and conference centre with a lively bar area. Though situated on a busy road, the rather small, modern rooms are sufficiently set back behind a crowded, bamboo-filled courtyard to avoid the noise. Also, there are handy self-catering apartments nearby. B&B N$$

Sonneneck Guesthouse 129 Eros Road, Eros Park ⓦ sonneneck.com.na. Immaculately kept establishment comprising seven light, spacious, well-appointed tiled rooms open to a private patch of patio with garden chairs and table. The communal grassy front garden and pool area are similarly inviting. B&B N$$

Tourmaline Guesthouse 10 Toermalyn St, Eros ⓣ 061 228922 or ⓣ 081 2831646, ⓔ olles@iway.na. The Astroturf mini-putting green and faux rock pool and water feature area are a little tacky. Still, you can't fault the service and excellent value: homely rooms with plenty of space to spread your belongings, a minibar, tea and coffee and ample bathrooms. B&B N$$

★ **Urban Camp** 2 Schanzen Rd, Klein Windhoek ⓦ urbancamp.net. This convenient, secure campground is in a residential area, within walking distance of a supermarket, an ATM and *Joe's Beerhouse*. It offers plenty of natural and artificial shade, clean hot showers, and a pleasant bar with a pool, picnic table and hammocks. Tents equipped with bedding are also available. Camping N$, tent provided for two N$$

Villa Moringa 111a Joseph Mukwayu Ithana St, Ludwigsdorf ⓦ villa-moringa.com. This upmarket guesthouse boasts six immaculate, well-appointed and tastefully designed standard doubles (with tea and coffee facilities and minibar), plus five larger and swisher VIP rooms and a few other combinations. There is a lovely, airy breakfast area and places to sit on the shady dining terrace or the poolside loungers. N$$–$$$

Villa Violet 48 Ziegler St, Klein Windhoek ⓦ villaviolet.

net. Smart guesthouse with accommodating hosts, comprising five immaculate rooms fitted out in contemporary design. As well as a shady garden and pool with sunloungers, there's a very comfortable breakfast-lounge area and good coffee and tea available round the clock. Breakfasts are highly recommended. N$$$

★ **The Weinberg** 13 Jan Jonker Rd gondwana-collection. If it's a hotel rather than a guesthouse ambiance you're after, this is arguably the city's top choice. A striking gleaming-white building featuring plenty of sparkling glass and 41 stylishly furnished rooms of various configurations – contemporary decor but some with retro touches, and some with private balconies or patios. The rooftop terrace lounge is a delight and while the food lives up to Gondwana standards, other high-quality restaurants are within the hotel complex. B&B N$$$

SOUTHERN SUBURBS, SEE MAP PAGE 91

Arebbusch Travel Lodge Corner of Golf and Auas roads, Olympia arebbusch.com. Efficient, modern and clean motel-like property a few kilometres south of town on the main road, with an array of good-value accommodation, from compact self-catering chalets with private patio and braai (no breakfast provided) to standard and superior rooms (some off site, in the city), or camping – standard or luxury. Book one of the quieter, more private chalets on the Eros Airport runway side, away from the busy main road. Other benefits include a pool, a decent restaurant (see page 98), good security and shaded parking. Camping per person N$, doubles B&B N$$, self-catering chalets N$$

Casa Blanca Hotel Corner of Gous and Fritsche streets, Pioneers Park casablancahotel.com.na. German colonial fort meets Spanish hacienda in this whitewashed confection with wrought-iron rail fixtures and some eclectic touches – a tiny gym, jacuzzi, small Moroccan-themed lounge and indigenous plant garden, for starters. Rooms are more conventional: even the standard rooms are spacious and light, with a minibar, DStv, a/c and a lounge area. B&B N$$

EATING

Culinary offerings in Windhoek are essentially a mix of **European** – with a predictable German bias – and **South African** fare. Meat features strongly, whereas **vegetarians** will have fewer menu options. Most restaurants are located in **Klein Windhoek**, many drawing a predominantly white clientele; some offer an alfresco dining experience; others opt for an air-conditioned environment, while some have both. Restaurants in the **city centre** have a more mixed crowd, especially at weekday lunchtime. If you want the kind of **Namibian food** that the majority of the population eats, head for the *Xwama Traditional Restaurant* (see page 98) in Katutura or sample some street food at the market there; other African dishes feature at the Cameroonian-run *La Marmite Royale*, at the Zoo Park (see below).

CENTRAL WINDHOEK, SEE MAP PAGE 82

Café Schneider Carl List Mall, Independence Avenue facebook.com/cafeschneiderwindhoek. The self-proclaimed oldest café in Windhoek (established 1957) is a dependable lunchtime choice if you're in the city centre. The location is a little gloomy – in a shopping precinct – but the daily chef's specials of German-Namibian fare usually hit the spot. N$$

La Marmite Royale (Zoo Café) Independence Avenue at the Zoo Park 081 2445353. The central leafy setting is reason enough to visit, and the West and Central African menu adds to the draw. Tuck into a spicy beef stew with *jollof* rice or the signature Cameroonian curry. Spinach and okra feature strongly, and vegetarians will also find other joy in the menu. The quality can be uneven, but it's worth the risk. N$$–$$$

Crafts Bistro Old Breweries, 40 Tal St facebook.com/craftbistronamibia.com. This upstairs terrace is a handy spot for a healthy light bite – using mainly organic ingredients – or an indulgent home-made cake while shopping for crafts. It also does a range of breakfasts. N$–$$

★ **Old Continental Café & Takeaway** Continental Passage, off Independence Avenue 061 307176. This weekday daytime venue is an unlikely find in an uninviting alleyway close to the post office. Clean and cosy, with indoor and outdoor seating, plus newspapers to browse, it boasts an excellent value cosmopolitan menu presented as a humorous newspaper sheet. Freshly-prepared pickings range from deli burgers and gyros with crispy fries and curries to rolls, stir-fries, fruit smoothies, and daily specials. N$–$$

Sicilia Corner of Independence Avenue and Garten Street facebook.com/siciliarestuarants. This central Italian restaurant pulls in a mixed crowd for its congenial yet relaxed setting. Decent, inexpensive pizza and pasta dishes finished with home-made ice cream. Takeaways are also possible. N$$–$$$

WINDHOEK WEST, SEE MAP PAGE 82

★ **NICE** 2 Mozart St, corner of Hosea Kutako Drive nicenamibia.com. As it's a finishing school for chefs and hospitality staff at the Namibia Institute of Culinary Excellence (NICE), generally, everyone strives to impress. The changing three-course fixed-price lunch is a steal at N$166 or you can just have a course or two. Meals are served in a sophisticated interior or the courtyard by the koi pond. Incorporating organic local produce from their vegetable garden, dishes are delicious, and the menu is varied and creative, featuring offerings such as grilled oryx loin with poached pear and rocket pilaf rice. N$$

Pepata Pavlov Street, at the back of Casa Bem Vindo Guesthouse facebook.com/pepatacuisines. An opportunity to sample some traditional fare in no-frills

1

surroundings, though you'll need a strong stomach and a sense of adventure. Take your pick from mopane worms, platefuls of mealie meal (pap) with *kapana* (grilled beef strips) or even a goat 'smiley' – best not to know in advance. You can take away or eat in; though service can be slow, a memorable experience is guaranteed. N$$

EASTERN SUBURBS, SEE MAP PAGE 89

Cape Town Fish Market The Weinberg Estate, 13 Jan Jonker St ⓦctfm.com.na. Upmarket South African franchise, specialising in fish dishes, seafood and sushi, across from the *Weinberg Hotel*. The West Coast *poijkie* – a tasty fish and seafood stew served in a classic metal pot – is a winner. The attractive interior and balcony and buzzing atmosphere at weekends pull in the crowds – so book a table in advance, especially if you want one on the balcony, looking out across the sparkling city lights. But note that vegetarians and vegans will find little joy here. N$$$–N$$$$

The Fisher 21 Nelson Mandela Ave, Hidas Centre, Klein Windhoek ⓣ081 1661032, ⓔres@thefisher.com.na. A classy joint with an extensive menu of beautifully presented freshly sourced seafood from Namibian, South African and Angolan waters, with choice wines to accompany. The menu spans simple fish and chips to champagne-doused monkfish with prawns. N$$–$$$

Fresh 'N' Wild @ Utopia 64 Nelson Mandela Ave, Klein Windhoek ⓦfreshnwild.net. Freshly prepared healthy food, using plenty of locally sourced ingredients: breakfasts, snacks, tasty light meals, and some tasty thin-crust pizzas in a pleasant garden setting. N$–$$$

Garnish Sam Nujoma Avenue, City Plaza ⓦgarnish-indian-restaurant.business.site. A haven for veggies and vegans in Namibia's meat-dominated culinary landscape, this poplar dimly-lit Indian restaurant has the same menu as its sibling in Swakopmund and the same system of individually priced veggies, starches and other sides, which can add up, but there are frequent meal deals. N$$–$$$

★ Joe's Beerhouse 160 Nelson Mandela Ave, Eros ⓦjoesbeerhouse.com. This renowned, vast watering hole under thatch serves decent, moderately priced pub grub; pork and game meat feature strongly. Try the sosatie (kebab) of assorted game meats in mango-chilli sauce with mealie pap croquettes. Often buzzing even midweek, the place can be seething at weekends, with tour groups and locals alike, which inevitably takes its toll on the overworked staff. Weekly drumming and occasional live bands add to the place's popularity. Reservations are recommended. N$$–$$$$

The Olive Exclusive Restaurant The Olive Exclusive Boutique Hotel, 22 Promenaden St, Klein Windhoek ⓦtheolive-namibia.com. A small, seasonal menu (only three to four starters, mains and desserts) of mouthwatering fusion cuisine in a relaxed but chic minimalist setting; dine outside on the balcony overlooking the olive grove. N$$$$

Olivia's Kitchen The Weinberg Estate, 13 Jan Jonker St ⓦfacebook.com/oliviaswindhoek. A great daytime venue with indoor and outdoor seating serving healthy breakfasts, lunches and tea-time cakes. Offering locally sourced ingredients, with plenty of vegan and veggie options and a scrumptious soup of the day, it's easy to understand the place's popularity. N$$–$$$

Sardinia Blue Olive Corner of Sam Nujoma Drive and Klein Street, Klein Windhoek ⓦfacebook.com/sardiniablueolive. Authentic Italian food (and more besides) that goes beyond pizzas – though there are plenty – including home-made pasta, served in a no-frills environment, both inside and out on the deck. The place is frequently packed, especially at weekends. N$$$

★ Stellenbosch Wine Bar and Bistro Bougain Villas Shopping Centre, 320 Sam Nujoma Drive, Klein Windhoek ⓦfacebook.com/TheStellenboschWineBar. Though the menu features other inventive dishes, this place is all about meat – especially beef; various cuts and sizes are served flame-grilled with a choice of sides and sauces in a delightful colonial-style courtyard setting. Perfect for lingering over a bottle of wine from their extensive and reasonably priced wine list. Reservations are essential at weekends. N$$$–$$$$

SOUTHERN SUBURB, SEE MAP PAGE 91

Arebbusch Travel Lodge Restaurant Corner of Golf and Auas roads, Olympia ⓦarebbusch.com. The inexpensive, large portions offer good value for money. This, combined with friendly, if sometimes slow, service and secure parking, ensures the place draws a good local crowd and guests. There's plenty of seating under the *lapa* or out in the open air under umbrellas, with the place humming at weekends, including at the Sunday lunch buffet. N$$–$$$

KATUTURA, SEE MAP PAGE 80

Xwama Traditional Restaurant Xwama Cultural Village, corner of Omongo Street and Independence Avenue, Wanaheda ⓦxwama.com. It's a rather touristy set-up for some 'authentic' African cooking. Be prepared to be taken out of your culinary comfort zone and indulge in some goat's head, donkey meat or mopane worms (see page 62) – heavily disguised in pizza; alternatively, there's some more familiar but tasty chicken and plenty of spinach, *fufu* and okra to accompany the mains, which includes favourites from across the continent. It's worth phoning ahead to avoid the tour groups. N$$–$$$

DRINKING AND NIGHTLIFE

SEE MAPS PAGES 81 AND 91

Clubs come and go and relocate, mainly operating during the latter part of the week and at weekends. **Entry** is usually around N$50 or more for special events. Several nightclubs in Katutura are starting to pull in a more mixed crowd.

However, only go with someone who knows the place, and make sure you've transport back fixed up before you hit the nightlife. If you're in Namibia in October or November, look out for the annual **Windhoek Jazz Festival**, which attracts international artists, such as Letta Mbulu and Caiphus Semenya, as well as talented local acts (ⓦ facebook.com/cityofwindhoekjazzfestival.com.na).

★ The Brewer's Market Old Breweries Complex, 48 Tal St ⓦ facebook.com/.na. Multilevel cultural space showcasing art, fashion and music, with food and drink outlets. Most of all, it's the place to party downtown, with DJs and karaoke featuring strongly. The *Boiler Room* has something on every evening, from live jazz to quiz nights, plus the rooftop bar, *The Loft*. All venues draw a multicultural crowd of visitors and locals.

Club London Nasmith Road, Southern Industrial ⓦ bit.ly/clublondon1. Complete with ceiling drapes, giant video screens, laser lights and a range of dance beats from hip-hop to house, *kudoro* to *kizomba*, this is Windhoek's top dance venue, enticing the punters with foam parties, theme nights, drinks specials and occasionally dancers – cheaper entry before 10pm.

Nimms Independence Memorial Museum, top floor, Robert Mugabe Avenue and Fidel Castro Street ⓦ nimmsr.com. The city's ultimate panoramic vista, though you can sink into comfy sofas or prop up the slick bar in air-conditioned comfort, head for the terrace, cocktail in hand, to watch the sunset or admire the city's glittering lights. It's probably best to skip the food.

Sky Bar Hilton Hotel, Rev Michael Scott St ⓦ facebook.com/HiltonWindhoekSkyBar. This small rooftop bar by the pool is a prime spot for a sundowner: cocktails, draught beer and craft gin are very much in vogue and a DJ mixes the tracks on a Friday night. Tapas are available to help soak up the alcohol.

Windhoek City Night Market Windhoek Country Club Resort, Western Bypass, by Pioneers Park ⓦ windhoekcitymarket.com. Though a little out of town, this extremely popular fortnightly Friday night market has a convivial, family-friendly atmosphere, with food and drink stalls to choose from and accompanying live music. Entry charge.

ENTERTAINMENT

There's not an overwhelming amount going on in Windhoek regarding entertainment. Check out the listings on ⓦ whatsonnamibia.com and keep an eye on the entertainment pages of the local press.

THEATRE

National Theatre of Namibia 12 John Meinert St ⓦ ntn.org.na. A drama, dance and music menu, from local amateur performers to international artists. It also hosts the Windhoek Symphony Orchestra.

CULTURAL CENTRE

Franco-Namibian Cultural Centre 118 Robert Mugabe Ave ⓦ fncc.org.na. The centre offers a full programme of European and African films and a range of cultural events, from art exhibitions and poetry readings to live music and dance.

CINEMAS

Ster Kinekor The Grove Mall, Frankie Fredericks St, Prosperita ⓦ thegrovemallofnamibia.com. In the south of the city, Windhoek's newest, largest smart shopping centre offers a multiscreen cinema, a ten-pin bowling alley and a games arcade.

Ster Kinekor Maerua Mall, Centauraus Road ⓦ maeruamall.com/cinema. Two digital 3D screens.

SHOPPING

SEE MAPS PAGES 80, 82, 89 AND 91

The main **street markets** are in Post Street Mall and along Independence Avenue by the main car park, where even some Himba have set up a stall. Haggling is expected in both places, though cheaper curios can be found in Okahandja (see page 171). More expensive but often similar offerings are sold at fixed prices in the shops along Independence Avenue. Windhoek's three main **malls** – Wernhil Park (ⓦ wernhilpark.com), Maerua Mall (ⓦ maeruamall.com) and The Grove (ⓦ thegrovemallnamibia.com) – offer much the same diet as South African **chain stores** and **supermarkets**. The first two are centrally located, whereas The Grove is the newest, glitziest and largest addition to the retail scene and lies off the main road south out of the city.

BOOKS

The Book Den Puccini Street at Hosea Kutako ⓦ facebook.com/WindhoekBookDen. The largest privately-owned bookshop in Namibia with informed and friendly staff and a good selection of books in English and Afrikaans.

CNA Wernhil Park and Maerua Park malls. South African chain store carrying mainly international bestsellers and magazines.

Orumbonde Books Old Breweries Complex, 40 Tal St ⓣ 081 1488462. A snug shop crammed with books in English, German and Afrikaans, particularly strong on Namibian and Southern African culture and history.

Uncle Spike's Book Exchange Corner of Garten and Tal streets ⓦ facebook.com/unclespikesbookexchange. Don't be put off by the metal security grill. Just ring the bell, as this place is a real treasure trove full of second-hand books to swap or buy.

Windhoeker Buchhandlung 69–73 Independence

1

Ave whk-buch.com/main.html. It mainly stocks books in German, but there are some in English, too, particularly coffee-table books on Namibia. There is also a good selection of calendars and maps.

CAMPING EQUIPMENT AND OUTDOOR GEAR

Most local four-wheel drive car rental companies also rent out camping gear. However, if you are in need, a couple of Windhoek companies provide a solid service renting out gear; alternatively, you can purchase what you need from one of several outlets.

Adventure Camping Hire 33 Tacoma St, Suiderhof adventure-camping-hire.com Rents out individually priced camping items, including satellite phones and GPS for remote destinations.

Bushwhackers 32 Rhino St, Rhino Park, Windhoek North facebook.com/bushwhackersnamibia. Just off Hosea Kutako, north of the city centre, this large store is an Aladdin's den of camping, hiking and fishing gear.

Cape Union Mart Shop 6 Maerua Mall, corner of Jan Jonker Avenue and Centaurus Road; Shop 478 The Grove Mall, corner of Chasie Street and Frankie Fredericks Road capeunionmart.co.za. South African chain selling good-quality outdoor clothing, footwear and camping gear – from sleeping bags and rucksacks to cooler boxes and gas stoves.

Cymot Greensport 60 Mandume Ndemafayo Avenue cymot.com. The place to go for all your camping, fishing and cycling needs – from four-wheel drive accessories to tents and other outdoor gear.

Namibian Camping Solutions 15 Oponono St, Klein Kuppe namibiancampingsolutions.com. Various shapes and sizes of tents and camping gear for rent, from the basic camping kit for two to a host of individually priced items.

CRAFTS

House of Anin 19 Bougain Villas Shopping Centre, 78 Sam Nujoma Drive anin.com.na. This Nama village women's empowerment project has become a mainstream business, producing distinctive, high-quality embroidered bed linen, tablecloths, cushion covers and the like – some done by hand. They also have a stall in the Namibia Craft Centre.

Namcrafts Old Breweries Complex, 40 Tal Street craftingnamibia.com. With various outlets in Windhoek and elsewhere in Namibia, it offers a wide choice of crafts; some are made in Namibia, but there are plenty of imports from South Africa, too.

★ **Namibia Craft Centre** Old Breweries Complex, 40 Tal St namibiacraftcentre.com. There is a great collection of stalls offering an array of handmade crafts from all over Namibia and sometimes beyond – everything from baskets to stationery, jewellery, wood carvings, textiles, ornaments and paintings. Don't forget to check out the back courtyard of the old brewery, where there are some bigger shops.

Omba Arts Trust Namibia Craft Centre omba.org.na. It's worth seeking out this fair-trade craft stall, selling exquisite basketry, ostrich-shell jewellery and artwork made by Ju|'hoansi communities in northeast Namibia.

Penduka Goreangab Dam, Katutura penduka.com. Although their products are available in various outlets, it's worth getting out to Katutura to see this long-standing women's development project in action (see page 90). The shop sells household products made from embroidered or batik cloth, such as tablecloths, sponge bags and cushion covers and oven gloves. Also, recycled glass jewellery.

Windhoek Textiles No. 3 Simmentaler, Northern Industrial windhoektextile.com.na. If you like the pillowcases or duvet covers embroidered with wildlife that adorns many a lodge bed, this is where to find them.

DIRECTORY

Banks and money Namibia's four leading banks have branches with ATMs on Independence Avenue. The city's shopping malls and petrol stations also have ATMs. FNB, Nedbank and Standard Bank have ATMs that always accept Visa and MasterCard. There are also several bureaux de change on Independence Avenue and at Hosea Kutako International Airport. Novacâmbios, for example, has several branches in Windhoek, including on Independence Avenue and in Maerua Park, The Grove Mall and the Gustav Voigts Centre.

Hospitals and clinics The two state hospitals are oversubscribed, so you are better off going to one of the private hospitals, which offer 24-hour assistance: Rhino Park Private Hospital, Johann Albrecht Street, Windhoek West (061 375000, hospital-namibia.com); Medi-clinic, Heliodoor Street, Eros (061 4331000).

Internet Most hotels, hostels and guesthouses offer free wi-fi. Connectivity is reasonably reliable, but the speed varies. Internet cafés can usually be found in the main shopping malls.

Laundry Most guesthouses, hostels and hotels provide a laundry service but will probably need a whole day to oblige. If you're short of time or have filthy camping gear you're too embarrassed to hand over, take them to one of the following, which do both laundry and dry cleaning: Lana Dry Cleaners at Wernhil Park and Maerua Mall (among other locations), or Laundryland, 339 Sam Nujoma Drive, Klein Windhoek.

Pharmacies There are plenty of well-stocked pharmacists in Windhoek, with knowledgeable staff. In addition to those in medical centres and shopping malls, a couple of useful pharmacies to locate include Klein Windhoek Pharmacy, 341 Sam Nujoma Drive (061 227323), and Langerhans Pharmacy, 7 Independence Ave, Ausspannplatz (langerhanspharmacy.com).

Police The central police station is on the corner of Independence Avenue and Bahnhof Street (061 2093111, emergency 10111). Of greater use is the 24-hour number for the Tourist Protection Unit ⊕ 061 2092002.

Post office The main post office is on the corner of Independence Avenue and Daniel Munamava Street.

Swimming There's a fabulous Olympic-size outdoor swimming pool and a smaller children's pool on Tennis Road, Olympia (⊕ 061 2903089). Set in immaculately kept lawns with thatched shelters and sunloungers. Since the pools are unheated, they're best enjoyed late afternoon or early evening in the summer after they've soaked up a day of sun (closed June–Aug).

Around Windhoek

The nearest escape for city dwellers on hot summer weekends is the rolling hills of **Daan Viljoen Game Park**, a pleasant slice of the countryside and a perfect place to picnic a mere thirty-minute drive west of the city centre. On the other hand, if you're prepared to drive an hour or more out of the capital and fancy a gentle introduction to the Namibian outdoors – as experienced by white Namibians, at least – several **guest farms** provide the perfect answer, offering hiking or horse riding opportunities and some hearty farm cooking. On a contrasting note, if you're heading south out of the city on the B1, it's worth swinging by **Heroes' Acre**, which pays homage to those who lost their lives in the independence struggle.

Daan Viljoen Game Park

20km (12.4 miles) west of Windhoek, signposted off the C28 (an extension of Sam Nujoma Drive) • Daily sunrise–sunset • Charge • Guided walks available • ⓦ nwrnamibia.com/daan-viljoen.htm • No public transport, though transfers can be arranged

If you have transport and fancy escaping the city for a few hours, then there's no better place to head than **Daan Viljoen Game Park**. It's a delightful natural retreat, set among the hills of the Khomas Hochland Plateau, covered in highland shrub vegetation, including kudu bush, buffalo thorn and various acacias.

Although the 6km (3.7-mile) **game drive** is pleasant enough (high-clearance vehicle necessary, four-wheel drive when wet), with some well-sited viewpoints, the absence of predators in the park offers an opportunity to get much closer to the wildlife and experience the bush by exploring on foot. There are two self-guided walking routes: the 3km (1.9 miles) – there and back – **'Wag 'n' Bietjie' trail** is a simple stroll from the reception to the Stengel Dam and is popular with birdwatchers early in the morning; those wanting a more challenging hike should opt for the 9km (5.6-mile) circular **Rooibos Trail**, which heads uphill from close to the *Boma* restaurant, returning via the Augeigas Dam. If you look carefully enough amid the vegetation, there are still signs of the odd crumbling wall that once demarcated plots of the formerly resident Damara community, which was forcibly relocated by the South African regime in the late 1950s.

Wildlife to look out for includes a variety of antelope – springbok, oryx, kudu and eland – alongside other large mammals such as blue wildebeest and even giraffes. Smaller potential sightings include porcupines, yellow mongooses and rock hyraxes. And you can't fail to bump into the ubiquitous warthogs and baboons. Over two hundred **bird species** have been recorded, with plenty of water birds gravitating towards the muddy edges of the dams.

Day visitors are welcome to use the resort's lovely large circular pool and eat at the *Boma* after paying a deposit, redeemable against food and drink purchases.

ACCOMMODATION AND EATING — DAAN VILJOEN GAME PARK

The Boma In the park ⊕ 061 232393. The resort restaurant sits under a large thatched roof with indoor and outdoor seating by the pool. Continental buffet breakfast with hot options is available; otherwise, meat-heavy à la carte meals are provided with the usual international options, plus a kids' menu. Snacks and light bites can be ordered during the day.

Sun Karros Daan Viljoen In the park ⓦ sunkarros.com. Nineteen compact, modern chalets (most for two people), arranged fairly close together, are tastefully designed with all mod cons since the place is also a conference venue. Private patios boast a good braai site, with basic crockery and cutlery, comfortable outdoor furniture and pleasant views. A dozen flat and grassy camping pitches look out at the surrounding hills; though not very private, they have all the necessary amenities, including superior ablution blocks with nice ceramic sinks, arty mirrors and monsoon showers. Camping per person N$, chalets B&B N$$$

Heroes' Acre

10km (6.2 miles) south of Windhoek, signposted off the B1 • Daily 8am–4pm • Charge • No public transport

The controversial, vainglorious N$60-million monument that is **Heroes' Acre** is worth a visit if only to fully appreciate the grandiose monstrosity that is Stalinesque in both conception and scale. Designed and built by a North Korean firm, it was inaugurated in 2002 to foster a spirit of patriotism and nationalism to be passed on to the future generations of Namibia. The hillside memorial comprises a vast parade ground and a broad flight of steps, flanked by the tombstones and grave sites of current and future heroes and heroines, that leads up to a towering white marble obelisk, symbolising a sword. In front stands an 80m (262.5ft) bronze **statue of the 'unknown soldier'**, who resembles Sam Nujoma (see page 344), depicted carrying a Kalashnikov and brandishing a hand grenade. The strong likeness to the country's first president has fuelled criticism in some quarters that Heroes' Acre is more a glorification of SWAPO than a more general remembrance of Namibians who lost their lives in the struggle. However, the vast bronze frieze at the top of the steps carefully portrays the suffering, resistance and ultimate triumph of all Black Namibians, irrespective of ethnicity, political allegiance, age or gender. Once you've hauled yourself up the final step, turn around and soak up the stellar view of Windhoek in front of you before grabbing a cold drink at the on-site **restaurant**.

ACCOMMODATION — AROUND WINDHOEK

Though most people visiting Namibia are itching to head into the desert after finding their bearings in Windhoek, there are a few **guest farms** and **lodges** within an hour's drive of the capital that are pleasant places to spend a night at either end of a holiday. Midweek stays will likely prove quieter. Serious hikers should take note of the new **multiday hiking trail** (see page 103), which takes in several such farms and meanders over the scenic Khomas Hochland, providing a good reason to linger in the area.

Auas Safari Lodge Off the D1463, 22km (13.7 miles) east of the junction with the B1, south of Windhoek ⓦ auas-safarilodge.com. Well-run thatched lodge with sixteen tidy en-suite rooms (with fan/wall heater and private porch) in the Auas Mountains, an hour from Windhoek, 45 minutes from the airport. A relaxing place that attracts day visitors, it offers massages and manicures, a *lapa* and a restful pool area set in grassy surroundings from where you can gaze across the savannah. The more active can do guided or self-guided walks, hikes and birdwatching. Game drives are popular – the reserve is well stocked with giraffes, wildebeest and antelope, including waterbuck and eland. Sunday buffet lunch N$$$, DBB N$$$

Gästefarm Elisenheim 15km (9.3 miles) north of Windhoek, signposted east off the B1 ⓦ elisenheim-guestfarm.com. Welcoming German-Namibian hospitality and home cooking are the draw here, and it's in a lovely setting with a shady, grassy pool area to lounge around and dine. Carpeted rooms are fairly dowdy, though tidy. There are also eight camping pitches accessible by two-wheel drive. With Equitrails based on the property, this is a great place to saddle up. Camping N$, doubles (B&B) N$$

Hohewarte Guest Farm East of the C23, 15km (9.3

HORSE RIDING IN THE EROS MOUNTAINS

There's no better way to appreciate the rolling countryside surrounding Windhoek than by saddling up for a few hours and **exploring on horseback**. Equitrails (ⓦ equitrails.org), a highly experienced and professional outfit with well-cared-for horses – riders must not weigh over 90kg (14.2st), for example – organises a range of **excursions** to suit riders of all levels of experience, from a couple of hours on the farm to a two-hour ride topped off with a sundowner and a bush braai, or even a fully inclusive two-night **horse safari**, staying in the lodge and guest farm accommodation. The stables are based at Elisenheim Guest Farm (ⓦ natron.net/tour/elisenheim/main.html) in the Eros Mountains, 15km (9.3 miles) northeast of Windhoek; hotel transfers from the capital can be arranged.

KHOMAS HOCHLAND HIKING TRAIL

Visitors often overlook the rolling highveld surrounding Windhoek in their rush to clap their eyes on Namibia's more famous landscapes. Still, the opening of the new **Khomas Hochland Hiking Trail** (ⓦhikenamibia.com) may soon change that. Covering a **91km (56.5-mile) circular route over six days** (or 53km/32.9 miles over four days), the trail takes you across five farms, hiking through thornbush scrub, along kloofs and across grasslands, scrambling over boulders and even climbing down a rock ladder. It's physically demanding, but the rewards are ample: superb views at times, abundant wildlife and the chance to sleep out under the stars. You'll catch sight of plenty of kudu, oryx, mountain zebra, warthogs, klipspringer and baboons, as well as countless small reptiles; the birdlife is prolific, too, congregating round the Aretaragas and Otjiseva rivers, farm dams and precious sheltered pools of water in the kloofs, while the ever-elusive leopard keeps out of sight. For the hardcore version of the trail, you need to carry your pack with a sleeping bag (one for cold nights), food, extra clothing, utensils, torch or headlamp and all the usual extras – a walking pole is advisable too, as parts of the trail are heavy on the knees. However, if that all sounds like too much hard work for a holiday, worry not, as there's a **slackpacking** option too, in which you take a daypack with water, snacks, your camera and not much else; the rest of your gear – food and bedding (including mattresses, or even tents, if you want) – is transported for you from camp shelter to camp shelter.

Though basic, each campground has a toilet, wood- or solar-powered hot shower, braai facilities, a pot and a kettle, with the Monte Christo **treehouse** on the fifth night the standout overnight spot. Rather than confining yourself to light, easy-to-cook meals, you can tuck into a pre-ordered fresh farm meal pack from each night's host, which includes braai meat and veg as well as freshly baked bread, though you'll need to carry anything you want to spice up the food. It's even possible to request a few cans of beer to enjoy around the campfire. This is all at an extra cost, but the hike alone is strenuous enough; taking the weight off your back will maximise your enjoyment of the trail.

PRACTICALITIES

The trail starts and finishes at **Dürstenbrook Farm** (ⓦduerstenbrook.net), located 46km (28.6 miles) broadly north of Windhoek – 30km (18.6 miles) along the B1 before turning west. A minimum of three hikers (maximum twelve) is required, and the booking can be made online to do the trail between April and September (though experienced hikers may be allowed in October and March). Daily rates for slackpacking, rather than hiking carrying your gear, are inevitably much more expensive. Check the ⓦhikenamibia.com website for all the details.

miles) south of the junction with the B6 ⓦhohewarte.com. Former colonial police station, post office, and now working cattle farm, this striking, squat farmhouse has seven rooms (some with shared bathrooms). The lounge is particularly cosy, especially round the fire in winter. Don't leave without a hike up Bismarck Mountain. B&B N$$–$$$

Immanuel Wilderness Lodge 20km (12.4 miles) north of Windhoek, west of the B1 ⓦimmanuel-lodge.de. This old-style lodge under lofty thatch has cool stone floors and mosquito nets over the beds so you can keep the doors open at night, though there is a/c. The German owner-chef prepares top-notch meals, and you can pamper yourself with some massage therapy. Although the suburbs of Windhoek are close, you feel right in the bush. B&B N$$

Okapuka 32km (19.9 miles) north of Windhoek, east of the B1 ⓦgondwana-collection.com. On Windhoek's doorstep and convenient if you're heading north, this lodge gives you an early taste of the bush. Surrounded by hills, the thatched main lodge overlooks green lawns with camelthorn trees. Rooms are in thatched cottages or tiled bungalows, decorated in warm earthy tones and providing all the standard comforts. The reserve is packed with wildlife – antelope, giraffes and white rhinos. It is worth driving out here for the Sunday buffet lunch (N$$$–$$$$). N$$$

Ondekaremba Just north of the B6, 7km (4.3 miles) west of Hosea Kutako International Airport ⓦondekaremba.com. This is a perfect layover for those off a late flight or heading for an early one; airport transfers possible. Comfortable rooms and great meals are available in the main lodge and there are a handful of self-catering bungalows a five-minute walk away, plus three camping pitches. Day visitors welcome. The lodge sits next to a dry riverbed, boasts a nice pool, and is surrounded by savannah bush with trails; closed until 31 December 2024.

The southwest

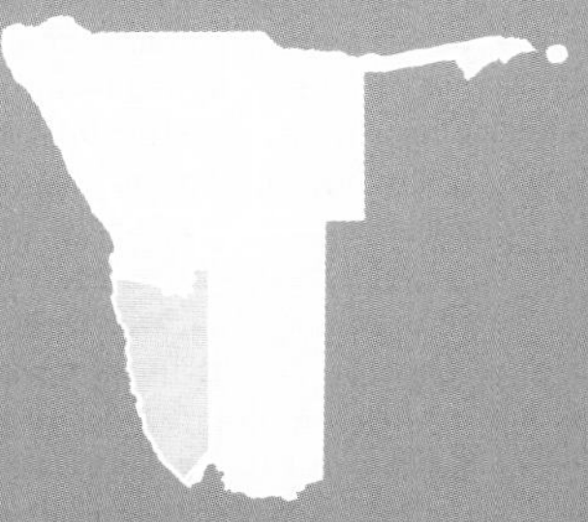

ORYX IN NAMIB-NAUKLUFT NATIONAL PARK

The southwest

2

Sandwiched between the cold Atlantic Ocean to the west and the rugged Great Escarpment to the east, southwest Namibia is a land of mountainous dunes, gravel plains and inselbergs. And the weather is just as varied as the landscapes; it's hard to believe, in the scorching midsummer desert heat, that the town of Aus, on the eastern fringes of the Namib, receives occasional winter snowfall. Much of southwest Namibia is inaccessible, but those reachable sights are among the most iconic in the country. The ever-changing Sossusvlei dunes deservedly hog their fair share of the limelight. Still, the anachronistic mining town of Oranjemund and the ghost mining towns of the Sperrgebiet simmer with intrigue. Lüderitz is also well worth visiting to glimpse Namibia's German colonial past.

Much of the Namib, one of the world's oldest deserts, is protected within the boundaries of the largely inaccessible **Namib-Naukluft National Park**, which includes the magical, richly coloured dunes around **Sossusvlei** – one of the country's most visited attractions – and the impressive **Naukluft Mountains**, home to the rare Hartmann's mountain zebra, and a popular hiking destination. Tucked away on the coast at the southwestern limit of the park sits the anachronistic German port town of **Lüderitz**, now an emerging tourist centre and the only point of access to the former diamond mining area that is now the **Tsau ||Khaeb (Sperrgebiet) National Park**.

Down in the far southwest corner of Namibia, right on the South African border, the Orange River empties into an avian-rich estuary at the former high-security diamond-mining town of **Oranjemund**, a little-visited, rather off-beat destination. Not far up the road from here, the booming mining settlement of **Rosh Pinah** sparkles with its pristine streets and shopping centre.

Namib-Naukluft National Park

Southern section access points: Sesriem for Sossusvlei and the dunes; 10km (6.2 miles) southwest of Büllsport on the D854 for the Naukluft Mountains • Sunrise–sunset • Charge (see page 112)

The **NAMIB-NAUKLUFT NATIONAL PARK** is one of Africa's largest protected areas. It has increased in size from a small game reserve in 1907 to a vast national park – larger than Switzerland – that now encompasses a huge tranche of the Namib Desert, including former restricted mining areas. However, only a fraction of this immense and unique landscape is accessible to the public.

As a tourist destination, the park is renowned above all for the desolate beauty of the vibrantly coloured **dunes** around Sossusvlei, on the eastern edge of a rippling dune sea, whose relentless progress is eventually halted by the Atlantic Coast to the west and the Kuiseb River to the north. Yet the **Naukluft Mountains**, which loom out of the gravel plains further east, prove an equally compelling destination for hikers, where the permanent water sources that lurk in the massif's deep ravines (kloofs) support a surprising diversity of **flora and fauna**.

A rockier desert landscape emerges in the northwest corner of the reserve, north of the Kuiseb River. It is interspersed with pockets of dunes, beyond which extend gravel plains strewn with specimens of the planet's oldest plant, the **welwitschia mirabilis** (see page 218). Along the northern section of the park's windswept coastline lie the

GERMAN COLONIAL ARCHITECTURE, LÜDERITZ

Highlights

❶ **Sossusvlei** The vibrant changing colours of Namib's loftiest dunes stand in stark contrast to the ghostly vleis, producing the country's most striking landscape. See page 112

❷ **Hot-air ballooning** Experience sunrise hovering high above the desert, followed by a sumptuous champagne breakfast. See page 113

❸ **Naukluft Mountains** One of the country's most scenic campgrounds provides an excellent base for some challenging hiking in the national park. See page 117

❹ **The NamibRand Reserve** Exclusive tented lodges in some of Namibia's most spectacular scenery, with glittering night skies. See page 118

❺ **Tiras Mountains** The D707, which skirts the muscular Tiras Mountains, is one of the country's most scenic roads. See page 121

❻ **Lüderitz** Home to Namibia's best-preserved German colonial architecture and the fascinating former mining town of Kolmanskop, which lies half buried in the sand. See page 124

HIGHLIGHTS ARE MARKED ON THE MAP ON PAGE 108

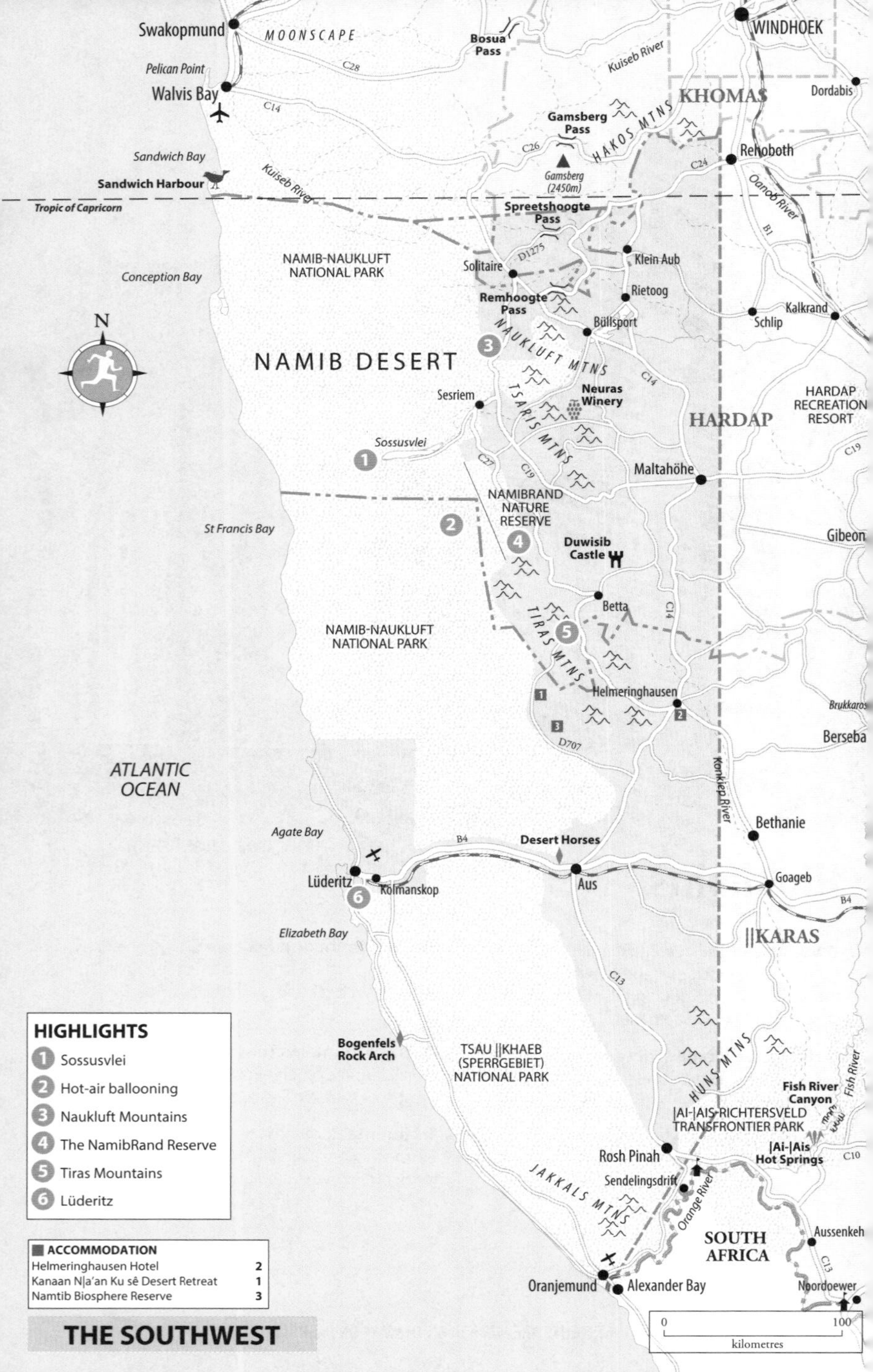

THE SOUTHWEST
HIGHLIGHTS
1 Sossusvlei
2 Hot-air ballooning
3 Naukluft Mountains
4 The NamibRand Reserve
5 Tiras Mountains
6 Lüderitz
ACCOMMODATION
Helmeringhausen Hotel 2
Kanaan N|a'an Ku sê Desert Retreat 1
Namtib Biosphere Reserve 3
Swakopmund
MOONSCAPE
Bosua Pass
WINDHOEK
Pelican Point
C28
Kuiseb River
Walvis Bay
C14
KHOMAS
Dordabis
Gamsberg Pass
HAKOS MTNS
C26
Rehoboth
Sandwich Bay
Gamsberg (2450m)
C24
Sandwich Harbour
Kuiseb River
Oanob River
Tropic of Capricorn
Spreetshoogte Pass
B1
D1275
NAMIB-NAUKLUFT NATIONAL PARK
Solitaire
Klein Aub
Conception Bay
Remhoogte Pass
Rietoog
Kalkrand
Büllsport
Schlip
N
NAMIB DESERT
NAUKLUFT MTNS
C14
Neuras Winery
HARDAP RECREATION RESORT
Sesriem
TSARIS MTNS
HARDAP
Sossusvlei
C27
C19
C19
Maltahöhe
NAMIBRAND NATURE RESERVE
St Francis Bay
Duwisib Castle
Gibeon
Betta
TIRAS MTNS
C14
NAMIB-NAUKLUFT NATIONAL PARK
Helmeringhausen
Brukkaros
Berseba
D707
ATLANTIC OCEAN
Konkiep River
Bethanie
Agate Bay
B4
Desert Horses
Lüderitz
Kolmanskop
Aus
Goageb
B4
Elizabeth Bay
||KARAS
C13
Bogenfels Rock Arch
TSAU ||KHAEB (SPERRGEBIET) NATIONAL PARK
HUNS MTNS
Fish River
Fish River Canyon
|AI-|AIS/RICHTERSVELD TRANSFRONTIER PARK
|Ai-|Ais Hot Springs
Rosh Pinah
C10
JAKKALS MTNS
Sendelingsdrift
Orange River
SOUTH AFRICA
Aussenkehr
C13
Oranjemund
Alexander Bay
Noordoewer
0
100
kilometres

constantly shifting contours of Sandwich Harbour – a shallow lagoon encircled by majestic dunes and a major wetland site for resident and migratory birds (see page 224). This northern section of the national park is accessed via, or en route to/from, Swakopmund and Walvis Bay and is covered in 'Chapter 5'. The southern section has two main access points: at Sesriem for the dunescape around Sossusvlei and southwest of the tiny crossroads and farm at Büllsport, where there is an entrance to the eastern side of the Naukluft Mountains.

The dunes

Flaunted in countless holiday brochures, wildlife documentaries and even car ads, the towering **dunes** of the Sossusvlei area constitute Namibia's most iconic landscape, epitomising the country's vast, arid and seemingly uninhabited expanses of wilderness and stark beauty. Yet, despite this overexposure, the dunes rarely disappoint when you finally get to see them for yourself, though at dawn in high season, the 65km (40.4-mile) access road from the Sesriem gate to the Sossusvlei car park can seem like a commuter highway, as a stream of vehicles race to catch the best sunrise shot or beat the crowds to the 325m (1066.3ft) summit of 'Big Daddy', the tallest dune in the area.

The **best time to visit** is early morning, as the rising sun causes the dunes to undergo dramatic colour changes, though you'll need several hours to explore the area thoroughly. Late afternoon, towards sunset, is also rewarding and usually less crowded since only visitors staying inside the park can stay that late. After 10am, with the sun high in the sky, temperatures soar above 40°C in summer and rarely dip much below 30°C in winter, although, at that time of day, you're almost guaranteed to have the place to yourself.

Elim Dune

5km (3.1 miles) from the Sesriem gate, signposted to the right off the road to Sossusvlei

Given its proximity to the main gate, **Elim Dune** is a popular spot to head for at sunset. Notable for its photogenic tufts of the Namib's endemic stipagrostis grass set against the rich ochre sand, the dune also offers dramatic views across the surrounding gravel plains to the Naukluft Mountains. However, it is a deceptively long climb to the top. Possessing relatively abundant vegetation, the dune is interesting to visit at dawn on a calm morning, as you'll see a multitude of criss-crossing tracks made by insects, reptiles and small animals that are supported by the grasses. Watch out for the aggressive Namib dune ant, which has a distinctive black-and-white-striped hairy abdomen and exceedingly long legs to keep its body well elevated from the hot sand.

Sesriem Canyon

4km (2.5 miles) inside the park, signposted off to the left as you enter the Sesriem gate

Sesriem Canyon is a narrow, shallow gorge consisting of sandstone and pebble conglomerate whose formation began some 10–20 million years ago when the Tsauchab River, which now only flows every few years after heavy rains, was a much more potent force, carving its way through the landscape. The layers containing larger rocks were formed during periods of strong water flow, whereas those composed of smaller pebbles and higher concentrations of sand were established when the current was less fierce. A continental uplift a mere 2–5 million years ago then set off a process of erosion that continues today. The name Sesriem derives from the *ses* (six) *riems* (leather thongs knotted together) that were needed to draw water up to the gorge rim. You can walk down into the canyon and along its sandy floor; it's only just over a kilometre (0.6 miles) long, around 30m (98.4ft) deep and only a few metres wide in places, flattening out as it heads towards Sossusvlei. In the rainy season, pools of water collect in the canyon's deep hollows.

2

Dune 45

Signposted left off the access road, 45km (28 miles) after the gate

Probably the area's most photographed dune, **Dune 45**, is, believe it or not, 45km (28 miles) from the entrance. Although only 85m (278.9ft) in height, this star dune proffers a classic curvaceous spine, with a perfectly situated gnarled camelthorn tree at its base, though it's getting progressively harder to capture a shot of it without vehicles parked in front of a stream of people toiling up the sand for sunrise.

Hidden Vlei

Follow the trail of posts 2km (1.2 miles) over the dunes to the left of the two-wheel drive car park

Tucked away behind rust-coloured dunes, **Hidden Vlei**, a ghostly clay pan dotted with dead acacia trees, is less visited than Dead Vlei (see page 110) but just as atmospheric. Look out for the oryx and springbok spoor across the pan.

Dead Vlei and 'Big Daddy'

To reach Dead Vlei, hike 3km (1.9 miles) south across the sand from the Sossusvlei four-wheel drive car park; take plenty of water

Eerily beautiful, **Dead Vlei** was once the endpoint of the Tsauchab River until the climate changed and the watercourse became blocked by dunes, leaving the camelthorn trees – some of which are estimated to be nine hundred years old – to wither and die. Their sun-scorched skeletal trunks remain due to the aridity of the climate and absence of wood-boring insects; protruding from the parched, white

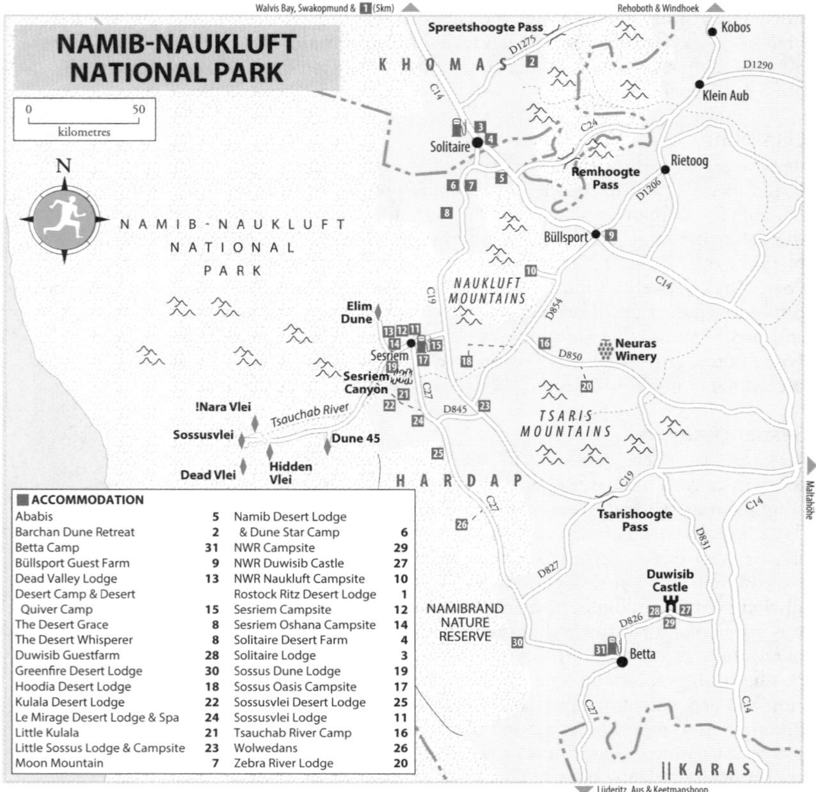

ACCOMMODATION			
Ababis	5	Namib Desert Lodge & Dune Star Camp	6
Barchan Dune Retreat	2	NWR Campsite	29
Betta Camp	31	NWR Duwisib Castle	27
Büllsport Guest Farm	9	NWR Naukluft Campsite	10
Dead Valley Lodge	13	Rostock Ritz Desert Lodge	1
Desert Camp & Desert Quiver Camp	15	Sesriem Campsite	12
The Desert Grace	8	Sesriem Oshana Campsite	14
The Desert Whisperer	8	Solitaire Desert Farm	4
Duwisib Guestfarm	28	Solitaire Lodge	3
Greenfire Desert Lodge	30	Sossus Dune Lodge	19
Hoodia Desert Lodge	18	Sossus Oasis Campsite	17
Kulala Desert Lodge	22	Sossusvlei Desert Lodge	25
Le Mirage Desert Lodge & Spa	24	Sossusvlei Lodge	11
Little Kulala	21	Tsauchab River Camp	16
Little Sossus Lodge & Campsite	23	Wolwedans	26
Moon Mountain	7	Zebra River Lodge	20

THE NAMIB SAND SEA

Undoubtedly, desert equals sand for most people, and there are few more spectacular examples of sand desert (erg) than the **Namib Sand Sea**, which stretches for most of Namibia's Atlantic Coast, pushing south into South Africa and north into Angola. The remarkableness of the 50,000 sq km (19305.1 sq mile) Namib dunes within the Namib-Naukluft National Park – about the size of Belgium – has now been internationally recognised as a UNESCO World Heritage Site. Though the Namib boasts some of the highest dunes in the world, at over 300m (984.3ft), it's the ever-changing palette of **colours** that most impresses – from gold to pink, cream to brick-red, apricot to maroon. The coastal dunes are generally paler, consisting of newer sand, much of which originates from sediments washed down the Orange River to be swept northwards by ocean currents and tossed onto the beaches. The colouration becomes deeper and redder towards the eastern limits of the sand sea due to the amount of iron oxide present in the predominantly quartz sand and the ways in which the dunes have weathered over time. Even so, the dunes magically alter in hue with the changing light and drifting fog (the only water source here).

Dune morphology, on the other hand, depends principally on the strength and direction of the **wind**; most kinds of dunes are longer on the windward side, where the wind pushes the sand up the dune, with a shorter 'slip face' in the lee of the wind, where the blown sand tips over. Here, occasional grasses take root, helping stabilise the dune, and wind-blown detritus collects, providing food for some of the Namib's extraordinary desert-adapted creatures (see page 9). Thus, it's worth being aware that racing down the slip face, in particular, causes damage to the dune ecology.

The following main dune formations are present in the Namib:

BARCHAN DUNES

Classic crescent-shaped dunes with two 'horns' facing downwind. The most mobile of dunes, forming in strong unidirectional winds; some in the Namib can migrate over 50m (164ft) per year. They are especially prominent around Lüderitz and Walvis Bay and up the northern section of the Skeleton Coast. Less common parabolic dunes are also crescent-shaped but with the horns trailing upwind and the slip face on the inside.

LINEAR (SEIF) DUNES

Converging winds push the sand into long lines or ridges parallel to the prevailing wind; some linear dunes in the Namib are over 32km (19.9 miles) long.

STAR DUNES

Many examples of these giant dunes are found around Sossusvlei. They are formed when several winds blow from different directions, resulting in three or more steep ridges radiating out from a central peak. Star dunes do not migrate but continue to grow vertically and in the Namib form in a south-to-north direction.

TRANSVERSE DUNES

Long, asymmetrical dunes that form at right angles to the prevailing wind in conditions of abundant sand, such as on the road between Walvis Bay and the airport; with steep slip faces, they appear like giant ripples from the air.

clay-pan floor, they provide a stark contrast to the surrounding golden dunes and cerulean sky. '**Big Daddy**' lies to the south of the vlei, and you'll be rewarded for the hour-long slog to the top by a spectacular panoramic view of the dune sea rippling away into the distance. This is often topped off by a five-minute adrenaline rush as you race down the dune slip face into the pan – though this can damage dune ecology (see box above).

Sossusvlei

65km (40.4 miles) from the Sesriem gate, 4km (2.5 miles) from the two-wheel drive car park, accessible only by four-wheel drive

The prized destination for most visitors is **Sossusvlei**, a large, elliptical-shaped, salt-rich pan surrounded by acacias, grasses and the odd shrub and enclosed by giant dunes. Look carefully in some of the camelthorn trees, where you may spot the parasitic mistletoe entwined around their branches. Once every five to ten years after exceptionally heavy rains, you may be lucky enough to witness the vlei transformed by a flash flood from the ephemeral **Tsauchab River**. The resulting shallow lake remains miraculously populated by water lilies and dragonflies for weeks, attracting a flurry of aquatic birdlife.

ARRIVAL AND DEPARTURE

By car There is no public transport to the Sesriem gate, which is the entry point for Sossusvlei. Access from the south or north along the high-quality dirt road C14 is well-signposted. Once in the park, you follow a tarred road for 60km (37.3 miles) to the two-wheel drive car park. Do not drive off the tarmac, whatever the temptation, as your tracks can remain for years. The final 5km (3.1 miles) to the Sossusvlei car park follows a broad sandy track for which you need to engage a four-wheel drive, preferably after letting some air out of your tyres. If you do not have a four-wheel drive vehicle or you are not experienced at driving in sand, it is recommended that you park your vehicle in the car park and take the regular Namibia Wildlife Resorts shuttle service to Sossusvlei (N$180 per person), rather than suffer the ignominy of being towed out by the park wardens once stuck – a common occurrence.

On a tour Most tour operators in Windhoek (see page 94) offer short overnight or two-night excursions to the area. Even if you drive yourself to your accommodation, consider taking one of the local tours offered by various lodgings, as the informative local guides are usually knowledgeable about the dune ecology and can point out some of the extraordinary but often overlooked small wildlife in the area.

INFORMATION AND ACTIVITIES

Park information The NWR park office is at the Sesriem gate (daily sunrise–sunset; ⓣ 063 293252), where you can buy your entry permits (charge). There's also a petrol station, shop and internet café just outside the gate. *Sossusvlei Lodge* and *Sossus Oasis Camp* have an ATM, but don't rely on them.

Activities Sossusvlei Lodge Adventure Centre, by the park gate (ⓦ sossusvleilodge.com/adventure.html), organises a range of activities, such as 'eco-friendly quad biking' (if that isn't tautological) and sundowner drives as well as the more usual guided excursions into Sossusvlei and Dead Vlei. NWR also runs guided excursions to Sossusvlei and around. The adventure centre can also arrange helicopter rides and hot-air balloon safaris (see page 113). Tsondab Scenic Flights (ⓦ tsondab.com), 100km (62.1 miles) north of Sesriem, offers one- to two-hour flights in a six-seater plane on various routes over the desert, including Sossusvlei. Check their website for rates.

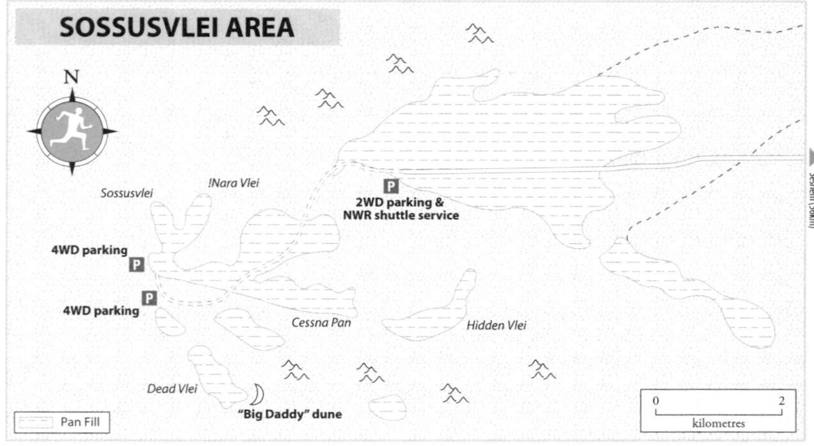

BALLOONING OVER THE DUNES

Of all the ways to comprehend the vastness of the desert and marvel at the play of light on the dunes, it's hard to beat the truly magical experience of witnessing sunrise over the Namib from a **hot-air balloon**. It doesn't come cheap, but if you only splurge on one activity during your trip, this should be it. Though you'll only spend around an hour in the air, the whole event lasts several hours, starting with a pick-up around an hour before dawn, followed by a safety briefing. The balloon envelope is inflated, and you clamber aboard and lift off. To the west, the dune sea ripples towards the coast while the Naukluft Mountains stand guard to the east. As you float upwards, you can make out the shapes of the various inselbergs below and track herds of springbok or solitary gemsbok as they trek across the desert. On landing, you can enjoy a sumptuous champagne breakfast before being driven back to your lodgings.

Namib Sky Balloon Safaris 21km (13 miles) south of Sesriem off the C27 Ⓦ balloon-safaris.com. Hot-air balloon rides (around N$8,000/person) typically fly over the Namib-Naukluft National Park and NamibRand Reserve, though the precise itinerary depends on the wind. Closed mid-Jan to mid-Feb.

2

ACCOMMODATION

SEE MAP PAGE 110

As arguably Namibia's top tourist area, places get booked well in advance for most of the year, and prices are higher here than in the rest of the country, especially for the more exclusive smaller lodges offering a greater wilderness experience. The **larger lodges** with more facilities get to see a lot of tour groups in the busy periods, which inevitably can sometimes detract from the desert feel, not to mention your sleep, as many set off pre-dawn to capture the sunrise experience. Note, too, that the back-to-nature **tented options**, while offering incomparable experiences, can be very chilly at night in the winter months beyond the blanketed warmth of your bed, as temperatures can drop below zero. Another consideration is whether your lodging has air conditioning (and heating) – a must for some to cool or heat the air but a noisy intrusion into the stillness of the desert for others. The places listed below are within an hour's drive from the park entrance.

INSIDE THE PARK

The only options actually inside the park are owned by NWR (Ⓦ nwr.com.na) or Sun Karros (Ⓦ sunkarros.com), which can be booked online or also, in the case of NWR, through the booking offices in Windhoek (see page 94) or Swakopmund (see page 214). Their chief selling point – and what makes them overpriced – is that they will enable you to set off before sunrise for Sossusvlei, thereby beating the crowds, and return an hour after sunset.

★ **Dead Valley Lodge** Inside the entrance gate Ⓦ sunkarros.com. Opened in 2019, the lodge comprises twenty sandy-coloured tented chalets (with a/c), which, in claiming their own fabulous views, have stolen the view from the NWR campsite. They exhibit earthy-toned modern chic, set on modern decking and share a lovely alfresco dining-lounge deck and swimming pool, looking towards Elim Dune. DBB N$$$$

Sesriem Campsite Inside the entrance gate Ⓦ nwr.com.na. This large campground provides an inexpensive base to get a head start on the sunrise chasers at Sossusvlei. With over forty pitches (plus an overflow area), there's little intimacy about the place, so get here early to grab a perimeter spot with a wall for shelter from the wind and away from the noisy staff quarters. Pluses include a pool to cool off in, an adequate bar-restaurant (6.30am–10pm), and most sites offer shade. The overflow site, without electricity or much in the way of facilities, does not offer the same value for money. N$$

Sesriem Oshana Campsite Inside the entrance gate Ⓦ sunkarros.com. These ten self-catering campsites opened in 2019 as part of the Sun Karros concession. Each has a private toilet, shower, washing-up facilities, electricity, and a braai site. Crucially, they are cheaper than the adjacent NWR site, yet you can still access the NWR facilities. N$$

Sossus Dune Lodge 4km (2.5 miles) inside the entrance gate Ⓦ nwr.com.na. Here you're very much paying for the chalet views and the in-park location: 25 desert chalets fashioned out of wood, canvas and thatch (no a/c) are strung out across the sand, with half facing the dunes, and the other half facing the mountains, connected by a wooden walkway. The higher-numbered chalets offer greater seclusion but entail more of a hike to dinner; conversely, you'll not get much sleep in the chalets nearer to the reception, as people traipse past from 4am onwards to catch sunrise in the park. As with many NWR properties, some of the chalets need attention. Dining (paid for in cash) can be hit or miss. Don't bother buying the wi-fi vouchers. Guided excursions are also on offer. B&B N$$$$

SESRIEM AREA

★ **Desert Camp & Desert Quiver Camp** On the D826, 5km (3.1 miles) from the entrance gate Ⓦ desertcamp.com; Desert Quiver Camp Ⓦ desertquivercamp.com.

2

Efficiently run twin camps offering similar, comfortable, good-value self-catering experiences. The former comprises 32 en-suite canvas and adobe camping units, with a/c and an extra foldout sofa for young kids. Each has a private open-air kitchenette and barbecue area complete with a fridge. The *Desert Quiver Camp*, boasting 24 units, gets the nod for the waterhole (units 8–12 get the best view) and the superior bar and pool nestled in a kopje – a fabulous sundowner spot, though, incongruously equipped with a large TV screen for sports. Bring your own food, pre-order a food box or braai pack online or at the reception; booking B&B or DBB – with meals at *Sossusvlei Lodge*, down the road – is also possible. Self-catering & B&B N$$–$$$

★ **Hoodia Desert Lodge** On the C19, 22km (13.7 miles) from the Sesriem gate. Modern but with a traditional feel, *Hoodia Desert Lodge* comprises eleven luxury thatched rondavel chalets (with a/c), family-owned and lovingly tended, in a spectacular setting surrounded by mountains. Expect fine dining and sundowners on the swimming pool deck. All the usual activities can be arranged. DBB N$$$$

Kulala Desert Lodge Down a dirt road signed off the C27, 15km (9.3 miles) south of Sesriem, just north of the junction with the D845 Ⓦ wilderness.co.za. Set in its own private reserve – alongside its even more exclusive sibling, *Little Kulala (see below)* – with superb views across to the dune sea, this thoughtfully designed lodge comprises 23 stylish semi-tented chalets with private rooftop terraces, which are arguably too many for the price tag. It's worth going all-inclusive to take the tour to Sossusvlei, as their vehicles can beat the crowds via their private park entrance (and the guiding's good), whereas self-drive vehicles have to go the long way round. Rates are considerably lower in the low season. DBB N$$$$

Le Mirage Desert Lodge & Spa On the C27, 21km (13 miles) south of the Sesriem gate, just south of Geluk Ⓦ mirage-lodge.com. You'll either love or loathe this extraordinary Hollywood-style 'Moroccan' palace, whose turrets – containing the most sought-after lodgings, with star decks to sleep out on – loom out of the desert. Spacious stone rooms remain cool though dark, with walk-in showers and vast four-poster beds. There's a nice shady pool area, classy dining and the usual trips on offer, as well as popular guided quad bike tours, a jacuzzi and a spa. Reductions for stays over one night. DBB N$$$$

Little Kulala Down a dirt road signed off the C27, 15km (9.3 miles) south of Sesriem, just north of the junction with the D845 Ⓦ wilderness.co.za. Stylish, minimalist chic reigns in this design-conscious solar-powered desert retreat, where the decking is dotted with objets d'art and the eleven state-of-the-art, a/c chalets boast gorgeous soft-toned furnishings and come complete with a private plunge pool, indoor and outdoor showers, and a candlelit rooftop bed deck. The opulence extends to a library and impressive wine cellar. Rates (significantly cheaper in low season) include two activities a day. AI N$$$$

Little Sossus Lodge & Campsite At the junction of the C19 with the D854, 35km (21.7 miles) southeast of Sesriem Ⓦ littlesossus.net. This hospitable homestead has twenty simple, fan-ventilated stone cottages for couples or families. An unpretentious bar-restaurant area spills over into a pleasant garden, where you can enjoy good home cooking if ordered in advance. Superior camping pitches privilege functionality over ambience with a serried rank of car shelters and private kitchens, plus shower blocks with electricity. But they offer views over a couple of waterholes in a reserve well stocked with wildlife. Camping N$–$$, cottages DBB N$$$

Sossus Oasis Campsite Opposite the entrance gate Ⓦ sossus-oasis.com. Owned by *Sossusvlei Lodge*, this efficient campground, offering individual and cheaper group campsites, is cheaper yet smarter than the NWR-run one over the road, though neither exudes charm. Each of the twelve individual sites has private ablutions, electricity and a braai site; the five group sites, popular with overlander and tour groups, share facilities. The place is bang next to the area's only petrol station, with an adjacent internet café and well-stocked shop. N$

Sossusvlei Lodge By the park entrance Ⓦ sossusvleilodge.com. Busy lodge with more of a hotel feel, comprising 45 spacious canvas and plaster rooms with tiled floors and a/c. Highlights include bountiful buffet dining and watching wildlife at the floodlit waterhole from the acacia-filled beer garden. The on-site adventure centre is good for arranging activities (see page 112). DBB N$$$

Solitaire and around

Just outside the national park boundary, flanked by the Naukluft Mountains to the east and scanning the flat grasslands to the west, the aptly named **SOLITAIRE** (meaning 'isolated' in French) is a classic middle-of-nowhere pit stop, the only source of roadside fuel, food and drink for many miles around. A clump of trees and a collection of rusted-out old vehicles surround this pinprick on a map consisting of a long-standing general dealer and a petrol station that does efficient tyre repairs and checks. Yet the place has now become a fixture on the tourist circuit; it even has its own website (Ⓦ solitairenamibia.com), due mainly to the widely advertised 'Moose' McGregor's Desert Bakery. Though its former larger-than-life patron is no more, his renowned

apple pie-cum-crumble recipe lives on amid a host of other sweet and savoury goodies, sold at tourist prices and of variable quality. A number of good lodges and guest farms lie in the area, several popular with tour groups, as they are within striking distance of Sossusvlei, around 80km (49.7 miles) south. However, they also provide a convenient base to explore the nearby mountain scenery. Moreover, Solitaire is a mere 10km (6.2 miles) from the turn-off to the **Spreetshoogte Pass**, arguably the most spectacular of the region's several breathtaking mountain roads that cascade off the Great Escarpment (see page 356).

ACCOMMODATION

SOLITAIRE AND AROUND, SEE MAP PAGE 110

Ababis At the junction of the C14 and the C24, 13km (8 miles) south of Solitaire ababis-gaestefarm.de. Conveniently located midway between the entrances to Sossusvlei and the Naukluft Mountains, this old colonial farmhouse oozes charm and history, packed with antiques and knick-knacks. Seven spacious rooms (most with a/c) are decorated in earthy, homely tones. Excellent dining, family-style, is on the long bougainvillea-draped veranda. Enjoy hiking on their reserve, followed by afternoon tea and cake on your return, or soak up sweeping desert vistas on the sundowner drive. It also offers a comfortably furnished two-bedroom self-catering house and a honeymoon chalet, which overlooks the (dry) Tsondab River; plus, there's a more distant mountain retreat and camping. Camping N$–$$, doubles (DBB) N$$$

★ **Barchan Dune Retreat** On the D1275, 15km (9.3 miles) from the junction with the C14 barchan.africa. Small hospitable guest farm at the foot of the Spreetshoogte Pass, offering seven modern bunker-like chalets half-buried in the earth and tastefully designed in stone and wood (the four newer rooms are smaller) with vast glass windows to maximise the mesmerising vistas. There's also a self-catering house for five. Still, the star attraction is Kuangu-Kuangu, a two-person romantic getaway with an outdoor bathroom, kitchenette and private braai, affording stunning views across to the Namib-Naukluft National Park, be it from your bed or your private patio. At five minutes' walk from the main lodge, you can choose to eat there if you prefer. The place affords good hiking, e-biking and birdwatching opportunities. AI is also available. No credit cards. DBB N$$$–$$$$

Moon Mountain East of the C19, 32km (19.9 miles) south of Solitaire moonmountain.biz. Seventeen commodious and ultra-luxurious tented chalets on stilts – including six suites with bidet and lounge – spread over the mountainside, offering stellar views across the plains to the Namib's petrified dunes from their private decks, each with a plunge pool. The common areas include a large restaurant, reading lounge and small cinema/conference room. Guided tours to Sossusvlei and sundowner drives are available. DBB N$$$$

GONDWANA NAMIB PARK

★ **The Desert Grace** gondwana-collection.com. Some 10km (6.2 miles) from the reserve gate, the austere exteriors of two dozen bunker-like modern chalets belie interiors affording supreme comfort and style, with inside and outside showers. With the trademark Gondwana quirkiness from the pink retro minibar to the basket of 'beachwear' for the private deck, loungers and plunge pool. The cuisine is excellent, topped off with home-made ice-creams. Self-guided walks, e-bike trails and a splendid sundowner make this place well worth at least two nights – more if you fit in a trip to Sossusvlei. N$$$$

The Desert Whisper gondwana-collection.com. Resembling an alien pod set into the mountainside, this is a special romantic retreat, affording breathtaking views across the desert plains – ones you can enjoy from your bed, patio or private pool. Every self-catering need is anticipated, or a private chef and attendant can spoil you. AI N$$$$

Namib Desert Lodge & Dune Star Camp West of the C19, 32km (19.9 miles) south of Solitaire gondwana-collection.com. Large lodge booked solid with tour groups in high season. Set at the base of a cliff with 65 cheerfully decorated, comfortable terracotta-tiled rooms (with a/c) of various configurations and shady patio areas. There are plenty of communal seating areas around the two decent-sized pools set in grassy tree-filled courtyards. Buffet meals are served in the cavernous thatched dining area. The more secluded *Dune Star Camp*, a short, guided hike away, is offered as a one-night escape for lodge visitors to get away from the crowds in nine solar-powered tented chalets atop a dune. They offer great views over yet more richly coloured sand and a chance to sleep under the stars on your private deck. Camping is also available, offering some shade and communal ablution blocks, as are eight supremely comfortable, spacious, well-equipped self-catering tents. Don't forget to visit the nearby fossilised dunes while there. Camping N$-$$, self-catering tents N$$, doubles (B&B) N$$$, dune chalets (B&B) N$$$$

Rostock Ritz Desert Lodge 7km (4.3 miles) east of the C14, 55km (34.2 miles) north of Solitaire rostock-ritz-desert-lodge.com. Nineteen distinctive and cool stone-and-cement igloos, equipped with mosquito nets and ceiling fans, offer fabulous views through sliding glass doors or from the private patio. The excellent restaurant draws visitors from lunchtime (11.30am–2.30pm), breaking the journey between Sossusvlei and the coast, though it only offers fine dining. It has well-preserved ancient rock paintings on the property, and after tiring yourself on one of several hiking trails, you can cool off in the pool. Four pitches are available, with superior stone braai sites under shade netting, nice stone ablutions, and a great communal viewing terrace and fire pit. Still, the flimsy fence partitioning offers little privacy. Camping N$, chalets (B&B) N$$$$

2

★ **Solitaire Desert Farm** Signed off by the Solitaire T-junction, 6km (3.7 miles) down a dirt road Ⓦ solitairenamibia.com. Set in delightfully landscaped desert gardens, which attract plenty of birdlife, this welcoming guest farm offers fifteen comfortable rooms (with a/c) and three deluxe camping pitches. This is a place for pet lovers, with various rescue animals and a plethora of dogs, rabbits, meerkats and peacocks. Hikes, wildlife drives and fat-tyre bike rental are on offer, plus there's a great swimming pool and high-quality evening meals. Lunch is not served. Camping N$, doubles B&B N$$$

Solitaire Lodge By the main road and petrol station Ⓦ solitairenamibia.com. Bang next to the frantic daytime comings and goings at the adjacent amenities, the lodge's courtyard desert garden with a swimming pool provides a surprising oasis of calm. It is enclosed by 25 spacious, cheerfully decorated rooms (with a/c), each with a small personal patio area and chairs. Dinner is a reasonably priced extra. N$$$

HIKING IN THE NAUKLUFT MOUNTAINS

There are a couple of reasonably demanding circular **day hikes** and an arduous **multiday trek** that takes eight or four days if you arrange a pick-up (or leave a vehicle) halfway. The two-day trails require no pre-booking and can be walked year-round, whereas the multiday hike has to be booked with NWR in advance (see page 112). All three hikes, clearly marked with painted footsteps, involve rocky terrain, requiring robust hiking shoes or boots. You'll also need to carry at least two litres of water per day.

OLIVE TRAIL

Probably the most popular trail, this 10km (6.2-mile) loop (4–5hr) starts from a car park 4km (2.5 miles) from the park office. It steadily winds up onto the plateau past many olive trees before descending via a gradually deepening valley – look out for the quiver trees – where, towards the end, you must use a chain bridge to navigate a canyon wall. The trail eventually joins a four-wheel drive track that leads back to the car park.

WATERKLOOF TRAIL

Starting near the campground, this more strenuous, and arguably more scenic, 17km (10.6-mile) hike (6–7hr) takes you up a narrow ravine dotted with pools (in the rainy season), onto an open, exposed plateau and then onto a ridge, which affords superb panoramic views. The trail then descends steeply past further pools and waterfalls (after rains) before meeting the usually dry Naukluft River and then a four-wheel drive track, which you follow back to the start.

MULTIDAY HIKE

This gruelling, eight-day, 120km (74.6-mile) trail (with a four-day option that avoids the most challenging sections) allows you to experience the full variety of the massif's rocky terrain but is not for the faint-hearted, those afraid of heights or the inexperienced. Moreover, while some sections of the trail lead you through impressive scenery, others take you along seemingly endless rocky ravines and riverbeds. Averaging around six hours of hiking a day, you'll stay in rudimentary shelters offering only water and toilets (no showers), and, with no fires allowed in the park, you'll need to carry a stove. The good news is that it is possible to leave a vehicle with supplies for the last four days at Tsams Ost, the shelter for the fourth night, thereby saving having to carry the extra kilos of food. Those doing the shorter four-day trail will also leave a vehicle here for transport back out of the park.

The Naukluft multiday hike is only permissible between 1 March and the third Friday in October (Tues, Thurs & Sat); buy a permit in advance from NWR in Windhoek (see page 94), for which you need a current medical certificate. The inexpensive trail fee (per person) is in addition to park entry fees. Three people (maximum twelve) are required to hike the trail.

NEURAS WINERY

One of Namibia's many striking curiosities is its desert wineries: one is situated outside Omaruru in the Erongo Region (see page 188), whereas the more visited **Neuras Winery** (Daily 10am–4pm; naankusecollection.com/establishment/neuras-wine-wildlife-estate) lies only a few kilometres off the D850 – an easy detour and perfect lunch stop if you're travelling between the Naukluft Mountains and Sossusvlei. Since this means it can also be popular with tour groups, it's advisable to phone ahead and time your visit accordingly. While the landscape at first glance would seem too harsh for successful viticulture, a guided tour soon puts you right, explaining the unique microclimate of the spring-fed estate, where the alkaline soil is perfect for planting and the mountainous backdrop protects the vines from the worst ravages of the desert winds. The first wine from Merlot and Shiraz grapes was produced in 2001, resulting in about three thousand bottles. Since then, the estate has expanded, various experimental grapes have been planted, and production is up to fifteen thousand bottles of red wine and brandy a year. Full tours of the vineyards and cellars take around an hour, culminating in a wine tasting of at least two reds and a cheese platter. If you want to skip the tour, you can still sample the wine per glass with the cheese plate or linger over a light lunch – wraps, salads, pasta, a plate of antipasti and the like – in their pleasant shady patio restaurant and savour a full glass or bottle. Though not up to the standards of wine in the Western Cape and pricier because of the challenging desert environment, Neuras wine is still surprisingly pleasant. Expensive rustic stone-chalet accommodation is also available (N$$$).

2

The Naukluft Mountains

Entrance on the D854 • Daily park fees payable in one of the MEFT offices in advance or at the park office, at the campground entrance

In a rush to experience what for most people is the 'real desert', namely the dunes around Sossusvlei, first-time visitors to Namibia often overlook the **Naukluft Mountains**, an impressive escarpment that falls off the Central Highlands and a rewarding, if challenging, hiking destination. This vast plateau boasts near-vertical cliffs in places that rise over 1,000m (3280.8ft) from the surrounding gravel plains. Formed 500–600 million years ago, it consists predominantly of porous dolomite and limestone rock, riddled with caves, galleries and ravines, sitting atop a solid granite base. Indeed, Naukluft takes its name from a Germanic corruption of the Afrikaans *nou kloof*, meaning 'narrow gorge' or 'ravine'. Where the underground water spills out in springs and streams in these fissures, crystal-clear pools support a surprising variety of **plant and animal life**, including around two hundred bird species. Look out for klipspringer, kudu, steenbok, oryx and Hartmann's mountain zebra, and soaring black eagles that nest along the cliffs.

ARRIVAL AND ACTIVITIES — THE NAUKLUFT MOUNTAINS

By car The signposted park entrance is located 8km (5 miles) along the D854 road, after the turn-off from the C14, just southwest of Büllsport.

Hiking Three hikes are available (see page 116).

Horse riding *Büllsport Guest Farm* (see page 117) owns a large portion of the mountains adjacent to the park, with horse riding activities, too, making it a popular alternative base to the NWR campground for exploring the mountains. They also accept day visitors for a reasonable entry fee.

ACCOMMODATION — SEE MAP PAGE 110

IN THE PARK

NWR Naukluft Campsite 16km (10 miles) along the access road from the D854 nwr.com.na. In a lovely setting, hemmed in by rocks and sheltered by thorn trees, this NWR campground boasts six smart 'bush chalets' overlooking a stream, 21 camping pitches and a small bar restaurant. Three-night maximum stay at peak periods. Park fees cost extra. Camping N$$, chalets B&B N$$$

OUTSIDE THE PARK

Büllsport Guest Farm By the junction of the C14 and the D1246, 8km (5 miles) north of the park entrance buellsport-naukluft.com. Well-established guest farm, offering twelve rooms, boasting a/c, heating, walk-in showers, fridge and private patio. Two wilderness campgrounds are located 3km (1.9 miles) from the lodge – ideal spots to hike from – with *lapas* for shade, no electricity, and simple ablution blocks with donkey-heated hot water (wood provided). Campers can book the set-menu meals at the guest farm, too, if bored of the braai. Activities include farm tours, self-guided mountain hikes, birdwatching and horse rides. Reductions for longer stays. Camping N$$, doubles (DBB) N$$$

2

★Tsauchab River Camp Signed 500m (0.3 miles) from the junction between the D850 and the D854 ⓦtsauchab.com. This is a fantastic place with thirteen basic stone-and-thatch chalets with barbecue outside and twelve camping pitches – some with open-air showers; none have power points; all are individually designed and spread over 15km (9.3 miles), so there's plenty of privacy for all. There's also a restaurant at the reception – a drive away. Sundowner drives, four-wheel drive and mountain bike trails, and self-guided hikes of up to 21km (13 miles) are all available on a property with freshwater pools and a giant fig forest – plus an ever-expanding quirky collection of iron art. Camping N$, chalets (DBB) N$$$$

★Zebra River Lodge 19km (11.8 miles) along the D850 from the junction with the D854, then a further 5km (3.1 miles) down a dirt track ⓦzebra-river-lodge.com. Looking across to the Tsaris Mountains, this welcoming lodge comprises charming, individually designed stone chalets – worth opting for – and some less fancy rooms. Tasty meals are served at the old farmhouse, inside or on the patio, to the sound of the whistling wind and singing cicadas at night. There are several good hikes on offer. DBB. Doubles N$$$$, chalets N$$$$

NamibRand Nature Reserve

One of the largest private reserves in Africa, the **NamibRand Nature Reserve** shares a 100km (62.1-mile) border with the southeastern section of the Namib-Naukluft National Park, thereby creating an important buffer zone. The reserve contains similar scenery to the national park: gravel plains, inselbergs, spectacular dunes and impressive mountains, and comparable flora and fauna, attracting over 170 bird species. However, the small handful of exclusive tourist concessions means you won't need to share this beautiful desert wilderness with hundreds of other tourists, as can be the case around Sossusvlei. The reserve is also the first designated **dark sky reserve** in Africa, so it's the perfect spot to indulge in stargazing. The southeastern section of the reserve hosts the only luxury multiday walking safari in Namibia, the Tok-Tokkie Trail, which provides a unique opportunity to get close to nature for an extended period without sacrificing too many comforts (see page 118).

ARRIVAL AND DEPARTURE — NAMIBRAND NATURE RESERVE

By car There are clear signs into the reserve from the C27; the entrance lies 70km (43.5 miles) south of Sesriem, 40km (25 miles) south of the junction between the C27 and the D845. All accommodation in the park will transfer you from reception to your actual camp.

THE TOK-TOKKIE TRAIL

Taking the nickname of the acrobatic Tenebrionid beetle (see page 359), the **Tok-Tokkie Trail** covers 20km (12.4 miles) of undulating vegetated dunes over one full and two half days of walking. The emphasis is on getting close to nature and learning about desert ecology from a knowledgeable guide while encountering some of the area's more intriguing, less obvious wildlife, from barking geckos to dancing spiders and fairy circles (see page 359) to the aforementioned beetle. The two nights are spent out under the stars on camp beds, and guests use hot-water bucket showers. Remember that while the cooler daytime temperatures of the high-season winter months are ideal for hiking, they can make for freezing cold nights, though the bedding will be as warm as possible. The walking is made easier – or as easy as is possible over sand – by only having to carry a light daypack, as a full backup crew transports the rest of your luggage from camp to camp and provides gourmet alfresco dining, complete with white linen tablecloths. This is serious glamping, though you do need to be reasonably fit to do the trip.

Since group sizes range from two to eight people, you need to make reservations well in advance (ⓦtoktokkietrails.com; AI N$$$$). The trail is closed Dec–Feb.

ACCOMMODATION **SEE MAP PAGE 110**

Sossusvlei Desert Lodge 4km (2.5 miles) off the C27, 40km (24.9 miles) south of Sesriem ⓦandbeyond.com. In a private concession within the reserve, this lodge – totally refurbished in 2020 – is the ultimate in exclusive desert chic: ten spacious, design-conscious split-level chalets in stone and glass, with sofas, rugs and cushions, all in earthy desert tones, plus fireplaces to ward off the night-time chill and private plunge pools. Stargaze through the skylight above the bed or the lodge telescope, aided by the on-site astronomer, and dine on your private patio, accompanied by fine wines from the extensive cellar, best digested with a loll in the spring-fed circular pool. The usual desert excursions, including e-biking, are available. AI N$$$$

WOLDWEDANS COLLECTION

Four of the five exclusive properties in the NamibRand Reserve belong to the Wolwedans Collection and are located in the northern section of the reserve. In keeping with the ethos of sustainability, the lodges are simple but stylish, blending in with the surroundings and running off solar-powered hot water but with no a/c or electricity – not even fans – which is why all but the Dunes Lodge are closed during the hottest part of the year. Each tented chalet has a private deck where you can sleep under the stars. All the lodges offer excellent guiding, top-notch levels of service and exquisite dining in stunning surroundings – at a price. Walking and vehicle safari activities are included in the rates, but hot-air ballooning, scenic flights, massage and horse riding are extra. Three nights are advised to make the most of the area. Rates include reserve entrance fees and contributions to the Wolwedans Foundation to help run its conservation and community development programmes. The reception is 20km (12.4 miles) from the reserve gate, signposted off the C27 70km (43.5 miles) south of Sesriem (ⓦwolwedans.com).

Wolwedans Boulders Camp Small tented camp that accommodates only ten people, set on wooden decking nestled among vast granite rocks. The common areas are similarly elegantly furnished, but, as the most remote of the camps, it is impossible to include a visit to Sossusvlei from here. Three-night package. AI N$$$$

Wolwedans Dune Camp A classic desert camp with half a dozen airy safari tents on private wooden decks atop a 250m (820.2ft) high dune connected by a walkway to the communal area, which boasts an open kitchen with alfresco fine dining. Two-night minimum. AI N$$$$

Wolwedans Dunes Lodge Slightly larger and more luxurious than *Dune Camp*, spread across a dune plateau, accommodating twenty in beautifully furnished wooden chalets – also with roll-up canvas walls – and plenty of social areas: a bar-lounge replete with leather sofas, a library, two dining rooms and a pool suspended above the sand and surrounded by sunloungers. AI N$$$$

OUTSIDE NAMIBRAND

★Greenfire Desert Lodge West of the C27, 100km (62.1 miles) south of Sesriem ⓦgreenfire.co.za/desert-lodge. Abutting the NamibRand reserve on its private concession, this modest, friendly place (part of a South African chain) boasts similarly mesmerising desert landscapes at a fraction of the price. Built from local stone that blends into the boulder-strewn backdrop, the lodge comprises six west-facing suites and six campsites. Sunsets on the patio by the pool are magical and the stargazing in the dry season is extraordinary. Rates include guided walks and game drives. Camping N$, doubles (AI) N$$$

2

Duwisib Castle

20km (12.4 miles) off the C27 from the junction with the D826 • Temporarily closed • Charge

Undergoing renovations, one of Namibia's more unlikely sights is the crenellated neo-medieval folly, **Duwisib Castle**, which, incongruously yet proudly, occupies a hilltop off the eastern fringes of the Namib. This sturdy sandstone fortress, erected in the early twentieth century by an eccentric German, 'Baron' – as he came to be known locally – **Hans Heinrich von Wolf**, is an anachronistic curiosity that promises more than it delivers. The tale of the mansion's construction and its owners, combined with the novelty value of its semi-desert setting, is of greater interest than the contents per se (see page 120).

Only a handful of rooms are open to the public, furnished with some original antique furniture, though labelling and explanations are scarce. You enter via the Knights' Hall – an early indication of the owner's over-ambition – presided over by a splendid chandelier and bedecked with von Wolf's sword collection, assorted weaponry and numerous pictures with a recurring equine flavour – incongruously sharing wall space with the obligatory portraits of Sam Nujoma and the current president. To the left is the dining room – note the burner to heat the curling tongs – whereas the private rooms lie to the right. Don't forget to pop upstairs and take in the flaking mural and the view outside before descending into the former wine cellar in the basement. While the castle does not merit a major detour, if you're in the area, it's worth dropping by, and once you've nosed around, enjoy a slab of cake with afternoon tea in the courtyard café shaded by two large jacarandas. The main niggle, which undermines the place's otherwise tranquil setting, is the constant daytime hum of the generator; luckily for guests choosing to stay overnight here, the place switches to solar power in the evenings.

ACCOMMODATION

DUWISIB CASTLE, SEE MAP PAGE 110

Betta Camp 37km (23 miles) southwest of Duwisib Castle, at the junction of the C27 and D826 bettacamp.com. An untouristy yet welcoming oasis, this no-nonsense camp makes a perfect one-night stopover, offering small self-catering stone chalets with two comfy single beds and a bathroom, braai area and a washing-up sink. Campsites also have braai and sink, picnic tables and a sundowner deck that provides welcome shade. On site are a thinly-stocked little shop selling fresh bread and cakes and a petrol station. Camping N$, doubles N$$

Duwisib Guestfarm 5min walk from the castle farmduwisib.com. There's nothing fancy about the rustic accommodation in this working estate's stone farmhouse; solar power means limited electricity – so no a/c. That said, the simple, brightly painted rooms are cool, clean and comfortable, and the hospitality is first-class, with excellent meals in a barnlike dining room. You can also pre-book dinner here if you're staying at the castle. Camping sites are not as scenically located as the NWR ones, but facilities are much better, and you can eat at the farm. A self-catering bungalow is also available. Camping N$, self-catering N$$, doubles B&B N$$–$$$

NWR campsite. Below the castle are ten delightful, well-spaced, shady pitches with shared ablutions and hit-and-miss water. No electricity. N$

NWR Duwisib Castle nwr.com.na/resorts/duwisib-

NAMIBIA'S DESERT FORTRESS

Duwisib Castle was the fantastical brainchild of **Hans Heinrich von Wolf**, a German from a military background, who had first visited German South-West Africa (as it was then) after volunteering to join the Schutztruppe and help contain the Herero threat. He was so taken by the country that he persuaded his wealthy **American bride**, Miss Jayta Humphrey, to set up a home and live the colonial dream in this improbable desert environment. Having succeeded in buying up several farms, he employed renowned architect Wilhelm Sandler – who had designed Windhoek's three castles (see page 88) – to create his fortified abode. No expense or pretension was spared: though the solid sandstone blocks were quarried in the area by a local workforce, everything else was sourced in Europe, from the furniture to the fitments and the **lavish furnishings**. These were shipped to Lüderitz and dragged the 300km (186.4 miles) across the desert by ox wagon to the site. Here, artisans from Italy, Sweden and Ireland set about realising Heinrich's fanciful 22-room creation. The solid, metre-thick walls, at least, were functional, keeping the desert heat at bay while providing some insulation against the cold winter nights, aided further by two large fireplaces. Their practicality ended as a lofty 'knights' hall', complete with a minstrel's gallery, was constructed, as well as a cloistered courtyard with a central fountain and wine cellar. Amazingly, the whole project took only a couple of years to complete. The farm was stocked with high-quality cattle and sheep, though Hans devoted most of his energies to his primary passion: horses. He built up an impressive **stud farm** from imported stock; it is believed that some of the feral Namib horses that cavort around Aus today may have originated from here (see page 123).

However, the baron's equine ambitions came to an abrupt end in 1914. He and Jayta were on their way to Britain to purchase yet more horses when World War I broke out; their ship was diverted to South America, where they were briefly interned, though as a US passport holder, Jayta managed to smuggle her husband back to Germany on a boat. Once back in the fatherland, Hans rejoined the army, was sent to France, and died in the **Battle of the Somme** in 1916. Jayta never returned to Namibia to reclaim her inheritance or sell the property.

castle. The main appeal is the cachet of spending the night in a castle. Five dark en-suite double rooms lead off the courtyard behind saloon-style swing doors, combining old-world charm with modern comforts such as tiled bathrooms. Occasional problems with food deliveries mean dinner offerings at the café can be limited sometimes, but the staff are accommodating. The small courtyard splash pool provides welcome relief in summer. N$$

The Tiras Mountains and around

The rugged, scenic **Tiras Mountains** rarely receive more than a photo stop from most travellers as they skirt their eastern flank, driving up or down the C13 on their way between Aus – and beyond, Lüderitz – and the dunes of Sossusvlei further north. Yet this beguiling range is worth lingering over for a couple of days as it lies at the convergence of several ecological zones, resulting in impressive plant biodiversity and varied landscapes, which transform their colours with the changing light. At the very least, consider a detour around the semicircular gravel D707 – just doable in a two-wheel drive when it's dry but better in a four-wheel drive – one of the most picturesque routes in southern Namibia. It picks its way around the southern and western edges of the mountains – giant rocky outcrops fringed with flaxen grasses, punctuated by hardy succulents – while affording mesmerising views across to the richly coloured pink and apricot dunes of the Namib to the west.

Helmeringhausen

To the northeast of the Tiras Mountains, where the C13, C14 and C27 converge, stands the small settlement of **Helmeringhausen** – effectively a single farm that has morphed into a quasi-village, with the same owners running a hotel (see below), a garage, a shop and a bottle store.

ACCOMMODATION **TIRAS MOUNTAINS SEE MAP PAGE 108**

Helmeringhausen Hotel Main Street, Helmeringhausen helmeringhausennamibia.com. Regrettably, the only place to stay in the area, this old stone hotel set in lush tropical grounds provides spacious rooms with stone floors and large windows, which are cool in summer but freezing in winter. Solar-powered electricity and water mean no electricity at the camping pitches, dimly lit rooms and no wi-fi. The dining areas are also dark, dinner is expensive and there's no cosy fire – or much of a warm welcome – to warm you in winter. Camping N$, doubles N$$$

Kanaan N|a'an Ku sê Desert Retreat Signposted west off the D707 45km (28 miles) from the junction with the C27 kanaannamibia.com. In this private reserve that abuts the Namib-Naukluft National Park, it's all about the wilderness feel and stunning desert vistas: grasslands, dunes and mountains can be appreciated from the deck of your simple tented chalet (one of eight) or camping pitch (also one of eight) with private canvas shelter, solar-powered ablutions and windbreak. Join a guided walk or scenic drive. N$, chalets (DBB) N$$$$

★ **Namtib Biosphere Reserve** 47km (29.2 miles) along the D707 from the junction with the C13, then a further 13km (8 miles) namtib.net. Friendly, family-run lodge and camping on a farm focused on sustainability – though strangely no solar power – nestled among boulders at the end of a valley. Five quaint, yellow bungalows and three other rooms are rustically but cheerfully furnished (without a/c or fans), with separate private bathrooms. Homely meals are served family-style. Don't miss the fabulous sunsets from the sundowner rock terrace, with an honesty bar. Five camping pitches enjoy similar surroundings, 3km (1.9 miles) from the lodge – with shade, a braai site and donkey-fuelled hot water but no electricity. Campers should be self-sufficient. All can enjoy the self-guided botanical trail or moderate-length hikes. Guided walks and drives are sometimes available. Camping N$, doubles B&B N$$$

Aus

Around 125km (77.7 miles) east of Lüderitz along the B4, a side road drops into a small valley that shelters the diminutive, historically significant town of **AUS**. As one of the main stations on the railway line between Lüderitz and Keetmanshoop, Aus was of strategic importance to the Germans during the colonial period, prompting them to build fortifications to defend the site, remnants of which are still visible today towards Klein Aus Vista. When, in 1915, the Germans eventually surrendered to the

South African Union troops, who took over the town, they were held in a prisoner-of-war camp just east of Aus (see page 122). As you enter the town, you'll see the recently renovated station just off the main street and the *Bahnhof Hotel* nearby; the hotel was established at the same time as the railway was completed, in 1906, although the original wooden structure burnt down, and the place was rebuilt in brick. The impoverished local populace hopes the railway's eventual reopening to Lüderitz will lead to jobs and the village's renaissance.

2

At the moment, Aus receives a steady trickle of people travelling by road who break off for a bite to eat between Keetmanshoop and the coast, though it's worth spending a night or two here to explore the varied flora and fauna in the surrounding **Aus Mountains.** Over five hundred plant species have been identified in the area, seven of which are endemic to the immediate vicinity, such as the pretty yellow Aus daisy. This biodiversity is due to the convergence of different biomes. At an altitude of almost 1,500m (4,921.3ft), Aus lies at the western limit of the Nama Karoo of the central plateau, at the eastern edge of the Namib Desert and at the top end of the Succulent Karoo (see page 153). The place is also affected by different weather patterns, making the weather unpredictable – some years, it even receives snow. Due to the Cape weather system, the rare years of winter rainfall (July–Sept) trigger a prolific flowering, particularly of succulents and herbaceous annuals, resulting in a multicoloured carpet of colour.

ARRIVAL AND INFORMATION — AUS

By car Aus is signposted off the B4, the main tarred road between Lüderitz (125km/77.7 miles west) and Keetmanshoop (215km/133.6 miles east).

By minibus Minibuses running between Lüderitz (see page 124) and Keetmanshoop (see page 145) can drop off passengers – and pick up when not full – on the B4 at the entrance/exit to town.

By rail It is hoped that the passenger service, which currently only runs between Keetmanshoop and Aus, will resume between Lüderitz and Keetmanshoop, stopping at Aus.

ACCOMMODATION AND EATING

There are a couple of decent enough accommodation options in the town centre, but another good option is the Klein-Aus-Vista private reserve, a few kilometres west of Aus. You can get a decent meal in both places.

TOWN CENTRE

★ **Bahnhof Hotel** 20 Lüderitz St hotel-aus.com. Though rooms are modern (some have wheelchair access), the hotel has kept its charm: lovely polished wooden floors and high ceilings. It also has a great dining deck overlooking the main street – and a fire-warmed lounge for winter nights – where you can choose from an extensive à-la-carte menu of light and more substantial dishes. With two modern self-catering houses a short walk away, the hotel also offers day trips into the surrounding area. B&B N$$–$$$

AUS' GERMAN POW CAMP

Signposted off the B4, a few kilometres east of Aus, a track leads northward to a Commonwealth War Graves **military cemetery**, just beyond the original **prisoner of war camp** that held more than **1,500 German soldiers** at one stage. The inadequate tented camp was exposed to the fickle and extreme weather of the area, as captives and captors alike withstood snow, scorching heat, sandstorms and bitterly cold nights. This prompted the industrious Germans – already cultivating their gardens to improve their diet – to start making sun-dried mud bricks to construct accommodations that would afford better protection against the elements. They were soon in more robust lodgings than their South African guards, to whom they even sold their bricks. The Commonwealth cemetery marks the deaths of over **sixty German prisoners of war** and a similar number of their **South African guards** who perished in the camp, not due to any military skirmish but because they succumbed to a bout of **Spanish influenza** that ripped through the population in 1918.

THE NAMIB'S WILD HORSE

Travelling along the tarred road between Aus and Lüderitz, you may be lucky enough to catch the incongruous sight of **wild horses** roaming across the desert's gravel plains. Failing that, there is now a strategically positioned viewing hide, just off the main highway, that allows visitors to get a closer look at these resilient animals – possibly the only herd of feral desert horses in the world. Their **origin** is a source of great conjecture, ranging from the view that they escaped from a shipwrecked cargo vessel on the coast to the notion that they belonged to Khoikhoi raiders who came north from South Africa. The ancestry of these athletic, lean-limbed horses would appear to have been of good stock, hence the current prevailing theory that they stem from a mix of stud and cavalry horses from the **German colonial period**. A stud farm was known to have existed nearby, and during World War I, a German pilot reportedly dropped a bomb on a South African encampment in the area, probably causing their horses to scatter. These horses may also have been joined later by steeds abandoned by the retreating Germans. In the turmoil of war, little effort would have been made to recapture the beasts; even after the conflict, being a diamond mining area, human access was restricted.

Now, a hundred years on, these feral horses are protected within the extended Namib-Naukluft National Park. Their numbers fluctuate between ninety and three hundred depending on climatic conditions. However, establishing a permanent water trough is likely to guarantee their continued survival, as is the fact that they've become a firm fixture on the tourist trail. The **viewing hide** is 100m (0.6 miles) off the main road, 20km (12.4 miles) west of Aus (and 90km/55.9 miles east of Lüderitz). The dirt track leading to the car park is manageable for an ordinary saloon car. The best time to see the horses is late afternoon, when a few oryx are also likely to use the water trough.

2

Namib Garage 52 Lüderitz St aus-namibia.com. An unlikely spot for good-value if unremarkable (semi-) self-catering – only microwave, kettle and toaster – accommodation, of various configurations, in modern tiled rooms with a/c. Breakfast can be arranged. Also, six cheap camping pitches with electricity, wi-fi, braai sites and shared water in a sandy compound over the road. Provisions are available at their general store while the garage provides petrol and repairs – truly a one-stop shop. Camping N$, self-catering units N$$

KLEIN-AUS-VISTA

Located on a private reserve that abuts the Sperrgebiet, the distinctive *Klein-Aus-Vista* (South of the B4, 3km/1.9 miles west of Aus; klein-aus-vista.com) offers a variety of well-maintained accommodation in a beautiful natural setting, which you can explore on foot, on a mountain bike (available for rent) or horseback along trails of varying length and difficulty. Though you'll get tour groups in high season, many independent travellers stopover, especially in the fabulous stone self-catering chalets. The buffet restaurant food is excellent and there's a cosy lounge bar (with fireplace for winter) and wraparound veranda, gift shop and a horseshoe-shaped pool, in keeping with the lodge's equine theme.

Desert Horse Campsite Ten well-spaced camping pitches are scenically situated a couple of kilometres from the lodge, each with solid braai and grill, tap, table with benches (no electricity) and some shade by a camelthorn tree. Bring your food or purchase a superior braai pack from the lodge reception. All pitches possess windbreaks. Shared ablutions. N$

Desert Horse Inn Four rooms in the original lodge building, where communal facilities are located, and ten more double chalets nearby. Fan-ventilated, with hot-water bottles for winter comfort. B&B N$$$

★ **Eagle's Nest Chalets** The pick of the accommodation: seven individually designed en-suite stone chalets built into the base of a rock face, offering uninterrupted views across pinkish desert sands to distant mountains – Eagle's View has the best vista. All are self-catering, with a kitchenette and braai area, or you can drive the 7km (4.3 miles) back to the lodge for dinner. Since breakfast is included, you can opt for a takeaway pack. B&B N$$$

Geisterschlucht (Ghost Valley) Named after a group of diamond thieves who were shot, trying to escape the chasing authorities – their rusted bullet-riddled car remains in the sand – and who are said to return when the moon is full in an attempt to reclaim their booty. This rustic, solar-powered, self-catering cabin is tucked away at the valley's end and is generally booked by groups or families; it can accommodate up to eighteen, with bunks and single beds spread over two bedrooms. Minimum booking for three. Per person N$

Lüderitz and around

Hemmed in by the wild Atlantic coast and the encroaching dunes of the Namib to the north and south, **LÜDERITZ** is undoubtedly Namibia's most isolated, and for many years forgotten, major town. It's also the country's windiest settlement – so unsurprisingly, home to the country's first wind farm – with gusts regularly topping 40km/h (24.9mph), especially during the summer months (Nov–Jan), and temperatures rarely topping 24°C. Yet, on the mornings when the wind drops and the sun gleams on the pretty, brightly painted colonial buildings that decorate the town's slopes, Lüderitz's charm is clear to see, and its dark colonial history easy to forget. There's enough to keep the visitor entertained for a few days: taking in the **Jugendstil** (Art Nouveau) **architecture**, making forays into the desert to the abandoned mining communities of **Kolmanskop**, **Pomona** or **Bogenfels**, exploring the lagoon-laden rocky peninsula to the south, or seeking out whales, flamingos or penguins on **boat trips** round the bay. The annual wind- and kitesurfing speed challenge (Oct–Nov) and five-day crayfish festival (April–June) – when accommodation prices will be hiked – are also major draws.

Brief history

The Nama had long inhabited the area before outsiders set up a coastal trading post buoyed by whaling, the seal trade and guano harvesting. The first European settlement was established in 1883 when an intermediary acting on behalf of German merchant **Adolf Lüderitz** effectively swindled the land from Nama chief Frederick II of Bethanie, who seemingly signed away five times more terrain than he realised. Once official backing for the colony had been granted (including from the British) and the German flag had been hoisted – making Lüderitz the first town of German colonial South-West Africa – Adolf Lüderitz set about acquiring more land for the colony. He then vanished – presumed drowned – on an expedition south searching for the mineral wealth he believed was needed to sustain the newly acquired empire. Despite this setback, the town began to expand as a major transit point and supply line for the Schutztruppe in the conflict with the Herero and the Nama; indeed, slave labour from the infamous concentration camp on Shark Island (see page 127) enabled the development of the town's infrastructure – the railroad, in particular – which in turn helped strengthen Germany's colonial grip on the land.

The colony's fortunes took a major step forward in 1908 with the discovery of **diamonds** (see page 132), which kick-started an eight-year boom period, during which most of the town's impressive colonial mansions were built. This was cut short by World War I, but even after the conflict had ended, Lüderitz continued to struggle as diamond prices fell. Richer pickings were found further south, initially at Pomona and Bogenfels, then eventually down at Oranjemund.

Today, after years of neglect and marginalisation, the prospects for Lüderitz's twenty thousand inhabitants are beginning to improve, with a reviving port, the establishment of a small waterfront, and the redevelopment of the old power station, set to feature a maritime museum. It is also hoped that the revival of the railway line to Keetmanshoop will create further jobs; although reopened briefly, constant encroachment by sand on the track has halted operations while plans are being drawn up to build a tunnel through the dunes.

Felsenkirche

End of Kirche Street • Mon–Sat: April–Aug 4–5pm; Sept–March 5–6pm • Free

Presiding over Lüderitz, the hundred-year-old Evangelical Lutheran **Felsenkirche** (Church of the Rock) is the town's most visible landmark. It is only open an hour

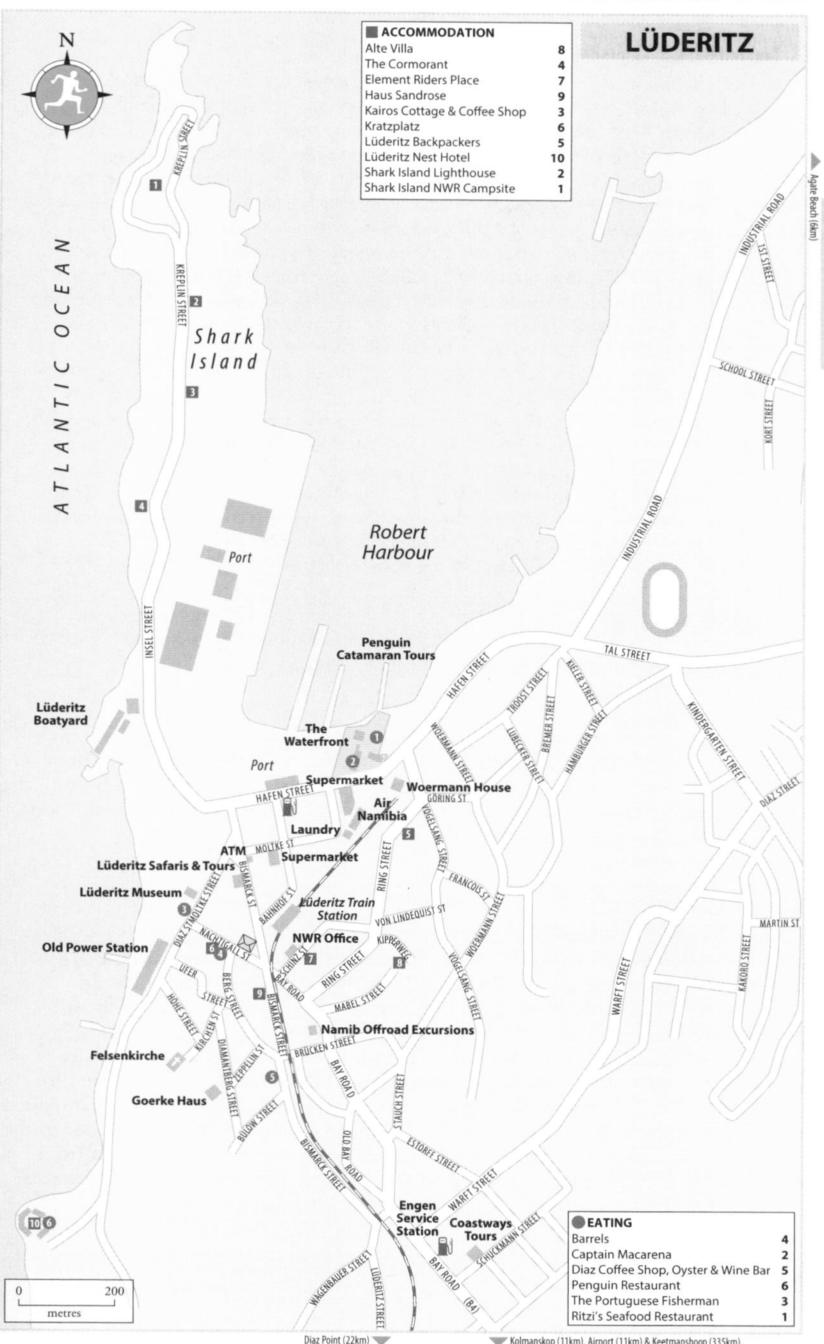
LÜDERITZ
ACCOMMODATION
Alte Villa 8
The Cormorant 4
Element Riders Place 7
Haus Sandrose 9
Kairos Cottage & Coffee Shop 3
Kratzplatz 6
Lüderitz Backpackers 5
Lüderitz Nest Hotel 10
Shark Island Lighthouse 2
Shark Island NWR Campsite 1
EATING
Barrels 4
Captain Macarena 2
Diaz Coffee Shop, Oyster & Wine Bar 5
Penguin Restaurant 6
The Portuguese Fisherman 3
Ritzi's Seafood Restaurant 1
N
ATLANTIC OCEAN
Shark Island
Robert Harbour
Port
Penguin Catamaran Tours
Lüderitz Boatyard
The Waterfront
Supermarket
Woermann House
Air Namibia
Laundry
ATM
Lüderitz Safaris & Tours
Lüderitz Museum
Lüderitz Train Station
NWR Office
Old Power Station
Namib Offroad Excursions
Felsenkirche
Goerke Haus
Engen Service Station
Coastways Tours
KREPLIN STREET
INSEL STREET
HAFEN STREET
INDUSTRIAL ROAD
1ST STREET
SCHOOL STREET
KORT STREET
TAL STREET
TROOST STREET
KIELER STREET
BREMER STREET
HAMBURGER STREET
LUBECKER STREET
WOERMANN STREET
KINDERGARTEN STREET
DIAZ STREET
GÖRING ST
VOGELSANG STREET
FRANCOIS ST
MOLTKE ST
BISMARCK ST
RING STREET
BAHNHOF ST
VON LINDEQUIST ST
MARTIN ST
KAKORO STREET
WARFT STREET
DIAZ ST
NACHTIGALL ST
KIPPERWEG
SCHINZ ST
UFER STREET
BERG STREET
HOHE STREET
KIRCHEN ST
DIAMANTBERG STREET
ZEPPELIN ST
BAY ROAD
MABEL STREET
BRÜCKEN STREET
STAUCH STREET
BÜLOW STREET
OLD BAY ROAD
ESTORFF STREET
BISMARCK STREET
WAGENBAUER STREET
LÜDERITZ STREET
SCHUCKMANN STREET
BAY ROAD (B4)
Agate Beach (6km)
Diaz Point (22km)
Kolmanskop (11km), Airport (11km) & Keetmanshoop (335km)
0 200 metres

2

2

NAMIBIA'S 'GUANO RUSH'

One of Namibia's lesser-known tales of colonial greed played out off the Namibian coast on a clutch of tiny islands near Lüderitz, with the discovery of large deposits of **guano** (bird or bat droppings). A corruption of the Quechua word *wanu*, guano had been cherished by the Incas as a **natural fertiliser** long before the colonisers in Peru cottoned on to its worth. They began shipping it wholesale back to Europe and North America in the early nineteenth century. This may have helped prompt the recollection by a retired British mariner of an old US sea captain's 1828 accounts of islands 'covered in birds' manure to the depth of 25 feet (over seven metres)' off the coast of Africa, thereby triggering Namibia's 'Guano Rush' some fifteen years later. The cold waters of the Benguela Current provide ideal conditions for the production of seabird excrement: nutrient-rich upwellings feeding vast quantities of fish, on which large colonies of gannets, cormorants and penguins feast, plus an arid climate that prevents these nutrients from being leached into the sea.

By 1843, Ichaboe Island, some 45km (28 miles) north of Lüderitz, had become a centre of frenzied 'white gold' harvesting. Only 15 acres (6 hectares) in size – the equivalent of seven football pitches – Ichaboe was soon home to around six thousand seamen and 350 vessels. Working conditions were appalling and extremely hazardous: constantly damp, squeezed into makeshift accommodations and without medical facilities, the workers frequently lacked fresh food and drinking water, much of which had to be shipped from Cape Town. Moreover, they suffered constant exposure to the stench of excrement and high ammonia levels. But the financial rewards – for the concession owners, at least – were huge. Within two years, the rush was all but over; the island had been scraped clean, with some 200,000 tonnes removed in two years. The seabirds have now reclaimed the rock, though in depleted numbers. However, small-scale sustainable guano harvesting continues in Namibia today, predominantly on artificial platforms dotted along the coast, most notably at 'Bird Island' just north of Walvis Bay (see page 220).

a day in the late afternoon to catch the sun's last rays, highlighting the building's main attraction: its beautiful **stained-glass windows**. Note the head of Martin Luther in a pane amid the biblical iconography. The other reason to climb up to the church is to soak up the **views** of the town and bay, though some recent additions to the skyline have undermined the panorama somewhat.

Lüderitz Museum

Diaz Street • Mon–Fri 3.30–5pm • Charge • T 063 202346

Eventually, to be rehoused in the adjacent power station development, the **Lüderitz Museum** currently consists of a single room – reminiscent of an old library – crammed with artefacts, photos and dioramas labelled in English and German. While you can take or leave the cabinets of taxidermy, mineral specimens and an assortment of whale bones, the museum's real value lies in its extensive **photographic collection**, which gives insight into German colonial fine living in Lüderitz in the diamond-mining heyday of the early twentieth century – gymnastics tournaments, horse racing, shows at the Turnhalle (gymnasium) – in contrast to the brutal working conditions of the several thousand labourers brought down from the north. Contracts were never longer than two years since it was thought that if workers stayed longer, they would wise up and start stealing the diamonds.

Goerke Haus

Although no longer open to the public, Lüderitz's most magnificent colonial building is still worth the climb to take a closer look at the exterior. Built in 1910 for the former soldier turned diamond mining magnate **Hans Goerke**, this private luxury mansion is the town's most opulent building, appropriately located at the top of Diamantberg (Diamond Hill). Goerke spared no expense in constructing and furnishing his residence, including importing sand from Germany for the cement. Delightful Art Nouveau features, such as decorative arches and friezes, incorporate local motifs, most notably the flamingos on the stained-glass window on the main staircase – all faithfully restored by Namdeb Diamond Corporation (the current owners) in the 1980s. However, modern comforts have been added to accommodate the VIPs the company occasionally lodges here.

Shark Island

A 10–15min walk from the centre of town; turn left at the port entrance below the fountain on Bismarck Street, then follow the road to the right

Pick a clear morning to visit **Shark Island** and wander around the far tip for splendid sea, harbour and town views as you watch the oystercatchers flit across the rocks. Then, focus on the array of **memorials** that serve as sobering reminders of the island's chequered past (see page 127) and the issues still to be resolved in Namibia's present.

ARRIVAL AND GETTING AROUND — LÜDERITZ AND AROUND

By car Lüderitz is at the western end of the tarred B4, 335km (208.2 miles) from Keetmanshoop and 125km (77.7 miles) from the last petrol station at Aus. When the wind gets up in the afternoons, the last 30km (18.6 miles) is dangerous as sand from the dunes frequently blows onto the road. Avis Car Hire has an office at 25 Bismarck St (W avis.com/en/locations/sw/luderitzbucht/lud).

By bus Minibuses depart from Nautilus (the suburb and former township), bound for Keetmanshoop and Windhoek. Take a taxi there from town. 'Aunt' Anna (T 081 252 0575) runs a shuttle service three times a week to/from Keetmanshoop (Wed, Fri & Sun) and occasional services to Windhoek when there is demand.

By plane Fly Namibia offers weekday flights between Windhoek (Eros Airport) and Lüderitz (1hr). Take a taxi to the airport 11km (6.8 miles) east of town.

By train At the time of writing, there was no train service to Lüderitz, though the service is due to reopen at some stage – but don't hold your breath.

On foot It's easy and safe to get around town on foot.

SHARK ISLAND CONCENTRATION CAMP

Taking the idea from the British, who had introduced the concept of the concentration camp in the Anglo-Boer war a few years previously, the Germans set up five **internment centres** for the Herero and, subsequently, the Nama, in their attempts to subjugate the local populace. The one at Shark Island was the most notorious of these camps, dubbed Todesinsel (Island of Death) even by the German troops. Herero prisoners – men, women and children – were initially transported there in 1905, both as a security move to isolate them from other Herero and to supply **slave labour** for the construction of the railway line to Aus – over 1,300 workers were estimated to have died in the process. They were joined the following year by almost 1,800 Nama prisoners.

Living conditions were appalling and mortality rates were high; although precise numbers and names were not recorded, there is widespread agreement that the vast majority never survived the incarceration. Malnourished prisoners were squeezed into barely adequate tents with inadequate sanitation on the tiny, windswept peninsula (there was a causeway joining the island to the mainland), which offered no protection from the fierce weather conditions. Disease was rife, as was rape, and prisoners were constantly beaten. On top of that, the work was dangerous and physically demanding – dynamiting rocks and being forced to work in icy-cold waters to build a new pier and wave-breaker. Most of the dead were given scant burial in shallow graves on the beach, their bodies washing out to sea once the tide came in, and there was a grisly trade in body parts to Europe – including Nama skulls – for medical experiments aimed at validating racist 'scientific' assumptions about racial superiority.

Lüderitz Safaris & Tours will provide you with a town map, which includes an informative walking tour of the many historical buildings.

By taxi If you want transport to Kolmanskop and don't want to go on a tour, there are plenty of registered taxis available with taxi signs on the roof, hanging around the main street and outside the supermarkets, which will quote a return fee, including one hour's wait time.

INFORMATION

Tourist information The de facto information centre is Lüderitz Safaris & Tours on Bismarck Street (Mon–Fri 8am–5pm, Sat 8.30am–noon, Sun 8.30am–10am; Ⓣ063 202719, Ⓔludsaf@africaonline.com.na). Very friendly and efficient, they can provide you with maps of the town and peninsula, a list of all accommodation options and current pricing, plus suggestions on what to do. They also issue the NWR passes to access Kolmanskop and run a well-stocked souvenir shop.

NWR office At the NWR office on Schinz Street (Mon–Fri 8am–5pm; Ⓣ063 202752), you can buy a permit for Kolmanskop or make last-minute bookings for Shark Island accommodation, but not for other NWR resorts.

ACTIVITIES AND TOURS

Boat trips Penguin Catamaran Tours (Ⓦpenguincatamaran tours.com) organise morning departures (8am; minimum of six needed) from the waterfront jetty on a motor-driven two-hour trip out of the bay, around Diaz Point to Halifax Island, home to a large colony of African penguins. Likely sightings include Heaviside dolphins, Cape fur seals and a wide variety of seabirds. Take binoculars and warm clothing with you.

Desert tours An increasing number of guided self-drive, off-road four-wheel drive camping trips are now being led into the Namib from Lüderitz. Ensure you make full enquiries about the company's environmental practices on the tour before signing up to any one provider (see 'Basics' page 68).

Windsurfing and watersports Call in at Element Riders Place (Ⓦelement-riders.com), where they can sort you out with lessons in kitesurfing, windsurfing or paddleboarding, as well as gear rental – though equipment is included in tuition prices – including wetsuits, which are strongly advised. There are also mountain bikes for rent.

ACCOMMODATION

SEE MAP PAGE 125

★ **Alte Villa** Mabel St Ⓦaltevilla.na. The clutch of gorgeous, individually decorated suites and apartments in this renovated colonial mansion please the eye and provide all the necessary comforts. Ample shared common areas ensure plenty of peace and quiet, whether in the lounge, garden, or sun deck. B&B N$$$

★ **The Cormorant** 627 Insel St, Shark Island Ⓦthe cormoranthouse.com. Outstanding oceanfront property with eight dazzling, modern, self-catering apartments. All are tastefully furnished with plenty of wood and cool stone tile floors, plus vast windows so you can make the most of the magnificent sea views. Bag one of the five best rooms with a private balcony. N$$

Element Riders Place Schinz Street Ⓦelement-riders.com. This lovely old house has been converted into a small classic backpackers hostel, popular with watersports enthusiasts. Basic facilities, including showers, are shared among the seven available rooms (doubles and triples). The kitchen is small but well-equipped, though further common areas are fairly limited. Camping space is only available for a couple of vehicles with roof tents. Camping & dorms N$, doubles N$$

Haus Sandrose 15 Bismarck St Ⓦhaussandrose.com. Centrally located and impeccably managed, these four

TOURS TO THE SPERRGEBIET

Coastways Tours, on the B4 on the way into town, behind the Engen station (Mon–Fri 8am–5pm; Ⓦcoastways.com.na), specialises in four-wheel drive day- and multiday trips into the desert. Coastways was the first operator with a licence to enter what is now the Tsau ||Khaeb National Park but is better known as the **Sperrgebiet** (meaning forbidden area' in German – a reference to the fact that it is an off-limits diamond-mining area) – and a copy of your passport will need to be submitted well in advance for approval. For its most popular (yet expensive) full-day tour, you'll spend several hours in the back of a four-wheel drive vehicle. Still, the experience is otherworldly as you cross dune fields studded with lichen and extraordinary succulents and visit the abandoned mining communities of Pomona and Bogenfels. There are also sobering views of dunescapes wrecked by mining, which you can see before the tour finishes at the gigantic Bogenfels Rock Arch on the Atlantic coast.

spotless self-catering units set around a pleasant courtyard with a shared shaded eating area offer excellent value for money. Discounts for multi-night stays. N$$

Kairos Cottage & Coffee Shop Kreplin Street, Shark Island kairoscottage.com. Superb value, well-appointed oceanfront B&B, though with some overly twee touches. Only five rooms – all offering sea views through large windows – so you need to book ahead. Be prepared to be serenaded on the piano by your host over breakfast. B&B N$$

Kratzplatz 5 Nachtigall St facebook.com/kratzplatz. Friendly, cosy guesthouse with twelve small rooms (each with fridge and DStv and some with decorative stone and shell bathrooms) overlooking a tree-filled courtyard with quirky ornamentation. The upstairs rooms that open onto a balcony are the nicest. B&B N$$

Lüderitz Backpackers 2 Ring St luderitzbackpackers.weebly.com. Friendly, old-style hostel in an old colonial home with high ceilings, large windows and polished wooden floors. Well-equipped kitchen, shared living room and sheltered outdoor area at the back for when it's warm enough to sit out. Try to get a room away from the kitchen for a quieter night's sleep. For a unique experience, rent out one of the two converted boat cabins – without a toilet – in the yard. All self-catering. N$–$$

Lüderitz Nest Hotel 820 Diaz St nesthotel.com. The town's upmarket modern resort hotel maximises its location on the bay, with almost all rooms – including some with wheelchair access – overlooking the sea. Lull yourself to sleep listening to the soothing sound of the waves. B&B N$$$

Shark Island Lighthouse Kreplin Street, Shark Island; book in Windhoek or the NWR office in town (see page 128) nwr.com.na. The pick of the NWR lodgings is the lighthouse, with two bedrooms, two bathrooms, a kitchen, a dining room and a TV lounge. True, the paint is peeling, the furniture is dilapidated and the bathroom has grimy grouting, but there are fabulous panoramic views from the roof terrace – and it's cheap. N$$

Shark Island NWR Campsite End of Kreplin Street, Shark Island; last-minute bookings can be made at the NWR office in town (see page 128) nwr.com.na. The campground at the head of the peninsula (facilities needing upgrading) offers great sea views – but few sheltered spots – with shared braai areas. However, it's sobering to be camping amid the gravestones on the site of appalling human suffering. N$–$$

2

EATING

SEE MAP PAGE 125

Barrels Kratzplatz, 5 Nachtigall St 063 202458. Though the streets of Lüderitz are often deserted at night, this cosy, rustic bar-restaurant is frequently packed to the rafters with folk of all ethnicities – locals and visitors alike. The waiting time for pizza, *eisenbein* and sauerkraut, the house speciality, and other pub grub can be long. There's occasional live music, and sport on the big screen also brings in the punters. N$$–$$$

Captain Macarena At the waterfront 063 203958. Great value take-away kiosk for fish 'n' chips, with calamari and kingklip kebabs to enliven the menu. It's all very inexpensive. N$–$$

Diaz Coffee Shop, Oyster & Wine Bar Bismarck Street 081 700 0475. No longer the corner café of old, this cheerful place is trying a bit too hard to be all things to all people, with a wine bar-cum-beer garden serving German specialities out back too. That said, the service is friendly, and the food is inexpensive. The fresh oysters are a definite must-try. N$$

Penguin Restaurant Lüderitz Nest Hotel, 820 Diaz St 063 204000. This is one of the few places open on a Sunday night, but a decent spot to dine at other times, too – bag a table with a sea view for lunch. There's a wide-ranging, if fairly pricey, menu. Light meals are offered at lunchtime, but dinner is a full à la carte service. Try the lobster or speciality abalone sea snails. N$$–$$$

★ **The Portuguese Fisherman** Diaz Street, 081 1478347. Succulent seafood and sushi platters are beautifully presented and served in cheerful, nautically themed surroundings, including an outdoor area on decking fashioned as the prow of a boat. The signature *cataplana* (a seafood stew) is a favourite and can be enjoyed as you gaze out at the ocean. Reservations are recommended. N$$–$$$

Ritzi's Seafood Restaurant Upstairs at the waterfront, Hafen Street facebook.com/ritzisrestaurant. With indoor and terrace seating offering great views across the harbour by day, candlelit dining by night, and decent food, *Ritzi's* is justifiably popular, though service can be interminable. In addition to the plentiful fish and seafood items on the menu – the seafood curry served in a *poijke* (three-legged pot) is a top choice. They also put on chicken and meat dishes, as well as pizzas and burgers and can even knock up a veggie stir-fry. Booking is essential on Fri & Sat. N$$–$$$

The Lüderitz peninsula

On a fine day with your own transport, a tour of the **Lüderitz peninsula** makes for a pleasant morning outing, with a sprinkling of sandy beaches and rocky inlets

2

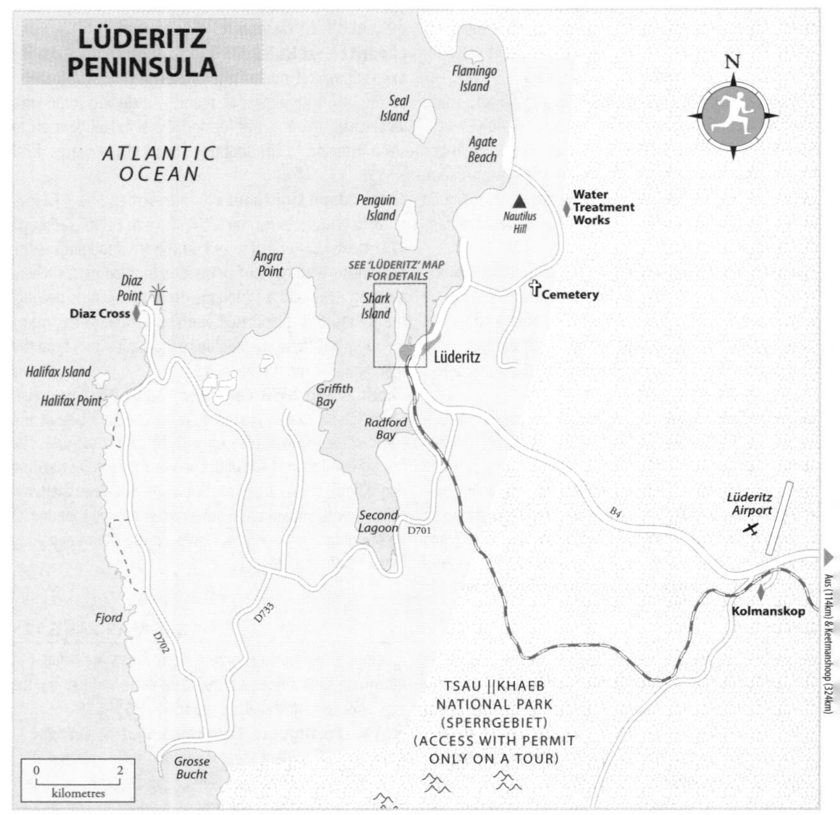

to explore and several salt pans favoured by flamingos. Most visitors head for the classic, red-and-white-striped lighthouse at **Diaz Point**, 20km (12.4 miles) by road from Lüderitz – take the B4 2km (1.2 miles) out of town, then turn right at the sign. Across a rickety wooden bridge, there's a replica of the granite cross erected by **Bartolomeu Diaz**, the pioneering Portuguese explorer credited with being the first European to visit the area in 1487. Continue round the headland, at least as far as **Guano Bay**, where, with a decent pair of binoculars, you can spot the African penguins across the water at **Halifax Island**, though you'll get a better view from a boat (see page 128). The colony is slowly recovering from the devastating bird flu epidemic that hit in 2019.

Agate Beach

Though often forbidding and blustery, on a calm, warm weekend, **Agate Beach**, 7km (4.3 miles) north of town, is a popular destination for a stroll along the sand and a barbecue; a collection of sheltered public braai sites is dotted along the back of the beach. Head out beyond Namdeb and follow the signs past the formerly segregated townships of Nautilus and Benguela – now suburbs with more mixed populations and merging with new developments. Consider pausing at the water treatment works, which is a choice location to spot springbok, oryx and a host of seabirds, including flamingos. The beach is pleasant but unremarkable, a stretch of tan sand strewn with mussels and other shells and strands of seaweed.

The Tsau ||Khaeb (Sperrgebiet) National Park

Despite its designation as a national park in 2008 and renaming as **Tsau ||Khaeb** (meaning 'deep, sandy soils' in Nama), the diamond mining **Sperrgebiet** ('Forbidden Area' in German) remains true to its colonial title as it's still pretty much a no-go zone except on a strictly controlled guided tour from Lüderitz (see page 128). The park stretches 320km (198.8 miles) northwards from the important Ramsar-protected wetlands at the mouth of the Orange River, encompassing vast sand sheets and dune areas, mountains, inselbergs and gravel plains, to some 70km (43.5 miles) north of Lüderitz. From the wild Atlantic coast, whose most photographed feature is the impressive 60m (196.9ft) Bogenfels Rock Arch, the park extends 100km (62.1 miles) inland.

Having been effectively off-limits for over a century, this whole environment has remained pristine, apart from the 5 percent exploited for mining, where the scars are all too apparent. In particular, the park is renowned for its outstanding **plant biodiversity**, boasting the greatest variety of succulents on the planet. After spring rains, they explode in a profusion of colour, enlivening the otherwise stark landscape. And nowhere is the desolation more tangible than at the abandoned mining towns of **Bogenfels** and **Pomona**, where a forlorn graveyard is gradually being engulfed by sand, and the wind speeds regularly top 60km/h (37.3mph) in the summer, generating ferocious sandstorms.

Kolmanskop

On the B4, 11km (6.8 miles) from Lüderitz • Mon–Fri 8am–1pm, Sat 8am–noon, Sun 8.30–10am; guided tours • Charge, including guided tour; photo permits granted for out-of-hours visits • Taxi from Lüderitz; the driver will wait for the return

For many, the main attraction of Lüderitz is the chance to poke around the eerie diamond mining 'ghost town' of **KOLMANSKOP** – the most accessible part of the Tsau ||Khaeb National Park – and witness the desert sands reclaiming the decaying buildings of what was once the wealthiest town in Africa. Every few months, diggers are sent into the ruins to excavate some sand so the area's main tourist attraction isn't totally buried beneath the dunes.

In 1908, Kolmanskop was merely an insignificant train station on the line out of Lüderitz until **diamonds** were discovered, triggering a mining frenzy that, in turn, fuelled an extravagant construction boom. Within three years, the settlement boasted electricity and a hospital, with the region's first X-ray machine – more to detect diamond smugglers than to serve medical purposes – a ballroom, theatre, casino, swimming pool and bowling alley, plus a wealth of luxurious houses to accommodate the three hundred white workers and their families resident in the town's heyday. There was even an ice-making factory to ensure the champagne stayed suitably chilled, though the freshwater needed for the ice still had to be shipped in from Cape Town. After World War I, when diamond prices dropped and richer deposits were found further south, Kolmanskop's star began to wane, and by 1956, the last remaining families had left, though mining had ceased some time before.

The tours are very informative, but make sure you take time afterward to look around the exhibits in the **smugglers' room** for tips in case you chance on a diamond. Back in the day, all manner of means were used to spirit the gemstones out of the area, as well as the more predictable methods, such as secreting the stone about the body, hiding it in a shoe or knife handle or sewn up in clothing, diamonds were also fired out over the security fence by crossbow or attached to a homing pigeon. For this reason, homing pigeons are still banned in Oranjemund to this day.

2

NAMIBIA'S DIAMONDS

On 14 April 1908, **Zacharias Lewala**, a Black labourer toiling on the railway just outside Lüderitz, discovered a rough **diamond** and showed it to his foreman, **August Stauch**. History doesn't relate what happened to Lewala, who had acquired his keen eye for the mineral while working in Kimberley. Stauch quietly resigned from his position with the railway and set himself up as a diamond prospector, becoming very rich almost overnight. The Germans immediately declared the 320km (198.8-mile) stretch of coastline (extending 100km/62.1 miles inland) from Lüderitz to the Orange River a Sperrgebiet (Forbidden Area) to control the diamond rush that ensued. Namibia was soon producing 1 million carats (200kg) annually, accounting for 20 percent of world diamond production and helping German South-West Africa to turn a profit by 1913.

Following the German defeat in World War I, the country's diamond mines, mainly along the Orange River, came under the control of Ernest Oppenheimer, founder of Anglo American and the man behind De Beers, who maintained a monopoly on the Namibian diamond trade right through the apartheid era until the 1990s.

Since 1994, the diamond trade has been controlled by Namdeb, a company set up by De Beers and the Namibian government, each with a 50 percent stake. Although not found in such quantities as in neighbouring Botswana and South Africa, diamonds continue to be a mainstay of the Namibian economy, with Namdeb, the country's largest taxpayer and biggest foreign exchange generator, contributing a fifth of the country's foreign exchange.

Namibia's diamonds have traditionally been found in alluvial and coastal deposits. Washed downstream over the centuries, into the sea and then back onto the coastline's raised beaches and dunes, the diamonds are small but crystal clear, resulting from centuries of erosion and weathering which have weeded out the imperfect stones. As a result, some 98 percent are of 'gem quality' (the highest proportion in the world) and are highly valued compared to diamonds from the land-based mines of South Africa.

In recent years, the biggest challenge for the industry has been the depletion of land diamonds, which are likely to run out entirely by 2030, and the increasing reliance on **marine diamonds**, which are now being dredged up from the bottom of the ocean at depths of over 120m (393.7ft). Debmarine, Namdeb's offshore arm, is now its most important asset, and in 2017, it invested N$2 billion in the world's largest diamond sampling and exploration vessel. The major downside to this marine mining is the obvious negative environmental impact of sucking up the seabed, sifting it for diamonds, then spewing the remains back into the sea. However, the industry argues that such activity is restricted to a relatively small area and that the seabed recovers naturally over time. The other threat to the diamond market is the arrival of cheaper synthetic diamonds of gem quality – industrial diamonds are nearly all synthetic now. The gem-quality synthetic diamonds are now so good that experts can't tell the difference without the help of expensive technology.

Oranjemund and around

Marooned at the far southwestern tip of Namibia, the anachronistic mining town of **ORANJEMUND** lies at the mouth of the Orange River – hence its name, which translates from German as 'Orange mouth'. Although unlikely to be on anyone's holiday hit list any time soon, given its isolation and the fact that the surrounding desert and the estuary still bear the scars of its mining history, it's an intriguing and incredibly leafy place to visit, full of mature trees, flower-filled gardens and green spaces. It's also a top spot for birdwatching as the river delta is a listed RAMSAR wetland site, supporting up to twenty thousand birds and over fifty species – when summer migrants pass through – including important populations of Southern African endemics such as the Damara tern, Hartlaub's gull and Cape cormorant.

Several hides and observation towers line the river, where you watch pelicans, flamingos and terns going about their business.

Otherwise, Oranjemund's principal draw is its erstwhile 'forbidden' status; a no-go area for the public for many years, in case they indulged in a little extracurricular prospecting on the beach, the town only finally opened its gates to all and sundry in 2017. Previously, a permit had to be secured to visit and nobody could enter or exit the town after 10pm.

The town's main, yet modest, sight is the museum, although, in 2019, the municipality opened the Hub Market, a new commercial area and community space. At the tourist office adjacent to the museum, you can rent fat-tyre e-bikes to explore the town and the surrounding area.

Arguably, however, Oranjemund's star attraction, which features on the town's crest, is the omnipresent oryx: nibbling at residents' herbaceous borders, trimming the parks or the greens at the golf course, lazing around outside the municipal offices or incongruously strolling around the town centre, window-shopping.

Jaspar House Heritage Centre

Main Street • Mon–Fri 11am–2pm, Sat 10am–noon • Free • ⓦ oranjemund-tourism.com

Crammed into a few small rooms of the home of the first general manager of Consolidated Diamond Mines (now Namdeb), the **Jaspar House Heritage Centre**'s focus inevitably is on the town's fascinating diamond mining history, explained through a collection of black-and-white photos and assorted memorabilia. Alas, no diamonds are on display, though a few other semi-precious stones feature. There's also an interesting section on the area's flora and fauna. The museum was completely renovated and displays were updated in 2021. However, plans to display previously unseen – by the public, at least – treasures from a 500-year-old Portuguese trading vessel, the *Bom Jesus*, have still to be realised. Laden with gold and silver coins, copper ingots, assorted weaponry and the like, it was shipwrecked on Namibian shores and unearthed in 2008. For the moment, a wooden sculpture featuring giant doubloons is the closest visitors will get to seeing these fascinating finds.

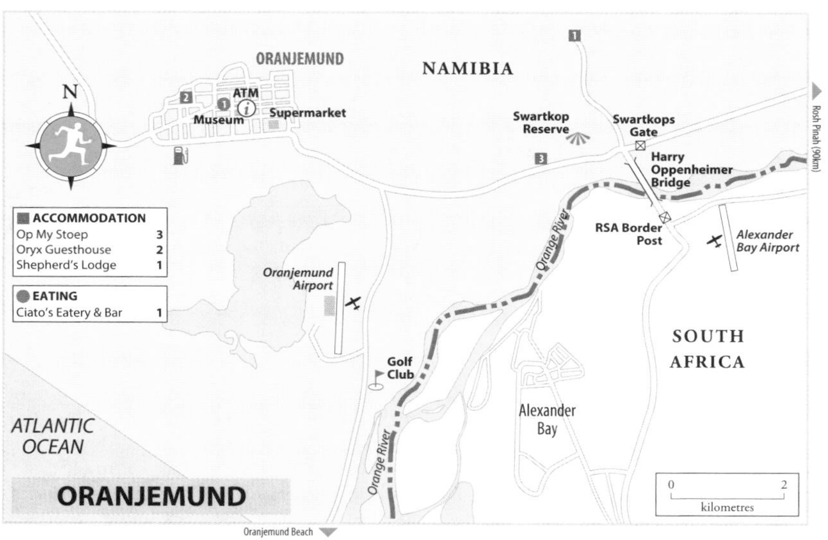

Swartkop Nature Reserve

Swartkop summit, signposted to your immediate right, after the security gate • 24hr • Free

Atop the hill of the same name, **Swartkop Nature Reserve** is no more than a patch of earth containing some non-too-apparent rare succulents fenced off from the public. It's the perfect spot to soak up fine views across the Orange River estuary and the Oppenheimer Bridge, named after the former gold and diamond magnate and anti-apartheid politician Harry Oppenheimer.

2

ARRIVAL AND GETTING AROUND — ORANJEMUND AND AROUND

By bus Several private bus companies provide transport to and from Oranjemund. They are listed on the tourist office website (see below).

By car The winding 80km (49.7-mile) road from the turn-off to Oranjemund from the C13 is completely paved.

By plane Fly Namibia operates weekday flights from Eros Airport, Windhoek, to Oranjemund (1hr 15min). The airport is 6km (3.7 miles) outside the town.

To/from South Africa Self-drive visitors bound for, or coming from, Alexander Bay in South Africa will cross the border on the Oppenheimer Bridge (daily 6am–10pm), 7km (4.3 miles) east of the town centre.

Getting around The centre of Oranjemund is compact and easy to walk around. The town's most established lodgings are close to the former security gate, 7km (4.3 miles) from the town centre, by the border bridge with South Africa. There's no public transport, though taxis do operate.

TOURIST INFORMATION

Tourist office The tourist office (Mon–Fri 9am–4pm; ⓦ oranjemund–tourism.com) is located next to the museum. Here, you can rent e-bikes.

ACCOMMODATION — SEE MAP PAGE 133

Op My Stoep 400m (0.25 miles) beyond the old security gate on the main road ⓦ opmystoep.com. This motel-like property – you park your vehicle outside your room – has sixteen functional tiled doubles, including four plusher rooms and several self-catering units. The bar-restaurant, complete with a TV and pool table, is a popular social hub for visitors and locals. Bedecked with baseball caps, car licence plates and assorted mining memorabilia, it serves excellent bar food. However, the fact that breakfast ends at 8am tells you that most visitors are here on business. Camping facilities are very rudimentary, with no shade or electricity. Camping N$ self-catering and doubles (B&B) N$$

Oryx Guesthouse 6 & 7 Ostrich Drive ⓦ facebook.com/Mariestoltz1023. Centrally located guesthouse named after the town's most famous inhabitant – frequently found in the garden – the place has thirteen comfortable rooms, furnished to modern tastes: half are self-catering, the rest singles or doubles, which can be booked without breakfast. A set menu dinner can be pre-booked. B&B and self-catering N$$

Shepherd's Lodge 1km (0.6 miles) beyond the security gate; turn right immediately after entering and follow the road over the hill ⓦ shepherds.africa. Tucked away in a shallow north of the Swartkop, this is a peaceful retreat, a tree-filled oasis with water features and appealing birdlife. The rooms, especially the new ones, are nice, and the semi-open bar-restaurant is pleasant. Service can be hit or miss. Camping on the grass is also possible. Camping N$, doubles N$$

EATING — SEE MAP PAGE 133

Ciato's Eatery & Bar Hage Geingob Avenue ⓦ facebook.com/ciatoseatery. This is the only place to eat with a bit of vibe – not counting *Op My Stoep* – with indoor and outdoor pub-style seating. Right by the ocean, you have oysters, calamari and kingklip to feast on besides the deli pizzas, burgers and steaks (including oryx) and a wealth of sides and extras. N$$–$$$

Rosh Pinah

In total contrast to faded Oranjemund, just down the road, the gleaming new centre of the small mining town of **ROSH PINAH** is bristling with confidence and money, boasting freshly painted cream houses with green roofs, neat, clean streets and a sparkling shopping centre. All this is mainly due to the booming Skorpion mine, 25km (15.5 miles) to the north. After opening in 2000, it has become one of the largest zinc mines in the world, though various rare and valuable minerals have also been found. There's nothing to the town itself, though the setting is attractive – once you disregard the slag heaps, which announce your arrival from the south – as it's overlooked by the Huns Mountains to the east and the Swartkloof Mountains that lie to the north and west, straddling the eastern limits of the Sperrgebiet.

The main reason to break your journey here is to use the ATM and get supplies from the well-stocked supermarket in the shopping centre – it's your best bet if you're heading south to camp along the Orange River or visiting the South African side of the Richtersveld park – and to refuel at the petrol station, as there's nowhere else for 150km (93.2 miles) in either direction unless you're bound for Oranjemund. Should you want or need to stay the night, there are a couple of decent guesthouses with restaurants aimed at visiting mining executives.

ACCOMMODATION — ROSH PINAH

Amica Guesthouse 306 Mukarob Close T 063 274043, E aguesthousevedantaresources.co.na. Comfortable mine-owned property in a quiet residential cul-de-sac. It has ten carpeted rooms with the usual business amenities: mini-fridge, phone, tea/coffee facilities, a pleasant plant-filled courtyard with a pool, and a two-storey *lapa* with a giant chess set and elevated sundowner deck affording desert views. B&B **N$$**

The southern Kalahari and the far south

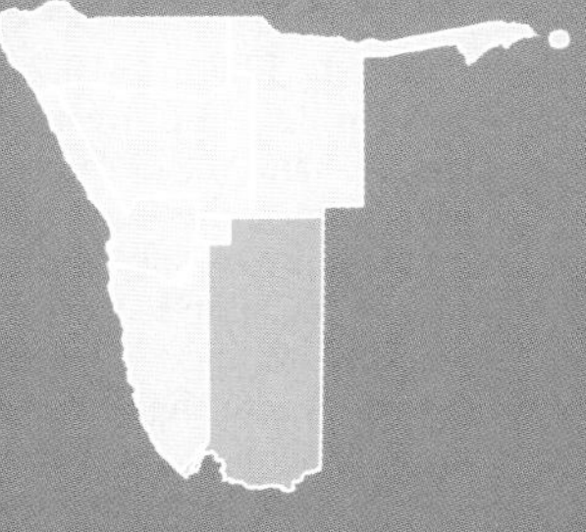

RED DUNES IN THE KALAHARI DESERT

The southern Kalahari and the far south

The vastness of the southern Kalahari and the far south of Namibia is daunting, as is the absence of people: only a fraction of the population lives here. The long, lonely road east of Windhoek passes through sparse thornveld to the Botswana border. While the road south from the capital stretches hundreds of kilometres to the South African border and the southern Kalahari. But the foray south is well worth the effort. Those who persist with the journey are rewarded with hugely enjoyable canoeing and birdwatching along the Orange River, unrivalled hiking opportunities in the vast Fish River Canyon, and rippling red dunes in the southern Kalahari.

Taking on the main road south of Windhoek promises some of the country's most incredible sights and spectacles. The tarred highway speeds through the unremarkable towns of **Rehoboth** – home to one of Namibia's proudest peoples – and **Mariental** before dividing at **Keetmanshoop**, the region's bustling administrative capital, and a good place to fill up with petrol and stock up with supplies. Northwest of the town, the Brukkaros 'false volcano' rewards hikers with beautiful views from the crater rim. And to the northeast of Keetmanshoop, the scenic **Quiver Tree Forest** is well worth the diversion.

Southern Namibia's great attraction is the spectacular **Fish River Canyon**. A 160km (99.4-mile-) long serpentine ravine, it hosts a challenging five-day hiking trail that ends in the popular hot-springs resort of **|Ai-|Ais**. The canyon lies within the **|Ai-|Ais/ Richtersveld Transfrontier Park**; extending into South Africa, this remote and rugged area has limited infrastructure but boasts extraordinary plant biodiversity. It's bisected by the scenic **Orange River**, whose meandering progress towards the Atlantic provides great opportunities for birdwatching and canoeing.

East of the B1, around Mariental, and along the picturesque 'back road' from Stampriet to the Mata Mata gate of the **Kgalagadi Transfrontier Park**, the rippling **red dunes** that gain in height and colour as you move further inland supply the attractive backdrop to a sprinkling of delightful lodges and campgrounds.

There's not much to lure visitors to the sparse land beyond the Eros Mountains east of Windhoek unless they're heading for the **Botswana border** or interested in visiting the bat-riddled **Arnhem Cave**.

The road south

It's a long 500km (310.7-mile) haul along the B1 between Windhoek, across the Hardap Region to Keetmanshoop, the capital of the vast ||Karas Region – the country's largest – and the de facto capital of southern Namibia. Once the B1 has wound its way through the Aus Mountains and flattened out in the unremarkable yet historically important town of **Rehoboth**, 100km (62.1 miles) down the road, there's little in the way of engaging scenery to keep your attention as you stare across the roadside fences marking off huge commercial farms at the never-ending flat savannah lands that stretch eastwards into the Kalahari. It's easy to be reduced to ticking off the 10km (6.2-mile) distance signs as you head towards your destination.

After Rehoboth, the next small town of note is **Mariental**, 180km (111.8 miles) further south, and then **Keetmanshoop**, another two hours' drive beyond that. To

QUIVER TREE FOREST

Highlights

❶ **Brukkaros** A hike up this false volcano is rewarded by some excellent birdwatching and breathtaking views across an endless, desolate landscape. See page 144

❷ **Quiver trees** Make sure you seek out the 'forests' of Namibia's most photogenic plant. See page 147

❸ **Kalahari Red Dunes** The less visited rippling red dunes of Namibia's second desert provide the perfect setting for some rest and relaxation. See page 149

❹ **The Kgalagadi Transfrontier Park** No need to do border formalities; pop over to South Africa for a couple of days and get your fill of vast herds of large mammals following ancient migration routes. See page 150

❺ **Fish River Canyon** Whether you marvel at this gaping chasm from the rim or take a gruelling hike along the canyon floor, this is a must-see attraction. See page 153

❻ **The Orange River** A chance to paddle for a day or more through lovely scenery, enjoying campfire dinners and nights sleeping out under the stars. See page 160

HIGHLIGHTS ARE MARKED ON THE MAP ON PAGE 140

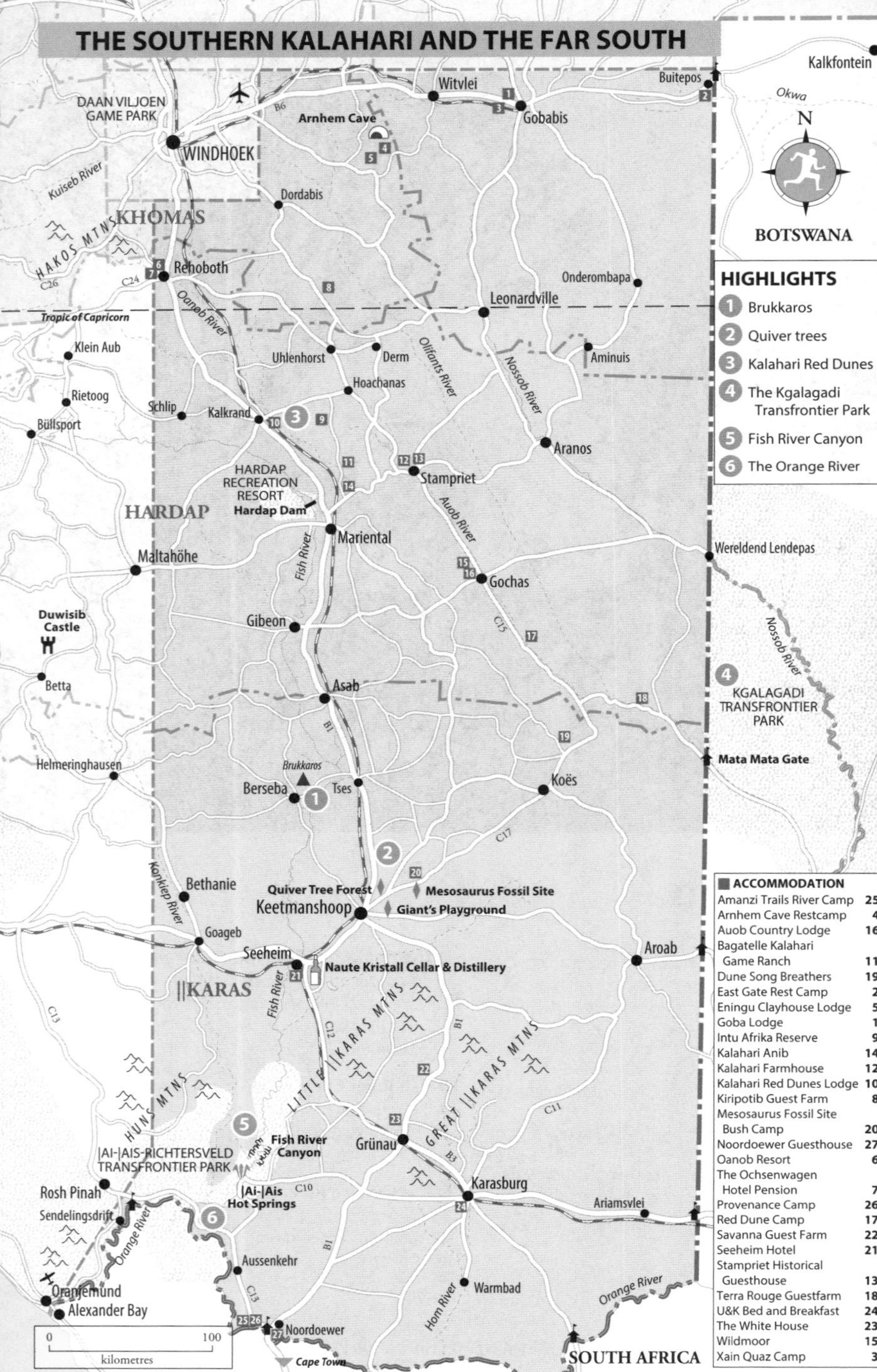
THE SOUTHERN KALAHARI AND THE FAR SOUTH
Kalkfontein
Buitepos
Witvlei
Gobabis
Okwa
N
BOTSWANA
DAAN VILJOEN GAME PARK
Arnhem Cave
WINDHOEK
B6
Kuiseb River
Dordabis
KHOMAS
HAKOS MTNS
Rehoboth
C26
C24
Onderombapa
Leonardville
Tropic of Capricorn
Oanob River
Klein Aub
Uhlenhorst
Derm
Olifants River
Nossob River
Aminuis
Rietoog
Hoachanas
Büllsport
Schlip
Kalkrand
Aranos
HARDAP RECREATION RESORT
Stampriet
Hardap Dam
HARDAP
Auob River
Mariental
Fish River
Maltahöhe
Wereldend Lendepas
Gochas
Duwisib Castle
Gibeon
C15
Nossob River
Betta
Asab
KGALAGADI TRANSFRONTIER PARK
B1
Helmeringhausen
Mata Mata Gate
Brukkaros
Berseba
Tses
Koës
C17
Bethanie
Quiver Tree Forest
Mesosaurus Fossil Site
Konkiep River
Keetmanshoop
Giant's Playground
Goageb
Aroab
Seeheim
Naute Kristall Cellar & Distillery
||KARAS
Fish River
C13
C12
LITTLE ||KARAS MTNS
B1
GREAT ||KARAS MTNS
HUNS MTNS
C11
Fish River Canyon
Grünau
|AI-|AIS-RICHTERSVELD TRANSFRONTIER PARK
B3
Karasburg
Rosh Pinah
|Ai-|Ais Hot Springs
C10
Sendelingsdrift
Ariamsvlei
Orange River
Aussenkehr
B1
C13
Warmbad
Hom River
Orange River
Oranjemund
Alexander Bay
0
100
kilometres
Noordoewer
Cape Town
SOUTH AFRICA
HIGHLIGHTS
1 Brukkaros
2 Quiver trees
3 Kalahari Red Dunes
4 The Kgalagadi Transfrontier Park
5 Fish River Canyon
6 The Orange River
ACCOMMODATION
Amanzi Trails River Camp 25
Arnhem Cave Restcamp 4
Auob Country Lodge 16
Bagatelle Kalahari Game Ranch 11
Dune Song Breathers 19
East Gate Rest Camp 2
Eningu Clayhouse Lodge 5
Goba Lodge 1
Intu Afrika Reserve 9
Kalahari Anib 14
Kalahari Farmhouse 12
Kalahari Red Dunes Lodge 10
Kiripotib Guest Farm 8
Mesosaurus Fossil Site Bush Camp 20
Noordoewer Guesthouse 27
Oanob Resort 6
The Ochsenwagen Hotel Pension 7
Provenance Camp 26
Red Dune Camp 17
Savanna Guest Farm 22
Seeheim Hotel 21
Stampriet Historical Guesthouse 13
Terra Rouge Guestfarm 18
U&K Bed and Breakfast 24
The White House 23
Wildmoor 15
Xain Quaz Camp 3

the west, not long after you cross the regional boundary into the ||Karas Region, the impressive massif of the **Brukkaros Mountain** looms out of the surrounding plains, dominating the horizon (see page 144).

Rehoboth

Surrounded by acacia woodland, the thirty thousand–strong town of **REHOBOTH**, situated just north of the Tropic of Capricorn, is of little interest to the casual visitor. However, it is home to the fiercely proud Baster people (see page 141), whose history is well explained in the local museum. The settlement had already had a couple of names before gaining its current biblical incarnation, thanks to a local missionary in 1844. Drawn by the natural hot springs in the area, a semi-nomadic Damara group that would visit periodically when water was scarce in the Kalahari dubbed the place

REHOBOTH BASTERS

The **Rehoboth Basters** are one of a number of groups of mixed heritage that emerged in the Dutch Cape Colony in the eighteenth century and were forced by their non-white status to live on the fringes of white colonial society – they were among the many people who were later designated as 'coloureds' in apartheid South Africa and Namibia. They primarily share a mix of Black African and European settler heritage reflected in the name they proudly bear (a corruption of 'bastard'). Originally settled in the Northern Cape, the Basters began their great trek north across the Orange River in 1868, when new laws prevented them from owning land. Led by their own 'Moses', the Basters' first *Kaptein*, Hermanus van Wyk, some three hundred or so Afrikaans-speaking, devoutly Calvinist Basters eventually set up the **Free Republic of Rehoboth**, 100km (62.1 miles) south of Windhoek, in 1872.

Initially, the Basters were careful to maintain their neutrality in the simmering conflicts of central and southern Namibia. But in 1884, they became the first group to sign a 'Treaty of Friendship and Protection' with the Germans and for the next twenty years, they threw their lot in with the newly arrived colonial power, even supplying troops and assisting in the genocide of the Nama and Herero during the Namibian War of Resistance (1904–09). With the outbreak of World War I, the Basters reasserted their neutrality, only agreeing to enlist after being assured that they wouldn't be asked to fight their South African neighbours. In April 1915, the Germans ordered the Basters to guard some South African prisoners of war and retreat north away from Rehoboth or be disarmed. Around three hundred Basters deserted their posts and, with their families, retreated to Sam Khubis, 80km (49.7 miles) southeast of Rehoboth. The Germans pursued them and, on 8 May 1915, confronted the Basters in the **Battle of Sam Khubis**. Outgunned all day long, the Basters were left without ammunition by nightfall, but their prayers were answered when, the very next day, the Germans were ordered to retreat in the face of the advancing South African army. It's a divine miracle celebrated every year by the Rehoboth Basters.

With the war's end, the Basters were keen to re-establish their autonomous republic but were thwarted by Namibia's new South African rulers. In 1924, the Rehoboth Basters revolted, appointing themselves a new *Kaptein* – the South African response was brutal, sending in troops, bombing the town into submission and arresting over four hundred Basters. From that low point, the Basters have been engaged in a long, hard struggle to try and reclaim and hold onto their unique status, applying to the UN for help; they even eventually made a deal with the apartheid regime to create a **Rehoboth bantustan** in 1979.

After independence, the Namibian government took control of many of the Basters' communal lands. Since then, they have been fighting an even more desperate rearguard action to try and win back the ancestral land, which they originally bought off the local Nama, to preserve their culture – a case that looks likely to fail.

|Gaollnāus (Fountain of the Falling Buffalo). A group of Nama later changed this to |Anes (Place of Smoke), referring to the steam rising from the springs. Even today, there has been an attempt to market Rehoboth as a spa town, though the baths have been closed for some time. Better recreational facilities can be found at the Oanob Dam, 7km (4.3 miles) outside town (see page 142).

Rehoboth Museum

Church Street • Mon–Fri 8am–5pm (closed for lunch) • Free • museums.com.na/museums/south/rehoboth-museum

The Rehoboth Museum building was originally the old postmaster's house built in 1927, adjacent to the post office, which was completed four years later. It became a museum in 1986, and its prime focus is to tell the story of the Baster community, including details of the Great Baster Trek from the Cape in 1868, which the knowledgeable curator will happily expand on. All of this is crammed into one main room. A second room has more eclectic displays on human evolution, the area's flora and fauna and even banknotes of the world used to educate visiting school children – hence the collection of chairs and desks in the middle of the room.

ACCOMMODATION — REHOBOTH, SEE MAP PAGE 140

Oanob Resort Oanob Dam off the D1280, 7km (4.3 miles) west of Rehoboth oanob.com.na. A surprisingly pleasant lodge resort comprising a collection of generous double stone-and-thatch chalets with shared balconies and freestanding fully equipped two- or three-bedroom family chalets dotted around the lake, facing the water through shady acacias. The bar-restaurant, which serves decent food, overlooks the dam too – though it's cold in winter as it lacks a fireplace. A popular getaway for Windhoek families on summer weekends, it's also a first-night stay for foreign tourists on their way to Sossusvlei. Plenty of campsites have electricity; prices vary according to location and shade. Day visitors are also welcome, which can result in a party atmosphere. Camping N$, doubles B&B N$$, family self-catering chalets N$$–$$$

The Ochsenwagen Hotel Pension B1 at the junction with the D1237 062 525910, ochsenwagen123@gmail.com. If you're heading north and too tired to make the last hour's drive to Windhoek, then this modern, fairly bland roadside establishment fits the bill. There's a sports bar restaurant, too. B&B N$$

Mariental

Rather like Rehoboth, to the north, **MARIENTAL**, the low-key administrative centre for the Hardap region, has little to detain the average tourist beyond the usual supermarkets and petrol stations for replenishing supplies and fuel. Indeed, it resembles a glorified industrial estate. The town has several acceptable places to stay if you need a bed for the night. However, the lodges and reserves in the red dunes of the Kalahari (see page 149), only an hour's drive away, are infinitely preferable if you're looking for recreation.

In classic colonial fashion, Mariental, meaning 'Marie's Valley', was named in honour of the wife of the first white settler, William Brandt. However, the notion of a valley was somewhat fanciful. In contrast, the Nama, who had been around for considerably longer, called the place Zara-gaeiba, meaning 'dusty', aptly nailing the location's defining characteristic. Indeed, on Sundays, the swirling dust is about the only sign of life in town.

That said, a 15km (9.3-mile) belt of lush commercial farmland west of Mariental runs parallel to the B1. The Fish River flows through the area from the Hardap Dam northwest of the town and provides further water for irrigation. The farms focus on sheep, goats, game – especially ostrich – and dairy and alfalfa production (more commonly termed lucerne).

Hardap Dam

Signposted west off the B1, 9km (5.6 miles) north of Mariental, 15km (9.3 miles) down the road • Daily 6am–11pm • Charge • Game drives and boat trips available

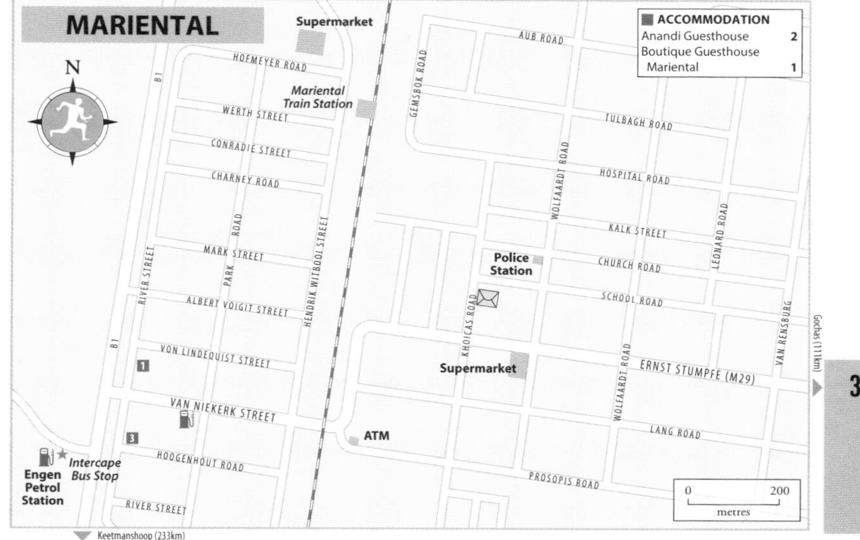

Just northwest of town is **Hardap Dam**, Namibia's largest reservoir. It draws its water from the Fish River and hosts an NWR resort, which reopened in 2016 after a multimillion Namibian-dollar, yet bland, facelift. Hardap is a Nama name for 'nipple' or 'wart', presumably how the surrounding area's conical hills appeared to the area's earliest visitors. The nature reserve, comprising the dam and its surrounding dwarf shrub savannah, supports an array of wildlife. Look out for black rhinos, Hartmann's mountain zebra, kudu, oryx, eland and red hartebeest. Over 280 bird species have been recorded in the area, with the fish-rich reservoir feeding cormorants, darters, spoonbills, fish eagles and even osprey, in addition to a breeding colony of great white pelican.

ACCOMMODATION

MARIENTAL, SEE MAP PAGE 143

Anandi Guesthouse 15 River St ⓦ anandiguesthouse.com. Cheerful lilac buildings and some greenery are secure within a lilac-walled compound. Staff are friendly and accommodating, while rooms are upbeat; some with fans, others with a/c. Gleaming, fully tiled bathrooms with fancy modern sinks (some with a jacuzzi bath). Bookable with or without breakfast. No dining restaurant. N$$

Boutique Guesthouse Mariental 65 River St ⓣ 081 229483, ⓔ reservations.boutique@travel-weaver.com. The most comfortable option in town, offering excellent value. Spacious modern rooms (the chandeliers apart) offer all comforts, including tea- and coffee-making facilities, a fridge and a microwave. Rooms open onto a private patio area overlooking a pleasant garden and you can choose English, Irish or vegetarian breakfast. N$$

Around Mariental

North of Mariental and east of the B1, several lodges set in private reserves make the most of their surroundings among the picturesque linear red dunes of the Kalahari (see page 149). These dunes, unlike those in the Namib, are generally vegetated and run northwest to southeast, interspersed with wider inter-dune valleys or 'streets' possessing the occasional pan and studded with acacia trees and shrubs and shimmering grasses after rain.

ACCOMMODATION

AROUND MARIENTAL, SEE MAP PAGE 140

★ **Bagatelle Kalahari Game Ranch** On the D1268, 25km (15.5 miles) north of the junction with the C20

3

BRUKKAROS – THE FALSE VOLCANO

Visible over 80km (49.7 miles) away, as you speed along the B1 north of Keetmanshoop, the forbidding massif of **Brukkaros** looms out of the surrounding flat, parched plains, dwarfing the nearby Nama settlement of Berseba (!Autsawises), one of the oldest villages in Namibia. The original name for the mountain was Geitsigubeb, the Khoekhoen word for a leather apron, which they thought it resembled; this led to the Afrikaans combination of 'broek' (trousers) and 'karos' (leather apron), which resulted in Brukkaros.

Despite its imposing stature, it is often overlooked by tourists. Still, it is well worth a detour if you like hiking, as it offers commanding **views**, fascinating **rock formations** and surprisingly good **birdwatching**. In the colonial era, the Germans used the crater rim as a heliograph station; then, in 1926, the National Geographic Society teamed up with the Smithsonian Institute and ran a solar observatory here for a few years.

For a long time, it was assumed to be an extinct volcano, suggested by its squat conical shape and the existence of a caldera. Yet it's now thought to be the result of an enormous gaseous explosion around **80 million years** ago: magma pushing upwards encountered groundwater, which then heated, vaporised and expanded while pressure from the magma continued to build. When the Earth's crust was welling up and could no longer take the strain, it exploded, spewing rocks forming the crater rim. Over time, the central area eroded, leaving a scree-encircled caldera floor 350m (1,148.3ft) below the rim. **Quiver trees** are present, hosting the inevitable sociable weavers' communal nest, and the area generally supports numerous bird species, particularly raptors; look out for black and booted eagles riding the thermals. The mountain also hosts the endemic Brukkaros pygmy rock mouse; though being nocturnal and minute, the chances of spotting one are not high.

HIKING TO THE CRATER

After passing under an unlikely gateway announcing your arrival at Brukkaros, the road bends around a hillock to the former lower campsite and car park; most visitors leave their vehicle here, though it is possible to take a four-wheel drive 2km (1.2 miles) further up the very rocky track to the upper campsite and parking area, but it's a very bumpy ride. From the upper camping area, a narrow, steep, meandering path takes you up a further 1.5km (0.9 miles) to the lip of the outflow, marked by a rock waterfall, where you'll only see cascading water after heavy rains. Here, you can explore the vegetated caldera or make a sharp left turn to scramble a further 500m (1,640.4ft) onto the rim and soak up the breathtaking views. The vertigo-hardened might want to navigate a further 4.5km (2.8 miles) along an increasingly indistinct path round to the northern side of the rim and nose around the decaying buildings of the abandoned research station before taking the same route back.

Don't hike alone since there's no mobile phone coverage and the walk involves a lot of boulder-hopping and rock scrambling, with the real risk of going over on your ankle. Make sure you have robust footwear, plenty of water and protection against the sun, as there's no shelter along the way.

ARRIVAL AND INFORMATION

Access is via the M98, signposted off the B1, 86km (53.4 miles) north of Keetmanshoop, and just south of Tses, signposted to the village of Berseba (!Autsawises in Nama), which lies 38km (23.6 miles) down the road, and where there are a couple of basic shops and a fuel station. About a kilometre (0.6 miles) before the village, a poorly marked dirt road, the D3904 (accessible by two-wheel drive), leads 10km (6.2 miles) up to the mountain. Theoretically, a community fee is payable upon entry. Still, there is rarely anyone there to take the money, as the community enterprise – including maintenance of the two campsites – has all but closed down.

bagatelle-kalahari-gameranch.com. This comfortable, converted old farmhouse contains communal areas, a pool and patio, and four rooms. An avenue of pricier savannah-facing chalets leads away to the choice and most expensive accommodation: a handful of superior tented chalets atop a high red dune, affording fabulous sunset views across a waterhole. Some have private plunge pools. All lodgings have a/c, and the food is high quality. Five individual campsites have private ablution blocks and provide a pony-and-trap transfer to the lodge if you prefer to eat there. There's lots to do: wildlife-viewing drives at morning, dusk and night – a chance to spot bat-eared foxes, porcupines, aardvarks and other nocturnal creatures; stargazing through a telescope; guided walks; a visit to a San community; and horseback safaris. The place also hosts three cheetah orphans. Camping N$$, doubles (DBB) N$$$, chalets (DBB) N$$$$

★ **Kalahari Red Dunes Lodge** 3km (1.9 miles) east of the B1, signposted 5km (3.1 miles) south of Kalkrand, and 70km (43.5 miles) north of Mariental ondili.com/en/lodges-en/kalahari-red-dunes-lodge. This tastefully designed lodge, run with efficiency and warmth, is not set among the dunes, though they feature in the reserve. Rather, the lovely stone-and-thatch chalets stand in a vlei, each with uninterrupted views across the Kalahari, through vast windows, or from your private porch, and connected by a series of raised wooden walkways. Lovely central *lapa* and an excellent range of activities: self-guided and guided walks, a mountain-bike trail, wildlife viewing – plains and mountain zebra, nyala, impala, springbok, blesbok, red hartebeest, oryx, kudu and steenbok are around – and sundowner excursions, plus a three-day dune-rambling hike on the reserve, staying in a tented camp en-route. DBB N$$$$

INTU AFRIKA RESERVE

Two lodges and one chalet camp share the 100 sq km (38.6 sq mile) Intu Afrika reserve, which holds giraffe, oryx, wildebeest, zebra, kudu, springbok and imported blesbok, as well as a host of smaller mammals, including bat-eared foxes. Though the lodges are managed separately, activities are shared. These include a morning walk with a San guide or a game drive. Strangely enough, the guides also lead quad-bike excursions, which tear around the reserve making a racket, but which they claim does not disturb the wildlife because they've become so habituated to it. The main entrance to Intu Afrika is on the D1268, 35km (21.7 miles) north of the junction with the C20; the entrance to Suricate Tented Lodge is 5km (3.1 miles) further south intu-afrika.com.

Camelthorn Kalahari Lodge is 5km (3.1 miles) from the reserve entrance. Good for birdwatching, this place has a lovely snug setting in a dune valley amid plenty of camelthorns, through which oryx and springbok wander at will. Eleven sparsely furnished, stone-and-thatch chalets encircle the pleasant two-storey main lodge with a pool and fire pit. DBB N$$$

Suricate Tented Lodge 5km (3.1 miles) south of the main entrance off the D1268 063 240846. Boasting the best views, this row of tented cabins is lined along a dune ridge overlooking a pan. Fan-ventilated tents are compact, with a minibar, open-air bathroom and private viewing decks. Dining is family-style in a rather featureless tented dining room or on the viewing deck. DBB N$$$

Zebra Kalahari Lodge & Spa 5km (3.1 miles) from the reserve entrance 063 240855. The main and most luxurious of the three lodges, this hotel-like complex, overlooking a waterhole, comprises eight spacious rooms flanking the main dining-lounge area with a pool and five larger, more private suites set apart. Accommodation is furnished in ebony, decorated with African masks, and possesses all the usual modern comforts: a/c, fridge, tea/coffee-making facilities, plus an additional outside shower. DBB N$$$$

3

Keetmanshoop and around

There's little of obvious attraction in **KEETMANSHOOP** – or Keetmans, as many Namibians call it – but it makes for a convenient break in the long haul up or down the B1 and is a good place to pick up supplies if you're heading out into the desert to camp. It's the administrative centre of the vast ||Karas Region, which covers most of southern Namibia and possesses a population of around eighty thousand. A former Nama settlement, it was named after Johann Keetman, a German industrialist who donated 1,000 gold marks to construct the first Rhenish Mission Church in 1869. After you've made a pit stop and eaten, you might swing by the church's more modern incarnation to check out the museum. Whereas Keetmans holds little appeal, several attractions within striking distance are worth a detour.

Rhenish Mission Church

Sam Nujoma Drive, 6th Avenue • Mon–Fri 7.30am–12.30pm & 1.30–4.30pm • Free; donations appreciated • museums.com.na/museums/south/keetmanshoop-museum

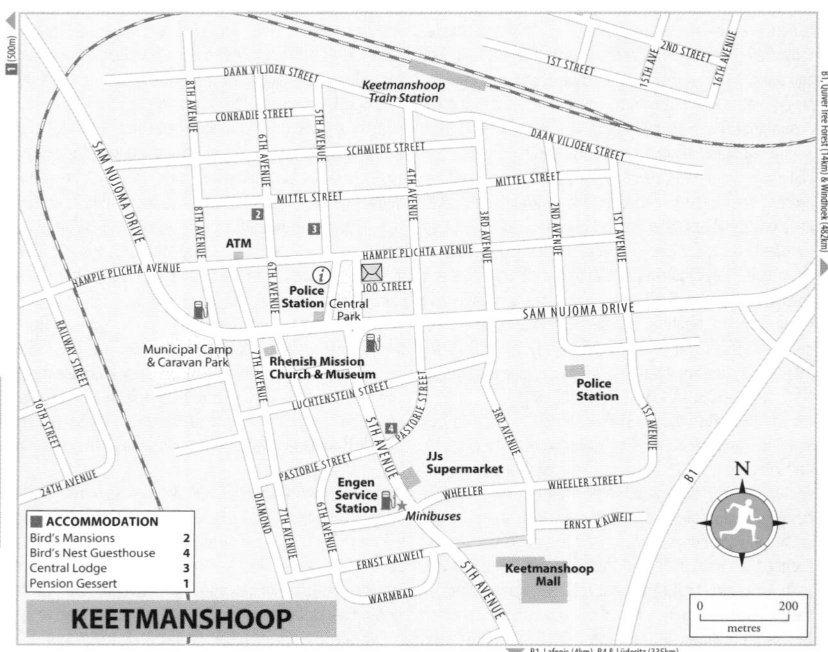

Dating back to 1895, the **Rhenish Mission Church** is the town's oldest building and houses a small museum collection in the Keetmanshoop Museum. The church is quite striking; made from stone brought by ox-cart from Lüderitz 337km (209.4 miles) away, it replaced an earlier wooden version that had been swept away in a flash flood in 1890.

Keetmanshoop Museum

The Rhenish Mission Church houses the **Keetmanshoop Museum**, a collection of modest and rather shambolic displays populated mainly by donations – offered, one suspects, by people cleaning out their unwanted junk: Singer sewing machines, coal irons, Bavarian crockery and the like. However, the collection of faded photos is of greater historical interest, documenting in part the War of National Resistance and the awful conditions of the Black population during colonial rule. Note the collection of brass passes that Indigenous peoples had to wear around their necks – part of the colonial powers' attempts to control their movements.

Quiver Tree Forest

Gariganus Farm, 14km (8.7 miles) northeast of Keetmanshoop on the C17, a good-quality dirt road suitable for two-wheel drive • Sunrise–sunset • Charge (cash only) • Ⓦ quivertreeforest.com • Call at the farmhouse first to pay the entrance fee; the Giant's Playground, also included in the price, is 2km (1.2 miles) further along the road

If you're looking for a worthwhile detour from the seemingly endless slog along the B1, the **Quiver Tree Forest** (Kokerboomwoud in Afrikaans), northeast of Keetmanshoop, is the spot to pick. This farm has an unusually high density of quiver trees, one of Namibia's most emblematic and photogenic plants (see page 147), which are best appreciated in the early morning or evening light. Enjoy scrambling around the rocks to get a good look at the plants before driving a couple of kilometres further down the road to the **Giant's Playground**. Another picturesque

QUIVER TREES

One of the most recognisable sights of southern Namibia, the magnificent **quiver tree** (*Aloe dichotoma*, or *kokerboom* in Afrikaans), is not a tree but a giant aloe. It gained its name from the Khoisan, who are said to use the hollowed-out branches as quivers to hold their poison-tipped hunting arrows. Perfectly designed to cope with the hot, arid climate, the quiver tree's distinctive crown of thick waxy leaves grows high from the ground – some reach 9m (29.5ft) in height – to escape the worst of the heat and help reduce water evaporation the pulpy fibrous tissue of its 'trunk' allows it to maximise water storage space, while its branches are coated in a thin white powder, to help reflect the sun's heat; the 'scales' on the cracked golden bark are thought to have a cooling effect too when there's a breeze. A slow developer, the *kokerboom* does not bloom until twenty or thirty years of age, but its pretty yellow flowers (June and July) attract numerous nectar-feeders, including eye-catching iridescent sunbirds. The succulent is also a popular host of sociable weavers who construct their haystack-like communal nest amid the rosettes of spiky blue-green leaves to protect the young from the heat and predators.

natural phenomenon, it comprises a vast array of dolerite boulders, weathered over millennia, which resemble piles of giant marbles that some alien colossus has stacked up. Camping and chalet accommodation are also available.

Mesosaurus Fossil Site

43km (26.7 miles) northeast of Keetmanshoop on the C17 • Daily 8am–5pm • Charge, including optional tour (cash only) • Ⓦ mesosaurus.com • High-clearance four-wheel drive needed to access the fossil site and bush camp

Less frequented than the Quiver Tree Forest, the **Mesosaurus Fossil Site** is set in a similar landscape, full of dolerite boulders, and claims to have the country's greatest density of quiver trees. While this is impossible to verify on a quick visit, there are undoubtedly a great many of them, enough to satisfy even the most ardent aloe enthusiast. Yet the sight's main attraction is **fossils**, specifically those of the **Mesosaurus**, a metre-long reptile with a small skull and long jaws – similar to a small crocodile – that frequented the freshwater habitats of Gondwanaland 290–270 million years ago. The farm owner and guide will show you various partial fossils during the guided tour, though the most complete and impressive specimen is on display in the National Earth Science Museum in Windhoek (see page 92). There are also a couple of Schutztruppe graves on the farm, and the guide's surprising star turn is to finish off the tour by bashing out a tune on 'musical' rocks.

When visiting the site, you can choose an unguided walk through the quiver trees or a guided hike that takes in the fossils and the graves too. Visitors staying overnight in the rustic accommodation can also do a self-guided trail (3–10km/1.9–6.2 miles) on the property, where you can catch the magical morning light on the quiver trees.

Nature Dam distillery

On the C 12, 17km (10.6 miles) south from the junction with the B4, 37km (23 miles) southwest of Keetmanshoop • Mon–Fri 8am–4pm, Sat & Sun 8am–2pm • Charge for a tasting • Ⓦ naute-kristall.com • Reservations preferred for groups, but drop-in is fine for self-drivers

Approaching from the north, you spot the serried ranks of date palms before you arrive at the roadside Naute Kristall Cellar & Distillery. This unlikely oasis provides the perfect pitstop for travellers heading to or from the Fish River Canyon and Sossusvlei or Lüderitz. The star product of this unlikely thriving distillery is its internationally award-winning Namgin, which features the medicinal Kalahari plant, devil's claw. Irrigated with water from the Naute Dam, grapes, prickly pears and pomegranates are also grown, forming the basis of other fine spirits. The dates are converted into the popular Dandy (date brandy), a fine spirit, and a pink gin liqueur, an enticing new product. Pack a picnic or order some *brötchen* or a platter to help absorb the alcohol before you hit the road again.

ARRIVAL AND INFORMATION KEETMANSHOOP AND AROUND

By car Keetmanshoop lies to the west of the B1, 482km (299.5 miles) south of Windhoek and 304km (188.9 miles) north of the border with South Africa.

By bus The Intercape service between Cape Town and Windhoek, as well as the bus between Johannesburg (change at Upington) and Windhoek, stops in Lafenis, 4km (2.5 miles) south of Keetmanshoop on the B1 at the Engen petrol station and Wimpy (for services to Windhoek, 4hr 50min; and for Cape Town, 14hr 45min; for Johannesburg, 20hr). In addition, minibuses leave from the Engen petrol station on 5th Avenue for Windhoek and less frequently for Lüderitz. Opposite, at JJ Supermarket, is the ticket office for the Intercape (intercape.co.za).

By train TransNamib runs an overnight train (Tue, Thurs, Fri & Sun) from Windhoek to Keetmanshoop and from Keetmans to Windhoek. However, at the time of writing, passenger services still hadn't been resumed following closure during the COVID-19 pandemic.

Tourist information A helpful tourist office is located in the Imperial Post Office (Kaiserliches Postampt) on 5th Avenue (Mon–Fri 7.30am–12.30pm, 1.30–4.30pm; 063 221266).

3

ACCOMMODATION SEE MAPS PAGES 140 AND 146

Bird's Mansions 6th Avenue birds-accommodation.com. Twenty-three small rooms with rather musty carpets but with good beds and cable TV. The shady, flower-filled beer garden-cum-restaurant (N$$) is inviting and the menu is quite extensive, offering the usual pizzas, burgers and salads as well as a variety of beef, pork, poultry, venison and mutton dishes. B&B N$$

Bird's Nest Guesthouse 16 Pastorie St birds-accommodation.com. Nice secluded environment comprising nine rooms – most newly renovated – with DStv and a fridge, opening onto a tree-filled courtyard, providing secure parking. Breakfast is provided, but you'll have to dine elsewhere. B&B N$$

Central Lodge 5th Avenue central-lodge.com. A pleasant enough hotel with 27 rooms facing towards a central lawn or the adjoining car park. Rooms are light, carpeted and fairly spacious, with cable TV, twin beds and a telephone. The on-site restaurant is popular, though the food is variable. B&B N$$

Mesosaurus Fossil Site Bush Camp At the Mesosaurus Fossil Site reception. Three rustic stone-and-thatch, twin-bedded self-catering cottages, plus one family cottage. All have semi-open kitchen areas. Six campsites are nearby with private water taps and braai sites but shared ablutions. Even nicer is the bush camp 3km (1.9 miles) into the farm, located by a riverbed between quiver trees. Cash only. Camping N$, chalet N$$

Pension Gessert 138 13th St 063 223892, gesserts1gmail.com. Seven homely, spotless rooms with a/c opening out onto a shady garden with a pool. Breakfast is a veritable feast and dinner can be pre-booked B&B N$$

DESERT OASIS: THE SEEHEIM HOTEL

Tucked away down a rocky ravine some 45km (28 miles) west of Keetmanshoop, the impressive **Seeheim Hotel** (seeheimhotel.com; B&B N$$) is an unlikely oasis, flaunting lush palm trees and a sparkling swimming pool. It dates back to the colonial era when the original stone building first served as a barracks for the Schutztruppe before being transformed into a hotel in the 1920s, becoming the centrepiece of a thriving town that was a major stop on the Lüderitz–Keetmanshoop railway line. Once road freight took over from the train, Seeheim's star faded and the hotel closed. Fast-forward to the twenty-first century, this magnificent three-tier stone-and-thatch structure retains some of the yesteryear feel while ensuring more than a modicum of comfort. The hotel also includes a carpentry workshop that produces high-quality, handcrafted furniture – examples of which adorn the hotel's large, cool, fan-ventilated stone rooms.

With a bar and respectable à-la-carte restaurant (N$$), Seeheim is a good place to break the journey between Lüderitz and the Fish River Canyon – a popular lunch stop for tour groups in the season and a charming place to overnight. It's well signposted off the C12, just south of the junction with the B4, with a steep rocky descent down to the car park; it's navigable with care in a saloon car when the road is dry, but high clearance is ideal.

The southern Kalahari

Forever in the shadow of the extraordinary Namib, the country's second desert, the Kalahari, is often neglected. Though technically a semi-desert on account of its greater rainfall – some areas receiving over 280mm (11in) per year on average – it's difficult to conceive of it as anything other than a desert, given that any precipitation immediately drains away through the porous sandy soils. Yet the higher levels of rainfall and the numerous ephemeral rivers that streak the Kalahari inevitably allow it to support more vegetation and more varied wildlife than the Namib. In particular, smaller mammals thrive on the shimmering grasses that follow the rain and on the greater availability of even smaller prey: aardwolves, porcupines and honey badgers are all possible sightings, so too are scurrying groups of meerkats, mongooses and suricates. Birders will be keen to watch out for the many raptors wheeling above: martial and snake eagles and lappet-faced vultures. Inevitably, snakes and scorpions are familiar denizens of the desert; keep an eye out for the puff adder and *Panabuthus raudus* – the largest scorpion in Southern Africa, which can reach over 12cm (4.7in), threatening with a particularly impressive tail. Some of the desert's more surprising inhabitants include tortoises and even frogs.

Yet the Kalahari is as much about the stillness and silence of the desert as it is about wildlife and – in this southern section – the visually stunning **red dunes**, made so by the high iron oxide content in the sand. In contrast to the towering dunes in the Namib, these are rippling vegetated linear dunes, running broadly northwest to southeast. They start just east of the B1 between Kalkrand and Mariental, where several private reserves make the most of this picturesque dunescape, and they cover much of the land between the B1 and the eastern border of Namibia, extending into the South African section of the **Kgalagadi Transfrontier Park**. The park is attracting increasing numbers of self-drive visitors entering via the **Mata Mata gate** on the Namibian border, roughly 200km (124.3 miles) northeast of Keetmanshoop, as the crow flies. Many take the scenic C15 from the agricultural centre of **Stampriet**, northeast of Mariental, which tracks the relatively lush Auob River valley 230km (142.9 miles) southeast to the park gate, sometimes stopping off at one of the new campgrounds that are sprouting up along the way.

Stampriet

There's not much to the small settlement of **STAMPRIET** that lies about 55km (34.1 miles) northeast of Mariental on the banks of the ephemeral Auob River. However, thanks to the area's abundance of artesian water, it's a surprising oasis in the Kalahari, complete with wafting palm trees and a gleaming whitewashed hillside church, where cypress trees and topiary hedges thrive. Importantly, it's a major area for fruit and vegetable production and, more recently, has become a stopover on the way to the Kgalagadi Transfrontier Park (see page 150). The village has a small supermarket, petrol station, and some good, inexpensive accommodation.

ACCOMMODATION

STAMPRIET, SEE MAP PAGE 140

Kalahari Anib Signposted north off the C20, 30km (18.6 miles) west of Stampriet and 21km (13 miles) east of the junction with the B1 gondwana-collection.com. With a hotel-like feel, this 52-room desert lodge, popular with tour groups, is set around a tree-filled grassy central area. Half the rooms look inwards over the pool, the other half face outwards across the bush. The main bar-dining area is an impressive glass-fronted structure with a large fireplace in the bar area, surrounded by red Kalahari sand. The excellent food attracts diners from Mariental for the evening buffet dinner (N$$$$). Three individual campsites have been joined by four new self-catering Camping2Go tents. Walking and e-bike trails, dune walks and sundowner drives are the main activities on offer. Camping N$–$$, self-catering N$$, doubles (B&B) N$$$

Kalahari Farmhouse South off the C20 at Stampriet, close to the stadium gondwana-collection.com. Incongruous oasis with eleven cheerful, rustic stone chalets, complete with wooden shutters set in lush grassy grounds shaded by wafting palm trees. The place is a training school for

KGALAGADI TRANSFRONTIER PARK

The **Kgalagadi Transfrontier Park** (Kgalagadi pronounced 'ka-la-khadi', the 'kh' as in the Scottish 'loch') is jointly run by South Africa and Botswana and stretches over 37,000 sq km (14,285.8 sq miles) – an area larger than Belgium. The South African section is bounded by two dry rivers, both of which originate in Namibia: the Auob River marks the park's southwestern boundary until it joins the south-flowing Nossob – delineating South Africa's national boundary with Botswana – at the aptly named Twee Rivieren. No fences exist along this line, allowing wildlife undisturbed access to the ancient migration routes so necessary for survival in the desert, and indeed, the park affords great opportunities to watch the seasonal movement of large herbivores such as blue wildebeest, springbok, eland and red hartebeest. It's also renowned for predator watching, with excellent chances of seeing cheetahs, leopards, brown and spotted hyenas and Kalahari lions. These commonly have much darker manes than those found in the bushveld, and studies have shown their behavioural and eating patterns to be distinctively well adapted to the semi-desert conditions here. Birdwatchers will be rewarded with some extravagant **birdlife**, including vultures, eagles, bustards and ostriches. There's also a good chance you'll see family groups of **meerkats** striking their characteristic pose of standing on their hind legs, looking around nervously for signs of danger.

The main roads follow the riverbeds, and this is where the game – and their predators – are most likely to be. Water flows rarely in the two rivers, but frequent boreholes have been drilled to provide water for the animals. Larger trees such as camelthorn and shepherd's tree offer a degree of shade and nutrition, and desert-adapted plants, including types of melon and cucumber, also provide moisture for the animals. Much of the park is dominated by vegetated linear **red dunes**, which lie strung out in long, wave-like bands and offer lovely photographic opportunities in the changing light when seen from the air.

PARK ENTRY

The park is open from sunrise to sunset, so gate hours change depending on the time of year. A daily entry rate per person is charged. Contact the park reception in South Africa (T 27(0)54 561 2000, W sanparks.org).

WHEN TO VISIT

In a place where ground temperatures in the **summer** can reach a scorching 70°C, timing your visit is everything. The best visiting period is between March and May, when there is still some greenery left from the summer rain and the sun is not so intense. **Winter** can be freezing at night, while **spring**, though dry, is a pleasant time before the searing heat of summer.

ARRIVAL AND DEPARTURE

If you arrive via the Mata Mata gate (daily 8am–4.30pm; T 063 252035) from Namibia and intend to return the same way, there are no border formalities or charges. However, visitors wanting to exit the park into a different country from the one they entered from should note that all immigration controls must be done at *Twee Rivieren* (daily 7.30am–4pm), the largest camp that houses the park headquarters. Also, note that a minimum two-night stay in the park is compulsory.

GETTING AROUND

The main park roads are gravel so that an ordinary saloon car can make it, but the higher the clearance, the better; entry to the Botswana section of Kgalagadi is four-wheel drive only. You need time to move between camps as the speed limit is 50km/h (31mph), and the distances are considerable: over 100km (62.1 miles) between *Mata-Mata Restcamp* and *Twee Rivieren* and around 160km (99.4 miles) between the latter and *Nossob Restcamp*. Fuel is available at all three camps but is inevitably more expensive within the park than at the petrol stations outside.

TOURIST INFORMATION AND ACTIVITIES

The visitor centre at *Twee Rivieren* (one hour after sunrise until one hour before sunset) is worthwhile, and an informative park guide is for sale at reception at the park office (South Africa ⓣ 27 (0)54 5612000; daily 7.30am–sunset). Although most people self-drive around the park, night and day game drives and day walks can be booked on arrival at the main camps. A four-day wilderness four-wheel drive 'eco-trail' involving bush camping runs monthly between Nossob and Twee Rivieren, departing on a Monday (approx R3,800 per vehicle).

ACCOMMODATION

It's vital to book park accommodation, even for campsites, as early as you can through South African National Parks in Pretoria (ⓦ sanparks.org), as places fill up months in advance. The two main types of sites are larger, fenced rest camps at *Twee Rivieren*, *Mata Mata* and *Nossob*, which have electricity (even in some campsites) and creature comforts such as kitchens, fans or a/c, braai areas, pools and shops, with some units wheelchair accessible; and six far more basic and remote unfenced wilderness camps, for which you need to be completely self-sufficient, but which are more appealing if you want to taste the raw flavour of the desert. There is also one community-owned lodge. Camping rates are per site for two people; each additional adult costs extra. A 1 percent community fee for community development is added to the accommodation total.

Bitterpan Wilderness Camp A peaceful spot near the centre of the park on a four-wheel drive trail between *Nossob* and *Mata Mata* (access by four-wheel drive only), with four unfenced reed cabins perched on the edge of a saltpan. R$$

Gharagab Wilderness Camp Four log cabins in an unfenced area in the remote far north, a four-hour drive from *Nossob* (access by four-wheel drive only), with elevated views onto a landscape of dunes and thornveld savannah. R$$

Grootkolk Wilderness Camp At the very northern tip of the South African section in prime predator country, it's booked up months in advance; its four chalets come fully equipped with cooking supplies, linen and fans. R$$

★ **Kalahari Tent Camp** Guarded by an armed guide, this unfenced site has comfortable, fully equipped, self-catering tents built of sandbags and canvas (including one luxurious 'honeymoon tent'), all decorated in desert tones with views over the Auob River. There's also a swimming pool. R$$

Kieliekrankie Wilderness Camp Just over 40km (24.9 miles) northwest of *Twee Rivieren*, is accessible to ordinary vehicles and consists of unfenced cabins sunk into a red dune, providing lovely panoramic views of the desert. R$$

Mata Mata Camp Right by the Namibian border post of the same name. Accommodation is in fully equipped chalets (sleeping two, four or six), including eight brand-new chalets overlooking the Auob River and a campsite. Other amenities include a waterhole lit up at night, a bird hide, a swimming pool, a shop and fuel. Camping R$, chalet R$$

Nossob Camp The most remote of the three fenced rest camps, on the Botswana border 160km (99.4 miles) north of *Twee Rivieren* along the Nossob River Road, has eighteen simple chalets for two to six people – the pricier riverfront ones are the nicest – plus a large campsite. There's also a supply shop, fuel, swimming pool, predator information centre (famed for nocturnal visits by lions, so night drives are on offer) and a waterhole with hide. Camping R$, chalet R$$

Twee Rivieren Camp The first and most developed of the three fenced rest camps (the only one with 24-hour electricity and mobile phone coverage) right by the South African entrance. Offers over thirty pleasant self-catering chalets with thatched roofs and nice patio areas, a sizeable campsite (with or without electricity), a mediocre restaurant, a pool, fuel, and a shop selling souvenirs and simple foodstuffs. Camping R$, chalet R$$

Urikaruus Wilderness Camp Roughly halfway between *Twee Rivieren* and *Mata Mata*, with an attractive setting among camelthorn trees overlooking the Auob River; the four two-person cabins and 'honeymoon cabin', all equipped with solar power and kitchen supplies, are built on stilts and connected by a plank walkway. R$$

!Xaus Lodge Signposted north 40km (24.9 miles) from Mata Mata gate, along a 30km (18.6-mile) sandy track over 91 dunes (four-wheel drive necessary) or transfers from Kamqua picnic site ⓦ xauslodge.co.za. Owned by San and Mier communities (who also jointly manage the national park), this is the only fully catered lodge in the park: twelve chalets aligned along the ridge of a red dune overlooking a pan and waterhole. Includes cultural engagements with your host communities, but park fees are extra. Stargazing opportunities abound; the reserve gained Dark Sky status in 2019, and your hosts have a wealth of Indigenous knowledge to pass on about the heavens. AI R$$$$

Gondwana staff and also hosts the company's self-sufficiency centre, which produces vegetables, meats and cheeses to supply Gondwana lodges countrywide, so much of the food here couldn't be fresher. Camping N$, chalets (B&B) N$$$

Stampriet Historical Guesthouse On the C20, village centre stamprietguesthouse.com. Enjoying a pleasant location on a hillside at the village entrance, this old-fashioned guesthouse is surprisingly popular, given its out-of-the-way location. Ten basic rooms with private porches are set around a pleasant shady garden dotted with memorabilia, such as milk churns and an ox-cart. The cosy lounge-dining area opens onto a breezy deck with a pool table and more comfy chairs, which is great for a sundowner. The hospitality is warm, the catering is decent, and the owner is an excellent potter. B&B N$$

The 'back road' to Mata Mata

From Stampriet, you can follow the Auob River valley, all 244km (151.6 miles) down the gravel C15, to the **Mata Mata** gate, which takes you into the Kgalagadi Transfrontier Park. The first 70km (43.5 miles) between Stampriet and the hilltop village of Gochas – which must surely claim the prize for the largest underused tourist office in the country – is particularly scenic; the road runs parallel to red dunes for a while before widening into a canyon enclosed by sandstone and shale cliffs. The river's artesian aquifer ensures plenty of greenery, featuring dense thickets of prosopis and a string of farms supporting sheep and cattle. Several places provide simple scenic stopovers.

3

ACCOMMODATION

THE 'BACK ROAD' TO MATA MATA, SEE MAP PAGE 140

Auob Country Lodge On the C15, 6km (3.7 miles) north of Gochas auob.com.na. Set in its own small reserve harbouring various antelope, this 25-room lodge has rather dark and austere communal areas but brighter, neat, clean, air-conditioned rooms. It's adequate for an overnight stay, though it's more popular as a lunch stop with groups doing a scenic tour of the dunes. The food is tasty, the pool in the courtyard pleasant, and the place offers walks and sundowner drives. There is plenty of camping space too, with electricity. Camping N$, doubles (DBB) N$$$

★ **Dune Song Breathers** Onze Rust Farm, 10km (6.2 miles) north on the D617 dunesong.net. A place to enjoy the views and the stars in these three chic, concrete self-catering 'bunkers' set atop a red dune, enlivened with some rustic wooden touches. Open-plan design with four single beds, well-equipped kitchen, fridge-freezer and wood-burning oven – to provide warmth at night – and a large veranda with seating and a braai area. Bush camping is also available. Four-wheel drive access, but the owners will provide transfers from the farm and braai packs if desired. Two-night minimum. Camping N$, equipped tents N$, chalets N$$

Red Dune Camp On the C15, 32km (19.9 miles) south of Gochas 063 250164 or 081 421 0927, reddunecamp@iway.na. Four sites on a fabulous dune ridge (four-wheel drive needed to access) affording magnificent sunset views – two have sundowner decks, one has a tent provided (and bedding on request) and one even has a consecrated wooden 'chapel' for weddings. Each has a flush toilet, bush shower and fire pit, though no electricity. Otherwise, you can pitch a tent in their shady, grassy garden at the farmhouse or book one of two simple rooms. Dune sites (up to four people) N$, doubles N$–$$

Terra Rouge Guestfarm On the C15, 45km (28 miles) north of the Mata Mata gate 063 252031 or 081 1290280, terrarouge@iway.na. Working sheep and cattle farm offering three snug, self-catering bungalows with a/c, equipped kitchens, braai areas and private porches. Also, five campsites in the Auon riverbed, under large shady camelthorns with braai sites, water and modern ablutions: flush toilets and open-air showers. Braai packs – from their farm – and firewood is available. Camping N$, bungalows N$$

Wildmoor On the C15, 51km (31.7 miles) south of Stampriet facebook.com/WildmoorNatureCamp. You can camp in the farmhouse garden, under large shady trees – just keep out of the way of the horns of the 'tame' springbok – or in one of the delightful, remote wilderness campsites: one built into the canyon wall, overlooking the valley; the other over the escarpment, deep in the farm. Donkey-fired hot water and open-air shower plus braai site, with firewood included. Camping N$

The Richtersveld and around

At Namibia's southernmost limit, the starkly beautiful, mountainous **|AI-|AIS/RICHTERSVELD TRANSFRONTIER PARK** – commonly known as the Richtersveld – straddles the border with South Africa, covering an area around four times the size of

Greater London. The park's main attraction is the genuinely awe-inspiring **Fish River Canyon**, about half of which lies within the park's boundaries. The canyon ends at **|Ai-|Ais** – meaning 'burning water' in Nama – Namibia's best-known sulphurous hot springs and a popular tourist attraction in itself. While the Fish River rarely flows, the **Orange River** (!Gariep, in Nama) – which demarcates the border between Namibia and South Africa and bisects the park – is a perennial water source, making it a bird lovers' paradise and a popular place to indulge in a day or more of gentle canoeing or kayaking (see page 160).

Importantly, the Richtersveld Park lies within the **Succulent Karoo Biome**. This biodiversity hotspot has the greatest variety of succulents on the planet, harbouring a third of the world's ten thousand species, 33 of which are endemic. They are at their most impressive between June and October, when – provided there has been sufficient rain – their flowers burst forth in a stunning carpet of colour.

The two succulents most associated with the area are the critically endangered giant or bastard quiver tree (*Aloe pillansii*) – distinguishable from its more common sibling by its towering, pale and statuesque trunk and fewer rosettes – and the more numerous halfmens (meaning 'semi-human' in Afrikaans; *Pachypodium namaquanum*). When outlined against the skyline, the spiny tapering trunk has been likened to a human trudging up the mountain, its head inclined slightly – always northwards, for some inexplicable reason – crowned with a single rosette resembling a mop of hair.

The succulents help nourish the animal life in this otherwise barren environment, including the park's fifty species of mammal and just under two hundred bird species, most of which inhabit the terrain close to the river. Lizards and snakes abound, but large mammals such as zebra, klipspringer and springbok are also in evidence, while leopards and other cats remain characteristically shy.

Though most of this vast park lies in Namibia, opportunities for wilderness camping and hiking (excluding the Fish River Canyon) and admiring the succulent-rich landscape are better in the South African section (see page 158), which is also home to a handful of **Nama** communities, who jointly manage the park south of the border. They still practise their traditional semi-nomadic lifestyle, moving their livestock according to the season and living in rush-mat domed huts (|haru om).

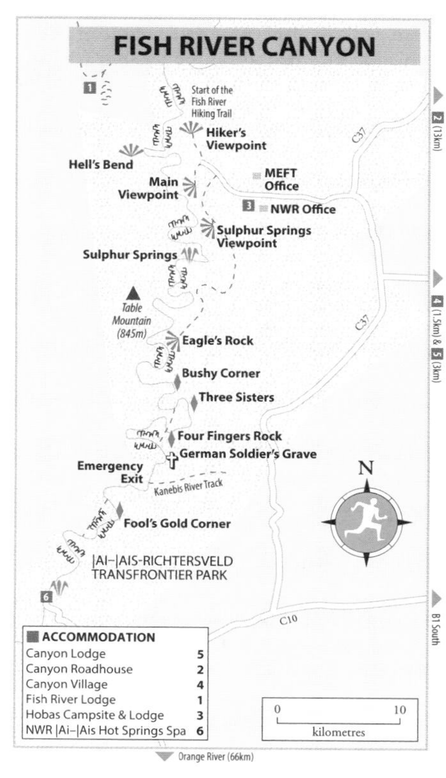

The Fish River Canyon

The main entrance to the Fish River Canyon is signposted off the C37 along a dirt road • daily charge, payable at the MEFT office at the park entrance (also valid for |Ai-|Ais) • T 063 266028

The Fish River Canyon is one of Africa's greatest natural wonders, a vast, sinuous chasm. It vies with the Blue Nile Gorge in Ethiopia for claiming to be the Earth's second-largest canyon (after the USA's Grand Canyon). At 160km (99.4 miles) in length, up to 27km (16.8 miles) in width and with a depth of 550m (1,804.5ft) in places, its grand scale can best be appreciated by gazing across the canyon rim or by climbing down the almost sheer rock to the valley floor and undertaking a gruelling five-day hike along the mainly dry river bed (see page 155).

Local Nama folklore has it that the deep meanders of the canyon were formed by the death throes of a giant snake killed by their warriors because it had been preying on their livestock. Modern science has a less evocative and more prosaic explanation, and one that stretches over millennia, starting when sediment and volcanic rock deposited around 1.8 billion years ago began to metamorphose under pressure. Around 700 million years ago, doleritic magma forced its way through fissures in the ground, forming the black dolerite dykes you can see today streaking the canyon walls. Periods of tectonic upheaval, the formation of a shallow sea, glaciation and erosion followed, creating much of the dramatic gorge visible today.

It was only around 50 million years ago that the **Fish River** began to flow, further deepening the tortuous ravine. Nowadays, the river only runs for a couple of months a year at the end of the rainy season (assuming sufficient rain); it is soon reduced to a trickle and most months merely consist of pools of water, which feed the occasionally sighted hardy populations of klipspringer, Hartmann's mountain zebra and kudu, as well as the more ubiquitous baboons and rock hyraxes. Some of the pools contain sizeable fish. This precious water source in such an arid region was known to Stone Age peoples, as several **archaeological sites** have been found in the canyon.

The canyon's main **viewpoint** is 10km (6.2 miles) west of the park entrance. From here, you can drive or walk a couple of kilometres northwards to Hikers' Viewpoint, which marks the start of the five-day trail and offers a different perspective on the canyon. The other two viewpoints involve longer drives southwards (signposted off the main access road) and are only possible in four-wheel drives: the first is to Sulphur Springs (6km/3.7 miles), and the second is to Eagle's Rock (another 6km/3.7 miles).

|Ai-|Ais Hot Springs Spa

At the southern end of the Fish River Canyon • Sunrise–sunset • Charge (also valid for the Fish River Canyon viewpoint at Hobas) • Ⓦ nwr.com.na/resorts/ai-ais-hotspring-and-spa

Spread across the valley floor and hemmed in by steep rock, **|Ai-|Ais Hot Springs Spa** marks the end of the five-day canyon hike. As such, it's the perfect place to soak your aching limbs in the lovely hot outdoor pool or the slightly disappointing indoor whirlpools and jacuzzis, where not all the nozzles work. There's also a massage parlour on site. Although lacking shade, the outdoor pool is open all night, too – a magical place to float on your back as you gaze at the stars. In season, the more energetic can book a guided hike a few kilometres back along the canyon to get a taste of the trail.

ARRIVAL AND ACCOMMODATION — THE FISH RIVER CANYON

By car There is no public transport that goes anywhere near the canyon. In your own vehicle, the easiest way to visit is via the park entrance at Hobas, signposted off the C37, the main dirt road that runs down the eastern side of the canyon (accessible in a saloon car in the dry season), around 15–20km (9.3–12.4 miles) from the canyon itself. Hobas has a restaurant, shop and the MEFT office, where you can get your park permit. Note that the *Canyon Roadhouse*, 13km (8 miles) north of the turn-off to the canyon on the C37, operates a petrol station.

On a tour Several tour companies in Windhoek (see page 94) include the Fish River Canyon on their itinerary. The nearby Gondwana Collection lodges also organise guided excursions to the canyon.

Tourist information There is an information centre at the main viewpoint at the canyon rim, which gives details on the geology, flora and fauna, and the human history of the canyon.

ACCOMMODATION — SEE MAP PAGE 153

Fish River Lodge Western rim of Fish River Canyon Ⓦ fishriverlodge-namibia.com. Boasting the ultimate

HIKING THE CANYON

You need to hike into the canyon for a totally different perspective on this giant chasm in the Earth's crust. The classic route is a four- to five-day, 85km (52.8-mile) hike, which has the reputation of being one of Southern Africa's most challenging trails. It is not to be embarked upon lightly, as you must carry all your gear, scramble over boulders, trudge through sand, and – at certain times of the year – wade through the river numerous times. Moreover, you only have two emergency exit tracks out of the canyon, once down at the bottom. There are one or two slightly easier ways to experience the valley floor. However, none could be classified as a stroll in the park since even the day-trip hike into the gorge involves a near-sheer descent and ascent, taking several hours and walking in extreme temperatures for much of the season.

The *Fish River Lodge* offers several day- and multiday **guided excursions** into the canyon for 2–8 people (Ⓦ fishriverlodge-namibia.com; N$9,500/person for a three-day hike). Their guided hikes include having your luggage transported along the way and the cooking is done for you. If you just want a taster of the riverbed, they have four-wheel drive access from the western edge of the rim, so you can be driven down to explore the rock pools on foot. Alternatively, you can hike down (and back if you still have the legs for it) in a day. Gondwana also offers several self-guided multiday hikes (mid-April to mid-Sept) along the northern reaches of the canyon covering 35km (21.7 miles) over three days, with four nights camping, including one at base camp (Ⓦ gondwana-collection.com; N$1,878 per person for a three-night hike). The advantage of the Gondwana and *Fish River Lodge* trails is the fact that your gear is carried for you. In the latter's case, a further bonus is that meals are far more appetising: a chef's campfire creations rather than the pot-noodle feasts of the backpacking trail.

PRACTICALITIES

Because of the extreme **temperatures** in the canyon (temperatures can rise into the forties in the summer months), the NWR hike can only be attempted between 1 May and 15 September. However, temperatures can still be debilitating at either end of this period. NWR **permits** cost N$535 per person, available from the NWR office in Windhoek (Ⓦ nwr.com.na; see page 94) upon presentation of a signed medical certificate (provided by them) that is no older than forty days. **Park fees** (daily charge) are payable at the MEFT office in Windhoek in advance or at the park entrance. **Hiking groups** must comprise at least three people, and there is a limit of thirty people on the trail per day. Remember to use biodegradable soap and take water-purifying tablets. The first detailed map of the Fish River Canyon was produced in 2017 (Ⓦ slingbymaps.com) and is excellent, though not essential, to complete the trail. A one-way shuttle (additional cost) can be booked to take you to Hobas or |Ai-|Ais at the start or end of the trail.

infinity pool on the canyon rim, this thoughtfully designed lodge comprises twenty chalets (including doubles, triples and family rooms) that blend in superbly with their rocky surroundings, maximising the beauty of the location with private decks overlooking the gorge and lots of light. Various activities exploring the canyon are on offer, on mountain bikes or on foot, and a masseuse is on hand to help soothe aching limbs. Four-wheel drive is needed to get there, though transfers are available. DBB N$$$$

Hobas Campsite & Lodge NWR Hobas park entrance, 10km (6.2 miles) east of the canyon rim Ⓦ nwr.com.na. Fifteen pitches within striking distance of the canyon mean this place fills up quickly. You need to be here early to bag one of the nicer, shadier spots by the dry riverbed at the far end of the camp. All sites have the usual braai facilities and electricity, and a pond-sized swimming pool is enough to bring the body temperature down in the summer. The six simple two-bed bush chalets (the lodge) are overpriced and hot in summer; the canteen-like *Quiver Taste Restaurant* does a brisk trade. The camp shop (daily 7am–7pm) has limited supplies, including wood and firelighters and serves snacks and hot drinks. Camping N$$, chalet B&B N$$$

NWR |Ai-|Ais Hot Springs Spa |Ai-|Ais, west end of the C10 Ⓦ nwr.com.na. Doubles are large and comfortable, with huge bathrooms and semi-private balconies opening onto a steep rock face; the slightly pricier river-view rooms have a more pleasant vista across the tree-studded campground (though many of the pitches lack sufficient shade). Better value are the two-bedroom self-catering bungalows, which have an enormous kitchen-dining lounge area with TV and music system, a large patio and braai area, and a private hot tub. The resort's downside is the catering: overpriced buffet breakfasts and indifferent dinners; à la carte is only available at lunchtime. Anyone self-catering should get supplies elsewhere if possible, as the shop is often low on stock. Rates exclude park fees. Camping N$$, doubles B&B N$$$, bungalows N$$$

Gondwana Canyon Park

Comprising 1,300 sq km (501.9 sq miles) of private reserve, the **Gondwana Canyon Park** is contiguous with the eastern flank of the |Ai-|Ais/Richtersveld Transfrontier Park and, therefore, provides a great base for exploring the canyon in relative comfort from one of the Gondwana Collection's lodgings. The land has made a remarkable recovery in the twenty years since it was formed from a collection of struggling sheep farms. There are now small populations of zebra, kudu, springbok, oryx, hartebeest and wildebeest, but it is the wilderness landscape that is truly captivating.

3

ARRIVAL AND ACTIVITIES — GONDWANA CANYON PARK

By car With no public transport available, you need to have your own vehicle, though two-wheel drive is adequate.

Activities All the accommodation options offer a guided three-hour excursion to the Fish River Canyon. In addition, you can sign up for enjoyable sunrise or sundowner walks. Don't miss the wonderful hike up the escarpment at the back of the *Canyon Village* (guided or self-guided), which affords spectacular views across the distant Huns Mountains.

ACCOMMODATION — SEE MAP PAGE 153

All accommodation in the park is owned and managed by the Gondwana Collection and is of good quality with excellent customer service, though each option is distinctive in style. Accommodation is around 20km (12.4 miles) east of the canyon.

★ **Canyon Lodge** 3km (1.9 miles) along the dirt road, signposted east off the C37, 6km (3.7 miles) south of the turn-off to the Fish River Canyon ⓦ gondwana-collection.com. The choice accommodation in the area, comprising over thirty chalets nestled among large granite boulders, with lush lawns (using recycled water) dotted with camelthorn trees. Chalets 25 and 28 offer the best views. Behind the old farmhouse, where excellent buffet food is served (dinner N$$$$), a delightful terrace is shaded by a huge pepper tree. Top of the treats, though, is the infinity pool set apart from the lodge, overlooking the desert plains – an idyllic spot for a sundowner. B&B N$$$

Canyon Roadhouse On the C37, 13km (8 miles) northeast of the turn-off to the Fish River Canyon ⓦ gondwana-collection.com. The quirky place makes an ideal lunch stop amid the quiver trees and antique cars. Light soups, salads and toasties are just some of the offerings, but the chef's selection for dessert is a must. Bang on the road, it's a less appealing place to spend the night, though the dozen tidy twin rooms are impeccably maintained, plus a small pool. The campground boasts superior washing facilities, though some sites lack shade. Camping N$–$$, doubles B&B N$$$

Canyon Village 1.5km (0.9 miles) along the dirt road, signposted east off the C37, 6km (3.7 miles) south of the turn-off to the Fish River Canyon ⓦ gondwana-collection.com. Have your luggage delivered to your chalet by horse and cart in this folksy, themed lodge popular with German tour groups. Colourful historical murals portray 'traditional' Nama life, and the bougainvillea-decorated terrace affords lovely views across a developing indigenous garden to the impressive escarpment beyond – a morning climb is a must, followed by a cool-off in the decent-sized pool. N$$$

To the South African border

South of Keetmanshoop, the relentless B1 skirts the forbidding Great ||Karas Mountains to the east for about 100km (62.1 miles), while the sibling Little ||Karas Mountains keep their distance, west of the flat, sandy valley that separates the two ranges. A couple hours' drive south, the road divides at **GRÜNAU**, a small, predominantly Nama and Afrikaner settlement of a few hundred. The roadside petrol station, just north of the junction, is of interest to the weary traveller, which can also provide an injection of caffeine. Despite its seeming insignificance on the ground, Grünau marks an important crossroads: north, the B1 heads towards Windhoek and beyond; west, a gravel road leads to the Fish River Canyon; while south, the B1 continues another 140km (87 miles) to the 24-hour border post with South Africa at Noordoewer, then onwards to Cape Town. Turning west, just before the border, takes you on a very scenic drive along the Orange (!Gariep) River – where you can stop off for some gentle kayaking – which meanders a further 250km (155.3 miles) until it slides into the Atlantic Ocean at Oranjemund (see page 132).

Eastwards from Grünau, the B3 follows the railway for 177km (110 miles), through **Karasburg** to the other main border post with South Africa (also 24hr), just beyond Ariamsvlei. This busy crossing serves traffic travelling between Namibia and the Johannesburg area. Karasburg, beyond being a useful refuelling pit stop, is the gateway to the important historical settlement of Warmbad, a forty-minute drive south.

Because of Grünau's strategic location, several hospitable guest farms lie in the vicinity, providing a convenient stopover for long-distance travellers keen to break their journey but also worthy of more extended stays. Some visitors make a day trip to the Fish River Canyon (only 100km/62.1 miles) from here.

ACCOMMODATION

GRÜNAU, SEE MAP PAGE 140

★ **Savanna Guest Farm** Just off the B1, 40km (24.9 miles) north of Grünau savanna-guestfarm.com. Built in the colonial era to billet German troops – the crenellations are a giveaway – this lovely stone-built working sheep farm at the foot of the ||Karas Mountains offers modestly priced, warm hospitality in self-catering units and large double rooms (with a/c and heating). Hike around the farm, climb the kopjes, look out for various antelope, or lounge by the heated pool. Bountiful breakfasts are provided, and hearty home-cooked candlelit dinners (on individual tables) on request. Breakfast and dinner can be pre-ordered. Self-catering and doubles (B&B) N$$

The White House Just off the B1, 11km (6.8 miles) north of Grünau withuis.net. Visible from the B1, this gleaming white colonial farmhouse clamours for attention. Old pine floors, wide verandas and high ceilings transport you back in time, as do the heavy blankets (in winter). Located in the yard are compact, modern, self-catering units and four spaces to camp. Although the pre-order dinner (N$$) is tasty, it arrives with the next day's breakfast wrapped in foil and prepared in the owners' kitchen 3km (1.9 miles) down the road. Activities are plentiful: birdwatching in their hides, self-guided walks, day and night farm drives, seeking out succulents and wildlife and visiting a rose quartz mine. Camping N$, self-catering units & doubles N$$

Karasburg

Fifty kilometres (31 miles) from the junction at Grünau, the B3 passes through the unremarkable town of **KARASBURG**. With a population of four thousand, it's the

THE BORDER WITH SOUTH AFRICA

There are four **border posts** with South Africa along the Orange River. By far, the most important one is on the B1, 2km (1.2 miles) south of Noordoewer (signposted to Vioolsdrift if you're approaching from South Africa). As the major transit point between Cape Town and Windhoek, it is open 24 hours. Two minor border posts lie some distance away either side: 160km (99.4 miles) due east, reached via the gravel C10 from Karasburg, is the **Velloorsdrift** border (Onseepkans, on the South African side; daily 8am–4.30pm), whereas around 100km (62.1 miles) due northwest, the border post at **Sendelingsdrift** (daily 8am–4.15pm) lies on the western limit of the |Ai-|Ais/Richtersveld Transfrontier Park, and at the only entrance into the park on the South African side. The Sendelingsdrift border is crossed on a pontoon ferry (charge), which does not operate if there are strong winds, high water levels, or insufficient water. It is, therefore, advisable to ring and check in advance (Namibia 063 274760; South Africa 27 (0)8311506). The fourth border post straddles the mouth of the river between the two diamond-mining towns of **Alexander Bay** (South Africa) and **Oranjemund** (daily 6am–10pm). Note that visitors arriving from South Africa can continue to spend rand in Namibia; however, if you're crossing into South Africa, your Namibian dollars will no longer be accepted.

CAMPING AND HIKING IN THE |AI-|AIS/RICHTERSVELD NATIONAL PARK

Though remote and inaccessible, the **|Ai-|Ais/Richtersveld National Park** offers some starkly beautiful, rugged scenery and the opportunity to undertake some challenging wilderness hiking. Names such as Hellskloof, Skeleton Gorge, Devil's Tooth and Gorgon's Head indicate the austerity of the inhospitable brown desert mountainscape, tempered only by a broad range of hardy succulents, mighty rock formations, the magnificence of the light cast at dawn and dusk, and the glittering canopy of stars at night. It's also a place to test your four-wheel drive skills – saloon cars are not admitted into the park –another reason why travelling in a convoy of at least two vehicles is advisable.

In summer, the daytime heat can be unbearable – temperatures over 50°C have been recorded – while on winter nights, temperatures drop below freezing. For this reason, hiking is only permitted between April and September, and only then with a guide. The **best time to visit** is usually August and September since they are generally the peak months for the succulents to bloom.

The three multiday hiking trails on offer are pretty challenging and should only be attempted by experienced wilderness hikers. They are the **Vensterval Trail** (four days, three nights), the **Lelieshoek–Oemsberg Trail** (three days, two nights) and the **Kodaspiek Trail** (two days, one night). Most overnights on the trails are in the Hiking Trails Base Camp in the Ganakouriep Valley within the park, which has bunks, gas stoves, fridges and hot showers. At the time of writing, the hikes can only be attempted if led by a qualified guide, though it is not always guaranteed that a qualified guide will be available in the park. To check the current status and make a reservation, contact South African National Parks (W sanparks.org).

For those less inclined to hike, there are a couple of restful camps with chalet accommodation, camping pitches and four very rudimentary and remote sites where you can soak up the stillness and the eerie beauty of your surroundings.

PARK ENTRY

Park hours are daily 7am–6pm. Entry fees (per person per day) are payable in South African rand at the park reception in Sendelingsdrift (South Africa T (0)27 831506; 8am–4pm).

largest settlement south of Keetmanshoop and a commercial hub for the surrounding sheep farms, yet there's still not much to it. Once boasting the busiest railway station in southern Namibia, the town has been struggling since the trains stopped running to Upington in the Northern Cape, though with two supermarkets and several petrol stations, it's an important pit stop for truck drivers travelling to and from South Africa, and handy for travellers too. Town morale was dealt a further blow in 2010 when Karasburg's municipal status was revoked because of spiralling council debts, epitomised by the headline-grabbing news that they could not afford to buy a ceremonial chain for the mayor.

ACCOMMODATION

KARASBURG, SEE MAP PAGE 140

U&K Bed and Breakfast 88 Kalkfontein St T 081 2795190, E ukbedandbreakfast@gmail.com. Excellent-value, newly renovated, no-frills accommodation run by accommodating and knowledgeable hosts. Simple but immaculate en-suite rooms are tiled, with a/c. For dinner, you can barbecue or pre-order a meal. B&B N$$

Warmbad

Just under 50km (31 miles) south of Karasburg lies the forlorn, parched settlement of **WARMBAD** (|Aixa-aibes), home to the Nama ‡Gami-!un, more widely referred to as the Bondelswarts. The Nama were already well established, successfully rearing cattle and hunting game, before Jacobus Coetzee rolled up in 1760 and decided to call the

GETTING AROUND

As stated above, ordinary cars are not allowed inside the park; the only way to explore is in a four-wheel drive or a pick-up with a high enough clearance to handle the sandy riverbeds and rough mountain passes between the designated campsites. Pay particular attention along the track linking the Richtersberg and De Hoop campsites, covered with thick sand and treacherously jagged rocks.

ACCOMMODATION

It's advisable to pre-book accommodation; reservations should be made through South African National Parks in Pretoria (W sanparks.org). For camping and late bookings, contact reception directly. Camping rates below are calculated for two people on a pitch; each additional adult is extra. Prices are slightly higher if you want electricity (where available). For the larger chalets, the park charges per extra adult. A 1 percent community fee for community development is added to the accommodation total. There is no restaurant in the park, but fuel (only leaded petrol and diesel) and limited supplies (cold drinks and dried and tinned food) are available at the park headquarters at Sendelingsdrift (daily 8am–4pm). Thus, it's advisable to stock up and fill up on the way in Rosh Pinah (11km/6.8km north in Namibia; see page 134) and in Alexander Bay (73km/45.4 miles west in South Africa). The same is true for money; although the café at Sendelingsdrift has an ATM, getting cash out in Alexander Bay or Rosh Pinar is advisable.

Gannakouriep Wilderness Camp Seriously remote, these two simple canvas cabins have two single beds, a solar-powered fridge, a shower, a stove (no oven) and an outside braai. No power point or drinking water. Wheelchair-accessible. Cabins R$$

Sendelingsdrift Rest Camp By the entry gate at Sendelingsdrift. The camp offers ten decent chalets sleeping between two and four people, each equipped with a/c, fridges and small stoves. There are views over the Orange River from the front porches, a swimming pool, and a campsite. Camping R$, chalets R$$

Tatasberg Wilderness Camp Inside the park at Tatasberg, on the border. Picturesque, two-person reed cabins with cooking facilities, set among dramatic boulders and enjoying lovely views of the surrounding mountains. Showers are provided, but bring your drinking water or means of purification. Wheelchair accessible. R$$

Wilderness camps At Kokerboomkloof, Potjiespram, Richtersberg and De Hoop. There are four very basic wilderness campgrounds, each with eight to eighteen individual sites. All have cold showers except for *Kokerboomkloof*, which has no water available at all. You'll need to bring all your drinking water. Jerry cans can be filled at Sendelingsdrift. R$–$$

place Warmbad. The name in both languages, however, refers to the area's **hot springs**, which, together with the presence of the Hom River, were key to human settlement here. The area's main attraction is the hot springs around which spa facilities have recently been built. However, the spa has already fallen into disrepair, with the restored sandstone gateway of the old German fort in better condition. Warmbad's only site is a small **museum**; if it's closed and you can't contact the curator, try the library to find someone to open up and show you around – it's worth the effort. The spa hotel (no number) and restaurant are said to open up periodically, predominantly at weekends. The bottom line is that if you have time on your hands, your own transport, and are interested in history, then it's worth detouring to Warmbad to try your luck; otherwise, wait for better times.

Brief history

A renowned centre of Nama resistance to both German and South African colonisers (see pages 339 and 343), and home to the country's first Christian church in 1806, Warmbad is an important historical site. It lay on a major colonial-era trading route to and from the Cape Colony, but once bypassed by the road and rail links further north, its star began to fade. These days, the population struggles to survive on subsistence goat farming, pensions, or remittances from other family members, though a nearby tantalite mine provides some formal employment. Attempts by the government in

3

CANOEING ON THE ORANGE RIVER

Using inflatable 'croc' rafts or two-person Mohawk fibreglass canoes, several outfits offer multiday **canoe trips** down the Orange River: paddle through dramatic scenery, enjoy excellent campfire cooking and sleep out under the stars. Watch out for the Cape clawless otter cavorting in the water or the aggressive Cape monitor slithering along the riverbank.

The two operators listed below are experienced, with excellent reputations, and can rent out camping equipment. Over the Noordoewer border in South Africa, Bushwhacked Outdoor Adventures (W bushwhacked.co.za) and Umkulu Adventures (W umkuluadventures.com) run similar operations. Since all these companies cater primarily to school groups and South African families, high-season prices coincide with South African school holidays (generally Sept to mid-Oct, mid-Dec to mid-Jan and over Easter), when the camp accommodation (see page 161) is usually booked up, and you'd be well advised to stay clear of the mayhem. You can also organise to go canoeing for a day – generally spending about four hours on the river – at short notice, provided you avoid high season. Prices given below are for high season and approximate as they vary according to group size as well as month and (in the case of Felix Unite) on the level of accommodation.

Amanzi Trails 15km (9.3 miles) west of the B1, signposted off the C13 after 11km (6.8 miles) W amanzitrails.co.za. The standard four-day fully inclusive canoe trip costs N$5,500/person, but if you're feeling less energetic, a half-day paddle from the bridge at Noordoewer back down to camp will give you a taster, or you can rent a canoe to paddle around near the camp.

Felix Unite 10km (6.2 miles) west of the B1, along the C13 W felixunite.com. Offers half-day excursions (around four hours' paddling, no refreshments included) and four- and six-day camping (and glamping) canoeing trips on set dates. Four-day trips from around N$6,000/person.

2006 to reinvigorate the economy through tourism have foundered: several million Namibian dollars were spent on establishing a spa round the thermal baths – having repurchased them off a private investor – and a country lodge, building tourist bungalows and converting the old German's officers' quarters into a restaurant. But with a rudderless community – they have disagreed on a *Kaptein* since the previous one passed away several years ago – and a lack of trained personnel, most structures are already in disrepair.

The museum

Behind the new library • Mon–Fri 9am–5pm, Sat 9am–1pm • Charge • T 081 2057504 (Custodian Loraine Rooi)

The town's small **museum** is housed in the old prison, where many of the Bondelswarts arrested after their failed insurgence against the South African regime in 1922 were incarcerated. Indeed, Nama uprisings are the subject of many somewhat musty exhibits – colonial maps, German weaponry, Nama genealogies and even the old telephone exchange – the significance of which only becomes apparent on a guided tour.

The Orange River

Marking the border with South Africa, the **Orange River** – sometimes referred to by its Nama name !Gariep – carves its way west through ancient rock to the Atlantic. Just before the border post on the B1, the tarred C13 heads west to Aussenker, 50km (31 miles) downriver. The settlement is surrounded by a vast and ever-expanding emerald carpet of grape farms, which provides a striking contrast to the otherwise desolate but scenic desert hinterland. Many of the reed huts empty at the end of the grape harvest in December, with workers mainly from northern Namibia returning the following June.

In the dry season in particular, it's easy to be put off by the barren landscape, though the verdant ranks of grapes, butternut and peppers hint at the lush riverine environment that lies beyond. Reed-lined banks hide warblers and fluorescent bishops, while kingfishers, fish eagles, cormorants, darters and herons gorge on the fish-rich waters. On the opposite bank, in South Africa, a metamorphic escarpment overlooking the river provides a picturesque backdrop, making it a perfect spot to enjoy a day or more of birdwatching or canoeing.

Noordoewer

Blink, and you'll miss the ramshackle collection of houses and sandy tracks that constitute **NOORDOEWER**. Signposted to the west off the C13, it lies nearer to Cape Town than Windhoek, just under 800km (497 miles) away. This small settlement has grown as Namibians have migrated here from across the country in search of work on the lush fruit and vegetable farms that line this section of the Orange River. Here, you'll find a bank, a bottle store and a small supermarket with limited offerings and very little fresh produce. The *Noordoewer Guesthouse* (see page 161) also operates a farm shop, where you can stock up on biltong, home-made biscuits and preserves. The overall message is to get supplies elsewhere if you intend to self-cater here.

ARRIVAL AND DEPARTURE

By car Noordoewer is 2km (1.2 miles) north of the border with South Africa, just west of the B1 at the junction with the tarred C13. If you're going to the river camps, fill up at the petrol stations on the B1 (both with ATMs) and continue down the C13; the camps are well signposted from the B1/C13 junction and accessible in a two-wheel drive.

By bus The Intercape bus (ⓦintercape.co.za) between Windhoek and Cape Town drops off and picks up passengers at the border (to Cape Town, 12hr; to Windhoek, 10hr 20min). Both canoe operators can arrange a pick-up/drop-off at the bus stop for a fee.

ACCOMMODATION

SEE MAP PAGE 140

Even if you don't intend to paddle on the water, it's worth travelling the extra kilometres to the nicer riverside camps. Otherwise, the two places to stay in Noordoewer are perfectly comfortable, though you can hear the intermittent rumbling of trucks on the main road.

IN NOORDOEWER

Noordoewer Guesthouse On the C13, 200m (0.1 miles) from the junction with the B1, by the Engen garage ⓦnoordoewerguesthouse.com. The restaurant terrace overlooks the vineyard at the back, while the rooms have sliding glass doors that open onto private porches around an unprepossessing yard. The rooms are well-appointed – especially the new ones by the pool below the restaurant terrace – and have a modern, sophisticated feel. B&B N$$

ALONG THE ORANGE RIVER

★ **Amanzi Trails River Camp** 15km (9.3 miles) west of the B1, signposted off the C13 after 11km (6.8 miles) ⓦamanzitrails.co.za/orange-river-camping. This quiet riverside spot boasts prolific birdlife and is immaculately kept, with 24 spacious, shady, flat grassy camping pitches, electricity and sheltered braai sites, protected from the wind by cane divides. There's a bar where breakfast can be pre-ordered and braai packs purchased, but if you don't want to cook at night, you'll need to drive down the road to the restaurant at Felix Unite's *Provenance Camp*. A tent with bedding can be provided if you don't have your own and there's one basic chalet. Cash only. Camping N$, chalet N$$

Provenance Camp Felix Unite, 10km (6.2 miles) west of the B1, along the C13 ⓦfelixunite.com. Popular with overlander groups, this efficient and friendly camp-cum-resort comprises twenty rustic stone-and-thatch chalets with a/c and fan, fridge and tea-making facilities, each with a private patio and seating overlooking the river. Chalets 5–9 are the most secluded and have the best views. Highlights include a riverside swimming pool, a sun-lounging area, and an open-sided bar area with a pool table. Good camping facilities are also available. There's an ATM, camp shop and restaurant (daily 7–10am & noon–10pm), with a small but varied menu, including burgers, salads and pasta (N$$) and a handful of more substantial dishes. Camping N$, rooms and chalets (room only) N$$

To the Botswana border

After snaking its way through the Eros Mountains east of Windhoek, past the airport – after which the traffic drops off – the B6 straightens and flattens out, heading for **Gobabis**, Namibia's last sizeable town of note before the Botswana border some 316km (196.4 miles) away on the western fringes of the Kalahari. The B6 forms part of the Trans Kalahari Highway. This paved road continues eastwards across the desert to **Gaborone** (around 800km/497 miles), the capital of Botswana, with onward connections to South Africa. It's a dull slog through dry, dusty and relatively featureless thornveld unless there's been some seasonal rain to soften the harsh landscape. The only relief comes from the occasional wildlife sighting: a troop of baboons lolloping over the road, a family of warthogs scuttling away from the wide-trimmed verges or a swooping hornbill heading for a tree. On the way, branching off south of the main road, there are a handful of guest farms and Namibia's longest **cave** system.

Arnhem Cave

124km (77 miles) east of Windhoek, off the D1801, on a private farm • Daily tours at 7.30am & 4.30pm • Charge • Ⓦ arnhemcaves.com • No public transport • Turn south onto the M51 just after Hosea Kutako International Airport, then after 66km (41 miles) turn left onto the D1506 (10km/6.2 miles), and then right onto the D1801, where it is signposted from the road

If exploring subterranean bat-infested chambers appeals, visiting **Arnhem Cave** makes for a worthwhile day or overnight excursion from Windhoek or a diversion en route to Botswana. This system of narrow tunnels and large caverns was formed through a solution of dolomitic limestone between layers of quartzite and shale, which then collapsed; the result is the country's longest known cave system, at over 4.5km (2.8 miles). While the absence of stalagmites, stalactites and other such interesting features might disappoint casual visitors, bat enthusiasts will be well satisfied. Six species cling to the caves and passageways, including the largest insectivorous chiropteran, the giant leaf-nosed bat (*Hipposidrus vittatus*), with a wingspan of over 60cm (23.6in). You'll likely see or feel them whizzing past your face at close quarters, though their honed echo-location skills should ensure no physical encounters. Other smaller residents of the caves include various beetles, spiders, false scorpions and shrews.

Once 'discovered' in 1930, the cave was initially heavily mined for guano, and although it is still periodically harvested for fertiliser, tonnes of the substance remains below ground. Tours can last two to three hours, depending on levels of interest. However, no crawling on your hands and knees is necessary to explore the underground labyrinth; you should wear old clothes, closed shoes, and perhaps a handkerchief to protect your mouth, as it is usually very dusty. Torches can be rented on site.

ACCOMMODATION

ARNHEM CAVE, SEE MAP PAGE 140

Arnhem Cave Restcamp On the D1801, 57km (35.4 miles) south of the B6 Ⓦ arnhemcaves.com. The farm has a pleasant shady rest camp with an array of attractive accommodations, including four neat air-conditioned thatched chalets with fridges and braai or camping under camelthorn trees (electricity and hot water), with private or shared ablutions. The pleasant pool is set in a grassy lawn (well-trimmed by resident livestock). Tasty home-cooked meals are available but need to be pre-booked well in advance. Camping N$, doubles and chalets N$$–$$$

Eningu Clayhouse Lodge 65km (40.4 miles) southeast of the airport, just south of the junction between the D1471 and the M51 Ⓦ eningulodge.com. Often a stopover at the beginning or end of a tour, this delightfully original lodge is a great spot to unwind for a couple of nights, offering unusual diversions: archery, volleyball and badminton; a visit to a renowned local sculptor; a nature trail and bird hide overlooking an illuminated waterhole, where porcupines are frequent visitors; plus a large-ish sparkling swimming pool. Arnhem Cave is also nearby. The use of clay bricks makes for cool, fan-ventilated rooms with hand-painted stone floors and various arty touches. Inventive, healthy dining. Airport transfers are possible. DBB N$$$

Kiripotib Farm

10km (6.2 miles) east along the D1448, from the junction with the C15 (M33) • **Shop and workshop** Mon–Sat 8am–4pm • Ⓦ kirikara.com

There's a surprising amount of activity at the isolated **Kiripotib Farm**, which offers a pleasant overnight stay and is a great place to stop for lunch if you're heading south into the Kalahari. The main draw is the karakul weaving workshop, where you can watch the workers in action at the spinning wheel or loom, though the rosy-faced lovebirds flitting around the shady trees are also engaging. One of the owners is a goldsmith with her atelier on the premises; some of her designs, along with weavings and other high-quality crafts from various parts of Africa, can be found in the craft gallery and shop. Advance notice for visits is preferred, though there's usually someone around if you drop in. There's also an observatory on site, which attracts keen astronomers.

ACCOMMODATION — KIRIPOTIB FARM, SEE MAP PAGE 140

Kiripotib Guest Farm ⓦkiripotib.com. Comfortable, reasonably-priced accommodation is in light, airy rooms with front porch or slightly more private brick chalets overlooking the flat savannah. The pleasant restaurant sits under a *lapa*, with a tasty menu relying mainly on locally sourced ingredients. Plus, there's a swimming pool. Guided walks and sundowner drives are possible, stargazing or even a day's gliding. Discounts for stays of two or more nights. B&B luxury tents, doubles and chalets N$$$

Gobabis

Namibia's only sizeable town on the B6 between Windhoek and the Botswana border, **GOBABIS**, has an estimated population of about twenty thousand. It's the administrative centre of the Omaheke Region – a broad expanse of flat sandveld, as the Otjiherero name indicates, historically home to the Mbanderu and the Ju|wa San. The statue of the gleaming white Brahman bull at the town entrance announcing 'Cattle Country' alerts you to the main business of Gobabis, which is further reinforced by billboards and signs relating to abattoirs and butcheries. However, the nickname 'Little Texas' might be stretching matters somewhat. Still, Friday is cattle auction day, when the place is humming with activity.

Gobabis is thought to be a corruption of a Khoekhoegowab name that means either 'elephant's lick' or 'place of strife'. Indeed, the area has seen plenty of conflict over the

CROSSING INTO BOTSWANA

The border post at **Buitepos** lies 316km (196.4 miles) east of Windhoek and 111km (69 miles) east of Gobabis. Since 2023, the border has been open 24/7. However, travelling onward in the dark is inadvisable because of the dangers of hitting wildlife, especially in unfenced Botswana. While the Namibian side of the border offers overnight accommodation at the *East Gate Rest Camp*, the nearest place to park up in Botswana is Ghanzi, 210km (130.5 miles) away, so make sure you fill the tank in Namibia if you're heading that way.

Don't forget that if you're entering Namibia with a car registered outside the country, you'll need to pay cross-border charges to **import your vehicle** into Namibia. Conversely, if you are entering Botswana with a Namibian-registered vehicle, similar costs will have to be met in Pula (see page 52). In addition, if the vehicle is rented, you must inform the rental firm in advance and pay the relevant supplement. The Botswana firm Monnakgotla Transport and the Namibian firm Tok Tokkie Shuttle run bus services between Windhoek and Gaborone, Botswana.

ACCOMMODATION, SEE MAP PAGE 140

East Gate Rest Camp 400m (0.25 miles) before the border ⓦeastgate-namibia.com. This is the place to crash near the border. A predominantly self-catering rest camp – with grassy campgrounds (or a bush camp) cabins that share ablutions, and well-equipped bungalows for two or four. It may be short on style, but it is inexpensive, well-managed and has all the basics: a restaurant, shop, fuel station and a pool to wash off the desert dust. They'll even exchange limited amounts of currency. Camping or simple cabins N$, bungalows N$$

years: between Khoikhoi and Mbanderu, then the Indigenous populations and the German colonists – who made Gobabis a garrison settlement – who, in turn, were later replaced by the South Africans.

As you enter the town, the main road morphs briefly into an attractive tree-lined quasi-boulevard with a surprising number of four-way stops, where the main supermarkets, banks and petrol stations are located. A pretty pink Catholic church is also at the western edge of the main street. The once bustling information centre, accommodation and restaurant at the Ui Wilderness Centre – also on the main street – has not recovered from a fire a few years ago and is only partially functioning. The town's museum has also been closed for several years, and the **Omaheke San Craft Centre** on Roosevelt Street, which is well worth dropping in on, has irregular hours.

ARRIVAL AND INFORMATION — GOBABIS

3

By car It's an easy two-hour drive along the B6, a good tarred road from Windhoek, or along the Trans Kalahari Highway to/from Gaborone.

By shared taxi Shared taxis leave when full from the town centre, bound for Windhoek.

By bus The long-distance weekly bus/shuttle services between Windhoek and Gaborone will drop off or pick up passengers in Gobabis en route, but you need to get in touch in advance (Tok Tokkie Shuttle, shuttlesnamibia.com).

Tourist information The friendly Ui Wilderness Centre on the main street has an office and a small café (where you can get a cup of coffee, but not much else). It can provide some information on the area and is the office for Uakii Wilderness Safaris & Cultural Tours (see below) (Mon–Fri 8am–5pm, Sat 8am–1pm; 062 564743).

Tours Uakii Wilderness Safaris & Cultural Tours (uakii.info). Run by an experienced Namibian guide, the company offers half- to four-day immersive package cultural experiences with San, Damara and Herero communities in the area. It also operates a wilderness campsite east of Gobabis.

ACCOMMODATION — SEE MAP PAGE 140

Goba Lodge Well signposted north off the B6, 1km (0.6 miles) west of Gobabis facebook.com/GobaGobabis. There's no real reason to stay in Gobabis, but if you get stuck here, this charming lodge (with cheaper rest camp rooms) on the edge of town has a friendly vibe and is a good deal. Rooms have all the conveniences, the restaurant is fine ($$) and the place possesses a small pool, plus neat gardens overrun with guinea fowl. B&B N$$

★ **Xain Quaz Camp** 10km (6.2 miles) west of Gobabis on the B6 062 562688 or 081 218 9800. A fabulous oasis in the Kalahari and just the ticket after slogging across the desert: sparkling new air-conditioned modern chalets with fridge, kettle and patio furniture, plus eight great campsites with flat, shady pitches. Enjoy the verdant grounds, pool and bar or indulge in a buffet breakfast feast or a well-cooked evening meal at the restaurant. Camping N$, chalets (room only) N$$

Central-northern Namibia

THE SPITZKOPPE, DAMARALAND

Central-northern Namibia

Central-northern Namibia, encompassing large chunks of Otjozondjupa, Erongo and Kunene regions, contains some of the country's most compelling natural landscapes, with a range of comfortable lodges and campgrounds making the most of the dramatic scenery. To the west, gravel roads wend through an impressive array of striking geological formations, containing some of the finest examples of ancient rock art, towards remote wilderness areas, where desert-adapted elephants and rhinos roam. In contrast, Namibia's main artery, the B1, speeds north of Windhoek through more vegetated, flatter terrain. After 250km (155.3 miles), on the eastern limit of the Central Highlands, you reach Namibia's very own table mountain, the majestic sandstone Waterberg Plateau, presiding above the savannah plains, which are prime cheetah country.

Heading north from Namibia's capital city, the B1 passes through the historically important town of **Okahandja** before streaking through endless savannah plains. Several large **private reserves** in this region contain healthy populations of large mammals, though arguably the biggest attraction, some three hours' drive north of Windhoek, is the **Waterberg Plateau**; an impressive sandstone escarpment and scenic national park, it is a nurturing ground for rare animal species, such as black rhino and sable antelope. The surrounding bush is also cheetah country, with the nearby **Cheetah Conservation Fund centre** a compulsory detour if you're interested in these majestic felines. At **Otjiwarongo**, the regional capital of Otjozondjupa, the road divides: heading northwest along the C38 takes you to the small farming town of **Outjo**, an increasingly popular staging post for forays into Etosha National Park, whereas the B1 veers northeast towards the former mining centres of **Tsumeb**, **Grootfontein** and **Otavi**, otherwise known as the **Triangle**, which possess a handful of low-key attractions, including the world's largest extra-terrestrial rock, the **Hoba Meteorite**, set against the attractive backdrop of the **Otavi Mountains**.

Northwest of Windhoek, the landscape becomes decidedly drier and harsher as you head into flat semi-desert savannah, out of which rise dramatic granite inselbergs produced through volcanic activity millions of years ago: the domed **Erongo Mountains**, the distinctive **Spitzkoppe**, and the vast, brooding **Brandberg**, which shelters thousands of stunning **rock paintings** and boasts impressive biodiversity and endemism. All three areas contain fascinating rock formations and superb **hiking** terrain. Moving further north into southern Kunene, you reach the globally significant collection of San rock engravings at **Twyfelfontein** in a hauntingly beautiful landscape. The scenery continues to impress as the road carves through the flat-topped basalt plateaus of **northern Damaraland**. However, visitors are often drawn more by the prospect of encounters with **free-roaming elephants** and **black rhinos** in the area's dry riverbeds.

The road north

As Windhoek continues to expand northwards, the town of **Okahandja**, 70km (43.5 miles) away, seems ever nearer, an impression likely to be felt more strongly once the interminable road-widening project between the two urban centres is complete. Once past Okahandja, where the two nearby resorts of **Gross Barmen** and **Von Bach Dam** attract Windhoek's middle classes at weekends, urban life is left behind; the

HIKING TOWARDS THE WATERBERG PLATEAU

Highlights

❶ **Waterberg Plateau** This splendid and luxuriant sandstone escarpment, hosting abundant birdlife, offers great savannah views from the plateau top. See page 174

❷ **Erongo Mountains** A sprinkling of rustic campsites, homely guest farms and comfortable lodges offer the perfect base for exploring these slabs of burnished granite. See page 190

❸ **Brandberg** The country's largest massif, containing the highest peak, looms out of the desert landscape, a challenging hike rewarded by pristine rock paintings, quiver trees and stunning vistas. See page 193

❹ **Twyfelfontein** Learn the secret meanings of ancient rock engravings on an informative guided tour. See page 195

❺ **Ugab Terraces** Scenically eroded flat-topped pillars and mini table mountains make a great day trip. See page 199

❻ **Desert-adapted wildlife** Several lodges and wilderness camps in Damaraland offer the chance to get close to desert-adapted rhinos and elephants. See page 200

HIGHLIGHTS ARE MARKED ON THE MAP ON PAGE 170

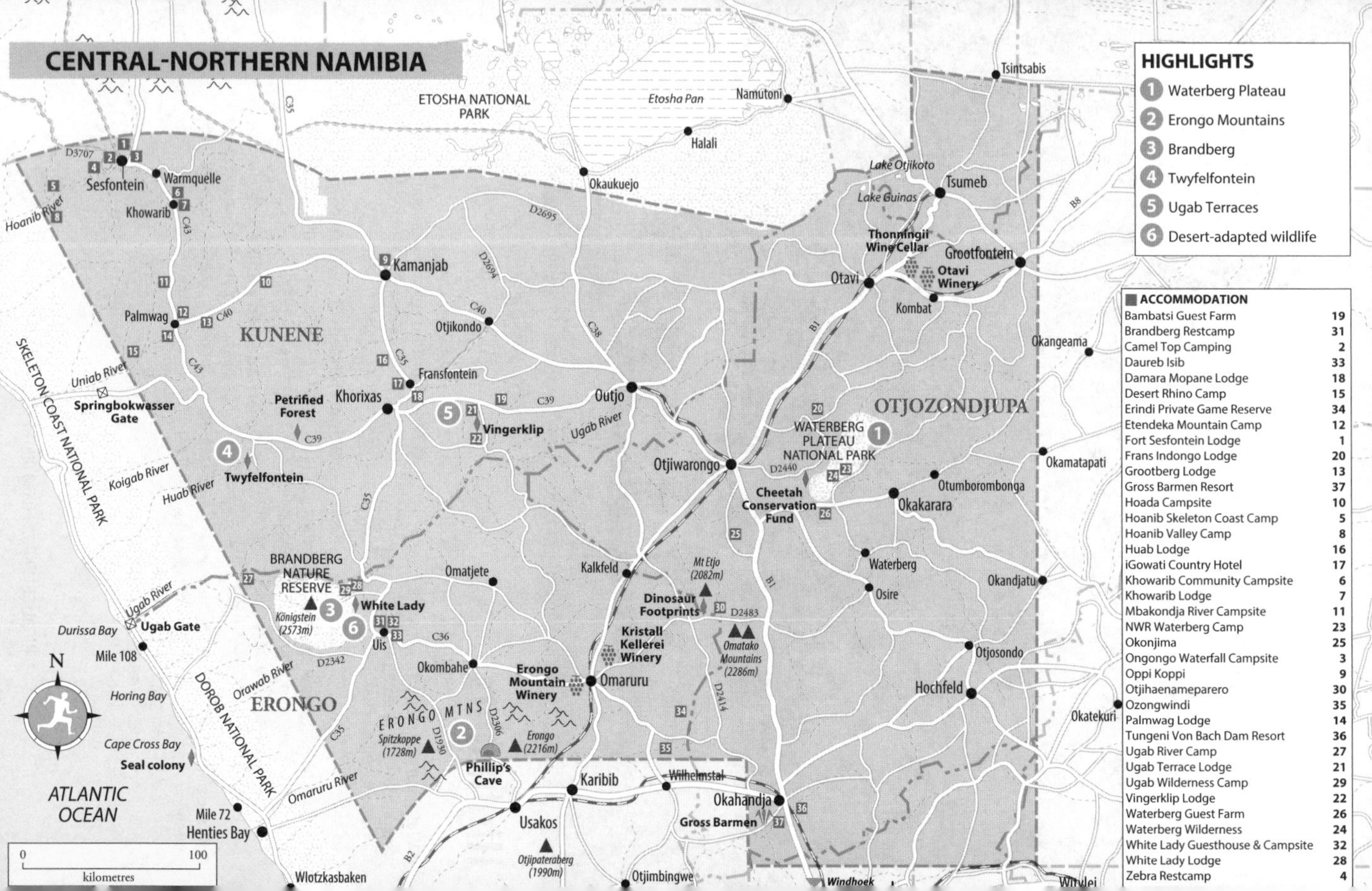
CENTRAL-NORTHERN NAMIBIA
HIGHLIGHTS
1 Waterberg Plateau
2 Erongo Mountains
3 Brandberg
4 Twyfelfontein
5 Ugab Terraces
6 Desert-adapted wildlife
ACCOMMODATION
Bambatsi Guest Farm 19
Brandberg Restcamp 31
Camel Top Camping 2
Daureb Isib 33
Damara Mopane Lodge 18
Desert Rhino Camp 15
Erindi Private Game Reserve 34
Etendeka Mountain Camp 12
Fort Sesfontein Lodge 1
Frans Indongo Lodge 20
Grootberg Lodge 13
Gross Barmen Resort 37
Hoada Campsite 10
Hoanib Skeleton Coast Camp 5
Hoanib Valley Camp 8
Huab Lodge 16
iGowati Country Hotel 17
Khowarib Community Campsite 6
Khowarib Lodge 7
Mbakondja River Campsite 11
NWR Waterberg Camp 23
Okonjima 25
Ongongo Waterfall Campsite 3
Oppi Koppi 9
Otjihaenameparero 30
Ozongwindi 35
Palmwag Lodge 14
Tungeni Von Bach Dam Resort 36
Ugab River Camp 27
Ugab Terrace Lodge 21
Ugab Wilderness Camp 29
Vingerklip Lodge 22
Waterberg Guest Farm 26
Waterberg Wilderness 24
White Lady Guesthouse & Campsite 32
White Lady Lodge 28
Zebra Restcamp 4
ETOSHA NATIONAL PARK
Etosha Pan
Namutoni
Halali
Okaukuejo
Tsintsabis
Lake Otjikoto
Tsumeb
Lake Guinas
Thonningii Wine Cellar
Grootfontein
Otavi
Otavi Winery
Kombat
Okangeama
OTJOZONDJUPA
WATERBERG PLATEAU NATIONAL PARK
Okamatapati
Otumborombonga
Okakarara
Cheetah Conservation Fund
Otjiwarongo
Waterberg
Osire
Okandjatu
Otjosondo
Hochfeld
Okatekuri
Okahandja
Gross Barmen
Windhoek
Witvlei
Wilhelmstal
Karibib
Usakos
Otjipateraberg (1990m)
Otjimbingwe
Mt Etjo (2082m)
Dinosaur Footprints
Omatako Mountains (2286m)
Kalkfeld
Kristall Kellerei Winery
Omaruru
Erongo Mountain Winery
Erongo (2216m)
Phillip's Cave
ERONGO MTNS
Spitzkoppe (1728m)
Okombahe
Omatjete
Uis
White Lady
BRANDBERG NATURE RESERVE
Königstein (2573m)
ERONGO
Outjo
Ugab River
Vingerklip
Fransfontein
Khorixas
Petrified Forest
Twyfelfontein
Otjikondo
Kamanjab
KUNENE
Palmwag
Sesfontein
Warmquelle
Khowarib
Hoanib River
Uniab River
Springbokwasser Gate
Koigab River
Huab River
SKELETON COAST NATIONAL PARK
DOROB NATIONAL PARK
Ugab River
Ugab Gate
Durissa Bay
Mile 108
Orawab River
Horing Bay
Cape Cross Bay
Seal colony
Omaruru River
ATLANTIC OCEAN
Mile 72
Henties Bay
Wlotzkasbaken
N
0 100
kilometres
C35
C38
C39
C40
C43
C36
B1
B2
B8
D3707
D2695
D2694
D2440
D2483
D2414
D2306
D1930
D2342

traffic thins out and the land flattens out as the savannah takes over once more. The B1 speeds northwards with scarcely a bend in sight for the next 180km (111.8 miles) before eventually arriving at the next main town and capital of the **Otjozondjupa Region**, **Otjiwarongo**. As you drive north, you'll notice the landscape transitioning into thornbush savannah, with taller shrubs and trees and denser cover than is evident in southern Namibia due to the relatively higher levels of rainfall and more fertile soil. Termite mounds are also visible along this stretch of road, and warthogs' families are often seen at dusk.

Okahandja and around

An hour's drive north of Windhoek, where the main road divides – continuing north as the B1 and veering off west to the coast as the B2 – sits the important historical town of **OKAHANDJA**. Its 24,000-strong population is rapidly expanding, bolstered by growth in light industry, the relocation of some government offices, and an improving road link with Windhoek, making it a commuter town for the capital.

Okahandja has a long history of trade and strategic importance. The Herero were the first to settle here, around 1800, before it became an important mission station and trading post and a site of conflict between the Herero and Nama, and later, the Germans. Today, the town is still the administrative centre of the Herero people, as well as containing the burial sites of many of their former chiefs, notably Samuel Maharero, who led the uprising against the German colonial forces (see page 339), and Hosea Kutako, a pivotal figure in the independence movement (see page 344). These and others are honoured in the annual **Herero Day commemoration** (see page 72). Jonker Afrikaner, the Oorlam-Nama leader, is also buried here (see page 339), but these graves are not open to the general public. Nor is the expensive military museum, which has stood behind iron railings on the main street since 2004 but remains off-limits to the public for unclear reasons.

However, what the town lacks in tourist sights it makes up for in its fine **craft markets**; two occupy either end of the main road into and out of town. Though basketry, painted gourds, gemstones and the like are on display, the markets are predominantly about **wood**. The array and size of some of the carvings are phenomenal, from beautifully polished masks to sculpted life-size Himba women, giant giraffes and even dugout canoes – not easily stuffed into your luggage. Be prepared to be hassled if the stallholders are short of custom when you arrive.

Less well known to tourists is the town's reputation for high-quality

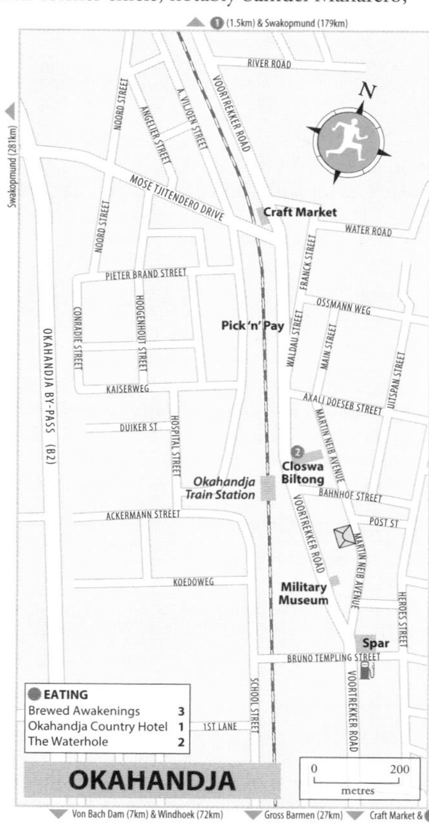

biltong – not to be missed, provided you're not vegetarian; head for the Closwa Biltong Factory Shop and Butchery on Vortrekker Street (see *The Waterhole*, page 172). A few kilometres away, two resorts – the hot springs of Gross Barman and the serene Von Bach Dam – have long been a favourite weekend getaway for urbanites needing some R&R.

ARRIVAL AND DEPARTURE — OKAHANDJA

By bus Intercape services (intercape.co.za) from Windhoek heading north all pass through Okahandja (1–3 times daily; 1hr). The bus stop is at the Engen and Wimpy garage on the B1. Alternatively, minibuses heading north from Windhoek and passing through Okahandja leave from the Monte Christo Service Station in Katutura. The shuttle services between Swakopmund and Windhoek can also drop off and pick up in Okahandja if pre-booked (see page 212).

By train The very slow TransNamib train between Windhoek and Walvis Bay, via Swakopmund, passes through Okahandja every day except Saturday (departure from Windhoek 7.55pm; 2hr).

EATING — SEE MAP PAGE 171

Brewed Awakenings Martin Neib Avenue, opposite the craft market, by the Shell garage brewcoffeeshop.business.site. This inexpensive café is a handy pit stop – grab a pick-me-up coffee for the road or a full fry-up breakfast, a light lunch, or an afternoon cuppa with a muffin. N$$

Okahandja Country Hotel 2km (1.2 miles) north of Okahandja on the B1, after the turn to Otjiwarongo okahandjahotel.com. This garden oasis makes the perfect lunch stop with its manicured lawns and bird-filled trees, surrounded by whitewashed stone and thatch. Besides, the food is decent: well prepared and in large portions – the steaks are particularly recommended. N$$$

★ **The Waterhole** Closwa Biltong Factory Shop, 2456 Vortrekker St closwa.com. Small café set in the factory outlet for this famous biltong producer, butchery and deli. Sample a biltong *brötchen* before stocking up on some of their superb cured meat and game for your journey or fresh cuts for your campfire braai. It also serves surprisingly good hot chocolate. Free wi-fi.

4

Gross Barmen

25km (15.5 miles) southwest of Okahandja, down the D1972 • Daily sunrise–sunset • Charge; day visitors also welcome

Just north of the Swakop River are the sulphurous springs that the Herero – the area's first settlers – called Otjikango, meaning 'big fountain'. On most tourist maps, however, the place is marked as **Gross Barmen**, a name given to it by Rhenish missionaries, after the small German town where the mission had its headquarters. The reason to visit is to indulge yourself at the NWR-run Gross Barmen **resort**, which boasts two glorious thermal pools fed by the springs: an expansive outdoor one that stays at a pleasant 25°C and an indoor one that can exceed 40°C, depending on the time of day, and should only be experienced in small doses. Don't be put off by the designer post-apocalyptic cement and rust-effect main building; inside is a **spa** offering a variety of treatments in what looks like time capsules, and the resort's location by a reed-fringed dam makes it prime **birdwatching** terrain. After a four-year closure and a multimillion-dollar refurbishment, the place reopened in 2014 and is once again a popular weekend and holiday getaway for Windhoek residents (with chalets and camping available), so aim to visit midweek and off-season.

ACCOMMODATION — GROSS BARMEN, SEE MAP PAGE 170

Gross Barmen Resort nwr.com.na. A range of lodgings is available, from luxury chalets sharing a jacuzzi to family self-catering units and regular doubles. They're all rather bland and some are not so well situated. However, a handful overlook the dam (chalet 25 has a nice view), as does the grassy outdoor pool area and pleasant restaurant deck: buffet only in peak periods; otherwise, à la carte is available. The campground has all the facilities you need but lacks shade and appeal, especially when the music from the day-visitor picnic area takes over. Camping N$, bush chalets (B&B) N$$

Von Bach Dam

2km (1.2 miles) along the D2102 from the junction with the B1, 4km (2.5 miles) south of Okahandja • Daily 6am–7pm (summer), 7am–6pm (winter) • Charge • No public transport

Supplying much of the water for Windhoek and Okahandja, **Von Bach Dam**, which lies on the Swakop River, is also a relaxing recreational resort. Like Gross

Barmen, Von Bach is geared up for weekending Windhoekers, keen to picnic or party, engage in watersports, enjoy a meal out, or even overnight in the good-value accommodation. The eleven campsites by the water double up as daytime picnic spots with braai sites, shade and ablutions, so if you pick a weekend or holiday period, you'll have the accompanying sounds of a boombox rather than the bush. Activities include walking, boating and canoe trips, jet-skiing or windsurfing. Alternatively, loll by the pool and admire water-skiers showing off their skills – Namibia's two clubs for the sport are based here. For the average holidaymaker, Von Bach will probably only serve as an overnight stop if you are too tired to return to Windhoek from a trip up north.

ACCOMMODATION **VON BACH DAM, SEE MAP PAGE 170**

Tungeni Von Bach Dam Resort Ⓦ tungeni.com. Some 22 stone-and-thatch chalets in two tiers facing the dam: the upper terrace holds two-storey chalets accommodating four, while on the bottom tier, smaller two-person chalets reign (Nos 4–19 have good views across the water). The pool, though nicely situated, is relatively small, given the number of weekend guests in the summer. Campsites are in variable condition, and the restaurant ($$–$$$) serves buffet and à la carte meals. Camping N$, chalets B&B N$$

Between the B1 and the C33

West of the section of the B1 that stretches between Okahandja and Otjiwarongo and east of the tarred C33, which heads north from Omaruru, joining up at Otjiwarongo, there are several major private reserves stocked with large mammals and offering comfortable accommodations that attract many visitors.

4

Dinosaur footprints

Otjihaenameparero Farm • Daily sunrise–sunset • Charge

A minor attraction, worth a short detour if you're in the area, is the **Dinosaur footprints** on Otjihaenameparero Farm, midway between the two main roads. Don't expect anything as exciting as Jurassic Park, but they are pretty remarkable, nevertheless. A larger set and smaller set of around thirty imprints of clawed, three-toed, two-legged dinosaurs – moving in a similar way to a modern-day ostrich – are visible on two separate slabs of sloping red Etjo sandstone; you can follow the larger set of prints for 30m (98.4ft) across the rock. It is thought that the imprints were formed around 190 million years ago in wet sediment, which was then covered by dry wind-blown sand and compressed, preserving the trace fossils until they were exposed once more several million years later due to erosion.

ACCOMMODATION **BETWEEN THE B1 AND THE C33, SEE MAP PAGE 170**

ERINDI PRIVATE GAME RESERVE

Set in a vast private reserve (over 700 sq km/270.2 sq miles) and a bit of a conveyor belt, this is canned luxury safari tourism, which you'll either love or hate, where a sometimes-resident group of CwiCwi (San) families also lives. The reserve is full of large mammals, from cats and wild dogs to rhinos and hippos; there are also crocs. A number of beasts, such as aardvarks, cheetahs and elephants, are electronically tagged for research purposes. There's even a pack of wild dogs. There are four entrances: 50km (31 miles) north from Okahandja on the B1, turn west onto the D2414 for another 40km (24.9 miles; Ⓦ erindi.com). Day visitors are not allowed and self-drive permits are issued for certain areas of the park, whereas guided wildlife viewing safaris take place in other areas, generally where more high-profile wildlife hangs out.

Old Trader's Lodge Ⓣ 081 621 7029. As the name suggests, the lodge harks back to colonial times, with large leather sofas and teak furniture in 47 suites of varying degrees of opulence. There's a vast viewing deck at the long thatched semi-open restaurant (where day-long music can niggle). A vast array of activities (at extra cost) ranges from standard game drives to cheetah and leopard conservation project walks. DBB N$$$$

OKONJIMA

This private nature reserve is home to the heavily marketed AfriCat Foundation (Ⓦ africat.org), which organises many lodge activities, such as leopard, rhino or pangolin tracking. These can feel a little staged and don't come cheap. Plenty of other wildlife abounds and can be seen on slightly less expensive wildlife-viewing drives. These activities are heavily promoted at the camp, though you can do a self-guided walk in the wilderness area (away from dangerous predators). Varied accommodation includes the main *Plains Camp* lodge, the more exclusive *Bush Camp*, and a couple of luxurious accommodations for small groups attended to by a private chef and attendant staff. 10km (6.2 miles) west of the B1 and 50km (31 miles) south of Otjiwarongo (ⓦ okonjima.com).

Bush Camp An intimate camp comprising an expansive main lodge overlooking a waterhole, and nine gorgeous open-sided thatched rondavels, decorated in earthy colours. The cuisine is fantastic. AI N$$$$

Omboroko Campsite There are four over-manicured but well-equipped (and expensive) private pitches with a shared pool. Camping N$$

Plains Camp There are various accommodations, but the best are fabulous glass-fronted chalets with private porches that allow you to gaze across the savannah and watch antelope graze; dining takes place in a glorified air hangar offering more views, but the high turnover of guests has a factory-like feel. DBB N$$$

Dinosaur Tracks Guestfarm Otjihaenameparero, signposted off the D2414, 29km (18 miles) from the junction with the C33 at Kalkfeld (not to be confused with signs for the Dinosaur Campsite) ⓣ 081 4622983. To accompany the dinosaurs' footprints on the property, a small, peaceful campground-cum-picnic area has five simple sites offering limited shade under acacia trees, stone tables and seats, braai pits (but own grill needed) and donkey-fired hot-water showers. A small guesthouse operates – a whitewashed block of three spacious, light guestrooms with a private patio and shared kitchen-lounge. You can also pre-order dinner at the farm. The place is unlikely to be busy, so you can just pitch up. Camping N$, doubles N$$

Ozongwindi 6km (3.7 miles) south of the D2110, 75km (46.6 miles) west of the B1, 20km (12.4 miles) east of the C36 ⓦ ozongwindi.com. Ten seriously luxurious, thatched chalets (a/c), with private wooden decks overlooking the (dry) River Khan, plus four self-catering rooms (no a/c) in an old farmhouse. The main lodge has a pool, library, bar-restaurant and satellite TV. Very relaxing place with great birdwatching. Lower rates for two nights or more. Self-catering N$$, doubles DBB N$$$

★ **Roidina Safari Lodge** Entrance gate 20km (12.4 miles) northeast of Omaruru on the C33 ⓦ roidinasafarilodge.com. An extremely welcoming and homely lodge comprising seven spacious stone-and-thatch self-catering chalets set around a delightful landscaped cactus garden (with pool) brimming with birdlife. A range of antelope – from dik-diks to eland – inhabit the reserve alongside zebra, wildebeest and even giraffes. You can watch visitors to the waterhole while enjoying a drink. With no predators, the place is perfect for relaxed bush walks, birdwatching and sundowners. Chalets N$$

4

Waterberg Plateau National Park

1km (0.6 miles) off the D2512 • Daily sunrise–sunset • Charge • Guided drives; book at an NWR office in advance or at the camp reception

An impressive table mountain popular with hikers and nature lovers, the extensive **Waterberg Plateau National Park** is located 60km (37.3 miles) southeast of Otjiwarongo; to the east, it surveys the arid Omaheke Desert – part of the Kalahari – to the west, acacia-covered savannah. The sheer sandstone cliffs that top the plateau glow a glorious deep reddish-orange in the late afternoon sun; they are surrounded by a sloping 'skirt' of scree and boulders, with patches of dense vegetation clinging onto the rock face. Water is relatively plentiful, hence the name Waterberg ('water mountain' in Afrikaans). Rain filters through the porous sandstone on top, but upon reaching the impervious lower layers of mudstone and siltstone, it re-emerges as springs through fissures in the southern slopes of the plateau. Unsurprisingly, water and the resulting abundant wildlife have attracted human populations for many years. **San rock art** near one of the plateau's waterholes testifies to their having passed through the area for thousands of years. Towards the end of the nineteenth century, the **Herero** settled in the area with their cattle, and it was here, on 11 August 1904, that the decisive **Battle of Omahakari** (or Waterberg) was fought between the Herero, who were defying colonial rule, and the German army (see page 341).

The trails

Since the threat of rhino poaching put paid to the multiday hike across the plateau, for which Waterberg was once famous, hikers are restricted to a handful of **shorter**

FLORA AND FAUNA OF THE WATERBERG PLATEAU NATIONAL PARK

Because of its inaccessibility, the park is used to reintroduce and breed **rare species** transferred to other protected areas. These include white and black rhinos, eland, tsessebe, roan and sable antelope, and Cape buffalo. They join other **large mammals** in the park, such as giraffes, wildebeest and kudu. The **birdlife,** too, is impressive, with over two hundred recorded species, including a number of rarities. Namibia's only breeding colony of Cape vultures inhabits Waterberg's southwestern cliffs, while other notable avian residents include Verreaux's (black) eagles and large numbers of peregrine falcon. But wildlife is not just confined to the mixed wood- and grassland of the plateau top; even around the campground, you'll catch sight of paradise flycatchers flitting around the trees, hoopoes probing the soil and Damara dik-diks picking their way delicately round tents. At dusk, if you're lucky, you might spot the bulging eyes of a lesser bushbaby. Regular visitors you can't miss are the baboons; make sure you keep food stowed away, all chalet and car windows closed and tents zipped up.

trails (maximum 3km/1.9 miles) leaving from the camping or chalet areas. The forty-minute hike to the plateau rim for sunset is well worth the effort, while the Fig Tree Walk is a favourite with birders. Visitors are not allowed to drive themselves around the park, so the only way to get to know the top of the plateau is by signing up for one of the twice-daily **wildlife-viewing drives**. However, the ready availability of food and water, plus the dense vegetation, means that wildlife sightings are often disappointing.

4

ARRIVAL — WATERBERG PLATEAU NATIONAL PARK

By car Around 30km (18.6 miles) south of Otjiwarongo, take the tarred C22, signposted to Okakara. After 41km (25.5 miles), take the gravel D2512 for another 17km (10.6 miles) to the park entrance. It is accessible in an ordinary saloon car, though parts of the D2512 can be rough after rain. There is both petrol and diesel available at the NWR camp.

By bus and hitching There is no scheduled bus service. You may be able to catch some sporadic transport to Okakara from Otjiwarongo – ask at a fuel station – but you would still need to hitch from the junction with the D2512.

ACCOMMODATION

SEE MAP PAGE 170

NWR has a monopoly on accommodation in the national park itself. Still, several lodges, with camping facilities too, are located in private buffer reserves around the fringes of the plateau.

IN THE PARK

NWR Waterberg Camp nwr.com.na. This resort is wonderfully situated on a vegetated slope below the sandstone cliffs. A shady campground is on flattish land by reception, at the foot of the escarpment, near the thinly stocked camp shop. Almost sixty chalets and a handful of self-catering units lie higher up the escarpment with simple but comfortable accommodations for two or four – some with outside braai and seating. Some sit on the cliff edge, offering glimpses of thorn tree-covered plains below through the undergrowth; Chalet 57 has a good view. A decent à la carte restaurant and bar, which occupy the former German police station, have terrace seating, with a lovely shallow pool in an adjacent shady area. Camping N$$, doubles B&B N$$, bush chalets (B&B) N$$$

OUTSIDE THE PARK

Waterberg Guest Farm On the C22, 22km (13.7 miles) east of the junction with the B1 waterbergnamibia.com. Personalised service and gourmet family-style dining on a cattle and horse stud farm that affords spectacular views of sunrise above the Waterberg Plateau. Four rooms are offered in the farmhouse, opening out onto a veranda. Still, it's worth splashing out on the even nicer, more private 'bush bungalows' (including a family unit) with rustic exteriors and light, airy contemporary interiors, offering indoor and outdoor showers. Some offer fine views across to the Waterberg from the patio. Birdwatching is excellent here (250 species have been recorded) and an illuminated waterhole attracts larger fauna. It would be best if you were a dog-lover as the owner has several that wander freely. Guided or self-guided hikes and horse riding are available, as well as excursions to Waterberg and the cheetah foundation. The only downside here is the proximity to a main road that can be busy during the day. B&B. Doubles N$$$, bush bungalows N$$$

Waterberg Wilderness 10km (6.2 miles) beyond the park entrance on the D2512 waterberg-wilderness.com. A former cattle farm turned private reserve that abuts the national park has now been restocked with wildlife, including giraffes and white rhinos, with several short trails. Still, it's worth doing the longer guided plateau hike for the superlative views. Rhino tracking is the most popular activity, so it is worth booking ahead. Solar-powered accommodation (so no a/c) is spread across three simple lodges – each with a pool and restaurant serving set menus – and a couple of campsites.

Waterberg Valley Lodge Five canvas 'chalets' with stone bathrooms cater to the budget traveller and offer the best value-for-money in the reserve but they are still pricey. DBB N$$$

Waterberg Wilderness Lodge Ten comfortably furnished, if overpriced doubles and four family rooms populate the two buildings of the lively main lodge – sandstone buildings set among mature trees and well-tended grounds. DBB N$$$

Waterberg Plateau Lodge It's all about the view in these eight furnished stone chalets, each with a private patio and plunge pool, perched along a rock terrace. DBB N$$$$

Waterberg Camping Twenty-four sites are spread across two areas, each with a small pool, offering secluded, shady spots with ablutions in a central block. Try to book one of the four pitches at the more secluded Andersson campsite. Campers can dine at the lodge restaurant, but only if there's space. N$$

Otjiwarongo

As you enter **OTJIWARONGO**, the road broadens into a dual carriageway punctuated by traffic lights, leading you to expect a town of some size. But blink, and you'll miss the town centre and find yourself heading back into the bush. That said, Otjiwarongo is the regional capital of the Otjozondjupa Region, and when the jacaranda and flamboyants lining the main street are in bloom, the place exudes a cheery feel.

4

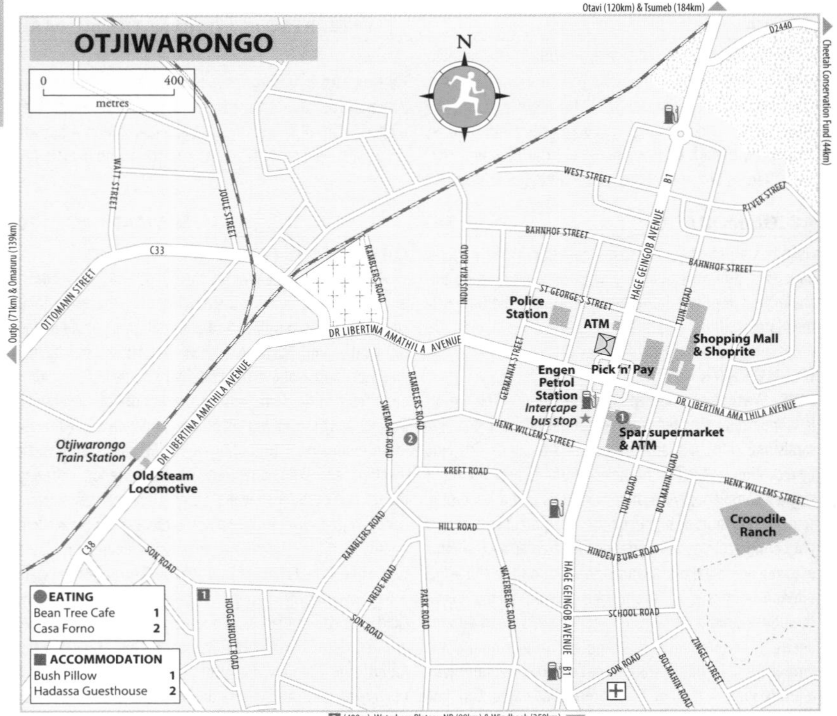

Otjiwarongo's newest attraction is the **Namibian Museum of Fashion**, which opened in 2022 and is worth swinging by. Attractions are otherwise thin on the ground, though railway buffs should swing by the station to look at the splendid retired old German steam locomotive. The only other place that draws visitors is the crocodile ranch, which gives guided tours of what is effectively a battery crocodile farm providing skin for the European and Asian leather markets – something to consider before paying the entry fee.

For tourists bound for Etosha or Caprivi, Otjiwarongo is a natural pit stop, providing a selection of well-stocked supermarkets and several petrol stations. The town is also within striking distance of the Waterberg Plateau (see page 174), Namibia's premier cheetah research and education centre (see page 178) and the AfriCat Foundation at Okonjima (see page 173).

Brief history

As with many places in central-northern Namibia, there are traces of nomadic San and later Damara presence in the area, though the first to settle here and push out any competition were the Herero, whose Chief Kanzambezi eventually allowed a Rhenish mission to be established in 1891. The Herero uprising in 1904 that resulted in their forced 'retreat' into the Omaheke Desert and thousands of deaths (see page 341) enabled the Germans to take over the town, establish a garrison and claim much of the land. The town was officially founded in 1906, when the narrow-gauge railway line between Swakopmund and the mines in Otavi and Tsumeb became fully operational, allowing the place to thrive. Otjiwarongo means 'place where fat cattle graze' in Otjiherero, which denotes a pleasant location for a cattle-loving society. Cattle are still the mainstay of the town's growing economy, aided by its excellent rail links with the coast and road connections with Windhoek and with Oshakati and Ondangwa, the main population centres in the north. In the last few years, the opening of the Otjikoto open-cast gold mine, midway between here and Otavi, and the hard-to-ignore new cement factory – a Namibian–Chinese venture that started operations in 2018 – which looms out of the savannah as you head north out of town have given the economy a further boost. Yet, the emergence of new businesses and jobs still cannot keep pace with the influx of rural migrants.

4

Namibian Museum of Fashion

12001, ERF 235 Park Road • Mon–Fri 8am–1pm, 2–5pm • Free • Ⓦ namibianfashion.com

This six-room gallery focuses variously on historical aspects of traditional clothing, from cloth or animal skins to accessories from shells, beads, metal or bones and their cultural meanings. There is a strong post-colonial lens in the museum, which also gives space and aims to inspire new designers whose creations inevitably draw on traditions. Although some of the clothing sits awkwardly on the stylised grey mannequins, this is a thoughtfully produced exhibition with space to grow and worth a visit. There is also a **craft shop** and online store.

ARRIVAL AND DEPARTURE — OTJIWARONGO

By car Otjiwarongo is right on the B2, 248km (154 miles) from Windhoek, on the road north. Several fuel stations, banks with ATMs and supermarkets lie on the main street.

By bus Intercape buses (Ⓦ intercape.co.za) stop at the Engen service station opposite Spar on the main street en route from Windhoek to Oshakati or Katima (several daily; 7hr 15min). The return buses to Windhoek from the north pass Otjiwarongo in the middle of the night and early morning (3hr 30min).

By minibus Minibuses leave the Monte Christo service station in Katutura for Otjiwarongo. For the return journey, catch one from the Engen station opposite Spar on the main street. Minibuses also leave here for Oshakati.

CHEETAH CONSERVATION

Almost half of the world's **cheetahs** – around 3,500 – roam the savannah lands of Namibia, predominantly on communal and commercial farms. In Namibia, Africa's most endangered cat is a protected species, but there are ongoing conflicts between these mighty hunters and people when livestock is threatened or killed. Loss of habitat and prey is another problem cheetahs face, as the increase in livestock rearing and subsequent overgrazing have resulted in bush encroachment. The recent expansion of game fencing has also affected the availability of food.

At the forefront of conservation efforts in Namibia and the global leader in cheetah research and education is the **Cheetah Conservation Fund** (daily 8am–5pm; charge; Ⓦcheetah.org), 44km (27.3 miles) east of Otjiwarongo, which is well worth a visit; if driving, turn east off the B1, onto the sandy D2440, just north of Otjiwarongo. The entry fee includes an excellent two-hour **guided walking tour** around the large enclosures, where around fifty rescue cheetahs are kept. However, good sightings of these splendid beasts depend on whether they happen to be prowling or lounging close to the perimeter fence. Arriving at feeding time (2pm on weekdays, noon at weekends) will increase your chances, as will signing up for the hour-long **cheetah drive** or the morning **cheetah run**. You'll also be taken to see the veterinary clinic and **livestock dogs**, one of the centre's most successful programmes, in which Kangal and Anatolian Shepherd dogs are trained to live among livestock and bark to scare off predators, thus safeguarding the farmer's livelihood, while saving the cheetah from a likely bullet. Around five hundred dogs now live on farms, with impressive results.

4

Another highlight is the **Dancing Goat Creamery** – one of several model farms used to help share predator-friendly management practices. Make sure you stock up on some of their superb feta or goat's cheese; they even produce fudge. Then, after trying to absorb all the information in the new interactive **cheetah museum**, you'll probably be ready for a cup of coffee and a bite to eat in the café. If you've not had your fill of cheetahs for the day, you can overnight here (Ⓦcheetah.org/cheetah-ecolodge). The luxurious *Babson House* overlooks a cheetah pen and can accommodate up to six in two rooms with four-poster beds (AI N$$$$). Alternatively, *Cheetah View Lodge* offers five suites, with private porch areas and large windows that gaze across the savannah towards Waterberg (DBB, N$$$). The profits from both go to support the foundation.

ACCOMMODATION

Though most visitors prefer to stay out of town, closer to Waterberg, or in one of the private reserves further south, some good, inexpensive accommodation in town would fit the bill for a comfortable one-night stopover.

IN TOWN, SEE MAP PAGE 176

Bush Pillow 27 Son Rd Ⓦbushpillow.co.za. Eco-focused smart guesthouse (run on solar power, emphasising recycling and supporting environmental projects) aimed at the 'discerning tourist' and business clients (hence the offer of an ironing board!). Possesses a handful of bright, elephant-themed rooms, secure parking and a small garden and pool. It also runs multiday tours. Room only or B&B. N$$

Hadassa Guesthouse 36 Lang St Ⓦhadassaguesthouse.com. Upmarket guesthouse catering to business folk and travellers alike, with seventeen stylishly designed rooms with all modern comforts. Comfortable common areas and a delightful garden with a sparkling pool. Massage is available and lunch or dinner can be pre-ordered. B&B N$$

NORTH OF TOWN, SEE MAP PAGE 170

Frans Indongo Lodge 17km (10.6 miles) along the D2433, whose turn-off is 43km (26.7 miles) north of Otjiwarongo Ⓦindongolodge.com. Established by Namibia's most successful Black entrepreneur, this well-run lodge pays homage to his roots with an Owambo homestead theme – mopane palisades dividing off the various sections and everyday artefacts as ornaments. However, the smart thatched chalets (for couples and families) are thoroughly modern, with comfortable interiors in earthy tones with all conveniences (a/c, phone, fridge, hairdryer, DStv, kettle). Only two chalets directly face the savannah plains, which can otherwise be enjoyed from the stone-paved pool or viewing deck. Substantial fixed-price lunch and dinner (N$$$–$$$$) available, plus walking trails, game drives and a visit to the former Otjiwarongo township. N$$$

EATING

SEE MAP PAGE 176

Bean Tree Café Spar supermarket, 47 Hage Geingob St. Ideally suited to a quick pit stop on the road, this supermarket café provides efficient service and good-value hot cafeteria meals and snacks all day long. Whether it's a decent coffee and croissant, a full breakfast fry-up, a bowl of pasta, a filling stew, or a tasty *brötchen*, you should find something to suit you. N$$–$$$

Casa Forno 21 Ramblers Rd casaforno.com. This trendy, shady beer garden with play area reels in local families, business folk and passers-by with their wood-fired pizzas – there's even a breakfast one – and game specialities such as oryx stroganoff and marinated game kebabs. N$$–$$$

Outjo

With a small population of about six thousand, the ranching town of **OUTJO** – meaning 'little hills' in Otjiherero – sits on the pleasantly undulating fringes of the Fransfontein Mountains, just north of the Ugab River. It's a surprisingly leafy town, which has recently taken on a new lease of life as a staging post for tourists trekking up to Etosha, a fact exemplified by the transformation of the high-street bakery from a small-town shop into a slick two-storey glass-fronted operation with restaurant, large shop and playground.

Beyond stopping for lunch and wandering down the pleasant main street, which boasts a quasi-town square and several tourist shops, there are a couple of German historical monuments worth a cursory glance before moving on since Outjo was one of the German colonial army's most northerly, and short-lived, outposts; it was established initially to control the rinderpest in the areas of white settlement (see page 341), but then to try and win over the Owambo kings. One of the first structures they built was a water tower to pump and supply water to the soldiers, their horses and the hospital. Though the wooden windmill has long gone, the square stone base can still be seen on the east side of town off the northern end of Sonop Street.

4

Outjo Museum

Corner of Meester Street with Tuin Street • Temporarily closed • Charge • 067 313402

The **Outjo Museum** is an extremely modest affair displayed in Outjo's oldest and most nicely restored building, the **Franke Haus**. It is named after the German commanding officer Major Victor Franke, for whom it was built in 1899 – he also has a tower named after him in Omaruru (see page 188). The museum's collection comprises an exhibition on his exploits and displays of antique artefacts and locally mined gemstones.

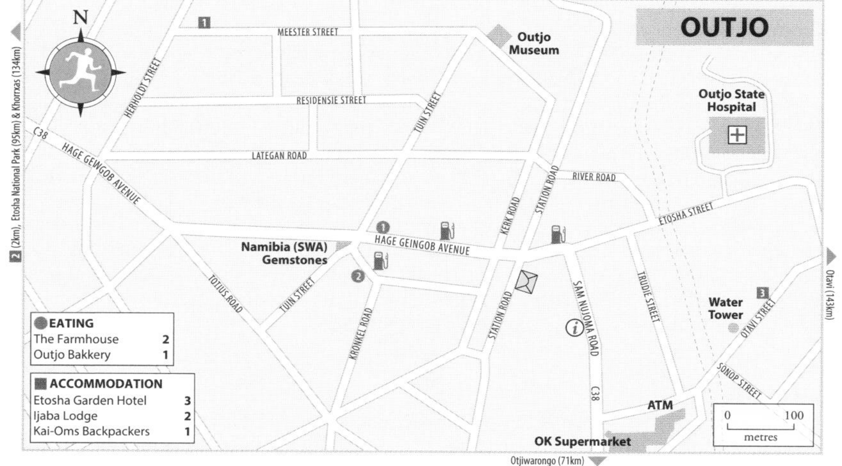

ARRIVAL AND INFORMATION — OUTJO

By car Easily reachable on the tarred C38 from Otjiwarongo and with good connections to Etosha, Damaraland and the Kaokoveld.

Tourist information A large modern municipal tourist information centre sits on Sam Nujoma Road (Mon–Fri 7am–4.30pm, Sat & Sun 7am–2pm), which also hosts a restaurant, a couple of craft stalls, and a local tour operator. If the information desk is not staffed (not an uncommon occurrence), enquire at South West Africa Gems (Mon–Fri 9am–5pm, Sat 9–1pm) on Hage Geingob Avenue on the square, which has served as the de facto tourist information centre for many years, with knowledgeable and helpful staff; they also sell guides to Etosha and postcards.

ACCOMMODATION — SEE MAP PAGE 179

Etosha Garden Hotel 6 Otavi St ⓦetosha-garden-hotel.com. This century-old building is set in a luscious tropical garden filled with jacaranda, palm trees and bougainvillea – a good spot for an indulgent lunch. Twenty large rooms (often filled with tour groups) are fairly basic – some with a/c, others with fan & TV – but generally clean and good value for the price. N$$

Ijaba Lodge 2km (1.2 miles) north of town on the C38 ⓦIjaba-lodge.com. Six compact, nicely decorated themed chalets, with braai facilities, are set in tree-filled grounds attracting good birdlife. There's also a small pool with a bar-restaurant under a *lapa*. The six campsites, not especially private, but grassy, are agreeably situated and with electricity. Camping N$, chalet (B&B or DBB) N$$

Kai-Oms Backpackers 2 Meester St ⓣ081 375 0152, ⓔinsurancegirl299@gmail.com. Old-style shoestring backpackers, providing basic accommodation: private rooms, dorms and a space to pitch a tent amid the pot plants, quirky ornaments and pond in their courtyard garden, with shared kitchen, braai and outdoor seating (less fun in winter) and with friendly owners. Breakfast costs extra. Camping per site (up to four people) N$, dorms, N$, doubles N$$

EATING — SEE MAP PAGE 179

4

The Farmhouse 7 Kronkel Road ⓦfarmhousenamibia.com. This place offers a vast, eclectic menu, from mopane worms to goulash, burgers to burritos. It's great for breakfasts, light lunches and vast slabs of home-made cakes to devour indoors or in the delightful shady beer garden at the back. Dinner can be a bit more hit-and-miss. N$$–$$$

Outjo Bakkery 75 Hage Geingob Ave ⓦfacebook.com/OutjoBakkery1947. This modern, expanded bakery captures much of the lunchtime tourist traffic to and from Etosha. While still serving up apfelstrudel, doughnuts and home-made bread, a fully-fledged restaurant serves pizzas, burgers, pies, and salads with various steaks. There's also a chill cabinet with canned drinks, as well as biltong, rolls and other snacks to go, plus excellent-value daily lunch specials. N$$

The 'Triangle'

Viewed on a map, the roads linking the northern towns of **Tsumeb**, **Otavi** and **Grootfontein** form an isosceles **triangle** enclosing the scenic Otavi Mountains, which provide welcome topographic relief to anyone travelling down from the flatlands of the far north. It's one of Namibia's most prosperous areas, rich in minerals and agriculture – thanks to fertile soils nurtured by annual rainfall that usually tops 500mm (19.7in); maize cultivation is particularly widespread, resulting in the sobriquet of the **Golden** or **Maize Triangle**. Located on the way to Etosha's eastern gate, as well as the lush game reserves in the Zambezi Region, many visitors pass through these small towns. Of the three, Tsumeb is the most attractive and has the best facilities, followed by Grootfontein; both are good places to withdraw money, stock up on supplies and top up your fuel, with Otavi a rather forlorn third. In terms of sights, the museum in Tsumeb and the Hoba Meteorite – the world's largest – west of Grootfontein are worth a brief detour, while a few lodges and guest farms in the area make the most of their scenic surroundings and offer enjoyable overnight stops.

Otavi

The smallest and most down at heel of the Triangle towns, **OTAVI** seems forgotten. Most of the action happens outside town, at the flagship Total petrol station and major truck stop, complete with ATM, neighbouring bar-restaurant and biltong shop, on the main crossroads east of the centre. Here, the B1 divides: heading northwest to the population centres of Oshakati and Ondangwa or northeast along the B8 towards the Trans Caprivi Highway. Note the heavily irrigated areas along this initial stretch of the B8, where the town's original springs – long known to nomadic Hai||om and Damara groups – are located.

Dominating the skyline as you drive into the nondescript town are the gleaming grain silos of the maize and millet mill across the railway track. The arrival of the railway from Swakopmund in 1906 marked the town's boom period. The German colonial mining company, the Otavi Minen und Eisenbahngesellschaft (OMEG), completed what was the longest narrow-gauge track in the world at the time – on the back of enslaved people or enforced labour – to transport the copper being mined at Tsumeb and Kombat down to the coast and onto ships bound for Europe. Once the copper deposits were exhausted, the town's fortunes slumped. So far, the new gold mine and cement factory in the area do not seem to have had the economic impact on Otavi that its four thousand inhabitants were anticipating, with Otjiwarongo appearing to benefit more from the mine.

A few kilometres north of town, signposted off the B1, stands the unremarkable **Khorab Memorial**. Of interest only to colonial history buffs, as there's little to see, it marks the site where in World War I, on 9 June 1915, the Schutztruppe, under the ubiquitous Lieutenant-Colonel (by then) Victor Franke, finally surrendered to Louis Botha's South African Union troops, signing the Khorab Peace Treaty six days later.

Otavi Mountains

4

Even if you do not have time to stay in the area, a drive through the scenic **Otavi Mountains** is a refreshing diversion, especially if you're arriving from the flat arid areas around Etosha. Formed about 700 million years ago, this stratified dolomite and limestone range has numerous **caves**, the most accessible of which is the **Ghaub Cave**, on the guest farm of the same name (see page 182), where you can arrange to go on a two-hour tour (ghaub-namibia.com). It's 38m (124.7ft) deep with 2.5km (1.6 miles) of chambers and passageways. Although it lacks large stalactites, stalagmites and ancient rock art, there are petrified waterfalls, organ pipes, rock

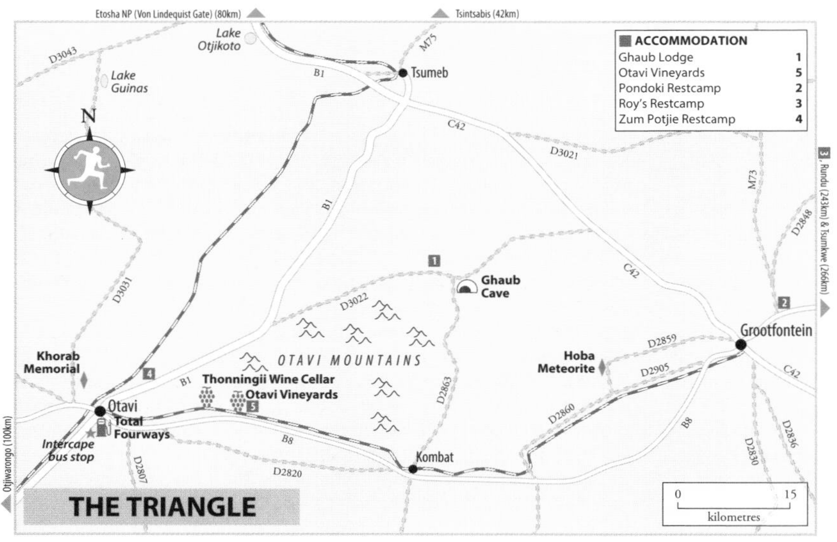

curtains and other interesting crystal growths to interest the casual cave-goer. The place, which is not suitable for the claustrophobic, is dark, slippery and dusty, so dress appropriately.

Thonningii Wine Cellar

11km (6.8 miles) east of Otavi, just north of the Grootfontein road • Mon–Sat 9am–5pm • ⓦ facebook.com/thonningii • Turn west off the main road, crossing the railway tracks and follow the signs right

This fantastic family-run enterprise is a must when in the area. They are currently producing three reds – Barbera, Syrah and Tinta Barocca, a fruity white blend, a dry rosé and a potent grappa-style spirit. Made only from the farm's grapes, harvested by hand, they are tended as naturally as possible. The wine is matured in French new oak barrels and stored in older barrels or stainless-steel containers. The farmhouse is a delight, full of family artwork and the odd heirloom. The whole lunch platter of home-made goodies produced on the farm, with wine-tasting, costs N$320; a sample of a few wines is currently free, provided you buy a bottle or two afterward.

Otavi Vineyards

13km (8 miles) east of Otavi, just north of the Grootfontein road • Mon–Sat 9am–5pm • ⓦ boshoffwines@gmail.com • Turn west off the main road, crossing the railway tracks and follow the signs

4

Just up the road from Thonningii, Gilmar Boshoff also produces wine on his neighbouring farm. More recently established, it still produces around seven thousand bottles of organic wine per harvest from twelve different cultivars. Wine tasting can be done here, too, with an equally scrumptious snack platter, which needs to be pre-ordered. The place also offers basic camping and self-catering accommodation (see below) – an easy solution to drink driving, as you can stumble to your bed for a siesta after the tasting. You can also hike across a field filled with antelope to Thonningii (see above) and stagger back to your tent after a wine-laden lunch.

ARRIVAL AND DEPARTURE — OTAVI

By bus The Intercape service from Windhoek (ⓦ intercape.co.za) stops at the Total Fourways petrol station in Otavi on the way between Windhoek and Oshakati (daily; 4hr 45min).

By minibus Local minibuses bound for Tsumeb or Grootfontein also leave from here, as do minibuses bound for Windhoek.

ACCOMMODATION — SEE MAP PAGE 181

★ **Ghaub Lodge** 24km (14.9 miles) along the D3022 from the junction with the B1, 25km (15.5 miles) north of Outjo ⓦ ghaub-namibia.com. Tucked away in the Otavi Mountains, this well-managed and welcoming former mission station has twelve airy chalets overlooking expansive lawns, a real treat. So, too, are the three private luxury campsites with their own stone ablutions, table and braai and superlative views. The main house retains many original features, and the shady terrace garden is an ideal spot to linger over a well-prepared meal. Trips to the Gaub Caves, a drive around their modest nature reserve (containing rhinos, blesbok and eland) or guided walks are on offer. Camping N$$, DBB & afternoon tea N$$$–$$$$

★ **Otavi Vineyards** 13km (8 miles) north-east of Otavi, just west of the B1 ⓦ facebook.com/people/Boshoff-Family-Wines/100063697622019. A relaxed and relaxing spot at the foot of the Otavi Mountains, surveying the vineyard. Accommodation is in simple, solar-powered, self-catering brick cottages with quirky decorations and four delightful campsites with shared ablutions. There's plenty of shade for eating out and barbecuing and greenery that attracts birdlife. The location is perfect for guided or self-guided walks, but don't forget to fit in some wine tasting. Camping N$, self-catering N$$

Zum Potjie Restcamp 8km (5 miles) northeast of Otavi, signposted off the B1 ⓦ zumpotjie.com. Easy access and simple, inexpensive lodgings in a friendly farm environment; five neat bungalows with fans can be booked self-catering or B&B, or there are campsites with or without power points. The farm's crammed full of old artefacts and memorabilia, and the flavoursome potjie stews are not to be missed. Camping N$, bungalow (B&B) N$$

Tsumeb

The largest and most populous of the Triangle towns, **TSUMEB** is also the most attractive, its main roads lined with mature trees, including palms, jacarandas and flamboyants – which provide splashes of lilac and red when in bloom, and brightly coloured bougainvillea hedges. There is even a sizeable leafy park, the town's fulcrum, overlooked by several of Tsumeb's main buildings and off which the high street leads. On the park's south side stands an excellent museum (see page 184) next door to the town's oldest existing building; erected in 1913, the striking **Saint Barbara Catholic Church** was aptly named since Barbara is the patron saint of miners. From the outset, mining has been the town's raison d'être, though the disused mineshaft that dominates the west end of President's Avenue is a reminder of its more recent decline. Nevertheless, Tsumeb is a pleasant enough place to spend a night, with a choice of accommodation that generally serves decent food. If you're just passing through en route to Etosha, this is the last stop for groceries in one of the town's well-stocked supermarkets. At the end of October, the town parties during the annual **Tsumeb Copper Festival**, essentially a trade fair centred on the United Nations Park, but also with the usual food and drink stalls and musical and cultural entertainment.

Brief history

Mining and smelting copper had probably been happening in the area for several thousand years before the London-based South-West Africa Company began prospecting in 1895. The Bergdamara had mined and smelted copper, whereas the Hai||om probably dug out the ore and traded with the Owambos for them to smelt. The Hai||om called the place 'Tsomsoub', meaning 'to dig a hole in the loose ground (that collapses)', which gave rise to the town's modern name, Tsumeb. In the second half of the nineteenth century, tensions grew over land ownership and rights in the Triangle as its mineralogical value became increasingly apparent, and there was much wheeling and dealing among different Owambo and Herero groups,

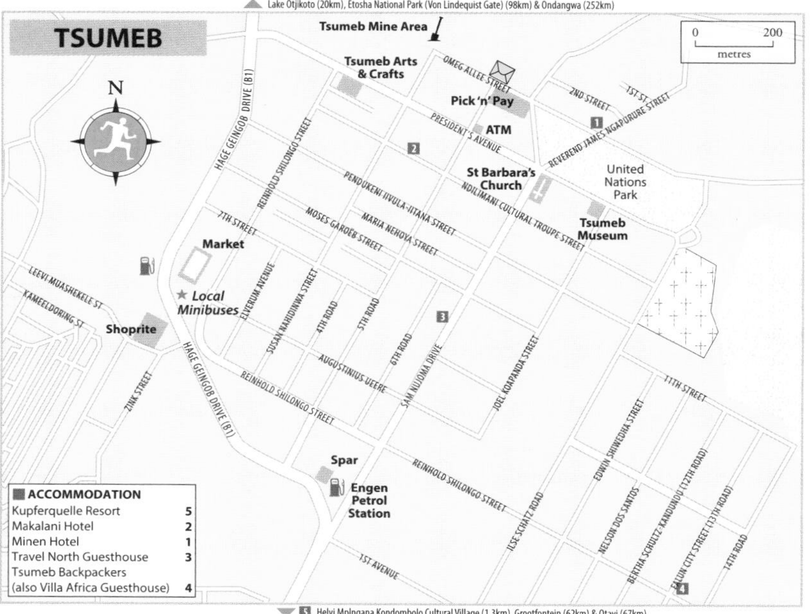

European traders and other interested parties, while the Bergdamara and Hai||om were gradually squeezed out. The first 9 tonnes of ore were transported to the coast via ox-cart in 1900, but once the railway line arrived from Swakopmund in 1906, mining production took off in a big way under the auspices of OMEG initially, and later the Tsumeb Mine Corporation. It created a boom era that lasted decades – with hiatuses during the two world wars – until copper prices sank in the 1990s and the mine was forced to close in 1998. Though more recently, small mining operations have started up again, they are nowhere near the scale that saw 24.6 million tonnes of ore extracted. What made the Tsumeb mine stand out, however, was also the variety of minerals it yielded: over 227 recorded, forty of which were unique to the mine; gemstones such as tourmaline, malachite and dioptase were also important finds.

Tsumeb Museum

President's Avenue, opposite the park • Mon–Fri 9am–noon, 2–5pm, Sat 9am–noon • Charge • T 067 220447

Unlike some provincial museums, the well-curated **Tsumeb Museum** merits a visit; it contains a rich collection of well-labelled artefacts, photos and explanatory text in English and German over several rooms. After the obligatory ethnography room, looking at the cultural artefacts and traditions of Namibia's various peoples comes the Khorab Chamber. Here, the star exhibits include some lovingly restored cannons, a machine gun, an ammunition wagon and assorted weaponry from the much larger cache that the Germans hurled into Lake Otjikoto in anticipation of losing World War I. Other war memorabilia includes a military stretcher, discovered up a tree some 65 years later. The third room narrates the town's mining history, with copious examples of rock crystals; don't miss the lump of Hoba Meteorite or the velvet malachite, which really does look as soft as velour. Ignoring the exhibits resulting from a clear-out of residents' attics, so beloved of Namibian museums – typewriters, cameras and crockery – philatelist enthusiasts can linger in the final room, which details the history of Namibia's postal service, complete with an immaculately displayed collection of stamps.

Helvi Mpingana Kondombolo Cultural Village

2km (1.2 miles) from the town centre on the main road to/from the B1 • Mon–Fri 7.30am–4.30pm, Sat 8am–1pm • Charge • W hmkcv.business.site

Although it has potential, the **Helvi Mpingana Kondombolo Cultural Village** currently disappoints. The aim is to showcase Namibia's various cultures, particularly the traditional homesteads, reconstructed with the appropriate materials and dotted around a pleasant patch of bush. However, unless there is an attendant free (rarely the case) who can take you on a guided tour, there is little to be gained from a visit since information boards, labels and brochures are lacking, though there are plenty of hornbills to enjoy in the surrounding scrubland.

ARRIVAL AND DEPARTURE — TSUMEB

By bus Intercape buses (W intercape.co.za) from Windhoek bound for Oshakati or Katima Mulilo stop at the Engen station, at the town entrance most days, as well as on the way back south to Windhoek (5hr 30min). Local minibuses tend to leave from around the market area to Windhoek and Grootfontein.

INFORMATION

There is no official tourist office in town, although the *Travel North Guesthouse* is very helpful and has a range of leaflets, while *Tsumeb Backpackers* also offers good advice.

ACCOMMODATION — SEE MAP PAGE 183

Kupferquelle Resort 1.5km (0.9 miles) from the park, on the main road to/from the B1 W kupferquelle.com. This large, pricey modern resort just outside town may resemble a shopping mall from the outside but boasts immaculate if rather bland, rooms and chalets set in lovely grounds, complete with velvety lawns, an Olympic-sized pool, majestic trees and even a duck pond. By far, it is the best camping option in town. The South African steakhouse franchise offers a standard menu, which is decent enough, though service is slow, and the restaurant has more of a dark evening-time bar vibe unless you bag a table on the terrace. Camping N$, room or chalet only N$$

Makalani Hotel Ndilimani Cultural Troupe Street Ⓦ facebook.com/MakalaniHotel. Great value, this bright yellow hotel exudes cheerfulness and friendly efficiency: well-maintained rooms are arranged on two floors around the poolside courtyard bar-restaurant (so the noise percolates a little) populated by palm trees, though not a makalani in sight. The preferred venue for a meal out for locals as well as hotel residents, with an adjacent sports bar. B&B N$$

Minen Hotel 7 OMEG Allee Ⓦ minen-hotel.com. The original mine hotel for visiting executives has had a full revamp. While it's lost much of its original charm and character, it is still the top place to stay in town, with a pleasant tree-filled terrace, nice pool, good food – the pepper steak's a solid choice – and smart, business-style rooms. B&B N$$

Travel North Guesthouse Dr San Nujoma Drive (opposite Telecoms) Ⓦ travelnorthguesthouse.com. The modern, compact guesthouse offers nine neat, comfy en-suite rooms, a pleasant on-site coffee shop and breakfast room, skincare, and even a hair salon. B&B N$$

Tsumeb Backpackers (also Villa Africa Guesthouse) 1713 13th Rd Ⓦ tsumebbackpackers.com. This backpackers ' pad occupies a small converted house, fifteen minutes' walk from the Intercape bus stop (they'll pick you up if arranged in advance) and a supermarket. There are seven small twin rooms with en-suite bathrooms, a family suite and a mixed dorm. A spacious, well-equipped modern kitchen, pool table and lovely, shady garden with a barbecue area and a small pool round out the picture. The friendly, laid-back owners also offer local tours. B&B. Dorms N$, doubles N$$

Lake Otjikoto

20km (12.4 miles) north of Tsumeb on the B1 • Daily 8am–5pm • Charge

A somewhat neglected site right by the main road, **Lake Otjikoto** is more interesting for what you can't see than for what you can. A sinkhole lake formed by the collapse of a vast underground cavern in the dolomite and limestone rocks, it's like an inverted mushroom, with sheer walls that widen out underwater, creating overhangs. Measuring 100m (328ft) in diameter, its depth is less certain, in part because it does not descend vertically. Some believe the lake is bottomless and connected via underground passages to the less accessible – as it's on private farmland – nearby sinkhole, **Lake Guinas**. Others claim it's closer to 55m (180.4ft) in depth, as colonial-era explorers Galton and Andersson (after whom two of Etosha's gates are named) earlier surmised while camping here in 1851. When the sun is shining, the lake gleams an attractive deep blue-green colour, but when overcast, the water appears murkier, and it's easy to see why the San dubbed it 'Gaisis', meaning 'very ugly'. Otjikoto, however, is a Herero name, which loosely translates as 'too deep for cattle to drink'.

The lake's main interest lies in its history as the resting place of many of the retreating German army's munitions, hastily dumped here in 1915 just before the army's surrender to South African troops to prevent the arsenal from falling into the enemy's hands. Many items, including some cannons, have been retrieved over the years and are displayed in the Tsumeb Museum (see page 184). Legend has it that a chest of gold bullion is also lurking somewhere in the water among the remaining weaponry, which might partly explain why it's the most popular of Namibia's cave diving locations (experienced divers only; Otjikoto Diving Enterprises, Ⓣ 081 129 5318, Ⓔ sviljoen@mweb.com.na). While the story itself is quite improbable, the part about the existence of abundant fish is true, including the extraordinary dwarf bream (*Pseudocrenolabrus philander dispersus*), whose female protects her eggs and young by carrying them around in her mouth.

Grootfontein

On a sloping hillside at the northern extreme of Namibia's central plateau, **Grootfontein** is quite attractive in September and October once the jacaranda and flamboyants bloom; even so, it has a slight frontier feel, in part due to the increasing numbers of informal Kavangan street traders in the town centre. Grootfontein is set on fertile agricultural land – producing meat, dairy products, sorghum, maize, ground nuts, sunflowers and leather goods. Below and to the east stretches the endless Kalahari, while to the north, the flat, dry lowlands extend as far as the Okavango River at Rundu, some 250km (155.3 miles) away. The Otjiherero name for the place, Otjiwandatjongue, meaning 'hill of the leopard', was eschewed by the first white colonisers in favour of the earlier Hai||om and Bergdamara designation, Gei-|ous, meaning 'big spring', giving rise to the Afrikaans name Grootfontein that persists today. The town has little to do except drop by the old German fort that now houses the **museum**.

Brief history

The area's productive potential in terms of grazing and copper deposits attracted both Owambo and Herero groups to settle here. However, the Bergdamara were thought to be the first to introduce copper smelting to the area. The Indigenous populations were soon displaced in 1893, once the South-West Africa Company – initially a British-German enterprise – established its headquarters here. In a short-lived, somewhat bizarre historical episode between 1885 and 1887, a group of Dorsland Trekkers also put down roots here (see Box page 187).

Grootfontein was formally established in 1907, and the railway link was completed a year later. In 1943, the headquarters of the South-West Africa Native Labour organisation was established in the town to recruit workers – primarily Owambo – for the diamond mines in the south but also the local mines. In the 1970s, the South Africans built a military air base here. Given its history, Grootfontein's 25,000-strong population is unsurprisingly culturally diverse. However, most farms are still owned by German- or Afrikaans-speaking white Namibians. In contrast, many Black people reside in the former township Omulunga, or the informal settlement Blikkiesdorp, in far less favourable conditions.

Old Fort Museum

Upingtonia Street • Mon–Fri 8.30am–3.30pm • Charge • Ⓦ altefortmuseum.de

The old German fort, which now houses the **Old Fort Museum**, was built in 1896, strategically positioned on a hilltop, with a good view of any impending trouble; the crenellated tower was a later addition. Before its present incarnation in 1975, the building was a school hostel. It's worth swinging by to have a look at the museum's

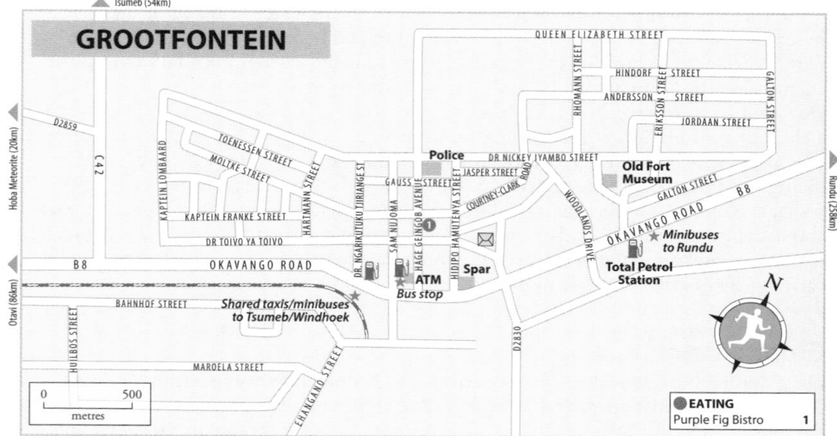

DORSLAND TREKKERS

The **Dorsland Trekkers** were originally granted free land in the area that went on to become Grootfontein by a certain W.W. Jordan, an adventurer and trader, who claimed to have bought a vast tract of land from Ndonga King Kambonde, in exchange for some cash, weaponry and brandy. In 1885, the Dorslanders declared the area the **Republic of Upingtonia** (later Lydensrust) after the prime minister of the Cape Colony at the time, whom they thought would offer support. None was forthcoming, however, leaving them reliant on protection from the Germans. The republic was doomed from the outset, as the Boers were variously challenged by Herero, San and Owambo groups, who disputed their claim to the land, and when Jordan was killed by Owambo King Nehale in 1887, the republic crumbled and was absorbed into German South-West Africa.

eclectic collection: standing in the courtyard is a range of colonial-era machinery, including a complete smithy, a steam engine, wood lathes and the obligatory ox-cart – particularly relevant given the town's association with the Dorsland Trekkers, who also feature prominently inside. Add to that displays of German military memorabilia, local gemstones, Kavango basketry and a room dedicated to the Himba, featuring an impressive photo collection and samples of jewellery and apparel, which make the place worth a quick stop.

ARRIVAL AND DEPARTURE — GROOTFONTEIN

By minibus Minibuses leave for Rundu from the Total garage north of the town centre. Minibuses heading south to Windhoek via Otavi and Otjiwarongo and local buses bound for Tsumeb leave from the Puma station at the other end of town, close to the junction between the B8 and the C34.

ACCOMMODATION

SEE MAP PAGE 181

Pondoki Restcamp 5km (3.1 miles) north of Grootfontein 081 3106795. A handy, untouristy overnight pit stop on the way to/from the Zambezi Region. The campsite suffers from noise from the main road, though the no-nonsense brick chalets more readily block out any noise. Still, the grassy pitches, with table, braai, light and electricity, are real pluses and the restaurant serves great food. Camping N$, chalets N$$

Roy's Restcamp 55km (34.2 miles) north of Grootfontein on the B8 067 240302 roys-rest-camp.com. This well-run place is a popular stopover, especially for overlanders and camping groups, with a rustic offbeat vibe reflected in the chalets (though they do have a/c and mosquito nets) and the campground decorations, from wood carvings to rusting vehicles. Sites are pretty close together and the chalets are quite pricey, given that you're in a rest camp, not a lodge. However, the pleasant bar serves filling meals (dinner N$$$); book in advance. The local wildlife can be watched at an illuminated waterhole, and excursions are organised to the Ju'|Hoansi Living Village at Grashoek. Camping N$, chalet (B&B) N$$$

EATING

SEE MAP PAGE 186

Purple Fig Bistro 19 Hage Geingob St facebook.com/PurpleFigBistro. At the back of the private health centre, spa and beauty salon is Grootfontein's only restaurant where you'd want to linger, whether over breakfast, a mid-morning latte and a slice of cake, or a light lunch. Snacks, tasty schnitzels, steaks and the like are served in a shady garden or inside. Affordable lunch specials are under N$100. N$$

Hoba Meteorite

20km (12.4 miles) down the D2859, signposted west off the C42, 1km (0.6 miles) from the junction with the B8 • Daily sunrise–sunset • Charge • Note that it's also signposted off the B8 between Grootfontein and Otavi, but this gravel road is much rougher • facebook.com/HobaMeteoriteNHC

The most popular attraction in the area is the **Hoba Meteorite**, the planet's largest single known meteorite; measuring just under 3m (9.8ft) across and around 1m (3.3ft) thick, it weighs approximately 60 tonnes – almost five times heavier than a laden double-decker bus. Though its age is estimated at anything between 190 million and 410 million years old, it can more accurately be said to have fallen to Earth less than 80,000 years ago. This lump of alien rock is primarily made up of iron (82.3 percent) and nickel (16.4 percent), with small amounts of other minerals. It was revealed to the outside world in 1920 by Jacobus Hermanus Brits, a farmer out hunting on his land, when he noticed a strange, black, rocky protrusion that stood out from the surrounding pale limestone. He chiselled a chunk off and took it for analysis, which confirmed its extra-terrestrial nature. After it became clear that Namibia would lose its 'fallen star' to enthusiastic vandals keen to chip off a space souvenir, the meteorite was declared a national monument in 1955. Once you've marvelled at the lump, which sits in a sunken stone surround, there's a pleasant picnic area to enjoy and a kiosk selling souvenirs, information leaflets and cold drinks. And you can even spend the night there in basic chalets if the urge takes you.

Omaruru

Sited at the crossroads between the C33 – the shortcut between Swakopmund and Otjiwarongo on the main road north – and the less frequented C36, which leads to the Brandberg, **OMARURU**, a small, somnolent town, makes a good stopover. It's also within easy striking distance of the scenic Erongo Mountains (see page 190). Established in 1868 by Wilhelm Zeraua, the first Herero White Flag chief, it later became a mission town – the old mission house is now a small, rather uninspiring **museum** (Mon–Fri 8am–5pm) – and was repeatedly the focus of battles between the Nama and Herero, then later the Herero and the German army. The distinctive, cylindrical **Franke Tower memorial**, which lies across the Omaruru River in a street parallel to the main drag, is a remnant of the latter. Over the weekend closest to 10 October, Herero flock to the former township of Ozondje to mark **White Flag Day** in commemoration of those who died fighting colonialism.

These days, Omaruru is garnering a reputation as a centre for arts and crafts – check out the shops on the attractive, shady main street, inevitably named after Wilhelm Zeraua. In particular, don't miss the Tikoloshe workshop and souvenir store (Ⓦ tikolosheafrika.com; daily 8am–5pm) at the western end, where you can watch the Kavango **root-carving** artists at work and peruse the craft shop, which sells their work, as well as all kinds of crafts from all over Africa. If you're in the area in August or September, look out for the increasingly popular annual arts and cultural **festival** (Ⓦ facebook.com/omaruruartsfestival), which involves exhibitions and workshops.

The Kristall Kellerei Winery

4km (2.5 miles) northeast of Omaruru on the D2328, a dirt road accessible in a saloon car • Mon–Fri 9am–4pm, Sat 9am–2pm • Charge • Tour of the estate, wine tasting (with spirits too) and lunch should preferably be pre-booked • Ⓦ kristallkellerei.com

An unlikely but exceedingly pleasant place to while away a couple of hours is the **Kristall Kellerei Winery**, one of Namibia's rare vineyards and a real entrepreneurial venture. Have a half-hour **tour** of the vines and the fermentation shed, followed by a generous **tasting** in the delightful, tree-filled garden full of birdlife. Everything's hand-processed with great invention, underscored by the need to keep wine temperatures constant in the desert heat. In addition to their popular white and red wines, they produce some knock-out schnapps and an award-winning nappa, Namibia's answer to grappa. Plus, you can sample some of their spirits. It's worth ringing ahead to avoid clashing with a tour group, and lunch needs to be pre-booked.

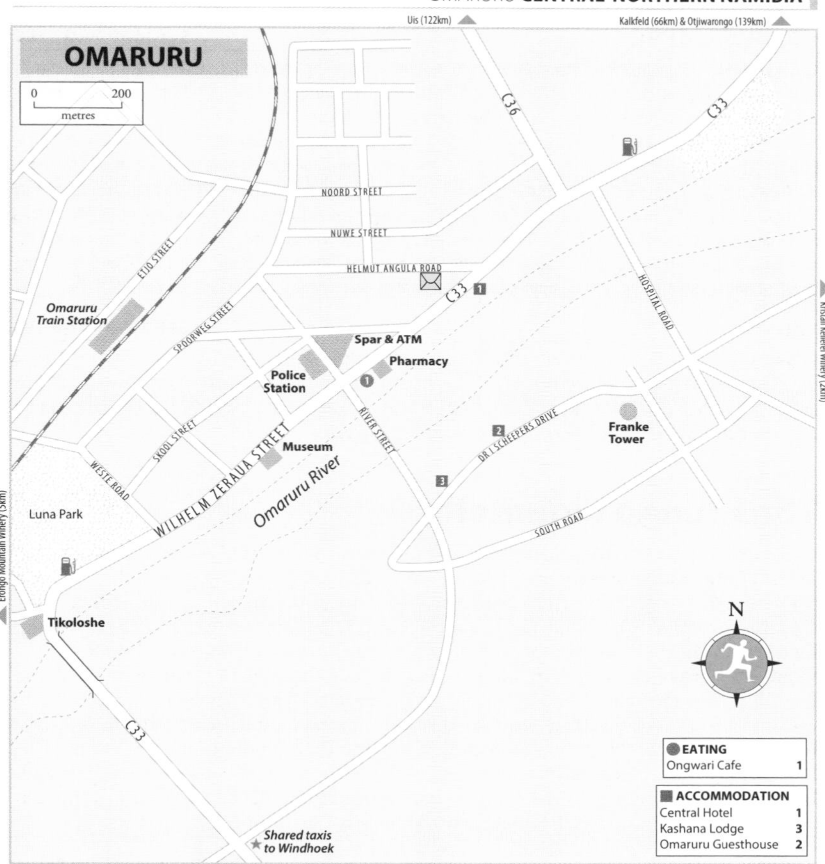

4

The Erongo Mountain Winery

5km (3.1 miles) southwest of Omaruru, on the northern bank of the Omaruru River • Mon–Sat 9am–5pm • Charge for wine-tasting, tour and a light lunch • Ⓦ erongomountainwinery.com • Accessible by saloon car along a dirt road

A newer vineyard that has only recently opened its doors to the public, the **Erongo Mountain Winery** is a more ambitious operation with more sophisticated equipment. What's more, it imports most of the grapes to add to the produce from its vines to make four red wines, four whites and four spirits. The smart new purpose-built building on the estate includes a tasting room and gourmet restaurant, which can be booked for à la carte dining or a set menu, including wine pairing.

ARRIVAL AND DEPARTURE — OMARURU

By car Easily accessible on the C33, a good tarred road that runs between Otjiwarongo (see page 176), which lies on the main road north, and Karibib, which lies on the B2, between Windhoek and Swakopmund.

By taxi/minibus Shared transport frequently leaves for Windhoek from the junction between the C33 and the road leading into Ozondje, south of the Omaruru River. Ask around the Monte Christo Service Station in Katutura for transport to Omaruru; otherwise, you might have to take a minibus bound for Swakopmund, getting off at the C36 turn-off north, midway between Okahandja and Karibib on the B2, from where you will then have to hitch the remaining 70km (43.5 miles).

ACCOMMODATION

SEE MAP PAGE 189

Central Hotel Wilhelm Zeraua Street centralhotelomaruru.com. This hundred-year-old hotel is a solid bet, possessing spacious rooms with gleaming tiled floors and a decent restaurant and bar where you can watch football. Dining N$$–$$$, B&B N$$

Kashana Lodge Dr Ian Scheepers Drive kashana-namibia.com. A converted casino for Canadian miners is now a good deal for a bed in town, with a decent restaurant under shady trees and a popular, buzzing bar. Offering standard and slightly larger, ambitiously named 'luxury rooms', there's plenty of space, though bathrooms are small, and rooms come with DStv, a ceiling fan and a/c. Doubles and chalets B&B N$$

Omaruru Guesthouse 305 Dr Ian Scheepers Drive omaruru-guesthouse.com. Larger than it looks, this homely guesthouse offers excellent value in twenty inexpensive air-conditioned rooms (singles, doubles, triples & family), with faux-wood floors, firm mattresses and the necessary amenities: fridge, satellite TV and tea/coffee. Outside, there's a shady veranda and pool. B&B N$$

EATING

SEE MAP PAGE 189

Ongwari Café 96 Wilhelm Zeraua Street facebook.com/p/Ongwari-Café-Omaruru-100082840977430. An unlikely annex to the local pharmacy, this garden café is the nicest place for breakfast – English or German – lunch or an afternoon coffee and cake. The home-made bread and *brötchen* are great to accompany a selection of nicely prepared salads and schnitzels, pasta and pizza, plus the usual snacks.

The Erongo Mountains

4

Only a couple hours' drive northwest of Windhoek, the splendid rounded summits of the **Erongo Mountains** loom out of the landscape, a draw for hikers and those interested in San rock art. The eroded remains of a volcanic magma chamber that collapsed around 110 million years ago, the Erongos comprise vast granite domes – the highest ones in the west topping 2,200m (7,217.8ft) – and collections of boulders weathered into fascinating formations, which glow in the late afternoon light. With the Namib Desert to the west and semi-arid savannah to the east, they lie in an important transition zone and, therefore, host an impressive diversity of **plant and animal life**, including almost two hundred bird species. In addition to kudu, mountain zebra, klipspringer, steenbok and dik-dik, keep a look out for the rare black-faced impala and black mongooses, as well as the chattering rosy-faced lovebirds or the quieter Rüppell's parrots. Black rhinos have also been reintroduced in recent years.

ARRIVAL AND DEPARTURE

THE ERONGO MOUNTAINS

By car The only way to explore the Erongos is with your own vehicle. The main access road, the D2315, runs 60km (37.3 miles) east–west across the northern edges of the range, where it meets the north–south-running D1395, which gives access to the Erongos from the west, and connects with the B2, the main Windhoek–Swakopmund highway. The turn-off for the D2315, a good-quality gravel road, is on the C33, a couple of kilometres south of Omaruru. Several accommodation options are signposted off the D2315. After about 10km (6.2 miles) on this road, heading west from Omaruru, you pass through a conservancy gate, where you may need to give your details, but there is no charge.

ROCK ART IN THE ERONGOS

The Erongos are rich in **San rock paintings**; several of the guest farms and lodges in the area possess examples on their land and offer guided or self-guided walks to view them. As with most other San rock art, figures include animals and humans, seemingly engaged in hunting or rituals related to fertility and community harmony (see page 197). The most celebrated example is **Phillip's Cave**. Located on the land of the *Ameib Guesthouse* – which welcomes day visitors (charge) – it is known for its giant white elephant with a superimposed red antelope, among other identifiable animals: ostrich, giraffe, rhino and various human figures. The cave, a thirty-minute hike from the parking area, is an impressive overhang, affording extensive views across the desert plains.

ACCOMMODATION **SEE MAP PAGE 192**

★ **Ai-Aiba: The Rock Painting Lodge** North of the D2315, 38km (23.6 miles) west of the conservancy entrance gate ⓦaiaiba-namibia.com. Scenically set amongst piles of granite boulders, a dozen stylishly yet comfortably furnished thatched chalets gaze across the savannah. As the lodge name suggests, the big draw is the many San rock art sites on the property, but hiking and mountain biking (though surprisingly, you need to bring your own bike!) are also popular, with or without a guide. The food and service are top-notch. B&B and guided sundowner walk N$$$

Ameib Guesthouse At the end of the gravel D1937, 30km (18.6 miles) north of Usakos ⓦameib.com. Remote old farmhouse with nine no-frills doubles (renovated in 2019), plus a wholly solar-powered campground in truly spectacular scenery. There's abundant birdlife in the tree-filled grounds and a small pool. The fenced campground offers some shade and shared picnic tables, though each site has a braai. No electricity points. A couple of basic cement cabins are also available. Camping N$, cabins N$, doubles B&B N$$

★ **Camp Mara** Just off the D2315, 10km (6.2 miles) west of the conservancy entrance gate ⓦcampmara.com. This is a relaxed, informal place, with lots of character and five individually designed tasteful yet rustic rooms looking out at the thorn trees, where rosy-cheeked lovebirds and Rüppell's parrots flit around, and across to the impressive Erongo Mountains. The owner provides seeds for the birds daily around 8.30am, attracting three types of hornbills, but the lovebirds steal the show. Dinner is also available. Cash only. Camping N$, self-catering N$$$, double (B&B) N$$

Erongo Plateau Campsite On Guest Farm Eileen ⓦerongo.iway.na. Four pitches – so book ahead – on the edge of a slight plateau offer stunning views across the plains. There's no electricity but good hot showers, which you can take by candlelight, and a braai site and cement 'table', sheltered from the sometimes chilly wind. A 5km (3.1-mile) self-guided trail is available. A high-clearance vehicle is necessary. Wheelchair-accessible bathroom. Camping N$

Hohenstein Lodge 25km (15.5 miles) along the D1935 from the junction with the B2 ⓦhohensteinlodge.com. This lovely, simple lodge boasts fourteen squat rooms with private patios to enjoy superlative views of the Spitzkoppe and the Erongos. Guided hikes, birdwatching and sundowner drives are on offer. DBB N$$$

Omandumba On the D2315, 40km (24.9 miles) west of conservancy entrance gate ⓦomandumba.de. This place is spread over two farms, offering a range of accommodations in a warm, family environment. There are eight rustic old-style rooms, one self-catering bungalow (for six) and a basic bush camp: safari tents pitched under a shelter with patio and stone bathrooms at the back, which are rather overpriced. But the secluded camping pitches are the star attraction here, snuggled in among the boulders, with donkey-fired water, open-air toilet facilities, and a private braai site, but no electricity. Only four spots are available, so book ahead. A San living museum is on the property and open daily. Camping N$–$$, doubles DBB N$$$, bush camp N$$$$

Damaraland

In western Erongo, flattish semi-desert savannah stretches northwards, the horizon interrupted by the distinctive domed peak of the **Spitzkoppe**, much favoured by rock climbers. Beyond is the vast massif of the **Brandberg**, home to the country's finest collection of San rock paintings. This area is known as **Damaraland** – a colonial and apartheid-era term that has seemingly stuck – which comprises some of the country's most beguiling landscapes and is still predominantly inhabited by the Damara people, after whom it's named.

As you cross the ephemeral Ugab River – a linear oasis of luxuriant vegetation and a vital source of nourishment for elusive desert-adapted elephants – into **southern Kunene**, the undulating landscape becomes hauntingly beautiful. Expansive grasslands are interspersed with colourful escarpments of layered sediment and endless kopjes of burnished granite, embellished by the occasional dazzling white trunk of the five-lobed sterculia tree clinging onto a boulder. In the middle of all this is one of the continent's largest collections of ancient rock engravings at **Twyfelfontein**.

Spitzkoppe

On the D3176, 11km (6.8 miles) north from the turn-off from the D1918 • Day visitors should check-in and pay at the campground reception

One of Namibia's most recognisable landmarks and a magnet for rock climbers, the **Spitzkoppe** has been featured on the cover of many a holiday brochure. Its distinctive pointed peak – which has earned it the nickname, the Matterhorn of Africa – measures 1,728m (5,669.3ft) and towers around 700m (2,296.6ft) above the surrounding desert plains. This granite bornhardt – a bald, rounded, steep-sided inselberg – was formed about 130 million years ago through volcanic activity and shaped over time as its surroundings eroded, resulting in fascinating **rock formations**, including several rock arches. Its giant granite domes and exfoliating boulders glow like burnished gold in the late afternoon or early morning light.

Between the Spitzkoppe and the equally impressive neighbouring Pondoks, a fenced area holds a thinly stocked **game reserve** – which you can only visit with a guide – a remnant of when the Hollywood flop *10,000 BC* was filmed here. The hiking possibilities and the chance to see some fine examples of rock art are of much greater appeal. Sadly, the most well-known site, Bushman's Paradise, no longer lives up to its name, having been damaged by over-enthusiastic tourists and vandals; however, there are plenty more pristine rock paintings to discover in less accessible spots if you arrange to hike with a guide from the local Damara conservancy.

ARRIVAL AND TOURS — SPITZKOPPE

By car Turn north off the B2, 23km (14.3 miles) west of Usakos, onto the gravel D1918 bound for Henties Bay, then north 12km (7.5 miles) up the D3716.

By bus and hitching The nearest place a bus passes to the Spitzkoppe is the turn-off from the B2, 23km (14.3 miles) west of Usakos; any of the transport that runs between Windhoek and Swakopmund can drop you off, but from there, you'd have to hitch, and traffic is sparse.

Guided hikes Three strenuous guided hikes are available (4–8hr), which take in various rock art sites. Guides are all from the local community (and vary in quality) and should be booked at the campground reception. Costs are calculated for every two hours of guiding.

ACCOMMODATION — SEE MAP PAGE 192

Spitzkoppe Campsite Ⓦspitzkoppe.com. This back-to-nature community campground is now a joint venture with a private enterprise, so facilities are gradually being upgraded. Currently, 31 pre-bookable basic pitches are nestled among the boulders, offering varying degrees of seclusion and shade. There is no electricity, long-drop toilets, and no water-fill cans at the tap by the communal open-air showers adjacent to the costly bar restaurant.

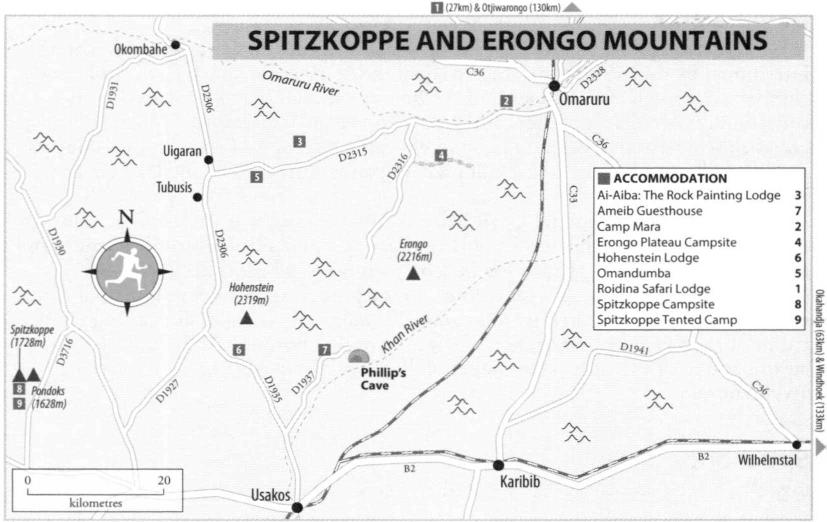

Here, you can book meals and purchase wood and braai packs. N$

Spitzkoppe Tented Camp In the Spitzkoppe reserve, 5km (3.1 miles) beyond the camp entrance Ⓦspitzkoppenlodge.com. A community venture, this modest, sensitively designed camp comprises a row of fifteen fan-ventilated tented chalets raised on stilts, each with a private porch so you can gaze across at the Spitzkoppe itself. Similar hiking and free-climbing activities at the campsite are available, plus mountain bike availability. The restaurant offers a great sunset view and a naturalistic rock pool to cool off in. N$$$$

The Brandberg

Namibia's most magnificent massif, the **Brandberg**, is visible from miles around, towering close to 2km (1.2 miles) above the desert plains and shimmering like a pink mirage through the heat haze. Not only a fabulous and little-explored **hiking** destination, the Brandberg is Namibia's pre-eminent site for **rock art**, boasting around nine hundred sites and 43,000 paintings and engravings, many in pristine condition.

Reaching 2,573m (8,441.6ft) at one point, the granite massif contains the highest peak in Namibia – **Königstein** – though its mass is equally impressive; formed from the eroded granite remains of a collapsed magma chamber over 130 million years ago, this almost circular inselberg measures nearly 140km (87 miles) round the base. Deep ravines slice through the rock in several places, where precious water collects and vegetation thrives.

The name Brandberg ('Fire Mountain' in German, and Dâures or 'Burning Mountain' in Damara) alludes to the glowing effect of the sun on the rock at sunrise and sunset. In contrast, the Otjiherero name – Omukuruvaro – means 'Mountain of the Gods', and indeed it is believed to have been a site of spiritual importance for the early San, whose art adorns its numerous overhangs, rock faces and even boulders. Archaeological remains also indicate that groups of migrating San often stayed in the Brandberg's upper reaches, probably drawn by the availability of shelter and water.

4

The 'White Lady'

At the end of the D2359, 20km (12.4 miles) from the junction with the C35 • Daily 8am–5pm • Charge; entry includes a guided walk

Most visitors to the Brandberg only venture as far as the **'White Lady'**, the area's most famous rock painting, which is tucked away beneath a rock overhang an easy 45-minute hike up the Tsisab Ravine on the northeastern side of the massif. The picture got its name from the mainly white central figure in a frieze that seems to depict some kind of procession, whom renowned rock art authority Henri Breuil, back in the 1940s, concluded was a woman. Later, scholars decided the figure was not a woman but probably a young man, possibly undergoing some initiation ritual or a traditional healer. Whatever the interpretation, the painting is worth a visit, even if its condition doesn't compare to some of the art secreted higher up the mountain.

Half the pleasure is the **walk** past Brandberg acacias, mustard and ironwood trees. Keen birdwatchers should aim for an early morning start, when you may be rewarded with a display of colour in the form of bee-eaters, rosy-cheeked lovebirds, Rüppell's parrots and bokmakieries.

ARRIVAL AND DEPARTURE — THE BRANDBERG

By car From the south – to access the 'White Lady' on the Brandberg's eastern flank – take the C35 north from Uis towards Khorixas; after 13km (8 miles), take the well-signposted turn-off west onto the D2359. From the north, take the C35 south from Khorixas. Access is possible in a saloon car and fuel is available in Uis.

ACTIVITIES AND TOURS

Guides Pay your entry fee to the staff member at the 'White Lady' entry kiosk, who will assign a guide from the Dâureb Mountain Guide Association, one of the country's more successful community-based tourism projects. It is appropriate to tip the guide if they do a good job.

Hiking If you want to do one of the multiday hikes up the Brandberg, you need to get the relevant permit from the National Heritage Council in Windhoek, at Lazarett House,

CLIMBING THE MASSIF

Though not a technical ascent – unless you want it to be – **climbing the Brandberg** is not a light undertaking. The heat is intense, you need to carry food, water and bedding, and the constant boulder scrambling gets tiring. Still, it's an unforgettable experience: the chance to sleep under the stars, peer at some stunningly vivid rock art that few people have seen in modern times, and truly feel on top of the world. However, you need to acquire a **permit** and hire a **guide** from the Heritage Council in Windhoek (see page 94) – an attempt by the government to regulate visitors and protect the rock art and the area's outstanding biodiversity, including many scorpion species. The guiding is generally excellent, undertaken by a member of the highly trained local conservancy guide association (see page 192).
The usual trip starts from Uis and lasts three days. Although the fee covers the site entrance, guiding, and food for the guide, some extra food to share would go down well. The first day, the most arduous, you hike and scramble up the mountain (6–8hr); the second day is spent exploring rock art sites and soaking up the jaw-dropping views before descending again on the third. Ascents of Königstein can also be organised. If you want to avoid the organisational hassle, some tour operators in Windhoek and Swakop can organise the trip.

on the corner of Lazarett Street (T 061 244375, E info@nhc–nam.org), usually giving two days' notice. However, the guiding association continues to push for the right to sell the permits on the spot.

ACCOMMODATION

SEE MAP PAGE 170

Ugab River Camp End of the D2303, northwest of the Brandberg T 064 403829; email reservations preferred but not essential: E srt@rhino-trust.org.na. Isolated, basic – think communal showers and long-drop toilets – wilderness camp in the dry riverbed, with some sites fenced off with reed partitions. You'll need to bring your own firewood and drinking water. The site is mainly used by four-wheel drive campers exploring the Messum Crater. Camping is currently free, but donations in aid of the Save the Rhino Trust (W savetherhinotrust.org) are appreciated. Beware of elephants.

Ugab Wilderness Camp 8km (5 miles) north of the D2359, 6km (3.7 miles) before the 'White Lady' T 081 336 3202. Well-managed community campground that can get busy in high season. Flush toilets and hot-water showers but no running water or electricity. Best of all, it is a magical location and a good place to start a hike up the Brandberg. Camping N$

★ **White Lady Lodge** Signed 27km (16.8 miles) off the D2359 W brandbergwllodge.com. This place is all about location: at the foot of the majestic Brandberg and on the banks of the scenic Ugab River, with a good chance of seeing desert elephants, especially in the dry season, when the lodge runs tours. Other than the nicely landscaped grounds, with two pools, everything's pretty rustic and tired in places: stone rooms and basic campground chalets. But the simple riverside campground (with safari tents if you want) is a nature lover's dream, spread out among huge ana trees. Be prepared for elephant visitors. The two tented 'tree houses' might feel safer in this respect. Four-wheel drive is necessary. DBB or bed-only rates are also possible. Camping N$$, safari tents (B&B) N$$, doubles, chalets and tree houses (B&B) N$$$

Uis

UIS, 30km (18.6 miles) southeast of the Brandberg, flourished for several decades as a town. The tin-mining industry prospered – the large slag heap that greets you when approaching the town from the south is a testament to that – but the dwindling population of around four thousand has struggled since the operation closed down in 1990. The ultimate insult came in 2010 when the place was downgraded from a village to a settlement. These days, there's a down-at-heel feel to the place, yet Uis still sees quite a lot of tourist traffic, stopping to refuel and calling in at the supermarket while travelling between the Spitzkoppe and the Brandberg. Should you wish to break the journey, there are some decent, inexpensive places to overnight here, including the *Brandberg Restcamp*, on the site of the mine's former recreation club.

ACCOMMODATION **UIS, SEE MAP PAGE 170**

Brandberg Restcamp Main road brandbergrestcamp.com. The star attraction of this otherwise no-frills rest camp is the glittering 25m (82ft) swimming pool in the central courtyard – a leftover from the local tin mine's recreational facilities. There are functional doubles (with fan or a/c), self-catering (up to six) and camping facilities. The bar-restaurant is decent enough and tours can be arranged through reception. Camping N$, self-catering N$$, doubles (room only) N$$

Daureb Isib Corner of 3rd Avenue and the golf course daurebisib.com. Pleasant five-pitch campground (plus one for overlander groups), each with private wood-and-palm shelter, table and chairs, braai site and ablutions, and a shared pool. There is also a simple stone two-bedroom fan-ventilated cottage. The on-site *Cactus and Coffee Tea Garden* (N$$) offers breakfasts, tasty savoury snacks and light bites as well as smoothies, cakes and coffee, and is surrounded by succulents from the ground's tree nursery. Camping N$, cottage N$$

White Lady Guesthouse & Campsite 3rd Avenue uiswhiteladyguesthouse.com. A neat and tidy guesthouse – nothing fancy, but with twelve simple thatched rooms with mosquito nets and a/c and a sheltered campground (twelve sites) set in a high-walled sandy yard. The small pool is a welcome bonus. Camping N$, doubles (B&B) N$$

Twyfelfontein and around

At the end of the D3214 • Daily 8am–5pm • Charge; entry includes a guided tour of the petroglyphs; more extended tours include the Zieben Plateau, the Organ Pipes and Burnt Mountain

At the head of the shallow Huab Valley in southern Kunene, large sandstone slabs that have broken off the flat-topped escarpment lie in jumbled piles, their smooth surfaces covered with one of the continent's greatest concentrations of **rock engravings**. They are collectively referred to as **TWYFELFONTEIN**, meaning 'uncertain spring' in Afrikaans, reflecting a farmer's fears about the local water source. However, the local Damara name |Ui-||Aes (meaning 'place among the rocks') is now also used in recognition of the earlier nomadic Damara communities that made seasonal use of the land. Many of the petroglyphs date back to six thousand years ago when San hunter-gatherers inhabited the region, drawn by the availability of water. Note that the name Twyfelfontein is also often used to refer to the general area, which encompasses several other geological curiosities; the **Organ Pipes** and **Burnt Mountain** are worth a quick detour if you've got your own transport and forty minutes to spare.

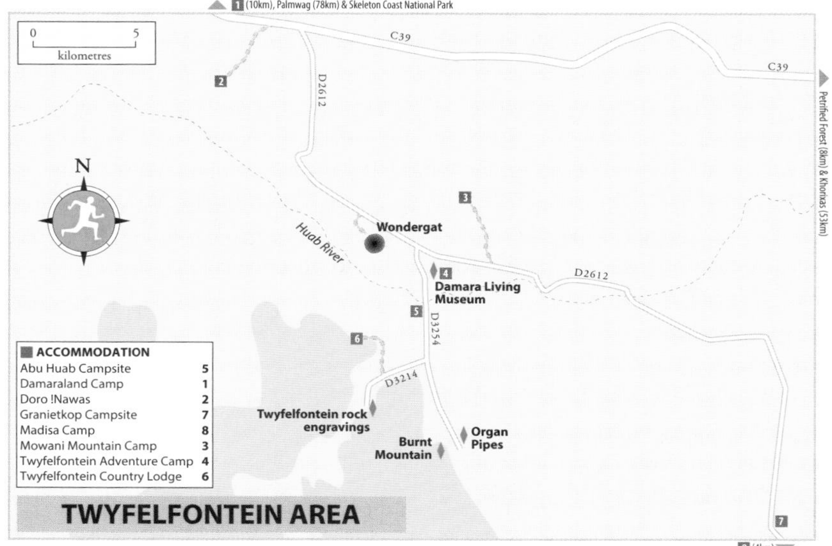

4

The rock engravings

An estimated 2,500–5,000 **rock carvings** and a few paintings were created, though the latter are not for tourist consumption and only a small proportion of the rock engravings can be visited. These predominantly depict humans or animals and animal spoor – including images displaying a mixture of animal and human features – as well as geometric shapes. The choice of **imagery** and the **siting** of the petroglyphs and paintings are now thought to relate to the belief systems, shamanic rituals and the spiritual world that shamans had access to while in a trance, rather than straightforward depictions of the world around them (see page 197).

As a UNESCO World Heritage Site, the rock engravings of Twyfelfontein are firmly on the tourist trail, attracting around fifty thousand visitors annually, so to miss the crowds and the heat, you should aim for early morning (though some of the rocks are in shadow then), or late afternoon when the light is at its best. Since there's no shade at the site, avoiding the midday sun, especially in summer, is imperative. To visit, you need to take a **guided tour**: the generally well-informed guides offer three circuits involving varying degrees of physical exertion, lasting thirty, sixty or eighty minutes. There is also an excellent information centre and a small café.

Damara Living Museum

On the D3214 • Daily 8am–5pm • Charge for 30min tour or tour & bushwalk • Ⓦ lcfn.info/damara/home

A few kilometres back up the valley is one of Namibia's living museums (see page 60): the **Damara Living Museum** gives some insight into traditional Damara skills, crafts and practices, though if a large tour group is visiting, it can make you squirm. The traditional village tour includes talks and demonstrations on blacksmithing, leather tanning, jewellery and other craft-making.

4

Organ Pipes

On the D3254 • Daily sunrise–sunset • Free • Coming from the rock art site at Twyfelfontein, turn right down the D3254, from where it's a 4km (2.5 mile) drive. Parking is on the left

The **Organ Pipes**, which, with a bit of imagination, vaguely resemble the eponymous church instrument, are actually two walls of densely packed polyhedral dolerite pillars at the bottom of a shallow sandy gorge. They make a good subject for photos – mid-morning and mid-afternoon are the best times to catch them. Peer over the edge of the parking area and you'll see the path that leads you down into the ravine.

Burnt Mountain

On the D3254 • Daily sunrise–sunset • Free • Coming from the rock art site at Twyfelfontein, turn right down the D3254, from where it's a 5km (3.1-mile) drive

A kilometre (0.6 miles) further along from the Organ Pipes, on the opposite side of the road, the **Burnt Mountain** can often be less impressive: the compacted shale resembles a bleak, black industrial slag heap for much of the day, though the manganese coating gives it a purplish hue in the early morning or late afternoon light, which, together with the golden glow of the neighbouring sandstone, can sometimes make the mountain appear to be on fire – hence the name.

Petrified Forest

Signposted north off the C39, 45km (28 miles) west of Khorixas • Daily 8am–6pm • Charge; entry includes 30–40min guided tour

If you're expecting something akin to a scene from *Lord of the Rings*, you will be disappointed, as the **Petrified Forest** is not a forest per se but a fascinating collection of some two hundred fossilised tree trunks, some fully exposed, others partly buried in sandstone – it's the most extensive collection in Southern Africa. Only two are almost full length, at around 45m (147.6ft); the rest are in segments, but they are incredibly lifelike – you can see the bark and even count the growth rings. The petrification process began over 200 million years ago, when the trees are thought to have been

SAN ROCK ART IN NAMIBIA

When you've climbed, scrambled and sweated your way over endless boulders in the hot afternoon sun and are finally confronted with a crumbling cave wall of barely discernible smudges and shapes, it's easy to wonder why so much fuss is made about **ancient rock art**. But when face to face with some of its more vivid depictions, it's hard not to be moved, especially considering the thousands of years it may have survived the elements.

Of course, interpreting the art helps deepen your appreciation, though theories come and go about what it all means and why it was done. More recent thinking, informed by anthropological work with existing San communities about their beliefs and ritual practices, considers most rock art related to **San religious cosmology**. Thus, what earlier theorists took to be straightforward representations of hunting scenes, interpreted as narratives of actual hunts or messages to other San groups about where to find food, are now thought to relate to rainmaking rituals, which involved animals, or to the symbolic association of particular beasts. The oft-represented eland, for example, was frequently led to a hilltop and sacrificed in the belief that rain would fall there; a buffalo may be the 'Rain Bull', controller of rain but also sickness and health and, therefore, a death deity. A cornerstone of San religious beliefs is the ability of the shaman to enter the spirit world through a **trance dance**, and many of the figures and scenes suggest their trance visions – understood as symbols and metaphors rather than literal depictions – probably linked to San mythology. The high number of half-animal and half-human paintings may relate to the widespread San **creation myth** that all animals were once human; alternatively, they may embody the physical transformation the shaman undergoes when entering the spirit world.

Rock art falls into two categories that are rarely found together: **rock paintings** (pictographs), for which the Brandberg is most renowned (see page 193), and **rock engravings** (petroglyphs), found in abundance in Twyfelfontein. Increasingly, the **context** of the art is considered to be significant: many paintings or engravings are located near fissures and crevices in the rock, which would serve as entrances to the spirit world; some paintings are situated in dark caves, where shamans were thought to concentrate their energies.

Not all rock art found in Namibia is of San origin: the Apollo 11 Cave, in the inaccessible Huns Mountains west of the Fish River Canyon – and one of the most ancient known sites in Africa, estimated to be around thirty thousand years old – is also thought to contain art by the **Khoikhoi**. Their art differed from that of the San, generally displaying more handprints, dots and geometric shapes, and drawn with their fingers rather than with brushes.

washed down the valley in a flood and buried in alluvial deposits. Over time, deprived of air and under extreme pressure, rather than decay, the trunks were permeated by aqueous silica, which gradually replaced the organic matter; then, as the water was lost, the wood was finally petrified.

On the compulsory **guided tour**, you'll also take in a number of welwitschia specimens (see page 218). Note that a few local entrepreneurs have also established their own petrified forest sites in the area, signposted off the C39, but this one has an official sign and operates with trained guides. A craft shop is also on site.

ARRIVAL — TWYFELFONTEIN

By car Twyfelfontein is at the end of the D3214, well signposted off the D2612, 73km (45.4 miles) west of Khorixas, off the C39. There's no public transport to the area.

Tourist information The information centre at the rock engravings site is the place to direct your enquiries.

ACCOMMODATION — SEE MAP PAGE 195

Abu Huab Campsite D3254, 2.6km (1.6 miles) south of the junction with the D2612 ⓣ 081 1290410, ⓔ abahuabreservation@iway.na. Located by the dry river of the same name, a short drive from Twyfelfontein, this community campground needs some investment. Apart from the main building, which boasts a bar with a pool table and one modern shower block, many pitches are rather run-down. Camping N$ (plus extra for the vehicle), tent and mattress provided, but no bedding N$$

Damaraland Camp 5km (3.1 miles) south of the C39, 2km (1.2 miles) west of the junction with the D2612 wilderness.co.za. Pioneering joint luxury venture with the local conservancy: ten raised chalets – a mix of adobe, thatch and canvas with all the usual Wilderness Safari comforts – in a scenic rocky location, with welwitschias down the riverbed. AI N$$$$

Doro !Nawas South Africa wilderness.co.za. Looming like a hilltop fort as you approach, the main building of this well-run wilderness camp offers panoramic views of the surrounding mountainscape. As convenient for self-drive visitors as for the more customary all-inclusive package clients, the place comprises sixteen spacious stone-and-canvas units under thatch, arranged at the foot of a kopje, with glass doors and veranda, where you can sleep under the stars. Activities include visiting Twyfelfontein – which you could easily do yourself – and tracking desert-adapted elephants. DBB N$$$$

★ **Granietkop Campsite** On the D2612, 45km (28 miles) east of Twyfelfontein 081 2006991 or 081 7273163. Four lovely private pitches in this community venture (now managed pro bono by Ultimate Safaris) are tucked beside a granite kopje with wonderful views across the mopane plains, though little shade. Donkey-fired hot water, individual ablutions, nicely made shower and flush toilet, and a shaded washing-up area. Reception is often unstaffed, but set up camp and someone will turn up eventually. N$

★ **Madisa Camp** On the D2612, 50km (31 miles) east of Twyfelfontein madisacamp.com. Set among mopane trees, nine individual pitches overlook the Gauntegab River, where desert elephants roam. You'll get the best view from your private, open-air shower-toilet on stilts, powered by a donkey, fired by your substantial braai hearth. Sites 5–9 offer greater privacy and less generator noise (6–9pm), though it's a longer walk to the bar and swimming pool area, nestled among the granite boulders. Meals on request. It also has simple safari tents for rent and cheaper dome tents with mattresses and linen at the overlander site. Camping N$, safari tents (tent only) N$$

★ **Mowani Mountain Camp** 3km (1.9 miles) north of the D2612 and 3km (1.9 miles) east of the junction with the D2354 chiwani.com. Blending in with the granite boulders, this tasteful, upmarket eco-lodge with a genuine commitment to community development comprises a dozen canvas-and-thatch rondavels. Comfortably furnished with colonial-style wicker and wood furniture, they also have viewing decks, some with spectacular vistas. Other attractions include intimate dining, a waterhole and a pool with a sundeck built into the rocks. Excursions to Twyfelfontein and guided hikes are on offer, as well as two- or three-night all-inclusive packages. A rustic campground is outside the main gate, without access to lodge facilities; seven sites have nice private cooking and washing facilities. Camping N$$, doubles (DBB) N$$$$

Twyfelfontein Adventure Camp Off the D2354, just south of the junction with the D2612 ondili.com/en/lodges-en. Conveniently situated east-facing camp nestled among the boulders of a large kopje, with accommodation and the central bar, dining and lounge area on raised decks affording great views of the glowing sun on the surrounding hills. Snug standard tents squeeze in two comfortable single beds with an open-air bathroom shower at the back. The larger superior tented chalets have semi-tiled bathrooms, lounge furniture and a more spacious viewing deck beyond the glass sliding doors. DBB. Standard tents N$$$, premium tents N$$$$

Twyfelfontein Country Lodge Huab Valley, 4km (2.5 miles) from Twyfelfontein twyfelfonteinlodge.com. You can't get any closer to the rock engravings than here – in fact, the place has rock art at the entrance – but you pay for the convenience. Pricey, rustic, high-ceilinged rooms (with fans) are arranged in blocks under thatch with shared terraces. The big plus is the raised, thatched bar-restaurant, dramatically set against the escarpment with great views, though at lunchtime, it can be overrun with tour groups – it's the only place to eat in the area – who pay tourist prices for average food. DBB N$$$$

Khorixas

Even when dusty **KHORIXAS** was the administrative centre of Damaraland before independence, it was never exactly throbbing with life. Since then, however, regional offices –with them, government jobs – have slowly been moving up to the new capital of the Kunene Region, Opuwo. Now more forlorn than ever, the town's six thousand–strong, mainly Damara population suffers from high levels of youth unemployment and its associated social ills. You don't need to stop long before being pestered by some desperate soul trying to flog a sub-standard curio you don't want. On the north side of the main tarred road on the eastern side of town, there's a small square hosting a supermarket, a bank and ATM as well as a petrol station – a busy pit stop for travellers heading north to Etosha, or west to Twyfelfontein.

ARRIVAL **KHORIXAS**

By minibus Weekend minibuses come from Henties Bay on Friday afternoons, returning on Sunday. Minibuses also leave for Windhoek when full from the petrol station/ supermarket area.

By car Khorixas lies on the C39, about 110km (68.4 miles) west of Outjo on a tarred road and about 80km (49.7 miles) east of Twyfelfontein on a good gravel road.

Information There is no tourist information office in Khorixas. Your best bet is to make enquiries at the reception in the *iGowati Country Hotel*.

ACCOMMODATION AND EATING **SEE MAP PAGE 170**

Damara Mopane Lodge 20km (12.4 miles) east of Khorixas, signposted off the C39 ⓦgondwana-collection.com. A large lodge comprising concentric semicircles of quaint rustic brick chalets with their own vegetable gardens tended to by folksy metal sculptures – providing for the buffet dinner. The chalets are set around a large mopane-studded pool area. B&B N$$$

iGowati Country Hotel Justus Garoeb Avenue ⓣ067 331592, ⓔigowati@afol.com. A surprisingly leafy oasis in the centre of town, adequate for an overnight stop: 29 rooms in two semicircular stone-and-thatch buildings overlooking the grassy pool area and semi-open *lapa* bar-restaurant, which can rustle up a reasonable steak, burger or pasta dish all day long. Camping sites, too, are popular with overlander groups. Camping N$, doubles (B&B) N$$

Ugab Terraces

Turning off south down the D2743, 52km (32.3 miles) east of Khorixas, takes you into the spectacular scenery of the **Ugab Terraces**. This broad, flat-bottomed valley, flanked by plateaus rising 160m (524.9ft) on either side, holds a collection of buttes and mesas – striking, steep-sided, flat-topped pillars of rock, reminiscent of Monument Valley in Arizona, so much so that you half expect John Wayne to appear on horseback at any moment. These harder sandstone conglomerate protrusions have been formed over the last 20 million years as the surrounding softer sedimentary deposits of the Ugab River floodplain have gradually been eroded. While the **Vingerklip** is as far as most people venture along this valley, it's worth completing the 68km (42.3-mile) semicircular detour along the D2743, which wends through picturesque mopane woodland.

4

Vingerklip

22km (13.7 miles) along the D2743, from the turn-off from the C49 • Charge; free if you're staying or eating at *Vingerklip Lodge* • Daily 8am–5pm

The best known of the Ugab Terraces is the 35m (114.8ft) high phallus known as the **Vingerklip** (Finger Rock), whose dramatic presence is enhanced by its location, perched precariously on top of a knoll. The rings on this butte, which has a 44m (144.4ft) circumference, tell a geological tale of rising and falling sea levels and the changing force of the Ugab River's flow that helped carve this natural sculpture.

ACCOMMODATION **UGAB TERRACES, SEE MAP PAGE 170**

Bambatsi Guest Farm 55km (34.2 miles) east of Khorixas, signposted north off the C39 (5km/3.1-mile track) ⓦbambatsi.com. Old-style guest farm on a fabulous hilltop, overlooking vast expanses of mopane woodland. Simple, no-frills painted brick bungalows with crazy-paving stone floors. Family-style dining inside or on the delightful plant-filled terrace, you'll also be treated to afternoon tea and cake. Also, there are two basic campsites – you pay slightly more for the hilltop one. Camping $, doubles (DBB) N$$$

Ugab Terrace Lodge Signposted off the D2743, 14km (8.7 miles) south of the turn-off from the C39 ⓦugabterracelodge.com. Crowning one of the terraces, this place has stunning views: from your private chalet terrace (eight offer sunrise view, eight sunset view) or the vast restaurant deck overlooking the Vingerklip, or even the gorgeous pool, set in the rock. For the more active, there are hiking and mountain bike trails (bikes not provided) and even a zipline, but you'll have to descend the terrace to participate. Three campsites lie amid giant boulders and mopane trees at the escarpment foot. Camping N$, chalets (B&B) N$$$

★ **Vingerklip Lodge** On the D2743, 22km (13.7 miles) south of the turn-off from the C39 ⓦvingerklip.com.na. It is a delightfully relaxing spot with thatched chalets dotted over a hillside among rock gardens full of succulents.

The chalets (with a/c) are cosy: chock-full of furniture and artwork (though overdosing on chrome and with small bathrooms), they afford mesmerising views from the private stone patios – topped only by the one from the *Eagle's Nest* restaurant, a short hike up the hillside to build up an appetite. The less mobile or energetic can hang out in the regular bar-restaurant by reception, which is popular with day-trippers. For pure indulgence, book the sublime Heaven's Gate luxury chalet on top of a terrace, with surround glass to maximise the panorama, plus a private plunge pool. Lodge visitors get to stroll to the Vingerklip for free. DBB N$$$

Kamanjab

Little more than a glorified crossroads, **KAMANJAB** has seen an increase in tourist traffic since the Galton Gate on the west side of Etosha opened up to the public in 2014. With two petrol stations and a couple of well-provisioned general stores – not to mention a handy break-down mechanic – it's a place to restock and refuel before driving north into the national park or beyond to the Kaokoveld or west into Damaraland. Note that the ATMs here are unreliable.

ACCOMMODATION **KAMANJAB, SEE MAP PAGE 170**

Huab Lodge 32km (19.9 miles) down the D2670, signposted off the C35, midway between Khorixas and Kamanjab huab.com. Wonderful wilderness spot off the tourist trail, on the banks of the ephemeral Huab River, sometimes frequented by desert elephants. The owner-managed lodge provides eight glorious brick-and-thatch chalets with private patios. Top-notch guiding (for guided hikes or drives), cuisine – dining family-style in the cavernous main *lapa* – and a hot spring to soak in, plus a telescope for stargazing. It's worth staying at least two nights. AI rates are also available. DBB N$$$$

★ **Oppi Koppi** 29 Gemsbok St oppi-koppi-kamanjab.com. The undistinguished chalet exteriors belie surprisingly comfortable twin-bed or family-size rooms with kettle, tea/coffee, fridge and a/c. The campsites have electricity and you can buy wood, ice and braai packs on site. Nice à la carte bar-restaurant under a *lapa* by a welcome pool. Camping N$, chalets (B&B) N$$–$$$

Northern Damaraland

Leaving the Huab Valley of Twyfelfontein, the well-graded C39 heads northwards into what is generally called **NORTHERN DAMARALAND**. The first half of the

WILDLIFE OF NORTHERN DAMARALAND

Though lacking the large numbers of Etosha, further east, **northern Damaraland** nevertheless has plenty of **wildlife** to seek out. Above all, it is associated with the proudly cited statistic of possessing the world's largest number of **free-roaming black rhinos** (see page 9). Several lodges offer whole-day excursions to try and track these magnificent beasts. However, you should bear in mind that the emphasis is always on rhino conservation rather than tourist satisfaction: human interference is kept to a minimum, and so, even assuming your guide manages to locate one, you may not get as close to a rhino as you would in a national park or private reserve. **Desert-adapted elephants** are sparsely scattered across the area (more visible in the dry season, as they seek out water holes in the dry riverbeds); **giraffes** are also sighted, and, very rarely, desert-adapted **lions**. You'll commonly come across hardy oryx, springbok, Hartmann's mountain zebra, klipspringer, kudu, steenbok and possibly hyenas. However, in the eastern fringes, nearer Kamanjab, you should keep your eyes peeled for the near-endemic **black-faced impala**. Cheetahs and leopards are in evidence, but rarely glimpsed, in the uplands further inland. Bird lovers will be keen to spot Monteiro's hornbill (see page 44) or Rüppell's korhaan strutting across the gravel plains. Meanwhile, the rockier hillsides and escarpments are prime raptor territory, featuring imperious Verreaux's (black) eagles.

82km (51-mile) drive to **Palmwag** is exceptionally scenic, as the road is framed by flat-topped escarpments, shored up by the odd unexpected dune. This striking landscape is part of the Etendeka Plateau, one of the planet's largest sheets of ancient lava, which extends as far north as the Hoanib River at **Sesfontein** and was formed millions of years ago when, following the break-up of Gondwanaland, the South Atlantic opened up and spewed forth volcanic rocks. Different hardness among the basaltic layers resulted in stepped plateaus, as the surrounding semi-desert plains were eroded. About halfway to Palmwag, the C39 peels west to the Skeleton Coast and the C43 takes up the baton. At Palmwag – essentially a road junction in a relatively featureless patch of semi-desert plain but with a crucial petrol station – the road divides; east takes you over the dramatic Grootberg Pass on the C40, towards Kamanjab some 115km (71.5 miles) away, whereas the C43 crosses the veterinary fence, travelling a similar distance northward, to the next sizeable settlement at Sesfontein. On the way, you pass through the sparsely populated communities of **Khowarib** and **Warmquelle**, which offer a few campsites and one very agreeable lodge between them.

Palmwag and around

Just under 500 sq km (193 sq miles) of the **Palmwag Concession** (pronounced 'Palumvag') spread westwards towards the Skeleton Coast, a stark and, at times, bleak semi-desert wilderness of reddish-brown rock-strewn earth dotted with euphorbias and distant plateaus. The southern entrance to the reserve coincides with the veterinary fence, where you can fill up at the adjacent petrol station and grab a drink at the shop.

4

ACCOMMODATION

PALMWAG AND AROUND, SEE MAP PAGE 170

Desert Rhino Camp 15km (9.3 miles) southwest of Palmwag wilderness.co.za. As the name indicates, the draw here is black rhino tracking (in partnership with the Black Rhino Trust, so you will keep your distance), though birding and guided walks are also on offer, with the usual high standard of service, cuisine and accommodation, in eight classy, elevated Meru-style safari tents with decks where you can gaze at the expansive desert vistas. AI N$$$$

★ Etendeka Mountain Camp 10km (6.2 miles) north of Palmwag etendeka-namibia.com. Set in the rock-strewn foothills of the Grootberg massif, this award-winning owner-managed eco-camp seeks to minimise its environmental footprint, so you'll need to eschew some comforts: accommodation in ten no-frills, old-style Meru safari tents with a couple of beds, camp chairs, and a solar-heated outdoor bucket shower. The small pool is the only real concession to 'luxury'. Expect bush camping over a fire, top-quality guiding about flora and fauna, and stargazing through a telescope. AI N$$$$

★ Grootberg Lodge South Off the C40, 23km (14.3 miles) east of Palmwag grootberg.com. This community-owned lodge is all about the view, which is breathtaking – though it can be windy – perched on the plateau edge, which plunges into the Klip River valley. Sixteen pleasant stone-and-thatch chalets are ranged along the precipice, with a communal bar-dining area, which is a tad short of space when full. Steep access road – you can get picked up at the bottom if you're unsure of driving. Various excursions, including rhino or desert elephant tracking (extra charge), are available. DBB N$$$$

★ Hoada Campsite 8km (5 miles) south of the C40, 40km (24.9 miles) east of Palmwag hoadacampsite.com. Community campground administered by *Grootberg Lodge*. It is a fabulous spot amid giant granite boulders and mopane woodland, with a pool carved out of the rock. Each of the six private sites has a toilet and outdoor shower with braai-heated donkeys. Also, two sites for larger groups, four tents with beds and bedding for a spot of glamping, and a light breakfast and braai pack included. Desert-adapted elephants and rhinos are occasionally sighted, and the campsite offers culturally guided walks around the Damara conservancy. Camping (own tent) N$–$$, equipped tent (B&B) N$$

Palmwag Lodge 6km (3.7 miles) along the C43 after the junction with the C40 palmwaglodge.com. This is a fabulous oasis by a spring in the Uniab River – where elephants visit – in a rather desolate plain. It is a popular lunch stop so the pleasant pool-bar restaurant can get busy. When Gondwana took over in 2019, they brightened up the previously gloomy thatched stone chalets, adding a/c. Well-equipped self-catering safari2go tents were a further addition. The guiding is top-notch and you can camp out in the wild for a night in the Palmwag Conservancy or go rhino tracking on foot. Great campsites with private ablutions overlook the riverbed. Camping N$, chalets (B&B) N$$$

Khowarib and Warmquelle

Eleven kilometres (6.8 miles) apart, along the C43, south of Sesfontein, in the small, predominantly Damara and Herero settlements of **Khowarib** and **Warmquelle**, respectively, you can find some simple community campgrounds and one standout lodge. Both communities lie on the ephemeral Hoanib River, with Khowarib enjoying a more imposing setting at the mouth of the Khowarib Gorge, where the dense aquifer lying close to the surface nurtures large mopane trees and attracts various large animals, including the local cattle, searching for water. The attraction in Warmquelle, 11km (6.8 miles) further north, as the name indicates – 'Quelle' meaning 'spring' in German – is the spring-fed **Ongongo Waterfall**, which tumbles over a rock into an idyllic crystalline pool, a great place to cool off on a scorching day. The local community runs a campground here but also accepts day visitors. A small store and a bakery are other points of potential interest on the main road.

ACCOMMODATION

KHOWARIB AND WARMQUELLE, SEE MAP PAGE 170

Khowarib Community Campsite Just beyond the Khowarib Lodge ⓣ 081 4079539. Well situated just above the riverbed, with the first plot boasting the best views. Wood-thatch shelters provide shade, and donkeys heat the private showers. Braai sites. Camping N$

Khowarib Lodge 1km (0.6 miles) east of the C43 at Khowarib ⓦ khowarib.com. Delightful location by a spring-fed river towered over by cliffs, with comfortable, rustic tented chalets possessing lovely open stone bathrooms and private shady decks – great for birdwatching. The main terrace offers atmospheric alfresco dining, a fire pit with cushions for evening relaxation and a grassed, shaded pool area. Service is friendly and efficient, dining is good and the place offers worthwhile half- or full-day excursions, from a couple of hours birding to a full-day tracking rhinos, but the place is expensive compared to similar lodges. Campers can use the lodge facilities if the place isn't full. Camping N$, chalets (DBB) N$$$$

Mbakondja River Campsite Signposted off the C43, 50km (31 miles) north of Palmwag. Rudimentary campground down a rocky track, offering little shade but warm hospitality from a Damara–Herero family for whom the campsite is a lifeline. Traditional cow-dung-and-adobe open-air ablutions. Camping N$

Ongongo Waterfall Campsite Warmquelle, 6km (3.7 miles) off the C43; turn east north of the Independence Bar, past the football pitch and then follow the pipeline ⓦ ongongo.com. This sprawling community campsite boasts nine luxury sheltered pitches, down by the luscious reed-encircled spring, which attracts good birdlife. Each has private ablutions with hot showers and a nice shaded area. The place is great when the water's flowing but less appealing when it's really low. Note that day visitors are also welcome, which can mean it's a little overcrowded in peak season. Camping N$$

Sesfontein and around

Marking the northernmost limit of Damaraland and serving as the gateway to the Kaokoveld, **SESFONTEIN** – named after six nearby springs – lies roughly midway between Palmwag and Opuwo, the regional capital of the Kunene Region. This pleasantly relaxed, if slightly soporific place, on the banks of the ephemeral Hoanib River, is home to a mix of around seven thousand Herero, Damara, Himba and Owambo people. The old German fort, set among tall wafting palm trees, is the main attraction for visitors. Following the rinderpest epidemic, the Germans initially set up a series of checkpoints in the north, of which Sesfontein was the most westerly, to control stock movement. However, they were then used to monitor illegal arms smuggling and poaching. The fort's days as a military station were limited, however, as it was handed over to the police a few years later and then abandoned altogether in 1914. Its new lease of life came just before independence when it was faithfully restored to become a hotel. It's an ideal spot to stop off for lunch, and the fuel station at its entrance is the only one for over 100km (62.1 miles).

ACCOMMODATION

SESFONTEIN AND AROUND, SEE MAP PAGE 170

Camel Top Camping Signposted off the main road 2km (1.2 miles) west of town ⓣ 081 7766076. Probably the best basic camping options, this community-run venture offers six well-spaced, simple, shady sites with electricity and hot water. Open-air rustic showers and a braai site (no grill); accessible by two-wheel drive. Camping N$

Fort Sesfontein Lodge Just off the main road as you enter the town fort-sesfontein.com. A well-restored hundred-year-old fort with a dozen cool rooms containing wood and rattan furniture opened onto a shady palm- and bougainvillea-filled courtyard. Dine in the former officers' mess or on the terrace by the large swimming pool. Half- or full-day tours are offered. B&B N$$$

Hoanib Skeleton Coast Camp Border of the Skeleton Coast Park around 75km (46.6 miles) west-south-west of Sesfontein wilderness.co.za. Wilderness Safari's latest luxury offering: a stunning, exclusive camp with state-of-the-art, modern safari tents in a unique wilderness environment on the Hoanib River, bordering the Skeleton Coast National Park. Three-day stays include a trip to the coast. Fine dining, efficient service, top-notch guiding and an unforgettable experience, but it doesn't come cheap. AI N$$$$

Hoanib Valley Camp 40km (24.9 miles) southwest of Sesfontein naturalselection.travel. Like Wilderness Safari's camp 'downriver', this exclusive new camp boasts a handful of solar-powered eco-luxury tents. Despite the remoteness, there's still a high degree of comfort and pampering. Still, the emphasis is on quality guiding and tracking large desert-adapted beasts, including giraffes, as it's a joint venture with the Giraffe Conservation Foundation. AI rates available. DBB N$$$$

Zebra Restcamp Main road 1km (0.6 miles) west of town 081 614 1410, zebrarestcampcc@gmail.com. Four basic, sandy sites under good shade, a fire pit but no grill, and solar-powered showers and toilets that could be better maintained. Camping N$

4

The central coast and hinterland

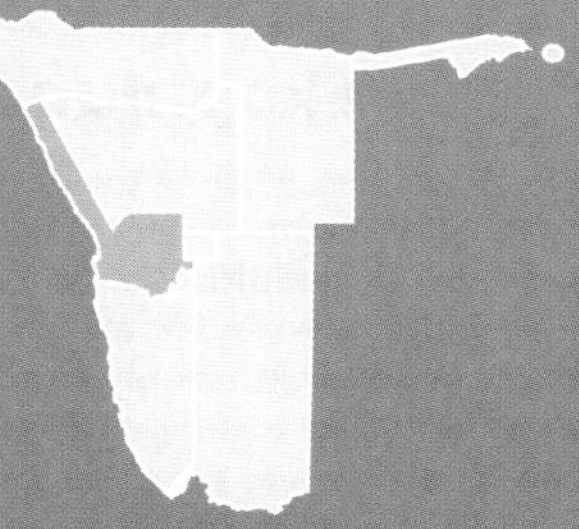

THE DUNES AT NAMIB-NAUKLUFT NATIONAL PARK

5

The central coast and hinterland

It's along Namibia's central coast that visitors can make the most of what the country offers, from exploring desert and marine wildlife to visiting former townships and rural communities and from road trips through dramatic coastal landscapes to a host of adrenaline-pumping adventure sports. All these activities can be enjoyed in the colonial-era towns of Swakopmund and Walvis Bay. Both can be reached from Windhoek in under four hours via the tarred B2 that follows the railway line west, passing through the former mining towns of Karibib and Usakos. Yet far more scenic back routes take you via the dramatic, tortuous Gamsberg or Bosua passes, dropping down onto the flat gravel plains of the Namib, affording opportunities to stop off at a hospitable guest farm or a wilderness campground along the way.

Around 350km (217.5 miles) west of Windhoek, the pretty seaside resort of **Swakopmund**, with its German colonial architecture and moderate coastal climate, has long been a holiday playground. Boasting comfortable accommodations, excellent cafés and restaurants and a relaxed vibe, it has more recently acquired a reputation as a centre for adventure activities. In contrast, **Walvis Bay**, a thirty-minute drive down the road, is Namibia's main port, home to a vibrant fishing industry, though its wildlife-rich lagoon is now the focus of a burgeoning tourist scene.

Both towns are surrounded by stunning dune scenery – some of which lies within the northern section of the **Namib-Naukluft National Park** and the contiguous, newly formed Dorob National Park – which can be explored in any number of ways: on the back of a camel, a horse or a quad bike, or from the air, either in a plane or skydiving out of one. Popular destinations include the fabulously isolated dune-enclosed **Sandwich Harbour**, an avian paradise south of Walvis Bay. Equally appealing is **Welwitschia Drive**, just outside Swakopmund, which takes in a variety of desert landscapes, as well as one of the planet's oldest specimens of the eponymous plant (see page 218). Further north, the mythical **Skeleton Coast** stretches 680km (422.5 miles) to the Angolan border. Most visitors only go as far as Namibia's largest seal colony at **Cape Cross**, 120km (74.6 miles) north of Swakopmund. Still, with your own wheels and a permit, you can head inland to explore the otherworldly **Messum Crater** or follow the coast road another 200km (124.3 miles) to experience the desolate desert landscapes of the Skeleton Coast National Park.

Swakopmund and around

Wandering along the orderly main streets, past half-timbered colonial-era buildings and pavement cafés, where German is spoken at every turn, it's easy to see how **SWAKOPMUND** – or Swakop, to use its more familiar name – is sometimes jokingly referred to as 'Germany's most southerly Baltic seaside resort'. German-Namibians may constitute only a small percentage of the town's 45,000 population, but German influence is still omnipresent in Namibia's only real **seaside resort**. However, you only need to gaze across the dry Swakop River at the rippling golden dunes or experience a savage sandstorm on a winter morning to be brought back to the more defining presence of the desert. Indeed, the recent exploitation of this desert – and the dunes

FLAMINGOS AT WALVIS BAY

Highlights

❶ **Colonial architecture** Take a stroll around central Swakopmund and check out the colonial-era buildings that still abound. See page 209

❷ **Adrenaline activities** There are endless ways to set your pulse racing in this unique desert landscape, from sandboarding to skydiving, quad biking to paragliding. See page 214

❸ **Seafood dining with sundowners** Both Walvis Bay and Swakopmund have their share of excellent seafood restaurants; the fresh fish is best enjoyed with a cocktail in hand as you watch the sunset. See pages 217 and 224

❹ **Explore desert ecology** Head out into the dunes and gravel plains with a knowledgeable guide and learn about Namibia's 'Small Five'. See page 219

❺ **Walvis Bay Lagoon** Get close to nature as you kayak among playful seal pups and marvel at diving pelicans. See page 222

❻ **Sandwich Harbour** Towering dunes meet crashing Atlantic waves on this exhilarating trip to an avian wetland paradise. See page 224

❼ **Wilderness camping** Head into the northern section of the Namib-Naukluft National Park to soak up the expansive desert vistas and eerie silence, with only the odd Cape fox or jackal for company. See page 232

HIGHLIGHTS ARE MARKED ON THE MAP ON PAGE 208

5

in particular – as a location for adventure activities- is helping attract more foreign tourists and a younger crowd.

Though midweek in winter, Swakopmund can seem like a ghost town; the place comes alive in the summer holidays (Dec–Jan) when half of Windhoek decamps here to enjoy the **cooler coastal climes** and get some respite from the hot desert interior. The downside is that guesthouse rooms and restaurant tables are hard to come by. At other times of the year, the place is less busy, though long weekends can attract crowds too.

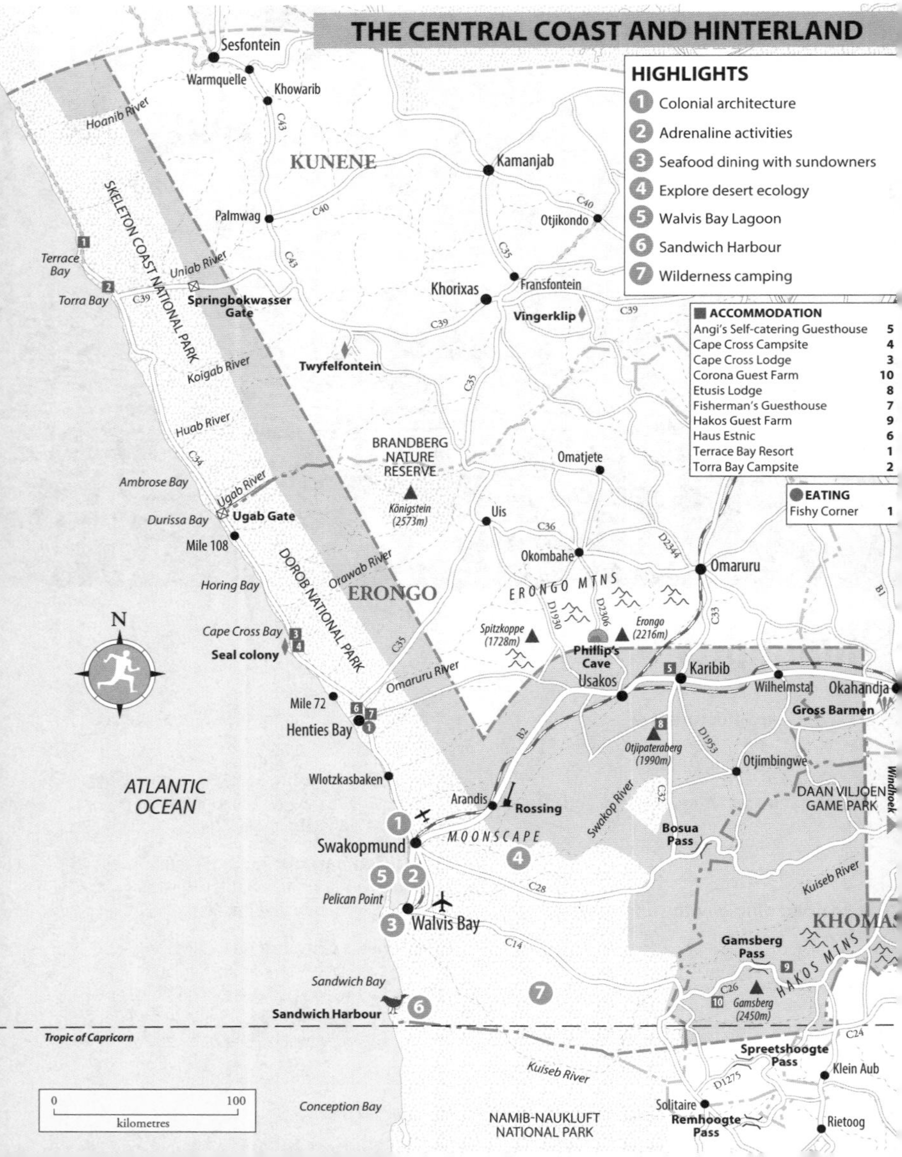

Brief history

Swakopmund is a corruption of the Khoekhoen Tsoaxub-ams (*ams* and *mund*, meaning 'mouth') – a clear indication that Indigenous people had been passing through the area long before the first colonisers put down their roots. Yet Germany's desire to establish an alternative port to Lüderitz led to the establishment of Swakopmund as a permanent settlement. Since the natural harbour of Walvis Bay had already been grabbed by the British, the Germans were forced to look elsewhere for a port, finally opting for a site at the **Swakop River mouth** – a decision based more on the presence of freshwater than because it afforded any protection to boats. Undeterred, in 1892, a German gunboat, the *Hyäna*, landed, and a couple of beacons were erected on the shore, officially founding Swakopmund. However, the first arrivals had to dig themselves shelters on the beach until the barracks had been built. The tricky part, which soon became apparent, was to achieve an effective trade link between the coast and German interests in the interior. The impractical hauling of goods by ox-cart across the desert was dealt a final hammer blow by the rinderpest epidemic (see page 341), underlining the need to construct a railway between Swakopmund and Windhoek. The loss of livestock due to the rinderpest forced many Black Namibians from the north to seek waged labour further south, where many were forced to work in appalling conditions on the railway. Within five years, it was complete, and in 1902, the first train from Swakopmund rolled into Windhoek.

The new port, however, had numerous teething problems: failure to consider the longshore drift meant that it soon silted up. A wooden jetty was constructed in 1906, a few hundred metres down the shore, but that scarcely lasted any longer, and work on a metal replacement began in 1911, only to be curtailed by the outbreak of **World War I**. Following the German surrender to the South Africans in 1915, the town's fortunes slumped as all maritime trade was transferred to Walvis Bay. The advent of **apartheid** led to the creation of the former 'Black' and 'Coloured' townships of **Mondesa** and **Tamariskia**, respectively. The town had to wait until the 1970s and the start of operations at the Rössing uranium mine, around 60km (37.3 miles) inland before its economic prospects began to improve. **Tourism**, too, began to take off in a small way and is now a significant source of income for many local residents.

The town centre

Despite the proliferation of informal settlements and low-cost housing, not to mention smart holiday homes, extending northwards, the town centre of Swakopmund remains small. It centres on the main **shopping street**, Sam Nujoma Avenue, and a few blocks on either side and ends at the **seafront** with the town's delightful ocean promenade, where the evenly spaced palm trees stand to attention. The hub of seafront activity is the recently revamped **Mole** – the colonial-era sea wall now topped with a swanky hotel and smart restaurants that protect the only safe, if cold, swimming spot at Palm Beach. Behind is the lighthouse, built a mere 11m (36ft) high in 1902 but given an extra 10m (32.8ft) a few years later. The building beside it, constructed at the same time, is the Kaiserliches Bezirksgericht; this was originally the district magistrate's court and is now the president's official residence when visiting. Below, the **craft market** offers a bewildering selection of woodcarvings, whereas a short stroll southward takes you past the renovated original jetty and down to the beach overlooking the Swakop River mouth, which marks the southern boundary of the town. One of the most impressive colonial buildings in the town centre is the **Höhernzollen building**, on the corner of Tobias Hanyeko and Libertina Amathila, a neo-Baroque colonial pile topped with an image of Atlas holding up the planet; it served as a hotel for much of the German colonial era.

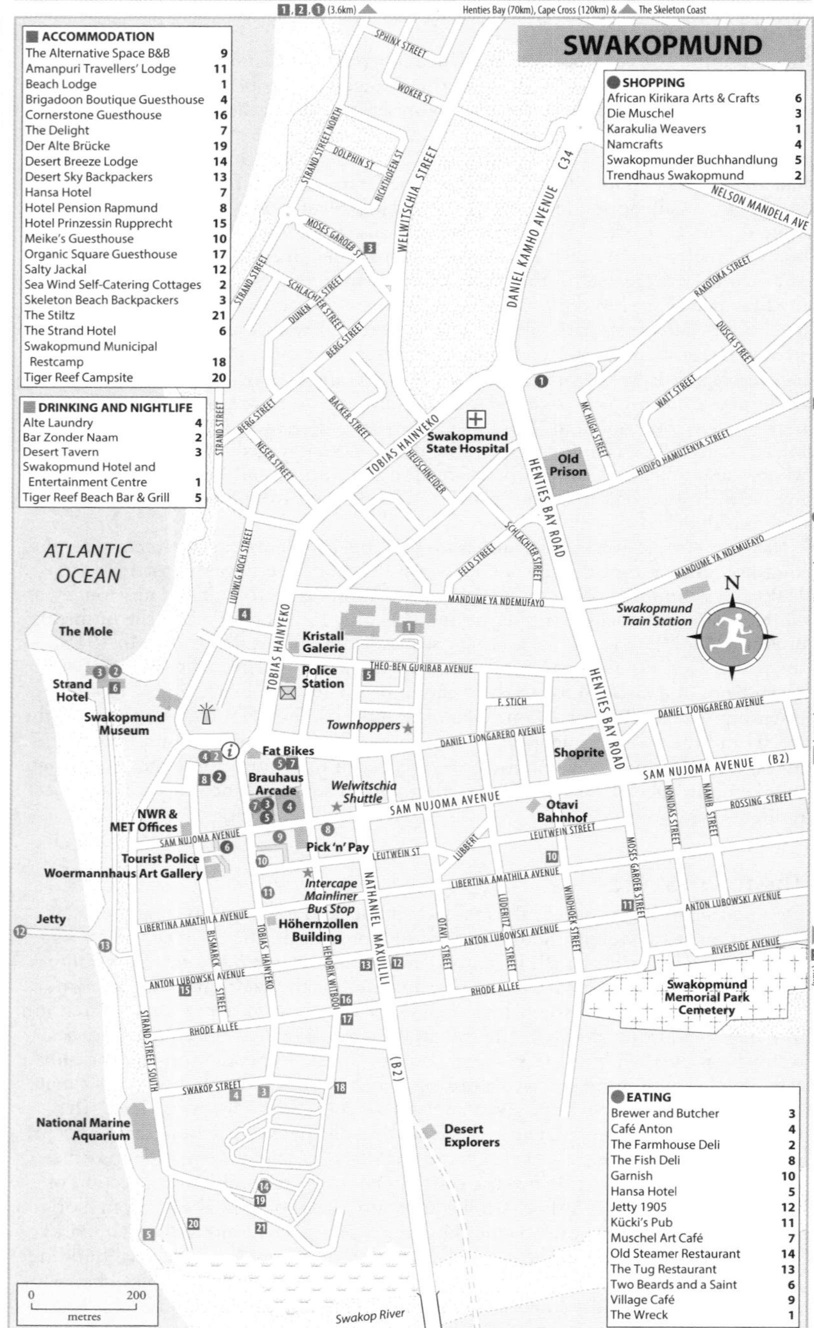
SWAKOPMUND
ACCOMMODATION
The Alternative Space B&B 9
Amanpuri Travellers' Lodge 11
Beach Lodge 1
Brigadoon Boutique Guesthouse 4
Cornerstone Guesthouse 16
The Delight 7
Der Alte Brücke 19
Desert Breeze Lodge 14
Desert Sky Backpackers 13
Hansa Hotel 7
Hotel Pension Rapmund 8
Hotel Prinzessin Rupprecht 15
Meike's Guesthouse 10
Organic Square Guesthouse 17
Salty Jackal 12
Sea Wind Self-Catering Cottages 2
Skeleton Beach Backpackers 3
The Stiltz 21
The Strand Hotel 6
Swakopmund Municipal Restcamp 18
Tiger Reef Campsite 20
DRINKING AND NIGHTLIFE
Alte Laundry 4
Bar Zonder Naam 2
Desert Tavern 3
Swakopmund Hotel and Entertainment Centre 1
Tiger Reef Beach Bar & Grill 5
SHOPPING
African Kirikara Arts & Crafts 6
Die Muschel 3
Karakulia Weavers 1
Namcrafts 4
Swakopmunder Buchhandlung 5
Trendhaus Swakopmund 2
EATING
Brewer and Butcher 3
Café Anton 4
The Farmhouse Deli 2
The Fish Deli 8
Garnish 10
Hansa Hotel 5
Jetty 1905 12
Kücki's Pub 11
Muschel Art Café 7
Old Steamer Restaurant 14
The Tug Restaurant 13
Two Beards and a Saint 6
Village Café 9
The Wreck 1
1, 2, 1 (3.6km)
Henties Bay (70km), Cape Cross (120km) & The Skeleton Coast
Mondesa (1km)
9 (1km), Martin Luther (1km), 6 (2km), Airport (4km), Welwitschia Drive & Windhoek (352km)
14 (1km)
Langstrand (20km) & Walvis Bay (35km)
ATLANTIC OCEAN
The Mole
Strand Hotel
Swakopmund Museum
NWR & MET Offices
Tourist Police
Woermannhaus Art Gallery
Jetty
National Marine Aquarium
Kristall Galerie
Police Station
Townhoppers
Fat Bikes
Brauhaus Arcade
Welwitschia Shuttle
Pick 'n' Pay
Intercape Mainliner Bus Stop
Höhernzollen Building
Desert Explorers
Swakopmund State Hospital
Old Prison
Swakopmund Train Station
Shoprite
Otavi Bahnhof
Swakopmund Memorial Park Cemetery
Swakop River
SPHINX STREET
WOKER ST
STRAND STREET NORTH
DOLPHIN ST
RICHTHOFEN ST
WELWITSCHIA STREET
DANIEL KAMHO AVENUE
C34
NELSON MANDELA AVE
MOSES GAROEB ST
STRAND STREET
SCHLACHTER STREET
DUNEN STREET
BERG STREET
RAKOTOKA STREET
DUSCH STREET
BACKER STREET
NESER STREET
TOBIAS HAINYEKO
HEUSCHNEIDER
MC HUGH STREET
WATT STREET
HIDIPO HAMUTENYA STREET
HENTIES BAY ROAD
FELD STREET
MANDUME YA NDEMUFAYO
LUDWIG KOCH STREET
THEO-BEN GURIRAB AVENUE
F. STICH
DANIEL TJONGARERO AVENUE
SAM NUJOMA AVENUE
(B2)
NONIDAS STREET
NAMIB STREET
ROSSING STREET
LEUTWEIN STREET
LEUTWEIN ST
LUBBERT
LIBERTINA AMATHILA AVENUE
ANTON LUBOWSKI AVENUE
RIVERSIDE AVENUE
NATHANIEL MAXUILILI
OTAVI STREET
LUDERITZ STREET
WINDHOEK STREET
BISMARCK STREET
HENDRIK WITBOOI
RHODE ALLEE
STRAND STREET SOUTH
SWAKOP STREET
N
0 200 metres

Swakopmund Museum

Strand Street South • Daily 10am–5pm • Charge • ⓦ en.sciswk.com/swakopmund-museum

Housed in an old customs warehouse, the excellent **Swakopmund Museum** has plenty to keep you busy for at least a couple of hours. As well as the standard museum fare, such as displays of Namibia's mineral wealth, desert flora and fauna – including the inevitable taxidermy specimens – and German military memorabilia, there are more surprising exhibits, such as a vast collection of model cars and a selection of 1930s Shell furniture – so-called because it was crafted from old paraffin and petroleum packing crates – mainly used by impecunious colonial newlyweds. Above all, the artefacts and photographs document **German colonial life**, including a few period rooms, reproducing the interior of a house, an apothecary and a dental surgery, complete with vicious-looking implements, made all the more scary by the thought that anaesthetic was not available at the time.

To offset the heavy colonial bias of these collections, an interactive **ethnology** wing focuses on the history and culture of Namibia's main ethnic groups. Importantly, information is also given in Indigenous languages, not just colonial ones. Among the artefacts, look out for the Kavango sand sledge, the San oracle discs – thrown to determine the direction of a hunt – and the twin horn-and-leather 'cosmetic boxes' of the Himba women, containing the necessary ochre and butter fat they mix to produce their body 'make-up' (see page 254).

Woermannhaus Art Gallery

Bismarck Street, between Sam Nujoma and Libertina Amathila avenues • Daily 10am–noon, Mon–Fri 3–5pm • Free; donations appreciated • ⓔ info@artswakopmund.com

Half the joy of visiting the **Woermannhaus Art Gallery** is the chance to wander around the wood-panelled rooms of Swakopmund's pre-eminent colonial building. Built in 1894 and named after the Woermann Brock trading company, which is still very active in Namibia, its most distinctive feature is the **Damara Tower**, which served as a lookout both for ships and for ox wagons arriving across the dunes, as well as functioning as a water tower. The **art collection** on the first floor comprises a few rooms, primarily showcasing evocative desert landscapes by immigrant painters; however, there are also a handful of pieces by Indigenous artists, including a couple of linocuts by **John Muafangejo**, Namibia's most internationally renowned artistic talent.

Kristall Galerie

Corner of Tobias Hainyeko Street and Theo-Ben Gurirab Avenue • Mon–Sat 9am–5pm • Charge • ⓦ namibiangemstones.com

Essentially an enticement to purchase gemstones in their shop, the **Kristall Galerie** is nevertheless highly informative and contains some outstanding samples of Namibia's quartz riches, including the largest **crystal cluster** in the world, which is over 520 million years old, took five years to excavate, and weighs in at over

COASTAL FOG

For around half the year, especially in summer, you'll head out of your hotel after breakfast to find Swakopmund or Walvis Bay enveloped in thick **fog**. As the prevailing southwesterly winds are further cooled over the Benguela Current, the air condenses to form clouds and fog. Blown inland, the humid air becomes trapped beneath the less dense hot air, creating an inversion layer. This compact white blanket of low-lying fog is an extraordinary sight as it creeps over the mainland, hovering over the desert, generally reaching around 60km (37.3 miles) inland (though sometimes twice that distance) until it's dissipated by the strengthening sun. Though responsible for many shipwrecks on the Skeleton Coast, this coastal fog helps maintain the **milder temperatures** at the coast and, crucially, is the lifeblood for much of the Namib Desert's **flora and fauna**, providing five times more water than is provided by rain.

5

14,000kg (2,204.6st) – heavier than a double-decker bus. You peer through a replica of the mineshaft where the crystal was found before emerging into the atrium to be confronted by the giant cluster itself. Upstairs, illuminated cabinets display a host of precious and semi-precious stones; don't miss the gypsum, resembling crushed rose petals, the green and pink of the aptly named watermelon tourmaline, and the canary-yellow sulphur crystals of pietersite.

National Marine Aquarium

Strand Street South • Tues–Sun 10am–4pm; feeding time 3pm • Charge • ⓣ 064 4101000

The small **National Marine Aquarium** offers insight into the marine life that thrives in Namibia's cold Atlantic coastal waters. The well-labelled small tanks display a variety of fish, lobsters, sea anemones, starfish and other aquatic life, highlighting some of their more curious features. Still, the star attraction is a walk-through tank affording close-ups of enormous dusky cobs and mean-looking sand sharks. Popular with school groups, it's best avoided if you see a school bus parked outside.

Vineta

Once a separate community established in the 1950s, **Vineta** is now a posh residential suburb that unfurls 4km (2.5 miles) up the coast from the Mole to a swanky new mall and waterfront. Here, seafront mansions are worth several million Namibian dollars, and in the streets behind, a handful of comfortable guesthouses and self-catering units have sprung up, aimed at holidaying Windhoekers. It's a pleasant enough stroll up here along the strand or the windswept beach.

Mondesa and the DRC

In total contrast, to the northeast of central Swakopmund lies the suburb and former apartheid-era **township of Mondesa**, where around half of the town's population lives. A product of apartheid segregation from the 1950s, specific areas are demarcated for particular ethnic groups – Owambo, Nama and Herero areas remain largely intact – although, over time, boundaries have become more blurred. The place is far more vibrant than restrained downtown Swakop, with kids playing in the streets, people trading in the **market**, and neighbours sitting outside chatting and cooking. That said, Mondesa suffers from high unemployment or underemployment – Rössing Mine (see page 220) is the biggest employer; others get casual work in the endless construction boom that has enveloped Namibia's main seaside resort.

On the fringes of Mondesa sprawls the **Democratic Resettlement Community**, or DRC, an ever-expanding informal settlement, which some township tours also visit. Taking one of these tours with people who have grown up in the area should enable you to meet and interact with various community members, learn about the area's history and experience its present. You may visit a preschool or development project, browse the open market, sample some local food – *mahangu* or *oshifima* most likely – and maybe visit a shebeen. As with any other tour, you should establish the itinerary before signing up and ascertain what is included in the price.

ARRIVAL AND DEPARTURE — SWAKOPMUND AND AROUND

BY CAR

Swakopmund lies on the coast, 351km (218.1 miles) west of Windhoek. Reachable in under four hours by the tarred B2. A slower, more scenic route can be taken along the C28 (see page 231).

BY BUS

Shuttle services Two air-conditioned shuttle services operate the Windhoek–Swakopmund route: Town Hoppers (Mon–Fri 8am–5pm; ⓦ namibiashuttle.com) and Welwitschia Shuttle (Mon–Fri 8am–7pm, Sat 8am–1pm;

THE MARTIN LUTHER

In a rather unprepossessing, brick-and-glass shed 1.5km (0.9 miles) outside Swakopmund, on the B2, stands one of the town's more curious monuments, a replica of the **Martin Luther steam traction engine** (daily 8.30am–4.30pm). It was the country's first such machine, imported from Germany in 1896 to replace the ox wagons used to transport freight, but the venture was doomed from the outset. Since the port facilities in Swakop were not up to unloading such a weight, the engine was diverted to Walvis Bay, where it idled in the port for a few months. It then took three more months to struggle the 30km (18.6 miles) to its destination because it kept sinking into the sand. In 1897, after a few outings, it ground to an inglorious halt in a dune outside Swakop, on the spot where it is currently housed. Its curious nickname came from the apocryphal words of the Protestant reformer Martin Luther, who, when asked to renounce his beliefs or be charged with heresy, responded: 'Here I stand; I cannot do otherwise. God help me. Amen.' That said, the steam engine is scheduled to be relocated.

welwitschia-shuttle.com). Both have daily early-morning departures from Swakop, with the return trip from Windhoek in the afternoon. Connecting transfers to and from Windhoek's international airport can also be booked. The Welwitschia bus stop in Swakop is Woolworths' car park in the centre of town, while the Windhoek stop is the Christuskirche car park. Town Hoppers pick up outside their office on Otavi Street in Swakop and leave from outside Windhoek train station.

Minibuses Minibuses leave the Monte Christo Service Station in Katutura, Windhoek. Minibuses bound for Windhoek and other long-distance destinations depart from the taxi rank in Mondesa.

BY TRAIN

An extremely slow and rather uncomfortable night train runs from Windhoek to Walvis Bay (Tues, Thurs, Fri & Sun at 7.15pm). This service is scheduled to reach Swakopmund by 5.30am, though they frequently arrive late. The return train to the capital leaves at 8.45pm on the same day. The passenger service was suspended during the COVID-19 pandemic and, at the time of writing, had yet to resume service.

BY PLANE

Swakopmund Airport, 4km (2.5 miles) along the B2 towards Windhoek, operates charter flights and Fly Namibia's safari flights (flynamibia.com); most scheduled flights leave from Walvis Bay Airport, around 45 minutes' drive from Swakop town centre.

INFORMATION

Tourist information There are two private tourist information centres where you can book tours and get information. Namib I (Mon–Fri 8.30am–1pm & 2–5pm, Sat 9am–1pm, Sun and public holidays 10am–noon; facebook.com/NamibInfoBureau) is the more established, better-informed venture on Sam Nujoma Avenue. However, Swakop Info, on Tobias Hainyeko, has slightly longer Sunday opening hours (Mon–Sat 9.30am–5pm, Sat & Sun 9am–1pm; facebook.com/swakopinfo).

NWR office The NWR office on Bismarck Street can book accommodation and activities in all the national parks (Mon–Fri 8am–5pm; 064 402172).

MEFT office The MEFT permit office is in the same building as the NWR office in Bismarck Street, upstairs, where you can purchase your permit for the Namib-Naukluft or Skeleton Coast national parks and wilderness campsite permits (Mon–Fri 8am–5pm, Sat, Sun & public holidays 9am–1pm; 064 404576).

GETTING AROUND

On foot Swakop has a small town centre and most accommodation is within walking distance of sights, shops and restaurants. The centre is also reasonably safe to stroll around at night, though the usual precautions apply, such as not walking down dimly lit side streets or being alone.

By taxi During the day, taxis can be found hanging around outside supermarkets; if you want a taxi to get home after going out in the evening, get your accommodation or the restaurant to call someone reliable.

By car Unless you're on a self-drive holiday with your own vehicle (in which case choose accommodation with secure off-road parking), you've a choice when it comes to reaching most out-of-town attractions, such as Welwitschia Drive, Cape Cross seal colony, or popping down the coast to Walvis Bay for the day. You can either go on a tour (see below) or rent a car for the day.

5

TOURS AND ACTIVITIES

In addition to the **adventure activities** (see page 214), for which Swakopmund is justifiably renowned, the town offers a number of half- or full-day **excursions**, many of which take you out into the Namib Desert east of Swakop, to seek out some of the desert-adapted wildlife. The day tours usually combine the above with Welwitschia Drive (see page 219). **Cultural tours** to the former township of Mondesa are also gaining in popularity. Some operators also run excursions to Walvis Bay lagoon and/or Sandwich Harbour; more details are given under the Walvis Bay listings (see page 222). Tours range from N$800–1,000 for a half-day activity, N$1,600 plus for a full day – around N$3,000 if you're travelling as far as Sandwich Harbour – and several thousand Namibian dollars if you want to go skydiving.

Batis Birding batisbirdingsafaris.com. Specialising in birding tours, they also offer other excellent eco-safaris during the day and at night, from inexpensive nature walks in the desert to full-day tours to Spitzkoppe, Brandberg or Sandwich Harbour. A minimum of four is needed for most excursions.

Charly's Desert Tours Brauhaus Arcade, Sam Nujoma Avenue charlysdeserttours.com. Half-day trips to the desert to explore the flora and fauna, as well as full-day tours, which include Welwitschia Drive. It also offers short guided tours around Swakopmund, a half-day tide-dependent outing to explore rock pools and beach life, and excursions to Sandwich Harbour.

Fat Bike Tours 6 Henrik Witbooi St swakopfatbiketours.com. The most ecologically sound way to visit the desert, these two-hour tours go up the Swakop riverbed, then onto the dunes, for which you need to be reasonably fit, though e-bikes make the task easier. A less energetic alternative is to do the beach ride at low tide or rent a bike to explore on your own (town bikes, fat bikes or e-bikes available).

Hata Angu Cultural Tours facebook.com/hata.angu. The name means 'Let's get to know one another' in Damara, and they specialise in tours to Mondesa, the former township, and the Democratic Resettlement Community (DRC) informal settlement, both during the day and in the evening, when you can relax into the shebeen experience. They also offer sandboarding excursions.

Mondesa Township Tours mondesatownship.com. As well as the township tours, during which you'll visit Herero, Owambo and Nama families, and while trying out an Owambo dish, you'll be serenaded by some a cappella singing. It also offers half-day and full-day cycling tours and the usual day trips from Swakopmund, such as Cape Cross.

Namibia Tours and Safaris Hans Kriess Building, 42 Nathanial Maxuilili St namibia-tours-safaris.com. Organises highly acclaimed multiday tours around Namibia and Southern Africa, including self-drive and fly-in safaris.

Okakambe Trails okakambe.iway.na. Established stables with well-cared-for horses offering outings of a couple of hours or a full day, with multiday camping trips

ADVENTURE ACTIVITIES IN SWAKOP

Swakop is gradually gaining a reputation for **adventure sports**, thanks to inventive ways of enjoying the dunes, from the more established quad biking to sand-surfing, power-kiting or skydiving, for the ultimate adrenaline rush. Below are some of the recommended specialist outfits that work to minimise their impact on the delicate desert environment (see page 68).

Alter Action Sandboarding Amanpuri Travellers' Lodge alter-action.info. A guaranteed morning of action as you build up to speeds of between 60–80km/h (37.3– 49.7mph) on your final runs, racing down the dunes. It's good value, and you can choose whether to lie down (for most novices) or stand up (if you can surf on water or snow). The rates include transfers, a light lunch and drinks.

Desert Explorers Nathaniel Maxuilili Street namibiadesertexplorers.com. Desert Explorers focuses on racing around the desert on a quad bike but includes combo tours with sandboarding and you can book other activities, too. Manual or automatic quad bikes are available (helmets provided). They also offer budget accommodation in a converted shipping container.

Ground Rush Adventures (also known as Swakop Skydive) corner of Moses Garoeb and Anton Lubowski Street, Amanpuri Traveller's Lodge skydiveswakop.com. This place offers similar rates to Swakopmund Skydiving, with tandem jump rates depending on the height you jump from. Videoing your exploits will cost extra. Take-off is from the old Swakopmund airport.

Salty Jackal 37 Anton Lubowski Avenue saltyjackal.com. Individual or group lessons for beginners or intermediate surfers and guided surf trips.

Swakopmund Skydiving Club Based at the old Swakopmund airport skydiveswakopmund.com. Highly experienced outfit offering tandem skydives with an instructor – ideal for a novice – from 10,000ft or solo dives for the more fearless or experienced. The static line course finishes off with a drop from 3,000ft. Prices include pick-up, training, the plane out and the dive, after which you can return to the bar to watch a DVD of your exploits (additional fee) over a well-earned beer.

for more experienced riders. Prices assume a minimum of two people and include pick-up in town. No credit cards.

Pleasure Flights and Safaris pleasureflights.com.na. Given the clear skies, spectacular scenery and inaccessibility of much of Namibia, this is one country where it's worth splashing out on a flight. This is an experienced, reputable operator with over twenty years in the business. Prices depend on flight length and number of passengers. Assuming the maximum of four passengers, they range from N$3,730/person for a 1hr 30min flight along the coast to N$10,890 for a full day's excursion taking in Sossusvlei, the Fish River Canyon and a city tour of Lüderitz, before returning via Sandwich Harbour.

Swakop Cultural Tours facebook.com/SwakopCycleTours.com. A great way to visit the former township, Mondesa, is by bike, though walking tours are also offered, as are shorter tours of Swakop town centre. Daily bike rental is available, too.

Tommy's Tours and Safaris livingdeserttours.com.na. The original living desert tour was developed in the 1990s. Tommy's offers a similar half or full-day itinerary (minimum two people) to Charly's Desert Tours. Cash or bank transfer only.

Turnstone Tours turnstone-tours.com. At the higher end of the price range, but with superior guiding. Turnstone offers exclusive full-day excursions to Sandwich Harbour, Cape Cross, and Messum Crater. The company also operates acclaimed multiday camping trips (maximum of four) with a special four-day tour to *Mundulea Bush Camp* (mundulea.com), in a private reserve in the Otavi Mountains, which you explore on foot.

ACCOMMODATION

SEE MAP PAGE 210

Swakopmund boasts a wealth of accommodation to suit most budgets; though mid-range **B&Bs** and **guesthouses** predominate, a couple of **backpackers** and **campgrounds** exist for budget travellers and there are a couple of larger smart hotels. Generally, rooms are without a/c – it is not usually hot enough – though some have heating for the colder nights. During the main **school holidays** (mid-Dec to mid-Jan), when rates are generally higher, booking is a must. During the season for European visitors (late July and August), rooms are also in short supply.

IN TOWN

The Alternative Space B&B 167 Anton Lubowski St thealternativespace.com. This long-standing anti-establishment art gallery provides a cerebral, aesthetic retreat boasting a handful of whitewashed stone rooms laden with artwork, vintage bathtubs – outside, under a tree in one case – and a secluded courtyard garden. Breakfast is self-service, with the kitchen and barbecue facilities available to prepare other meals. B&B N$$

Amanpuri Travellers' Lodge Corner of Moses Garoeb and Anton Lubowski streets amanpurinamibia.com. With a motel-like feel, this place is popular with overlanders and tour groups, providing spotless, basic, yet comfortable tiled dorms and doubles. Good value. B&B dorms N$, doubles N$$

Brigadoon Boutique Guesthouse 16 Ludwig Koch St ondili.com/en/lodges-en/brigadoon-boutique-guesthouse. Having been taken over by Ondili, totally renovated and reopened in 2023, Brigadoon is now a 'boutique'. It's a cut above the other guesthouses, boasting stylish furnishing with nautical touches and a delightful breakfast and lounge area. The seven rooms each have a semi-private patio area to sit out – ask for one that overlooks the garden rather than a wall. N$$$

Cornerstone Guesthouse Corner of Rhode Allee and Hendrik Witbooi streets cornerstoneguesthouse.com. Superior B&B with five doubles and two family rooms, each immaculately kept, with a private entrance and patio overlooking the garden. Depending on the weather, a sumptuous breakfast is served indoors or on the shaded terrace. Three luxury self-catering apartments with three bedrooms and two bathrooms (sleeping up to six) are also available for rent in town. Doubles (B&B) N$$$, apartments N$$$

★ **The Delight** Corner of Theo-Ben Gurirab and Nathaniel Maxuilili streets gondwana-collection.com. This hotel lives up to its name, flaunting an upbeat modern design with retro touches in aquamarine and scarlet; enlarged photos of local scenes decorate the walls and nice touches include an espresso machine with a cookie tin, plus a hot-water bottle for winter. The scrumptious champagne breakfast includes fresh oysters. The only niggle is with the rooms overlooking the Entertainment Centre; you'll hear people spilling out of the casino in the early hours at weekends. Wi-fi signal is strongest in the cosy bar-lobby area and upstairs restaurant but weakens in the rooms further away. B&B N$$$

★ **Der Alte Brücke** Strand Street South altebrucke.com. What it lacks in character, this resort makes up for in value for money: over thirty modern, well-equipped, fully serviced self-catering units (for two to six) with patios and palm trees, plus deluxe camping pitches. Wind-protected, these have manicured lawns to pitch the tent, private ablutions, a dining area and a vast braai hearth for a heart-warming blaze on chilly winter nights. The buffet breakfast is available for campers (at additional cost). Camping N$$, self-catering units (B&B) N$$

Desert Sky Backpackers 35 Anton Lubowski Ave, at the corner with Nathaniel Maxuilili desertskylodging.com. This friendly, efficient backpacker makes a great base

5

for campers, backpackers and families on a budget; you can choose from rooms with shared or en-suite facilities and use the well-equipped kitchen and braai facilities (breakfast not included). The large walled garden makes a pleasant spot for an early evening beer before you hit town. Camping is a little cramped and can be noisy. Camping N$, dorms N$, doubles N$$

Hansa Hotel 3 Hendrik Witbooi St hansahotel.com.na. From the marble foyer to the Neoclassical columns and heavy drapes, the *Hansa* announces itself as 'Namibia's finest and oldest hotel'. Rooms are good-sized and comfortably furnished, though nothing special, offering all the services you'd expect from an upmarket business establishment. The underfloor heating is particularly welcome in winter. The breakfast buffet is a veritable Teutonic feast, while there's fine dining in the silver service restaurant (see below). B&B N$$–$$$

Hotel Pension Rapmund 6–8 Bismarck St hotelpensionrapmund.com. With double and family rooms, this well-established twenty-room hotel is a solid choice, offering reasonable rates in a central location. Bag one of the upstairs rooms with a private balcony, and don't miss out on the tasty German buffet breakfast. B&B N$$

Hotel Prinzessin Rupprecht 15 Anton Lubowski Ave en.hotel-prinzessin-rupprecht.com. A former German military hospital, sharing its formal grounds with the neighbouring retirement home, the hundred-year-old building inevitably has long corridors and high ceilings, with most rooms decent-sized, if rather stark, with fridge and kettle. Though renovated, it can't quite shake off its austere image but often has space (doubles, triples and family rooms) when others are full and offers good rates for children. B&B N$$

★ Meike's Guesthouse 23 Windhoek St meikes-guesthouse.net. This eco-friendly, solar-powered guesthouse run by experienced hosts offers five spotless, well-appointed doubles and six family rooms (sleeping four) with home comforts: TV, fridge, tea- and coffee-making facilities, plus private verandas and walk-in showers. Most rooms are wheelchair accessible. B&B N$$

Organic Square Guesthouse 29 & 56 Rhode Allee guesthouse-swakopmund.com. Modern, stylish guesthouse with fifteen rooms of various sizes spread over two properties: rustic chic reigns in grey and lime green, with modern artwork inside and out. Rooms have DStv, fridge-minibar and spotless bathrooms, and each opens onto a private patio-garden space. The healthy organic continental breakfasts are a treat. B&B N$$

Salty Jackal 37 Anton Lubowski Avenue saltyjackal.com. Cosy, friendly surfers' hostel – though you don't have to surf to stay – centrally located, with a handful of tidy rooms pleasantly decorated with wooden furniture. Rooms include a couple of dorms and privates with shared or en-suite bathrooms and a communal kitchen, lounge, and small garden area. B&B. Dorms N$, singles and doubles N$$

★ The Stiltz Strand Street South thestiltz.com. Unique accommodation comprising nine raised wood-and-thatch chalets overlooking scrubland and connected by elevated wooden walkways; No. 7 has a standout beach view. Spacious, with large windows and creative use of wood and rustic touches, each chalet has a fully stocked minibar, tea/coffee facilities and a safe. Here, you can feel close to nature while being a short hop from town. B&B N$$

The Strand Hotel The Mole strandhotelswakopmund.com. The swanky spot in town (complete with presidential suite) at suitably elevated prices, in a top location, on the Mole surrounded by the ocean. Apart from the evocative historical photos, the well-appointed rooms (all with sea views) are smart if lacking character. There are also three distinctive on-site restaurants and a decent spa. B&B N$$$$

Swakopmund Municipal Restcamp End of Henrik Witbooi Street swakopmund-restcamp.com. A sound budget choice, this place has been going for years, offering affordable, functional units accommodating from two to six people, all with kitchen and braai sites. The basic Fisherman's cabin with two single beds is the cheapest. It also has an on-site restaurant. N$–$$

Tiger Reef Campsite Strand Street South facebook.com/tigerreefcampsite. Smallish but secure, private and sheltered camping plots are arranged in a circle around a large expanse of grass. Each pitch has a thatched *lapa* and picnic table, braai area, electricity and water, and shared ablutions. You can hear the ocean waves but sometimes feel the biting ocean wind despite the cane shelters. Discounts in low season. Camping N$

OUT OF TOWN CENTRE

Beach Lodge 1 Stint St, Vogelstrand beachlodge.com.na. The ship design might have gotten somewhat lost in translation, but the place lives up to its name, being bang on the beach, 4km (2.5 miles) north of town. Light and spacious modern rooms boast sea views – through a large porthole in the case of the first-floor accommodation – and come with a ceiling fan, heater, satellite TV, fridge and private patio or balcony from which to admire the sunsets. The family rooms offer the best value. B&B N$$$

★ Desert Breeze Lodge 5min drive east of Swakopmund desertbreezeswakopmund.com. Perched above the dry Swakop River, these twelve distinctive luxury studio bungalows (plus a villa for six) offer a superb alternative to staying in town. Vast windows and a private viewing deck maximise the expansive desert vistas, while a cosy wood-burning stove staves off the evening chill. You'll need transport to get into town. B&B N$$$

Sea Wind Self-Catering Cottages 1 Aragoniet St seawind.com.na. Located in north Swakopmund, a block from the beach, they are not exactly cottages but rather self-catering suites catering for couples or families. But rather than the usual functional units, these are enlivened by cheerful maritime-themed decor. Kitchenettes include hobs and microwave (but no oven) and outside braai areas; plus, there's daily cleaning if you want and secure parking. Altogether, it is good value. N$$

Skeleton Beach Backpackers 14 Moses Garoeb St Ⓦskeletonbeachbackpackers.com. A stiff fifteen-minute hike north of town, this converted house in a quiet residential area is a good deal, if a little cramped when full. Dorms include a shipping container, which is freezing in winter. Doubles are en suite with TV (Room 8 even has a balcony). Other amenities include cable TV in the communal lounge, all-day tea/coffee and a laundry. The shared semi-open kitchen is well equipped, and the delightful garden with a braai area is a bonus. Camping N$, dorms N$, doubles N$$

EATING

SEE MAP PAGE 210

CAFÉS

Café Anton Hotel Schweizerhaus, 1 Bismarck St Ⓦschweizerhaus.net/cafe_anton.htm. A Swakop institution whose reputation does not always stand up to the test. The patio terrace is perfectly situated, and you can't beat the incongruity of biting into a slice of Black Forest gâteau as you gaze at the palm trees. Tasty buffet breakfasts. N$$

Muschel Art Café Brauhaus Arcade Ⓣ81 849 5984. Tucked away in the pedestrian precinct, this sheltered café catches the late afternoon sun when it's a prime spot to unwind with a coffee and a fresh-filled roll or slice of cake and even mulled wine in winter. N$

Two Beards and a Saint 5 Einstein St Ⓦ2beardscoffee.com.na A surprisingly buzzy café–bistro on an accessible road in the industrial estate, with craft gin and beer production happening across the road. Eat indoors or outdoors in the garden, complete with a water feature. A mix of gourmet and familiar comfort food is served, but coffee is the main event. Beans from all over the world are freshly roasted each day. N$$–$$$

Village Café 23 Sam Nujoma Ave Ⓦvillagecafenamibia.com. This quirky café is popular with locals and travellers alike. There's well-prepared, inexpensive food, including all-day breakfasts (and grub for visiting dogs), plus good service with a mellow vibe. N$$

RESTAURANTS

Brewer and Butcher The Mole Ⓦstrandhotelswakopmund.com. The pick of *The Strand Hotel*'s three restaurants, with its warming fires, unobtrusive sports screens and buzzing atmosphere, caters for lovers of meat and craft beer – note the two large copper brewhouses on show. Sample the generous tasting tray of three beers to accompany the house oxtail or any of the succulent steaks or deli burgers on offer, but leave room for the melt-in-your-mouth chocolate-and-banana Malva pudding. N$$$–$$$$

The Farmhouse Deli The Mole Ⓦstrandhotelswakopmund.com. As it serves The Strand Hotel's breakfast, this airy place opens early and stays open late. Even non-guests can choose between à la carte or the full-on buffet breakfast – worth splurging on. Throughout the day, there's plenty of home-made breads, cheeses and cold cuts, with a full Italian menu of freshly made pasta and pizzas. But if Italian's not to your liking, an alternative menu offers steaks, chops, burgers or salad. It is also an enjoyable spot for a cocktail sundowner in the conservatory area. N$$$–$$$$

★**The Fish Deli** 29 Sam Nujoma Ave Ⓦfishdeli-swakopmund.com. A fishmonger's, deli, take-away and restaurant all rolled into one, which is especially busy at lunchtimes, offering the best fresh catch straight from the boat and sushi. Try one of their mouthwatering stir-fries: mango and prawn or red curry calamari in coconut sauce. N$$–$$$

Garnish Corner of Tobias Hainyeko and Libertina Amadhila streets Ⓦfacebook.com/garnishswakopmund.com. Inevitably pleasing vegetarians, this Indian restaurant is also popular for groups of friends and families to share several dishes. However, the cost can mount up as sides, rice, naans and rotis are priced separately. It also does takeaways. N$$–$$$

Hansa Hotel 3 Hendrik Witbooi St Ⓦhansahotel.com.na. This is the place if you're after refined dining and old-world elegance. Sink into your upholstered chair and soak up the white-glove service, damask tablecloths, silver cutlery and crystal decanters – not to mention exquisite cuisine: try springbok loin in red wine with apple-infused red cabbage. N$$$$

★**Jetty 1905** End of the pier Ⓦlighthousegroup.com.na/jetty1905.com. Hidden at the end of Swakop's restored pier, this chic, modern restaurant is all about the view. Surrounded by glass, you can gaze at the ocean from all angles as you tuck into sushi or a plate of baked garlic oysters (a must) or sip a cocktail as the sun sinks over the sea. N$$$–$$$$

Kücki's Pub 22 Tobias Hainyeko St Ⓦkuckispub.com. A long-standing culinary institution in Swakop, which has grown in size and price but still succeeds in pleasing the palate. Specialising in grilled game meat and seafood – try the seafood platter, served with spätzle, rösti or fried potatoes (extra) – this Bierkeller provides large portions of pub grub at tourist prices, washed down with draught beer and wine by the glass. Upstairs is a louder sports bar, but even downstairs is humming when packed with tour groups. N$$$–$$$$

★**Old Steamer Restaurant** Der Alte Brücke Resort,

Strand Street South 081 4303923. A place to dispel any misgivings about buffet food, this sumptuous buffet feast is a real treat in a cosy fire-warmed room: all pipes, portholes and other steamship paraphernalia plus candlelit tables. A wide range of wines and excellent service accompanies the varied and changing spread. Reservations are advised. N$$$

The Tug Restaurant Swakop Jetty the-tug.com. Iconic, upmarket restaurant spilling out of a beached tugboat, with superlative vistas across the sea from the upstairs 'deck'. Seafood predominates, including crayfish in season, local oysters and the mountainous Tug Seafood Extravaganza for two, but vegetarians need not despair as there are several veggie options, too. If you can't get a table, a cocktail at sundown will at least let you admire the view. Reservations are strongly advised. N$$$–$$$$

★ **The Wreck** Beach Lodge, 1 Stint St, Vogelstrand (4km/2.5 miles north of the town centre) the-wreck.com. One of the top places for fine dining. Imaginative international dishes, such as snails wrapped in blue cheese filo parcels or grilled kingklip with creamy lentils and slow-roasted tomato, are beautifully presented at this elegant restaurant. It makes the most of its second-floor beachside location, with floor-to-ceiling windows and 'portholes' that afford stunning sea views – so get there before sunset. N$$$–$$$$

DRINKING AND NIGHTLIFE

SEE MAP PAGE 210

★ **Alte Laundry** 15 Swakop St 064 402135. Swakop's most happening venue attracts a multiracial crowd most nights. There's a pool table, weekend DJs that get a crowd on the dancefloor, a grill, and a beer garden hung with fairy lights that hosts occasional live music. The place is open from 10am but doesn't get going until late. Cover for events.

Bar Zonder Naam 1 Tobias Hainyeko St bznwinebarswakop.com. A cosy little wine bar with an outdoor terrace lined wall to ceiling with bottles of wine and featuring craft beer and gin, too. The dimmed lighting and candles add to the mellow mood but even indoors can be chilly on a winter evening.

Desert Tavern 2 Swakop St facebook.com/deserttavern/?locale=en_gb. Featuring a brick-and-wood interior, this is a warm and cosy spot once the fires are blazing at night. It comes alive when there's live music (usually jazz or rock) on a Friday or Saturday evening. Serves large burgers and other pub grub.

Swakopmund Hotel and Entertainment Centre 2 Theo-Ben Gurirab Ave swakopmundhotel.com. The brashest, glitziest place in town inhabits a conversion of the colonial-era railway station. There's a casino (daily 10am–4am) and the town's only cinema here.

Tiger Reef Beach Bar & Grill End of Strand Street South, on the beach lighthousegroup.com.na/tiger-reef. A relaxed, thatched place to kick off your shoes, sink your toes into the sand and watch the sunset, though it can be chilly on windy evenings. Order at the bar, grab a seat on the beach and let the drinks – or the indifferent pub grub – be brought to you.

SHOPPING

SEE MAP PAGE 210

Outside Windhoek, Swakopmund is the best place to shop for **souvenirs** in Namibia, including skincare products made locally with some of the country's natural wonders such as !nara melon, baobab and marula. The Brauhaus Arcade on Sam Nujoma is a good place to start. Swakopmund also has a wide choice of supermarkets and deli shops to load up with supplies if you're self-catering here or heading back into the desert.

WELWITSCHIAS

Appearances can sometimes be deceptive: what may look like a mangled giant cabbage run over by a truck is most likely to be Namibia's most remarkable desert survivor, the aptly named **welwitschia mirabilis** – 'mirabilis' being Latin for marvellous or wonderful, while 'Welwitsch' was the surname of the Austrian botanist who stumbled over some in the mid-nineteenth century. Featuring on Namibia's coat of arms and nicknamed the 'living fossil', welwitschias can live over 1,500 years; its most celebrated specimen – rumoured to be one of the oldest and largest – is located inland from Swakopmund and attracts thousands of visitors annually, though the plant's withered and dishevelled appearance can be an initial disappointment.

Welwitschias are endemic to the arid, coastal **gravel plains** that extend 1,000km (621.4 miles) northwards from the Kuiseb River south of Walvis Bay to southern Angola. They survive on very little water and some years get none at all.

Strangely, the welwitschia – a dioecious plant with female and male specimens – only possesses two grey-green leaves that shrivel and shred over the years. Though the leaves can reach 2–4m (6.6–13.1ft) in length, this extraordinary plant rarely grows higher than 1.5m (4.9ft).

BOOKS

Die Muschel Brauhaus Arcade, Tobias Hainyeko Street ⓦmuschel.iway.na. Probably the country's best bookshop, it has a wide selection of books in German and English, especially on art and history, as well as a selection of music and calendars.

Swakopmunder Buchhandlung 22 Sam Nujoma Ave ⓦfacebook/swakopmunder.buchhandlung. A decent enough selection of novels, as well as books on Namibia, in English, plus a more comprehensive selection of books in German and stationery.

ARTS & CRAFTS

African Kirikara Arts & Crafts Am Ankerplatz, Sam Nujoma Avenue ⓦkirikara.com. A Swakopmund outlet for Kiripotib Farm karakul weavings, jewellery, and other arts and crafts.

Karakulia Weavers 2 Rakotoka Street, NDC Centre ⓦfacebook.com/karakuliaweaversswakopmund. This thriving community development workshop produces top-quality karakul rugs and weavings (with made-to-order designs, too). Watch the spinning and weaving first-hand or drop in at the smaller outlet in the Brauhaus Arcade in the town centre.

Namcrafts Brauhaus Arcade, Tobias Hainyeko Street ⓦcraftingnamibia.com. The Swakopmund outlet of the popular Namibian chain with locally produced crafts and South African imports.

Trendhaus Swakopmund Otto Günther Courtyard, 2 Tobias Hainyeko St ⓦfacebook.com/TrendhausSwakopmund. An airy barn-like structure with an outside patio space showcasing Namibian arts and crafts, from ceramics to skin products, photography to weaving and fashion, with a small café.

DIRECTORY

Banks and money All the major banks with ATMs are in the town centre. There's also a branch of NovaCâmbios (ⓦnovacambios.com) on Hendrik Witbooi Street by Pick 'N' Pay.

Bicycle repairs Cycles 4U on Hidepo Hamutenya Avenue sells parts and repairs bicycles (ⓦfacebook.com/cycles4u2013/).

Car rental There are both local and international car rental agencies in Swakop. Avis (ⓦavis.com.na) and Budget (ⓦbudget.com/en/locations/sw) share an office in the Swakopmund Hotel and Entertainment Centre on Mandume Ya Ndemufayo Street, charging around US$70-80 per day for a small manual saloon car (over double that for a four-wheel drive); Swakopmund Car Hire, 202 Sam Nujoma Ave (ⓦswakopmundcarhire.com), is a reliable local outfit, also with an office in Windhoek, but only offers minimum three-day rental and driving on gravel roads is not permitted.

Hospitals and clinics Since the state hospital is always oversubscribed, head for the Mediclinic Swakopmund on Franziska van Neel Street for serious matters (ⓣ064 412200, ⓦmediclinic.co.za); to see a doctor, call in at the Bismarck Medical Centre on 17–20 Sam Nujoma Ave (ⓣ064 405000).

Laundry Alte Laundry, 15 Swakop St (ⓣ064 405618). It is in the same building as the sometimes-functioning nightclub and bar of the same name, so you can enjoy a beer while your clothes wash.

Internet Free wi-fi is available in almost all lodgings and various cafés. Still, if you need a PC, there's an internet café on Hendrik Witbooi, opposite Pick 'N' Pay, which scans documents and does photocopies.

Pharmacy Try the central, reliable Swakopmunder Apotheke at 26 Sam Nujoma Ave (reduced hours at weekends and public holidays; ⓦswakopmunder.webs.com).

Police The Central Police Station is on Tobias Hainyeko Street (ⓣ064 402431; emergency ⓣ064 10111).

Post office The post office is next to the police station on Tobias Hainyeko Street.

Vehicle repairs Auto Fix, Einstein Street (ⓦfacebook.com/autofixswakopmund), does basic repairs.

Welwitschia Drive

As the circuit takes place in the northern section of the Namib-Naukluft National Park, you need to purchase a permit from the MEFT office in Swakopmund (see page 213), which comes with a map of the route

A long-standing favourite excursion from Swakopmund is along **Welwitschia Drive**, a marked interpretive route across the desert that starts a few kilometres from town and can be done either as a four-wheel drive self-drive (3–4hr) or a half-day tour (see page 214). The route traverses **gravel plains**, where you can stop and peer at **lichen fields** (see page 227) and drought-resistant plants, such as the dollar bush, with waxy coin-shaped leaves that give it its name. Other highlights include the otherworldly '**moonscape**' – an area of undulating granite mounds that pushed through the Earth's surface around 460 million years ago and was eroded by the wind and the changing course of the Swakop River over time. Last but not least, you will see **welwitschias** – including Namibia's presumed largest and oldest specimen (see page 218).

Rössing Mine

60km (37.3 miles) northeast of Swakopmund, near Arandis • Half-day tours given the first Fri of every month, leaving at 10am outside Swakopmund Museum • Tickets available from the museum • No open shoes, and no admittance if you've been drinking; the mine reserves the right to breathalyse you

It's not everyone's idea of a fun day out. Still, if mineralogy or chemical engineering is your bent, then you may fancy a visit to **Rössing Mine** – one of the largest and longest-running open-pit **uranium mines** in the world. At the very least, you'll be staggered by the scale of the operation: the chasm is currently 3km (1.9 miles) long and 1.5km (0.9 miles) wide, and as you peer into the abyss – almost 400m (1,312.3ft) deep – the huge trucks that remove the blasted rocks appear like ants below. Uranium was first identified in the area in 1928, though extraction did not begin until 1976. The mine now looks set to continue until at least 2032. As with any mining behemoth, especially one involving uranium, there are many questions about its operations. Concerns about environmental degradation, water usage, working conditions of labourers and health effects periodically bubble to the surface. Despite the hard work by Rössing's PR department – including this guided tour – which includes spending millions of Namibian dollars annually on social development projects, many issues remain shrouded in mist and spin.

Swakopmund Salt Works

At Mile 4 – around 8km (5 miles) north of Swakopmund by road – off the C34 to Henties Bay, the **Swakopmund Salt Works** provide some tremendous early morning **birdwatching** opportunities. You need to get there before the workers arrive (or after they leave) to increase your chances of being rewarded by sightings of greater and lesser flamingos, a variety of terns, plovers, avocets, oystercatchers, cormorants and pelicans.

Walvis Bay

As a major **fishing port** possessing a rather dispersed town centre and lacking the more attractive colonial-era architecture of Swakopmund, **WALVIS BAY**, Namibia's second-largest population centre, attracts few overnight visitors. Tourists usually come on a day trip from Swakopmund to do some activity on the **lagoon**. However, the town's very ordinariness and down-to-earth nature can be pretty appealing after the surreal, toy-town nature of Swakop. What's more, tourist-oriented accommodation and decent dining options, clustered around the lagoon and new waterfront, are on the increase, and the town makes a better base for the highly worthwhile excursion to **Sandwich Harbour** (see page 224). Beyond the lagoon, the only sight – and a very modest one at that – is the town's one-room **museum** in the library basement, which contains some interesting photographs of colonial life in Walvis.

Brief history

Archaeological evidence shows that the semi-nomadic **Khoikhoi** – and the **‡Aonin**, particularly – have inhabited central coastal zones for thousands of years. They even kept cattle in this harsh desert environment, which they traded with traders and **whalers who** started to arrive in Sandwich Harbour and Walvis Bay ('Whale Bay' in Afrikaans) in the late seventeenth century. The ubiquitous Portuguese explorer

Bartolomeu Diaz (see page 338) had drifted into the bay searching for a route to Asia. Still, it was only later, as the 'Scramble for Africa' (see page 339) gained momentum, that the various competing imperial powers began to recognise Walvis Bay's strategic importance as the only decent-sized **natural harbour** on the coast, and Indigenous interests were increasingly marginalised. After briefly being bagged by the Dutch in 1793, the British soon seized the port – keen to safeguard their ships around the Cape – before eventually being annexed to the Cape Colony in 1878. At the outbreak of World War I, Walvis was briefly overrun by the Germans before they, in turn, were ousted by South African troops, who eventually took control of the port as part of their **League of Nations mandate** to govern South-West Africa.

Walvis Bay continued to thrive, especially once its international **fishing industry** took off in the 1950s. Such was the strategic and economic importance of the port, however, that South Africa attempted to cling onto it even after Namibian independence until they were forced to relinquish sovereignty in 1994, once apartheid had ended in South

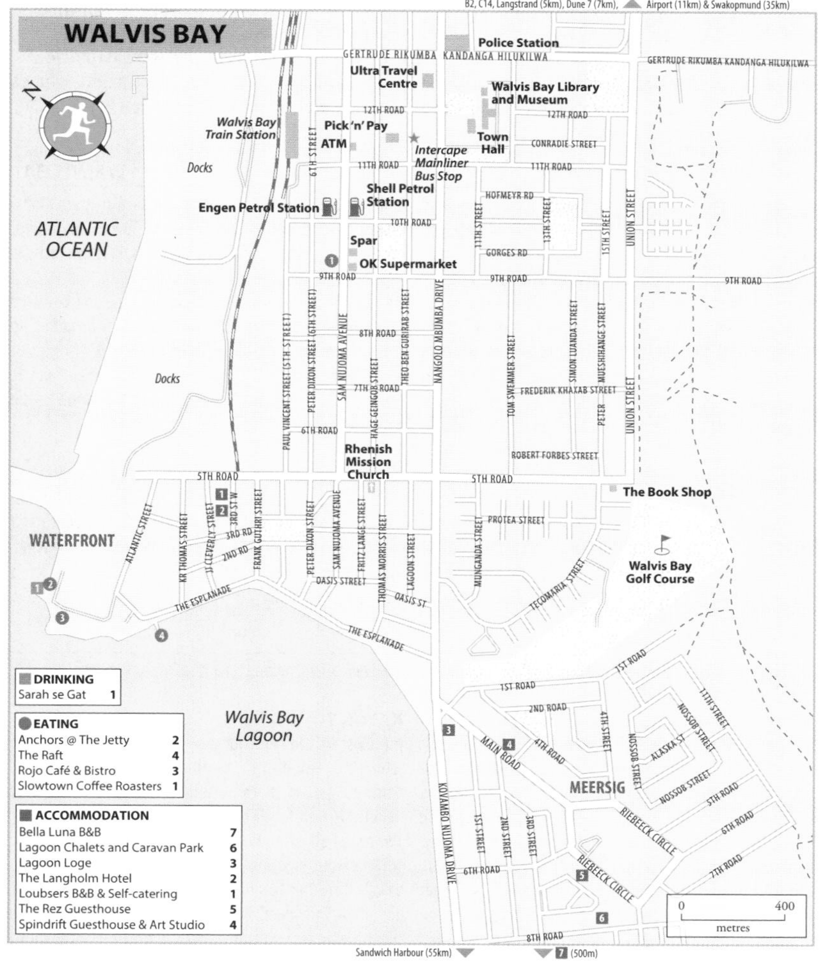

5

Africa. However, since the South African authorities had exhausted fish stocks over many years, there followed a major slump in the industry. After enforcing stricter controls, fishing has only recently enjoyed a resurgence, being the main earner of foreign exchange after mining and a major contributor to GDP. The industry employs around eight thousand people in fishing or fish processing, mainly in Walvis Bay. The N$20 billion port expansion that is currently underway is likely to bring further prosperity to the city.

The lagoon

As Southern Africa's most precious coastal wetlands, **Walvis Bay lagoon**, together with the adjacent tidal mud flats and salt pans, has long been a top destination for keen birders, hosting over one hundred thousand birds in summer – notably thousands of **flamingos**, but also masses of pelicans, terns, plovers, grebes and cormorants – and around fifty thousand in winter. More recently, more casual wildlife lovers have begun to enjoy the lagoon, on catamaran cruises or kayaking tours, gliding among dolphins and Cape fur seals, which have colonised the sandspit known as **Pelican Point** that extends a protective arm across the bay, sheltering the lagoon from the wild Atlantic waves beyond. Further out, in season (July–Nov), humpback and southern right whales are regularly sighted from boats, and even the occasional leatherback turtle (Feb–March) or killer whale.

ARRIVAL AND INFORMATION — WALVIS BAY

By car The tarred B2 from Windhoek to Swakopmund continues along the coast to Walvis Bay. Alternatively, you can pick the faster dual carriageway (D9184), which runs parallel to the coastal road and cuts through the desert.

By bus and shuttle McClunes Shuttle Service has twice-daily daily departures from the same location, which is also outside its office, and also does airport transfers (mcclunes.com). Minibuses also leave early morning from Kuisebmund bound for Windhoek.

By plane Walvis Bay Airport lies 11km (6.8 miles) outside Walvis Bay. Air Namibia (airnamibia.com) has daily flights to and from Windhoek's Hosea Kutako International Airport (40min) and to and from Cape Town (2hr 10min). South African Express (flysaa.com) has daily connections with Johannesburg and Cape Town.

By taxi Shared and private taxis run regularly between Swakopmund and Walvis Bay. Taxis can easily be picked up in the centre of Walvis, opposite Spur's car park.

MEFT office The MEFT office, 643 Heinrich Baumann St (Mon–Fri 8am–5pm; 064 205971), sells permits for the national parks.

GETTING AROUND

By taxi Walvis Bay is relatively spread out and it's a stiff twenty-minute hike from the lagoon area to the centre of town along Sam Nujoma Avenue, so you might find it easier at times to hop in a taxi, which is perfectly safe during the day. At night, you're best off calling one out, which will cost extra as most drivers have to come from Kuisebmond, the former township. Ask your accommodation for a recommended driver.

ACTIVITIES AND TOURS

Most activities focus on the **lagoon wildlife**, which you can explore in a kayak (N$1,000–1,300) or on a catamaran or other motorised vessel. The other main excursion is a four-wheel drive to **Sandwich Harbour** (see page 224). Several 'combo' tours (around N$3,200–3,500) visit the lagoon in the morning, either in a kayak or on a boat, and tackle the dunes of Sandwich Harbour in the afternoon, which can make for quite an exhausting and rushed day. Plus, Sandwich Harbour is well worth a full-day tour. Company charges vary slightly, but so do the details of what you're paying, so shop around. Most companies can arrange transfers from Swakopmund. Activities must be booked well in advance if you intend to visit in July or August.

KAYAK TOURS

Tours last around four hours and leave early in the morning to make the most of the weather conditions, as the wind tends to get up in the afternoon. It takes about fifty minutes to transfer clients around the bay to Pelican Point; you spend about an hour and a half on the water with a guide before enjoying a snack on the beach. Operators usually take between two and twelve clients per guide and offer double and single kayaks. The companies below come highly recommended and can organise a combined excursion with Sandwich Harbour, for which you are picked up en route rather than returning to the town in between excursions.

Eco-marine Kayak Tours ecomarinekayak.com. High-quality owner-operator kayaking on the lagoon. Can organise a combo tour to Sandwich Harbour with one of the four-wheel drive operators.

Namibia Kayak Tours Walvis Bay Angling Club, Atlantic Street namibia-kayak-tours.com. Kayaking tours from Pelican Point plus the combined kayaking and Sandwich Harbour tour. You can also organise birdwatching.

Pelican Point Kayaking Jettyshoppe, Waterfront pelican-point-kayaking.com. Kayaking with seals from Pelican Point. You'll get a discount if you drive to meet the guides (but note you'll need a four-wheel drive and know how to drive on sand).

CATAMARAN TOURS

The catamaran tours visit the oyster farms, lighthouse and the wreck at Pelican Point while on the lookout for whales (June–Oct), dolphins (year-round), leatherback turtles and other marine life. Unfortunately, they also usually feed fish to tame seals and pelicans that come on board, which may not be to everyone's taste. The classic bay tours usually last around three hours, and a light buffet, including fresh oysters and sparkling wine, is served on the boat (from N$1,300–2,600).

Mola-Mola Safaris Waterfront mola-namibia.com. Well-established company with several speedboat catamarans (and one more leisurely one) offering the usual three-and-a-half-hour cruise around the bay or a longer one with a beach barbecue lunch. It also offers a half-day Sandwich Harbour tour and a packed bay cruise, kayak, barbecue and Sandwich Harbour combo tour.

Sun Sail Catamaran Atlantic St sunsailnamibia.com. Tries to use the sail as much as possible. It does the lagoon favourite and offers a combo tour with a trip to Sandwich Harbour in the afternoon and private charters.

TOWNSHIP TOURS

Walvis Bay Tour Guides Wooden office by Mola-Mola, Waterfront walvisbay-eco-tourism.com. The only Black-owned operation in town, run by the engaging and experienced Owambo guide, Fried Fredericks; in addition to dolphin and seal cruises in the bay, it also offers its signature cultural tours to Kuisebmund.

SANDWICH HARBOUR TOURS

Sandwich Harbour 4x4 Jettyshoppe, Waterfront sandwich-harbour.com. Full-day tour to Sandwich Harbour, or a half-day there combined with a morning boat trip on Walvis Bay lagoon looking at the seals. They also conduct cultural excursions to visit a community of Indigenous ǂAonin, who live in the Kuiseb Delta, and birdwatching excursions. All tours need a minimum of three or four people.

ACCOMMODATION

SEE MAP PAGE 221

Bella Luna B&B 12 Hesko St, Meersig bellalunabnb.com.na. A stone's throw from the lagoon, this place offers spacious modern rooms with walk-in showers and comfortable beds piled with ample bedding for the chill nights. The decor is simple but tasteful – grey and white with the occasional splash of colour – and the low rates make Bella Luna excellent value. N$$

Lagoon Chalets and Caravan Park 8th Road West, Meersig lagoonchaletswb.com. Well-run, secure site four blocks from the lagoon offering a range of accommodation, from dorms to chalets and VIP suites, most with DStv. Units are generally drably painted concrete, and some are a little aged and uninspiring inside, but they're clean, cheap and with the necessary facilities, including a café. The good-value campground has sheltered private plots with their own washing line, braai facilities, and power point. The on-site restaurant with wi-fi is a plus. Dorms N$, camping N$$, doubles N$$, chalets N$$

Lagoon Loge 88 Kovambo Nujoma Drive lagoonloge.com.na. Visible across the lagoon, this canary-yellow beacon has eight capacious rooms, each amply supplied with eclectic furnishings and artwork. The friendly French owners (hence 'loge') help organise tours and activities. There's also a great rooftop sundeck – a prime spot for birdwatching – and a delightfully furnished, comfortable, sunlit lounge. B&B N$$–$$$

The Langholm Hotel 18–20 JJ Cleverly St langholmhotel.com. Sparkling green-and-white hotel popular with tourists and business folk, offering reliable service and light, clean rooms with all the usual amenities: fridge, DStv, tea/coffee facilities, safe. There's a pleasant lounge bar – bedecked with baseball caps – a garden and secure parking. Good value for money. B&B N$$

Loubser's B&B & Self-catering 11 3rd St West loubseraccommodation.com. Slightly cramped accommodation in a converted house around a yard: three double rooms, two small four-bed dorms with en-suite bathrooms and handy kitchenette, and a self-catering unit. The decor is bland, bordering on the chintzy, but you can't beat the price. Shared braai and TV area, with a pool table and darts board. Dorms N$, doubles N$$

★ **The Rez Guesthouse** 16 Mandume Ndemufayo Circle therez.com.na. Eclectic is the word in this superior guesthouse that exudes character. The individually decorated suites are a riot of colour and styles – crammed with a carefully curated assortment of lighting, mirrors, artwork and soft furnishings. The spacious and comfortable lounge area is laden with artwork and outside seating around a fireplace. N$$$

★ **Spindrift Guesthouse & Art Studio** 22 Main Rd,

5

SANDWICH HARBOUR

A long-standing birding hotspot, isolated **Sandwich Harbour**, which lies 55km (34.2 miles) south of Walvis Bay, has recently begun to attract more casual visitors, drawn by the stunning wilderness scenery as the rolling golden dunes of the Namib meet the wild Atlantic coast. The 'harbour' is a lagoon, a mix of fresh and saline water, and an important site for migratory and resident seabirds and waders, spreading over the nearby tidal mud flats. Numbers can top fifty thousand in summer and twenty thousand in winter. Even non-birders will be amazed at the colourful carpet of huge flocks of flamingos and pelicans, vast numbers of grebes and the immense variety of terns and waders, dramatically enclosed by the dunes.

Though theoretically, anyone with a high-clearance four-wheel drive can get a permit from the MEFT office in Swakopmund and drive themselves here, it is not advised, even for experienced four-wheel drive motorists, as the driving conditions are treacherous. The route constantly shifts with the sand, plus you will only add more eyesore tracks to the sand (see page 68). It is better to leave your vehicle behind and take one of the **organised day trips** (see page 222). Even then, research the **tide timetable** thoroughly before booking, as access to the lagoon itself depends on it being low tide so that vehicles can drive along the beach.

Meersig Ⓦ spindrift3.wixsite.com/spindriftguesthouse. Delightful, homely B&B set in a small tropical garden with charming hosts just a couple of blocks from the lagoon. Each of the nine double or family rooms is individually decorated and full of artwork by the owner. B&B N$$

EATING SEE MAP PAGE 221

★ **Anchors @ The Jetty** The Esplanade, Waterfront Ⓦ anchors-the-jetty-restaurant.business.site. This nautically themed restaurant does a brisk trade throughout the day, on account of its location and decor, as much as for its moderately priced succulent seafood. The calamari are highly praised, but try their breakfasts too; this is one of the few places that offers a healthy alternative and the usual fry-ups. NSS–$$$

★ **The Raft** The Esplanade Ⓦ theraftrestaurant.com. This unmissable large structure on stilts, jutting out into the lagoon, is the ideal spot to laze away an afternoon watching the sea life. Warm wooden interiors and winter log fires make for a relaxed ambience. The usual spread of salads, pasta, seafood and flame-grilled meat dishes, including tasty veggie options, is available. The quality is consistently high, and the prices are moderate. N$$–$$$

Rojo Café & Bistro Walvis Bay Yacht Club Ⓦ rojobistro.com. A cheery, nautically-themed venue, serving light salads, savoury pancakes, burgers and wraps to more substantial fish, surf 'n' turf and steak mains – all freshly prepared. There's also sushi and a kids' menu, but the seafood platter for two is a real draw. N$$–$$$

Slowtown Coffee Roasters 95 Sam Nujoma Ave Ⓦ slowtowncoffee.com/stores/store-walvisbay. This successful Swakopmund enterprise opened in Walvis, offering a cosy coffee shop on the main street with comfy seating indoors and a pleasant garden outside. The ideal spot for a cappuccino or a latte with a large slab of cake. Bags of speciality coffee for sale too. N$$

DRINKING SEE MAP PAGE 221

Sarah se Gat The Boardwalk Ⓣ 081 122 0181. This is a serious drinking den and a good sundowner spot, especially in the summer when you can lounge the wooden benches and tables on the rooftop terrace and soak up the panoramic views of the bay. There is a decent cocktail menu and live music, usually on Friday and Saturday evenings from 8pm and Sunday afternoons.

North of Swakopmund

North of Swakopmund, the increasingly wild and seemingly barren coastline stretches towards the **Kunene River**, which marks the border with **Angola** about 680km (422.5 miles) away. Travelling along the compacted salt and gravel coastal road affords you views of endless gravel plains, flat sandy **beaches** pummelled by the Atlantic waves, and, eventually, pale, distant **dunes** that creep closer as you drive further north. This is punctuated by the occasional flecks of lichen fields, which transform into a colourful tapestry in the early morning mist.

Theoretically, this whole strip of land (reaching only around 40km/24.9 miles inland) is protected by Namibia's most recently formed reserve, the **Dorob National Park** (formerly the West Coast Recreational Area). The park extends southwards to the Kuiseb River Delta, south of Walvis Bay, and northwards to the Ugab River, where the **Skeleton Coast National Park** begins. The ultimate aim is to create a coastal mega park that extends the entire length of Namibia's coastline. For the moment, the incipient Dorob National Park is more of a paper park, with various excluded areas (where development has already taken place) and no real facilities; as a result, no park fees are charged yet, except to enter the **seal reserve** at **Cape Cross**.

Henties Bay

Once little more than a tiny fishing village, **HENTIES BAY** is expanding: new construction is very much in evidence, and everywhere you look, there are road signs to self-catering chalets, guesthouses and B&Bs. Though still primarily geared towards the fishing fraternity, many of whom trek here annually from South Africa, the municipality is keen to attract other tourists and has invested in a sizeable new tourist centre, which can furnish keen walkers with a map of a couple of lengthy unmarked **hikes** (18 or 20km/11.2 or 12.4 miles): one goes inland along the Omaruru River – with an unpromising un-scenic start through a sand-mining operation – the other heads down the coast to some wetlands. You'd need to set out early in the morning with plenty of food and water. More popular are the **four-wheel drive trails**; again, the tourist office can provide you with the relevant information, including satellite maps, though having a GPS is also advisable. Destinations include the impressive **Messum Crater** (see page 227), a vast natural amphitheatre containing welwitschias and ancient rock art, and the **Ugab Menhir** – an interesting megalith. Don't miss the impressive **lichen fields** east of the road, 4km (2.5 miles) north of Henties Bay.

ARRIVAL AND INFORMATION — HENTIES BAY

By car Follow the C34 70km (43.5 miles) north up the coast from Swakopmund. The compacted salt and gravel road is hard and smooth, for the most part, but can be slippery in the early morning fog and has one or two bumpy moments.

By minibus There are daily minibuses between Henties Bay and Swakopmund and weekend departures to Khorixas on Friday, returning to Henties Bay on Sunday.

Tourist information There is a large municipal tourist office building (T 064 501143, W hentiesbaytourism.com) offering free high-speed wi-fi, with some occasionally open curio stalls and a coffee shop. Here, you can get your free MEFT permits for the four-wheel drive trails and purchase the relevant satellite map; otherwise, you need one from the MEFT office in either Swakopmund (see page 213) or Walvis Bay (see page 222).

ACCOMMODATION — SEE MAP PAGE 208

Fisherman's Guesthouse Auss Street 2007 W huntandfishnamibia.com. Friendly, cheerful, fishing-themed guesthouse, primarily catering to fisherfolk but offering warm hospitality to all, close to the beach. It has fourteen tidy, well-kept rooms (Room 4 has a sea view), twin beds, tea/coffee facilities and TV, and it can provide gourmet meals (host Louis was a former full-time chef). N$$

Haus Estnic 1417 Omatako St W hausestnic.weebly.com. Though you might feel overly enclosed, personalised service is guaranteed as this place only has three double rooms – all en-suite with fridge, tea/coffee-making facilities and TV. They open onto a plant-filled patio with shade and a braai hearth to warm you when it's chilly. N$$

EATING

Fishy Corner 19 Benguela St, next to Spar T 064 501059. Festooned with fishing tackle and possessing quaint painted wooden furniture, this cosy, friendly place prepares decent-sized portions of fresh fish and other seafood at modest prices. Choose from hake, steenbras, calamari, kabeljou or kingklip. N$

5

Cape Cross

Charge payable at the MEFT office

A pinprick on the map around 120km (74.6 miles) up the coast from Swakopmund, Cape Cross is home to the world's largest colony of Cape fur seals. Though the landscape is bare and unremarkable, the seals draw a surprising number of visitors. The walkway allows you to get close to the action: belligerent bulls tussling for supremacy and mating rights, trying to take chunks out of each other, and female seals and pups squabbling, playing, dozing off in the sun, or struggling to get out of the surf as it lashes against the rocks.

Nearby is the Cape Cross itself – or rather a replica – which marks the spot where, in 1484, Diago Cão, a Portuguese explorer, erected a *padrão* (stone cross) in an attempt to claim the land for the king of Portugal. The original cross, taken to Germany by the colonisers, was returned to Namibia in 2019.

ARRIVAL AND INFORMATION — CAPE CROSS

By car Access is easy even in a saloon car; Cape Cross is accessed via a dirt road signposted off the C34, 48km (29.8 miles) north of Henties Bay – 70km (43.5 miles) north of Swakop – which has the only fuel between Swakopmund and the reserve.

On a tour Several tour operators in Swakopmund (see page 214) include Cape Cross on a half-day or full-day itinerary.

MEFT office Pay your entrance fee at the MEFT office (daily 8am–5pm, but opens at 10am during the seal-culling season: 1 July–15 Nov; T 064 694037), 5km (3.1 miles) from the turn-off to the seal colony; the seals lie a further 3km (1.9 miles) down the dirt road.

ACCOMMODATION AND EATING — SEE MAP PAGE 208

Cape Cross Campsite Halfway between the MEFT office and the seal colony T 064 694037. This exposed and frequently windy site has only minimum facilities: a long-drop latrine and a braai area, but no water or electricity. It's hard to imagine why you'd want to stay here unless you fish, especially as Cape Cross Lodge campground offers far better

THE CAPE CROSS SEAL COLONY

You're likely to smell it before you see it: the world's largest breeding colony of **Cape fur seals**, which sprawls over the windswept beach at **Cape Cross**. Fur seals (family *Otariidae*), endemic to southern Africa, are commonly known as 'eared seals' as they are distinguished from 'true seals' (family *Phocidae*) by their visible external ears.

Out in the ocean for much of the year, the vast, blubber-bloated **bulls** heave their 360kg (56.7st) bodies onto shore around mid-October, losing almost half that body weight over the next few weeks as they scrap with other bulls to establish and defend territory and secure a decent-sized harem. The heavily pregnant **cows** arrive a few weeks later but enjoy very little breathing space: no sooner are the pups born (late Nov–early Dec) than the dominant bulls mate with each female in their harem. Development of the fertilised egg is delayed for three months, followed by a nine-month gestation period, which results in females giving birth at the same time each year. **Pups** suckle from their mother for almost a year, though progressively, they hunt for more extended periods away from home. Just under one in three pups survives – some drown, some are abandoned or lose their mother, or get trampled on by other seals; around a quarter fall prey to brown hyenas and black-backed jackals, which can be spotted at dusk, lurking on the fringes of the colony, awaiting their chance to snatch their prey.

Numbering between eighty thousand and one hundred thousand, the size of the seal colony is kept more or less constant by the highly controversial **annual culling** between July and November, during which thousands of seals are slaughtered. The Namibian government maintains that the cull is necessary to protect fish stocks, provide seasonal jobs and as a means of generating income through fur sales; counter-arguments put forward by the increasingly vocal national and international anti-culling protest movement claim seals do not threaten fish stocks and that more jobs and better revenue could be generated through eco-tourism activities involving seals.

LICHENS

By the side of the salt road up the Skeleton Coast and en route to the Messum Crater on the Namib's gravel plains lie some of the world's most extensive (foliose) **lichen fields**. One of Namibia's more overlooked treasures – especially since to the uninitiated, they resemble shrivelled, dead bits of plant for much of the time – they warrant closer examination. In contrast, on overcast mornings, when there is moisture in the air, they show their true colours, '**blooming**' and producing kaleidoscopic shades of purple, orange, black, green or reddish-brown, only to shrivel up once more as the sun burns more to reduce transpiration. If you happen to miss the show in the morning fog, at any time of day, you can stop, sprinkle a little water on a patch, wait a few minutes, and watch the transformation.

Lichens are extraordinary: plant-like but not plants, but instead **organisms** that are combinations of algae living among the filaments of a fungus in a symbiotic relationship. The alga absorbs light and moisture from the air to photosynthesise and provide food and energy; the fungus also absorbs and stores moisture, draws nutrients from the ground, and usually acts as an anchor. For this reason, lichen is an important stabiliser in the Namib, helping prevent erosion. However, a relatively common sight is the *Xanthomaculina convoluta*. This free-flowing foliose lichen blows around and collects in hollows and dry river beds, with a charcoal-grey appearance when sheltering from the sun; it turns green when absorbing moisture.

Of the world's twenty thousand known lichen species, the Namib hosts around 120, many endemic to the area. One of the most visually striking is *Teleschistes capensis*. This relatively large bushy specimen can grow several centimetres high and resembles a piece of terrestrial coral the colour of burnished gold when open. Some lichen is thought to be **thousands of years old** – even older than welwitschias (see page 218), growing at a glacial pace of only 1mm per year. This makes them incredibly fragile; a thoughtless bit of off-road driving over a seemingly featureless desert can destroy centuries of growth.

facilities for a little extra cost. Closed 1 July–15 Nov. N$

Cape Cross Lodge 4km (2.5 miles) north of the seal colony on the coast, South Africa ⓦ capecross.org. Spacious, comfortably furnished rooms overlooking the desolate coast; you get your own balcony upstairs, whereas, on the ground floor, you can step directly onto the beach. Day visitors are welcome at the reasonably priced restaurant, where you can watch the restless waves. The well-sheltered pitches have high-quality ablutions and braai facilities. Camping N$, doubles (DBB) N$$$

Messum Crater

46km (28.6 miles) northeast of Cape Cross • Permits should be purchased from the MEFT office in Swakopmund (see page 213), Walvis Bay (see page 222) or Windhoek (see page 94); alternatively, en-route in Henties Bay tourist office (see page 225) • There are three entrances/exits to the Messum Crater that all need four-wheel drive: approaching from the south, a well-graded gravel road is signposted off the C34, 2km (1.2 miles) north of Cape Cross; another enters/exits the northwest edge of the crater along the Messum River and connects with the C34 at Mile 108; the third exits at the northeast edge of the crater and joins the Messum River, heading eastwards until you join the D2342 that skirts the southern edge of the Brandberg

Straddling the eastern boundary of the Dorob National Park lies the mesmerising **Messum Crater**, the centre of a collapsed volcano that erupted some 132 to 135 million years ago and the probable source of much of the basalt that forms the neighbouring Goboboseb Mountains, to the north. The shallow flat **caldera**, around 20km (12.4 miles) in diameter, is surrounded by two non-continuous concentric rings of heavily eroded igneous rocks, forming a surreal, eerie wilderness worthy of a science fiction film. The routes to and from the crater also provide opportunities to explore other fascinating natural and human phenomena: **lichen fields** (see page 227) and **welwitschias** lie along the well-graded gravel track from the Skeleton Coast side (see page 218); **archaeological remains**, such as stone circles used by ancient nomadic Damara groups, are also visible; and taking the northeastern exit out of the crater, the vast massif of the Brandberg looms as you draw closer, glowing pink and gold when bathed in the afternoon sunlight.

Make sure you're well prepared for the drive here. In addition to the satellite map you can purchase from the Henties Bay tourist office, a **GPS** is advisable (and a satellite phone if you're travelling alone and not up to basic breakdown repairs) since it's easy to get lost.

Skeleton Coast National Park

Ugab Gate (main entrance) daily 7am–3pm (last entry), last exit 7pm; Springbokwasser Gate (eastern entrance) daily 7am–3pm (last entry), last exit 7pm • The MEFT offices in Windhoek, Swakopmund and Walvis Bay sell entry permits (daily charge per person and for the vehicle), or they can be purchased at the Ugab Gate

At the Ugab River, the larger-than-life skull and crossbones on the gates herald your entry to the **Skeleton Coast National Park**, evoking images of whalebones strewn along the shoreline, giant rusting hulls of shipwrecked vessels half-buried in the sand, and the twisted skeletons of the unfortunate crew members who struggled and failed, to make it out of the desert alive. While some of these images hold true, most **shipwrecks** have been consumed by either the sand or the sea, and those that remain are to be found in the most northerly section of the park, only accessible on a **fly-in safari** (or in the equally inaccessible Sperrgebiet), and not the southern section open to self-drive visitors.

As a result, it's easy to be underwhelmed by the Skeleton Coast, especially when driving across never-ending and seemingly empty gravel plains in thick **coastal fog** flanked by a beach scene reminiscent of the North Atlantic in November. There are few actual sights – a couple of small and unimpressive wrecked fishing boats and some abandoned mining equipment. However, if you adjust your expectations, appreciate the stark beauty of the landscape, and take time to stop along the way and seek out some of the smaller pleasures of the desert – the **insect life** and multicoloured carpets of lichen fields, which are only apparent when soaking up the morning moisture from the fog – then the park will still mesmerise you.

If you persist as far as the last 58km (36 miles) between Torra and Terrace Bay, the **dunes** reach the road; a 7km (4.3-mile) dune drive affords you a closer exploration. Some 166km (103.1 miles) after the Ugab Gate, the fairly bleak collection of exposed cement cabins that comprises Terrace Bay marks the end of the road; part of a former mining operation, this isolated **outpost** is now favoured by fishing enthusiasts.

A further 80km (49.7 miles) north lies **Möwe Bay**, known for its gemstone-rich beaches. Not accessible to independent travellers, it is the pick-up point for guests bound for the isolated, exclusive *Shipwreck Lodge* (see page 263), though most choose to fly in.

ARRIVAL AND DEPARTURE — SKELETON COAST NATIONAL PARK

By car The only way to visit this southern section of the park is in your own vehicle (a saloon car will manage most parts, but four-wheel drive is necessary to reach Terrace Bay). However, several overlander tours drive through the bottom corner of the park en route to Damaraland. The main entrance is the Ugab Gate on the C34, at the Ugab River, whereas the eastern entrance/exit, the Springbokwasser Gate, lies on the C39, which eventually leads northeast to Khorixas. The distance between the two gates is around 180km (111.8 miles). Visitors to the park are only allowed to drive through the park leaving by the other gate, whereas overnight visitors who will need to produce their reservation slip on entry can arrive and leave by the same gate.

On a tour You can only visit the northern section of the national park on a fly-in-safari (see page 262), though some of the Damaraland wilderness lodges do day trips into the central area of the park.

ACCOMMODATION AND EATING — SEE MAP PAGE 208

Terrace Bay Resort nwr.com.na. Experience the pounding surf backed by the dune sea in this desolate and frequently windy spot, only really frequented by keen fishermen. The cabins (sleeping six or ten) are basic, with much-needed hot water and comfy beds. Amazingly, there's a snug bar, an excellent restaurant on site, and a table-tennis table, making the whole visit a surreal experience. It also has a fuel station and a small shop. Doubles (DBB) N$$–$$$, cabins N$$

Torra Bay Campsite nwr.com.na. An extremely basic, exposed fishing camp only open seasonally (Dec–Jan). Camping per pitch N$

The hinterland

The longest yet quickest route to the central coast from Windhoek is via the tarred B2, which peels off the B1 at Okahandja (see page 171), some 66km (41 miles) north of Windhoek, heading west via the small towns of Karibib and Usakos to complete the remaining 280km (174 miles) to Swakopmund. The journey should take at most four hours. However, some diversions can be made along the way, for example, by venturing south into the **Otjipatera Mountains** south of Karibib or exploring the bronze boulders and rock art of the **Erongo Mountains** (see page 190) to the north of Usakos or even the dramatic **Spitzkoppe**, slightly further to the west. Avoid driving west along this road late Friday afternoon, especially on holiday weekends, as it's prime time for accidents: the traffic is inevitably heavy and travelling fast, and the dazzling setting sun will be directly in your eyes.

For quieter, more adventurous back roads to both Swakopmund and Walvis Bay, you need to head west and southwest out of Windhoek, along the C28 and C26, respectively – gravel roads that are devoid of shops, petrol stations and, for much of the way, human habitation. Both take you down **scenic passes** as the roads plunge off the central highland plateau, down onto the gravel plains of central Namib below, across increasingly desolate landscape until you reach the coast.

Karibib

Blink, and you can easily miss **KARIBIB** – a small town of around five thousand – as you speed along the B2 towards the coast. Although there's little specifically to detain you, it's worth pausing to pick up a cold drink and stroll around some of the surviving colonial buildings that bear witness to the small town's former importance that was assured once the first train reached here from Swakopmund in 1900. Much of Karibib's high-grade marble from the local quarries, which started in the early twentieth century, is exported to Europe. The Karibib Marble and Granite Works still support around three hundred jobs, while a more recently opened gold mine in the vicinity employs a further four hundred workers. Other small-scale gemstone mining occurs in the area.

ARRIVAL AND INFORMATION — KARIBIB

By shuttle or minibus The daily air-conditioned shuttle services that run between Windhoek and Swakopmund or Walvis Bay stop to pick up passengers at Henckert's Tourist Centre and charge the same price whichever way you're bound (2hr). Regular, cheaper minibuses between the two population centres also drop off/pick up passengers.

By train The very slow overnight train between Swakopmund and Windhoek stops off here in the middle of the night, so it's not an especially convenient way to travel.

Tourist information Henckert's Tourist Centre, on the main street (Mon–Fri 8am–5pm; 064 550700), is both an information centre and a rather depleted curio shop – the main operation moved to Swakopmund.

ACCOMMODATION — SEE MAP PAGE 208

Angi's Self-catering Guesthouse 315 Fracht St 064 550126, angis@iway.na. Perfectly respectable, if uninspiring, place to bed down for the night; ten functional, mainly twin rooms behind sliding glass doors, with a/c, TV, fridge and kitchenette, plus an on-site bar-restaurant serving pub grub if you don't fancy cooking. B&B N$$

★ **Etusis Lodge** Signposted west off the C32, 16km (10 miles) south of Karibib, plus another 16km to the lodge etusis.de. In a lovely location at the base of the Otjipatera Mountains, set in a private reserve, this delightful

5

rustic lodge is surrounded by fascinating rock formations. The scenery can be explored on foot or horseback, watching out for kudu, zebra, impala, klipspringer and the like. Accommodation is in neat stone-and-thatch bungalows with a/c and fridge or basic Meru-style tents. Expect hearty home cooking with locally sourced ingredients. Reductions for two-night stays. Some 20km (12.4 miles) from the lodge, the camping is a real treat, with six immaculately kept sites, each with shade and windbreaks, overlooking a dry river bed. Camping N$, self-catering farmhouse (min stay two nights) N$$, safari tent or bungalow (DBB) N$$$

Usakos

Though **USAKOS** has a pleasant aspect, spread across the hillside overlooking the Khan River, with the burnished granite domes of the Erongo Mountains in the background, there's little happening here to disrupt the town's torpor these days. During its heyday as the centre for Namibia's rail network, men were kept busy servicing the engines that came down on the Otavi line from the Tsumeb mine. When the mining tailed off in the 1960s, and with it the railway, Usakos' importance faded too. A graffiti-covered old steam locomotive sits forlornly outside the station as a poignant reminder of better days. Apart from dropping in at the popular **farm shop**, stopping in Usakos is to stock up with provisions if you're heading off to camp in the Erongo Mountains or the Spitzkoppe. The small **supermarket** on the main street is your only option. Should you miss the sharp right-angled turn in the high street, if you're heading towards the coast, carry on a block, and you'll come across some surprising topiary and a couple of dignified colonial-era buildings.

ARRIVAL AND DEPARTURE — USAKOS

By shuttle and minibus The daily air-conditioned shuttle services that run between Swakopmund or Walvis Bay and Windhoek drop off and pick up passengers at the farm shop by the Shell petrol station, 1km (0.6 miles) west

!NARA MELONS

Across the Namib's dunes and dry riverbeds sprawl the tangled spines of the desert's most valuable food source – the **!nara melon** (*Acanthosicyos horridus*). Several of these spiky green fruits the size of a grapefruit can be found on a single plant, which can live for over a hundred years. Fossil evidence points to its vital role in human and animal survival for over 40 million years. As well as being a major **source of water and protein**, the !nara's vicious thorn-like leaves – so modified to reduce water loss – afford protection to countless insects, spiders, rodents and reptiles, as well as to its fruit, while the plant's deep and extensive root system is a vital stabiliser of fragile dunes. The ! Nara exists in a symbiotic relationship with the black-backed jackal, which feeds on the pollinated nutrient-rich seeds of the fleshy fruit and then disperses them through its faeces.

The name ! Nara derives from '!na', meaning 'more than enough food' in Nama, the language of the **‡Aonin** – more commonly referred to as the Topnaars (see page 350) – who primarily inhabit the Lower Kuiseb River, and whose livelihoods and culture are inextricably entwined with this extraordinarily versatile fruit. Lauded in the ‡Aonin's traditional tales and praise poetry, !Nara melons are **harvested** annually (Aug–Sept & Dec–March). Nothing is wasted. The fruit's orangey, proteinous pulp is boiled and eaten as a porridge or then dried and made into !nama cakes (‡hoagaribeb) to store for future consumption, while the seeds, rich in fat and oil, are dried to provide a tasty snack, traded, or used to make natural cosmetics or cooking oil – you'll find the last two for sale in tourist shops in Swakopmund. Even the rind is dried and used as fuel or donkey feed, while its roots are said to have medicinal properties. Traditionally, ‡Aonin families had exclusive harvesting rights to specific !nara plants, though, in recent times, regulations have been relaxed, which has led to disputes. Like the ‡Aonin, the !nara melon faces major **survival challenges**, particularly decreasing groundwater levels due to increased water usage from dams along the Kuiseb River.

of the town centre. Regular, cheaper minibuses also pass through and stop in town.

By train The very slow overnight trains between Swakopmund and Windhoek wait for each other here in the middle of the night to exchange drivers and conductors before continuing on their way.

EATING

Namib Oasis Farm Stall & Deli 064 530283. A popular place to break the journey on the B2, either to grab a bag of freshly sliced biltong and a take-out coffee or to order something more substantial from their café: burgers, salads, sandwiches and the like. Camping is also possible, though there are much nicer sites in the nearby Erongos.

Travelling the C28

The 300km (186.4-mile-) long **C28** takes the back route from Windhoek to Swakopmund via some delightful **scenery**, initially across the highland savannah plateau of the Khomas Hochland. Around 45km (28 miles) out of Windhoek, a few kilometres after the turn-off for the D1418, look up through the scrub to your right to spot the ruins of Curt von Francois' **fort**, a small squat stone construction on a hilltop, established after the colonial administration had settled in Windhoek, to protect the trade route to the coast. It later became a rehab clinic for alcoholic soldiers.

Otjimbingwe

Some 125km (77.7 miles) west of Windhoek, the D1953 turns north off the C28, arriving, after 46km (28.6 miles), in the historical **Herero** settlement of **OTJIMBINGWE** – worth the detour if you have time. The site of **natural springs**, acknowledged in the Herero name Otjzingue (meaning 'refreshing place'), was the seat of the Herero Royal House of Zerua. It also contains Namibia's **oldest church**, consecrated by the Rhenish missionaries in 1867 after Chief Zerua had donated ten thousand bricks to build it. The church is still quite an impressive structure, with a lofty bell tower – added later – that you can look up into and a fine wood-panelled ceiling and pews. Otjimbingwe was also the seat of the colonial administration before it was moved to Windhoek.

The Bosua Pass

Around 150km (93.2 miles) after leaving Windhoek on the C28, you cross into the Erongo Region before the road falls off the escarpment in dramatic fashion at the **Bosua Pass**. The 1:5 gradient and the winding descent are not to be undertaken lightly – check your brakes first – and preferably not driven after heavy rains, as the gravel becomes treacherous, though some of the worst section is paved. Don't forget to pause periodically to take in the breathtaking **views**.

Once the land flattens out, the road streaks away across the more desolate and sparsely vegetated pre-Namib plains towards the **Atlantic**. As it does, you enter the northern section of the Namib-Naukluft National Park; provided you drive straight through, no park fees are necessary. However, there are a couple of **four-wheel drive trails** off to various rudimentary **wilderness campsites**; if you want to stop over, you must organise **permits** and camping **fees** in advance in a MEFT office (see page 233).

Travelling the C26

To travel the back way from Windhoek to Walvis Bay, you take the C26 southeast out of the capital, which eventually swings west through the **Hakos Mountains** towards the spectacular **Gamsberg Pass** (the 'g' is pronounced 'ch' as in the Scottish 'loch'). Here, the rugged folds of seemingly endless mountains ripple into the distance; while the daytime views are awe-inspiring, they are equally impressive at night since the Gamsberg area is one of the world's top sites for **stargazing**.

THE NORTHERN NAMIB-NAUKLUFT WILDERNESS CAMPGROUND

While most people confine their camping in the Namib-Naukluft National Park to the popular, **well-provisioned sites** at Sesriem (see page 113) and in the Naukluft Mountains (see page 117), lesser-known opportunities for **wilderness camping** exist in the very northern section of the park, in the hinterland behind Swakopmund and Walvis Bay. The settings may not be as dramatic in these isolated spots. Still, by stopping over at several of these locations, you can get a feel for the desert's variety: shallow and deep watercourses, granite inselbergs with fantastical stone sculptures due to erosion, flat gravel plains and burnished dunes. Moreover, you may not have to share the wilderness with anyone else except possibly a visiting hyena or jackal and a handful of lizards. Then, the sky can appear like a diamond-encrusted black velvet cape at night.

The most popular route is the one that curves north off the C28, taking in the **Tinkas** and **Bloedkoppie** sites, with **Rock Arch** out on a limb. The other camps are accessed via the C14. The ten campgrounds listed below have only the most rudimentary facilities – some in a poor state of repair, generally only long-drop toilets and the occasional concrete braai site, picnic table or rubbish bin (though you should take all rubbish out with you). You will also need to be self-sufficient in fuel, firewood and drinking water. In summer, it can be unbearably hot; in winter, it is freezing at night; the best time is just after the rains, when there should still be enough residual moisture and vegetation to take the harsh edge off the landscape, and the daytime temperatures, though still hot, are more bearable.

AROUND THE C28

Bloedkoppie (Blood Hill) North of the C28. No battle site, the 'blood' refers to the rich red colour of this granite outcrop at sunset, less appreciable if you happen to be sitting on top enjoying a sundowner. Saloon car drivers must camp on the solid, harder ground on the southern and eastern sides; the shadier sites in the dry riverbed on the northwestern side of the inselberg are only accessible to four-wheel drive vehicles.

Ganab Just south of the D9812. It is named after llGanab, the Nama name for the camelthorn trees that sparsely populate this shallow watercourse and provide some shade in an otherwise exposed area. Look out for the stately Rüppell's korhaan and possibly a Cape fox at night.

Great Tinkas Between Bloedkoppie and Rock Arch. Several campsites are set amid the kopjes and some good hiking trails. There's also an unlikely dam nearby, which, when full following a rare rainfall, attracts a variety of birds and mammals. Four-wheel drive only.

Rock arch 30km (18.6 miles) east of Bloedkoppie. The shade at this campground is provided by its main feature, the eponymous rock arch, like a miniature version of the one at the Spitzkoppe. There is also a short nature walk. Only accessible by four-wheel drive, the track leading here is very rocky.

Swakop River Between the B2 and C28. This most northerly campground is also a popular picnic site

Once you reach the pass – the tortuous 30km (18.6-mile) descent requires concentration – before you plunge off the escarpment and cross the **Kuiseb River** for the first time, look to the south, at the Gamsberg itself. Namibia's **third-highest peak**, at 2,347m (7,700.1ft), is an extraordinary **table mountain** whose smooth, flat top appears to have been sliced off with a sharp knife. At the bottom of the pass are a few nice **guest farms** – perfect places to break the journey and make the most of the mountain scenery.

Shortly after the C26 joins the C14 – which leads southwards to Solitaire – you enter the Namib-Naukluft National Park and find yourself descending into the **Kuiseb Canyon**, a deep incision in the otherwise flat, bleak desert crust, though on a rare stretch of tarred road.

Kuiseb River

The ephemeral **Kuiseb River** rises in the Khomas Hochland, beginning a 500km (310.7-mile) journey towards the Atlantic. Like the Tsauchab River at Sossusvlei (see page 112), the Kuiseb fails to reach the ocean – except in the rare years of exceptional rains, when it manages to push through the dunes blocking the way. Instead, it filters on the well-visited Welwitschia Drive trail (see page 219), so it may not be as isolated or clean as you hope. However, the relatively lush riverine vegetation provides good shade.

AROUND THE C14

Homeb 60km (37.3 miles) south of the C28, at the end of the D2186. Striking camping area for its location by the Kuiseb River, at a point where it separates the dunes to the south from the grey granite folds (reminiscent of the 'moonscape' near Swakopmund; see page 113) and gravel plains to the north. The riverine vegetation, which includes ana, wild tamarisk, figs and false ebony, provides excellent shade. It's a good place for spotting raptors, and if you walk over into the dunes, you may be lucky to spot the elusive dune lark. There is a small ‡Aonin (Topnaar) settlement with assorted livestock nearby.

Kriess-se-Rus 8km (5 miles) west of the turn-off for the D1198. This campground in a dry watercourse just north of the C14 is neither especially attractive nor particularly popular, though the exposed schist rocks provide some shelter.

Kuiseb Bridge Where the C14 crosses the Kuiseb Canyon. What should be one of the most attractive campgrounds, deep in the shady, sandy Kuiseb Canyon, can suffer from the rumble of traffic, especially in high season, as it lies on the Sossusvlei–Swakopmund desert 'highway'.

Mirabib On the way to the desert research station at Gobabeb, west of the D2186. This isolated inselberg rises out of the desert plains, its weathered granite overhangs providing the only decent shade, which you may share with the bats, with a couple of other sites tucked in among the boulders and rock sculptures. Great views of the dune sea in the distance.

Vogelfederberg Just south of the C14. A smallish granite inselberg (translating as 'Bird-feather Mountain') with stunning views from the top. Being around 40km (24.9 miles) from the ocean, it is susceptible to the Namib's early morning fog.

PRACTICALITIES

Permits must be purchased in advance from an NWR or MEFT office (in Sesriem, see page 112; Swakopmund, see page 213; Walvis Bay, see page 222; or Windhoek, see page 94). Permits cost modest daily rates per person and vehicle, with camping fees per pitch. Park wardens periodically patrol these areas and you will be fined if found driving along one of these minor gravel roads or camping without the relevant permits. When you get your permit, you'll be given a rudimentary map of the area; though the roads are generally well marked and straightforward, a Tracks4Africa map and GPS are always good backups. Most tracks are driveable in a high-clearance saloon car, except where stated, though obviously, you should not drive into any riverbeds if you only have a two-wheel drive vehicle. Even with a four-wheel drive, you should always resist the temptation to drive off the marked tracks and help preserve the fragile desert ecology (see page 68).

away into the sand just south of Walvis Bay. Even after heavy rains, it rarely flows for more than a few weeks, though precious life-giving pools of water remain in more sheltered parts for much longer. The Kuiseb ploughs a deep furrow of the escarpment and then carves its way across the desert. Satellite imagery shows how crucial the river is to halting the northerly progress of the marching Namib sand sea. Nearer the Kuiseb's 'delta', ‡Aonin people, more widely known as Topnaars, a Nama group, inhabit the sandy riverbed, where they are heavily dependent on the !nara melon (see page 230) for survival.

The **Kuiseb Canyon** formed some 20 million years ago and is 200m (656.2ft) deep in places. It was made famous in the book *The Sheltering Desert*, an account by German geologist Martin Henno of how he and a companion, Hermann Korn, survived there for two years during World War II to avoid internment. The **Carp Cliff Viewpoint**, signposted off the C14, 1km (0.6 miles) east of the descent into the ravine, allows you to peer over the edge at one of the shelters the Germans used, as well as affording great **all-round views** of the valley and the surrounding otherworldly landscape.

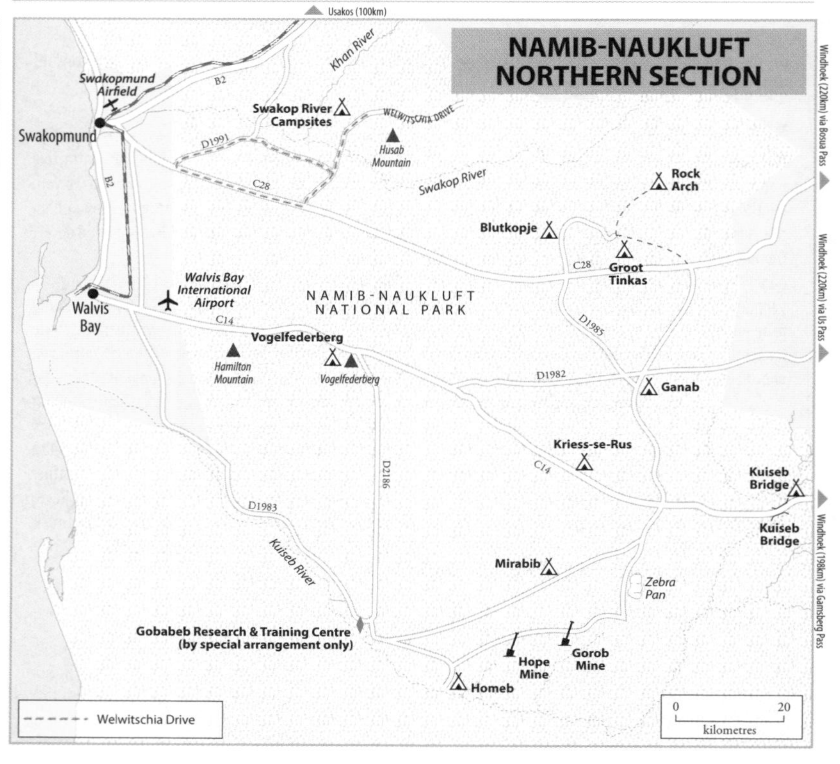

ACCOMMODATION

GAMSBERG, SEE MAP PAGE 208

Corona Guest Farm Signposted east off the C26, 16km (10 miles) from the junction with the C14 (another 16km/10 miles from there; four-wheel drive required) coronaguestfarm.com. Heavily themed guest rooms are chock-full of eclectic furnishings and ornaments – many antiques and animal skins from when the place was a hunting farm. The place enjoys a lovely garden setting, with a superb pool area and dining terrace (food is delicious and beautifully presented), and hiking trails are available. Reduction for more than one night. DBB N$$$

Hakos Guest Farm Signposted 7km (4.3 miles) north off the C26, just before the Gamsberg Pass hakos-astrofarm.com. The country's number one astro-venue enjoys a spectacular setting, imperiously perched on a mountain at the top of the Gamsberg Pass. However, the place is rather austere, and the 14 single/double rooms feel institutional. But the stargazing is what it's about (at extra cost) and the area is great for hiking. Camping N$, doubles (DBB) N$$$

Etosha and the far north

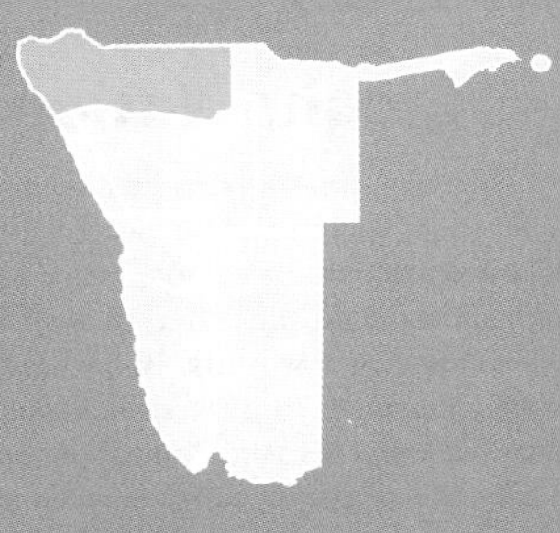

BURCHELL'S ZEBRA IN ETOSHA NATIONAL PARK

Etosha and the far north

6

The far north of Namibia holds some of the country's most-visited and least-explored landscapes. In the former category is the vast expanse of Etosha National Park, which receives over two hundred thousand visitors annually, drawn by almost guaranteed sightings of large numbers of big mammals and abundant birdlife. In contrast, the evocative mountainous wilderness of northern Kunene – lacking in decent roads and largely devoid of people – remains inaccessible to most. However, it provides an unforgettable experience for those who make it that far.

Centring on a vast salt pan, Etosha National Park is the main reason visitors venture to the north of Namibia, enticed by the prospect of coming face to face with a lion, glimpsing a leopard at dawn or gazing at herds of zebra and wildebeest sweeping across the savannah. As there is limited accommodation inside Etosha, many stay in the more comfortable lodges and campgrounds just outside the park boundary, often in private reserves offering outstanding wildlife-viewing opportunities. North from Etosha, the predominantly flat, sandy scenery extends to the urban and rural developments in the so-called '**Four O's**' – the small but densely populated regions of Oshikoto, Omusati, Ohangwena and Oshana, home predominantly to the **Owambo** peoples. **Oshakati** is the main commercial hub of the chaotic conurbation, a helpful pit stop to stock up on supplies and witness life outside the tourist bubble. There are a handful of modest cultural attractions in the area worth taking in if you're passing through: the traditional royal homestead at **Tsandi**, a giant baobab in **Outapi**, or **Lake Oponona**, a large dusty depression for much of the year, which transforms into an avian wetland paradise after good rains.

Heading west into the sparsely populated **northern Kunene** region, the landscape alters dramatically as you enter the **Kaokoveld**, as does the population density – only 1.7 people per sq km. From the dramatic **waterfalls** at **Ruacana** and **Epupa** on the Kunene River, striking, reddish-brown stony earth gives way to rugged, mountainous areas interspersed with desolate valleys at Marienfluss and Hartmann's. Yet further west, the Wilderness Area of the **Skeleton Coast National Park** – only accessible by fly-in safari – eventually melts into rippling dune fields before hitting the Atlantic coast. This remote, starkly beautiful region is home to desert-adapted elephants, black rhinos and even lions – and to the semi-nomadic **Himba**, one of Namibia's most recognisable and resilient Indigenous peoples. The small, underdeveloped and isolated regional capital of **Opuwo** is the place for independent travellers to start their explorations. However, it's not until you spend time in one of their remote settlements that you'll begin to learn more about the people and their environment.

Etosha National Park

Sunrise–sunset • Daily charge per person and vehicle (children under 16 free)

Located in the far northwest of the country, and covering an expanse of around 22,000 sq km (8,494.2 sq miles), **ETOSHA NATIONAL PARK** is Namibia's premier wildlife-viewing destination, stuffed to zoo-like proportions with a host of large mammals and some spectacular birds. In Indigenous languages, it is variously known as 'great white place', 'place of mirages' or 'lake of a mother's tears', which all refer to the park's defining feature, **Etosha Pan**, a vast saline pan that covers a fifth of its surface area. Around 110km (68.4 miles) long and more than 50km (31 miles) wide in places, it is Africa's largest salt pan and is even visible from space. In the dry season, it is a seemingly endless expanse of

BAOBABS AT EPUPA FALLS

Highlights

❶ **Etosha National Park** The undisputed crown jewel of Namibia's parks in terms of wildlife. Etosha is full of megafauna and has a vast, unworldly, saline pan at its core. See page 238

❷ **Visiting an open market** Feel the buzz in Oshakati, Ondangwa or Ongwediwa, where stalls overflow with pulses, grains, fruits and vegetables you'll struggle to identify, alongside clothing, crafts and household utensils. See page 251

❸ **Visiting a Himba community** With a good guide, and the right sensibility, interacting with Namibia's distinctive semi-nomadic pastoralists is an unforgettable experience. See page 258

❹ **Epupa Falls** Stunning sunsets, basking crocs and glorious cascades of water have helped put this remote outpost firmly on the tourist trail. See page 258

❺ **Marienfluss** If you don't have the necessary vehicle convoy and four-wheel drive experience to drive to this hauntingly beautiful desolate valley, consider a tour with a specialist operator. See page 259

❻ **Puros** Only accessible by four-wheel drive, this Himba-run campground lies on the banks of the Hoarusib River, where permanent springs attract desert-adapted elephants, rhinos, giraffes and lions. See page 263

HIGHLIGHTS ARE MARKED ON THE MAP ON PAGE 240

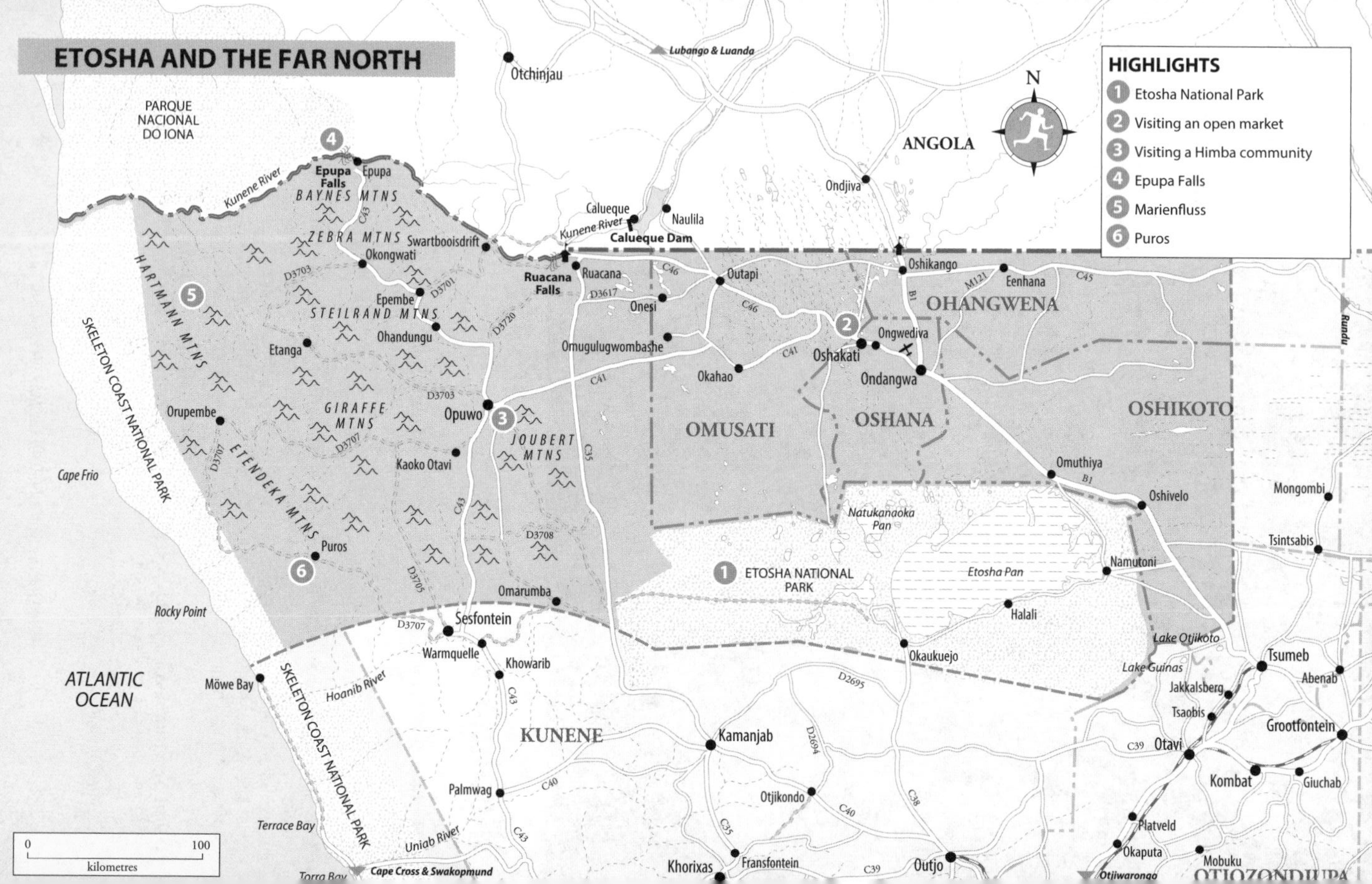

ETOSHA AND THE FAR NORTH
HIGHLIGHTS
1 Etosha National Park
2 Visiting an open market
3 Visiting a Himba community
4 Epupa Falls
5 Marienfluss
6 Puros
N
ANGOLA
PARQUE NACIONAL DO IONA
Otchinjau
Lubango & Luanda
Ondjiva
Calueque
Naulila
Calueque Dam
Kunene River
Epupa Falls
Epupa
BAYNES MTNS
ZEBRA MTNS
Swartbooisdrift
Okongwati
Ruacana Falls
Ruacana
Outapi
Oshikango
Eenhana
OHANGWENA
Rundu
Epembe
STEILRAND MTNS
Ohandungu
Etanga
Onesi
Omugulugwombashe
Okahao
Oshakati
Ongwediva
Ondangwa
HARTMANN MTNS
GIRAFFE MTNS
Opuwo
JOUBERT MTNS
OMUSATI
OSHANA
OSHIKOTO
Orupembe
ETENDEKA MTNS
Kaoko Otavi
SKELETON COAST NATIONAL PARK
Cape Frio
Omuthiya
Oshivelo
Mongombi
Natukanaoka Pan
Tsintsabis
Puros
ETOSHA NATIONAL PARK
Etosha Pan
Namutoni
Omarumba
Halali
Rocky Point
Sesfontein
Warmquelle
Khowarib
Okaukuejo
Lake Otjikoto
Lake Guinas
Tsumeb
Abenab
ATLANTIC OCEAN
Möwe Bay
Hoanib River
Jakkalsberg
Tsaobis
KUNENE
Kamanjab
Grootfontein
Otavi
Kombat
Giuchab
Palmwag
Otjikondo
Platveld
Terrace Bay
Okaputa
Uniab River
Mobuku
0 100 kilometres
Torra Bay
Cape Cross & Swakopmund
Khorixas
Fransfontein
Outjo
Otjiwarongo
OTJOZONDJUPA
C43
D3703
D3701
D3720
D3617
C46
C41
C45
M121
B1
C35
D3707
D3705
D3708
D2695
D2694
C38
C39
C40

WHEN TO VISIT ETOSHA NATIONAL PARK

The best time to visit is during the drier **winter months** (May–Oct) when more animals are concentrated around the waterholes, predominantly scattered around the southern edges of Etosha Pan. Viewing is easier because the vegetation is sparser, while the lower temperatures make a stakeout at a waterhole a more pleasurable experience. On the other hand, when the wind gets up, the landscape can become enveloped in dust clouds. Visitor numbers are inevitably higher in winter, especially during European and Namibian school holidays. However, the park is so large and the waterholes so numerous – 86 in all – that it never gets unbearably busy. In the wetter **summer months**, however, the lusher vegetation is much easier on the eye, and the water-filled pans attract an abundance of migratory birdlife, especially between November and April. In the rare years when the rains are really heavy (usually Jan or Feb) and the water lingers, Etosha Pan becomes a vast pink-and-white carpet of pelicans and flamingos, which flock here in their hundreds of thousands to breed.

shimmering white, tinged with olive green, which, in years of exceptional rain, briefly morphs into a shallow lake resembling a giant mirror. This transformation harks back to the pan's origins millions of years ago when it was probably a much larger, deeper inland lake fed by northern rivers – including the Kunene. When tectonic shifts altered the lie of the land, forcing the rivers to change course, the lake dried up.

Brief history

The establishment of Etosha as a '**game reserve**' by the governor of German South-West Africa in 1907 was as much, if not more, about safeguarding an economic resource for the colony as it was about wildlife conservation. Earlier incursions by European missionaries and traders from the 1950s opened trade routes, resulting in a major depletion of wildlife. However, after years of conflict, the Owambo chief Nehale Mpingana and his followers had succeeded in driving most settlers away. German troops arrived in 1896, initially to control the rinderpest (see page 341). Three years later, they built a fort at Namutoni, which was attacked and destroyed by the Owambo but rebuilt the following year – and still stands today. A second outpost was added at Okaukuejo in 1901.

Initially, an area of almost 100,000 sq km (38,610.2 sq miles) was envisaged for the park, stretching to the coast. Over the years, the controversial boundaries have been altered and the area reduced to its present size, though inevitably, large numbers of people – specifically Hai||om San, Herero and Owambo – have been dispossessed of their land in the process.

During **German colonial times,** the nomadic Hai||om San population was allowed to stay in the reserve, provided they continued to hunt with bow and arrow, but in 1954, under the South African regime, most were forcibly removed to work on nearby farms; a small percentage have remained as park employees, but they, and other communities, continue to press the government for the return of their land and greater benefit from the park's income.

Flora and fauna

Etosha is a wonderful haven for **wildlife**, boasting the continent's largest concentration of black rhinos and other large mammals in abundance: elephants, giraffes, lions, leopards, cheetahs, wildebeest, kudu, oryx, eland and hartebeest, to name but a few. Round every second corner, you bump into herds of Burchell's zebra, impala and springbok – the park's most numerous antelope. The rarer black-faced impala and Hartmann's mountain zebra are only found in the reserve's western reaches. **Birdlife,** too, is prolific: 340 species have been recorded in the park. Large bateleurs and martial eagles wheel above, while ostriches, kori bustards and secretary birds stride across the plains; rollers, bee-eaters, sunbirds and orioles provide brilliant flashes of colour; and others fascinate with their extraordinary appearance. Two such birds are the marabou stork, a huge, seemingly bald character with a particularly pendulous gular pouch, and the southern ground hornbill, a turkey-sized creature with distinctive crimson throat and eye patches, whose unearthly booming call can carry for 3km (1.9 miles).

Mopane woodland savannah and grassland predominate in the areas surrounding Etosha Pan, with the occasional clump of elegant makalani palms conferring around some water sources. However, some 30km (18.6 miles) west of Okaukuejo, the ghostly, contorted forms of moringa trees, dubbed the 'fairy-tale forest' – over ambitiously, given their depleted numbers – form a striking contrast. In the western section of the park, which until 2014 was closed to the general public, the landscape is markedly different: hillier terrain is covered with rich reddish-brown earth, peppered with rocky dolomite outcrops and covered with smaller mopane shrubs.

ARRIVAL AND INFORMATION — ETOSHA NATIONAL PARK

By car There are four points of entry into Etosha, all accessible in an ordinary saloon car via good roads: the Von Lindequist Gate, on the eastern edge, lies 19km (11.8 miles) west of the B1 between Tsumeb and Ondangwa; the little-used King Nehale Lya Mpingana Gate is on the northern park boundary, only 17km (10.6 miles) from the B1; the Andersson Gate is on the south side of the park, on the C38, 114km (70.8 miles) north of Outjo; and the Galton Gate is tucked away in the southwest corner, on the C35, 59km (36.7 miles) north of Kamanjab.

Park information The website ⓦetoshanationalpark.org is a good source of information and has detailed maps of the park that can be downloaded. Otherwise, enquire at reception in the rest camps; guides and park staff can advise you on the best places to head to see particular animals, which change seasonally and from day to day. There is sometimes a visitors' book in which recent sightings are recorded. NWR also produces a decent booklet containing maps and identification charts for some of the more common or sought-after species. This is usually available at camp shops and in Windhoek, Swakopmund and Outjo shops.

GETTING AROUND

By car The extensive road network consists of good-quality gravel roads, and all camps, except *Onkoshi* (where they can arrange a pick-up from *Namutoni*), are accessible in a saloon car. While the speed limit within the park is 60km/h (37.3mph), you need to be travelling more slowly in most places if you want to spot any wildlife and not risk flattening some of it on the road; it's commonplace to go around a bend and find tussling wildebeest or loping giraffes blocking your

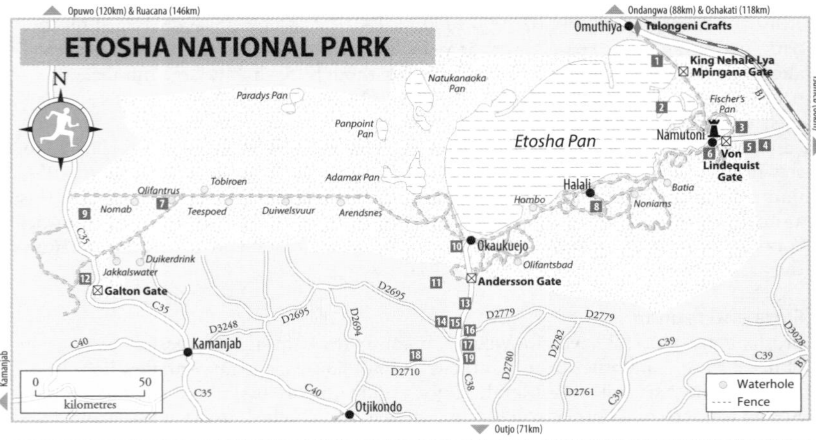

ACCOMMODATION

Dolomite Camp	9	Halali Camp	8	The Mushara Collection	4	The Onguma Game Reserve	3
Etosha King Nehale Lodge	1	Hobatere Lodge	12	Namutoni Camp	6	Onkoshi Camp	2
Etosha Safari Camp	15	Mokuti Etosha Lodge	5	Okaukuejo Camp	10	Toshari Lodge	17
Etosha Safari Lodge	14	Mondjila Safari Camp	19	Olifantrus Camp	7	Vreugde Guest Farm	18
Etosha Village	13	Mopane Village Etosha	16	Ongava Game Reserve	11		

6

ETOSHA GAME DRIVES

Etosha is predominantly about wildlife viewing or **game drives**. If not in a tour group, you will inevitably spend some time cruising around the park on your own, taking in waterholes and lookout points. However, even if you're driving yourself, it is worth considering booking one guided excursion. For a start, the **guides** are knowledgeable about the animals, though it's pot luck what you will see, beyond the ubiquitous springbok and zebra. They also have a better idea of what might be spotted in which areas. NWR guides can enter the park before sunrise, ensuring an early stakeout at a waterhole – peak viewing time – and a greater likelihood of catching a lion on the prowl. Moreover, the raised seating of the **safari vehicles** provides better vantage points from which to spot and watch wildlife. **Night game drives** are a different, almost ghostly, experience, where the animals' eyes give them away in the vehicle's search lamps.

All game drives organised by NWR within the national park last three hours, leaving at 5.30am, 3pm and 8pm. Daytime drives cost N$650, whereas night drives cost N$750. As spaces are limited, you must book a drive well in advance, especially at *Okaukuejo* and *Namutoni* in high season.

The private reserves **outside the national park** also offer excursions into Etosha and sometimes in their own reserves as well. Their rates vary tremendously; a half-day tour can cost N$800–1,200, including park entry fees, cold drinks or just water. Some lodges also organise whole-day trips, which may or may not include a picnic lunch.

path. You, therefore, need to plan your route carefully and leave plenty of time, as distances are considerable and the camps are strict about gate closures. If you misjudge the time and get locked in, you must pay a substantial fine before being allowed out. Fuel is available at the three main camps and payment by credit card is accepted, provided the machines are working.

ACCOMMODATION

SEE MAP PAGE 242

INSIDE THE PARK

All accommodation inside the park is provided by NWR, bookable at their offices in Windhoek and Swakopmund or online (Ⓦ nwr.com.na), though walk-ins can pay on the spot if there's availability. This is only an option in the low season (Nov–Feb, excluding the Christmas holiday). If you are staying in the older 'big three' camps (*Okaukuejo*, *Halali* and *Namutoni*) and are self-catering, stock up on supplies before you arrive since offerings at the camp shops are pretty paltry. Otherwise, dining is à la carte in the smaller camps – high quality but with a limited menu – and a mixture of overpriced, average buffet and à la carte fare is available at the larger camps, depending on numbers. Note that while the camps accept credit card payments, the machines are often not working.

★ **Dolomite Camp** Atop a lofty dolomite outcrop, cosy safari tents and private viewing decks are spaced along the ridge, with 1 to 12 facing west for the spectacular sunset views and 13 to 20 enjoying the sunrise. Premium chalet 13 also overlooks a waterhole, and several possess a private plunge pool. The view from the infinity pool is stunning and the food is excellent, though the tented dining, lounge and bar areas fail to make the most of the fabulous hilltop location. B&B **N$$$$**

Halali Camp Smaller and more intimate than the other two camps of the 'big three'. It is distinctive for its kopje with an antenna and a great sunset-viewing area above the waterhole, where black rhinos are regular visitors. Another draw is the pool – long enough to do a few lengths and adjacent to the restaurant and bar. The air-conditioned rooms are a little cramped, furnished with armchair and fridge. More enticing, pricier bush chalets have a kitchenette, while self-catering family rooms enjoy a private braai hearth to keep you warm in the winter. The campground, with its own bar, offers more shade than *Okaukuejo*; most pitches have stone tables, seating, electricity and braai stands. Camping per person **N$$**, doubles (B&B) **N$$$**, chalets B&B **N$$$**

Namutoni Camp This camp's 24 large rooms are stylishly furnished, with bathrooms containing a sunken bath and shower and a 'bush shower' outside; the twenty bush chalets are larger and plusher, though all rooms show signs of wear. The pick of the NWR campgrounds offers a fair degree of shade. The old fort that constitutes the resort's hub currently looks like it's relived the Battle of Namutoni: beyond the gleaming white exterior, there are signs of disrepair, though renovations are frequently rumoured. The pool area is less inviting than the other two camps, though the bar-restaurant area is more appealing. Game drives are good here, as they have access to several

6

restricted waterholes; there's also a shaded viewing area for the waterhole at the camp. Camping N$$, doubles (B&B) N$$$, chalets B&B N$$$

Okaukuejo Camp The park's administrative hub, and the largest camp, also has a shop and post office; during the day, it is always heaving with vehicles coming and going. For an extra N$1,000, you can have premium two-storey waterhole accommodation (chalets W31–35), with upstairs verandas overlooking the action. The distinctive central tower is another great vantage point (free for all to climb) to view the animal goings-on across the pan. Another plus is the pleasant shady pool area, with three pools and a bar. The kiosk offers burgers and toasted sandwiches during the day (9am–5pm); breakfast and dinner are at the main restaurant. The campground could do with an overhaul. Camping N$$, doubles (B&B) N$$$, chalets B&B N$$$

★ **Olifantrus Camp** Opened at the end of 2014; this is a fenced campground on the site of an old abattoir (whose shell remains) used in a controversial elephant-culling operation in the drought of the late 1980s. Ten basic pitches offer very little shade, sandy spots to pitch your tent, electricity, and cement slabs on which to build a fire. Cooking can also be done in a shared kitchen area. The big draw – shared with day visitors – is the fabulous two-tier hide overlooking a waterhole, plus the sounds of the bush at night. An on-site kiosk sells drinks and snacks. Camping N$$

★ **Onkoshi Camp** Fifteen stilted chalets made from canvas, wood and thatch peer over the eastern edge of Etosha Pan, with views extending to the horizon and fabulous sunsets: gaze out from the comfort of your pillow-piled bed through folding glass doors or from your private deck. The stylish, rustic design is similar to that of *Sossus Dune Lodge* (see page 113), with indoor and outdoor showers, lovely wooden floors and a raised walkway leading to the chalets. The wildlife viewing from the camp may not be as prolific as elsewhere, but the views more than compensate. Access is by four-wheel drive or by transfer from Namutoni. B&B N$$$$

WEST OF ETOSHA

★ **Hobatere Lodge** West of the C35, 5km (3.1 miles) north of the Galton Gate, 16km (10 miles) down a signposted track ⓦ hobatere-lodge.com. This community-owned lodge's friendly and enthusiastic staff make this place a real treat, plus the opportunity to get close to wildlife in the 88 sq km (34 sq mile) private concession. There are two waterholes, one with a hide, plus walking safaris and game drives on offer. Megafauna such as lions, cheetahs, elephants and giraffes are present, but the night safaris offer a chance to spot smaller mammals: bat-eared foxes, aardvarks and genets. The thatched main lodge is new, with plenty of comfortable seating indoors and out. The accommodation is in a row of stone-and-thatch double rooms or half a dozen individual rondavels, some with private verandas. Day trips into Etosha are also offered. DBB N$$$–$$$$

SOUTH OF ETOSHA

Etosha Safari Camp C38, 10km (6.2 miles) south of Andersson Gate ⓦ gondwana-collection.com. Down the hill from the *Etosha Safari Lodge*, this heavily themed main camp area celebrates the freedom of New South Africa and Namibian independence with quirky decor touches, such as tyre and wheelbarrow seating in the enclosed garden, where the shebeen is situated (live music in the evenings). The campground is a refreshing carpet grass, though shade's at a premium. Forty basic but functional brick chalets with a/c are scattered among the thorn trees, and if you don't want to fork out for the buffet dining, you can use the braai at the campground. Offers similar, though cheaper, excursions to those at *Etosha Safari Lodge*. Eight spacious self-catering tents are also available. Camping N$, self-catering tents N$$, chalets (B&B) N$$$

Etosha Safari Lodge C38, 10km (6.2 miles) south of Andersson Gate ⓦ gondwana-collection.com. Occupying a prime site on top of a ridge and offering commanding views across the national park, this large lodge has 65 chalets on either side of the elevated main building. Still,

WHERE TO STAY

The main decision to make when visiting Etosha is whether to stay **inside or outside** the park – assuming you book early enough to have a choice. Ideally, you should try to spend two or more nights inside the park and then a couple of nights outside. There are various advantages to staying **inside the park**: you can be at a waterhole just after sunrise and wait until just before sundown. The main three camps (*Okaukuejo*, *Halali* and *Namutoni*) overlook waterholes, which attract a host of animals in the dry season and are illuminated at night when they also attract wildlife. On the other hand, some of the lodges and campgrounds **outside the park** offer greater levels of comfort, are more intimate, and provide better catering and service than the three main camps. Those within well-stocked private reserves can also provide comparable wildlife-viewing experiences in terms of variety (if not in numbers). In any event, most lodges also run excursions into the national park.

you're never far from one of the three refreshing swimming pools. The air-conditioned chalets are simply but tastefully furnished with French windows that open onto your private patio. However, the vista's even better from the main lodge's extensive terrace, where you can tuck into some of the best buffet food you're ever likely to taste. Half-day or full-day safaris into the national park are available. The latter includes a picnic. B&B N$$$

Etosha Village C38, 2km (1.2 miles) from Andersson Gate ⓦetosha-village.com. Well-spaced among the thorn trees are distinctive, superior safari tents (with a/c), making intriguing use of stone, metal and branches in their rustic design. Each has an open kitchenette with a hob, fridge, kettle, braai and picnic table under the shade. Seven shadeless concrete-platform camping pitches have recently been added, with communal braai and dining area more suited to groups. Breakfasts and superior dinners are available, and there's a TV at the bar. Run by the Taleni group, so the service is friendly and efficient. As well as the usual drives into Etosha, you can stargaze through a telescope and take a guided morning walk. Camping N$, safari tents (DBB) N$$$

★ **Mondjila Safari Camp** 3km (1.9 miles) down a gravel road, 32km (19.9 miles) south of the Andersson Gate ⓦmondjilasafaricamp.com. Affordable, friendly, no-frills camp offering excellent value. Set on a rocky ridge, the place makes the most of its location, with lovely sunset views from the main stone-and-thatch lodge – which serves tasty meals – and the grassy pool area below, as well as from the private patios of eleven simply furnished, twin-bedded safari tents set on concrete bases. Only a small fan to cool you, but roll up the flaps and let the breeze do the rest. Also, with eight grassy camping pitches, each has a power point, light and braai stand, with shared ablutions. Local hiking trails and relatively inexpensive Etosha game drives are another plus. Camping N$, safari tents (DBB) N$$$

Mopane Village Etosha C38, 14km (8.7 miles) south of the Andersson Gate ⓦmopanevillage.com. This no-frills camp has bags of character. The ten tunnel-shaped safari tents are spacious and fan-ventilated, with a nicely designed stone bathroom at the end. Some have braai facilities for self-catering. Ten bush chalets, made from a mix of materials with private porches, are also available. Otherwise, meals are served at a simple, open-sided restaurant or alfresco in a beer-garden-like environment. The four campsites are a good deal, each with shade netting, private shower and toilet facilities, a braai site, sink and electricity. Camping N$, safari tent or bush chalet (B&B) N$$

Toshari Lodge Off the C38, 25km (15.5 miles) south of the Andersson Gate ⓦquiverandco/toshari-lodge. The communal areas make this place: an atmospherically illuminated cavernous *lapa* for dining, complete with a well-stocked bar and a two-tier swimming pool, both set among well-tended grass and trees. Fanning off a central *allée* lined with giant white cement urns are freestanding air-conditioned rooms with a contemporary feel. Campers can enjoy three glorious compact pitches on soft grass, under shady mopane trees, with private open-air ablutions, a power point, and braai wood provided, and can enjoy the lodge facilities. Guided day trips into Etosha are on offer. Good value. Camping N$, doubles (B&B) N$$$

Vreugde Guest Farm 9km (5.6 miles) down a gravel road, signposted off the C38, 44km (27.3 miles) from Andersson's Gate ⓦvreugdeguestfarm.com. Hospitable working sheep and cattle farm with a handful of cool, painted fan-ventilated brick bungalows – some semi-detached, others freestanding, with sliding glass doors opening out onto a lush, well-tended garden that attracts good birdlife. A sparkling, circular pool is well-used in the summer. This pleasant, affordable alternative to some of the overpriced lodges around the park offers excursions on the farm, as well as into Etosha, plus birdwatching tours. DBB N$$$

6

ONGAVA GAME RESERVE

One of Namibia's largest and exclusive private reserves, Ongava Game Reserve (ⓦongava.com), covers over 300 sq km (115.8 sq miles) abutting Etosha's southern perimeter. It has four lodges and is filled with tourist-enticing wildlife: the big cats, including lions, black and white rhinos, plains and mountain zebra, black-faced impala, giraffes, elephants and even wild dogs. Activities include game drives, birdwatching, guided walks and rhino tracking.

Andersson's at Ongava What was once the 'poorer' relative is now equally exclusive, accommodating a maximum of eighteen guests, who are accorded a dedicated private guide for the duration. The striking, luxurious stone chalets in contemporary style are replete with conservations and science-focused reading matter to complement the on-site scientific research centre. Another big plus is a sunken hide at the waterhole – great for close-up shots of drinking animals. DBB N$$$$

Ongava Lodge 10km (6.2 miles) from the reserve entrance. The most affordable of the Ongava options, this luxury venue has a great location atop a kopje, with a classic safari lodge feel: large open thatched main building with a pool and plenty of deck space, looking down on a waterhole (floodlit at night) and offering great views across the savannah. Fourteen top-notch stone-and-thatch chalets with a/c and fans, comfortable furniture, plus plenty of deck space. DBB N$$$$

★ **Ongava Tented Lodge** 20km (12.4 miles) down the gravel drive. Back-to-nature feel in this intimate, stylish, unfenced bush camp: eight stylish Meru-style tents on wooden decks – a place to keep the tent flaps open, the fan on, and fall asleep to the sounds of lions roaring. Enjoy top-quality dining while watching the floodlit waterhole almost under your nose. Make the most of the guided walks and tracking activities included. The even more exclusive and expensive *Little Ongava* also offers fully inclusive packages. DBB N$$$$

EAST OF ETOSHA

Etosha King Nehale Lodge 5km (3.1 miles) north of the King Nehale Gate ⓦ gondwana-collection.com. Developed in conjunction with the King Nehale Conservancy, Gondwana's newest lodge (opened in 2022) offers exclusive access to a hide overlooking a waterhole in a less frequented part of the national park. It boasts forty sumptuous chalets stylishly decorated with Owambo cultural artefacts, each with a private plunge pool. In addition to the guided wildlife viewing in the park, excursions are offered to Ondjumba village and a traditional homestead. B&B N$$$

Mokuti Etosha Lodge 2km south of the D3028, just outside the Von Lindequist Gate; ⓦ mokutietosha.com. Refurbished and upgraded in 2023, this is a large hotel resort-style lodge (over 90 rooms) with tennis courts, pool tables, a spa, large swimming pools, all-day dining, manicured lawns and even a snake park. Beneath the thatch, contemporary design reigns in the rooms, with standard four-star hotel facilities: a/c, DStv, hair dryer and safe, comfortable sofas and armchairs, and furniture on the outside porch. Indigenous Hai//om guides lead guided walks. N$$$$

THE MUSHARA COLLECTION

The Mushara Collection (south of the D3028, 8km/5 miles east of the Von Lindequist Gate ⓦ mushara-lodge.com) is made up of three main properties (plus one luxury villa) – with separate entrances off the main road – in a small reserve. However, activities are centred on Etosha, with twice-daily game drives.

Mushara Bush Camp This is a relaxed, family-friendly place with toys, a playground, a kiddies' menu and a child-minding service. A traditional thatched communal area overlooks a small lawn for dining, enjoying a drink or relaxing. The sixteen light and airy safari tents (four with pull-out couches for families) are nicely kitted out, with a generous, cool stone bathroom, plus a porch looking into the bush, with deckchairs. Book Tent 5 or above to escape the main lodge noise. Good value. DBB N$$$

Mushara Lodge This smart lodge offers top-of-the-range accommodation in two opulent villas (private plunge pool and fabulous furnishings), but fairly luxurious lodgings in the so-called 'standard' chalets: large en-suite rooms are generously furnished and decorated in chic, modern African style. The tasteful designs extend to the ample bar-restaurant area. *Bomas* are held every few nights. DBB N$$$$

The Mushara Outpost The most exclusive option: eight elegant canvas tents on raised wooden decks boasting modern amenities (minibar, intimate lighting, safe). You can gaze at the sun-baked bush through sliding glass doors from the comfort of your air-conditioned retreat, which also has a cosy fireplace for winter nights. Fine dining takes place in a sophisticated setting, where cushioned sofas are perfect for enjoying a digestif. There's also a nearby waterhole and viewing hide. DBB N$$$$

THE ONGUMA GAME RESERVE

The Onguma Game Reserve (7km/4.3 miles north of the D3028, signposted just outside the Von Lindequist Gate ⓦ onguma.com), covering some 340 sq km (131.3 sq miles), contains a range of accommodation from lodge rooms to tents, chalets and bungalows, plus two camping areas on the eastern side of Etosha. The most recent addition, *Camp Kala*, is a specially designed exclusive camp for small groups, where each suite has its own private butler. The reserve borders Fischer's Pan, with lots of plains animals, including black rhinos. Sundowner drives and guided walks are offered on the reserve and twice-daily excursions into Etosha.

The Fort A forbidding exterior belies an extravagant themed interior, mimicking a North African palace, with cascading water features, hanging lanterns, velvet cushions galore and heavy drapes. But the stunning view from the lodge's raised terrace is pure African bush. Alongside, twelve sumptuous mini-suites continue the theme: cavernous stone rooms contain fabulous fireplaces, while each private deck includes a plunge pool and sun loungers. DBB N$$$$

Forest Camp An assortment of bungalows plus *Tamboti*, a newish, substantial campground, offers a more luxurious experience than the campground at *Onguma Bush Camp*. Comprising 25 well-equipped sites, it also has a pool and a snack bar/restaurant overlooking a waterhole (meals should be pre-booked). Camping N$$, bungalows B&B N$$$

Onguma Bush Camp The collection's only fenced camp is more modestly priced than the other options, aimed at families – some accommodation comes with a loft room for kids – and groups. Eighteen thatched rondavels and rooms (with fans and a/c) in earthy colours are spread out among well-tended grounds, with a games room, pool and large waterhole. There are also half a dozen campsites here set on compacted ground under shady leadwood trees. DBB rates are also available. Camping N$$, doubles (B&B) N$$$–$$$$

Onguma Tented Camp An intimate camp comprising seven luxurious tents – a blend of stone, wood and canvas, with a touch of glitz – centred on a waterhole. Indoor and outdoor showers, fine dining and plenty of space to lounge and chill, watch wildlife or curl up with a book by the infinity pool. Guided walks and night drives are organised on the reserve and game drives into Etosha. Offers the same activities as *Onguma Bush Camp*. DBB N$$$$

The 'Four O's'

North of Etosha, around 40 percent of the population is squeezed into under 10 percent of the country's landmass across four small regions – **Ohangwena**, **Oshana**, **Omusati** and **Oshikoto** – more readily referred to as the 'Four O's', or even Owamboland, the former apartheid-era designation for the homeland for the Owambo peoples. It's the SWAPO heartland, where during the 1970s and 1980s, resistance against South African rule was at its fiercest, resulting in its conversion into a heavily militarised zone (see page 345). Though development and reconstruction money has poured into the region post-independence, the emotional scars will take longer to heal, not helped by high unemployment and poverty – despite some pockets of wealth in evidence – with many people still having to migrate south in search of permanent or seasonal labour.

The urban agglomeration of **Ondangwa**, **Ongwediwa** and **Oshakati**, strung roughly 30km (18.6 miles) along the B1 and C46, is the commercial fulcrum of the north's economy. Unprepossessing, flat towns with little to interest the tourist beyond browsing the open markets, though they are the **gateway** to a handful of interesting cultural sights in the vicinity. What's more, they are good places to visit a bank and stock up on food supplies and fuel, though you'll need to keep your wits about you and remain streetwise when parking your vehicle and going about your business. Most services are dotted along the dual carriageways in Ondangwa and Oshakati that scythe through the dust, lined with a seemingly endless stream of warehouses, car showrooms, service garages, tyre repair enterprises and *cuca* shops – shebeens (that also sell necessities) named after the Angolan beer that was illegally stocked here in the 1970s and 1980s, and with alluring names such as *Hot Stuff Bar*, *Nice Time Shebeen* or *Happy Life Number 2*.

The rural landscape here is strikingly different; expanses of flat, loamy sands are noticeably lacking in tree cover beyond the emblematic clumps of makalani palms that stand sentinel and pockets of mopane, fig and marula trees. Homesteads fill the countryside, though the traditional mopane palisades and conical thatched rondavels are gradually incorporating more aluminium, breezeblock and plastic sheeting in their construction. Hot, dry and dusty for much of the year due in no small part to the insidious downward spiral of overgrazing, land degradation and deforestation – now exacerbated by **climate change** – the region's harsh aridity is blunted somewhat once the *iishana* (shallow pools) fill with water and the seasonal rains arrive.

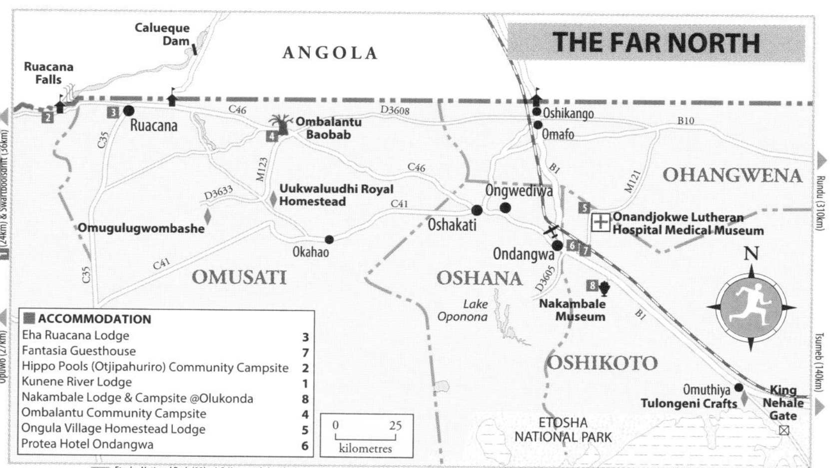

IISHANA AND OMETALE – NORTHERN NAMIBIA'S VITAL WATER SOURCES

Central to northern Namibia's agro-ecology is the existence of the **Cuvelei-Etosha Basin**, a large water catchment area in the Highlands of Angola, whose perennial rivers filter down across the border into Namibia spreading into 7,000 sq km (2,702.7 sq miles) of a delta-like network of seasonal watercourses and shallow pools known as **iishana** in Oshiwambo (though the anglicised term 'oshanas' is commonly used). The **oshana system** is critical to the subsistence crop and livestock farming that sustains the rural populations. This flooding or *efundja*, as it is known, depends on the rainfall in Angola but occurs most years, and even in seasons when the water inflow is low, local precipitation can fill the *iishana*. The water can reach as far south as the Etosha Pan in years of exceptional rainfall. Crops are planted in anticipation of the floodwater's arrival or the first rains, which can trigger the emergence of aestivating bullfrogs, crustaceans and other invertebrates. In good years, fish are washed into the pools, adding welcome protein to the local diet. The grasses and reeds that sprout around the edges are used for basketry, including the basket-fishing nets you'll see women using as they wade through the shallow pools, alert to trapping the day's meal. Once the water arrives, the landscape is transformed: dotted with bushy marula trees and haughty makalani palms, the pale, dusty, overgrazed flatlands are replaced by mirror-like lakes, where white lilies burst open and a wealth of wetland birds are drawn to feast on this temporary food source. Though the wet season usually runs from November to April, the wettest months are December to February. Many of the more rural communities dig *ometale* (earth dams), which are effectively excavated *iishana* so that they can retain the water for longer. Despite the high evaporation rates in good years, these communally managed water resources can last much of the dry season, providing a vital lifeline to communities in this challenging environment.

Ondangwa

ONDANGWA is the first sizeable town you encounter after crossing the veterinary cordon fence at Oshivelo, north of Etosha's Von Lindequist Gate. Slightly less frenetic and less populated than neighbouring Oshakati – it has a population of about 23,000 – it was established in 1890 as a Finnish mission station at the western edge of the Ondonga Kingdom. Following World War I, the British decided to base their administration here; the South African colonial government then followed suit, and from 1918, Ondangwa became the main assemblage point for labourers being recruited to work in the mines and farms in the Police Zone or South Africa. Once the apartheid regime established Oshakati as the new capital of Owamboland in the mid-1960s, which became the regional capital post-independence, Ondangwa's political importance faded. However, commerce in the town is still growing and likely to expand further, given Ondangwa's strong rail and air links and strategic location on the main transit route between Namibia and Angola – the busy main junction in the town centre sees the B1 turn northwards to Oshikango, Namibia's main border with Angola (see page 249) 60km (37.3 miles) away.

Onandjokwe Lutheran Hospital Medical Museum

Along the M121 to Eenhana, a few hundred metres after the bridge over the railway • Mon–Fri 8am–5pm • Charge • Key kept at the reception of the private ward • Ⓦ museums.com.na/museums/north/onandjokwe-medical-museum

The town's one recognised attraction is the well-signposted **Onandjokwe Lutheran Hospital Medical Museum**, located in said hospital, which was the first to be built in northern Namibia, set up by the Finnish Missionary Society in 1911. The gleaming white adobe building draped with bougainvillea is the original clinic, which stands out from the less well-maintained surroundings of the current hospital. While the exhibition rooms contain some interesting photos of early medical care and of the role of the hospital (and Lutheran Church) during the independence struggle, the insights into the challenges facing present-day healthcare provision that you'll gain from wandering around looking for someone to let you into the museum are likely to leave a more lasting impression.

ARRIVAL AND GETTING AROUND — ONDANGWA

By car Ondangwa lies on Namibia's main road, the B1, around 100km (62.1 miles) north of the King Nehale Gate into Etosha National Park and 50km (31 miles) south of the Angolan border. It's also 30km (18.6 miles) southeast of Oshakati.

By bus Intercape (Ⓦ intercape.co.za) runs an overnight service from Windhoek to Oshakati (10hr), stopping off in Ondangwa, and a similar overnight service to Windhoek from Oshakati, picking up in Ondangwa at the Engen Olunkono Centre on the C46 daily. In addition, minibuses shuttle between the two Engen service stations in Ondangwa and Oshakati. They also leave from the Puma petrol station in Oshakati, bound for Windhoek.

By air The airport lies 3.5km (2.2 miles) along the C46 towards Oshakati after the B1 turn-off to Oshikango. Fly Namibia (Ⓦ flynamibia.com) operates flights to and from Eros Airport in Windhoek (five days a week; 1hr).

ACCOMMODATION — SEE MAP PAGE 247

Fantasia Guesthouse Brian Simita Street, Ondangwa Ⓔ edduplessis@gmail.com. A secure location, with spotless en-suite rooms with a/c, TV and kitchenette. The decor's rather chintzy, but the place is good value. Eight cramped camping pitches are squeezed into the yard. Camping N$, doubles (B&B) N$$

Ongula Village Homestead Lodge Eembahu, on the D3670, signposted west off the M121 to Eenhana Ⓦ ongula.com. A lodge with a difference – a clutch of comfortable, cheerily decorated thatched rondavels in a genuine Owambo homestead and a few basic shaded camping pitches with shared ablutions. In addition to organised excursions to Nakambale Museum or Oshakati markets, you have a chance to join in everyday activities: pounding mahangu (pearl millet), clay-pot-making, or visiting a *cuca* shop, plus local dishes are served at mealtimes. The lodge also supports a local technical skills training academy. Camping N$, chalets DBB N$$–$$$

Protea Hotel Ondangwa Main Street at the junction between the B1 and the C46 Ⓦ marriott.com. It may not be anywhere near the four-star establishment it purports to be. However, the area's premier business hotel is still surprisingly pleasant, with well-furnished, light carpeted double rooms, acceptable buffet food – though only a limited à la carte menu – a pool and a small casino. With decent wi-fi. B&B N$$

Nakambale Museum

Olukonda village, 14km (8.7 miles) southeast of Ondangwa • Mon–Fri 8am–1pm, 2–5pm, Sat & Sun by appointment • Charge for entry to the museum and the homestead, plus extra for a tour of the homestead • Ⓣ 065 240472 • To reach here, take the D3629 signposted west off the B1, about 4km (2.5 miles) south of Ondangwa

CROSSING THE ANGOLAN BORDER

Oshikango, a somewhat sketchy frontier town, is 60km (37.3 miles) due north of Ondangwa and is one of Namibia's five **border crossings with Angola**: the others are at Ruacana (8am–6pm), Omahenene, near Outapi (8am–6pm), Katitwe, some 160km (99.4 miles) west of Rundu (6am–6pm), and the floating pontoon at Rundu (6am–6pm; see page 278). Oshikango's hours are 8am–6pm, but travellers should note that Namibia's daylight saving between the first Sunday in September and the first Sunday in April means times are an hour earlier. Oshikango is the busiest Namibian–Angolan border because it connects to the main tarred road to Luanda, so you can look forward to long queues of trucks and lengthy procedures. Ensure you're well acquainted with the latest visa regulations, as you'll need to get a tourist visa in advance, for which plenty of supporting documentation and a yellow fever vaccination will be required. However, in 2018, online applications were introduced (Ⓦ smevisa.gov.ao). Intercape, which provides a regular overnight service between Windhoek and Ondangwa and Oshakati, also connects to Oshikango (Ⓦ intercape.co.za; 11hr 30min). The bus stop in Oshikango is on the main road in front of Spar.

The very underused **Ruacana border post** with Angola, right by the falls, can only be accessed by four-wheel drive vehicles since, on the Angolan side, the initial road, which leads to the small village of Culueque by the dam, is very rough. A slightly better road continues to Xongongo, just under 100km (62.1 miles) further north, with tarred connections to Luanda.

Nakambale is the local name given to Finnish missionary Martti Rautanen because of the skullcap he liked to wear that was thought to resemble a basket – *okambale* in Oshindonga. The **Nakambale Museum** is situated in the old mission station – which was also Rautanen's home – established in 1880 and one of the earliest in the north. The modest exhibition has plenty on the missionary's life, including photos, clothing, medical instruments and everyday artefacts. At the same time, there is information on Indigenous traditional cultural practices, including a collection of artefacts, such as hunting bows and musical instruments. Next door, a **Ndonga homestead** has been re-created; while the museum exhibition is pretty self-explanatory, it is worth taking a guided tour of the homestead to make sense of the various partitioned areas and their significance. You can also engage the services of a guide here to go to Lake Oponona (when it has water) or to the markets in Oshakati and Ondangwa.

ACCOMMODATION

NAKAMBALE MUSEUM, SEE MAP PAGE 247

Nakambale Lodge & Campsite @Olukonda ⓦ scadvlodges.com/southern-cross-adventure-lodges-map/namibia-lodges/nakambale-lodge-olukonda. The adjacent tented lodge is basic, rustic (though tents have a/c) and inexpensive but offers a chance for more community interaction. 'Glamping' units in small traditional rondavels and five campsites are also available, with electricity, shared ablution blocks with hot and cold water and a kitchen and braai area. The on-site restaurant offers traditional meals and offerings from the brick pizza oven. Camping and glamping N$, safari tents N$$

Lake Oponona

Broadly, at the end of the D3605, approx 25km (15.5 miles) southwest of Ondangwa, depending on how high the flood levels have risen in any given year

The largest *oshana* in the Cuvelei Basin, **Lake Oponona** transforms into a glorious wetland in years of *efundja* (see page 248), when it increases its surface area several times over and lasts through most of the dry season, thus attracting a wealth of birdlife. This process of expansion gave rise to its name, which means 'the one that swallowed up all the water' in Oshindonga. Greater and lesser flamingos, white pelicans, saddle-billed storks, knob-billed ducks – even the critically endangered blue crane – and a host of other migratory birds flock here once other *oshanas* have dried up.

Oshakati and Ongwediwa

Established in 1966 by the South African colonial administration as the capital of the newly designated Owamboland, **OSHAKATI** means 'the place where people meet' or 'that which is between' in Oshiwambo – perhaps a reference to its deliberately central location, chosen so that the authorities could further their political and commercial interests. Today, with a population of just under forty thousand, Oshakati is Namibia's fourth-largest town; it's the capital of the north and a major commercial centre and transport hub. Along the main dual carriageway, punctuated by traffic lights and lined with the occasional pavement, new supermarkets, warehouses and shopping malls gleam in the sunlight; at the same time, rusted old cars still decorate the waste-ground and the odd herd of goats will slow down the traffic, while battered combis slither on and off the road at will, to pick up or drop off passengers.

Just south of Oshakati, but soon to be sucked into the conurbation, lies the quiet, mainly residential town of **ONGWEDIWA**; established initially to house workers in Oshakati and Ondangwa, the place hosts a faculty of the University of Namibia plus a teachers' education college; more pertinently, it also offers a couple of pleasant places to stay.

Brief history

Oshakati's rapid infrastructural development in the late 1960s was prompted by the immediate militarisation of the area as the independence struggle escalated into full-scale war the year the town was founded. For much of the 1970s and 1980s, Oshakati was a heavily fortified encampment, with watchtowers, barbed wire, bullet-proof walls and a heavy army and police presence. There soon followed an influx of people from rural areas fleeing poverty and/or the fighting, including large numbers of Angolans, who arrived in the mid-1970s once the civil war started north of the border; many such migrants still live in informal or shanty settlements on the town's fringes. In 1970, the population numbered under three thousand; by the late 1980s, it had swelled to 37,000, more or less matching present-day figures. Since independence, much money has been pumped into the place for redevelopment.

Dr Frans Aupa Indongo Open Market

On the corner of the C46 and the C45 • Daily 6am–6pm • Free

If you happen to be passing through Oshakati, take some time to wander around the sparkling new **Dr Frans Aupa Indongo Open Market** – named after the pre-eminent Namibian entrepreneur – adjacent to the new bus terminal. You'll pass baskets piled high with pulses, grains, fruit, vegetables, dried fish and mopane worms; rails of modern 'traditional' Owambo dresses wafting in the breeze while women beaver away on Singer sewing machines; and the sale of all kinds of artefacts and crafts, from fly whisks to carved walking sticks, reed mats to wooden masks and clay pots. Don't forget to visit the stallholders grilling *kapana* – sizzling strips of seasoned meat washed down with some *oshikundu* (fermented mahangu). The centrepiece of the N$80-million-dollar market renovation is a twelve-storey **observation tower**, resembling a spaceship when illuminated at night. Since the market was inaugurated in 2016, the local authorities have been searching for an investor to develop the tower into an attraction.

ARRIVAL AND DEPARTURE — OSHAKATI AND ONGWEDIWA

By car Oshakati lies 708km (439.9 miles) north of Windhoek; after turning west off the B1 onto the C46 at Ondangwa, it's a further 30km (18.6 miles).

By bus Intercape (intercape.co.za) operates an overnight service from its terminal in Bahnhof Street, Windhoek, to Oshakati (daily 6pm; 11hr), picking up passengers for the return to Windhoek (daily at 7.30pm) at the Engen Oneshila service station on the main road in Oshakati. Large buses and minibuses on no fixed timetable leave the Monte Christo Service Station in Katutura, Windhoek, bound for

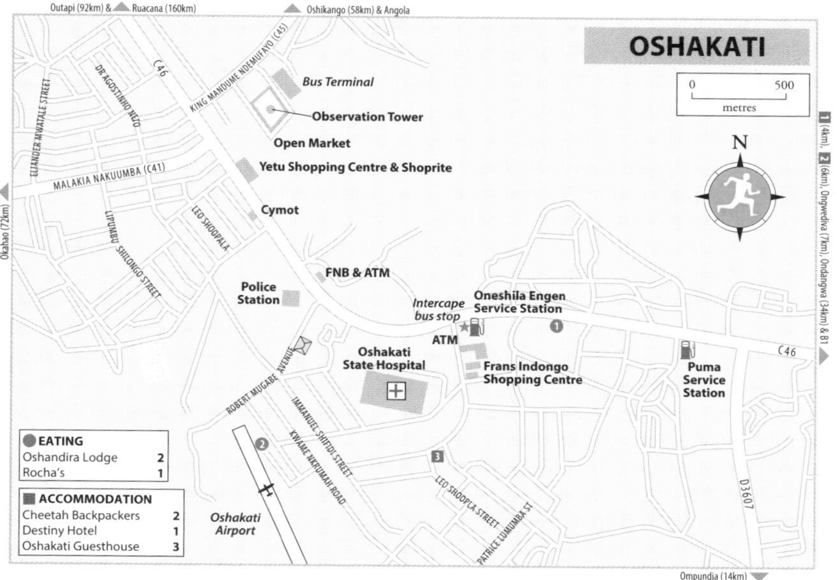

Ondangwa and Oshakati (8hr). The inexpensive twice-weekly (Tues & Fri) Orange Bus service, operated by Namib Contract Haulage (kalahariholdings.com), runs between Soweto Market, Katutura and Oshakati (8am or 5pm). Other private bus companies also occasionaliy serve this route.

By minibus In Oshakati, minibuses (and sometimes shared taxis) fan out to other major centres in the north, such as Opuwo (3hr) and Rundu (5hr), as well as shuttling back and forth between the two Engen petrol stations in Oshakati and Ondangwa. Buses usually leave from the new bus terminal adjacent to the open market at the junction between the C46 and the C45. However, some transport still uses the more traditional service station – enquire at the bus terminal.

By air Oshakati Airport only accommodates charter flights. Andimba Toivo ya Toivo Airport (formerly Ondangwa Airport) is the nearest commercial airport.

6

INFORMATION AND TOURS

There is no official tourist office yet in Oshakati. Still, the amiable staff of Cheetah Backpackers and Safaris based in the Shoprite Complex on the main C46 in Ongwediwa, a few kilometres south of Oshakati, are helpful (Mon–Fri 8am–5pm; cheetahbackpackers.com). The company runs some interesting, inexpensive day tours, including one around the local towns, taking in a market and a *cuca* shop. Though tours are primarily aimed at the local market, this is a great way to meet Namibians outside the foreign tourist circuit.

ACCOMMODATION

SEE MAP PAGE 251

Cheetah Backpackers Reception at the office in the Shoprite Complex on the main C46 in Ongwediwa cheetahbackpackers.com. Located in a residential neighbourhood, a range of functional, inexpensive accommodation options, from a well-equipped self-catering unit to dorm beds, singles or regular double rooms, and spots to pitch a tent. All in a compound with secure parking on a residential street a few blocks east of the main road. Camping N$, doubles N$$

Destiny Hotel Turn east off the C46 at Ongwediwa open market, then take the second left and follow the signs hoteldestiny.com.na. Welcoming budget business hotel comprising 31 small but spotless tiled rooms, which still manage to pack in all you need: a/c, DStv, phone, hair dryer, desk, tea/coffee-making facilities, and, best of all, a monsoon shower. N$$

Oshakati Guesthouse Corner of Sam Nujoma Road and Leo Shoopla Street, Oshakati oshakati-guesthouse.com. Efficient, friendly, mid-range business hotel with en-suite tiled rooms and DStv. Bag one of the lighter upstairs rooms. N$$

EATING

SEE MAP PAGE 251

Although the two hotels below have respectable accommodation, their restaurants are the main draw.

Oshandira Lodge Airport Road oshandira@iway.na. Tucked away in a quiet spot, this is probably the best place to eat in town, so it gets busy at weekends. Choose from pub-style seating on the veranda or a table under a fan-ventilated thatch. The menu has the usual international regulars: schnitzels, pasta, pizzas and steaks, or more local dishes, such as mahangu with Owambo-style chicken, or various potjies – justifiably their most popular orders. N$$–$$$

Rocha's West side of the C46 065 222038. A veritable oasis, with wooden tables and benches arranged in a leafy paved courtyard around a small pool, where you can forget about the dust and noise outside while enjoying some authentic Portuguese cuisine, from *prego* rolls to their famous *bacalhau* (cod) or regular burgers, steak and pork dishes with pap or rice. If you can't take the heat, there's also a tiled dining room with a/c. N$$–$$$

West of Oshakati

West of Oshakati takes you into the heart of the Cuvelei-Etosha basin and countryside full of *oshanas* and mahangu plantations (see page 248). Most travellers are passing through for Ruacana, Opuwo and the Kaokoveld. However, it's perfectly feasible to plan a circular day trip from Oshakati, all on good tarred roads, which can give you a glimpse of small-town and village life and a chance to visit some modest sights of cultural and historical interest. First, you take in the famous **Ombalantu Baobab** in the rapidly growing town of **Outapi** and capital of the Omusati Region, some 92km (57.2 miles) further west along the C46. A half-hour drive south along the little-used M123 then takes you to the small community of Tsandi, where you can stop off to visit the **Uukwaluudhi Royal Homestead.** Those interested in the War of Independence might consider a 20km (12.4-mile) detour southeast down the D3633 to the monument at **Ongulumbashwe**, though there is not much to see. Back on the M123, returning eastwards towards Oshakati, you pass through the small town of **Okahao**, which also possesses a large baobab and campsite (T 081 270 6006), before completing the last 70km (43.5-mile) stretch back to base. Look out on the south side of the road, some 17km (10.6 miles) outside Oshakati; in the afternoons, you will often see women selling large clay pots (left under a cloth if they are absent), though the cooperative they were part of is no more, they still do business on an individual basis, and the pots are worth perusing.

Ombalantu Baobab Heritage Centre

Outapi, behind the open market just after the junction with the M123 to Tsandi • Daily 8am–6pm • Charge • T 081 438 4705

Though not the only such tree in town, the **Ombalantu Baobab** is nevertheless an impressive specimen: it is rumoured to be 800 years old, 28m (91.9ft) tall and with a girth almost as wide, 26.5m (86.9ft). Its hollowed-out centre has served many purposes over the ages. Initially able to hold 45 people, it was used in the early 1900s as a shelter to hide and protect the community's women and children whenever they were attacked. In calmer times, it served as a storage facility and then, in 1940, as Outapi's first post office. Later, it became a church – indeed, it still retains two pews and an altar. After the SADF had established a base in Outapi, the baobab's belly hosted a bar and was also used to detain people.

The site also has a **craft shop**, selling miniature baobabs, among other items, and is a **community campsite**.

ACCOMMODATION — OMBALANTU BAOBAB HERITAGE CENTRE, SEE MAP PAGE 247

Ombalantu Community Campsite By the baobab tree T 081 4384705. Four simple pitches with braai facilities and shared ablutions offering warm showers. Camping N$

Uukwaluudhi Royal Homestead

On the M123, just opposite the turn-off to Omugulugwombashe • Charge • Mon–Fri 8am–5pm • T 081 301 2739

In 1978, King Josia Shikongo Taapopi of the Uukwaluudhi – one of the seven Owambo groups – moved out of the traditional mopane-palisaded royal palace (*ombala*) into a modern brick construction with glass windows next door. He then decided to open the old palace to the public as the **Uukwaluudhi Royal Homestead**. After digesting the writing on the information boards that contextualise the homestead within Uukwaluudhi history and culture, you are then taken on a walk around the labyrinthine complex, a series of fenced-off areas and separate wooden huts, made deliberately confusing to confound enemies and discourage wild animals. To the uninitiated, many of the huts and enclosures look much the same. However, each of the 35 areas has its purpose, which is carefully explained: places for warriors to gather before battle or for grain to be stored; royal sleeping quarters, with widely spaced poles to allow for air circulation, or a hut with a calabash in which the milk is churned. In the main forecourt, before entering the palace proper, spreads a magnificent marula tree, where it was customary to wait for an audience with the king. That is theoretically possible for visitors, but he likes to have advance notice.

State Cemetery

At the end of the D3633

A relatively innocuous patch of bush hosts the **Omugulugwombashe State Cemetery**, the country's second such cemetery after Heroes' Acre, just outside Windhoek (see page 102), and one which thankfully is a lot less grandiose. Six PLAN fighters who died when the SADF attacked their camp here on 26 August 1966 are buried at this site. An evocative bronze sculpture of them strategising now sits under a tree. There's also a more general monument to those who lost their lives in the struggle and the compulsory bronze statue of Sam Nujoma, this time waving a rifle.

Ruacana

On the westernmost limit of the Omusati Region lies the near-deserted town of **RUACANA**, which came into being to house workers for the construction of the dam and underground power station on the Kunene River in the 1970s before hosting a SADF base during the war for independence – the dam and power station were bombed by the Cubans in 1988, just as the South Africans were retreating from Angola. Despite its elevation to 'town' status in 2010, Ruacana has a population of just three thousand. There's nothing to detain visitors here, but since there's no fuel for miles around, you should fill up at the busy petrol station, which also has a well-stocked shop with an **ATM**, though a nearby supermarket offers greater choice. The border post here is underused and suitable for four-wheel drive vehicles only.

Ruacana Falls

Well signposted off the C46, 20km (12.4 miles) west of Ruacana • Daily 8am–6pm, but dependent on Angolan border post hours • Free • Note that the right-turn to the falls, 500m (0.3 miles) before the access road ends, is not signposted; then you need to go through the Angolan border post into the neutral land – the border guard will point out the dirt road leading to the viewpoint

The **Ruacana Falls** was once a truly spectacular sight, a 600m (1,968.5ft) wide wall of water plunging 120m (393.7ft) into the gorge below, making it one of the largest falls in Africa. However, a hydroelectric power station and **dam** built in the late 1970s – now Namibia's main source of power – soon put an end to this natural wonder. Yet, on the rare occasions that heavy rains produce too much water, the sluice gates are opened upriver in Angola (generally Feb–April), and the dramatic aquatic show is resumed, albeit only temporarily. However, even in the dry season, the bare, sheer rock face and the impressive gorge below are worth the short detour if you're in the area, provided you ignore the heavily littered viewpoint.

THE IMPORTANCE OF APPEARANCE IN HIMBA CULTURE

Himba women in traditional attire have graced many a magazine cover and featured in documentaries galore with their distinctive reddish-brown body '**paint**' and goatskin 'miniskirts'. While the Himba's physical appearance often brings out the worst voyeuristic tendencies in tourists (see page 70), appearance is, nevertheless, very important to Himba culture; women spend several hours on their toilette each day. Their body **'paint'** (*otjize*) is a mix of ground red ochre and animal butter or fat, scented with resin, and used to cover their skin, hair, clothing and jewellery. It has functional, symbolic and aesthetic value, protecting their skin from the burning sun while keeping insects at bay; its reddish-brown hue evokes both the earth and life-giving blood. Since water is scarce, women often have a smoke 'bath' and similarly 'wash' their leather clothing by smoking it over incense.

Hair is similarly important: various styles indicate different life stages for both males and females. Toddlers often have shaven heads, but as they grow, girls have two plaits pulled over their faces once they hit puberty (to show modesty), while boys maintain one plait at the back, which becomes two at puberty. The style of the plaits indicates the *oruzo* (the patrilineal descent) of the wearer.

Once married, men bundle their hair into a head wrap, only removed for funerals or when they are widowed. Puberty for young women entails sporting numerous plaits smeared with *otjize*. Once married, women incorporate a tanned sheep or goatskin headpiece, which is replaced by a different headpiece (*erembe*) after they have been married a year or given birth to their first child.

Traditionally attired women and men are heavily adorned with a collection of **jewellery** – necklaces, collars, bracelets and anklets, which also serve as protection against snakebites. The jewellery is fashioned from metal, shell, beads, leather and woven grass and sometimes weighs several kilos. Inevitably, as westernisation encroaches and traditions become eroded, Himba apparel is becoming more hybrid or abandoned altogether.

ARRIVAL AND DEPARTURE **RUACANA**

By car Easily accessible by good tarred roads from Oshakati, 160km (99.4 miles) to the east, and from Opuwo, 140km (87 miles) to the southwest. A challenging but scenic track runs westwards alongside the Kunene to Epupa Falls (317km/187 miles), much loved by four-wheel drive fanatics. Much of this is impassable in the rainy season. As far as Swartbooisdrift, the first section is pretty straightforward, whereas the longer stretch through the Zebra Mountains to Epupa requires greater four-wheel drive expertise. There are several basic community campsites along the way, as well as the delightful *Kunene River Lodge* (see below).

By minibus Minibuses between Ruacana and Oshakati pull in at the Puma garage.

6

ACCOMMODATION **SEE MAP PAGE 247**

Eha Ruacana Lodge Ruacana village, on the C46 ruacanaehalodge.com.na. A functional motel-like place with a surprising array of facilities: a moderately priced restaurant, bar-lounge area, a swimming pool, and even a gym and squash courts. The clean, bland tiled rooms are perfectly adequate if you get stuck for the night, while the campground also contains some small domed budget chalets if you crave a little a/c and a fridge. Camping N$, budget chalets N$–$$, doubles (B&B) N$$

Hippo Pools (Otjipahuriro) Community Campsite On the banks of the Kunene, 4km (2.5 miles) west of the turn-off to the Ruacana. Simple, back-to-basics, shady campground with ten pitches in an idyllic location, affording views across to hilly Angola; here, you can hear the cry of the fish eagle and the grunting of the eponymous hippos in the river below. There is no electricity; basic washing and long-drop toilet facilities are run down. Guided walks and village visits can be arranged. Camping N$

★ **Kunene River Lodge** 45km (28 miles) west of Ruacana Falls on the D3700 kuneneriverlodge.com. A long-standing favourite with a relaxed, away-from-it-all feel. The camping pitches take pride of place along the riverbank, under a shady canopy of mature trees, with braai sites, sink, electricity and shared ablution block. Further back, spacious rooms (with a/c) and cheaper rustic chalets (with fans) overlook a tropical garden, which hides a sheltered pool area. Meals (which need to be pre-ordered) are served on the riverside deck. It's the perfect spot to unwind for a few days, given the wealth of activities: birdwatching (almost three hundred species), canoeing, excursions to a Himba village, whitewater rafting down a local gorge or chugging along the river by boat for a sundowner. Four-wheel drive access only. Cheaper for two-night stays. Camping N$–$$, chalets (B&B) N$$, doubles (B&B) N$$$

Northern Kunene

Occupying the northwest corner of Namibia, **northern Kunene** is a predominantly mountainous wilderness area, accessed by few roads and sparsely populated even by Namibian standards. The **Baynes Mountains**, which overlook the picturesque **Epupa Falls** on the Kunene River, rise to over 2,000m (6561.7ft). Elsewhere, the land consists of rock-strewn, reddish earth covered in acacia trees and flat-topped escarpments. Often referred to as **Kaokoland**, the former bantustan name that is still commonly used, or the **Kaokoveld** – designating the geographical area – it is home to the vast majority of the fifty thousand **Himba**, who are very much in evidence in **Opuwo**, the Kunene region's unlikely capital. Stretching from the **Skeleton Coast** in the west a few hundred kilometres inland towards Etosha, northern Kunene is bounded by the perennial Kunene River in the north, which marks the border with Angola, and the dry Hoanib River in the south. Here, along the sandy riverbeds of the Huab, Hoarusib and Khumib rivers, desert-adapted elephants and black rhinos wander, seeking out vegetation in the scarce, spring-fed waterholes.

Opuwo

There's a touch of the Wild West about **OPUWO**, a frontier feel that exists nowhere else in Namibia. During the day, there's a purposeful bustle of tourists, NGO workers and the occasional film crew passing through on their way to somewhere else – usually Epupa Falls, lesser-explored parts of the Kaokoveld or a Himba village – pausing only to stock up with supplies. Indeed, most tourists are drawn to Opuwo – though relatively few ever reach this remote region – to interact with and learn about the Himba.

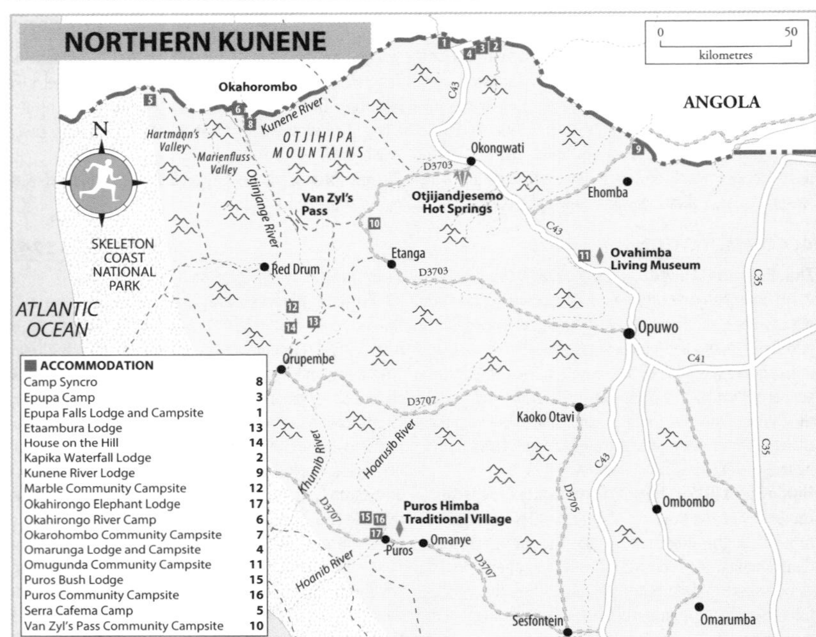

Only officially declared a town in 2000, Opuwo is now the regional capital of Kunene. For many years after independence, it was a neglected backwater, in no small part because many Himba and Herero – related to the Himba and relatively well represented in the town – were on the wrong side in the independence struggle (see page 345). Opuwo's town centre still consists of little more than a couple of paved roads converging at a T-junction, a collection of government buildings and ever-expanding, informal Himba settlements. Indeed, when many Himba lost cattle and other livestock in Namibia's worst drought for thirty years in 2013, they saw little alternative than to migrate to Opuwo in the hope of some relief. These days, pavements are crammed with Himba camping out, the women surrounded by crawling babies, swigging out of large bottles of Fanta, while the older men sit in deckchairs or on makeshift stools, surveying the scene. Himba from remote villages also periodically come into town to visit the hospital, stock up at the wholesalers or sell crafts to tourists.

There are no tourist attractions as such, but pick your way through the rubble and rubbish dumped by the roadside and the thriving shebeens to take a wander around the **Himba market** behind the main shopping complex or seek out the Kunene Conservancy Indigenous Natural Products Trust processing plant, **Scents of Namibia**, southwest of the T-junction, which manufactures Himba cosmetics made from traditional ingredients, and can offer **guided tours** with advance notice (Mon–Fri 8am–5pm; Ⓦ scentsofnamibia.com).

ARRIVAL AND DEPARTURE — OPUWO

By car From the south, the quickest route to Opuwo is via the tarred C35 from Kamanjab (237km), turning west onto the signed C48 for the final 56km. Although the road to Opuwo is wholly tarred, you'll come across many animals north of the veterinary fence, just north of Kamanjab. There is also no petrol available between the two.

By bus or shared taxi To reach Opuwo from Windhoek, you need to enquire at the Monte Christo Service Station in Katutura. Alternatively, ring Davi (Ⓣ 081 2586186) in Opuwo to find out when the return transport will return north.

In Opuwo, to get a ride out of town, ask at the Puma filling station, next to the OK supermarket complex; minibuses and shared cars leave regularly for Oshakati (3hr) and less frequently for Windhoek, Swakopmund or Walvis Bay (7–8hr).

INFORMATION

Kaoko Information Centre On the C41, entering town, 500m (0.3 miles) before the junction facebook.com/ovazemba. Run by HIPO (Hizetjitwa Indigenous People's Organisation), this very helpful office can provide you with lots of information about the area's various Himba, Herero, Zemba and Hakaona communities. They can also organise a trained local guide to accompany you in your vehicle on day or overnight trips to various villages, including as far as Marienfluss or Hartmann's Valley. Costs vary depending on time, distance and demand, but are usually around N$400/person for a day trip to a settlement, plus food to take to the village, and N$800/person for an overnight excursion; food for you and the guide would be on top. Daily 8am–5pm.

ACCOMMODATION

SEE MAP PAGE 257

Aameny Rest Camp 50m (0.03 miles) off Mbumbijazo Muharukua Avenue, 300m (0.2 miles) north of the T-junction 065 273572 or 081 275 0156, aamenylodge@yahoo.com. The town's backpacking option is a pleasant, secure and shady spot with rondavels, twelve basic twin rooms (some with fans, some without) and grassy pitches, though the town's noise can permeate the place at night. Camping N$, doubles N$$

Abba Guesthouse Mbumbijazo Muharukua Avenue, 500m (0.3 miles) north of the T-junction, by a school abbaguesthouse.com. Good-value, simple guesthouse with neat and tidy rooms. The budget rooms (with fans) are en-suite. Still, with little more than two beds and a kettle, it's worth splashing out the extra for the upstairs air-conditioned 'luxury' rooms that open onto a shared balcony, each with a fridge, kitchenette, tea/coffee-making facilities, and even DStv. Secure parking too. The owners are heavily involved in supporting the adjacent church, school and orphanage, towards which a percentage of the guesthouse income goes. Breakfast on request. Budget rooms N$, luxury rooms N$$

Okahene Guesthouse Mbumbijazo Muharukua Avenue, 200m (0.1 miles) north of the T-junction 081 7081648, ohakene@rise-in-africa.com. Tucked behind the disused Shell petrol station, an unprepossessing exterior belies a pleasant, tropical oasis – a small lawn dotted with palm trees and a tiny pool, around which a dozen tidy tiled rooms (a/c and DStv) are arranged. The small terrace restaurant, which serves nicely cooked, inexpensive dishes, is open to the public, though they need advance notice. B&B N$$

Opuwo Country Lodge On the ridge, on the west side of town, signposted off Mbumbijazo Muharukua Ave 500m (0.3 miles) north of the T-junction opuwolodge.com. Surveying Opuwo like a feudal lord, this hotel is by far the best lodging in town, though it isn't as good as it thinks. The main thatched lodge boasts enviable views across the surrounding countryside from its terrace and infinity pool deck. However, only the small 'luxury' rooms – crammed with nice furniture – share this view. Even smaller standard rooms sit behind, with shared porches and noisy a/c units under the tables. 400m (0.2 miles) away, the campground lacks shade and has rocky and uneven pitches, but it's quiet (unlike in town), and the big plus is access to the lodge's facilities, including its fabulous infinity pool. Camping N$, doubles (B&B) N$$

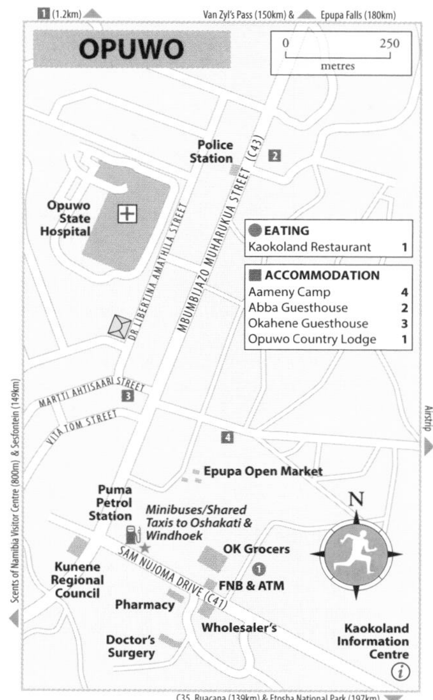

EATING

SEE MAP PAGE 257

★ **Kaokoland Restaurant** Main road, close to the OK supermarket facebook.com/bestinopuwo. This is the only place to eat in town outside the hotels and market stalls. It does decent breakfast fry-ups, sandwiches, burgers and salads, and more substantial chicken, goat and meat dishes with mealie-pap, rice, chips or salad.

6

Epupa Falls

Before the Kunene River empties into the Atlantic on the Skeleton Coast, it fans out across a broad valley, forming numerous channels that skirt round islands and trip, tumble and cascade over a series of cataracts before plunging into a chasm. This is **Epupa Falls** – Epupa means 'falling water' in Otjiherero. The main cataract is a mere 35m (114.8ft) and only captures a third of the river's flow. Still, the whole scene is truly magical: set against the backdrop of the Baynes Mountains, lofty makalani palms interspersed with majestic jackalberries and sycamore figs fringe the riverbank, while stout baobabs and silvery moringa trees balance precariously on the rocks above the ravines. Though at their fullest and most impressive in April and May, when the water thunders and the spray obscures your view, the falls are picturesque even in the dry season, when expanses of attractive reddish-brown rock and tiny grassy islets are exposed.

Birdlife is abundant – including the localised endemic Cinderella waxbill and rufous-tailed palm thrush – and a walk upriver from the falls is likely to yield sightings of watchful crocs half submerged in the shallows or lazing on the riverbanks. One of the most delightful places to **camp** in Namibia, Epupa also attracts visitors whose main aim is to interact with the semi-nomadic **Himba**, one of Africa's most resilient – and most photographed – Indigenous peoples (see page 254).

ARRIVAL AND DEPARTURE — EPUPA FALLS

By car Epupa is around a 180km (111.8-mile) drive northwest of Opuwo (3hr), on a gravel road, which becomes

VISITING HIMBA COMMUNITIES

Activities in Opuwo and northern Kunene generally centre on visiting **Himba communities**. Your first port of call should be the Kaoko Information Centre. However, visits can also be arranged through English-speaking Himba such as Western, the owner of *Aameny Camp* (see page 257), or 'Queen Elizabeth' (T 081 213 8326), usually found with the other Himba jewellery sellers close to the OK supermarket. Alternatively, you can arrange a visit through your accommodation or book with a tour operator. Before deciding, make sure that your visit is likely to involve a small group, be culturally sensitive and benefit the community. Whatever you do, avoid giving tobacco, alcohol or sweets to individuals or communities. Establish what the parameters are in advance. When visiting a village or even meeting Himba on the way, merely handing money to adults or sweets to kids is not helpful, as it has already encouraged begging, which is growing among some of the populace along the route to Epupa. Similarly, photo-taking is a sensitive issue; permission should be sought before taking a photo, but better than that is to interact with people during an activity or on a visit with an interpreter, and maybe after spending time together, you might ask to take a photo of you all together, to share among the group. The snap-for-cash culture that has dominated interactions between Himba women and tourists for some time now is not helping to develop intercultural understanding or positive relations.

Kunene Conservancy Safaris (KCS; W kcs-namibia.com.na) is Namibia's most successful conservancy-based tourism company, with great ethical and environmental credentials, running a range of small-group tours (two to ten people) led by experts for eight days or more. Around N$10,000/day per person for a group of up to three; reduced rate for larger groups). All profits go to the five conservancies involved and some tours include staying at *Etaambura*, the first Himba-owned lodge (see page 260).

Another option for travellers who wish to visit independently is to drop in on the **Ovahimba Living Museum** (call manager John T 081 3713884; W lcfn.info/ovahimba), which is next door to the community campsite at Omugunda (N$), 42km (26 miles) along the gravel road towards Epupa. As with the other living museums (see page 60), each activity is paid separately in cash. Here, you can choose from an hour's bushwalk or body painting to a general cultural introduction to the village or a whole day during which you participate in a whole range of activities with a guide/interpreter on hand.

THE KUNENE DAM CONTROVERSIES

Since the mid-1990s, when the first feasibility studies were conducted, the Namibian and Angolan governments have been attempting to **dam the Kunene River** and build another hydroelectric power station (in addition to the one at Ruacana) to satisfy the countries' ever-increasing demand for power. The favoured site for the dam, initially, was at **Epupa**. Still, the Himba, whose ancestral lands would have been flooded and whose way of life was threatened, protested vociferously, supported by national and international human rights and environmental agencies. Bowing to sustained pressure, the Namibian government eventually shelved the plan in 2007 but is now pushing for the construction of a dam 40km (24.9 miles) downstream in the **Baynes Mountains**. Once again, this would flood Himba lands, including gravesites, entail the forced resettlement of some communities, deprive settlements of an important riverine resource for people and cattle, and lead to the inevitable influx of construction workers and a likely increase in crime. All of which would threaten the Himba way of life. As an alternative, most Himba favour developing **solar power** in the region. In 2012, the Himba took their case to the African Union and the United Nations, followed by protest marches in Opuwo. Pressure to construct the dam has been building once again, with allegations of bribery and corruption of some of the Himba leadership by some government and Chinese agents to persuade them to agree to the project. Other Himba leaders and communities continue to voice their opposition while the current economic crisis in Namibia has seemingly pushed the project into abeyance once more, though it is unlikely to be the end of the saga.

increasingly sinuous as it nears Epupa. Stock up on camping supplies and fuel in Opuwo.

On a tour Lodgings in Opuwo (see page 255) run tours to Epupa, including day trips, though an overnight stay is preferable to catch the sunrise and sunset, which are often magical.

ACCOMMODATION

SEE MAP PAGE 256

★ **Epupa Camp** 1km (0.6 miles) upriver from the falls ⓦepupa.com.na. This is a delightful location, with ten stone-enclosed safari tents lined along the riverbank; you can watch the water flow from your private porch. Dinner and drinks are served on the deck, with a small splash pool to cool off. Make sure you visit the tiny private island, where you can loll on a swing bed while sipping your sundowner. The adjacent campground lies further upriver, with six quiet, spacious plots boasting private ablutions, though there's less shade than at *Epupa Falls Campsite*. It also has simple dome tents with beds and linen. Camping per person N$, dome tents N$$, safari tents (DBB) N$$$

★ **Epupa Falls Lodge and Campsite** On the river, at the top of the falls ⓦepupafallslodge.com. When the river's full, you can see the spray from this shady camp with six camping pitches and rustic solar-powered stilted en-suite cabins, which afford great views across the river and are good value. The raised terrace-restaurant deck offers similar vistas and a pool to cool off in. Half-day Himba village visits are the main activity, though guided river walks and birdwatching can also be organised. Camping N$, chalets (B&B or DBB) N$$$

Kapika Waterfall Lodge On the ridge, 1km (0.6 miles) upriver from the falls ⓦepupalodge.com. Perched high on the hillside, affording commanding views of the river from the restaurant deck, this lodge is a prime spot for a sundowner. The ten stone chalets with open-plan bathrooms and semi-private porches are large, though rather bare and bland. Two appealing private campsites also have the views and own facilities. Camping N$$, (B&B or DBB) N$$$

Omarunga Lodge and Campsite 500m (0.3 miles) upriver from the falls ⓦgondwana-collection.com. Shaded under wafting makalani palms, this nicely maintained riverside lodge offers fourteen safari-tent chalets; numbers 1–5 directly overlook the water. The decent-size pool has a nice shaded area for lounging around, and each spacious campsite has a light (but no power point), tap and fireplace, with a spotless shared ablution block and kitchen area. Camping N$, chalets (DBB) N$$$

Marienfluss and Hartmann's Valley

In the far northwestern corner of Kunene, **Marienfluss** and **Hartmann's Valley** constitute one of Namibia's most remote wilderness landscapes, receiving few visitors beyond the semi-nomadic Himba with their cattle and goats, alongside herds of springbok and

ACTIVITIES AT EPUPA FALLS

All four established accommodation options offer much the same activities – **sundowners**, gentle river **rafting** (when there's enough water), birdwatching, **guided walks to look for crocodiles** and **visits to Himba villages**. For village visits, prices usually include the guide and transport but do not include the 'payment' to the village. Generally, food is taken, in agreement with the villagers: sacks of ground maize, cooking oil, sugar and the like, which can be purchased at the village store in Epupa. Before signing up for an excursion, check what is included and what is expected of you.

oryx. Few tourists make it this far, except for a trickle of determined, hardy four-wheel drive adventurers or a select few who can afford a fly-in safari (see page 262). Tracks are sparse, mobile phone coverage non-existent, and the main reference points are painted oil drums. More self-drive visitors stop in Marienfluss, but if you have the time, the fuel and the water – there's nowhere to replenish stocks en route – you should try to visit both valleys. Marienfluss is arguably the more beautiful of the two, being lusher – if there's been rain – coated with flaxen grasses and home to carpets of fairy circles (see page 261) along its broad, flat sandy floor, flanked by the Otjihipa Mountains to the east and Hartmann's Mountains to the west. Moreover, there's a gorgeous riverside campsite to reward the dusty drive, though don't be tempted to jump in the water, as this is prime croc territory. These days, there's even a tiny Himba store selling cold beer. Reaching the end of Hartmann's Valley is a rougher ride, 70km (43.5 miles) of more arid conditions that will take you well over two hours, but its moonscapes have a desolate beauty: vast expanses of flecked cream- or rust-coloured sand, interspersed with endless domes of seemingly barren grey rock; as you approach the Kunene, the huge dunes to the west separate you from the Skeleton Coast, some 50km (50 miles) away.

The best-known entrance into Marienfluss is the dramatic descent over the **Van Zyl's Pass**, a precarious, rocky affair, not for those suffering from vertigo or lacking in four-wheel drive experience. You will have to get out and inspect the terrain as you go and move the odd rock, but before focusing your attention on not overturning the vehicle or toppling over the edge, don't forget to pause at the viewpoint and absorb the stunning panorama. However, if you approach the valleys from the comparatively easier route via Red Drum, in the south (which still demands good four-wheel drive experience, GPS, possession of spare parts, some mechanical know-how, a satellite phone and driving in convoy), you will have to return the same way as far as Orupembe, since you are only allowed to cross the Van Zyl's Pass from east to west.

ARRIVAL AND DEPARTURE — MARIENFLUSS AND HARTMANN'S VALLEY

By car Van Zyl's Pass is reached via Opuwo along the well-graded C43 road to Epupa, turning off at Okongwati after around 110km (68.4 miles), from where it is slow going along a rocky track to Otjitanda. Most people camp here before tackling the pass the next day; allow at least three hours for it and another two to reach camp at the Kunene. From the south, most people access the area via the D3707 from Sesfontein, via Puros (see page 263) and Orupembe.

ACCOMMODATION — SEE MAP PAGE 256

Community campsites are constantly springing up; some are very rudimentary, but even those that are more developed, with better facilities, may still lack water for one reason, especially after several years of drought. Wood may also be hard to come by, so you should bring both water and wood with you or use a gas stove for cooking. Moreover, if something breaks, it's a long way to go to buy a spare part, so you need to be patient and understanding should facilities not function quite as you might hope.

Camp Syncro Kunene River, Marienfluss. Four lovely riverside campsites are augmented by two rustic stone-and-thatch chalets, with an outside braai site to cook on. A good place if the community campsite is full. Expect sometimes-functioning showers and a warm welcome. Camping N$, self-catering N$$

Etaambura Lodge Onjuva, 25km (15.5 miles) north of Orupembe, in the direction of Marienfluss. Contact Kunene Conservancy Safaris kcs-namibia.com.na/

etaambura-camp.html. Pioneering joint venture between KCS and several Himba communities, this self-catering lodge (though you can pay to have your food cooked for you) boasts spectacular 360-degree views from five imaginatively designed tent-and-thatch chalets with sliding glass doors to maximise the views. En-suite bathrooms are carved into the marble outcrop. Donkey-heated water and solar power do the rest. Great main lodge made of rock gabions and domed thatch. Opportunities for informal learning about Himba life through organised activities with English-speaking Himba guides. Camping is only allowed if chalets are full. N$$$

House on the Hill Onjuva, 26km (16.2 miles) north of Orupembe houseonthehillnam.com. A Namibian artist working with the local conservancy has applied his artistic talents to transforming the old marble quarry manager's residence into three solar-powered self-catering units (one for four people, two for two). It is a good base for forays into Marienfluss or Hartmann's Valley. Great quirky stone-and-wire sculptures around the building. N$$

Marble Community Campsite Onjuva, 26km (16.2 miles) north of Orupembe openafrica.org/participant/marble-community-campsite. Close to a disused marble quarry from which it takes its name, this spot is well organised. It has five delightful secluded campsites with private sinks and food preparation surfaces, a braai site and lovely stone ablution blocks with solar-powered hot water. Cold beer is for sale when the freezer's working – a real treat. It's often full in high season, so get there early. N$

Okahirongo River Camp Kunene River, Marienfluss sanctuaryretreats.com/namibia-camps-river-camp. Five luxury tented chalets hosting up to fourteen guests in style – solar-powered but without sacrificing comfort – lots of sofas and cushions to lounge on while watching the crocs in the Kunene doing much the same on the sandbanks, plus

6

THE NAMIB'S MYSTERIOUS FAIRY CIRCLES

One of the Namib's many curious natural phenomena is that of '**fairy circles**'. From the air, they appear like a giant polka-dot pattern across a vast sheet of scorched cloth along the eastern fringes of the desert. A closer inspection reveals **discs of bare earth** fringed with lush grasses, which are higher and healthier than the ones between the circles. Measuring between 2–20m (6.6–65.6ft) in diameter, the larger circles have an average lifespan of forty to sixty years as they appear, mature – growing in some cases – and then fade.

To the Himba, they are simply the **footprints** of their deity, Mukuru; scientists, needless to say, have been looking for other explanations, though they have so far failed to solve the puzzle. Over the years, many **theories** have been put forward – from ostriches taking dust baths to poisonous underground gases, not to mention the inevitable intervention by aliens – but most ideas have eventually been dismissed. The two most persistent explanations relate to sand termites and grasses competing for scarce natural resources. For a long time, the **sand-termite** theory held sway, the notion that these busy subterranean insects were eating the roots of grasses and therefore killing them; with no remaining plants to suck up the water, it pools below the surface, allowing the termites to survive the dry season and the grasses on the periphery to thrive. However, critics point out that while termite presence is generally high in fairy circles, termites have not been found in *all* the circles. Moreover, the theory would not seem to explain the regular, almost honeycomb-like spacing of these circles, so clear from aerial surveys, nor the fact that these apparent carpets of bronze coins only occur in a very limited geographical range, in the arid transitional zones between grasslands and true desert.

What threw the termite theory up into the air was the realisation in 2014 among experts that fairy circles, which for years were thought to be unique to Namibia, also exist in the outback of **Western Australia**, in similarly arid conditions but without the number of termites. This would seem to lend greater weight to the notion of grasses in arid conditions 'organising' themselves to maximise scarce water and nutrients. While an even carpet of plants would be unsustainable in such conditions, the argument is that hardier grasses survive, sucking up the water, leaving their neighbours to die; the gap between the vegetation widens and the barren circle of sandy soil is then too hard to take seed but rather acts as a repository for any moisture, like an oasis, which further nourishes the stronger and healthier plant life encircling the bare earth. Further evidence supports this reasoning: the circles seem to grow after dry years and shrink after wet ones. In 2019, a study of fairy circles in Australia suggested that the circles were due to **weathering**: heavy rainfall followed by evaporation. The bottom line, however, is that whatever the most plausible theory is, the mystery is far from being unequivocally solved.

6

SKELETON COAST FLY-IN SAFARIS

Hemmed in between the wild Atlantic and the rugged Hartmann Mountains, the remote northern section of the **Skeleton Coast National Park** – the **Wilderness Area** – is the stuff of National Geographic documentaries. Its few visitors are privileged to experience an immense, desolate beauty of unworldly landscapes: a scalloped sea of huge **'roaring' dunes** (sound waves thought to be produced by the friction of sand particles); the **moonscape** and **'clay castles'** – striking sand formations – of the Hoarusib River Valley; and the endless bleak **coastline** pounded by surf and sprinkled with bleached whalebones, rusting shipwrecks and scuttling ghost crabs.

In refreshing contrast stands the avian-rich riverine strip along the **western Kunene River** as it carves its way towards the coast, separating Namibia from Angola. **Fly-in safaris** to the region – the only way to access this isolated wilderness – are not focused on big game; they're about marvelling at the vast and varied desert scenery, seeking out smaller creatures and the extraordinary plants that have adapted to the unforgiving arid environment; and learning about Indigenous people – from the Himba, who still inhabit some areas, to the early Khoisan beachcombers, whose ancient ruined shelters and rock art give clues to their way of life. That said, you're still likely to spot the odd loping hyena or black-backed jackal on the scrounge – especially near the Cape Frio seal colony – as well as the perennially hardy oryx, and, with luck, a herd of desert-adapted elephants. Visiting this region is not cheap – expect to pay US$4,200–5,500 per person sharing for an all-inclusive four-day safari (flights extra) for a wilderness camp experience and over US$12,000 for a fully inclusive fly-in safari. But the experience will be unforgettable.

TOUR OPERATORS

Natural Selection naturalselection.travel. The arresting *Shipwreck Lodge*, 45km (28 miles) north of Möwe Bay, is the ultimate Skeleton Coast wilderness retreat: a row of ten solar-powered eco chalets spread atop a dune. Strikingly designed as shipwrecked hulls, complete with portholes looking across the sand to the wild sea, they possess wood-burning stoves to counter the cold nights. As with other such wilderness safaris, activities focus on both the otherworldly scenery and the unique desert ecology while affording likely opportunities to glimpse rare desert-adapted wildlife. Although guests can drive to Möwe Bay for a transfer, many fly in, often combining a stay with the *Hoanib Valley Camp*.

Skeleton Coast Safaris skeletoncoastsafaris.com. This operation is run by the members of the pioneering Schoemann family, who have been exploring the Skeleton Coast for over forty years and have legendary knowledge and guiding skills. The classic four-day safari – by plane, Land Rover and on foot – flies out of Windhoek and spends a night in each of their three comfortable but basic camps (expect small domed tents, bucket showers and dining under the stars). Groups of two to eight people. They also run tours that take in Etosha and the Namib around Sossusvlei. Drop-off/pick-up fees are extra, plus an additional cost per aircraft.

Wilderness Safaris wilderness-safaris.com. If you want more luxurious, *Out of African*–style accommodation, a higher level of pampering and fine dining, consider one of Wilderness Safaris' two remote, exclusive tented camps – only accessible by plane. Though both lie just outside the national park boundary, they are effectively 'next door', set in similarly awe-inspiring scenery, and travel into the park itself. *Serra Cafema* is the more established camp, overlooking the Kunene, while the newer *Hoanib Skeleton Coast Camp* lies in the broad valley of the same name – a prime spot for spotting desert-adapted elephants and rhinos. Flights are additional to advertised rates.

a fabulous pool and deck area offering yet more splendid views. Walking and riverboat (when water levels permit) safaris are available. Accessible by road or fly-in. N$$$$

Okarohombo Community Campsite Kunene River, Marienfluss conservationtourism.com.na/what-to-do/4x4-routes-and-camping/okarohombo-community-campsite. Five lovely spacious sandy sites under spreading ana trees by the Kunene. Good communal solar-powered hot showers and flush toilets when working. N$

Serra Cafema Camp Kunene River, Hartmann's Valley wilderness-safaris.com. Long-standing wilderness lodge comprising eight luxury wood-and-canvas thatched chalets amid lush riverine trees, where you can gaze across to Angola from your private deck. It stands in stark contrast to the arid surroundings, which you can explore on a guided quad bike excursion. Himba village visits and boat trips on the river are also on offer, fortified by fine cuisine. Airstrip nearby for fly-ins, not included in the otherwise fully inclusive rates. AI N$$$$

Van Zyl's Pass Community Campsite 20km (12.4 miles) before the pass, near Otjitanda conservationtourism.com.na/where-to-go/north-west/van-zylspass-campsite. Three spacious, shady sites set along a sandy riverbed, with private ablutions offering a basin, mirror and donkey-fired hot water. N$

6

Puros

Heading south from Orupembe along the D3707 eventually brings you to the mixed Himba and Herero settlement of **PUROS**, some two and a half hours later. It boasts a magnificent setting at the confluence of the Goatum and Hoarusib rivers, surrounded by dark ripples of striated rock offset by banks of pale sand. The small settlement is aptly named, being a corruption of the Otjiherero word *omburu*, meaning 'fountain'. The impressive **Hoarusib River**, with its dramatic cliffs and gorges, has permanent springs that ensure pools of water exist year-round. They are fringed by mature vegetation, a magnet for an abundance of **wildlife**: desert-adapted elephants, giraffes, zebra and a host of varied antelope are regular visitors to these areas, in turn, pursued by less visible cheetahs, hyenas and leopards. Even the occasional desert-adapted lion frequents the riverbed. Birdwatchers have the chance to spot the likes of near-endemics such as Monteiro's hornbill, Carp's back tit, and Rüppell's korhaan. Still, the oasis pools sometimes attract more surprising avian visitors, such as hamerkops and Egyptian geese.

This is an excellent area to explore for a couple of days by engaging a trained English-speaking community guide who can take you to the permanent springs in the river, twenty minutes from the campsite, where you'll likely be rewarded by good wildlife sightings in the dry season. The **Puros Traditional Village** – a conservancy-managed Himba demonstration settlement – is within walking distance of the camp. However, you'll need a guide to interpret and help you learn a little about their culture. Crafts are also for sale. Guides can be arranged at the campsite or the bush lodge (see page 263).

ARRIVAL AND DEPARTURE — PUROS

By car Four-wheel drive is essential. From the south, the D3037 criss-crosses the Goatum River before taking you across the unworldly Giribes Plains to Sesfontein – around a three-hour drive – where there is fuel. From the north, the D3037 carries you the 100km (62.1 miles) from Orupembe, a straightforward drive, though the corrugations can be bothersome. Experienced four-wheel drive travellers in convoy and with all the necessary gear prefer to take the spectacular four-wheel drive trails down the Khumib and Hoarusib rivers (only in the dry season).

INFORMATION AND ACTIVITIES

Information Enquiries about the area can be made at the campground or the bush lodge reception. Mobile phone coverage can be unreliable in this area; you may need to contact the Puros Conservancy Office (T 081 3836811) on their satellite phone (T 870 762711719). Note that firewood can be purchased at the campground or bush lodge but should be used sparingly as it's in short supply.

Activities These can be booked at the campground or the bush lodge: half-day Himba village tour or nature walks; full-day excursions including some hiking – you'll need to take lunch for you and the guide; a half-day game drive (in your vehicle) down the Puros Canyon in search of elephants. Guiding fees for longer excursions to Marienfluss or Orupembe can also be negotiated.

ACCOMMODATION — SEE MAP PAGE 256

Okahirongo Elephant Lodge W sanctuaryretreats.com/namibia-camps-elephant-lodge. The box-like structures ranged along the hillside belie distinctive, designer-chic interiors painted in earthy tones to blend into the surroundings. The lodge is laden with expensive African artefacts and stuffed with sofas overflowing with cushions. Take in the astounding scenery while lolling in the infinity pool. Discounts for four-night stays or more. Most guests fly in (see page 262). AI rates are also available. DBB N$$$$

Puros Bush Lodge 2km (1.2 miles) north of Puros W puros.wild-exp.com. This is an inexpensive alternative to a night in a tent. Six no-frills brick-and-thatch en-suite chalets, a few hundred metres from the camping, with glass windows, screen-netting but no fan. Braai facilities. N$$

★ **Puros Community Campsite** 2km (1.2 miles) north of Puros T 081 716 2066 (signal intermittent) or T 081 383 6811 (Puros Conservancy Office) or contact the Puros Bush Lodge. Six secluded, shady, sandy sites (No. 2 is the most private) spread out among giant ana and camelthorn trees on the banks of the Hoarusib River. Each has a private toilet, hot shower, sink and braai site. Elephants frequent it – so don't leave food around. N$$

The northeast

JU|'HOANSI SAN MAN SETTING AN ANIMAL TRAP

The northeast

Namibia's vast size means that most first-time visitors fail to reach the country's northeast corner, encompassing the remote areas of Otjozondjupa and the Kavango and Zambezi regions – which includes Namibia's idiosyncratic panhandle. In so doing, they miss out on a great deal: a chance to experience the Kalahari through the eyes of the Ju|'hoansi San and to explore Khaudum, one of the country's most untamed national parks requiring good off-road skills and a sense of adventure; and a chance to immerse themselves in a lush subtropical environment. The five rivers – including the mighty Zambezi – are surrounded by a handful of small national parks, each promising abundant wildlife, including hippos, crocodiles and buffalo – not generally found in Namibia's other national parks – unparalleled birdwatching, serene boat trips and glorious sunsets.

The vast area between Grootfontein and Rundu, to the east of the B8, is sparsely inhabited, home only to a couple of thousand **Ju|'hoansi**, scattered across the flat sandveld of the **Kalahari**. Primarily, they live in the Nyae-Nyae Conservancy, the 9,000 sq km (3475 sq mile) area that was the former apartheid-designated Bushmanland and is now part of the Otjozondjupa Region. Its isolated centre, Tsumkwe, sits at the end of the area's only road out by the Botswana border. If you're interested in learning more about **San culture**, both past and present, this is the place to do it; approached with sensitivity, it can be an informative and enriching experience.

Back on the B8, heading north, you enter **Kavango East**. However, there's still little evidence of human habitation: 80 percent of the region's population live in the 10km (6.2-mile) strip by the Kavango River, which comes as a welcome relief after so many hours driving through rather uninspiring, arid landscapes. On a bluff above the river lies **Rundu**, the region's rapidly growing capital and the gateway to what was previously known as the Caprivi Strip (see page 270), but which these days is shared between Kavango East and the Zambezi regions and traversed by the Trans Zambezi Highway. The few visitors to Namibia who make it this far north often consider this 500km (310.7-mile) sliver of land as a place to overnight between Etosha and Victoria Falls. Yet the region merits a much longer sojourn as it is unlike anywhere else in Namibia: verdant, humid and tropical, boasting mature forests, free-flowing rivers and swampland, home to large populations of elephants and buffalo and prolific birdlife.

Moving eastwards from Rundu, well-equipped and experienced four-wheel drive adventurers might divert southwards to undeveloped **Khaudum National Park**, where the sense of achievement from getting through the endless deep sand without incident should compensate for any shortfall in animal sightings. For most, though, the first port of call is **Popa Falls Reserve**, a picturesque, if not spectacular, series of rapids on the Kavango River, which forms the western boundary of the **Bwabwata National Park**, the region's largest and most diverse protected area, which extends right along the strip. Two sections are open to the public, giving access to wonderful wildlife-rich riverine environments: the **Mahango Core Area** and the **Kwando Core Area**, at the park's eastern limit. From here, the Kwando River meanders south to the region's southernmost tip, providing opportunities for seeking out antelope, other large mammals, and some colourful birds in **Mudumu and Nkasa Rupara national parks**. The latter comprises Namibia's main wetland area, and it is here that the Kwando makes a

CAMP KWANDO

Highlights

❶ Visiting a Ju|'hoansi community Approached with sensitivity and an open mind, a day or two in the company of the Ju|'hoansi San is an unforgettable learning experience. See page 272

❷ The Nyae-Nyae Pans in flood A rare sight – only following good rains – makes this experience all the more precious: delightful lilies and waterbirds in the Kalahari bush. See page 274

❸ Popa Falls More a series of rapids than a falling torrent of water, Popa Falls are nevertheless extremely picturesque. See page 280

❹ Encounters with elephants Wait long enough at the oxbow lake in the Bwabwata National Park and herds of elephants will surround you. See page 282

❺ Relaxing in a riverside lodge Whether overlooking the floodplains of the Chobe or Kavango rivers, the reed-lined Kwando or the sweeping grandeur of the Zambezi, there are lodges to suit all budgets. See page 284

❻ Browsing markets and craft stalls Displayed in roadside stalls, craft centres or town markets, you'll find great crafts. See page 286

❼ Sunset cruise on the Zambezi An evening boat trip on any of the region's rivers is a treat, but a sunset cruise along the Zambezi is genuinely magical. See page 289

HIGHLIGHTS ARE MARKED ON THE MAP ON PAGE 268

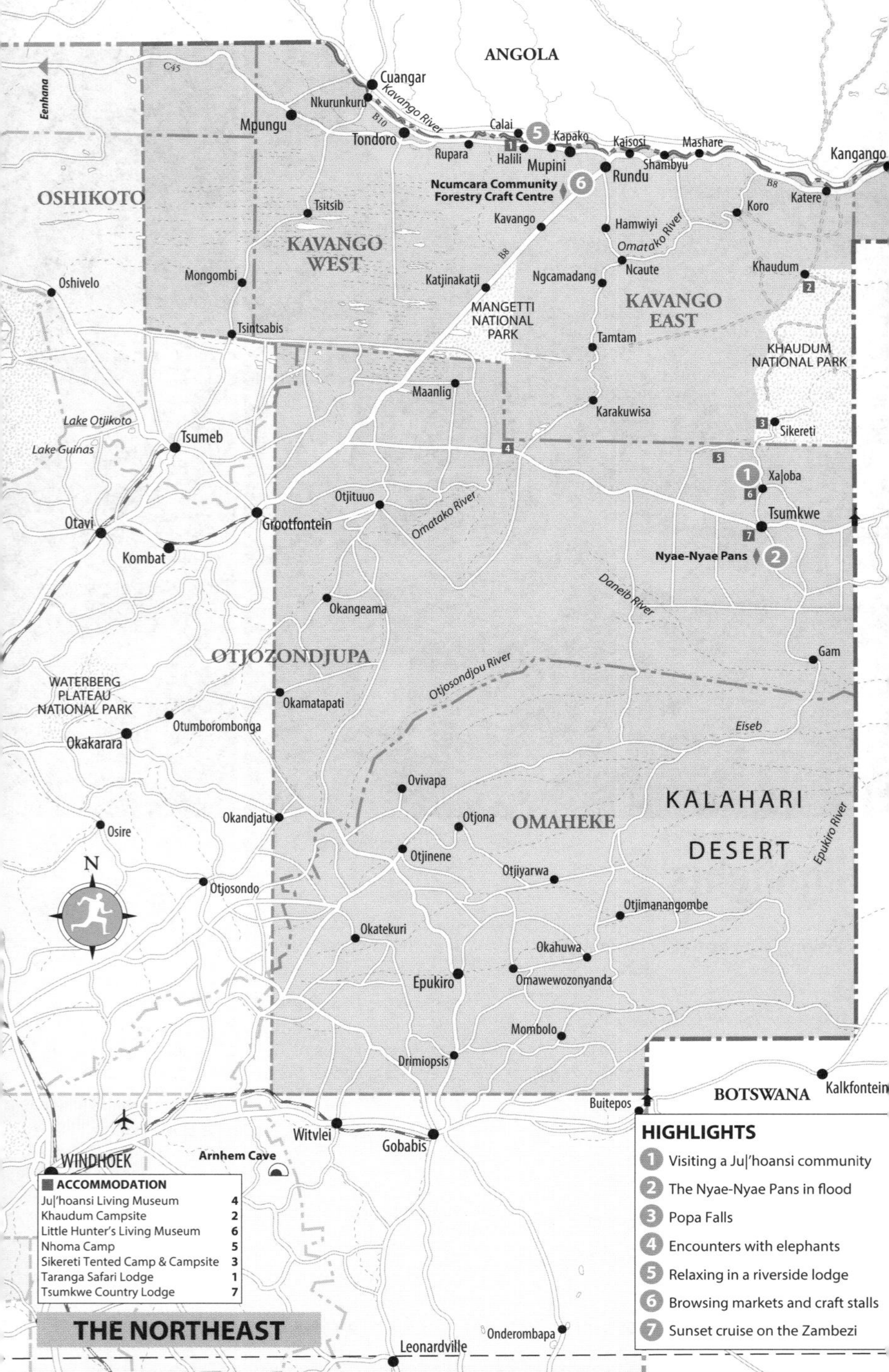
ANGOLA
Eenhana
C45
Cuangar
Kavango River
Nkurunkuru
Mpungu
B10
Tondoro
Calai
Kapako
Kaisosi
Mashare
Kangango
Rupara
Halili
Mupini
Shambyu
Rundu
B8
Katere
Koro
OSHIKOTO
Ncumcara Community Forestry Craft Centre
Tsitsib
Kavango
Hamwiyi
Omatako River
KAVANGO WEST
B8
Ncaute
Khaudum
Mongombi
Katjinakatji
Ngcamadang
Oshivelo
MANGETTI NATIONAL PARK
KAVANGO EAST
Tsintsabis
Tamtam
KHAUDUM NATIONAL PARK
Maanlig
Karakuwisa
Lake Otjikoto
Sikereti
Lake Guinas
Tsumeb
Xa|oba
Otjituuo
Tsumkwe
Otavi
Grootfontein
Omatako River
Kombat
Nyae-Nyae Pans
Daneib River
Okangeama
OTJOZONDJUPA
Gam
Otjosondjou River
WATERBERG PLATEAU NATIONAL PARK
Okamatapati
Otumborombonga
Eiseb
Okakarara
Ovivapa
KALAHARI
Okandjatu
Otjona
OMAHEKE
Osire
DESERT
Epukiro River
Otjinene
N
Otjiyarwa
Otjosondo
Otjimanangombe
Okatekuri
Okahuwa
Epukiro
Omawewozonyanda
Mombolo
Drimiopsis
Kalkfontein
BOTSWANA
Buitepos
Witvlei
Gobabis
Arnhem Cave
WINDHOEK
ACCOMMODATION
Ju|'hoansi Living Museum 4
Khaudum Campsite 2
Little Hunter's Living Museum 6
Nhoma Camp 5
Sikereti Tented Camp & Campsite 3
Taranga Safari Lodge 1
Tsumkwe Country Lodge 7
HIGHLIGHTS
1 Visiting a Ju|'hoansi community
2 The Nyae-Nyae Pans in flood
3 Popa Falls
4 Encounters with elephants
5 Relaxing in a riverside lodge
6 Browsing markets and craft stalls
7 Sunset cruise on the Zambezi
THE NORTHEAST
Onderombapa
Leonardville

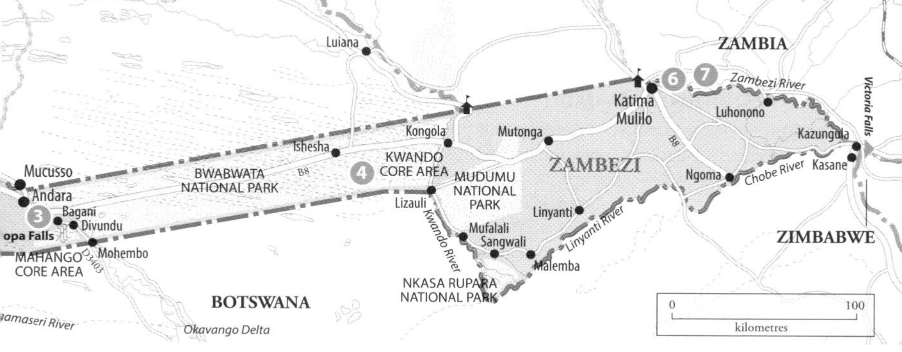

ninety-degree turn eastwards, as the Linyanti, before heading into Botswana, where, as the Chobe River, it eventually flows into the Zambezi. Around 110km (68.4 miles) west of this confluence lies the bustling capital of the Zambezi Region, **Katima Mulilo**. After browsing the town's outstanding craft centre, most visitors head eastwards to the secluded riverside lodges and camps tucked along the leafy banks of the Zambezi. Malaria is endemic in the region year-round and appropriate preventive measures should be taken (see page 63).

Brief history

Just as the riverine environments of the northern **Kavango** and **Zambezi** regions are distinct from the rest of Namibia, so too are the people. Moreover, the area's major towns, Rundu and Katima, founded by the South African administration after German colonial rule had been and gone, are both border towns with a more cosmopolitan African vibe.

The two hundred thousand Namibians who identify themselves as Kavangans were originally river-dwellers – Kwangali, Mbunza, Shambyu, Gcriku and Mbukushu – Bantu-speaking groups that migrated down from East Africa, settling in the Upper Zambezi before moving southwards to the Kavango at different times between the sixteenth and eighteenth centuries. Scarcely touched by German colonial influence, they were more affected by the arrival of the Portuguese across the river and later by the South Africans, who founded Rundu in 1936 as an administrative base for the Kavangos. At the frontline of SWAPO's lengthy struggle for independence in southern Angola, Rundu had to accept a SADF base. This led to the town and surrounding villages suffering violence from both sides. Waves of Angolans followed this – now a large percentage of the town's population – fleeing first from the Namibian conflict and later from their civil war.

Most of the people further east towards the Zambezi are Lozi and, therefore, culturally closer to Lozi populations in Zambia, Botswana and Zimbabwe than most other Namibians. In fact, until the end of the nineteenth century, the area was known as Itenge, or Linyanti, and was part of the Lozi Kingdom of Barotseland, which covered a large chunk of present-day Zambia. The colonial wrangling that followed resulted in the curiously shaped 450km (279.6-mile) panhandle that stands out on maps of the region today (see page 270). More reminiscent of a guitar head than a kitchen utensil, its forested 200km (124.3-mile) 'neck' is only 20km (12.4 miles) wide, squeezed between Botswana and Angola, while its 'headstock' fans out into lush wetlands that border Botswana and Zambia and are within easy striking distance of Zimbabwe.

The northern Kalahari

Namibia's slice of the **northern Kalahari** is very different from the southern Kalahari east of Mariental and Keetmanshoop (see page 145). There, a series of linear red

THE ORIGIN OF NAMIBIA'S PANHANDLE: THE CAPRIVI STRIP

The reason the anomalous **Zambezi Region** – formerly the **Caprivi Strip** – belongs to Namibia goes back to a **colonial barter** in 1890, in which Germany persuaded Britain to accept the islands of Zanzibar and Heligoland (a small archipelago off northern Germany) in exchange for this sliver of land, which was then part of Bechuanaland (present-day Botswana). Keen to gain access to the Zambezi and create a riverine trade route connecting with the Indian Ocean, the Germans seemingly overlooked the very substantial obstacle to such a plan: the Victoria Falls. This stumbling block, however, turned out to be irrelevant since defeat in World War I meant the Germans had scarcely set foot in the area before they were forced to hand it over to **South Africa** – though not before naming the strip of land after the then German Chancellor, General Count Georg Leo von Caprivi di Caprara di Montecuccoli, which was mercifully shortened to Caprivi.

Given its location at the confluence of five countries, the strip's strategic potential repeatedly put it at the forefront of a succession of conflicts and led to the development of the region's eventual capital, Katima Mulilo (see page 287), which soon became a garrison town. In 1964, in opposition to South Africa's apartheid policies, the Caprivi African National Union (CANU) – a movement pushing for Caprivi self-governance (see page 347) – joined forces with SWAPO to fight for Namibian independence with the proviso (so they say) that once it was secured, Caprivi could itself be **independent** – a deal that SWAPO vehemently denies. Discontent about alleged discrimination against Caprivians and repeated calls for Caprivi self-rule simmered throughout the independence struggle and beyond, though matters didn't boil over into full-scale **conflict** until 1999 when an attack on Katima by the **Caprivi Liberation Army** (CLA) – the military wing of the secessionist movement – provoked intervention by the security forces. Several deaths resulted, both sides committed abuses, and many civilians were forced to flee. In the end, 121 separatists were arrested and put on trial for treason – a trial that dragged on for around twelve years and received much criticism from human rights groups. A verdict was finally reached at the end of 2015; the final tally was 79 not guilty, 30 guilty, while 12 had died in custody. Most of those found guilty have appealed against their sentencing to the Supreme Court, while some of those acquitted have reached out-of-court settlements for compensation. In turn, the Namibian state has appealed against the acquittals, which is ironic given their lack of interest in pursuing similar crimes committed during the independence struggle. The Caprivi Concerned Group (Ⓦ capriviconcernedgroup.com) continues to press for the release of all political prisoners and a referendum on Caprivi's independence.

In 2014, Caprivi was controversially renamed **Zambezi**, arguably part of the ongoing erasure of colonial names, though opponents of the name change argued that it was another attempt by SWAPO to undermine Caprivi identity and stifle any further secessionist ambitions.

dunes ripple towards the border, receiving an average annual rainfall of less than 250mm (9.8in), which results in shorter, scrubbier and sparser vegetation, typically grey camelthorn and shepherd's tree. In contrast, as you move up into central and northern areas of the **semi-desert**, the duneveld gives way to flatter, paler sandveld, with more savannah grassland and greater coverage of acacia trees and shrubs. Even further northwards and eastwards, the increase in rainfall – albeit erratic and localised – is aided by a network of *omiramba* (water courses) and a smattering of pans to create a landscape of taller trees and a denser canopy. There are also more broad-leaved species, such as purple-pod terminalia, wild teak, wild syringa, mopane or marula. While some visitors are here to tackle this inhospitable environment – usually in convoys of four-wheel drive vehicles armed with GPS, satellite phones and all manner of equipment to get you out of a scrape – most come to interact with the semi-deserts most resilient inhabitants, the **Ju|'hoansi San**.

Along the C44

Seventy kilometres (43.5 miles) along the B8, just after the veterinary cordon fence, there's a sign-off to the **Ju|'hoansi Living Museum**. The road then dips into the **Omatako Valley**, the region's main *omuramba*, which eventually wends northwards to the Kavango River. There is a community campground here, at the Kano junction; at the time of research, it was in a state of disrepair, though it may have been renovated by the time you pass. Once the road has climbed back out of the valley, it's almost 90km (5.9 miles) before the signed turn-off to *Nhoma Camp* (see below) and Tsumkwe, another 40km (24.9 miles) beyond.

ACCOMMODATION — ALONG THE C44, SEE MAP PAGE 268

Ju|'hoansi Living Museum 7km (4.3 miles) north of the C44, along the road to Grashoek, just after the veterinary fence Ⓦlcfn.info/juhoansi. This original living museum receives more visitors than the one at ||Xa||oba, north of Tsumkwe (see page 272), which can be a disadvantage if you coincide with a group from *Roy's Restcamp* (see page 187). It also offers a greater range of experiences, from a two-hour bush walk to a three-day immersion. The simple community campground has three sites, each with an individual bucket shower, long-drop toilet, fire pit and tap. Camping N$

Nhoma Camp 185km (115 miles) along the C44, then 40km (24.9 miles) north along the D3301 Ⓦnhomasafaricamp. An opportunity to spend time with members of the N||hoq'ma community and learn about aspects of traditional culture and current challenges, mediated by Arno Oosthuysen, the camp owner, who has many years' experience with the community. Guests sleep in ten simple Meru-style tents with partitioned or semi-partitioned bathrooms. Activities can also include guided excursions into Khaudum National Park. Minimum two-night stay and walk-ins not permitted. Campers can book activities. Camping N$, safari tents (Al; minimum two-night stay) N$$$$

7

Tsumkwe and around

After driving on autopilot along the C44, a seemingly interminable gravel road, for 220km (136.7 miles), it's easy to drive right through **Tsumkwe** before you even realise you've arrived. You certainly expect the place to be more substantial than the glorified crossroads that it is – enhanced by a short stretch of asphalt – though possibly no less forlorn. It's a place where you do your business as fast as possible and get out into the far more appealing surroundings. The main reason tourists trek out here is to interact with the Ju|'hoansi (San), though, for some, it's a stopover on the way to Khaudum National Park. Yet there are also a couple of scenic attractions in the area.

The **Nyae-Nyae Conservancy Office**, which should be your first port of call (see page 274), is hidden behind a chain-link fence and a large tree on the right-hand side as you approach the crossroads, the ersatz village centre. Next to the office, **G!hunku Crafts** sells jewellery and artefacts from various settlements and is worth supporting. Demand for Ju ostrich-shell jewellery is now so great that the conservancy has to import most of its ostrich shells from a farm in South Africa.

Despite having a fluctuating population of five hundred to eight hundred, Tsumkwe possesses a secondary school, which serves the 1,500–2,000 wider conservancy population, though few of the Ju|'hoansi complete their education.

THE BOTSWANA BORDER AT DOBE

Fifty-two kilometres (32.3 miles) east of Tsumkwe, a small hut constitutes the **Dobe border post** (daily 6am–6pm), as they only see around half a dozen vehicles a day; if that, you'll have their complete attention. After a quick anti-foot-and-mouth spray of the wheels and maybe getting you to wipe your feet in disinfectant, you can head off towards Nonakeng, 135km (83.9 miles) away, though the nearest fuel is a lot further. The first 10km (6.2 miles) are slow going; after that, it's now a decent enough gravel road.

VISITING A JU|'HOANSI COMMUNITY

There are several ways to visit a **Ju|'hoansi community** as an independent traveller. A major consideration is language. Within the Nyae-Nyae Conservancy, only three communities currently have English-speaking guides: at Doupos and Mountain Pos, around 8km (5 miles) and 12km (7.5 miles) south of Tsumkwe, respectively, as well as at the *Little Hunter's Living Museum* in ||Xa||oba, 23km (14.3 miles) north of Tsumkwe (see page 271). The conservancy office can give you directions. In addition, the living museum near Grashoek, off the C44 by the veterinary fence (see page 271), was the first such set-up to be established in Namibia in 2004 and is used to receiving visitors. The **living museums** both have set prices for activities, given on their website, for bushwalks or a half- or full-day of mixed activities, which will generally be carried out in traditional animal skin clothing. **Activities** include tracking, learning about medicinal plants, setting snares, hunting, making ostrich-shell jewellery, preparing food, storytelling and dancing. You'll get the most out of your visit by being willing to join in and learning at least a few phrases in Ju|'hoan from your hosts. Each museum has a 'demonstration village' with the kind of 'beehive' grass-covered wooden domed huts the San constructed when they practised a nomadic lifestyle. However, if you stay a night or two, you may also be invited to their modern settlement. Be prepared for jeans and T-shirts, and makeshift shelters from sheets of plastic, as well as clay bricks, or breezeblocks and empty Coca-Cola bottles. Each living museum has a few nicely located **campsites** with well-maintained long-drop toilets, a tap, bucket showers and a fireplace. For both of these places, you need no prior reservation.

Alternatively, you can stay at *Nhoma Camp*, where the lodge owners have lived and worked among the **N||hoq'ma community** for many years, and the experience is organised much more around the rhythm of the Ju|'Hoansi's daily activities, rather than tourists picking and choosing what to do from a menu. There is no demonstration village and residents wear their everyday clothes.

In addition, several villages in the Nyae-Nyae conservancy have established community campsites – a couple under giant baobabs – though some have no facilities, not even a latrine. On arrival, you should ask permission to camp from one of the community elders. Traditionally, the Ju|'Hoansi's non-hierarchical social structure does not entail a headman.

A couple of thinly stocked stores, a petrol station, a courthouse, a police station, a clinic, a handful of churches and shebeens, and a sprinkling of houses make up the rest of Tsumkwe.

Brief history

Though various San groups have been ranging over southern Africa for twenty thousand years or more as nomadic hunter-gatherers (see page 337), over the last couple of centuries, their traditional !nores, or hunting grounds, have gradually been eroded, and their lifestyles challenged. However, it was the establishment of Tsumkwe in 1959 by order of the South African apartheid Native Affairs Department that accelerated the process and forced a period of unprecedented change on the Ju|'hoansi, the effects of which are still felt today. A borehole was dug, a gravel road was built, and the Ju|'hoansi were invited to come in from the outlying areas to receive schooling, health care, agricultural training and food handouts. The formal establishment in 1970 of apartheid **Bushmanland** placed further restrictions on the Ju|'hoansi's land and lifestyles. In the late 1970s and well into the 1980s, as the Namibian War of Independence gathered momentum and the SADF established themselves in Tsumkwe, Ju|'hoansi men were employed as trackers. Catapulted fully into a cash economy, gripped in a stranglehold of dependency, the Ju|'hoansi became prey to jealousies regarding individual acquisition of wealth – so alien to their culture – exacerbated by the ready availability of alcohol, which often resulted in violence and

However, pressure from outsiders wanting to negotiate with leaders has, over time, pushed some into these leadership positions. Establish the camping rate in advance (usually N$60–80/person). Note that wild camping is forbidden. Many of these settlements (which may only consist of around 20–25 people) with campsites are also beginning to invite tourists to join in foraging, hunting, cooking or craft-making activities. Women do the foraging, whereas men hunt. There may not, however, be anyone in the village who speaks English, so unless you have some Afrikaans, which some of the older Ju|'hoansi can speak, you'll be reduced to sign language, though you could make enquires about engaging an interpreter at the conservancy office in Tsumkwe in advance. The conservancy has given the villages general guidelines about payment, which generally relate to fees for groups: N$1000 for a day's activities and N$750 for a half-day.

When **camping** at a community site, take all the rubbish away. You should also bring sufficient water, preferably firewood, as they may not be available, or cook on gas. Where there is a tap, be sparing with the water, and if the wood is not available for purchase, you should not collect it from their precious supply. Alcohol is another sensitive issue; be discreet if you're having a beer and do not drink in the presence of your hosts, as alcohol dependency is a problem in many Ju|'hoansi communities. All services and activities currently need to be paid for in cash; bringing some food to share with your hosts, such as nuts and dried or fresh fruit, is welcome. Sweets are not helpful, given the lack of dental care available, though you'll find sugar, tea and tobacco are common purchases in the general store. Excessive tipping is also ill-advised as it disturbs the economic equilibrium within and among communities, creating jealousies and raising expectations that subsequent visitors may be unable to fulfil. Photography is another delicate topic; if you want to take photographs, ask about the etiquette before you bring out your camera.

A visit to almost any community almost always concludes with an invitation to purchase some **crafts**; these usually have labels with fair, set prices; haggling is not customary. Choose from exquisitely made ostrich-shell necklaces and bracelets, bows, quivers and arrows, small leather pouches decorated with more shells, and, best of all, love bows. These miniature blunt arrows are traditionally fired at a young woman's buttocks by an aspiring suitor. She indicates her response either by picking up the arrow and clasping it to her bosom or letting it lie in the dust.

7

damaged social relations. Tsumkwe – or Tjum!kui, as the Ju|'hoansi call it, became a rural slum and has variously been referred to as the 'place of death' or 'place where problems follow one around'.

With the establishment of a farmers' cooperative in the mid-1980s and then the **Nyae-Nyae Conservancy** in 1998 (Namibia's first), prospects for the Ju|'hoansi began to look up, and many started to move back to their !nores. Though the wholesale hunter-gatherer lifestyle is now a thing of the past, most communities have members who still forage and hunt to some extent. This is now supplemented by small-scale livestock rearing and crop cultivation, encouraged by the conservancy. However, the recent arrival of squatter Herero families, who have moved in from the south with their cattle, poses a new threat. Though the conservancy's biggest money-earner is trophy hunting, ethno- and safari tourism, including visits by researchers and film crews, is increasing, providing a steady trickle of cash.

Baobab trees

The area possesses some majestic **baobabs**, well worth seeking out, along the main road to the Botswana border, some 15km (9.3 miles) east of Tsumkwe, and to the south down the sandy track to |Gam. For many years, the largest baobab in the area was the aptly, if unimaginatively, named Grootboom (Afrikaans for Big Tree). Though it has now keeled over, it's still impressive, with some parts seemingly still growing. Halboom (Hollow Tree), near the settlement of Djokhoe, is possibly even larger and is commonly visited on local tours. Having collapsed outwards, leaving an empty core, it resembles a shipwrecked galleon. Be careful if you clamber around since snakes like deadly black mambas may be hiding inside. North of Tsumkwe, on the way to Khaudum, is the so-called Dorsland baobab, which displays some Dorsland Trekker graffiti carved into the bark in 1891 when they were en route to Angola (see page 278).

Aha Hills

Straddling the Botswana border, to the southeast of Tsumkwe, lie the **Aha Hills** – apparently named after the sound of the barking gecko. Though only rising modestly above the surrounding sandveld, these eroded remains of a dolomitic limestone and marble plateau, which formed some 700 million plus years ago, present an agreeable if tricky clamber, rewarded by some fine views. Easily accessible (by four-wheel drive) from the Tsumkwe–|Gam road, they are best explored with a local guide.

Nyae-Nyae Pans

An extensive, interconnected system of saline pans and water, the **Nyae-Nyae Pans** form a large crescent shape that stretches southwards from around 15km (9.3 miles) south of Tsumkwe. When flooded, they transform into Edenic wetlands – some vegetated, others not – that draw thousands of birds, notably Namibia's largest concentration of wattled cranes and a breeding colony of slaty egrets, but also a host of stilts, rails, crakes, ruffs, grebes, sandpipers and, in exceptional years, flamingos. As the pans start to dry up, and other water sources have already disappeared, elephants, various antelope and other mammals come here to drink.

ARRIVAL AND GETTING AROUND — TSUMKWE

By car To reach Tsumkwe, you turn off the B8, 50km (31 miles) north of Grootfontein; it's then a further 220km (136.7 miles) along a gravel road. It is manageable in a standard saloon car in the dry season, though there are one or two sandier patches further east. However, once in Tsumkwe, if you intend to visit any of the villages, you will need a four-wheel drive and sand-driving experience to get around. Traveling in more than one vehicle is a good idea, especially in the rainy season, when the deep sand becomes mud, and some roads become impassable. Note that, although there is a petrol station here, it occasionally lacks fuel, and even when available, it is limited to old diesel and leaded petrol.

INFORMATION

Nyae-Nyae Conservancy Office C44 just before the crossroads on the right-hand side ⓦ nndfn.org Though it is a community development office, not a tourist office, the staff are very helpful. They can advise you on where to go and how you might engage a guide, assuming you have not organised anything in advance (see page 272). Moreover, they will want you to pay your N$30/day conservancy visitors' fee. Mon–Fri 8am–5pm.

ACCOMMODATION — SEE MAP PAGE 268

★ **Little Hunter's Living Museum** ||Xa||oba, 23km (14.3 miles) north of Tsumkwe ⓦ lcfn.info/hunters. The best option, as there are fewer groups and everything is well organised and run by the community, with minimal outside interference. The camping facilities are well maintained, and the campsite is an idyllic spot a few hundred metres from their village. Camping N$

Tsumkwe Country Lodge 1.5km (0.9 miles) south of the crossroads in Tsumkwe ⓦ tsumkwelodge.com. Unless you're heading out to stay at one of the communities, this is the only place to bed down. Enclosed by an unconvincing low stone wall, ostensibly aimed at keeping elephants out, the lodge comprises 21 simple, small safari tents with chipboard panelling; it's supposedly a training institution for the local Ju|'hoansi community (only a few of whom now work there). The main dining *lapa* is dark and uninspiring, though the staff try hard to enliven the place. Six campsites, each with light, power point, barbecue and grill, share ablutions while four sites have private ablution blocks. It offers full-day village visits – though it's unclear how much money the village receives – and excursions to Khaudum or the pans and baobabs. Camping N$, safari tent (B&B) N$$

Khaudum National Park

65km (102.5 miles) north of Tsumkwe and 44km (27.3 miles) south of Katere on the B8 • Sunrise–sunset • Daily charge per person and vehicle

A wild, unruly reserve, undeveloped for tourism, **Khaudum National Park** is probably the least frequented of Namibia's protected areas – outside the Skeleton Coast Wilderness Area – visited more by elephants than people; just the place if you want a real **wilderness adventure**. Clinging to the Botswana border, this 3,842 sq km (1483.4 sq mile) expanse of Kalahari sandveld is, for the most part, a dense tangle of tree and shrub savannah streaked with *omiramba*. These life-giving sandy valleys generally run west to east across the park, feeding into the Okavango in Botswana. Along the two main omiramba, you have the best chance of seeing wildlife from late August to October – once the water has dried up in the clay pans and before the rains have started. There are twelve artificial waterholes and two natural springs, many of which have hides, where you can wait in safety for the animals to show up.

Hosting a wide variety of trees, in addition to the ubiquitous camelthorn and other acacias, Khaudum boasts substantial teak forests, patches of evergreen false mopane, leadwood, wild syringa and the occasional unmistakeable baobab. The thickness of the vegetation, however, makes wildlife-viewing tricky, though the occasional grassy clearing can be particularly rewarding as vast numbers of **large mammals** – including elephants (with a reputation for aggression) but also the less common roan antelope, eland and tsessebe – inhabit the area. Khaudum is also rich in predators, with plenty of leopards, lions and even wild dogs, though catching sight of them is a wholly different matter.

7

Birdlife is similarly prolific, with over 320 species: look out for colourful racket-tailed rollers, the russet belly of the African hobby falcon or the extraordinary turkey-size ground hornbill; further brightly coloured delights arrive in summer (Nov–April), including African golden orioles and carmine and blue-cheeked bee-eaters.

Progress through the park is glacially slow, as you have to force your way through deep sand the whole way – or mud if it has rained – probably having to clear away trees that have blown down or been uprooted by elephants. Khaudum is also heavy on fuel. Only if you are experienced at driving in these conditions and fully armed with a GPS (preferably a *Tracks 4 Africa* map and satellite phone), and are travelling in a convoy with plenty of fuel, water and food should you consider driving here. If all the above seems like too much work or beyond your skills level or comfort zone, consider visiting on an excursion from *Nhoma Camp* or *Tsumkwe Country Lodge* (see pages 271 and 274).

ARRIVAL AND ACCOMMODATION — KHAUDUM NATIONAL PARK

By car There are two entrances to the park, only accessible by four-wheel drive: in the south, follow the D3315 65km (40.4 miles) from Tsumkwe; in the north, turn off the B8 at Katere (there's a sign); and follow the track 44km (27.4 miles) southwards.

Information Given the wild nature of Khaudum, it's a good idea to contact MEFT in advance to check on conditions: the regional office (T 067 244017). Only four-wheel drive vehicles in a convoy of at least two vehicles are allowed into the park. Wardens will also check that you have food for at least three days per person, 100 litres of water, and plenty of fuel – 120 litres minimum – before letting you proceed. Since you are not permitted to collect firewood in Khaudum, you should bring wood with you. You'll also need the skills and the tools to repair your vehicles should disaster strike.

ACCOMMODATION — SEE MAP PAGE 268

There are currently two campgrounds in the park; one was renovated and managed for a while by a private company but has subsequently been abandoned; the other remains under MEFT management and is in a state of disrepair.

Khaudum Campsite T 084 0009178. Six sites in a nice spot by an *omuramba*, with wooden shaded tables, a braai site and private ablutions with warm water, 14km (8.7 miles) south of the park's northern entrance. N$$

Sikereti Tented Camp & Campsite 12km (7.5 miles) north of the southern park entrance W khaudum.com.

na. Revamped in 2022–23, this tented camp at the park's south end offers eight spacious, raised self-catering units made from a mix of canvas, stone and wood, with ensuite bathrooms. Also, four shady private campsites with space for up to four vehicles (travelling in convoy) and private ablution blocks with donkey-powered hot water showers and flush toilets. Camping N$$, tented chalets N$$

The road from Grootfontein to Rundu

There's little joy to be had from what is effectively a tedious 258km (160.3-mile) slog along the B8 from Grootfontein to Rundu, where even a stop at the veterinary fence checkpoint, at roughly the halfway point provides welcome relief. Shortly afterward, to the east, lies the entrance to **Mangetti National Park** (daily 6am–6pm), which abuts the main road and sounds much grander than it is. A joint government-community venture, the reserve still used for trophy hunting was only elevated to national park status in 2014. It needs more infrastructural development before it holds any real appeal. Although it contains over four hundred eland and two hundred wildebeest, as well as sable antelope and three waterholes, the bush is exceedingly dense, the sand is deep and the tracks are unmarked. Hence, the chances of seeing anything are slim, whereas the chances of getting lost are high.

Along the B8, and with increasing regularity once you near the Kavangan capital, you'll see **woodcarvings** displayed along the roadside. The Kavangans have a reputation for high-quality furniture making and woodcraft, with wild teak, or kiaat, the favoured material, usually taken from sustainably managed community forests in the region. Around 28km (17.4 miles) south of Rundu, look out for the Ncumcara Community Forestry Craft Centre.

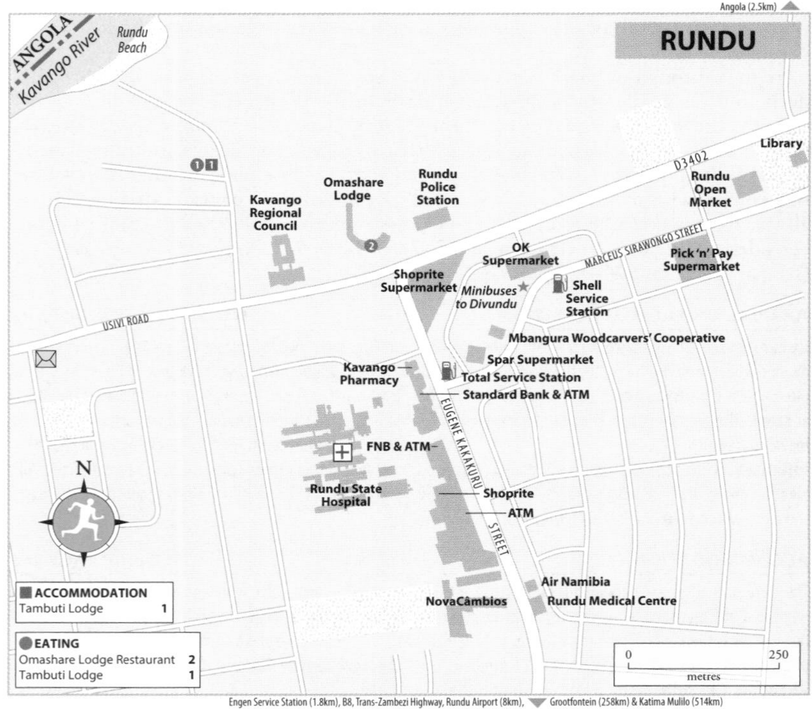

MBUNZA, MAFWE AND KHWE LIVING MUSEUMS

Three active 'living museum' communities (see page 60) give insight into some of the past and present practices of Kavango, Mafwe and Khwe-San cultures, respectively. On the shores of Lake Samsitu, the **Mbunza Living Museum** (daily 8am–5pm; Ⓦlcfn.info/mbunza) offers tours of varying lengths, allowing you to learn about and experience traditional fishing and agricultural techniques and a whole host of skills, from basketry and mat-weaving to drum-making. Indeed, if crafts are your main interest, you can undertake a craft workshop and focus on making an item to take away with you. The village is 14km (8.7 miles) west of Rundu, signposted off the road to *Hakusembe River Lodge* (see page 278).

The **Mafwe Living Museum** (daily 8am–5pm; Ⓦlcfn.info/mafwe), located on a hillside overlooking the scenic Kwando River, offers a similar interactive programme: you can learn how to use an animal trap or weave a fishing net or go on a bush walk. They also have a community **campsite**. The village is signposted north off the B8 just west of Kongola and is located 19km (11.8 miles) along the D3509, close to where the Namibian, Angolan and Zambian borders converge.

The **Khwe Living Museum** (daily 8am–5pm; Ⓦlcfn.info/khwe) lies just south of the B8, around 10km (6.2 miles) east of Divundu. The focus is on teaching about hunter-gatherer culture and learning to forage, craft bows and arrows or make jewellery from papyrus.

Community tours range from an hour-and-a-half programme to a full-day (four hours) session. You'll also find a range of well-made **crafts** for sale at all three locations.

Rundu and around

Sprawling along a bluff above the Kavango River, subtropical **RUNDU**'s rapidly expanding population – an estimated eighty thousand – has doubled over the last fifteen years. With the Trans Caprivi Highway speeding east to Zambia and improving links with Angola, the town is developing as a commercial and transport hub, prompting the municipal website to declare optimistically that it is 'much more than a refuelling stop'. Most tourists, however, have yet to be convinced, rarely spending more than a few hours, or a night, here en route to somewhere else. Yet outside the town, along the river, there are several relatively inexpensive lodges where you can unwind for a couple of days. However, the setting and wildlife are not as spectacular as that offered by some accommodation further east. Their main appeal is getting on the water in a boat, watching the birds flit along the riverbank and soaking up the glorious sunsets. However, note that at the height of the dry season (Sept–Nov), there's rarely enough water in the river to float a rubber duck, never mind a motorboat.

Rundu itself has little in the way of tourist sights and is trying hard to shrug off its frontier-town feel: hawkers have been banned from flogging their wares along the pavements – though some are defiantly resisting the 'clean-up' – and a relatively swanky new shopping mall, with the predictable South African chain stores, has now replaced the older shops on the main street.

For more local flavour, wander around the **open market**, laden with fruit and vegetables, on Usivi Road. Or call in at the **Mbangura Woodcarvers Cooperative**, next door to the Spar supermarket – the Kavango inhabitants of the region are renowned for their woodcarving and here you can see artisans at work. Down at the river, **Rundu Beach** is another community focal point, where folk wash, play in the water, and party to loud music on the sand.

ARRIVAL AND DEPARTURE — RUNDU

By car There's easy access along the tarred B8, 250km (155.4 miles) northeast of Grootfontein and 510km (316.9 miles) west of Katima Mulilo.

By minibus Daily minibus services run to Oshakati,

Otjiwarongo, Katima Mulilo and Windhoek from the Engen station at the junction of the B8 and the main road into town. Minibuses to Divundu leave from beside the OK supermarket in the centre of town.

By plane Fly Namibia flies between Eros Airport, Windhoek, and Rundu Airport three times a week (Mon, Wed, Fri; 1hr 5min).

ACCOMMODATION

IN TOWN, SEE MAP PAGE 276

★**Tambuti Lodge** Above Rundu Beach ⓦtambuti.com.na. This delightful lodge, which aims to maintain a low carbon footprint and boasts an excellent restaurant (see below), is set on a slope above the river, offering eight light, well-equipped bungalows (a/c, minibar, tea- and coffee-making facilities) sprinkled around a lush tropical garden. Nos 1 and 8 have wonderful freestanding baths as well as showers. Breakfast is served on a terrace overlooking the river and boat cruises and canoe rental are available. The only downside is the loud music and partying during holiday periods at Rundu Beach. B&B N$$

OUT OF TOWN, SEE MAPS PAGES 268 AND 280

★**Hakusembe River Lodge** Off the B8, 10km (6.2 miles) west of Rundu, 5km (3.1 miles) down a dirt road ⓦgondwana-collection.com. Twenty immaculate African-themed chalets are spread around well-tended, tree-filled grounds that attract abundant birdlife. Though all the same price, the more spacious riverside stone chalets (Nos 2–6) are the most desirable; the older wooden chalets, though wholly refurbished, are slightly smaller. Two lovely family-size villas and four lovely private riverside camping spots are also available. The food is excellent, and the service is friendly and efficient. The morning coffee brought to your private porch is a pretty nice touch. Fishing trips and sundowner boat cruises are on offer, too. Camping N$$, B&B N$$$

Kaisosi River Lodge 7km (4.3 miles) east of Rundu ⓦkaisosiriverlodge.com. This pleasant lodge set in verdant surroundings has more of a rest camp feel – though with added peacocks and sheep. Camping is good value, if not especially private, on grassy pitches with private ablution blocks and brick braai sites; the comfortable, modern glass-fronted rooms overlooking the river have a/c and DStv. Champagne breakfast boat cruises are organised for N$235/person. Camping per person N$, doubles (B&B) N$$

Mukuku Restcamp 60km (37.3 miles) east of Rundu on the Kavango River ⓦmukukurestcamps.com. Overlooking the Kavango and with bags of shade, this delightful low-key fishing camp – though open to all – has an intimate but mellow vibe. It comprises a collection of small brick or (nicer) all-wood self-catering cabins (fan-ventilated) with a simple but appealing lounge bar, where breakfast can be pre-ordered. There is also a pool and a handful of pleasant grassy campsites with communal facilities. Camping N$, chalets N$$

N'kwazi Lodge 21km (13 miles) east of Rundu on the Kavango River ⓦnkwazilodge.com. A very relaxed, no-frills, family-run place committed to local community development. Dark, cool, thatched stone-and-wood chalets fronted with mosquito netting have twin beds and a bathroom separated by a saloon door. The sunken lounge-dining area is also dark – cosy around a fire at night in winter but rather gloomy at other times – and serves tasty home cooking. The grassy campground has abundant shade and shared ablutions, with some sites more private than others. Restaurant meals can be booked. Boat trips and guided village tours are on offer, plus there's a refreshing small pool. Camping N$, chalets (B&B) N$$

Samsitu Camping Off the B8, 10km (6.2 miles) west of Rundu, 5km (3.1 miles) down a dirt road ⓦopenafrica.org/participant/samsitu-riverside-camp. Also known as 'Andy's place', this spot shares the same access road as *Hakusembe Lodge* (bear left at the lodge security gate). It comprises five camping pitches with power, lights on the

THE BORDER WITH ANGOLA

There is a makeshift **border crossing into Angola** at the eastern end of Rundu, though the traffic is mainly the other way, with Angolans coming to the Namibian town to shop. To get to the border (6am–6pm), take the signed turn-off to *Sarasungu River Lodge* and the 2.5km (1.6-mile) sandy road will take you to the riverbank, where a couple of tents serve as customs and immigration. There's a passenger ferry across the river and a more infrequent car ferry – when there's sufficient water in the river. While crossing over for the day is an enticing prospect, you'll still need a visa. Most nationalities require a **visa** to visit Angola. Still, thankfully, there is now an online application system (ⓦsmevisa.gov.ao) where you can get pre-approval within 72 hours and pick up the physical visa at the border.

water's edge, and a riverside bar and pool. Note that while it can be a lovely chilled spot, it is aimed at large groups, and if you stay in late November and December, you may find yourself with thumping music as it is popular with partying day visitors at weekends and year-end work functions. Boat trips are offered. N$

Taranga Safari Lodge Halili village, 35km (21.7 miles) west of Rundu along the B10 ⓦtaranganamibia.com. Lovely setting on a bend in the Kavango, overlooking wetlands that are brimming with birdlife, this stylish tented lodge has eight indulgent tents, set high on stilts, embellished with cream drapes, cooled with fans, and each with fridge and tea and coffee making facilities. Camping, too, is superior: mature riverine trees ensure constant shade and seclusion for eight grassy sites. The pontoon bar is the perfect spot for a sundowner, and when there's sufficient water, you can glide up and down from dawn to dusk, watching the birds and the local lads fishing. Camping N$, tented chalet (DBB) N$$$

EATING

SEE MAP PAGE 276

Omashare Lodge Restaurant Marie Mwengere Street ⓦomasharehotel.com. Times have been better in the town's main business lodging, but lunch overlooking the garden is still pleasant enough, and the food is reasonably tasty. N$$–$$$

★ **Tambuti Lodge** Above Rundu Beach ⓦtambuti.com.na. A decent steak and chips can be had here, but you'd be missing out on what this place is about traditional African cuisine using local produce. The menu offers detailed descriptions of the dishes' ingredients, origins and nutritional value. Choose from *maafe* (chicken stew in groundnut sauce) with cassava or *sorghum* and wild spinach, or, for the more adventurous diners, crocodile or oryx steak, washed down with sorghum beer or hibiscus flower juice. You can then finish off your meal with marula nut ice cream or mousse. It's a culinary experience not to be missed, but order your meal in advance and be prepared to wait. N$$–$$$

Between Rundu and Popa Falls

From Rundu, the B8 speeds east 200km (124.3 miles) to the sizeable village of **Divundu**, which marks the western gateway to Namibia's panhandle. Here, the Kavango River sweeps southwards, tumbling over Popa Falls before heading into the delta in Botswana. The road also divides: the D3430 peels off and shadows the river 32km (20 miles), passing signs to various lodges and camps before cutting through a section of the Bwabwata National Park (see page 282) to the Botswana border at Mohembo. Meanwhile, the B8 continues its trajectory, crossing the Kavango, past a police checkpoint, into the narrow corridor leading to Katima Mulilo.

As the only place to fill up with fuel and stock up with food for a couple of hundred kilometres in either direction, the Divundu 24-hour Engen service station and adjacent supermarket (Mon–Sat 7am–7pm, Sun 9am–6pm; ⓣ066 259048) and take-away, just west of the junction, are a constant hive of activity. There's even a post office. If necessary, minibuses pick up and drop off passengers here and lodges in the Popa Falls area will provide a transfer (at extra cost).

Parallel to the B8 and much closer to the river, the gravel D3403 provides a more interesting but much slower drive between Rundu and Divundu, meandering through a stream of pretty impoverished villages, which bore the brunt of the Angolan civil war spilling over into northern Namibia over a number of years. Subsistence farmers live off a mix of livestock and crop farming and fishing. The bright blue and red structures resembling oversized post boxes that you'll see along the way are VIP (ventilated, improved, pit) latrines – part of an ongoing countrywide government plan to improve sanitation and provide employment in their installation.

Places of mild historical interest en route include the old Catholic mission stations of Nyangana and Andara, in villages of the same name, 100km (62.2 miles) and 170km (105.6 miles) east of Rundu, respectively. They can be visited from a couple of the pleasant lodges and camps sprinkled along this stretch of the Kavango. In contrast to the camps around Popa Falls, the only large animals you'll see in these parts are grazing cattle, but the prolific birdlife and relaxing scenery more than compensate.

ACCOMMODATION **BETWEEN RUNDU AND POPA FALLS, SEE MAP PAGE 280**

★ **Mobola Island Lodge & Campsite** 33km (21.7 miles) west of Divundu, signed north off the B8 to Shadikongoro ⓦ mobolo-lodge.com. Five tastefully designed, well-equipped, and spotlessly maintained self-catering stone-and-thatch chalets in a scenic spot overlooking an island in the Kavango. Plus, there are inside and outside showers, cooking areas and lovely wooden decks, where a splendid breakfast can be served if you fancy being pampered. Across a swing bridge on the island stands three stunning safari tents, each with a private viewing deck. Campers, too, can enjoy one of six wonderful campsites set on immaculate grounds. Offers village visits, game drives or river trips. No credit cards or wi-fi. Reduction for two-night stays. Camping N$, chalets N$$

★ **RiverDance Lodge** 31km (19.3 miles) west of Divundu, signed north off the B8 to Shadikongoro ⓦ riverdance.com.na. Classy lodge overlooking the Kavango, with generous use of wood and glass in five cosy, romantic cabins. There are lots of private and communal deck areas to recline and read a book or watch the river. A telescope for birdwatching, too. Four fabulous shady campsites on grassy pitches along a bluff surveying the river, with glorious private ablutions, a braai site, but no grill. Camping N$, chalets (DBB) N$$$

Shamvura Camp 110km (68.4 miles) east of Rundu, signposted north up the D3413 ⓣ 066 264007, ⓔ shamvura@iway.na. Popular with birders (owner Mark is a renowned ornithologist), this no-frills place offers a great nature-lovers bush-camping experience (in your own or made-up tents), with secluded pitches offering private or shared facilities in mature woodland. Though the tents don't offer river views, a great communal observation deck overlooks the Angolan floodplains. Cottage rooms are available for the camping-averse. Small boat rental is available; rates include a guide. Camping N$, equipped tents (B&B) N$$, cottage N$$

Popa Falls Reserve

West bank of the Kavango River, 5km (3.1 miles) south of Divundu • Sunrise–sunset • Charge; free if you're staying at Popa Falls Resort

If you've come from Victoria Falls or even Epupa in northwest Namibia, you're likely to be underwhelmed by the **Popa Falls Reserve** – essentially a series of rapids on the Kavango River that gush over quartzite rocks and scurry their way around banks of reeds and papyrus. Moreover, the reserve is small: it can be explored in under half an hour on foot via raised wooden walkways and viewpoints unless you book yourself on a river cruise. For all that, Popa Falls is a scenic spot where the cascading water stretches almost 1km (0.6 miles) across at its widest and is set in a lush riverine forest frequented by hippos, crocs (see page 281) and a host of water birds. It is also a convenient place to break the journey between Rundu and Katima Mulilo and a popular stopover for travellers

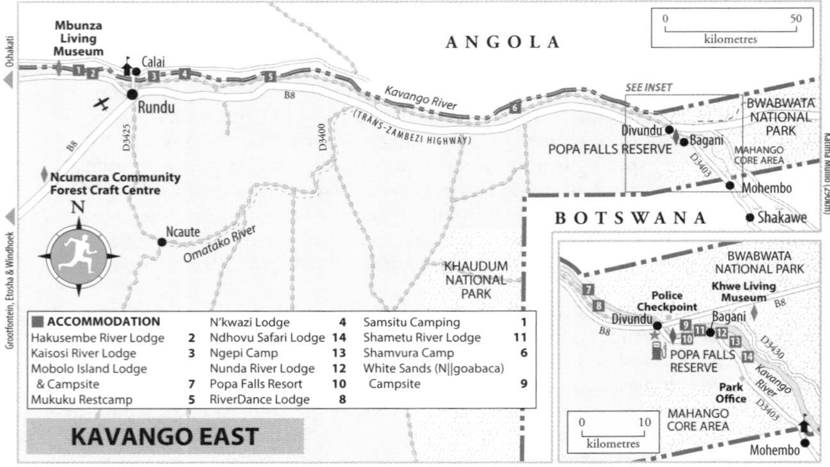

BEWARE OF THE HIPPOS AND CROCS

Hippos and crocs annually vie for the dubious distinction of being the animal responsible for the largest number of deaths in Africa (the mosquito aside). The bottom line is that both are very dangerous and are plentiful in the rivers and wetlands of the Zambezi Region. **Hippos, in particular,** wander freely through many camps at night. Though herbivores, they can be particularly aggressive in the water and on land when they come out to graze, usually at night. If you encounter one, ensure you are not between them and water. Males, on average, weigh in at 1.5 tonnes (236.3st), and they can reach speeds of almost 30km/h (18.6mph), so don't try to outrun one. Nile **crocodiles**, on the other hand, are carnivores and see humans as legitimate food. Remain vigilant when walking along riverbanks, giving areas of long grass a wide berth.

heading to or from the Okavango Delta in Botswana. The varied accommodation in and around the falls also makes the area a good base for exploring the nearby, easily accessible Mahango section of the Bwabwata National Park (see page 282).

7

ARRIVAL AND DEPARTURE — POPA FALLS RESERVE

By car At Divundu (approximately 200km/124.3 miles east of Rundu and 310km/192.6 miles west of Katima Mulilo), take the D3403 southeast off the B8 towards the Botswana border. The reserve lies 5km (3.1 miles) along this road. There is a fuel station at Divundu.

By bus Minibuses run between Rundu (from the Engen garage) and Divundu; transport between Rundu and Katima can also drop you off. After that, you'll need to hitch, though some lodgings offer transfers.

ACCOMMODATION — SEE MAP PAGE 280

The only accommodation inside the Popa Falls Reserve is operated by NWR (Ⓦ nwr.com.na). However, several lodges and campgrounds are close to the reserve, further south along the bank of the Kavango River. All offer two-hour sunset river cruises and guided drives into Bwabwata National Park. Other activities include *mokoro* and fishing trips or visits to a local village or the Khwe Living Museum (see page 277).

Ndhovu Safari Lodge 20km (12.4 miles) south of Divundu along the D3403 towards the Botswana border Ⓦ ndhovu.com. The location here is the big draw, offering the best views on this stretch of the river, right across into the national park, where the wildlife viewing can be superlative in the dry season. The two-hour boat trips are worth doing. The camp is simple but pleasing, with ten no-frills Meru-style safari tents with shower cubicles, toilets and shady private decks overlooking the water. Also, two glorious suites (renovated in 2023) with lovely wooden decks accommodating four. The large observation deck at the main lodge allows you to keep an eye on the nearby hippo pool while sipping your sundowner, but communal dining (set menu) takes place in a rather gloomy *lapa*. The main secluded riverside camping pitch is a treat – pre-booking is essential; a second smaller site is behind. It also offers trips to Botswana. Camping N$, safari tents (DBB) N$$$

★ **Ngepi Camp** 4km (2.5 miles) from the signed turn-off, 10km (6.2 miles) south of Divundu on the D3403 Ⓦ ngepi.com. With its trademark quirky open-air bathrooms, this legendary backpacker and overlander stopover with sound eco-credentials (all solar-powered) caters to all sorts of visitors, offering semi-open rustic accommodation that gets you close to nature. The grassy, well-equipped riverside campsites are lovely, and while only two treehouses are actually up trees, the others incorporate the woodland landscape into their design. Thatched bush huts (lacking a river view) are also available. Decent home cooking is available at the bar restaurant, and bags of activities are on offer. The occasional generator noise from the park wardens across the river is the only downside, audible from the more southerly accommodation. It also supports a worthwhile tree sponsorship programme. Camping N$, bush huts and treehouses (B&B) N$$

Nunda River Lodge 9km (5.6 miles) south of Divundu along the D3403 Ⓦ nundaonline.com. Possessing a more manicured feel – thanks in part to the hippos that 'mow' the grass at night – than its neighbours, this classic thatched lodge has a comfortably furnished main building and dining area, plus a lovely pool. For accommodation, choose from chalets (pay the extra for a slightly larger one on the riverfront), a handful of somewhat worn-looking Meru-style tents (avoid Nos 1 and 2, which are close to the kitchen), and some delightfully shady camping pitches – some on the river – with superior ablution blocks. DBB rates, too. Trips on the river can be by boat (with an engine) or canoe. Camping N$, safari tents and chalets (DBB) N$$$

THE KAVANGO–ZAMBEZI TRANSFRONTIER CONSERVATION AREA

The **Kavango-Zambezi Transfrontier Conservation Area**, officially established in 2011, is now the world's largest transboundary reserve, encompassing the Zambezi and Kavango river basins, and spanning **five countries**, namely Angola, Botswana, Namibia, Zambia and Zimbabwe. Incorporating around 36 **protected areas**, including the Okavango Delta, Chobe National Park and Victoria Falls, it aims to open up traditional **wildlife migration routes**. Many fences have already been taken down, allowing the 250,000–300,000 elephants in the region, for example, to wander freely – all the more reason to take care at dawn and dusk when driving along the Trans Caprivi Highway. Through improved and regionally coordinated conservation efforts and greater community engagement, communities will likely derive greater benefits from the anticipated increase in tourism opportunities. In the meantime, however, there remain tensions between conservationists and some villages, which are losing increasing numbers of inadequately protected livestock, prompting them to kill the predators responsible (see page 360).

Popa Falls Resort 5km (3.1 miles) south of Divundu, down the D3403 nwr.com.na. This recently refurbished resort offers very smart river chalets with chic modern furnishings; large windows open onto a private deck overlooking the riverine forest (Nos 5 and 10 offer the best views). To gaze at the falls, book one of the four larger luxury units with vast windows that allow you to fully appreciate the views (opt for Elephant or Rhino). The campground lies at the back of the chalets, and though it has a superior ablution block, the rocky pitches currently lack privacy and shade. The pleasantly situated restaurant is decent enough, but the sundowner bar deck, which offers the best view of the falls, steals the show. However, there's often nobody there to serve you. River cruises and game drives are available. Camping N$, chalets (B&B) N$$$

Shametu River Lodge 7km (4.3 miles) south of Divundu along the D3403 towards the Botswana border shameturiverlodge.com. This fancy lodge makes the most of its gorgeous setting, though it doesn't exactly blend in with the surroundings. That said, the spacious canvas chalets and airy communal areas boast enviable river views – especially the luxury ones, with excellent cuisine and service. Up the bank, the deluxe camping pitches don't have the same view, nor are they secluded. Still, they have everything else: grassy pitches, electricity, firewood, and private ablutions that even have towels. Camping N$, chalets (DBB) N$$$

White Sands (N||goabaca) Campsite 4km (2.5 miles) down a sandy track signposted off the D8, 800m (0.5 miles) east of the bridge whitesands.com.na. Overlooking Popa Falls from the northern river bank, this joint private–Khwe San community venture offers nine secluded pitches, some with platforms affording good views across the top section of the falls. Each has private, rustic, semi-open ablutions, water, power points, and a thatched shelter with a sink and food preparation area. Down where the new bar area is being developed, you get the best view of the falls in the whole area from a lovely white-sand beach – hence the name. Several air-conditioned chalets have been built, with more accommodation planned, which can be rented on a self-catering or half-board basis. Wheelchair accessible. Day visitors are welcome. Camping N$, chalets self-catering or DBB N$$$

Bwabwata National Park

Re-declared a national park in 2007, following years of conflict and unrest in the region, the **Bwabwata National Park** is still in its infancy, with facilities virtually non-existent. Yet, its scenic riverine environments are wonderful for wildlife viewing. Though the protected area stretches 200km (124.3 miles) along the entire neck of the Zambezi Region, the only two areas open to tourists lie at either end of the strip: at the western end, the **Mahango Core Area** borders the Kavango River, while at the eastern end, the **Kwando Core Area** borders the river of the same name. These two reserves require separate permits despite being part of the same national park. In between these two areas, yet still within the national park boundaries, the tarred B8 – the main artery that traverses the whole region – is punctuated with traditional villages of reed-thatched rondavels, from where cattle and goats occasionally wander onto the highway.

Mahango Core Area

Park entrance on the D3403, 22km (13.7 miles) south of the turn-off from the B8 at Divundu • Sunrise–sunset • Daily charge per person and vehicle; no charge if you are travelling directly to or from Botswana

The main entrance to the **Mahango Core Area** lies on the through gravel road to the Botswana border, which cuts through the park. Visitors to the reserve proper can choose between two circuits. The shorter 15km (9.3-mile) **river route** to the east runs along a decent dirt road (accessible in a saloon car) and is preferred by most visitors, as the more open grasslands, floodplains and stretches of the Kavango River afford more varied scenery – including a couple of giant baobabs – and better wildlife-viewing opportunities, especially in the dry season. Hippos and crocodiles lurk in the river, with elephants and buffalo regular visitors in the heat of the day. You're likely to spot sable and roan antelope grazing alongside the more commonly sighted antelope, while tsessebe and wildebeest are also present. The two 'picnic sites', where you can get out of your vehicle and stretch your legs, lack benches and tables.

The longer 30km (18.6-mile) meander **west of the main road** is only for four-wheel drive and takes you through denser broad-leaved woodland, where it's harder to spot animals, though, in the dry season, the Thingwerengwere waterhole can attract thirsty visitors. The park is a favourite with bird lovers, with over 450 species recorded – more than any other park in Namibia.

7

ARRIVAL AND DEPARTURE — BWABWATA (MAHANGO AREA)

By car The park entrance lies 22km (13.7 miles) south of Divundu on the D3403. Two-wheel drive is possible for the more popular drive east of the road and along the Kavango River. West of the road, four-wheel drive is necessary.

By bus Minibuses run from Rundu and Katima to Divundu. After that, you'll have to hitch a ride to the Popa Falls Reserve, a neighbouring camp that offers guided excursions into the park.

Kwando Core Area

Park entrance on the B8, 1.5km (0.9 miles) west of the Kwando Bridge • Sunrise–sunset • Daily charge per person and vehicle

Unlike its western counterpart (see page 282), this eastern section of Bwabwata National Park, the **Kwando Core Area**, is only accessible by four-wheel drive. It consists of low-lying vegetated dunes covered in deciduous woodlands of wild syringa, Zambezi teak and copalwood and areas thick with acacia and combretum species. The main, poorly signed sandy track twists and turns for several kilometres before reaching the **wetland** areas, where your efforts will most likely be rewarded. And the rewards can be substantial, especially along the banks of the **Kwando River** – where stunning carmine bee-eaters nest (Aug–Nov) – and at **Horseshoe Bend**, an oxbow lake that lies some 10km (6.2 miles) into the park. Here, resident hippos snort and wiggle their ears while vast herds of elephants can be seen converging on the water in the afternoon to bathe, drink and play. Buffalo and impala are also

THE BOTSWANA BORDER AT MAHANGO

The **Mahango-Mohembe border crossing** (daily 6am–6pm) lies just south of the Mahango Core Area entrance, 35km (21.7 miles) down the D3403, which turns off the B8 just west of the bridge at Divundu. In addition to the usual form-filling formalities, you'll need to pay from Pula 152 (or the Namibian dollar/Rand equivalent) if you're 'importing' a **vehicle** into Botswana. You'll need to pay road tax when entering Namibia with a foreign vehicle as a tourist. The tarred road into Botswana follows the Kavango River into the Okavango Panhandle to the large village of **Shakawe**, 13km (8 miles) southeast, where vehicles can refuel, and there is onward public transport to **Maun**, the main access point to the Okavango Delta proper.

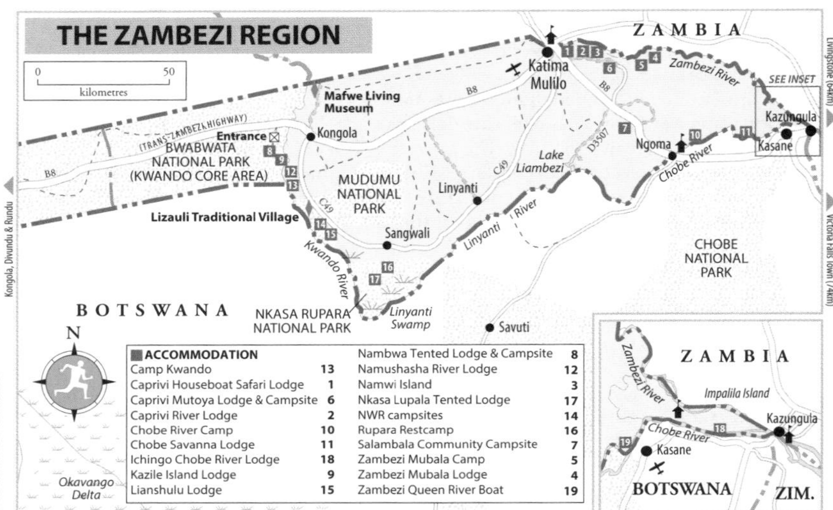

present in large concentrations in the reserve, alongside roan and sable antelope, while the elusive sitatunga – a strange swamp-dwelling antelope – can also be spotted. You'd have to be very lucky to encounter **wild dogs**. However, the park is one of the last refuges in Namibia for these endangered animals; only a handful are estimated to inhabit the area. You may also catch occasional glimpses of leopards, lions and hyenas.

ARRIVAL AND INFORMATION — BWABWATA (KWANDO AREA)

By car The park entrance is on the B8, 1.5km (0.9 miles) west of the police checkpoint at the bridge over the Kwando River and 6.5km (4 miles) west of Kongola. You will be given a makeshift sketch map and information sheet on the park. A four-wheel drive vehicle is essential.

ACCOMMODATION — SEE MAP PAGE 284

There is an unfenced campground and one new luxury lodge inside the park, which needs four-wheel drive through the sand to access, but they'll do transfers from the park entrance; the other accommodation lies on the east bank of the Kwando River, which demarcates the eastern boundary of the national park. All accommodation offers excursions into the national park by boat or on a game drive.

IN THE PARK

AFRICAN MONARCH LODGES

This collection of lodgings (ⓦ africanmonarchlodges.com) constitutes the only accommodation in the park (so daily park fees are additional to accommodation costs) and is a joint venture between a private consortium and the local Mashi Conservancy that is promising to deliver on community development. The Sijwa Project – the focus of future village visits from the various accommodations – involves permaculture projects to grow food for the lodges, training, and an innovative recycling centre that melts down tin cans and plastic bottles to refashion as crafts and a sewing workshop.

★ **Nambwa Tented Lodge** 1km (0.6 miles) from Horseshoe Bend. Along a tributary to the Kwando, this fabulous tented treetop lodge comprises ten well-ventilated, sumptuous safari-tent suites affording wonderful vistas (Nos 8, 9 and 10 have the best river views), connected via a raised walkway. The bar-restaurant deck, where mouth-watering meals are served, is located above a waterhole overlooking the savannah to maximise sunset and wildlife viewing. Lots of activities are on offer, from guided bush walks, boat cruises or game drives to village visits, plus there's a pond-sized pool to cool off in. DBB N$$$$

★ **Nambwa Campsite** Away from the main camp, under mature trees, overlooking the floodplains, are four fabulous wilderness campsites – so expect wildlife wandering through the camp at night. Each has its own high-quality kitchen and bathroom areas under expansive wooden shelters, beautifully decorated with recycled glass and other materials from the Silwa Project. Booking is essential. N$$

Kazile Island Lodge Smaller, more intimate and less fancy on a tiny island downstream from Nambwa, accessible only by boat. The comfortable common social and dining area on an impressive raised deck is fabulous. The ten tents are also elevated on stilts, five offering river views and five plains views, with slightly less generator hum and better wildlife-watching opportunities. DBB N$$$$

EAST OF THE PARK

Camp Kwando 25km (15.5 miles) south of Kongola on the C49 (MR125); a dirt road is signposted off to the west, follow this for 3km (1.9 miles) to the river campkwando.info.na. This relaxed and low-key place with rustic facilities is in a beautiful location amid the water lilies and papyrus, with tremendous sunsets from the (not especially) private shaded decks of the modest, rustic riverside safari tents. The four marginally more upmarket tents lack the river view. Four private campsites are spread around a grassy area behind, with private braai sites and ablution blocks. There is a handful of hammocks, sunloungers, and a small relaxing pool. The three airy *lapas* of the small main lodge are simply decorated with traditional African artwork. There is also a private bush camp for up to eight people 5km (3.1 miles) before Kongola, approaching from Rundu, with a swimming pool and sun deck. Camping N$$, safari tents (B&B) N$$$

Namushasha River Lodge 24km (14.9 miles) down the C49 (MR125), south of Kongola gondwana-collection.com. Popular with groups, this large lodge comprises around thirty simply furnished but comfortable stone-and-thatch chalets spaced along a bluff above the Kwando River, with views across the floodplains into Bwabwata National Park – chalet 23 has the best view, while Nos 7 and 8 are the only two not overlooking the river. Mature trees shade private balconies, and intimate candlelit dining takes place on the airy bar-restaurant terrace high above the water. Even campers should splash out one night on the excellent buffet dinner. Nine splendid grassy camping pitches have superior private ablution blocks, plus the usual amenities, and four family-size self-catering safari tents have well-equipped kitchenettes. With vehicles permanently stationed in the national park, a game drive is only a short water transfer away. Boat cruises, fishing trips and guided walks are also available, and service is good. For full-on pampering and superlative deckchair wildlife-viewing, a luxury self-catering floating villa is the latest addition; anchored in one of the nearby river channels: an exquisitely-designed romantic hideaway, it has a fully stocked bar, ice-making machine, and plenty of wildlife guides to help you identify your neighbours. Camping N$, chalets (B&B) N$$$, floating villa (AI) N$$$$

7

Mudumu National Park

Park entrance at Nkatwa Camp, approximately 35km (21.7 miles) down the C49 (M125) • Sunrise–sunset • Daily charge per person and vehicle

The small, flat **Mudumu National Park** covers the eastern riverbank and floodplains of a meandering channel of the Kwando River. Signposting is virtually non-existent and there is only a handful of sandy tracks – some of which peter out into the bush – that weave their way through mopane, wild syringa, leadwood and mangosteen, nearly all within the strip of land between the main road and the river itself. That said, you're likely to have the place to yourself – apart from the police, who occupy a small outpost to keep a watchful eye on cross-border activity – especially if you spend the night in one of the three bush camps (see below).

Birdwatching in the park is particularly rewarding; while dawdling along the river, watch out for African skimmers, cranes, storks, jacanas and ibis, while western-banded snake eagles can be sighted wheeling above. The water attracts larger visitors, too: elephants and buffalo come to drink in large numbers, and roan and sable antelope and eland are also present. If you're lucky, you might catch sight of a spotted-necked otter in the shallows. Consider visiting the nearby **Lizauli Traditional Village** – well signposted off the main road to the north of the park – to learn more about Lozi traditional culture; it's also an opportunity to purchase genuine local crafts (see page 286).

ARRIVAL AND DEPARTURE **MUDUMU NATIONAL PARK**

By car The only way to reach and explore this park is in your own vehicle. The park entrance is signposted off the C49 (MR125), approximately 35km (21.7 miles) south of Kongola. A four-wheel drive vehicle is essential.

ACCOMMODATION

SEE MAP PAGE 284

Lianshulu Lodge Just off the C49, at the southern park border caprivicollection.com. A rare concession inside a national park, this exclusive camp accommodates a maximum of 24 visitors in ten nicely appointed, if somewhat small – given the price – chalets, each facing a scenic channel of the Kwando River, looking into Botswana. The open, thatched main lodge offers more viewing space, a pool and plenty of comforts. Dinner is a set menu, with the occasional braai. Boat trips and game drives into the park are organised, as well as village visits. AI rates available. Chalets (DBB) N$$$$

NWR campsites Three unfenced bush campgrounds are located within the reserve, bookable at the park entrance (free). There is currently no charge since they possess no facilities beyond a pit latrine, though they make for a real wilderness experience.

Nkasa Rupara National Park

Linyanti Swamp, southwest corner of the eastern Zambezi Region, 10km (6.2 miles) south of Sangwali, off the C49 • Sunrise–sunset • Daily charge per person and vehicle

7

The many channels of water of the Kwando-Linyanti river system comprise Namibia's largest protected wetland, **Nkasa Rupara National Park** (formerly Mamili), a mix of marshland, high reed beds and woodland savannah that collectively offer visitors an area rich in **birdlife**, with over 430 species. Elephants, buffalo – over one thousand – red lechwe, reedbuck and puku wade or jump through the reeds, while huge crocodiles, hippos and water monitor lizards occupy the shallows. Lions are also very much in evidence. The park is mostly inaccessible as many of its 'tracks' are filled with water, and much of the area is flooded during the wettest months of the year – usually February and March – and when the floodwaters arrive from the Angolan highlands (which can be weeks later), and so is a true wilderness.

CRAFTS IN THE ZAMBEZI REGION

Like the neighbouring Kavango Region, the Zambezi Region is renowned for its **crafts**, especially **woodcarving** and **basketry**. Over the last few years, several centres have been established to showcase these skills and sell the fruits of the artisans' labours as souvenirs to tourists. The government has encouraged these as a means of sustainable development, though with varying degrees of success. However, the overall rise in visitor numbers to Namibia has increased the demand for crafts, resulting in more mass-produced items and fewer genuine, high-quality, individually crafted pieces. Indeed, the selection varies little from place to place: walking sticks, wooden animals, baskets, clay pots, soapstone carvings and tie-dye textiles abound, with a smattering of jewellery across the craft shops. Designs often reflect the surrounding environment, incorporating themes and techniques from Zambia and Zimbabwe, while some items are straight imports from these neighbouring countries.

CRAFT CENTRES

Mashi Crafts Junction of the B8 and the C49 (MR125), Kongola 0813878718. An easy stopover at the intersection opposite the Engen garage. Plenty of items are nicely displayed, including carvings, basketry, pots and jewellery, mainly produced by Zimbabwean and Zambian artisans from several nearby communities. There's another smaller, private venture next door.

Ngoma Crafts On the B8, 2km (1.2 miles) before the border post 0814156815. This unmissable, brightly painted thatched rondavel by the main road features attractive baskets and some ceramics. Now with a small café.

Sheshe Crafts Sangwali, just after the turn-off from the C49 towards Nkasa Rupara National Park 081 238 6366. You'll need to get someone to open up here to see the rather dusty collection of basketry and woodcarvings.

Zambezi Arts and Cultural Association Hage Geingob Road at Hospital Road, Katima Mulilo 066 252670. Probably the best regional selection of crafts, chock-full of the customary offerings but with some more unusual items hidden among them. Mon–Fri 8am–5pm, Sat 8am–noon.

THE ZAMBIA BORDER

Some 4km (2.5 miles) northwest of Katima, the kilometre (0.62-mile) -wide bridge at **Wenela** that spans the Zambezi marks the **border between Namibia and Zambia** (daily 6am–6pm). It is a short taxi ride from Katima to the border. The usual cross-border charges apply if you drive a private vehicle into Namibia or Zambia (see page 56). To enter Zambia, unless you're from Ireland, you'll need a **visa**, which, from many countries, costs US$50. However, in November 2022, Zambia waived visa fees for various countries, including the UK, US, Canada and Australia to help kickstart tourism after the COVID-19 pandemic. Check the latest before travelling. If you have to pay for a visa, you'll need to pay in US dollars, so you must change your money before you reach the border. From the border, you can easily hop in a shared taxi to **Sesheke**, a few kilometres away, from where there is reliable onward transport by bus to Livingstone (and **Victoria Falls**) and **Lusaka** (see page 331). If you're heading for Victoria Falls and intend to visit Zimbabwe and Zambia, consider travelling via Botswana. You can buy a Kaza visa at Kazungula but not at Wenela.

7

ARRIVAL AND DEPARTURE — NKASA RUPARA NATIONAL PARK

By car The park entrance is 10km (6.2 miles) down the dirt road signposted off the C49 at Sangwali towards *Nkasa Lupala Tented Camp*. A four-wheel drive vehicle is essential, and even then, the park is only accessible in the dry season. There is no regular public transport, though you might be able to hitch to Sangwali from Katima.

ACCOMMODATION — SEE MAP PAGE 284

★ **Nkasa Lupala Tented Lodge** 11km (6.8 miles) south of Sangwali on the park access road signed off the C49 (MR125) ⓦ nkasalupalalodge.com. A seriously committed, unfussy, proper eco-lodge with solar power and genuine community involvement, comprising ten lovely, simple, fan-ventilated tents on stilts high above the reed bed – unfenced, so you'll get elephants wading through the water right by your private deck and lions prowling around. The birdwatching is superlative, whether from the lodge, on a boat, in a safari vehicle, or even on foot (with an armed guard). Four-wheel drive is necessary or arrange for a pick-up in Sangwali. Minimum two-night stay. They also run the intimate four-tented *Jackalberry Tented Camp* (ⓦ jbcamp.com), tucked away even deeper in the reserve and have a fantastic two-storey observation tower-cum-lounge wrapped around a giant jackalberry tree. Nkasa Lupala (DBB) N$$$, Jackalberry (DBB) $$$$

Rupara Restcamp Just outside the park boundary, 10km (6.2 miles) south of Sangwali, down the dirt road ⓦ rupara.com. Nkasa Lupala Tented Lodge now manages this community campsite. Seven pitches are scenically located amid the reeds, with shared reed-and-thatch ablution blocks and cement braai sites, though no grill or electricity. Two private campsites – No. 1 has the best waterside location, surrounded by water lilies. Two simple canvas-and-thatch self-catering units are also available. Camping N$, self-catering units N$$

Katima Mulilo

Surrounded by lush forest, overlooking the majestic Zambezi, tropical **Katima Mulilo** – usually shortened to Katima, and meaning 'to quench the fire' in SiLozi, referring to some nearby rapids – has more in common with towns in Zambia and Zimbabwe than most of Namibia. Indeed, located 1,200km (745.6 miles) away by road from Windhoek, Katima is nearer to the neighbouring capital cities of Lusaka and Harare than to its own, a view soon confirmed by a wander around the vibrant **open market** and the sandy shortcuts between buildings, where women in *chitenges* crouch over makeshift stalls selling fruit, cloth, comics and sweets, and competing Sungura and Zed beat rhythms waft out onto the street.

The **town centre**, such as it is, primarily centres on Hage Geingob Street and its junction with Hospital Road, where there are several supermarkets, banks and a seemingly never-ending collection of strip malls. While here, be sure to call in at the **Zambezi Arts and Cultural Association** to browse their excellent selection of crafts (see page 286) and have a nose around the open market next door. In 2021, a new

Zambezi Museum (ⓦfacebook.com/zambezimuseum) opened its doors to the public; it focuses on the region's environmental issues and showcases cultural heritage.

If you find yourself anywhere near the suburb and former township of **Ngweze**, seek out the '**toilet tree**' outside the SWAPO office – a giant baobab hollowed out to accommodate said toilet.

The abandonment of the multimillion-dollar **Zambezi Waterfront Park** has meant that Katima has so far failed to make the most of its lovely waterside setting. For the moment, to fully experience the magic of the Zambezi, you need to head to the *Protea Hotel Zambezi River Lodge* or stay at one of the lodgings out of town.

Brief history

Though the Masubia and Mafwe dominate Katima's urban population, the majority of the people in the Zambezi River area are **Lozi** and, therefore, culturally closer to Lozi populations in Zambia, Botswana and Zimbabwe than to most other Namibians. In fact, until the end of the nineteenth century, the area was known as Itenge, or Linyanti, and was part of the **Lozi Kingdom of Barotseland**, which covered a large chunk of present-day Zambia. The colonial wrangling that followed resulted in Germany claiming the curiously shaped 450km (279.6-mile) panhandle – whose shape is arguably closer to that of a guitar head than a kitchen utensil – that stands out on maps of the region today. However, no sooner had the Germans gained this precious fluvial corridor than defeat in World War I forced them to hand it over to the South Africans. The latter is credited – by some, at least – with founding **Katima Mulilo** in

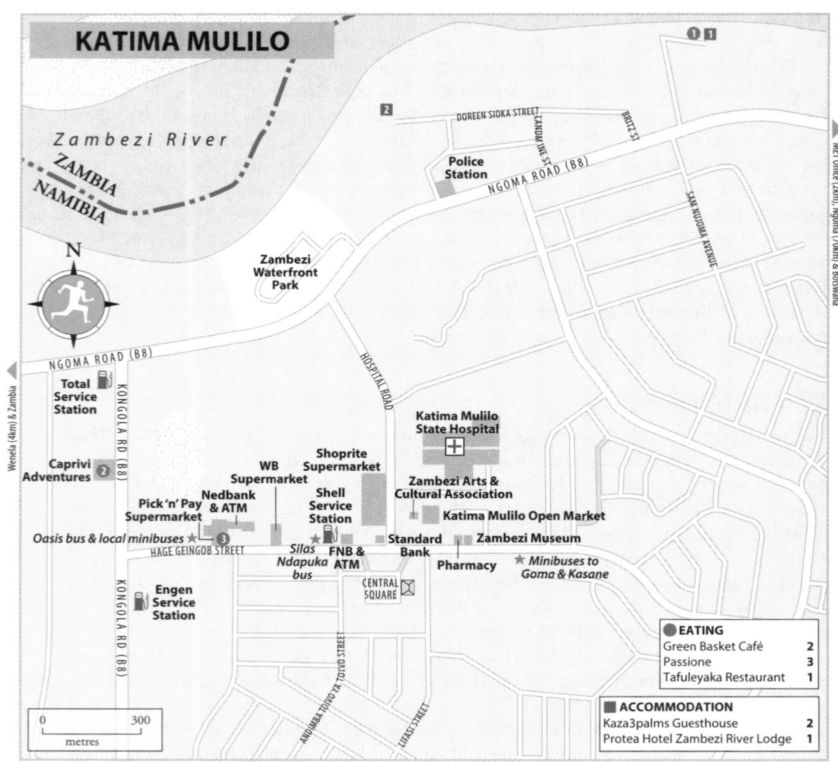

1935, transferring the Caprivi administration here from Schuckmannsburg (present-day Luhonono) in recognition of its geographically **strategic location**. This turned out to be a double-edged sword, as over the next sixty years, Katima was effectively run as a garrison town at the forefront of **conflicts**, with civilians constantly bearing the brunt of the violence from World War II through apartheid to the Bush War in Angola and finally the Caprivi secessionist uprising that ignited fully in 1999 (see page 270).

Since the **Katima Mulilo Road Bridge** opened in 2004, the Zambezi Region's capital has become increasingly cosmopolitan. Connecting the Zambian Copperbelt and even the distant Democratic Republic of Congo with Namibia's deep-water harbour at Walvis Bay, the re-emergence of this trade corridor has resulted in significant investment and development. Inevitably, as with any busy frontier town, it has fuelled its share of illicit business (including an increase in wildlife trafficking), sprawling shantytowns and accompanying social ills.

ARRIVAL AND DEPARTURE — KATIMA MULILO

By car Katima lies 510km (316.9 miles) east of Rundu along the tarred Trans Caprivi Highway (B8). It is also accessible by car from Botswana via the Ngoma border (see page 290) and from Zambia across the bridge at Wenela (see page 287).

By bus Intercape operates a service between Windhoek to Livingstone and the border with Zimbabwe at Vic Falls, via Katima. Two local bus operators also provide a daily service. The Oasis bus (T 081 7079957, E infobridgecrossinginv.com) leaves from the waste ground on Hage Geingob at the back of Pick 'N' Pay. It goes every day except Saturday (Tue & Fri 3pm; other days 5pm) and has a ticket booth at the stop. Return passage from Windhoek to Katima occurs daily at 3pm from outside Wernhil Park. Silas Ndapuka (T 081 469 4777) also runs a similar timetable with daily buses from Katima to Windhoek, returning from Wernhil Park to Katima around 3pm. There are also connections with Harare Zimbabwe.

By minibus Minibuses depart from the Engen station on the B8, at Hage Geingob Street, for Rundu, Oshakati and Windhoek. They also leave around 7–8am and 1–2pm for Kasane in Botswana via Ngoma from the areas of waste ground on Hage Geingob Street, east of Lifasi Street. If you're willing to pay a little extra, the minibus may drop you at the Zimbabwe border outside Kasane; otherwise, you must hail a taxi where you are dropped in Kasane town.

By plane M'Pacha Airport lies 18km (11.2 miles) southwest of town. Fly Namibia (W flynamibia.com) operates three flights per week between Windhoek and Katima (Wed, Fri & Sun; 1hr 30min). Taxi costs to town depend on whether the car was waiting there or had to be called out from town.

By taxi/shuttle *Caprivi Adventures* can organise cross-border transport to Livingstone, Zambia, Victoria Falls, Zimbabwe or Kasane, Botswana, but at great expense. A cheaper option is to contact Willy in Kalrose Tours in Kasane (T 267 7772 7899, E kalrosetours@gmail.com), who runs transfers from Katima to Kasane and Victoria Falls.

GETTING AROUND

On foot The town centre is very compact and easy to get around on foot.

Taxis Though there's no need around town, you might need one to get to/from the Zambian border or the airport.

INFORMATION AND TOURS

Tourist information Katima lacks a formal tourist office, but Caprivi Adventures (Mon–Fri 8am–5pm, Sat 8am–1pm; W capriviadventures.com), set back from Kongola Road, diagonally opposite from the Pick 'N' Pay supermarket, has helpful staff and is a good source of local information. They also offer various day tours to national parks, including Chobe (Botswana), as well as a sundowner cruise on the Zambezi, specialist birdwatching tours, and shuttle services to Livingstone (Zambia), Kasane (Botswana) and Victoria Falls (Zimbabwe), and can book lodge accommodation for you.

MEFT office Drop by the MEFT office on Ngoma Rd (T 066 262300) if you want to buy a permit in advance for one of the Zambezi Region national parks, though you can always buy it on the day at the park entrance.

ACCOMMODATION

IN TOWN, SEE MAP PAGE 288

★ Kaza3Palms Guesthouse 1 Doreen Sioka St W kaza3palms.com. Superior B&B with immaculate, well-appointed rooms, with access to private seating in the garden, where you can sip your sundowner overlooking the Zambezi, chill in the *lapa* or loll in the pool. B&B N$$

Protea Hotel Zambezi River Lodge Kongola Road ⓦ proteahotelzambeziriver.h-rez.com. The premier hotel in town, frequented mainly by business folk and tourists, stopping off for the night, but pleasant enough, with decent rooms containing the usual amenities and a good-sized pool set in manicured grounds. Standard international hotel fare is served at the riverside restaurant. The campground has decent facilities and lovely riverside views. Camping N$, doubles (B&B) N$$

OUT OF TOWN, SEE MAP PAGE 284

Caprivi Houseboat Safari Lodge Ngweze, 5km (3.1 miles) east of town, north of the B8 ⓦ caprivihouseboatsafaris.com. An informal, friendly rustic camp for nature and dog lovers – the owner has several large ones – comprising a handful of no-nonsense reed-and-thatch chalets facing the river, with mosquito nets and ceiling fans. One budget chalet shares the shower block and kitchenettes with the three camping pitches, which are not situated in particularly appealing locations. The small bar-restaurant, where you need to order meals in advance, has a pleasant veranda overlooking the Zambezi, though the food's indifferent. Two basic camper boats (sleeping up to six in rooftop tents and a bunk bed) can be hired with a guide to explore the rivers and wetlands within striking distance. Camping N$, chalets (B&B or DBB) N$$

Caprivi Mutoya Lodge and Campsite 25km (15.5 miles) east of town, signposted north off the B8 after 12km (7.5 miles). Overlooking Lake Liaviezwe are four stone chalets, with a handful of modestly equipped tented chalets (with a/c) set further back among the jackalberries. Ten sites are sprinkled across a grassy, shady area and a pool provides further respite from the heat. Afternoons can happily be spent cycling, paddling kayaks, fishing, birdwatching, or lazing by the pool. At the campground, a couple of budget tents are available if you fancy sleeping on a bed for a change. Camping N$, equipped tents (B&B) N$$, tented chalets (B&B) N$$$

Caprivi River Lodge Ngweze, 5km (3.1 miles) east of town north of the B8 ⓦ capriviriverlodge.com.na. This welcoming, well-organised lodge is set in lush grounds brimming with birdlife on the banks of the Zambezi. There are eight river-facing glass-fronted chalets with ceiling fans and a/c private porch. Meals are served in the pleasant lounge-dining *lapa* overlooking the Zambezi. Lots of activities are available, from day trips to Chobe and Victoria Falls to boat-based fun, including paddling in a kayak. B&B N$$$

Namwi Island 9km (5.6 miles) east of Katima Mulilo ⓦ namwiisl.com. Despite the fabulous location overlooking a good stretch of the Zambezi, this place feels a bit like a caravan park but offers excellent value for money. The rather gloomy and dated accommodation comprises fully equipped chalets for two (with a/c) or six people (with a fan) and budget chalets that share the camping facilities. Campers get solid braai stands and electricity. Boat and fishing trips are available. Camping N$, budget chalets N$$, chalets N$$

Zambezi Mubala Camp 37km (23 miles) east of Katima Mulilo, signposted north off the D3508, 14km (8.7 miles) southeast of Katima ⓦ gondwana-collection. A relaxed, shady environment under acacias and jackalberries is great for camping. Though only a few of the ten sites are actually on the riverbank, the communal lounge-dining deck provides ample space to watch the river glide past. Eight fully-equipped safari tents with full kitchens host up to four. Occasionally, the odd noise from the neighbouring rice plant disturbs the peace in some pitches. Camping N$, self-catering tents N$$

★ **Zambezi Mubala Lodge** 40km (24.9 miles) east of Katima Mulilo, signposted north off the D3508, 14km (8.7 miles) southeast of Katima ⓦ gondwana-collection. Connected by a couple of walkways, a row of spacious and stylish houseboat-themed chalets with private decks overlooking the Zambezi. Open your portholes and let in the sun and birdsong as dawn creeps over the river. The place is well set up for birding – as well as the stellar boat trips. Don't miss the breeding colony of visually stunning carmine bee-eaters (mid-Aug–Nov), with a viewing platform on the bluff 700m (0.43 miles) west of the lodge. B&B N$$$

THE BOTSWANA BORDER AT NGOMA

The **border with Botswana at Ngoma** (daily 7am–6pm; ⓣ 062 360002) lies 60km (37.3 miles) south of Katima Mulilo along a good, tarred road. Across the border, in Botswana, a decent tarred road runs through Chobe National Park to **Kasane**, 70km (43.5 miles) east, which has onward tarred road connections south to other major towns in Botswana and east to Victoria Falls, Zimbabwe. If you are transiting the park to Kasane, keeping on the main road, no park fees are charged. However, if you want to take your time along the more scenic route bordering the Chobe River (four-wheel drive is necessary) or even strike out southeast towards Savuti and the Okavango Delta, then park fees will apply. The usual cross-border **fees** apply to take a vehicle into Botswana or Namibia (see page 56). Note that if you're a motorcyclist, you'll have to find an alternative route, as motorcycles are forbidden in national parks in Botswana.

EATING **SEE MAP PAGE 288**

Green Basket Café Caprivi Adventures Kongola Rd/ B8. A few tables and umbrellas in a shady garden of sorts provide an unlikely oasis on a dusty main street. Various bacon and egg combos or healthy yoghurt and muesli are served for breakfast. Lunches are generally light and include sandwiches, wraps, salads, burgers steak or pie with pap or chips. But you can also treat yourself to a fillet of Zambezi bream. N$

Passione Hage Geingob, close to Pick 'N' Pay ⓦ facebook.com/passionerkm. It's probably Katima's best bet for a decent evening meal, though this upstairs air-conditioned restaurant with TV screens lacks ambiance. A mixture of Portuguese-inspired dishes, ubiquitous pizzas and options more familiar to the local palate: try the spicy beef strips with pap and local spinach. N$$–$$$

Tafuleyaka Restaurant Protea Hotel, Ngoma Road ⓦ proteahotelzambeziriver.h-rez.com. Different buffet breakfasts are offered, while lunch is à la carte. Dinner offers a full buffet or you can grab something from the menu – generally grilled meat, Zambezi fish, and game, including the standard international fare (steak and chips, club sandwich, pasta). The bar has a lovely riverside view from which to enjoy a sundowner from the decent cocktail menu. N$$–$$$

Lake Liambezi and Ngoma

From Katima, a decent, tarred road heads 70km (43.5 miles) southeast past a string of tidy, well-swept settlements and wandering cattle to the **Botswana border** at the village of **Ngoma**, home primarily to the Masubia and the location of a cheerfully painted roadside community **craft shop** (see page 286). Around 38km (23.6 miles) from Katima, there's a sign-off down the D3507 (around 25km/15.5 miles) to **Lake Liambezi**, a curious and constantly changing lake worth swinging by if you've time. Created in the late 1950s from a major flooding of the Zambezi, it was reduced to a dustbowl for many years in the mid-1980s, possibly due to the large-scale poaching of hippos, which used to keep the water channels open by trampling through them. Heavy rains for several years after 2009 allowed it to replenish, prompting a profitable seasonal fishing industry to mushroom around its edges, with villagers sending off their catch of tilapia, bream and catfish to neighbouring countries and even as far away as the DRC. Hippos and crocs, too, have now repopulated the lake, which also attracts good birdlife. However, the vagaries of climate change – more extreme droughts and flooding – mean that the lake will continue to disappear and reappear periodically.

ACCOMMODATION **LAKE LIAMBEZI AND NGOMA, SEE MAP PAGE 284**

★ **Chobe River Camp** On the Chobe River, 2km (1.2 miles) east of the B8 at Ngoma ⓦ gondwana-collection.com. A proper no-frills solar-powered eco-lodge overlooking the Chobe floodplains into the national park in Botswana, offering exceptional wildlife viewing – with well over four hundred bird species and regular sightings of wild dogs. The twenty simple tented chalets on stilts have solar-powered glass doors, affording pleasing river or floodplain views. The main rustic-design lodge offers similarly impressive viewing decks. Depending on water levels, affordable boat and walking safaris are available, and you can even paddle around in a Canadian canoe. The river usually floods from March to May, when the road may be inaccessible, necessitating pick-up by boat. The campground, a few hundred metres away, is regularly visited by elephants and has six pitches, with individual facilities – four facing the river – but no power. You can book tours and eat at the lodge (if there's space). Wi-fi is limited to the main lodge. Camping N$, chalets (B&B) N$$

Salambala Community Campsite Signposted west off the B8, 45km (28 miles) from Katima towards Ngoma ⓦ openafrica.org/participant/salambala-community-campsite. Follow the signs 5.5km (3.4 miles) along a sandy track from Salambala for this friendly, community-run camp with four basic pitches set among mopane trees. A nearby waterhole is visited by eland, giraffes and wildebeest, and the surrounding pan sometimes floods. Elephants pass through in April/May. N$

Impalila Island and around

At the confluence of the Zambezi and the Chobe rivers, over 100km (62.1 miles) southeast of Katima, sits **Impalila Island**, which marks the easternmost tip of Namibia.

Its unique and enviable position, overlooking scenic waterways and within easy striking distance of **Chobe National Park** in Botswana and **Victoria Falls** in Zimbabwe and Zambia, makes it the perfect spot for high-end **wilderness lodges**. Captivating scenery and glorious sunsets abound, and superlative wildlife safaris can be conducted on the water and land – in a motorboat or a *mokoro* (the traditional dugout canoe) or even from the deck of a houseboat.

The island's location, within sight of three of Namibia's neighbouring countries, also justified the island's former strategic importance as a military base for the SADF during the 1980s. Though the base has long gone and the barracks now house a school, the tarred airstrip remains to bring lodge visitors to Impalila – the only way to access the island without going into Botswana.

The eastern wetlands

7

Whereas the larger **Zambezi** flows inevitably eastwards towards Victoria Falls and ultimately the Indian Ocean, the **Chobe River** occasionally exhibits a curious phenomenon: on the rare occasions when the upper Zambezi floods, you can witness the Chobe River's flow being temporarily reversed, as it is forced to run westwards, as well as pushing water into Lake Liambezi (see page 291), until the floodwaters recede and it resumes its usual course once more, sliding into the Zambezi.

Between the two rivers, west of Impalila, their swampy **floodplains** extend, laced with deep channels of water lined with high reeds and clumps of papyrus. The area is more populated than you might imagine, with over two thousand **Lozi** making a living from subsistence farming, hunting and fishing, leading a semi-nomadic existence as they move with the rise and fall of the river levels, seeking higher land when the floodwaters swell (generally from March onwards). Significant quantities of large mammals are returning to the region, and the prolific birdlife is a further draw.

ARRIVAL AND DEPARTURE — IMPALILA ISLAND AND AROUND

The lodges listed below, although within Namibia's boundaries, are best accessed either via charter flight (in the case of Impalila Island) or via boat from Kasane in Botswana. Citizens from most Commonwealth and European countries and the US do not need a visa to enter Botswana. Check whether the inclusive rates include the transfer to/from Kasane.

By car and boat If you are self-driving, your accommodation can advise on where you can park your vehicle safely in Kasane, where a boat will pick you up.

By plane It's possible to take the luxurious option of chartering a plane to Impalila Island or Kasane (Botswana) from Eros Airport, Windhoek. Contact your accommodation for a recommended charter flight company.

By taxi If you don't charter a plane and you do not have a vehicle of your own, your best bet is to take a shuttle/taxi from Katima or Victoria Falls to Kasane (see page 320), where your accommodation will be able to arrange a pick-up, usually from the Kasane Immigration jetty.

ACCOMMODATION — SEE MAP PAGE 284

The location of the lodges, on or near the Chobe River and Chobe National Park in Botswana, which contains one of the largest concentrations of elephants in Africa, virtually guarantees sightings of these magnificent beasts, as well as a host of other large mammals and prolific birdlife. Prices for these lodges are high and given in US dollars on the websites.

Chobe Savanna Lodge Peninsula jutting into the Chobe River, 15km (9.3 miles) west of Kasane ⓦ chobesavannalodge.com. Cut off from the world of mobile phones and wi-fi; this sophisticated lodge provides opportunities for some serious armchair wildlife-viewing across the vast floodplains of the Chobe River, be it from the private veranda of one of the thirteen stylish brick-and-thatch a/c suites (each with a personal guide for the duration), or the comfortable open-sided bar area. Guided walks, canoe and boat safaris guarantee further wildlife wonders. Additional comforts include riverside fine dining and a delightful splash pool in a shady garden. AI N$$$$$

Ichingo Chobe River Lodge Impalila Island ⓦ ichingochoveriverlodge.com. A highly acclaimed fishing-focused lodge comprises eight large, well-appointed safari-tent suites (with a/c and new bathrooms), each with a private balcony tucked away in the riverine forest and overlooking the Chobe River. Communal meals are served in a high-ceilinged brick-and-thatch dining room. AI N$$$$

Zambezi Queen River Boat zqcollection.com. Spending a night or two aboard an opulent contemporary-design houseboat is a unique experience. Enjoy superlative game viewing from the top deck while dipping your toes in the plunge pool and sipping a gin and tonic. The boats range from the super-luxurious *Zambezi Queen*, boasting fourteen suites and serious pampering, to the smaller *Chobe Princesses*, each with four or five smart cabin suites, offering plenty of creature comforts. Owned by the same company that operates the *Ichingo River Lodge*, combining packages is possible. AI N$$$$

7

Victoria Falls

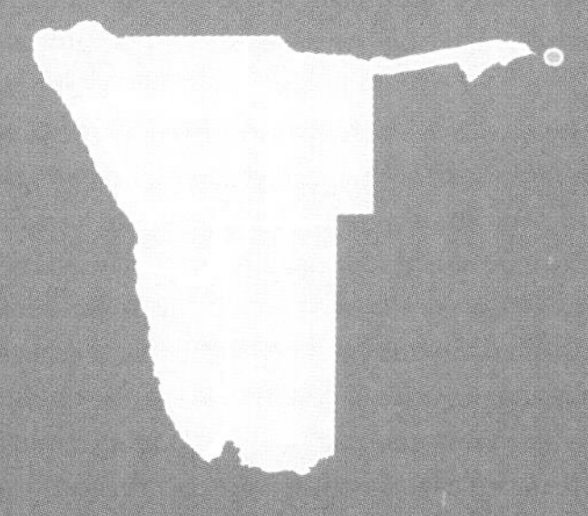

KAYAKING DOWN THE ZAMBEZI RIVER

Victoria Falls

Arrival and getting around

Most international visitors to Victoria Falls arrive by air, generally via Johannesburg, South Africa, since there are no direct international flights from Europe or North America to either Livingstone (see page 327) or Vic Falls Town (see page 313). Several airlines, however, now serve the destination via the East African hubs of Nairobi (Kenya) and Addis Ababa (Ethiopia), which offer direct flights on their respective national airlines. Livingstone and Vic Falls Town also connect several times a week with Cape Town. They also have connections with Nelspruit, the gateway to Kruger National Park in South Africa, and Maun, Botswana, the access town for the Okavango Delta.

Alternatively, there are cheaper, relatively comfortable long-distance buses to Livingstone and Vic Falls Town from the countries' respective capital cities and South Africa via Bulawayo. Intercape offers a regular bus service from Windhoek to Livingstone. Efficient shuttle services also run between Vic Falls Town and Livingstone and Kasane, a short hop over the border in Botswana and gateway to renowned Chobe National Park. Arriving by train is also inexpensive for those with a sense of adventure and bags of time and patience: from Bulawayo to Vic Falls Town and from Lusaka to Livingstone.

Border crossing

There are few more **impressive borders** than the one between Zambia and Zimbabwe (daily 6am–10pm) that spans the dramatic Victoria Falls Bridge, high above the raging Zambezi – the only pity is that scheduled trains no longer ply the route. **Shuttles** run by the various tour operators and lodgings in Vic Falls Town and Livingstone are allowed to provide cross-border transfers – the cost of a shuttle service between Livingstone Airport and Vic Falls Town varies widely from US$25–40 per person one way, and shuttles usually need a minimum of two people to run. No **taxis** or local **minibuses** are allowed to take customers into the other country, but some taxis cover the 1.5km (0.93-mile) stretch between the two border posts (private US$5). If travelling to Zimbabwe **from Zambia** (Livingstone), you can take a taxi, hotel shuttle or local minibus to the Zambia border, where you'll need to negotiate formalities – which may include paying for a **visa** (see page 296). Then, you can take a shared or private taxi to the Zimbabwe border or **walk** – pausing on the bridge en route to marvel at the view of the falls and the nerve of the bungee jumpers as they plunge into the void. Once through the Zimbabwe border, you can hike uphill to Vic Falls Town (1.5km/0.93 miles) during the day or grab a taxi. Don't try walking at dusk or night. Crossing into Zambia **from Zimbabwe** (Vic Falls Town), you'll find taxis to shuttle you between the two border posts (see page 317) and other taxis at the Zambia side of the border to drive you the 10km (6.2 miles) into Livingstone town; alternatively, during the day you can wait for the inexpensive local minibus (roughly every 20min), which will drop you off in the centre of town. In the unlikely event you contemplate walking, don't: it's unsafe.

There are also border charges to consider if travelling by **car**.

Car rental and driving

Car rental rates in both Zambia (see page 331) and Zimbabwe (see page 318), including basic insurance cover and limited mileage (usually 200km/124.3 miles), are **expensive** – from around US$600–700/week and over double that for four-wheel drive. Note that driving is **on the left** in Zimbabwe and Zambia and that if you intend to cross into any neighbouring country, you must inform the rental company in advance, for which there may be an additional charge. What's more, you will be liable for **cross-border fees** to 'import' the vehicle into the other country, as well as road tax, insurance, etc. These cross-border charges apply to all vehicles not registered in the destination country, not just rental cars. Petrol and diesel are available at Vic Falls and Livingstone fuel stations.

Visas

Visa regulations change in this part of the world as often as some people change their socks. A UNIVISA (or KAZA Visa; see Ⓦ kazavisa.info) is probably the most convenient option for most European, North American or Australasian nationalities. This allows tourists from around forty countries to pay a one-off US$50 on arrival at particular ports of entry, which affords thirty days of free movement between Zimbabwe and

VICTORIA FALLS HOTEL

Highlights

❶ **Whitewater rafting** Exhilarating and nerve-wracking in equal measure of the many adrenaline activities on offer, rafting the turbulent rapids of the Zambezi is the classic highlight. See page 303

❷ **The Victoria Falls** Soak up the spray while marvelling at one of the world's most spectacular waterfalls. See page 309

❸ **Victoria Falls Bridge** You may not fancy bungee jumping off it, but seek a vantage point to take in this outstanding feat of imperialist engineering. See page 313

❹ **Camping and canoeing** Spend an unforgettable night under canvas before witnessing sunrise over the Zambezi and paddling right up to the wildlife. See page 315

❺ **Walking safari** The only way to really experience the sights, sounds and smells of the African bush is on foot: consider tracking rhinos or birdwatching at dawn. See page 318

❻ **Sunset cruise** Glide past lazing crocs and grunting hippos on the Upper Zambezi as you sip your gin and tonic and watch the sun slip below the horizon. See page 318

❼ **High tea at the Victoria Falls Hotel** A chance to indulge in dainty sandwiches, cream scones and tea out of china cups while enjoying the view from Stanley's Terrace. See page 320

HIGHLIGHTS ARE MARKED ON THE MAPS ON PAGES 306 AND 310

Zambia (across the border at the bridge) and also to make day trips (not overnight) into northern Botswana to visit Chobe National Park (see page 320). Visitors at the following ports of entry are allowed to purchase a UNIVISA: the international airports in Livingstone, Harare and Victoria Falls; the Kazungula land and ferry borders that Zimbabwe and Zambia have with Botswana; and the Victoria Falls Bridge between Zimbabwe and Zambia. You cannot, unfortunately, buy a UNIVISA at Namibia's border with Zambia at Katima Mulilo, though there is talk of the agreement extending that far eventually. Of course, you are not obliged to buy a UNIVISA, but if you intend to stay in both countries to see both sides of the falls, it is likely to be the most cost-effective option. If staying in Zimbabwe, however, you can get hold of a day **activity visa** (US$20) at Zambian immigration on the bridge, which allows you to nip over for the day to Zambia from Zimbabwe, but not the other way round.

Of course, depending on your nationality, the visa fees demanded of you, and whether or not you intend to visit both sides of the falls, getting a regular visa may still be preferable. Most visitors likely to read this book will fall into the category of a country that can buy a visa on arrival; some may not even need a visa at all. Visa **rates** for Zimbabwe vary considerably depending on your nationality; when going to press, a visa to enter Zimbabwe for a UK/Irish national costs US$55 for a single entry, US$30 for a US citizen and US$75 for a Canadian. A double-entry visa for a UK/Irish citizen costs US$70. Single-entry ninety-day tourist visas for entry into Zambia cost US$50, irrespective of country of origin (with reductions for SADC residents). Double-entry visas cost US$80. That said, in November 2022, Zambia waived visa fees for various countries, including the UK, the US, Canada and Australia. The bottom line is that you should double-check with the relevant consular section before your trip. In the end, however, what you are charged may depend on the official you encounter since there is often confusion about which visa regulations are in effect. Note that you'll need US dollars in cash to pay for your visa at the border, though online visa applications are growing in popularity. These allow you to get a pre-approval letter and save you from carrying the extra cash, though they don't save much time at the border. For a Zimbabwean visa (excluding the Kazavisa at the time of writing), consult Ⓔ evisa.gov.zw. For Zambia, which also offers an online Kazavisa, consult Ⓦ eservices.zambiaimmigration.gov.zm.

8

Accommodation

When visiting the area, the big decision is where to stay: Zambia, to the north of the falls, or Zimbabwe, to the south. There's a greater choice of accommodation in or around Victoria Falls Town, and most of the activities are organised from this side, but it's possible to book activities from either side; for some, you may have to pay for the transfer and an extra visa, depending on the type of visa you have. So, which activities (see page 299) you're keen to do might affect where you choose to stay.

Another important consideration is that 80 percent of the lion's share of the falls lies in Zimbabwe, only a ten-minute stroll from the centre. However, in recent years, the town's rampant commercialism – including incessant hassle from desperate hawkers due to the country's economic and political crises has encouraged increasing numbers of visitors to shift over the border to the former Zambian capital, Livingstone (see page 327). One disadvantage of Livingstone is that it is 10km (6.2 miles) from the falls, although many lodgings provide free transfers at least once a day. The town also lacks the compact commercial

ACCOMMODATION PRICES

Most lodgings on the Zambian and Zimbabwean sides of the falls maintain the same **prices** throughout the year. The few properties that differentiate usually consider the high season to run from July to the end of December; some consider the high season to end at the end of November and then charge high-season rates again over the Christmas and New Year period. The prices given here are for the **cheapest double en-suite room in high season (or the year-round price, if consistent)**, which also includes breakfast unless otherwise stated. Prices are given in the advertised currency for that particular lodging – generally the US dollar. However, in practice, most places accept various currencies, so the exchange rates may not be favourable. Typically, children under 12 are charged half price.

SOME FACTS AND FIGURES

	ZAMBIA	ZIMBABWE
Time zone	GMT + 2hr	GMT + 2hr
Capital	Lusaka	Harare
Country size	752,610 sq km (290,584 sq miles)	290,760 sq km (112,263 sq miles)
President	Edgar Lungu	Emmerson Mnangagwa
Population	18 million (Livingstone: 110,000)	17.3 million (Victoria Falls Town: 35,000)
Main official languages	English, Chibemba and Chinyanja (also known as Chichewa); Silozi and Chitonga are also widely spoken in the Livingstone area	English, Chishona and Isindebele – the last being the main local language in the Vic Falls area
Currency	Zambian kwacha (but some accommodation here is given in and accepts US dollars)	RTGS dollar (but US dollar widespread)
Economy	Main industries: mining – copper (85 percent of all exports); agriculture – main export maize; floriculture is a growth industry, as is tourism	Main industries: mining – main exports gold, platinum, diamonds and coal; agriculture – main exports tobacco, cotton and sugar; tourism; manufacturing
Telephone dialling codes	Country +260 / Livingstone 0213	Country +263 / Victoria Falls 013
Mobile phone providers	Airtel, MTN, Zamtel	Econet, Telecel, NetOne
Electricity	220–240V / Plugs: 2 or 3 round pins, or three flat pins (as in the UK)	220–240V / Plugs: usually three flat pins (as in the UK); sometimes 2 round pins
Water	Tap water usually needs purifying	Tap water is generally drinkable

centre of Vic Falls Town, where everything you need is within a 100m (328ft) block, and mosquitoes are more prevalent. On the other hand, Livingstone feels more relaxed and a more 'authentic' place – albeit rather spread out – where, although tourism is increasingly important, people also go about other business. What's more, there's more of a nightlife scene in Livingstone, and you generally get more for your kwacha than for the US dollar over in Zimbabwe. Note that, in both countries, the backpackers' lodgings and less expensive guesthouses or B&Bs are in town. In contrast, the pricier lodges and hotels are nearer the falls, surrounded by bush, or along the banks of the Zambezi, set in scenic surroundings.

Activities

Beyond ogling the main event, visiting Vic Falls is all about activities. On both sides of the border, there is an ever-increasing array of ways to get your pulse racing and other more relaxing ways of enjoying the fabulous scenery and teasing out the wildlife. In recent years, cultural excursions have also been added to the menu for visitors to learn about contemporary village life. Most activities take place either around the falls, on (and off!) the Victoria Falls Bridge, on the Zambezi, across the Batoka Gorge further downstream, or in the two national parks on either side of the Upper Zambezi.

Note that **rates** for activities generally do not include the park fees (which range from US$15–100, depending upon the activity and the park) or visa fees (see page 296) if you are crossing the border for an activity. Since 2018, a bridge toll fee of US$2.50 per

8

person has been charged per crossing to help pay for the maintenance of the bridge. FUle surcharge fees have also been added to some activities. Additionally, be aware that with some half- or full-day excursions, you may not spend as much time as you were anticipating doing the actual activity, given time spent on pick-ups, drop-offs, transportation and briefing times. Most pursuits need at least **two people** to run; some activities are seasonal and depend on the river level (see page 308). Some contrived wildlife encounters are not in the animals' best interests – think before you book (see page 302).

Getting a good deal

Unsurprisingly, **prices** vary considerably – especially in low season – so it pays to shop around and to have a rough plan of what you want to do before you book anything since taking **multiple tours** with the same operator usually guarantees reduced rates. The bigger tour operators in Vic Falls Town and Livingstone also offer enticements such as free booze cruises on the Zambezi if you book two or more activities and free airport transfers, while '**combo packages**', such as half-day rafting combined with a bungee jump, can help cut costs. Getting several people together to make a group booking will also result in a better deal per person, and of course, bargains are more readily available when business is slack. First, you should compare what the **service providers** charge – such as the companies in Zimbabwe and Zambia that do the whitewater rafting – before comparing rates offered by the various tour operators or booking agents who sell these activities on commission. Of course, if you're not too worried about costs, you're short of time or want the organisational hassle taken out of your hands, then simply let your accommodation's **activity desk** sort everything out for you. The leading tour operators are listed under Vic Falls Town (see page 313) and Livingstone (see page 327); a list of almost all the activities on offer follows.

8

An A–Z (almost) of Vic Falls activities

Abseiling

See high-wire activities (see page 301).

Birdwatching

Discover Victoria Falls (see page 319), based in Vic Falls Town, is your best bet on the Zimbabwean side, whereas Savannah Southern Safaris (see page 332) fits the bill on the Zambian side.

Boiling Pot

For yet another perspective on the **Smoke that Thunders**, hike the 110m (360.9ft) down into the gorge, raft across the swirling Boiling Pot and get a first-rate hydro-massage under the falls before hauling yourself back out. Bundu Adventures (see page 331) offers this experience in the low-water season (generally late Aug–early Jan), depending on water levels.

Bridge tours

Fun and informative **historical tours** offering insights into the pioneering Victorian engineering skills that resulted in the construction of the Victoria Falls Bridge. This one-and-a-half-hour engagement starts with an actor in period costume entertaining you with tales of the times, followed by a **walk** across the gorge along the underside of the bridge. Though you'll be clipped into a safety harness and given a full safety briefing, this is not for anyone suffering from vertigo. No extra fees are required as it takes place in 'no-mans-land' between the two borders.

Bungee jumping

See high-wire activities (see page 301).

Canoeing and kayaking

Canoeing on the Upper Zambezi is a wholly different experience from rafting below the falls. With only the occasional bubbling rapid, the water is generally smooth, with lots of reed beds and channels to explore and abundant birdlife. Frequent pods of hippos will be your main sighting – and concern – plus crocs basking on sandbanks and possibly elephants. Adventure Zone organises **overnight** and **multiday** canoe trips on the Zimbabwean side (see page 318); Bundu Adventures and Makoro Quest – through Livingstone's Adventures – do the same on the Zambian side (see page 331). Safari Par Excellence does the same with inflatable rafts. Bank on paying around US$440 per person for a two-day canoe safari in Zimbabwe, involving **camping** in the bush, and paying a lot less in Zambia.

Canopy tours

See high-wire activities (see page 301).

Cultural tours

If you're keen to see a bit of **rural Zimbabwe** and visit a village, the big tour operators and various lodges run cultural tours. They can be somewhat contrived, especially if you're in a large group. Still, it depends on the guide, the rapport with the villagers concerned, and the number and sensitivity of the other travellers in the group. Expect it to last a couple of hours, during which you'll be shown around, taking in a market, school and perhaps invited into someone's home to sample a local dish, before usually being shown some **local crafts**, which you'll be encouraged to buy. Knowledge Nyoni of the Vic Falls Information Centre (see page 318) can arrange for a visit to the nearby village of **Mpisi**. The most popular excursion on the Zambian side is to **Mukuni Village** (see page 330), though Simonga Village is considered less touristy. Most operators can organise the trip; alternatively, you can pay a taxi driver to take you there or catch the local minibus heading to the falls and then change to one leaving opposite the *AVANI Victoria Falls Resort* bound for Mukuni. Both sides of the border now offer this kind of cultural tour. Consider taking one of the cultural **cycle tours**, such as Livingstone's Local Cowboy Cycle Tours, as the groups tend to be much smaller and the service more personalised.

Cycle tours

Wild Horizons offers two-hour guided cycle tours of Vic Falls with local guides several times a day. The route skirts the top of the Batoka Gorge, goes around **Zambezi Drive** (see page 316), stops at the Big Tree, and goes down to the bridge. Adventure Zone also offers the Zambezi Loop (as the route is known) but also takes you into the markets of Chinotimba. *Shoestrings Backpackers* (see page 320) also does cycle tours and rents bikes; Jollyboys in Livingstone also rents bikes. Most popular in Livingstone is Local Cowboy Cycle Tours (Ⓦcowboybicycletourslivingstone.com), a good-value, locally owned outfit, which comes highly recommended; its tours are a great way to get off the tourist trail for a half-day, taking in **local neighbourhoods**, a market and a village, enabling you to get much more of a sense of everyday life in Zambia while helping raise funds for a school that was started and is maintained from the proceeds.

Flights

Take to the air by **helicopter** or **microlight** – most awe-inspiring when the falls are in full flow and you can fly through the 'smoke'. When visitor numbers are high, it can feel like you're in a production line. The Shearwater-owned (see page 319) Zambezi Helicopter Company (Ⓦzambezihelicopters.com) offers two trips: the more popular is the 'Flight of the Angels' – a twelve- to thirteen-minute wow-factor spin in a helicopter over the falls and the gorges (around US$200). You also get to whizz over wildlife in the Zambezi National Park on an airborne safari for double the time and nigh on double the price. Ensure you don't get the middle berth at the back of the helicopter, or you might feel short-changed. On the Zambian side, United Air Charters (Ⓦuaczam.com), which flies from Baobab Ridge, just south of Livingstone, does the same two itineraries, only hovering above **Mosi-oa-Tunya National Park** and charging more for the shorter adventure and less for the longer one. In addition to helicopter flights, Zambia-based Batoka Sky (Ⓦlivingstonesadventure.com/helicopters) offers an exhilarating **microlight experience** (the only operator to do this), leaving you exposed to the elements as you soar over the falls for fifteen minutes with a private pilot. A thirty-minute flight takes in the gorges. Note that cameras are prohibited in case you drop yours and accidentally kill someone, but they will sell you pics of your flight at a vastly inflated price.

High-wire activities

Located midway across the bridge, Victoria Falls Bungee – owned by Shearwater (see page 319) – is the only operator (Ⓦshearwaterbungee.com) that offers you the chance to throw yourself headfirst 111m (364.2ft) towards the Zambezi rapids below. Single or tandem **bridge swings** allow you to look at the falls after you've jumped feet first and begun to swing'; you can also do a solo or tandem **zipline**. For an orgy of adrenaline, you can do all three. Note that you'll need your passport to go on the bridge. Wild Horizons (see page 319) offers a similar package of activities downriver across the Batoka Gorge, including relatively sedate **abseiling**, the 'flying fox', and a foofie swing, which is a zipline at a sharp angle that you zoom down at speed. There's also the genuinely terrifying **gorge swing**, while the Canopy Tour is a more conventional treetop glide along nine ziplines, finishing off with a slide across the gorge for good measure. You can do a combo of three or four activities. The best value, though, is from Zambezi Eco Adventures (see page 332), which provides a whole day of unlimited vertigo-inducing fun in the Batoka Gorge, followed by the **Devil's Pool Tour** (when water levels are low). The rates for individual thrills are more on a par with their competitors.

Horseback safaris

Zambezi Horse Trails (Ⓦzambezihorsetrails.com), an established owner-operated stables with horses to suit **all levels of experience**, offers rides in the Victoria Falls National Park. Those who've scarcely saddled up before can do a two-hour ride, while experienced riders can choose from a half-, full- or multiday horse safari. A cheaper option is the Zambia-based Victoria Falls Horse Safaris – now part of Livingstone's Adventure (see page 332) – which does a two-hour

THE ETHICS OF ANIMAL ENCOUNTERS

There is a constantly expanding repertoire of **animal encounters** in the Vic Falls area, from tracking rhinos to walking with and getting up close to lions, cheetahs and elephants or cage diving with crocs. While the more intrusive encounters have been scaled back in response to negative feedback by animal welfare groups and even some tourists, some of the currently available activities, to differing degrees, raise questions about the **ethics** of these types of interactions with wildlife. The operators themselves often argue that they are supporting conservation efforts to protect the animal in question and are rescuing and rehabilitating injured animals that would otherwise have died; some point to the educational value of such interactions, though opponents would argue that since they are wild animals, they would be studied more effectively in the wild. Further justification is the provision of local employment or the fact that the animals appear healthy and happy. Some of these conservation projects are making large sums of money, in part through enthusiastic volunteers who pay to come and help. Still, questions remain about the percentage of the profits that are ploughed back into conservation and education initiatives. **Critics** of these animal encounters are also concerned about the low percentage of animals that are reintroduced back into the wild and the destiny of those that become old and surplus to requirements when they are no longer capable of entertaining the tourists; there have been claims about some animals – lions in particular – being sold off for 'canned' hunting, as well as cases of animal mistreatment.

To satisfy yourself that an activity is in the interests of the animal(s) concerned, you should consider these issues and consult the wealth of articles and personal testimonies on the internet – some a little disturbing – which include several specifically on Vic Falls.

trail from the Falls Resort or a half-day one, including a light lunch back at the stables in the national park.

Livingstone Island and Devil's Pool

Zambia-based Green Safaris (Ⓦ greensafaris.com) is the only operator for this activity, which offers you the chance to **re-create** the moment the good doctor peered over the edge and 'discovered' the falls. Next, you jump into Devil's Pool (see page 326) at the lip of the chasm – the ultimate infinity pool. This is followed by a gourmet breakfast, lunch or high-tea picnic on the island, surrounded by plummeting water and incredible rainbows; it's a treat, though not for anyone suffering from vertigo. Numbers are limited to 24 – which is still a pretty large group for such a venture – and the tour is only possible when water levels are low (generally July till the end of Feb; late Aug–Dec/Jan for the pool swim).

Quad biking and segways

On the Zambian side of the falls, the Livingstone Quad Company, as part of Livingstone's Adventures (Ⓦ livingstonesadventure.com), operates two quad-bike routes: an hour-long '**eco-trail**' that blasts through the bush, promising views across the Batoka Gorge and **wildlife** sightings, though you'd think the wildlife would scarper at the din; and a more popular two-and-a-half-hour **village tour** (minimum four people), that takes in several villages. Helmets are provided and the minimum age is 12. If your kids are too young to clamber onto a quad, you may be able to persuade them to do a more sedate one-hour **guided segway tour** (minimum age 7) of the footpaths around Zambia's *AVANI Victoria Falls Resort* area.

River cruises

A cruise is one of the finest ways to experience the serenity of the Zambezi after the buzz of the falls – while keeping the hippos at arm's length. Boats of all sizes offer you the chance to have breakfast (the best time for birdwatching), lunch or dinner while gliding smoothly along the Zambezi. The most popular is the classic **sundowner booze cruise,** when the river can be chock-a-block with boats. Costs depend on the craft type, the cruise length and the quality and quantity of food and drink offered; on the whole, passengers on the less expensive boats tend to feel they have had better value for money. Excursions tend not to include the park fees. The most **exclusive** option is the *Ra-Ikane* (Ⓦ raikane.com; twelve passengers max), which offers the full-on luxury experience: polished teak panelling, club chairs, and superior canapés and cocktails. A further plus is that you can get closer to the action than in the bigger boats, but your view is more restricted for being lower in the water. At the other end of the scale, Pure Africa's *Zambezi Explorer* (Ⓦ pure.africa/zambezi-explorer) caters to 150 people, spread over three decks; for an extra fee, you can sprawl on the sofas of the 'signature' top deck. Wild Horizons (see page 319) and Shearwater (see page 319) have their own luxury and mid-sized boats, as do several hotels and lodges. For a gourmet dinner experience on the Zambezi, Pure Africa has two vessels and Bush Cuisine has three – offering fine dining for various size groups.

On the Zambian side, the triple-decker *African Queen* – without Humphrey Bogart at the helm – and the smaller *African Princess* take you round the Kalai and Siloka islands. The sleekest boat on this stretch of the river is the *Lady Livingstone* (Ⓦ davidlivingstone.co.za), which resembles a spaceship when illuminated. Backpackers tend to opt for the colourful thatched **party boat** run by Taonga Safaris (Ⓦ taonga-safaris.com), which accommodates thirty, has an on-deck barbecue and plenty of atmosphere.

Safaris

Classic game drives in open-topped safari vehicles are available in the Zambezi National Park for around US$80, plus park fees, or in the big game-rich, private Victoria Falls Private Game Reserve with a high chance of spotting a **rhino** – and the slightly smaller Stanley and Livingstone Private Game Reserve, which also hosts the Bear Grylls Survival Academy (Ⓦ beargrylls-survivalacademy.com). The main attraction of these private reserves is the existence of rhinos, the greater

RAFTING THE WORLD'S BEST WHITEWATER

Since the mid-1980s, Vic Falls has been synonymous with **whitewater rafting**, as the churning and tumbling rapids of the Zambezi squeeze through the dramatic cliffs of the Batoka Gorge, providing some of the world's finest and scariest whitewater. Boasting the highest concentration of **Grade V rapids** in the world, the Zambezi offers a roller-coaster ride of huge waves, steep drops, holes and whirlpools, yet the absence of large rocks protruding from the river makes this safer than it might otherwise be. Welcome to Stairway to Heaven, Terminator (I and II), Oblivion and the Gnashing Jaws of Death – the rapids' names are enough to remind you that, while the rafting can be truly exhilarating, it can also be terrifying and dangerous – while thousands make the descent every season without incident, there is the occasional accident, near miss, or, very rarely, a fatality. Not that you should be put off, as the outfits that run the rafting are highly professional and take **safety** seriously: you'll get a full briefing, be armed with a state-of-the-art helmet and high-flotation life-jacket, and be accompanied by safety kayakers with radio contact, who periodically help reunite tourists who've flown overboard with their dinghy – something you're likely to experience at least once. Besides, you should grab this opportunity while the rapids are still here; contracts are soon to be awarded to construct the long-standing, controversial plan to flood much of the gorge and build a hydro-electric power facility (see Ⓦ internationalrafting.com/2021/01/stop-the-batoka-gorge-dam/)

Once you've decided to take the plunge, there are various decisions to make. One choice to be made ahead of time is when to raft; the preferred **low-water season** generally runs from August to December (see page 308). During this time, most rafting companies start at the Boiling Pot below the falls and run rapids 1 to 18 or 19 – though the dinghies are carried round Rapid 9, the Grade 6 Commercial Suicide. The Zimbabwean companies charge around US$120 for a full day, plus a US$10 park fee; a half-day of rafting is also possible with some companies for not much less. In the **high-water season** (usually Jan–June, with a closed season usually at some point in April), which is not as hair-raising, though it's exciting enough for many, rafts are usually taken down rapids 11–23 or 24, often at a slightly lower cost. The next decision is whether you want to paddle yourself or be rowed. Most choose to **paddle themselves**, under instruction from the guide; here, you're more involved in the action, but some people prefer the guide to row them down, using giant oars, leaving them to concentrate full-time on staying in the dinghy. You must also decide whether to go with a Zambian or Zimbabwean firm. The main difference is that some Zambian outfits charge more (usually around US$140 for a full day).

Four **companies** operate from the Zimbabwean side (Adventure Zone, Shearwater, Shockwave and Wild Horizons; see page 319) and two from the Zambian side (Bundu Adventures and Safari Par Excellence; see page 331), usually offering more or less the same rates as their competitors on the same side of the falls.

PUBLIC HOLIDAYS

HOLIDAYS IN ZAMBIA AND ZIMBABWE

New Year's Day 1 January
Good Friday and Easter Monday March/April
Labour Day 1 May
Africa Day 25 May
Christmas Day 25 December
Boxing Day 26 December

HOLIDAYS IN ZAMBIA

Youth Day 12 March
Heroes' Day First Monday of July
Unity Day First Tuesday after Heroes' Day
Farmers' Day First Monday in August
Independence Day 24 October

HOLIDAYS IN ZIMBABWE

Independence Day 18 April
Heroes' Day Second Monday in August
Defence Forces' Day Second Tuesday in August
Unity Day 22 December

concentration of big game, and the more interactive – and controversial (see page 302) – animal encounters, such as walking with lions or elephants. **Game drives** are much more expensive and can only be done through a tour operator. To experience the African bush's sounds and smells, you can't beat a **walking safari** with a knowledgeable – and armed – guide. Most operators and the main lodges and hotels offer a range of safaris in various locations, either in a vehicle or on foot. Discover Victoria Falls (see page 319) does a highly recommended all-day safari involving walking and driving in the Zambezi National Park. **Night game drives** are also an option. Zambian tour operators (and also Wild Horizons, from Zimbabwe) take visitors into the Mosi-oa-Tunya National Park, where there are white rhinos, which you can track as part of a walking safari. Contact Livingstone Rhino Walking Safaris (Ⓦ livingstonerhinosafaris.com) or Savannah Southern Safaris (see page 332).

Steam train & tram

Another highly indulgent evening out from the Zambian side of the falls is to dine in style on the *Royal Livingstone Express* (Ⓦ bushtracksafrica.com/signature-products), a beautifully-restored **1920s steam train**, complete with polished wooden panelling and damask tablecloths, but with modern comforts, such as a/c and a glass observation coach, and large sparkling windows to maximise viewing opportunities. The trip takes you down to the **Victoria Falls Bridge** in time for a sundowner before moving on to enjoy a five-course meal. Departures depend on demand. From the Zimbabwean side of the falls, the slightly less opulent *Bushtracks Express* does a shorter rail journey offering a similar package and a more budget-conscious excursion offering canapés and drinks rather than the complete dining experience. In addition, Bushtracks provides an even less expensive tram excursion from Vic Falls down to the bridge, including drinks and a historical tour.

Swimming under the Falls

See Boiling Pot (see page 300).

Whitewater rafting, bodyboarding and jet boating

Rafting (see page 303), by Zimbabwean and Zambian companies, is the adrenaline activity that puts Vic Falls on the map as an adventure sports destination and remains as popular as ever. **Bodyboarding** can only be done on particular rapids, so you'll raft down the others, making it a combo trip and more expensive. If you want to get the adrenaline thrills and have a chance to experience the spectacular scenery, then consider one of the multiday rafting trips, which entails sleeping out on the sandbanks under the stars. As the pace of the river slows, you'll have the close company of crocs and hippos to keep your pulse rate up. A five- or six-day trip, including **riverside camping**, costs around US$1,300. When water levels are moderately low, a couple of companies offer the chance to whizz down the rapids on a jet boat.

Health and safety

Malaria is the main health risk in Vic Falls, alongside dehydration and sunburn, especially if you're spending a lot of time on the river, where the sun will be reflected off the water. For further information, see the main 'Basics' section of the guide (see page 62).

The centres of Victoria Falls Town and Livingstone are pretty **safe** places to walk around during the daytime. However, as elsewhere in the world, you should avoid wandering into backstreets and poor neighbourhoods at night. **Moneychangers** are also best avoided if possible; with so many currencies floating about, tourists are easy prey for simple deceptions. Go to a bank, exchange bureau or an ATM, though the banks and ATMs have lacked cash for several years in Zimbabwe. **Hawkers** and some stallholders are the main two-legged nuisance in Vic Falls Town during the day – especially when there are few tourists around – as they can be aggressive, partly due to the desperate financial circumstances many of them face. Local businesses now fund the **tourist police**, usually fairly conspicuous in their lime-green bibs, who are there to help visitors and protect them from harassment. In Livingstone, hawkers are less widespread and less insistent, but you should not walk or cycle any of the 10km (6.2 miles) to the falls on your own, as the occasional **mugging** has occurred. On the Zimbabwe side, it's inadvisable to go to or from the town and the falls or the border on foot at night for the same reason. An unwelcome **wildlife** encounter, however, is possibly a greater danger – especially with elephants – at dawn, dusk and night. The shortcut down from Vic Falls Town to the bridge is a prime site for encountering elephants, as is Zambezi Drive. If staying at any of the lodges along the Zambezi, be it in Zambia or Zimbabwe, you should think twice about striding off along the riverbank in case you run into a grazing hippo – quite likely at dawn or dusk – or trip over a lounging croc.

Introduction

Along with Mount Everest and the Grand Canyon, Victoria Falls – or Mosi-oa-Tunya ('the smoke that thunders') – ranks as one of the world's seven natural wonders. No matter how many pictures you've seen beforehand, nothing can prepare you for the awe-inspiring sight and deafening sound of the falls. The world's largest curtain of water crashes down a vast precipice, producing clouds of spray visible from afar, before squeezing into a zigzag of sheer-sided gorges as a torrent of turbulent rapids, carving its way to the Indian Ocean, well over a 1,000km (621.4 miles) away. Straddling the Zambezi between Zimbabwe and Zambia, the falls are only a few hours' drive from Katima Mulilo, at the northeastern tip of Namibia. Boasting regular bus and air connections with Windhoek and Johannesburg, they provide a fitting finale to a holiday in Southern Africa.

Their dramatic setting on the **Zambezi River** has also made Victoria Falls the undisputed **adventure capital of Africa**. There's an array of adrenaline-fuelled activities, from whitewater rafting and bungee jumping to zip-lining and bodyboarding or simply the chance to pick your way along the edge of the precipice to bathe and peer over into the abyss. Less touted are the **stunning wildlife viewing** opportunities Victoria Falls affords: the **national parks** that line the serene banks of the Upper Zambezi are home to large mammals, such as elephants, lions, buffalo, giraffes and leopards, as well as a variety of antelope and over 410 bird species. This abundance of wildlife can be observed on foot, from a safari vehicle or canoe, or while on a sunset cruise. Unsurprisingly, given its diversity of attractions, this iconic destination draws visitors from all over the world – partying backpackers, sedate sightseers, thrill-seekers or nature lovers can all find lodgings that suit their lifestyle and budget in or around the small town of Victoria Falls in Zimbabwe, or its Zambian counterpart, Livingstone.

When to go

Vic Falls is a **year-round destination**, but inevitably, some months are better than others depending on what you want to do, how much you want to spend, and how hot you

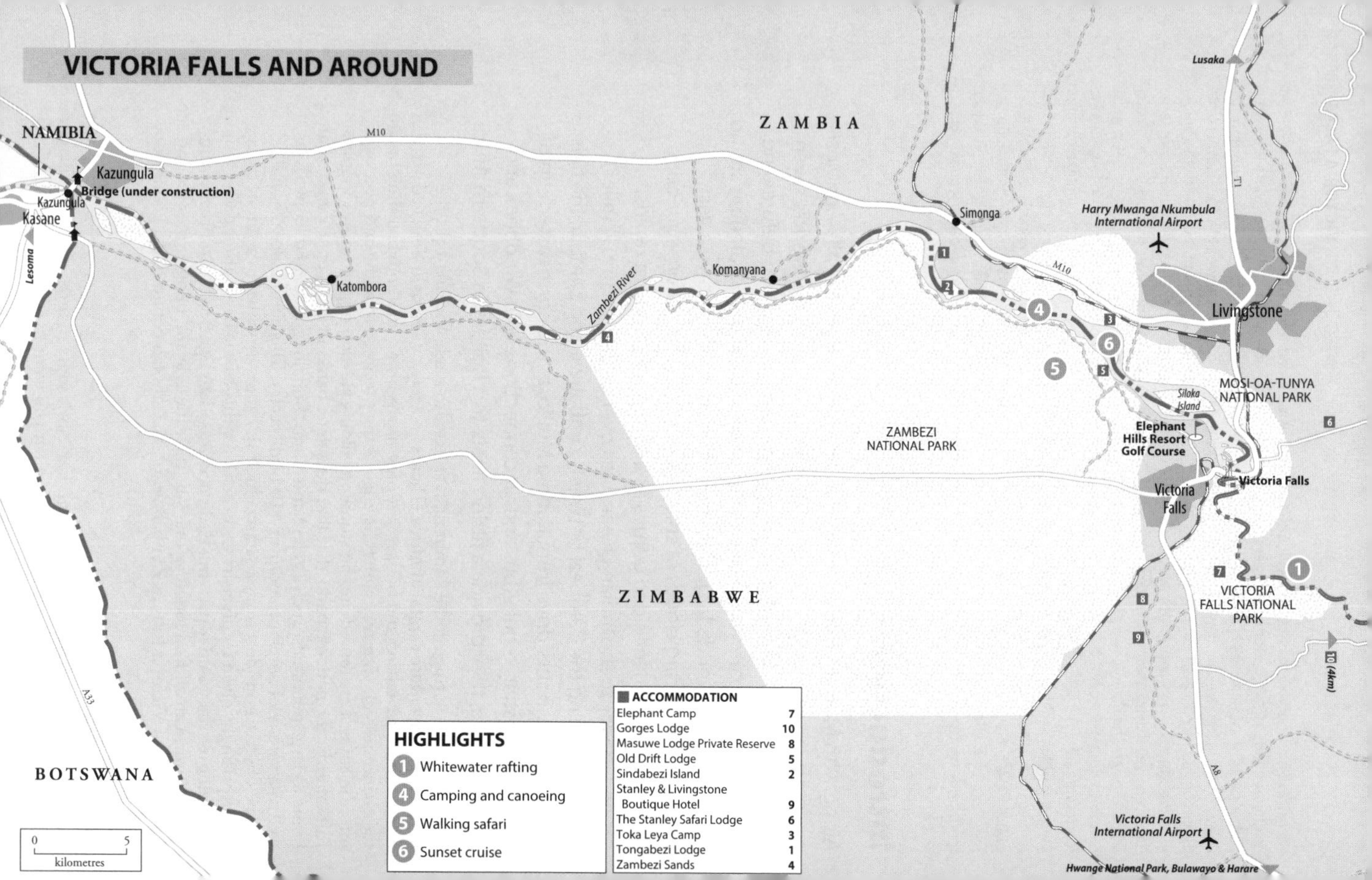
VICTORIA FALLS AND AROUND
ZAMBIA
NAMIBIA
ZIMBABWE
BOTSWANA
M10
T1
A33
A8
Lusaka
Kazungula
Bridge (under construction)
Kazungula
Kasane
Lesoma
Katombora
Zambezi River
Komanyana
Simonga
Harry Mwanga Nkumbula International Airport
Livingstone
MOSI-OA-TUNYA NATIONAL PARK
Siloka Island
Elephant Hills Resort Golf Course
Victoria Falls
Victoria Falls
ZAMBEZI NATIONAL PARK
VICTORIA FALLS NATIONAL PARK
10 (4km)
Victoria Falls International Airport
Hwange National Park, Bulawayo & Harare
0
5
kilometres
HIGHLIGHTS
1 Whitewater rafting
4 Camping and canoeing
5 Walking safari
6 Sunset cruise
ACCOMMODATION
Elephant Camp 7
Gorges Lodge 10
Masuwe Lodge Private Reserve 8
Old Drift Lodge 5
Sindabezi Island 2
Stanley & Livingstone Boutique Hotel 9
The Stanley Safari Lodge 6
Toka Leya Camp 3
Tongabezi Lodge 1
Zambezi Sands 4

are prepared to be. Taking **cost** first, most hotels and lodgings maintain the same prices for the whole year (see page 298). On the other hand, air tickets and hotel rooms are harder to come by and can be more expensive over Christmas and New Year, Easter, and the main summer holiday period for Europeans and North Americans (July–Aug).

The region's **winter** occurs between May and October, in the generally slightly cooler dry season; **summer** runs from November to April, which coincides with the rainy season. At the height of winter (May–Aug), daytime temperatures are also more pleasant, remaining in the mid- to late twenties, though you'll need to bring something warm for the cold nights. As the land continues to heat up after the rains stop, the temperatures rise, sometimes exceeding 35°C in October and November, until the arrival of the rains helps cool the place, albeit only very slightly; with the advent of rain, though, humidity levels rise and tropical thunderstorms are common.

The Zambezi's **water levels**, which vary throughout the year, are crucial to your experience of **viewing the falls** (see page 308) and other activities such as **whitewater rafting**. Low water levels (generally Aug–Dec) see the rapids at their most hair-raising, whereas when the river is swollen (usually Feb–May or June), some of the rapids get washed out in the surge of water or are too dangerous to raft down. The summer rains in Vic Falls (Dec–April, usually peaking Dec–Feb) may be insignificant to water levels in the Zambezi. Still, they affect the vegetation and conditions for **wildlife viewing**. The latter is much easier towards the back end of the drier winter months (July/Aug–Nov) when animals are forced to migrate to the river or congregate at well-established water holes to drink.

FACT FILE

- Victoria Falls is the **world's largest** curtain of falling water: at 1.7km (1 mile), it is one and a half times wider than Niagara and at 108m (354.3ft) is twice as high.
- When a 22-year-old Australian made the **111m (364.2ft) bungee jump** from Victoria Falls Bridge in 2012, the rope broke, plunging her into the rapids. With feet still bound, she managed to swim ashore, escaping with only bruises and cuts.
- In 1905, to celebrate fifty years of Livingstone's 'discovery' of the Falls, a **rowing regatta** was held on the Upper Zambezi, acclaimed, incredibly, by the *Evening News* as 'our new Henley [on Thames], the finest rowing water in the world'.
- **Travel and tourism** in Zimbabwe directly support around forty thousand jobs and contribute to about 10 percent of Zimbabwe's GDP, much of which is due to Vic Falls; for Zambia, the figures are 110,000 and just over 7 percent, respectively.

8

Brief history

Archaeological evidence indicates that people have lived close to the Zambezi for at least three million years, with particularly high concentrations of human artefacts discovered from the Middle and Late **Stone Ages** in and around the falls, especially where Livingstone is now located. Arguably, the first people to settle permanently in the area, around the seventeenth century, were the **Leya** (or Baleya, or Toka-Leya), as they call themselves now – though at the time when ethnic identities were more fluid, some people also identified themselves as Toka (Batoka) or Tonga (Batonga). Two of the more prominent Leya chiefs presiding over these small, decentralised communities, which made a living from subsistence agriculture, cattle herding and fishing, were Mukuni and Sekute (see page 325). They originally lived on Siloka Island (sometimes called Lwanda or Long Island) and Kalai Island, respectively. Though initially at war with each other, they eventually found peace through marriage but were squeezed between the more powerful **warrior kingdoms** of the Lozi (Silozi) – to whom they paid tribute – and Kololo (Makololo) north of the Zambezi and the Ndebele (or Matabele) to the south. With their detailed knowledge of the river, the Leya found themselves indispensable to these more powerful neighbours, helping them to cross the dangerous waterway to carry out raids on each other. However, Leya's assistance in such matters sometimes resulted in reprisals. Considered inferior to these peoples, the Leya were inevitably left out of the wars, negotiations, treaty-making and trickery that the **British** engaged in with the Lozi and Ndebele elites as they pushed for imperial dominance in the region during the latter part of the nineteenth century.

The colonial period

Britain's imperial and colonial ambitions in southern Africa were facilitated by the arrival of the railway from Bulawayo and the construction of the Victoria Falls Bridge in 1905, masterminded by arch-imperialist **Cecil Rhodes**, head of the British South Africa Company. While the railway was instrumental in kick-starting foreign tourism in the region, its main aims were to serve the development of settler communities and facilitate mineral extraction.

By the early nineteenth century, Britain had consolidated its grip on the land by forming the Protectorate of Northwest Rhodesia in 1891, north of the river, before amalgamating it with Northeast Rhodesia in 1911 to establish **Northern Rhodesia** (modern-day Zambia); at the same time present-day Zimbabwe became **Southern Rhodesia** in 1923, and the Zambezi was declared as the boundary between the two. The Leya and other riverine populations around the falls became split between the two areas. Though the Lozi royalty maintained some status in and around Livingstone, and Lozi were generally favoured for jobs in the colonial administration, the Black populations became increasingly physically, economically and politically marginalised. They faced onerous taxes, restricted access to the river – as game reserves and parks were formed to create a white playground – and eventually **forced evictions** from their lands as they were moved into reserves.

Though both protectorates developed different trajectories in the years between annexation by the British and independence, the common thread was one of **white privilege** in every sphere – land tenure, political rights and economic advantage – sustained through force if necessary, punctuated by periodic civil unrest, labour strikes and political protests by some of the Black African majority.

Struggle for independence

In Northern Rhodesia, the colonial government more readily recognised the 'winds of change' in Africa. Despite the usual period of jailing, persecuting and intimidating opposition leaders, the transition to **independence** was relatively smooth – the

VIEWING THE FALLS

Your experience of **viewing the falls** depends very much on the amount of water tumbling over the precipice: you could gaze at a lengthy, bare rock face with scarcely a trickle of water; alternatively, you may be drenched in thick spray, unable to see a thing. All this depends not on the rain in Vic Falls but rather on the arrival of the water that has fallen as rain in the Zambezi headwaters in the hills of Zambia and Angola. This usually peaks in late March to early May. When in **full flow**, the 'thunder' is deafening, aerial views of the spray are at their most dramatic, and rainbows abound. On the other hand, you will be constantly soaked with spray, visibility will be severely reduced, and photography – unless you have a fully waterproof camera – will be impossible. Conversely, from the end of October to December, as the **river level drops**, many of the falls dry up, exposing vast sheets of bare basalt; at this time of year, you get a much better view of the reddish cliffs, and a greater appreciation of the depth of the gorge, and the falls' geological formation. Thus, arguably, the **prime viewing times** are January, February, and July to September, when there is usually sufficient water for the falls to impress, but not so much that the thick cloak of spray obscures the falls themselves.

Republic of Zambia was established in 1964 – compared to the years of bloodshed that occurred across the Zambezi in Southern Rhodesia. Here, inspired by Zambia's independence, two rival factions – the military wing of the Shona-dominated Zimbabwe African National Union (ZANU), led by **Robert Mugabe**, and the Ndebele-dominated Zimbabwe African People's Union (ZAPU), led by **Joshua Nkomo** – took on the Rhodesian white-minority government, which was led by **Ian Smith** and backed by the apartheid South African government. The ensuing Liberation War (often referred to as the **Second Chimurenga**) lasted on and off for fourteen years. It was a brutal civil conflict involving periods of martial law, international sanctions, dirty tricks campaigns and covert assassinations. It resulted in the loss of around thirty thousand lives before independence was finally achieved in **1980** and Robert Mugabe was elected prime minister.

Post-independence

From the late 1960s and throughout the 1970s, **tourism** in the Vic Falls area suffered on both sides of the Zambezi on account of the conflict in Southern Rhodesia and the growing unrest in South Africa since most tourists were from those two countries. Once Zimbabwe gained independence and the political situation had stabilised somewhat, visitors began to flock back to Vic Falls and new hotels were built. However, tourism on the Zambian side remained neglected since the government was more concerned with exploiting the country's **mineral wealth** – copper in particular – than promoting tourism. By the mid-1990s, Vic Falls Town was packed to capacity while the Zambian side of the falls remained in the doldrums. Once copper prices had plummeted, however, the Zambian government began to promote tourism in the country – highlighting **Livingstone** in particular – as a means of diversifying the economy. Livingstone's emergence as a tourist destination was aided by the political and economic crisis unfolding across the border. Though the Zimbabwean economy was already struggling, it was dealt a further blow by the violence that erupted in 2000 due to the mismanaged fast-track **land reform programme**, which stipulated that white-owned farms should immediately be handed over to Black citizens. Land grabs by war veterans (both genuine and bogus) resulted in further political violence, ultimately spiralling into financial chaos and soaring unemployment, sending an already ailing economy into free fall, and pitching many Zimbabweans into yet greater poverty. Visitors and even some businesses fled across the border to Livingstone, whose fortunes were further boosted by two huge hotel investments. In 2017, having been president for thirty years, Mugabe was ousted in a coup by his party and former vice-president Emmerson Mnangagwa took over. Mugabe died two years later at the age of 95. Despite all these setbacks, and following the hosting of the **UN World Tourism Organization** general assembly in Vic Falls in 2013, Mosi-oa-Tunya is very much back on the global tourism map and flourishing on both sides of the Zambezi.

Zimbabwe

Victoria Falls National Park

Entrance on Livingstone Way, just before the bridge • Daily sunrise–sunset, 7–10pm • Charge • ☎ 013 42294 • A 10–15min downhill walk from Vic Falls Town or a short taxi ride

People from all over the world flock to this corner of Zimbabwe for the magnificent **Victoria Falls**; although also shared with Zambia, 80 percent of the river cascades into the gorge on the Zimbabwean side. In full flow, more than 500 million litres of water tumble over this 1.7km (1-mile) wide precipice every minute, providing a full-frontal assault on the senses. But the sight is breathtaking whether you witness this phenomenal spectacle at its peak or are confronted – when water levels are at their lowest – by a bare, 100m (328ft) high sheet of rock, laced only with a few dramatic cascades. If you want to **avoid the crowds** and the heat of the day, then arrive when the gates open at 6 or 6.30am; this is also the best time to stand a chance of glimpsing some of the park's shy **wildlife**. Rainbows can be seen at any time of the day when there's enough spray, though lunar rainbows are a different matter. It'll take a good

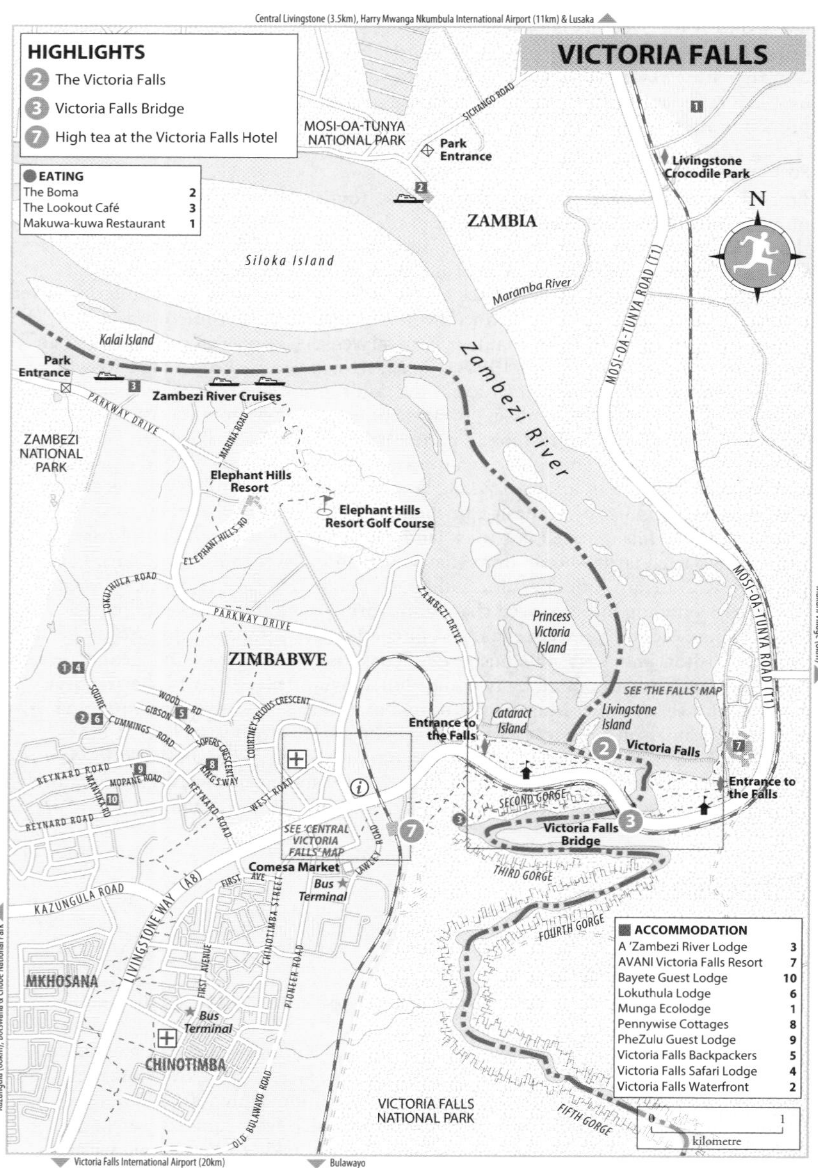

8

LUNAR RAINBOWS

The falls are famous for their rainbows – some are even double or full-circle – which are at their most magnificent when water levels are high and more spray is produced. If your visit coincides with a full moon on a clear night, you might even be treated to a **lunar rainbow**. Also known as a moonbow or white rainbow, the colours appear faded to the naked eye, though they will show up on a photo if taken with a long exposure. Provided the weather is favourable, the park stays open after sunset the night of the full moon (plus a night on either side). Bring a torch along, take the usual precautions regarding getting wet, and **organise transport** to and from the falls, which can be easily done via your accommodation. Do not try to walk there or back at that hour since it is unsafe. Lunar tours are now big business, costing US$100 on the Zim side and US$30 in Zambia, with obligatory guided tours.

couple of hours to meander around the various viewpoints. Be prepared for the **spray** to drench you – and anything you may be carrying – when water levels are high; ponchos can be rented at the entrance, but since they are not made of breathable material, you're likely to get just as wet from sweat on the inside.

Brief history

An aerial view of the present-day falls reveals that their current location is possibly their **eighth incarnation**, 8km (5 miles) upstream from where they were first located, as years of erosion by the mighty Zambezi have forced them to retreat.

The geological process that led to the falls' formation in the first place began in the **Jurassic period**, over 150 million years ago, following the breakup of the supercontinent Gondwanaland. In this tectonic upheaval, cracks in the Earth's crust allowed molten lava – basalt – to spew onto the surface, filling in these cracks and leaving a thin layer on top. As the hard basalt cooled, it contracted, revealing further fissures, which were filled and overlaid with softer sedimentary deposits over time.

When the Zambezi River, which millions of years ago followed a different course, was eventually forced to settle on its current route, the **erosion process** at the falls that is visible today started in earnest, probably several hundred thousand years ago. Over time, the falls have shifted as the Zambezi's force has carved its way through the softer rock in the wide cracks in the basalt – predominantly east-west and west-east, with some narrower ones running north-south. Today, the beginnings of new falls are already evident at the far western end, as a ravine is being worn at the lower-lying Devil's Cataract.

The falls

Although plenty of operators offer guided tours of the falls, they are easy to get to and visit **on your own**. Armed with the annotated map given on entry, you are perfectly equipped to start your circuit of the sixteen viewpoints, where you are protected from the cliff edge by the flimsiest of wooden fences, if at all.

At the entrance, head left, past the **statue of David Livingstone** (see page 326) – in explorer, rather than missionary, attire – over to the **Devil's Cataract**, which funnels the greatest volume of water in a year-round raging torrent. Make sure you descend the 56 steps, known as the chain walk, to get an even closer, eye-level view. Moving east, viewpoints 3–6 give you further perspectives on the Devil's Cataract before you reach **Main Falls**, an 800m (2,624.7ft) wide curtain of water that roars in full flow, throwing up vast plumes of spray that drench the visitor and nourishing the surrounding '**rainforest**'. Though not rainforest in the true sense, the microclimate produced by constant spray and sunshine nourishes some impressive ebony, fig and mahogany trees and a tangle of vines.

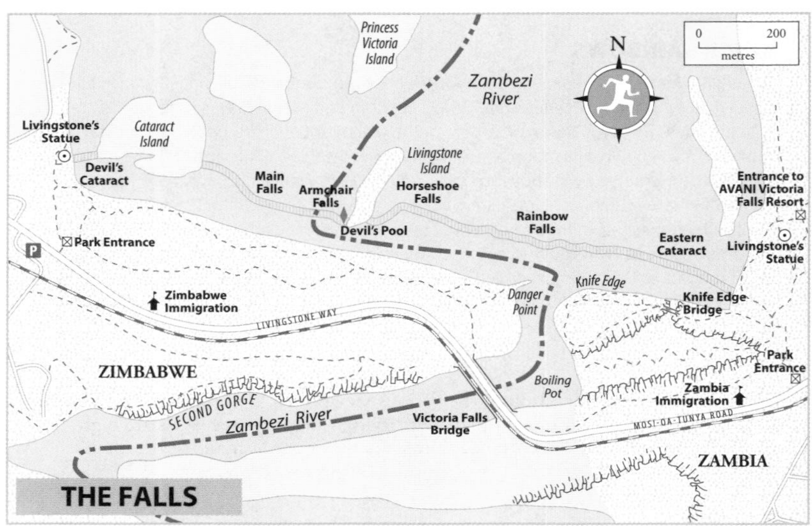

8

A couple of hundred metres further along the path, the vegetation falls away as you look across to **Livingstone Island** (viewpoints 9–10), where the explorer peered over the edge into the void 'to find out where the vast body of water went; it seemed to lose itself in the Earth'. These days, in the dry season, look out for tourists doing much the same thing while bobbing in the **Devil's Pool** (see page 326) to the west of the island. To the east of Livingstone Island, **Horseshoe Falls**, so named because of their shape, and **Rainbow Falls**, the highest at 108m (354.3ft), cascade into the ravine. Further east along the path, the bare unprotected ledge of rock that forms the aptly named **Danger Point** looks across to the Zambian side of the falls, taking in the **Eastern Cataract** and the rocky **Knife Edge** promontory. If you have the stomach for it, you can peer into the **Boiling Pot** below, where the churning water heads down into the second gorge and under the **Victoria Falls Bridge**. Watch the bungee jumpers plummet off the bridge before returning to the exit, where there is a good café and craft shop.

Zambezi National Park

Main entrance on Parkway Drive, 7km (4.3 miles) northwest of the town centre • Daily 6am–6pm • Charge

A small but scenic reserve, the **Zambezi National Park** may not compete with Chobe or Hwange (see page 320) for either quantity or variety of large mammals. Still, it is, nevertheless, a beguiling setting. The landscape, comprising a 40km (24.9-mile) stretch of the majestic Upper Zambezi, is lined with patches of riverine forest, becoming mopane woodland, scrub and open **savannah** further inland. There's enough wildlife in the park to keep you interested, too – provided you're not obsessed with seeing large herds of big game. Moreover, with the main entrance only a few kilometres outside Vic Falls Town, it makes an easy half or full-day outing.

The park is recovering from years of **neglect**, and the underfunded park authorities, aided by local conservation groups, are struggling to deal with the increasing threat from poachers – yet wildlife numbers are improving. Substantial herds of **elephants** can be seen drinking and bathing in the river, especially in the dry season; other large mammals you might see include giraffes, zebra, buffalo and wildebeest; antelope are pretty common – sable, impala, eland, kudu, waterbuck and bushbuck are all present. So too are lions, leopards and even wild dogs, though in small numbers and they

THE VICTORIA FALLS BRIDGE

Variously condemned as an act of 'engineering vandalism', a 'hideous monument to Victorian vanity', and a stain on the landscape's natural beauty, the **Victoria Falls Bridge** has become almost as big a tourist attraction as the falls themselves. Moreover, its construction was instrumental in bringing foreign visitors to Vic Falls in the early twentieth century, paving the way for the place to become the major international tourist destination it is today. The project was driven by **Cecil Rhodes** (see page 308), who wanted a bridge across the Zambezi to fulfil his expansionist dream of a Cape-to-Cairo railway. Various locations for its construction were considered, yet Rhodes – who died before ever seeing Mosi-oa-Tunya and before work on the bridge had even started – was adamant that it should span the gorge below the falls, '**where the trains, as they pass, will catch the spray**'. Designed by consultant engineer George Hobson, the structure's various components were built and assembled in sections in northern England for £72,000. After being shipped over 13,000km (8077.8 miles) to Mozambique, they were brought by rail to Vic Falls, where they were reassembled on site in a matter of weeks by a team of engineers and several hundred African labourers, most of whom were paid little more than US$1 per month. The **official opening** occurred on 12 **September 1905** amid much imperial pomp and fanfare. Remarkably, the project had taken less than a year and a half to complete, resulting in the world's highest bridge at the time, its signature parabolic arch – the world's widest then at 157m (515ft) – suspended 128m (420ft) above the Zambezi.

are seldom spotted. Pods of snorting **hippos** and watchful **crocs**, however, are almost guaranteed sightings in the river.

The reserve certainly offers excellent **birdwatching** – over 410 species have been recorded in the area – especially in the early morning as the mist lifts from the reed beds and sandbanks. Keep a lookout for African skimmers on the river's surface, the shy African finfoot hiding under overhanging vegetation, or the western banded snake eagle on the lookout for prey.

Tour **operators** lead walking or driving **safaris** into the park (see page 318). Still, two of the nicest ways to explore the area are to glide down the Zambezi in a **canoe** (see page 300) or to saddle up on a **horseback** safari (see page 301). If you decide to **drive** yourself (see page 296), note that four-wheel drive is necessary; after very heavy rains, the park roads may be closed altogether.

PRACTICALITIES — ZAMBEZI NATIONAL PARK

The reserve is bisected by the main road to the border with Botswana, dividing the park into **two distinct areas**. The more visited area north of the road is accessed via the **main park entrance** on Parkway Drive, 5km (3.1 miles) from Vic Falls Town. From here, the Zambezi River Game Drive leads you towards the river before following it upstream, with the occasional loop road off it. Dotted with riverside picnic sites, it's a popular weekend retreat for local families, but you can have the place to yourself midweek. The **southern section** is accessed along the 25km (15.5-mile) Chamabondo Game Drive, whose entrance is off the Bulawayo road. Initially taking you through the teak forest, the road then leads onto open grasslands punctuated by the occasional waterhole.

Victoria Falls Town

Given that Vic Falls is one of Africa's top tourist destinations, **VICTORIA FALLS TOWN** is surprisingly low-key in many respects. That's not to say it lacks the touristy hustle and bustle – and it's certainly not short of hawkers – but the legacy of what was essentially an apartheid development policy in Zimbabwe means that most of the town's Black population carries on their day-to-day lives in outlying 'suburbs'. In **high season**, however, there's an unmistakable buzz about the place – and plenty of toing and froing – as tourists hike to and from the falls or the bridge, nervous about their impending bungee jump, exhilarated and soaked by the spray from the falls, or flying high after a day's rafting. The town centre, moreover, comes alive in the early evening as folk compare tales about the day's events – but just as quickly, it quietens down: bars and restaurants close relatively early, with people returning to their lodgings to carry on partying there or to have an early night in preparation for the next day's early-morning activities. The exception to all this is three days of hedonistic excess at the end of April that is the **Victoria Falls Carnival** (vicfallscarnival.com), which draws a big crowd, and centres on a music festival that attracts big-name DJs and music artists from around Southern Africa; at the same time, major discounts are offered on the usual adventure activities.

The **town centre** is little more than a glorified T-junction, where Parkway Drive – the road that leads to the Zambezi National Park and many of the nicer lodges out of town – meets the main highway from Bulawayo, which becomes Livingstone Way as it enters the urban area. At the junction, there's an assortment of quaint, old-fashioned **shopping arcades** fronted by painted signs and stuffed with tour operators, curio (craft) shops and the occasional café or restaurant. Most major **services** are also located in this area. If you head steeply downhill from the junction, across the old railway line, and 1km (0.62 miles) further, you'll reach the entrance to the **falls**, where the deafening roar beyond the gate will set your pulse racing in anticipation. Beyond lies the Zimbabwe **border post** just before the Victoria Falls Bridge.

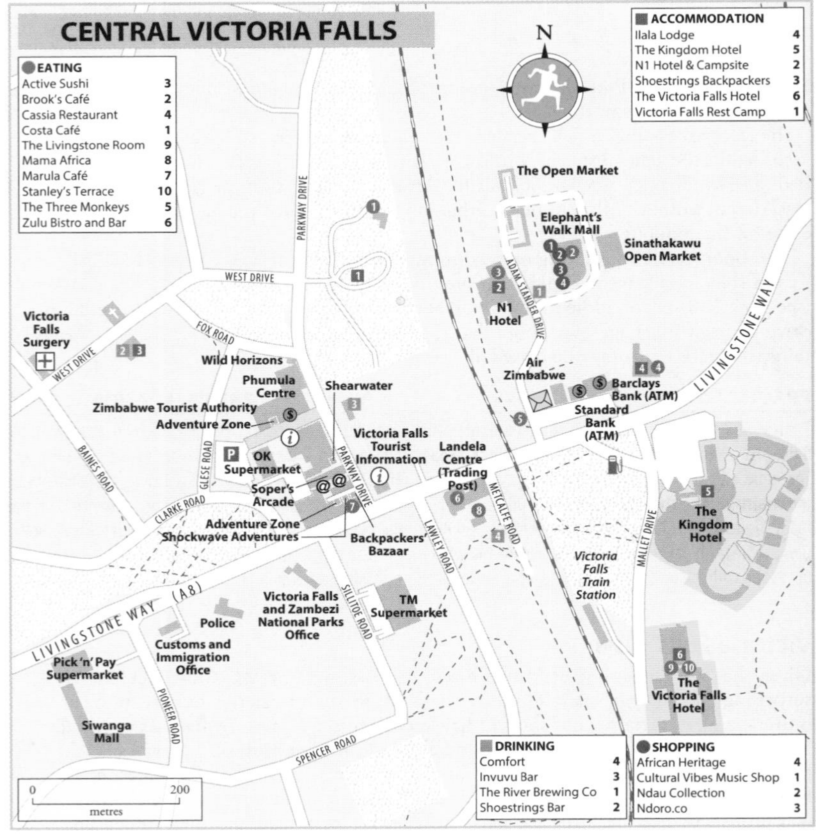

ZAMBEZI NATIONAL PARK CAMPSITES

If total immersion in nature is what you want, it's worth spending a night or two within **Zambezi National Park**. The self-catering accommodation has become so dilapidated that the chalets have now been leased to and renovated by Zambezi Crescent (zambezicrescent.com). However, the campsites remain in park hands, dotted along the banks of the great river in picturesque spots; the various accommodation options are surrounded by bush brimming with birdlife and home to plenty of other animals. The four unfenced bush **campsites** and three **fishing camps** – which have shelters but are rather run-down – lie some distance away (up to 46km/28.6 miles) from the main entrance and are even more rudimentary, possessing little more than a braai stand (barbecue) and a long-drop toilet (no water). Whichever you choose, you're guaranteed an incredible wilderness experience. Note that you may have camp visitors – including hippos, buffalo and elephants – especially during the dry season.

PRACTICALITIES

The main disadvantage of camping in the park is the hassle of booking the accommodation. The online system that the national parks office (zimparks.org) has been promising for some time is yet to function, and emails (bookings@zimparks.co.zw) often go unanswered. You can try phoning central reservations in Harare (04 706077). The Victoria Falls and Zambezi National Parks office on Victoria Falls Road (Mon–Fri 7.45am–1pm, 2–4.45pm, 013 42294 or 013 44566) will accept bookings on the day only, or just turn up at the park entrance (013 42294) where, if there is availability, you can pay on the spot. Campsites cost $100 per site (up to three people).

8

Behind the central shopping area, west of Livingstone Way sprawls a leafy, **middle-class neighbourhood**, home to Vic Falls' white and wealthier Black residents, where the backpackers' accommodation, B&Bs and smaller, less expensive lodges are located. On the other side of Livingstone Way, and further out, south of the road to Kazungula, lie the high-density poorer **townships** of Chinotimba and Mkhosana, home to most of Vic Falls' sixty thousand Black population.

Between these various locations and at the fringes of the developments, the **bush** encroaches on the town; so too do its inhabitants, as monkeys are often seen scampering across the road, while baboons lope nonchalantly and elephants frequently roam about at night. You are pretty likely to encounter some such wildlife, and more besides, if you take an early-morning wander around the 4km (2.5-mile) **Zambezi Drive loop** (see page 316), one of the few free attractions of Vic Falls Town.

Brief history

There were permanent settlements in the Victoria Falls area from around the **seventh century** – and humans have inhabited the place for a great deal longer – but Vic Falls as a **resort town** only came about after the building of the bridge and the arrival of the railway from Cape Town in 1905 (see page 313). Even then, it lagged behind development across the Zambezi in Livingstone. The first shop – Clark's Curios – was opened in 1903 by one of the early north-bank settlers, **Percy Clark**. An enterprising man, he soon expanded his business to include photography, tours of the falls, and even excursions upriver in Canadian canoes. By 1911, he had introduced the first

VICTORIA FALLS: A FLUID NAME

Note that Victoria Falls, or '**Vic Falls**', to use the standard abbreviation, can refer to the actual falls, the nearby Zimbabwean resort town, and the whole area surrounding the falls, which takes in the Zambian town of Livingstone too.

motorised launch on the Upper Zambezi, taking the genteel guests from *The Victoria Falls Hotel* (see page 320) – which had opened in 1904 – to sip their G&Ts on the deck while watching the sunset. As the falls' fame spread, tourist numbers increased in the 1920s and 1930s with the completion of a new **tarred road** from Bulawayo and interest from cruise-ship visitors to Cape Town. However, it wasn't until the era of relatively cheap air travel and the opening of the **airport** in 1967 that mass tourism began to take off.

Vic Falls remained relatively unaffected in the early stages of the Liberation War of the late 1960s and early 1970s. Still, by the middle of the decade, tourism had more or less come to a standstill until **Zimbabwean independence** in 1980 brought stability to the country.

Tourists soon flocked back to Vic Falls and numbers were increasing until the political and economic troubles from around 2000. Add to that the negative press **President Mugabe** and Zimbabwe were getting, and tourism collapsed once more. Vic Falls was the last place to feel the effects and was the first to get back on its feet, though it suffered further knocks during the COVID-19 pandemic; it is beginning to recover again, though Zimbabwe's economy, more generally, is still tottering.

Jafuta Heritage Centre

Elephant's Walk Mall • Daily 9am–5pm • Free

Tucked away among the shops of the Elephant's Walk Mall is one of the town's few real 'sights': the **Jafuta Heritage Centre**, a gem of a small private collection of cultural artefacts – tools, weapons, musical instruments, adornments and pieces of art from the Shona, Ndebele, Lozi and Tonga peoples, all beautifully displayed and accompanied by informative text. The museum's curator, Ephraim, often on hand to share his knowledge, is also a practising traditional healer.

ARRIVAL AND DEPARTURE — VICTORIA FALLS TOWN

BY PLANE

VICTORIA FALLS AIRPORT

International flights arrive at the recently expanded and upgraded Victoria Falls International Airport (VFA), 23km (14.3 miles) south of town. Facilities in the international terminal include an ATM but no money exchange, an Econet desk, where you can purchase a SIM card and airtime, and desks for several car rental firms (see page 318).

Getting into town There is no bus service from the airport into Vic Falls. Most lodgings, however, provide a shuttle, usually at extra cost and for much the same rate charged by various tour companies. Wild Horizons (wildhorizons.co.za) also runs a shuttle service (US$16). Otherwise, a private taxi costs around US$30, though they may do a cheaper deal if you agree to return to the airport with the same driver.

Flights and airlines There are no direct flights from Europe, North America or Australasia to Victoria Falls. Most international visitors fly in via Oliver Tambo International Airport, Johannesburg, from where there are daily connections to Vic Falls with Airlink (flyairlink.com) – often code-sharing with bigger airlines – and South African

THE ZAMBEZI DRIVE LOOP

A pleasant itinerary for a morning stroll is the 4km (2.5-mile) **Zambezi Drive loop**, which runs parallel to the Zambezi for a couple of kilometres before doubling back to join Parkway Drive and ultimately returning to town again. Along the way, you'll get glimpses of the quickening river as it slides unknowingly towards the falls, while the walk also makes for good **birdwatching**. At around the halfway point, you'll come across the '**Big Tree**', a giant baobab with a sizeable girth (though by no means the largest around) whose main claim to fame is that it once served as the meeting point and shelter for early travellers planning to cross the Zambezi to 'Old Drift', the area's original European settlement over the river in present-day Zambia. If you are doing the loop in the drier months (especially in the early morning or dusk), beware of **elephants** and **buffalo** going down to the water.

Airways (flysaa.com). Air Namibia (airnamibia.com.na) flies directly to Vic Falls from Windhoek, Namibia, six days a week. Return flights from Johannesburg to Vic Falls cost around R5,800, but better deals may be had by flying into Livingstone, over the border in Zambia (see page 330) – so check before booking. You must budget for a shuttle transfer and an extra visa if you are not applying for a Kazavisa (see page 296).

BY BUS AND MINIBUS

Extra City bus company operates buses four times a day between Harare and Vic Falls via Bulawayo (leaving Vic Falls at 5 & 7.30am, 9 & 11pm; 5hr 30min to Bulawayo; extracity.co.zw), where you can connect with transport from one of the two South African companies that offer long-distance bus services between Pretoria and Johannesburg and Bulawayo: Greyhound (greyhound.co.za) and Intercity (intercityxpress.co.za). Greyhound offers a slightly quicker, more expensive service (about 14hr). Extra City buses leave from Chinotimba bus station, east of Livingstone Way, as you enter town along the main road from Bulawayo and the airport. Minibuses bound for Bulawayo and Harare also leave from here throughout the day when full – or overfull – with music blaring. The minibuses are faster and cheaper, but the driving is prone to being more reckless and more uncomfortable.

BY SHUTTLE

A seat on a shuttle between Vic Falls and Kasane – airport or town – or Livingstone airport or town can be booked through the leading operators.

BY SHARED TAXI

Although there's no official transport between Vic Falls and Kasane, Botswana, shared taxis leave when full from the turn-off to Kazungula, a few kilometres outside town.

BY TRAIN

A daily overnight service runs between Bulawayo and Vic Falls. Cabins are available for three or six people in the second or two or four in the first class. Trains are in desperate need of refurbishment – including some beautiful 1950s wood-panelled carriages – so it's worth paying the extra for a first-class ticket to ensure a modicum of comfort – but don't raise your expectations too high; bedding, for example, is no longer provided. Trains depart from Bulawayo at 7.30pm, arriving around 9am in Vic Falls. From Vic Falls, trains leave at 7pm, arriving in Bulawayo at 9am. Both trains have a dining car, but the food can be limited, so it's advisable to take supplies too. Note, however, that safety may be a concern, as robberies have periodically been reported, so enquire about the current security situation before jumping aboard.

Tickets Tickets can be purchased at the Vic Falls station ticket office only on the day of travel (013 443902; Mon–Fri 7–10am & 2.30–6.45pm; Sat & Sun 9–10am & 4.30–6.45pm; or at Bulawayo train station (09 362284; Mon–Fri 8am–7.30pm, Sat & Sun 4–7.30pm).

BY CAR

You must present the vehicle's papers at all these borders and be liable for cross-border vehicle charges.

Within Zimbabwe Vic Falls is accessed via a fast, tarred road from Bulawayo, which lies 440km (273.4 miles) southeast (around a 5-hour drive).

From/to Zambia The town is also easily accessible by good roads from Zambia via Livingstone, 10km (6.2 miles) across the border on the Victoria Falls Bridge (daily 6am–10pm; see page 313). Note that the Victoria Falls Bridge now charges toll fees that go towards maintenance costs.

From/to Botswana The Kazungula road border with Botswana (daily 6am–6pm) lies only 70km (43.5 miles) west of Vic Falls on a good tarred road, with good road connections on the Botswana side of the border.

From/to Namibia The two access routes from Namibia both entail travelling via Katima Mulilo: one uses the Ngoma border with Botswana (daily 7am–6pm), through Chobe National Park, crossing into Zimbabwe at the Kazungula road border west of Vic Falls (see page 331); the other involves crossing into Zambia via the Katima Mulilo Bridge over the Zambezi (daily 6am–6pm), driving to Livingstone and then on to the border post at the falls. Note that the 6am opening time is Namibian time, which is one hour behind the time in Zambia, Zimbabwe, Botswana and South Africa for some of the year (see Basics page 73).

From/to South Africa Depending on where you are travelling from in South Africa and where you want to stay en route, you can drive on good roads to Vic Falls through Botswana or Namibia or cross the border into Zimbabwe at Beitbridge/Mzingwane, 320km (198.8 miles) southeast of Bulawayo, which is the route most transport from the Johannesburg/Pretoria area takes.

GETTING AROUND

BY TAXI

Taxis are plentiful but generally expensive. The standard rate from the Zambian border or the falls (within 100m/328ft of each other) to town is around US$8, depending on your negotiating skills and how brisk business is. It's about US$6 for anywhere around town. Rates are a little higher after dark. For the lodges several kilometres out of town, bank on paying nearer US$12–15 from the border, the falls or the town. A journey to or from the airport costs US$32–35.

MONEY MATTERS

Since 2016, the Zimbabwe government has officially recognised **nine currencies** in the country – from yen to euros, pounds to pula. To confuse matters further, an RTGS dollar – or zollar – was introduced in February 2019, though tourists will unlikely come across it too often. In practice, the US dollar is the most helpful currency for day-to-day living, with the fading South African rand more current near the South African border. In Vic Falls Town, where all activities are priced in **US dollars** and the ATM (when functioning) dispenses dollar bills, this currency is king, and others, though accepted, tend to get less favourable rates. That said, in June 2019, the Zimbabwean government banned trading in US dollars within the country with immediate effect. However, it is still business as usual in Vic Falls and it remains to be seen whether the ruling will ever be enforced. If the **ATMs** in Vic Falls Town are not working, the banks (see page 323) should **advance** money on your credit card (provided it is Visa or MasterCard) on the presentation of your passport. However, cash was unavailable in the ATMs or banks for some time at the time of writing, so bringing cash with you is imperative, including some small denominations. **Travellers' cheques** are no longer of use, but **credit cards** (Visa and, to a lesser extent, MasterCard) are now accepted by most of the major lodges, shops and tour operators. At the opposite end of the scale, you're bound to encounter young lads in the street trying to flog you an old Zimbabwean trillion-dollar note as a souvenir.

8

BY SHUTTLE BUS

Outlying lodges and hotels provide courtesy shuttles that will drop you off and pick you up in town. The service, which ranges from hourly to daily, deposits people in town, then goes down to the falls, dropping off or picking up passengers at the entrance before returning back through town, stopping outside Soper's Arcade or the main Wild Horizons office (see page 319), to whisk guests back to their accommodation. For most activities, hotel transfers are included in the rates.

ON FOOT

Since 'downtown' Vic Falls essentially consists of two roads and a couple of small shopping arcades, you can get everywhere easily on foot. The entrance to the falls, too, is a mere ten- to fifteen-minute walk downhill from the central T-junction, though the lengthier return slog uphill in the heat of the day might persuade you to succumb to a taxi. Although it is perfectly safe to walk during the day, you should take a taxi in the evening.

BY CAR

Car rental is very expensive in Vic Falls (see page 296) and petrol is scarce. Still, there's no real need (unless you're planning onward travel to other parts of Zimbabwe and Southern Africa): you can get around easily and more cheaply using courtesy shuttle services, taxis, tours and walking.

Rental companies Avis, Budget and Europcar have offices at the airport: Avis (W avis.co.zw); Budget (W budget.com); Europcar (W europcar.com). Hertz (W hertz.com) is in the Bata Building on Parkway.

INFORMATION

There is no municipal tourist information in Vic Falls.

Victoria Falls Tourist Information Centre Parkway Drive, at the corner with Livingstone Way T 013 44202. Managed by the aptly named Knowledge Nyoni, this private information office can get good deals on activities, has some fliers, and can sell you maps of the falls (the same one included in the falls entry fee!), Vic Falls and Zimbabwe. If you want to experience more of 'real' Zimbabwe, he can also arrange a half-day visit to the nearby village of Mpisi. Daily 8am–6pm.

TOUR OPERATORS

The biggest **tour operator** in Vic Falls is Wild Horizons, which runs several lodges, followed by Shearwater, the longest-established rafting company. These outfits operate most of the **activities** they offer, though they will also book **third-party** activities for you. Both advertise a wide range of attractions, including excursions to Chobe and Hwange national parks (see page 320). Other operators are **specialists** in just one activity or are general operators who book on behalf of the specialists.

Adventure Zone Shop 4, Phumala Centre W adventurezonevicfalls.com. This operator is mainly about adrenaline sports – and is one of the four rafting operators – though they also offer the usual tours and transfers, plus a cycling tour of the area. For example, a two-day safari to Chobe (minus transfers to/from the border) costs US$325 per person.

Backpackers' Bazaar Shop 5, Bata Building ⓦbackpackersbazaarvicfalls.com. *Shoestrings Backpackers* (see page 320) is a tour company which, along with the usual range of adrenaline, scenic and wildlife-viewing activities, organises one- to three-night budget camping trips to Chobe and Hwange national parks (see page 320) and tailor-made trips, even to Namibia.

Discover Victoria Falls ⓦdiscovervictoriafalls.com. Owner-operator Charles Brightman is an excellent professional guide, renowned conservationist and founder of the Victoria Falls anti-poaching unit. He leads affordable private birding or wildlife drives and walking safaris to the Zambezi National Park and further afield.

Shearwater Parkway Drive ⓦshearwatervictoriafalls.com. Highly professional, experienced operator. As well as being the rafting pioneers, they can book all manner of tours and activities and offer combination packages. They also run transfers within Zimbabwe, Zambia and Botswana and own several restaurants.

Shockwave Adventures Shop 6, Bata Building Parkway Drive ⓦshockwavevicfalls.com. A rafting outfit is known for its personalised customer service and multiday tours, such as the five-day trip to the Matestsi River. It also offers good deals on combo packages with other adventure activities and does transfers.

Victoria Falls Guide ⓦvictoriafalls-guide.net. This experienced Zimbabwean husband-and-wife team offers a personalised service and can organise everything from accommodation to tours and car rentals. Mon–Fri 8am–5pm.

Wild Horizons 310 Parkway Drive ⓦwildhorizons.co.za. The glitziest main office (and various smaller offices) for the biggest tour company, which can organise every aspect of your trip, if you want, from accommodation to transfers to activities. This major rafting operator offers various combo packages, runs highly acclaimed cruises in its boats on the Zambezi, and manages two of the most luxurious lodges in the area.

ACCOMMODATION

There are plenty of options in Vic Falls Town itself, from the historic *Victoria Falls Hotel* to a range of inexpensive accommodations, including campsites and backpackers' places. Several hotels and lodges are situated a few kilometres outside the town, off Parkway Drive that runs broadly parallel to the Upper Zambezi, and there's a growing number of small lodges, guesthouses and B&Bs sprouting up around Raynard Road in a quiet suburb about a forty-minute walk (or a short taxi ride) from town.

Rates and reservations Most places are overpriced, though you can often bargain a better rate in the low season (see page 298) when a lot of package deals are available. Even the inexpensive options are not as cheap as elsewhere in Zimbabwe. However, the number of places to stay does not match the demand in the high season when it's essential to book in advance. If you stay out of town, where some of the more luxurious accommodation is located, you must budget for taxis in the evening if you want to eat anywhere other than at your lodge. For the all-inclusive rates some lodges offer, check carefully what is included before committing.

IN TOWN, SEE MAPS PAGES 310 AND 314

★ **Bayete Guest Lodge** 584 Manyika Rd, off Reynard Rd ⓦbayeteguestlodge.com. This stylish thatched lodge is set in luscious gardens. It boasts 25 nicely decorated, spacious rooms leading into similarly design-conscious walk-in bathrooms with monsoon showers (and stand-alone Victorian-style baths in the executive rooms). There is a lovely pool area with sunloungers and a pleasant semi-open dining room. Set dinner on request. B&B **US$$$$**

★ **Ilala Lodge** 411 Livingstone Way ⓦilalalodge.com. Superbly located – central yet secluded, and a stone's throw from the falls, which you can hear from the lovely patio – this elegant, welcoming, family-run hotel provides 34 spacious, carpeted rooms tastefully done out in reclaimed teak. Gorgeous balconied suites sit under thatch, overlooking woodland. Count on superb food, efficient, friendly service and a pleasant pool area. B&B. Doubles and suites **US$$$$$**

The Kingdom Hotel 1 Mallett Drive ⓦthekingdomhotel.co.za. More in tune with Vegas and Sun City, this Great Zimbabwe-themed hotel and entertainment centre hosts a casino, food court and health spa. Beyond the ostentatious lobby lie surprisingly pleasant enclosed grounds, including ornamental ponds with reed beds, bridges, lawns and a nice pool area. Smart, if bland, business-style rooms, most with a patio or balcony that overlooks the grounds. A good option for families: rooms for four include bunk beds. B&B **US$$$$**

N1 Hotel & Campsite 266 Adam Stander Drive ⓦn1hotel.co.zw. The best-value central hotel in town is often full. It offers compact, modern rooms with a/c and TV, tea- and coffee-making facilities, and a four-bed dorm. Make sure you bag one of the newly renovated second-floor rooms. The secure grassy campsite at the back is the best place to pitch a tent in town, with a dozen braai stands, a pleasant pool area with sunloungers, plenty of shade and a sometimes-functioning bar. Breakfast US$7 extra. Camping **US$**, dorm **US$**, doubles **US$$**

Pennywise Cottages ⓦpennywise-cottages.business.site. Warm, hospitable budget accommodation in a quiet residential area. Six simple en-suite rooms with old-fashioned furnishing (yet with DStv, fridge and a/c) open out onto a small shaded patio with a smidgen of grass. Breakfast is included and you can use their kitchen too. **US$$**

8

TIPS TO CHOBE AND HWANGE NATIONAL PARKS

Two main excursions outside the Vic Falls area are to these nearby national parks. The most popular destination is **Chobe National Park**, just 70km (43.5 miles) away over the border in northern Botswana. Chobe is renowned for its vast quantities of large mammals (the world's greatest concentration of elephants), likely sightings of predators – including wild dogs – and fabulous river cruises. Some heading for Chobe make a **day trip** (around US$170–180), but this can be a tiring disappointment: you can spend three to four hours on hotel pick-ups and drop-offs, travel, border and other formalities, and you're likely to miss the best times of the day for wildlife viewing – dawn and dusk. Moreover, you'll not experience the magical sunsets frequently witnessed on a cruise along the **Chobe River**. A much better option is the acclaimed overnight or two-night basic **camping trip** that can be arranged through *Backpackers' Bazaar* (see page 319) or *Adventure Zone* (see page 318) in Vic Falls, or *Livingstone Backpackers* and *Jollyboys* in Livingstone (see page 332), which is usually cheaper. They all generally work with a third party in Kasane. An overnight stay, including two days of activities, will set you back around US$350–400 and usually includes a game drive or two and a river cruise. In some cases, visa fees are not included, nor are transfers to the border, but park fees usually are. Check the small print.

Potentially even more rewarding is an excursion to less well-known and less-visited **Hwange National Park**, Zimbabwe's largest reserve (US$20 international park fee), a two-hour drive away (but minus the border hassles). It, too, has a large elephant population and over four hundred bird species. Moreover, you can enjoy the **wilderness experience** of being largely alone in the bush, whereas Chobe in the dry season can be jam-packed with safari vehicles queuing up to see a lion kill. The big operators will only put on a trip to Hwange if you have a group of at least four together. The *Kingdom Hotel* offers a three-night safari package to the park. With your own vehicle, it's an easy drive and plenty of private and government accommodation (see Ⓦzimparks.org) in or around the park should you wish to spend the night here. As with Chobe, an overnight sojourn will likely result in a more rewarding experience.

8

★ **PheZulu Guest Lodge** 557 Mopane Rd Ⓦphezuluguestlodge.com. 21 smart, bright and cheerily decorated rooms with local basketry and large walk-in showers, set around a leafy green area with a pool, sunloungers and a semi-open bar-breakfast area. Staff are friendly and efficient – which altogether makes for a relaxing sojourn. US$$$

Shoestrings Backpackers 12 West Drive Ⓦshoestringsvicfalls.com. This is a classic party backpacker place – so sleep will be limited – with a renowned lively bar (open to locals and guests) serving decent pub grub and a shady garden with a pool and hammocks. Small, brightly painted rooms offer a good range of budget lodgings, with fan – or a/c, costing extra). Organises activities through its budget tour operator (see page 319). Camping US$, dorms US$, doubles US$$

Victoria Falls Backpackers 357 Gibson Rd Ⓦvictoriafallsbackpackers.com. Relaxed, friendly backpackers in a quiet residential area a fifteen–twenty-minute walk from town. Plenty of Zimbabwean art is in the leafy garden, plus a giant chess set, pool and nightly campfire. Accommodation is varied, but space is at a premium – the large dorm, in particular, is rather cramped. Self-drive camping plots are also available. Other amenities include an on-site café. Camping per person US$, dorms US$, doubles US$$

The Victoria Falls Hotel 2 Mallett Drive Ⓦvictoriafallshotel.com. A relic of a bygone era, this place exudes faded colonial splendour, from the framed historical photos and prints that adorn the walls to the original brass taps in the rooms and the chandelier-lit, carpeted corridors. That said, rooms are small, except the new, much pricier, stables rooms, which look towards the falls, though the grounds' huge trees can block the view. B&B US$$$$$

Victoria Falls Rest Camp Parkway Drive at the corner with West Drive Ⓦrestcampvicfalls.com. Secure, cheap and central – though it may be moving out of town – and with lots of room and shade, this rest camp attracts lots of overlander groups and end-of-year school parties (in Dec). In addition to camping, there are a couple of single-sex dorms, very basic chalets, some renovated but containing little beyond two single beds of varying quality. Bed linen is supplied, but not towels. Both chalet-dwellers and campers share the spotless camping ablution blocks. The self-catering chalets (two to four guests) are similarly basic with metal-frame beds, but some have a/c. The big plus is the lovely grassy pool area with plenty of shade, picnic tables, sunloungers and a good bar restaurant (see below). Camping and dorms US$, small chalets and self-catering US$$

OUT OF TOWN, SEE MAPS PAGES 306 AND 310

A 'Zambezi River Lodge 308 Parkway Drive ⓦrtgafrica.com/azambezi-river-lodge.com. With an enviable location on the banks of the eponymous river (though marred slightly by the many boats moored there), the longstanding *A 'Zambezi* is more hotel-like than lodge in feel. It comprises two large, semicircular, two-floor thatched buildings containing small, modern en-suite rooms with a/c, minibar and TV, which open out onto a long shared patio or balcony. Sit and gaze over the nicely maintained grounds – frequented by warthogs – which slope down to the water. À la carte and buffet dining available. B&B US$$$

Elephant Camp 10km (6.2 miles) from Vic Falls Town in the Victoria Falls National Park, off the road to Bulawayo ⓦtheelephantcamp.com. This is a luxurious safari experience, with twelve tents that offer fabulous views. Gaze across the bush to the spray from Batoka Gorge from your bed, bath or deck (including a private plunge pool and outdoor shower). Top-notch cuisine, service and facilities ensure that you'll want for nothing. AI US$$$$$

★ **Gorges Lodge** Batoka Gorge, 22km (13.7 miles) from Vic Falls, signposted off the Bulawayo Rd ⓦbatokaafrica.com/properties/gorges-lodge. Currently under renovation. In a stunning location, peering over a cliff 220m (721.8ft) above the Zambezi and set in butterfly-filled grounds, ten breezy stone-and-thatch chalets with private patios offer spectacular views over the rapids – as does the main lodge. Adjacent is the smaller luxury-tented *Little Gorges* camp (same contact details), with its separate bar-dining area. A joint private-community venture, its activities include school and village visits and seeking out the resident black eagles. AI US$$$$$

Masuwe Lodge Private Reserve 6km (3.7 miles) south of town ⓦmasuwe-lodge.com. Enclosed by bush in a small private reserve, this place exudes warmth and is a real treat. Perched on a hilltop, a handful of canvas-and-stone chalets on stilts gaze outwards across the bush. The thatched dining area, in particular, affords great views and looks down on a water hole frequented by elephants and antelope. Buffalo occasionally has to be coaxed out of the nicely landscaped gardens and pool area at night. AI US$$$$$

★ **Old Drift Lodge** Zambezi National Park, 7km (4.3 miles) northwest of Vic Falls ⓦolddriftlodge.com. Fabulous tented lodge occupying a prime site on the Zambezi within the national park, yet only a twenty-minute drive from town. You'll want for nothing in the vast safari suites, where you can fall asleep to the sounds of the bush or indulge in armchair game viewing from your private deck or outdoor shower. The main lodge is similarly luxurious, while service, guiding and cuisine are all first-rate. AI US$$$$$

Stanley & Livingstone Boutique Hotel Victoria Falls Private Game Reserve, 7km (4.3 miles) south of Vic Falls Town, off the A8 ⓦmore.co.za/stanleyandlivingstone. After a major revamp and change of ownership in 2022, this colonial-style, thatched lodge has morphed into a boutique hotel as safari-chic meets high-end hotel. Its sixteen sumptuous suites stuffed with quality furniture and furnishings combine with modern hotel comforts (TV, minibar, spa therapies, sunloungers around the pool), plus private patios overlooking the manicured grounds or the bush. Expect top-notch a-la-carte dining. Located in a well-stocked private game reserve, home to the 'Big Five', its safari drives and bush dinners are a major attraction, as is the busy waterhole overlooked by the terrace. B&B US$$$$$

★ **Zambezi Sands** Zambezi National Park, 1hr drive upriver from Vic Falls ⓦbatokaafrica.com/properties/zambezi-sands. Comprising eight vast, opulent, tented suites in an idyllic location overlooking the Zambezi, each has a private deck with a plunge pool and indoor and outdoor ablutions and is exquisitely furnished. The birdwatching is excellent, and as well as the usual game drives and river cruises, you can go whitewater canoeing or opt for a more sedate paddle. AI US$$$$$

VICTORIA FALLS SAFARI LODGE ESTATE

Spread over a hillside within a private reserve, abutting the Zambezi National Park, the *Victoria Falls Safari Lodge Estate* (471 Squire Cummings Rd, 3km/1.9 miles from Vic Falls ⓦafricaalbidatourism.com) contains several outstanding properties, all served by a regular shuttle service from town.

★ **Lokuthula Lodge** ⓦlokuthukla.com. These superior, thatched, self-catering chalets (two- or three-bedroom) are extremely well kitted out (though don't expect a TV), exuding tasteful design yet a homely appeal, and are surrounded by bush. The multilevel pool is a treat, and if you tire of cooking for yourself, stroll over to *The Boma* (see page 322) or the safari lodge for dinner. A B&B package is also possible. Two-bedroomed chalets US$$$$

★ **Victoria Falls Safari Lodge** ⓦvictoria-falls-safari-lodge.com. High on a hill, presiding over the Zambezi National Park, this flagship lodge is a large, multitiered, thatched construction boasting panoramic vistas across the bush, glorious sunsets, and a prime view of the waterhole below; perch at the bar, slouch in the lounge, or sprawl by the pool deck with a drink and enjoy nonstop wildlife viewing. Well-appointed rooms, award-winning restaurants and exceptional service make this lodge a top choice that is consistently voted as one of the best places to stay in the country. Don't miss the daily vulture feed at 1pm if you're here for lunch. B&B US$$$$

EATING

SEE MAPS PAGES 310 AND 314

Beyond the hotels and lodges, which predominantly offer buffet spreads or fine dining, there is a small but varied selection of restaurants in town, plus a handful of popular fast-food joints. Like everything else in Vic Falls, restaurants tend to be expensive and are often overpriced for what you get. There are a couple of supermarkets for self-caterers.

Active Sushi N1 Hotel & Campsite 266 Adam Stander Drive ⓦ activesushi.com. A South African chain, it may be, but it's the only place to indulge in a sushi craving – sashimi, tempura, spring rolls and other East Asian favourite soups and poke bowls. The casual grassy poolside venue at the back of the N1Hotel is an ideal spot. US$$–$$$

The Boma Lokuthula Lodge, 471 Squire Cummings Rd ⓦ theboma.co.zw. The hottest evening ticket in Vic Falls is a high-quality, interactive, touristy affair that allows you to sample some traditional Zimbabwean cuisine: expect sadza (thick porridge), mopane worms (actually caterpillars) and warthog, amid more familiar dishes. Dinner is a belly-filling barbecue buffet with good veggie options, served under a cavernous, semi-open thatch building. Be prepared to don a *chitenge* (traditional sarong), have your face painted, try out some drumming, and be wowed by Ndebele dancers. N$$$$

8

★ **Brook's Café** Elephant's Walk Mall ⓣ 077 5671574. A casual café with a gourmet touch: great breakfasts, light lunches, coffee and freshly baked cakes – all exquisitely presented. The Friday lunch 'local's special' dish from a different part of the world is a must. Daily 8am–4pm.

★ **Cassia Restaurant** Ilala Lodge, 411 Livingstone Way ⓦ ilalalodge.com. Enjoy lunch on the terrace to the sound of marimbas or a more formal candlelit dinner under their giant acacia, listening to the thunder of the falls. Delectable fine dining, with ostrich, kudu, warthog and crocodile served creatively, offering more inventive vegetarian cuisine than most places. US$$$

Costa Café Victoria Falls Rest Camp, corner of Parkway Drive and West Drive. Open-sided thatched restaurant in a relaxed poolside setting, with a couple of sports screens to entertain during the day. The drinks are cheaper than in most places, and meals are reasonably priced: try a filling potjie stew with rice or sadza or a full fry-up breakfast. Service is polite and efficient. US$$–$$$

The Livingstone Room Victoria Falls Hotel, 2 Mallett Drive ⓦ victoriafallshotel.com. Formal splendour served up on damask tablecloths, decked with crystal glasses and candles, accompanying exquisite, inventive cuisine. For sheer indulgence, get the whole table to order the seven-course tasting menu, comprising the restaurant's signature dishes. Mains are delicious and beautifully presented, but leave room for the chocolate tart with white chocolate mousse and salted caramel sauce. US$$$$$

★ **The Lookout Café** Top of Batoka Gorge, 400m (0.25 miles) downriver from the bridge. ⓦ thelookoutcafe.com. You can't beat the setting, perched on a clifftop overlooking the Zambezi rapids; install yourself at a table under a semi-open thatch or at a table in the garden, and feast on the spectacular view. As Wild Horizons owns it, you can watch the adjacent zipline action as you tuck into a breakfast platter, indulge in brunch or savour some freshly prepared comfort food for lunch: steak, ribs, kebabs, wraps or salads. Plenty of veggie and vegan options. Reserve a table for a full-moon dinner on a cloudless night in the dry season. US$$$

Makuwa-kuwa Restaurant Victoria Falls Safari Lodge, 3km ((1.9 miles) from Vic Falls, 471 Squire Cummings Rd ⓦ victoria-falls-safari-lodge.com. You can't beat this hillside location: glorious sunsets and (if you reserve early enough) a table overlooking the waterhole so you can watch the elephants guzzle as you tuck into your succulent warthog fillet or Zambezi bream – two of the house specialities. However, the sounds of the bush are likely to play second fiddle to some a cappella singing. US$$$$$

Mama Africa Back of the Trading Post complex ⓦ mamaafricaeatinghouse.com. This is a popular restaurant where you must book a table on the buzzy, candlelit terrace. Choose from a range of salads and grilled meats or plump for one of the house-specialty hotpots: try the *sadza ndiurae* (literally 'sadza kill me'), a Shona stew of spiced, mixed vegetables and steak, served in a three-legged pot (*potjie*), accompanied with sadza or groundnut rice. Be prepared to wait when it's busy and to endure a local group whose nightly numbers range from African tunes to Elvis and the ubiquitous Bob Marley. US$$$–$$$$

★ **Marula Café** Corner of Parkway Drive and Livingstone Way. This stylish modern corner terrace café (prime people-watching territory) is a popular mid-morning pit stop for a latte and a cake. Breakfasts are great, too: try the eggs Benedict or waffles. In the evening, sophisticated lighting on the wooden decor makes it an atmospheric place for a delicious dinner – choose from a wide-ranging menu including the usual international favourites and local dishes, all nicely prepared. US$$$

★ **Stanley's Terrace** The Victoria Falls Hotel ⓦ victoriafallshotel.com. This is a must for high tea (daily–5.30pm) or a cocktail sundowner. As you bite into dainty sandwiches, cakes and scones and sip tea out of fine bone china, you can gaze across the manicured lawn and soak up views of the falls, the bridge and the bungee jumping. Then, linger in the hotel's fabulous, sofa-filled main lounge on the way out and admire the beautiful, framed pressed flowers. High tea US$$

The Three Monkeys Corner of Adam Stander Drive and Livingstone Way ⓦ 3monkeys.co.zw. Vic Falls' top pizza place alongside a thriving bar. Tasty wood-fired, thin-crust pizzas, deli burgers and flame-grilled steak efficiently churned out at elevated prices. US$$$–$$$$

★ **Zulu Bistro & Bar** Landela Centre ⓦzulubistrobar.com. Despite the African-sounding name, there's no indigenous fare on the menu. A mixture of North American and Mediterranean comfort food prevails – but nicely prepared and tasty. Vegetarians can finally breathe out as there's plenty to please, from halloumi or quinoa salads to mushroom risotto or a veggie burger. But for carnivores, the melt-in-your-mouth slow-roasted pork ribs are the dish to choose from, with the pan-seared Zambezi bream a close second. US$$$

DRINKING

SEE MAP PAGE 314

Comfort At the back of the Trading Post complex by the railway tracks. This happening place for drinking and dancing is mainly populated by locals but friendly towards tourists. There's a pool table, cheap beer and inexpensive filling fare, such as chicken or burgers and sadza for next to nothing, enlivened by a DJ at weekends. The place doesn't get going until 11pm once the many hotel and restaurant staff knock off.

Invuvu Bar Parkway Drive, opposite Soper's Arcade. There is a popular watering hole in the centre of town – especially when there's a big football match on TV – because of the cheap beer and food. You'll pay a few dollars for a plate of sadza and chicken or bargain game meat such as buffalo or kudu. The game, procured from the park wardens (part of the regulated game culling), is often cooked up late afternoon and runs out fast. Be prepared to eat with your hands.

The River Brewing Co Adam Stander Drive ⓦriverbrewco.com. Vic Falls' first micro-brewery, with a beer garden and indoor seating (plus monster sports screen) – just the place to linger over a craft beer or a good-value beer paddle of six craft brews. There's also pub grub on sale: the predictable burgers, ribs, fish, and chips help the ale slip down. The gin tasting is less impressive, involving regular gin infused with botanicals and other flavours. Occasional live music at weekends.

Shoestrings Bar Shoestrings Backpackers, 12 West Drive ⓦshoestringsvicfalls.com. This is a popular bar to kick off the night, hosting occasional DJs, live bands, interactive drumming and theme parties, open mic and cocktail nights. It often attracts a mix of locals and tourists. The popular inexpensive pizzas help soak up the alcohol. Cover charge for events for non-residents.

NIGHTLIFE

Most mid-range and high-end hotels and lodges provide nightly entertainment, as do most restaurants. This usually entails one or more of the following: Ndebele a cappella singers, dancers and/or drummers dressed in traditional ostrich-feather finery or mellow marimba music. Nightlife is otherwise relatively low-key.

SHOPPING

SEE MAP PAGE 314

Most tourists are directed towards the ever-expanding Open Market (daily 8am–6pm), which boasts many stalls selling mass-produced soapstone or wooden crafts (whatever the stallholder might tell you). Don't forget to check out the **women's cooperative stalls**, specialising in basketry and cloth, in the rather gloomy sheds to the left. Most mainstream gift shops are located in the Trading Post Complex on Livingstone Way; Elephant's Walk Mall (ⓦelephantswalk.com; daily 9am–5pm), which hosts a collection of more varied, upmarket (and expensive) craft stores is also worth checking out. For a less touristy market, try the Comesa flea market (daily 8am–5pm), offering cloth, cheap goods and bags of local colour. For fresh fruit and veg, head for the Old Market in Chinotimba.

African Heritage Elephant's Walk Mall ⓣ0772254552. Superior gift shop with prices to match stocking quality goods from Zimbabwe and other parts of Africa, and with a fine collection of masks in particular. Daily 9am–5pm.

Cultural Vibes Music Shop Elephant's Walk Mall ⓦcultural-vibes.com. The place to come for Zimbabwean CDs: The enthusiastic and knowledgeable owner lets you sample the sounds and can guide you in your selection. Daily 9am–5pm.

Ndau Collection Elephant's Walk Mall ⓦndaucollection.com. Stunning, award-winning, hand-made designer jewellery and accessories inspired by nature, from dung-beetle earrings to rhino-tusk bangles. Prices range from US$100 to several thousand. Daily 9am–5pm.

Ndoro.co Elephant's Walk Mall. Stunning designer porcelain by internationally renowned Zimbabwean ceramicist Marjorie Wallace, alongside individually crafted cards, ceramic jewellery and fashion accessories. Daily 10am–5pm.

DIRECTORY

Banks and money Barclays Bank (ⓦzw.barclays.com) is set back from Livingstone Way, opposite the petrol station. So, too, is Standard Chartered (ⓦsc.com/zw). Both have ATMs that take Visa (US$5 charge). Banking hours are Mon–Fri 8am–3pm & Sat 8am–11.30am. At the time of writing, however, neither banks nor ATMs had had any cash for some time.

Hospital/clinic The Victoria Falls District Hospital, Chinotimba, is always overstretched, so you are better off going to the THB Private Hospital, 95 West Drive (ⓣ013 46634, ⓔvicfalls@thehealthbridge.org), a state-of-the-art private hospital aimed at tourists, which provides medical

CRAFTS GALORE

Zimbabwe is renowned for its **crafts** and you can shop till you drop for them in Vic Falls. The place abounds with gift shops (see page 323) and curio stalls – especially outside the entrance to the falls – and there's an ever-expanding craft market, too, named the **Open Market**, at the end of Adam Stander Drive, where you'll find a bewildering array of stalls, many offering much the same wares. **Woodcarvings** – from hardwoods such as olive, teak, ebony or mahogany – are ubiquitous; sculpted animals – everything from large elephants and hippos to small frogs and dung beetles – are the most common. Beyond the wildlife, you can find wooden bowls, masks, carved walking sticks and salad servers. **Shona sculpture** is internationally famous and there's plenty on display, commonly made from soapstone and serpentine, with the *ukama* or family sculptures portraying couples or groups of figures particularly popular. Equally renowned is Zimbabwe's distinctive **sadza batik cloth**. The women use sadza – just like the porridge you may have tasted on your plate – in much the same way as the wax is used in other traditions of batik-making to prevent colour from entering parts of the cloth. Look out also for the colourful Ndebele beadwork and their brightly painted **geometric designs** on everything from mugs to picture frames and cloth, as well as the distinctive, finely woven baskets of the Tonga women from the remote region of Binga. Many of the items on sale these days are mass-produced – don't be fooled by the ubiquitous assertion: 'I made it myself' – though you can still pick up the odd original curio.

8

and dental care.

Pharmacy Victoria Falls Pharmacy, Phumala Centre, Parkway Drive (T 013 44403; Mon–Fri 8am–5pm, Sat 8.30am–1pm & Sun 9am–noon).

Police Livingstone Way (T 013 42206). You are more likely to have contact with the tourist police, recognisable by their lime-green vests.

Post office Livingstone Way, opposite the Total garage (Mon–Fri 8am–4pm & Sat 8–11.30am).

Supermarkets OK Grocers, the main supermarket, is at the back of the Phumala Centre on Clark Drive (Mon–Sat 8am–8pm & Sun 8am–5pm) although a new Pick n Pay opened in 2019 in the new Sawanga Mall, on the corner of Pioneer Road and Livingstone Way (daily 8am–8pm); the small 7–11 store in the Phumala Centre is, as the name indicates, open daily 7am–11pm.

Telephones SIM cards cost around US$1 but were in short supply at the mobile phone service providers' shops on Parkway Drive at the time of writing. It should cost around US$20–30 for a phone to be unlocked, depending on the make.

Zambia

Mosi-oa-Tunya National Park

Entrance to the falls is on Mosi-oa-Tunya Road, 10km (6.2 miles) south of the town centre, just before the Victoria Falls Bridge and Zimbabwe; entrance to the game reserve is on Sichango Drive, signposted off Mosi-oa-Tunya Road, 3km (1.9 miles) south of the town centre • Both daily 6am–6pm • Charge

Encompassing both the Zambian side of the falls and a slender strip of protected land that extends for about 12km (7.5 miles) upriver along the northern bank of the Zambezi, **Mosi-oa-Tunya National Park** is much smaller than the combined area of Victoria Falls National Park and the almost contiguous Zambezi National Park on the Zimbabwean side. But the view of the falls from here is really special and definitely worth the outlay, even if you have seen them already from the Zimbabwean side. Although the Mosi-oa-Tunya game reserve does not boast as much in the way of **large mammals** as the Zambezi National Park across the river – there are usually no elephants, for example – the birdlife and river views alone make for a very pleasant drive.

The falls

Although more people flock to the Zimbabwean side of the falls (see page 309), where most of the water thunders into the chasm, you should try to visit **both sides**: the Zambian section affords completely different perspectives on the spectacle. It guarantees a quickening of the pulse as you cross **Knife Edge Bridge**, which connects the area surrounding the reserve entrance to the rocky peninsula known as Knife Edge Island. This **circular trail** affords fabulous views across the ravine to the **Eastern Cataract** – though when the water's tumbling at full throttle, you may only experience its deafening noise as you become lost – and drenched – in a thick fog of swirling spray. Arguably, the most spectacular vista is saved for **Knife Edge Point**, at the far western end of the rocky promontory. From this vantage point, you can gaze in awe down the entire length of the falls gorge (the **First Gorge**). Depending on the time of year, you will be treated either to pounding torrents of water and clouds of spray or – when water is low – to the sight of the vast, deep sheet of exposed basalt rock; you can also peer into the gaping chasm below at the churning waters of the **Boiling Pot** as they jostle their way downriver through the Second Gorge, and under the **Victoria Falls Bridge**. If you like to get your adrenaline rush by proxy, wait to catch sight of one of the **bungee jumpers** – you get a great view of them plummeting from the bridge from here. For a closer look at the Boiling Pot and a chance to marvel at the falls from below, head back towards the entrance and follow the signs down the **Palm Grove Trail**. This is an easy, though sometimes slippery, descent, though it can be a hard slog to climb the 100m (328ft) back out again in the heat of the day. You can also take a **tour** that ferries you across the Boiling Pot in an inflatable to stand under the falls (see page 300) when water levels permit. However, the latest craze is to swim below the falls, which is also inevitably a low-water activity. The Zambian **whitewater rafters** also start at this point (see page 303). A more sedate stroll along the reserve's **Photographic Trail** provides more perspectives on this natural wonder. It takes you parallel to the main road within touching distance of the Victoria Falls Bridge. A **statue of David Livingstone** stands proudly close to the entrance/exit.

8

SYUUNGWE NA MUTITIMA ('THE HEAVY MIST THAT RESOUNDS')

Mosi-oa-Tunya ('the smoke that thunders'), the Kololo and Lozi word for the falls, is widely promoted as its **Indigenous name** – thanks in no small part to the fact that the guides who led David Livingstone (see box, page 326) were Kololo – yet it is by no means the only one. The Mukuni Leya, who claim to be the original river settlers in the area, refer to it as *syuungwe na mutitima*, meaning '**the heavy mist that resounds**'. However, *syuungwe* also implies a place of rainbows. Legend has it that the resounding in question comes from a drum: it is said that in a battle between Leya chiefs Sekute and Mukuni, Sekute's drum – a potent symbol of his power – fell over the edge of the falls to become wedged at their base, and is now permanently pounded by the falling water. Mukuni Leya also refers to the falls as *syuungwe mufu* ('**mist of the dead**') since the area possesses important sites associated with worshiping ancestral spirits. One such place is the *katolauseka* ('make offerings cheerfully') – known by tourists as the **Boiling Pot** – into which valuable items were hurled as offerings to appease the ancestral spirits. Another ritual site is *sambadwazi* ('**cleanse disease**'), a pool by the lip of the Eastern Cataract. Ill or diseased people would bathe here and toss their clothes into the water, which would then be washed over the falls, taking the bathers' sickness away. A third place of significance is *chipusya*, a spot along the river still known to only a select few, where water would be drawn for rainmaking and other rituals. More generally, the falls are associated with the mythology of **Bedyango**, the original female Leya leader with presumed powers over land, rain and fertility, who is said to have agreed to rule the Leya jointly with the initial Chief Mukuni when he first arrived on the scene. Both the present-day chief and the current Bedyango – a title bestowed on one of the chief's female relatives – live in Mukuni Village outside Livingstone, which can be visited on a **cultural tour**.

Livingstone Island

Stuck in the middle of the falls on the brink of the precipice, with water pouring over the edge on either side for most of the year, is **Livingstone Island** – so named because it was where the failed missionary first set eyes on Mosi-oa-Tunya by peering into the abyss. Here, he is also supposed to have carved his name on a **tree**, in a fit of overexcited vandalism, and planted some fruit seeds, though evidence of either activity is absent today. The only way to visit the island is on a tour with *Tongabezi* (see page 333), generally **on foot**, picking your way precariously across the exposed rocks from the Zambian side when the water is low to get the ultimate thrill of jumping – or sliding tentatively – into the island's **Devil's Pool**, where the river is prevented from sweeping you over the edge by a rocky lip beneath the surface – dubbed the **Devil's Armchair**. Peek over the 100m (328ft) sheer drop if you dare; you'll feel as if you're peering into the bowels of the Earth.

The game reserve

Above the falls, the **game reserve** section of the national park comprises tall riverine forest along the Zambezi and, further inland, a mix of grassland, mopane and miombo woodland – miombo trees shed their leaves to reduce moisture loss in the dry season and grow new ones just before the onset of the rains. Although a relatively small protected area of around 66 sq km (25.5 sq miles), the reserve hosts abundant **birdlife**, especially along the riverbanks. Unfortunately, the number of **large mammals** has dropped in recent years following a series of droughts, which can make a game drive here rather disappointing. Even so, keep a lookout for antelope (including sable, eland

LIVINGSTONE: FROM FAILED MISSIONARY TO SUPERSTAR EXPLORER

It's easy to see why the Scottish missionary **David Livingstone** became one of the most popular national heroes back in Victorian Britain: he was a rags-to-riches story, combining strong Christian beliefs with a career as a glamorous explorer of 'Darkest Africa'. Born in Blantyre in 1813 to a teetotal Sunday School teacher, Livingstone worked fourteen-hour shifts in the local cotton mill from age 10, followed by several hours of schooling in evening classes. He went on to study medicine and signed up with the **London Missionary Society** (LMS) to go to China, but the First Opium War broke out and he was offered the West Indies instead. In the end, though, Livingstone opted for a post at the LMS mission station in Kuruman, South Africa, inspired by the idea of destroying the **African slave trade**.

It is fair to say that Livingstone was more or less a failure as a missionary, briefly converting just one man, Sechele, leader of the Kwêna people of Botswana. He did, however, succeed in marrying Mary Moffat, the daughter of the head of the mission. In 1849, disillusioned with missionary work, Livingstone gave up his post with the LMS and concentrated all his efforts on combating slavery, which he hoped to do by encouraging legitimate commercial trade. He believed in the three great Cs – '**Christianity, Commerce and Civilization**' – and was convinced that the key to unlocking trade in central Africa was the Zambezi River, which he believed was as yet unexplored by Europeans.

As an **explorer**, Livingstone was much more successful. Despite losing the use of his left arm after an early encounter with a lion, he was dogged and could endure the most terrible physical conditions. He was also adept at allaying the fears of Africans he met by travelling relatively lightly and without the usual team of armed soldiers. His first **Zambezi expedition** (1852–56) was his most successful, as he laid claim – possibly erroneously – to be the first European to cross Southern Africa from coast to coast, most famously 'discovering' Mosi-oa-Tunya, which he renamed the **Victoria Falls** after Queen Victoria.

Returning to Britain the following year, Livingstone published *Missionary Travels in South Africa* in 1857, a bestseller that sealed his status as a national hero. It also enabled him to get government backing for his second Zambezi expedition (1858–64), which proved something and impala), giraffes, buffalo, zebra and warthogs. Elephants wade across the river from the Zimbabwean side when river levels are low. For 'Big Five' fanatics, there is the chance to glimpse Zambia's few remaining **white rhinos**; there are ten individuals at the current count, and they are heavily guarded, but it's even possible to track them on foot (see page 299). If you adjust your expectations and focus on the tantalising views of the Zambezi through the trees, you can enjoy a relaxing drive here, although a **river cruise** through the park is often more satisfying.

Livingstone

In contrast to Vic Falls, **LIVINGSTONE** seems like a real town; as you enter from the south, past an unappealing stream of big trucks, Mosi-oa-Tunya Road becomes a broad, main boulevard lined with lilac jacaranda and flaming flamboyants at certain times of the year. The high street stretches north for a couple of kilometres, hauling itself uphill, away from the falls. The **Livingstone Museum**, on the west side of the road, heralds the start of the town centre and Livingstone's **business district**: a strip of banks, pharmacies, the post office and shops, which gives way to the well-ordered line of stalls that constitute the **curio market** (Mon–Sat 8am–6pm), where you'll be far less hassled than at Vic Falls. If you head a block east of the high street at the museum and walk northwards, parallel to the museum, you'll come across taxi ranks and **bus stations** interspersed with **market stalls** where women sell mounds of fruit, vegetables and pulses alongside blankets, cheap shoes and toasted sweetcorn. As you walk around, keep your eye out for a few flashes of faded Edwardian **colonial architecture**.

of a disaster: most of his team deserted him; he was accused of incompetence; and his uncomplaining wife, Mary, who had borne him six children, died of malaria shortly after joining him in 1862. On the other hand, he declared himself the first European to reach **Lake Malawi**. He uttered his most famous words, 'I am prepared to go anywhere, provided it be forward', while at the same time failing to establish a navigable route across the continent.

Livingstone's third and final expedition (1866–73) – partly funded by the Royal Geographical Society (RGS) – was an attempt to find the source of the **River Nile**, which he wrongly believed had so far been incorrectly identified. Once again, the expedition was plagued by disaster, with all but a few of his helpers deserting him or dying en route and Livingstone falling so ill that he had to be saved on several occasions by the **Arab slave traders** he was trying to oppose. Suffering from pneumonia, cholera and tropical ulcers, Livingstone found himself stranded in Bambarre, in eastern Congo, in 1869, just as the wet season began, and was forced to eat his meals in public for the entertainment of the locals in return for food.

Yet Livingstone's fame was assured when Gordon Bennett, publisher of the *New York Herald*, decided in 1869 to send the journalist **Henry Morton Stanley** out to Africa to seek out the explorer, who had been out of contact with the outside world for several years. After two years of searching, Stanley finally tracked him down to Ujiji – an Arab slave station on Lake Tanganyika in modern-day Tanzania – where, seeing the only white man for many kilometres around, he uttered the famous words, '**Dr Livingstone, I presume**' – or so the story goes.

Although Livingstone was very ill at this point, he refused to be persuaded to leave Africa, soldiering until 1 May 1873, when he died in the village of Chitambo in present-day Zambia. His heart and internal organs were buried in a tin box under a mpundu tree by Susi and Chuma, his long-suffering servants. They then **embalmed his corpse**, using salt and brandy, sun-dried it and wrapped it in calico, and spent the next nine months transporting it 1,600km (994.2 miles) to the Tanzanian coast. From there, the body was sent back to London, where it **lay in state** at No.1 Savile Row, headquarters of the Royal Geographical Society at the time, before being buried in the centre of the nave of Westminster Abbey.

Brief history

The area around Livingstone – as with Victoria Falls Town – has a long history of **African settlement** (see page 337), peopled by groups identifying themselves variously as Leya, Toka, Tonga and Kololo, while the eastern end of the pre-eminent Lozi Kingdom of Barotseland once also stretched this far. In about 1897, the first Europeans settled at **Old Drift**, 10km (6.2 miles) upstream from the falls, where the Zambezi was at its narrowest, providing the best crossing point. The river-dwelling **Leya** constantly navigated and ferried people across the river here. However, the colonisers later abandoned the swampy, malaria-infested area in favour of higher ground on **Constitution Hill**. This new settlement was named **Livingstone** after the good doctor, though it did not take off until the railroad arrived in 1905. Then, in 1911, once the British colonisers had strengthened their grip on the land, it became the capital of the **British Protectorate of Northwest Rhodesia** – and, therefore, a major administrative centre – until the capital was transferred to Lusaka in 1935. During this early colonial period, the **Indigenous populations** were gradually pushed out to the margins; even the

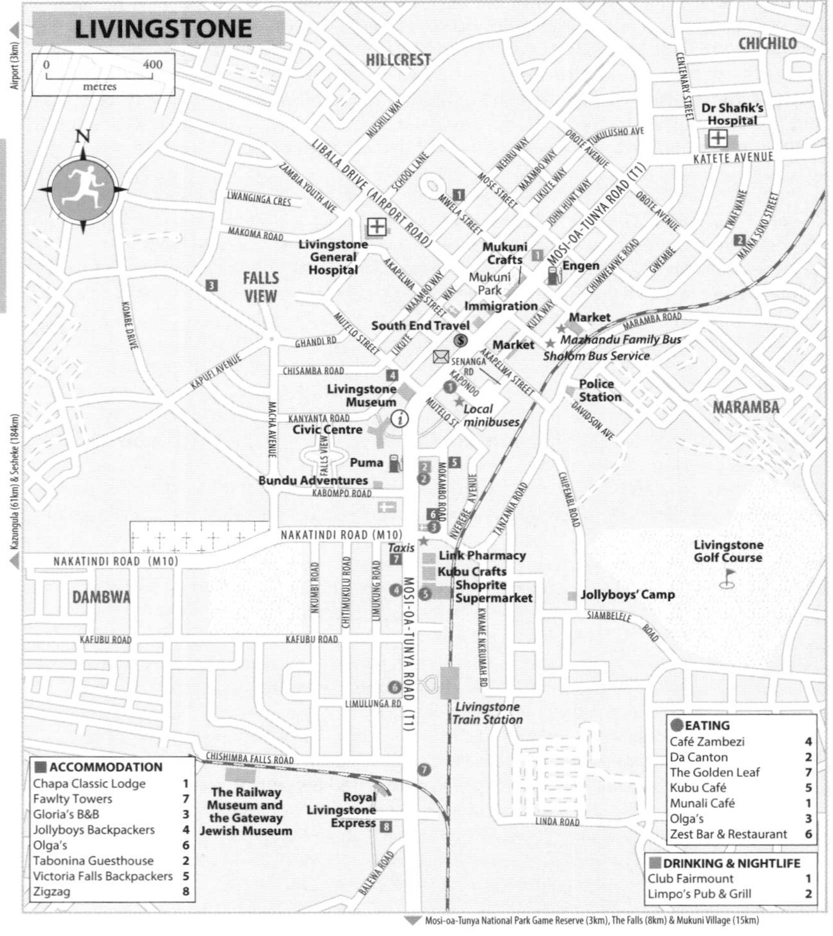

Lozi royalty, who initially enjoyed a relatively privileged relationship with the colonial administration, found their authority slowly eroded over the years.

In the 1970s, Livingstone thrived as a base for **textile production**, and a vehicle manufacturing plant was also established here. But by the mid-1990s, following the nosedive in the Zambian economy due to the crash in copper prices (see page 309), cars were no longer being made and all but two of the textile factories had closed down. It wasn't until the late 1990s, when the Zambian government started to recognise the potential of **tourism** to contribute to economic development, that Livingstone began to experience renewed growth, especially following the establishment in 2001 of the vast **Sun International resort complexes** (now the AVANI) at the gates of the falls. Other smaller hotels, backpackers and guesthouses followed, and tourism expanded. At the same time, the completion of the **Katima Mulilo Road Bridge** between Namibia and Zambia in 2004 – which provides Pacific port access to landlocked Zambia as part of the Trans Caprivi or Walvis Bay Corridor – has also helped improve tourist infrastructure, and the newly expanded airport looks set to attract more international flights. The waiver of visa fees for visitors from the UK, North America and Australia is another recent incentive to encourage tourism.

The Livingstone Museum

Mosi-oa-Tunya Road • Daily 9am–4.30pm • Charge • Ⓦ museumszambia.org

While the much-vaunted **Livingstone Museum** is Zambia's largest and oldest, it will certainly not set your pulse racing. Still, it is worth delving into, not just to learn more about the famed explorer (see page 326) – the reason most foreign tourists go – but also for what it says about the area's history and people. First established in 1935, the museum has occupied its current, rather ugly building since the 1950s and is organised into five sections. Things kick off in the **archaeology room**, where there is a plaster cast of the Broken Hill skull – the original having been spirited away to the British Museum – unearthed in 1921 and dates back some two hundred thousand years. Next is **ethnography**, in which idealised rural life is pitted against the 'mirage' of urban development. Aspects of traditional life are explained through the important life stages of birth, puberty, marriage and death through photos and artefacts; note the rather gruesome objects of witchcraft, such as the *ndile*, used to exhume corpses. An extensive taxidermy collection follows in the **natural history** section with animals set in their various habitats, but don't miss the impressive display of insects featuring a giant bush locust. A cardboard cutout of Henry Morton Stanley then announces the more recent **Livingstone wing**, which includes some extraordinary memorabilia, including a cast of his humerus, his remarkably well-preserved umbrella and his coat. The objects he collected on his travels were equally eclectic: look out for a portion of hippo jaw, a Nyasaland fishing net and a letter stand. A room detailing the various **peoples** of Zambia follows, tracing their migrations, the advent of colonialism, the subsequent struggle for independence, and post-independence politics, with these last two periods explored mostly through photos and news clippings.

The Railway Museum and The Gateway Jewish Museum

Chishimba Falls Road • Daily 9am–4pm • Charge, including guided tour • Ⓣ 0213 324281

Located on the site of the one-time sawmill of the Zambezi Sawmills Railways – for over fifty years, the longest private railway line in the world – Livingstone's **railway museum** is a somewhat neglected affair and the hefty entrance fee is likely to deter all but keen railway buffs.

The railway took off in 1925 as a cheaper way of transporting timber, which had previously been moved by oxen, then by barge, along the Zambezi. The trains soon began taking passengers as well, who initially made the journey perched precariously on piles of logs – photos of which are on display. However, the heart of the museum lies in the fourteen rusting engines and a handful of carriages in varying stages of decay spread around the grounds, which have been put out to grass; one dilapidated specimen even has a papaya tree growing inside. The hulking brutes on display are second-hand steam engines manufactured in cities like Manchester and Glasgow and shipped to Africa. The oldest engine dates from 1892. Don't miss out on the plush, wood-panelled and leather-seated general manager's carriage – a reminder of the lucrativeness of the timber industry.

A more recent and arguably more compelling on-site attraction is the fascinating, one-room **Gateway Jewish Museum**, which documents the early Jewish immigrant pioneers at the end of the 1800s, whose participation in Zambia's economic and political development is closely entwined with the development of the railway.

Around Livingstone

Tourists who have 'done' the falls, had their fix of adrenaline-fuelled activities and satisfied their wildlife-viewing ambitions are increasingly turning to culture-oriented excursions. Around Livingstone, several villages, such as Mukuni Village, Musokotwani and Simonga, welcome visitors and are willing to afford them glimpses of modern-day village life for a fee. While several operators offer tours, you can miss the crowds and increase your chances of having a less contrived experience by getting there under your own steam and arranging a private tour; better still, go on a bike tour to a less visited village with Local Cowboy Bike Tours (see page 301).

Mukuni Village

15km (9.3 miles) from Livingstone, signposted off the main road just north of the falls • Daily 9am–4pm • Charge including guided tour; tour operator packages also available • ⓣ 0213 324281 • Take a minibus bound for the falls from the town centre, then transfer to a minibus bound for Mukuni, across the road from the entrance to the AVANI; be prepared to wait, as buses only leave when full

About 10km (6.2 miles) southeast of Livingstone as the crow flies lies **Mukuni Village**, where Chief Mukuni, head of the six thousand Leya, holds court when he's not travelling. Forget any thought of seeing a 'traditional village', since its proximity to the falls and inevitably the influx of so many tour groups has left its mark. Even so, tours (1–2hr, depending on interest) are informative and will include the palace, provided the chief's not around, and the giant acacia tree outside, where Livingstone first met Chief Mukuni. The chief refused to greet the explorer in the palace since he was convinced that Livingstone's white skin meant he was a ghost or spirit. Since then, so the story goes, village gatherings have always been held under the tree.

ARRIVAL AND DEPARTURE — LIVINGSTONE

BY PLANE

International flights arrive at the Harry Mwanga Nkumbula International Airport (ⓦ nacl.co.zm) 6km (3.7 miles) northwest of the town centre. Facilities include a money exchange, a post office, an ATM, and desks for several car rental firms (see page 331). There is free wi-fi throughout.

Getting into town There is no regular bus service from the airport into Livingstone, but shuttles from many lodgings in town provide a free pick-up service. Otherwise, a private taxi costs around K100 (US$10) depending on your negotiating skills and whether you're going into town or to accommodation closer to the Zimbabwe border.

FLIGHTS AND AIRLINES

International flights There are no direct flights from Europe, North America or Australasia to Livingstone. Most international visitors fly in via Oliver Tambo International Airport, Johannesburg, from where there are daily connections to Livingstone with South African airline Airlink (ⓦ flyairlink.com). These flights take 1hr 45min and cost from around R9,000 return. The airline also operates a daily flight from Nelspruit, just outside Kruger National Park, South Africa to Livingstone a week (1hr 40min) from around R5,000 one way. Note that flights to and from Nelspruit will be transferred to the new international Kruger Mpumalanga International Airport during the lifetime of this guidebook. It is also possible to reach Livingstone from European destinations by flying via East African hubs such as Addis Ababa (Ethiopia) and Nairobi (Kenya), via the Zambian capital, Lusaka, and then transferring to a domestic flight (see below). Flying with Emirates via Dubai is another possibility. These itineraries are usually cheaper than flights via Johannesburg.

Domestic flights Zambia Airways (ⓦ zambia-airways.com), the country's flag-bearing airline resuscitated in 2021, fly between Lusaka and Livingstone several times a day (1hr 10min) from around K3,800 one way. Proflight (ⓦ proflight-zambia.com) also operates flights on the route.

BY BUS

From/to Lusaka The reliable Mazhandu Family Bus Service (ⓣ 0975 805064) runs several daily services, including an overnight bus, between Lusaka and Livingstone (7hr). The Shalom Bus Service (T097 0833235) also operates buses between Lusaka and Livingstone on a similar timetable. Both bus companies have offices by the market on the corner of Chimwemwe and Zambezi streets in Livingstone, from where their buses depart.

From/to Namibia and Botswana, Shalom and Mazhandu Family Bus Service (ⓣ 0977 805064) have two daily departures from Sesheke, a couple of kilometres from the Namibia border near Katima Mulilo, to Livingstone (3hr). The bus travels via Kazungula, the border with Botswana (from the Namibia border: 2hr). Some taxis connect with Kasane, the gateway to Chobe National Park, from the Botswana side of the Kazungula border.

From/to Zimbabwe Access from and to Zimbabwe is via the border on the Victoria Falls Bridge (see page 313), a few hundred metres downhill from Vic Falls Town, from where there is onward transport to Bulawayo and Harare and beyond to South Africa.

BY CAR

Relatively good tarred roads lead to Livingstone from Lusaka (480km/298.3 miles; 6hr) and from Sesheke (186km/115.6 miles; 3hr), 4km (2.5 miles) from the border with Namibia at Katima Mulilo (daily 7am–6pm). The route from Sesheke goes via the Botswana border at Kazungula (daily 6am–6pm), which lies 63km (39.1 miles) from Livingstone. This border crossing is via a new road bridge –inaugurated in 2021 – across the Zambezi River. The roads are good from Bulawayo and Zimbabwe, although fuel is expensive and hard to acquire, and the roads are now toll-paying. Note also that you will be liable for cross-border vehicle charges and must present the vehicle's papers if you bring a vehicle from another country (see page 296).

BY TRAIN

There are two passenger train services a week between Livingstone and Lusaka (ⓦ zrl.com.zm/passengers), which take forever – over sixteen hours – and are notoriously unreliable. Still, if you fancy an adventure and a chance to chat with people, this is one way to do it. Economy, Standard, Business and Sleeper services are available, and there is a buffet car – but take extra supplies just in case. Departures from Lusaka are on Tuesday and Saturday mornings and from Livingstone on Monday and Friday nights at 8pm. Enquire at the relevant train station (Livingstone: ⓣ 0213 321001; Lusaka: 0211 228023).

GETTING AROUND

By taxi Taxis are plentiful but can be expensive. From the Zimbabwe border or the falls (within 100m/328ft of each other) to town, which is 10km (6.2 miles) away, is US$15–20 per taxi, depending on your negotiating skills and how brisk business is. It's around K50–60 for anywhere around town. Rates are a little higher after dark. A journey between the town centre and the airport costs about US$15, depending on your bartering skills, the exchange rate, transport availability at the time, and where in town you are picked up.

By minibus Minibuses for the border (around every 20–30min, when full) leave from the bus station on Mokambo Road at the junction with Kapondo Street.

On foot It's perfectly possible and safe to wander around central Livingstone on foot during the day, but at night you should take a taxi.

By bike *Fawlty Towers* and *Jollyboys* (see page 332) do bike rental, as does Local Cowboy Cycle Tours (ⓣ 0977 747837; see page 301).

By car Europcar is based at the airport (ⓦ europcarzambia.com). Hemingways (ⓦ hemingwayszambia.com) specialises in four-wheel drive rental and vehicles for people with physical disabilities. Note that if you intend to take your rental car over the border into Botswana (for example), you will be liable for charges (see page 296).

INFORMATION

Livingstone Tourist Centre Mosi-oa-Tunya Road ⓦ zambiatourism.com. Good for a burst of a/c, a friendly face and a glossy brochure with a street map – but you'll probably find your accommodation's activities desk has all the information you need. Mon–Fri 8am–5pm.

ACTIVITIES

Unlike in Vic Falls Town, where most tour operators are concentrated in a block of a few hundred metres, the ones in Livingstone are far more strung out, often operating out of a lodge or hotel or otherwise without a physical address. Although most accommodations usually book activities for you, you might prefer to deal directly with one of the operators listed below to get a combo deal.

Bundu Adventures 1364 Kabompo Rd, at the Gemstone

Restaurant bunduadventures.com. Primarily a rafting company specialising in single- and multiday rafting trips, as well as the rafting and body-boarding combo, and more sedate drifting about in a dinghy above the falls. For US$1,100, you can get the most out of the Zambezi with a six-day trip to Lake Kariba. Also does the swim under the falls.

Livingstone's Adventure livingstonesadventure.com. A group of diverse specialist activity operators now operate under this umbrella organisation, which can offer a river cruise on the *African Queen* or a flight with Batoka Sky microlights. They also lay on canoeing with paddling specialists Makoro Quest (see page 300) and quad biking, fishing or horse riding.

Maano Rafting 5058 John Hunt Way maanoadventures.com. Relatively new locally owned rafting company (but with very experienced rafting guides) offering other activities and transfers, including to Chobe.

Safari Par Excellence Victoria Falls Waterfront Hotel, Sichango Drive safpar.com. Quality operator with experienced rafting team; also does well-regarded overnight and multiday trips. In addition to offering game drives, they have several river cruise vessels of different sizes and can organise transfers on both sides of the border.

Savannah Southern Safaris Olga's, 20 Makambo Rd savannah-southern-safaris.com. Small, community-focused outfit providing knowledgeable, personalised service for private tours, focusing on walking in the bush: birdwatching, nature walks and rhino tracking in the national park. Also does community visits, including to development projects they are involved with.

Zambezi Eco Adventures Victoria Falls Curio Centre zambeziecoadventures.com. The high-wire specialists on this side of the Zambezi will pick up clients from Zimbabwe at the border and include the day visa in the price. The menu includes abseiling, sliding, or swinging alone or in tandem high above the Batoka Gorge. A full day of unlimited fun that finishes off with a trip to Devil's Pool and high tea on Livingstone Island is undoubtedly the best value.

ACCOMMODATION

8

There is a good range of accommodation around – from backpackers' places and guesthouses in **central Livingstone** to high-end lodges and hotels south of town, **near the falls**, and lodges, self-catering and campgrounds further upriver along the Zambezi, **west of town**. Most will do free airport pick-ups, and the backpackers' lodgings nearly all do a free daily run to the falls and will pick up anyone hovering at the border for the return, though you may have to pay if you're not booked in with them. While hideaways west of Livingstone along the Zambezi are delightfully free of the whirring of helicopters, **transfers** to do activities at the falls can rack up. Note that most accommodation keeps the same prices all year round, but a few lodges have **peak season** rates (see page 298). Another point to remember is that you will hear the thumping sounds of *Limpo's Pub & Grill* on certain nights when staying anywhere in central Livingstone.

IN TOWN, SEE MAP PAGE 328

Chapa Classic Lodge 66 Nehru Way chapaclassiclodge.com. Pleasant and excellent value, this non-touristy, locally owned, old-fashioned hotel is spread around tree-filled grounds with an attractive pool area. The 27 tiled rooms are clean and cool (with a/c). Most have a vast TV screen, fridge, tea/coffee facilities and mosquito nets. Enjoy the hearty, full English breakfast. A more recent, less attractive forty-room annex offers pricier, more spacious (though bare) rooms. US$$

★ **Fawlty Towers** 216 Mosi-oa-Tunya Rd adventure-africa.com. The large leafy garden of this backpackers-cum-guesthouse is the real draw – plenty of space to find your quiet spot away from the lively poolside bar if you want. Its range of accommodations, all with mosquito nets, includes quality doubles (with a/c), twins, family rooms and dorms that cater to a range of visitors. The usual backpacker facilities include a kitchen, laundry, free afternoon pancakes and a bar. It offers a daily free shuttle to the falls and has an excellent activities desk. Dorms US$, doubles US$$

Gloria's B&B 19 Ghandi Ave facebook.com/gloriabedandbreakfast. Located in a quiet residential area a ten- to fifteen-minute walk from town (though take a taxi at night), this well-kept guesthouse has a handful of simply furnished rooms (with a/c and fridge), with kitchen available, and a couple of small self-catering bungalows. There's a small pool in the garden. Cash only. B&B US$$

Jollyboys Backpackers 34 Kanyanta Rd, behind the museum backpackzambia.com. Environmentally friendly and socially engaged backpackers with an extremely efficient activities desk and plenty of things to keep you entertained in their fruit tree-filled grounds: have a game of table tennis or pool or grab a paperback from the book exchange and sprawl on the fabulous sunken communal bed. The rooms are a little small: choose from dark, thatched, fan-ventilated A-frames with shared bathrooms or more expensive en-suite doubles with a/c. You can also squeeze in your tent. Plus, the food is tasty too. Camping and dorms US$, doubles US$$

Olga's 20 Makambo Rd olgasproject.com. Heavily involved in community development, *Olga's* is a worthy and pleasant place to stay. Comprising nine no-frills, spacious thatched rooms with ceiling fans, private bathrooms, and comfortable beds. The cons are the traffic noise, the sporadically loud church bells and the lack of a really comfortable communal area. Rates vary depending on the season. B&B US$$

Tabonina Guesthouse 3 Maisoko Rd taboninaguesthouse.com. Owned by a French-Zambian couple, this homely place is set around a delightful flower-filled garden with a small pool. A pleasant social area under thatch has a bar, pool table, darts board, and a small TV lounge. Spotless, compact double and family rooms with a/c have good mattresses and small bathrooms – some a little old. For the budget-conscious, a shared bathroom is possible, and they have an annexe down the street, offering cheaper fan-ventilated accommodation. Camping US$, doubles B&B US$$

Victoria Falls (formerly Livingstone) Backpackers 559 Mokambo Rd livingstonebackpackers.com. This great place has friendly staff, pleasant chill-out areas, and a pool and climbing wall. On the downside, the mattresses in the rooms are variable and some of the fans are tiny in the cheaper rooms with shared bathrooms. You can squeeze in a tent here or they'll lend you one (for free). Camping US$, dorms US$, doubles US$$

Zigzag Plot 239 Industrial Rd 0213 22814. An unpromising street address belies a welcoming guesthouse on a quiet road just off the main drag, a fifteen-minute walk south of town. The real draw is the lovely shady garden filled with mango trees (where you can eat lunch) and a pool and children's play area. Rooms are well maintained if small, dated and dark, but the a/c works well, and you can drink water fresh from their borehole. B&B US$$

SOUTH OF TOWN, SEE MAPS PAGES 306 AND 310

AVANI Victoria Falls Resort Formerly the Zambezi Sun; 393 Mosi-oa-Tunya Rd avanihotels.com/victoria-falls. A sprawling behemoth of a hotel with 212 smart business hotel-style rooms and suites with the usual amenities: a/c, Wi-fi, satellite TV, phone, safe, tea- and coffee-making facilities and vast beds. Despite the slightly sterile feel of the rooms, the resort's large-scale fantasy African decor and architectural touches remind you where you are. Dining options include two restaurants (one serving a huge buffet breakfast), two cafés and a bar beside a lagoon-sized pool. But the real plus is that it's bang next to the falls, with unlimited free access to the Smoke that Thunders. B&B US$$$

Munga Ecolodge Signposted east off Mosi-oa-Tunya Rd, 3.5km south of the town centre mungaecolodge.com. Surrounded by bush, this eco-lodge uses some solar power and has a naturally filtered swimming pool surrounded by reeds, bulrushes and waterlilies as the centrepiece. Five cosy stone-and-thatch chalets painted in earthy tones have outdoor showers and a private sun-bathing courtyard at the back, where you can sleep under the stars as the whim takes you. Full board is also possible. Reductions in low season. B&B US$$$

The Stanley Safari Lodge Off the road to Mukuni Village robinpopesafaris.net. Three kilometres (1.9 miles) from the falls as the fish eagle flies, this elegant lodge is about indulgence. When the Zambezi is in full flow, you can loll in the glorious infinity pool, sipping your cocktail and watching the distant clouds of spray. Choose from ten lovely stone suites and cottages. Eschew the comfort of the a/c for the open-sided accommodation that lets in the sounds of the bush. AI US$$$$$

Victoria Falls Waterfront (formerly the Zambezi Waterfront) Sichango Drive, 8km (5 miles) by road from the falls safpar.com/lodges/victoria-falls waterfront. Known affectionately as 'the Waterfront', this is the most affordable riverside option in the area. It offers camping (in your own or one of their tents) and chalet accommodation spread out in luscious grounds on the banks of the great river. A-frame chalets comprising three en-suite doubles are comfortable but simple; you pay for the location, which is worth forking out the extra cost for the riverside view. Their two-bed domed tents have a light, a padlock and a small fan, but they can still get very hot. Though camping rates are good, the bar-restaurant, which offers great sunset views and can get lively to rowdy, still charges tourist rates. The hotel is located in the park, so you must pay an extra US$10 park fee per night. Camping US$, dome tents (B&B) US$$, doubles (B&B) US$$$

8

WEST OF TOWN, SEE MAP PAGE 306

★ Toka Leya Camp Parks Road, Mosi-oa-Tunya National Park, 5km (3.1 miles) from Livingstone, off the M10m, South Africa wilderness-safaris.com. Twelve lovely, luxurious safari tents (with a/c) set back slightly from the Zambezi with inside and outside showers and private decks. However, the best views are from the fabulous communal areas and infinity pool, which are bang on the river. There's even a gym overlooking the rapids and a small spa. Top-notch service, dining, and plenty of activities, including a tour of the falls. AI US$$$$

TONGABEZI, SEE MAP PAGE 306

★ Sindabezi Island greensafaris.com/sindabezi. Brimming with romance and a short boat ride downriver from *Tongabezi Lodge* (same ownership), this private island hosts five idyllic open-sided thatched chalets on raised wooden decks; you can watch the water glide past without getting out of bed. Fine dining is by lamplight as you push your toes into the white sand. US$$$$$

★ Tongabezi Lodge On the Zambezi, 15km (9.3 miles) west of Livingstone, off the M10 greensafaris.com/tongabezi. A stunning setting for a collection of sumptuous, individually decorated cottages and houses featuring fabulous African furnishings and artefacts; each has a private deck overlooking the river and a personal concierge. Service and organic cuisine are top-notch, and the place oozes relaxed indulgence: private dining – even on a sampan on the river – outdoor baths and personal plunge pools. Then there's the *Lookout* – a delightful over-the-water lounge – perfect for sundowners and wildlife viewing. AI US$$$$$

EATING

SEE MAP PAGE 328

There aren't too many places to eat out in Livingstone, but the quality of what's available is good and the food is varied, though prices are on the high side.

★ **Café Zambezi** 217 Mosi-oa-Tunya Rd ⓣ 0978 978578. Expect a varied menu of African and Caribbean dishes – plus good music – in this vibey rear courtyard, where seating is at picnic tables that are candlelit at night. Choose from the likes of *jollof* rice, groundnut, goat stew or jerk chicken with *nshima* (like porridge), or excellent chips and veg for not much. Pizzas and burgers also feature. Good wi-fi. K$$

Da Canton Mosi-oa-Tunya Road ⓣ 0953 709666. The Italian owner orchestrates inexpensive pizzas and home-made pasta dishes, though he also offers a little goat or fish with *nshima* on the side. Pass through the unpromising-looking bar to a thatched barn-like structure laden with local artwork. Pick up an authentic home-made gelato on the way out. K$–$$

The Golden Leaf 1174 Mosi-oa-Tunya Rd ⓣ 0213 321266. This is a very popular Indian restaurant with the usual naan and roti accompaniments and a good spread of vegetarian options. There's both indoor and outdoor seating on a nice breezy terrace. K$$

Kubu Café Mosi-oa-Tunya Square ⓦ facebook.com/KubuCafe. Under a leafy trellis just outside Shoprite, the service is usually good, but the food quality is variable. In addition to the usual eggs, bacon and sausage fry-up, you can indulge in eggs Benedict or a healthy yoghurt, fruit and muesli mix. Lunchtime offerings include wraps, gourmet burgers and salads, while succulent flame-grilled meats and chicken curry are evening highlights. K$$

Munali Café 357 Mosi-oa-Tunya Rd ⓣ 021 320602. Centrally located, this basic cafeteria and bakery serving cheap food pulls in a steady flow of locals throughout the day. In addition to full-fried breakfasts and pastries, it has a surprisingly good variety of coffees, including espresso. N$

Olga's 20 Mokambo Rd ⓦ olgasproject.com. With profits going to support the Youth Community Training Centre, it's hard to resist the delicious, home-made pasta dishes and tasty thin-crust pizzas – try the crocodile one – or naughty breakfasts, such as chocolate crêpe with ice cream, all served under fan-ventilated thatch. N$$

★ **Zest Bar & Restaurant** 2616 Mosi-oa-Tunya Rd ⓦ facebook/zestbarandrestaurant. This is a very popular bar-resto, with a beer garden out back, a sports screen, table football, and some delicious food. The wide-ranging menu includes succulent *espetadas* – char-grilled skewers of meat marinated in chimichurri sauce – but also some appetising veggie options and local favourites. N$$

8

DRINKING AND NIGHTLIFE

SEE MAP PAGE 328

Most nightlife doesn't get going until the weekend, hotting up on Thursday and letting rip on Friday and Saturday. Though places are often open during the day, you'll need to wait until at least 10pm for much sign of life.

Club Fairmount New Fairmount Hotel, Mosi-oa-Tunya Road. This rather staid-looking hotel hosts the town's most enduring nightclub, with a laser and plasma-screen-filled disco and lounge bar drawing a clientele of varying ages and offering a bit of everything from *kwassa kwassa* through classic disco hits to hip-hop. DJs on Friday and Saturday. Entry charge from 11pm, though the price often increases as the night wears on! Thurs–Sat

Limpo's Pub & Grill Mosi-oa-Tunya Road ⓦ facebook.com/limpospubandgrilllivingstone. This is a semi-open venue, with a buzzing bar with beer on tap and a pool table under thatch, where you can get a Mosi or Castle for under a dollar. There are sports screens, a stage for live music or DJ and live music from Wednesday to Saturday, which you're likely to hear wherever you're staying in the centre of town whether you want to or not. There's even a barber's and car wash on site.

SHOPPING

For **souvenirs**, head for the line of Mukuni Crafts stalls at the northern end of Mosi-oa-Tunya Road by Mukuni Park. Most offerings are bought in bulk from Mukuni Village (see page 330), where you'll inevitably get a cheaper deal. The other place to pick up a curio is down by the falls; traders at the **curio market** by the entrance also source most of their goods from Mukuni Village, though some come from further afield, including from outside Zambia. Alternatively, browse the **shops** in some smarter hotels, which usually charge more but generally stock goods of more consistent quality. For a taste of market life, head for **Maramba market** down the road of the same name.

DIRECTORY

Banks and money Several of the big banks, including Barclays and Standard Chartered, are in the central area of Mosi-oa-Tunya Road, just north of the museum. They have ATMs, will advance your money against a Visa or MasterCard credit card, and can change currency. Banking hours are usually Mon–Fri 8.15am–3.30pm, Sat 8.15–11.30am.

Hospitals/clinics Livingstone Central Hospital, Akapelwa Street (T 0213 321475); Dr Shafik's Hospital Katete Avenue (T 0213 321130).
Internet Free wi-fi is widely available in accommodations, though it's not necessarily very fast.
Pharmacy Link Pharmacy (Mon–Sat 9am–6pm, Sun 10am–2pm; T 0213 324222), on Mosi-oa-Tunya Square next to the *Kubu Café*, is well stocked.
Police The police station (T 0213 323575) is on Maramba Road by Davidson Avenue.
Post office Mosi-oa-Tunya Road; Mon–Fri 8am–6pm, Sat 8am–2pm.
Supermarkets Shoprite in Mosi-oa-Tunya Square, opposite *Fawlty Towers*, is the main supermarket. For fresh fruit and vegetables, head for the market stalls along Mokambo Road and round the bus station on Chimwemwe Road.
Telephones If you have a locked mobile phone, find an MTN shop on the main street and they will unlock it for free if they can; otherwise, they will refer you to a specialist. Zambian SIM cards are readily available for next to nothing.

HEROES' ACRE, WINDHOEK

Contexts

History

Namibia's pre-colonial history is bound up with its geography, dominated by its arid landscape across which humans have migrated for thousands of years. Gradually, the central and southern regions became home to semi-nomadic foragers and pastoralists, while the more fertile north was characterised by small kingdoms based on agriculture and cattle farming. The opening up of trade in the mid- to late-eighteenth century and the arrival of Christianity had a profound effect on the country. Still, it was only with the 'Scramble for Africa' in the late 1880s that the modern borders of Namibia were drawn up. Ruled over with brutality first by Germany and then by neighbouring South Africa, Namibia's independence only came after a bitter and protracted struggle on 21 March 1990. Since then, it has enjoyed a relatively stable democratic political system, though widening inequalities in access to land and employment, exacerbated by increasing drought coupled with unaired grievances related to the independence struggle, may threaten this stability in the future.

The early settlers

The oldest evidence of human settlement in Namibia (and in Southern Africa) is the **rock art** of south Namibia, with the decorated slabs of the Apollo 11 Cave dating back more than 25,000 years. The original **Stone Age** inhabitants who arrived here after the last Ice Age (which peaked around 18,000 years ago) are assumed to have been nomadic hunter-gatherers, referred to as either **San** or Bushmen, who spoke languages from the Khoisan language group characterised by the use of click consonants (see page 365). The oldest examples of rock art from this period are the paintings and engravings in **Twyfelfontein (|Ui-|Ais)**, which date back at least six thousand years. Around 2000 to 2500 years ago, it's thought that **Khoikhoi** pastoralists (ancestors of today's Nama, known pejoratively in colonial times as Hottentots) migrated from present-day Botswana and settled in the area, bringing with them pottery and their sheep and cattle. The Khoikhoi produced the later rock art at Twyfelfontein. After the ninth century, the **Damara** people are known to have settled in the grasslands of central Namibia, although their origins are unknown.

In the north, in the rich agricultural land along the Kunene River, the **Owambo** and other Bantu-speaking groups gradually established centralised (mostly matrilineal) monarchies by at least the seventeenth century. They remained outside colonial control until 1909. Other Bantu-speaking groups, such as the **Herero**, only reached northern and central Namibia in the mid-sixteenth century. They kept cattle and were organised in decentralised clans, each under a leader whose power was heavily

Over 25,000 years ago	**Over 6,000 years ago**	**1486**
The earliest signs of human settlement in Apollo 11 Cave	Post-Ice Age, Khoisan speakers are the first to arrive: the San/Bushmen, followed by the Khoikhoi, then the Nama	Portuguese explorer Diago Cão, the first European in Namibia, lands at Cape Cross

circumscribed by the other clan leaders. Strong single leaders emerged only when groups such as the Oorlam migrated northwards into Namibia from the Cape in the early nineteenth century. But by this point, the impact of colonialism and the trade in enslaved people, ivory and cattle, not to mention arms and alcohol, was already beginning to cause tensions within southwest Africa.

Early European contact

The coastline of Namibia first became known to Portuguese explorers in the 1480s. First, **Diago Cão** landed north of Walvis Bay in 1486 and erected a limestone cross at Cape Cross (see page 226), then **Bartolomeu Dias** anchored at Walvis Bay and Angra Pequeña (Lüderitz). However, Namibia's famously bleak coastline successfully deterred Europeans from attempting to settle (or even trade) until the second half of the eighteenth century. 'So inhospitable and so barren a country is not to be equalled except in the Deserts of Arabia' was the opinion of the captain of HMS *Nautilus* in 1786 while scouting the coastline for a suitable place for a penal colony. It wasn't until 1793 that the first land grab took place when the Dutch annexed **Walvis Bay**. Two years later, the British took the Cape Colony from the Dutch and, the following year, claimed Walvis Bay for themselves. Africans along Namibia's coastline had traded with European shipping for some time. Still, the advent of whaling off Namibia – which started in the late seventeenth century but peaked between 1790 and 1810 – led to a significant increase in the volume of trade centred on Walvis Bay.

The arrival of the Oorlam

From the 1790s, the **Oorlam** began to emerge, migrating north in ever-greater numbers. The Oorlam were of mixed heritage, the descendants of Khoikhoi, European and enslaved peoples, who, through acculturation in the Cape, now dressed as Europeans and spoke Afrikaans and Khoisan. They had ceased to be exclusively pastoralists, possessed guns, oxen and wagons and engaged in cattle raiding. Their influence on Indigenous peoples in the area was far greater at that time than that of any European missionaries or traders. Namibia's oldest systematically designed and built structure is at ||Khauxa!nas. It was erected around 1795 by the leader of the Oorlam, **Klaas Afrikaner**, who had fled the Cape Colony, accused of murder. The Oorlam inhabited the settlement until the 1820s before moving further northwards.

Meanwhile, in 1806, two missionaries from the London Missionary Society built the first **church** in Namibia, in Warmbad (|Aixa-aibes). This didn't initially go down well with the local Oorlam, and the missionaries had to flee after an attack by Jager Afrikaner (Klaas' son) in 1811. After numerous setbacks, the German Protestant Rhenish Missionary Society (RMS) emerged as the dominant mission society in the region, having established their first mission in Bethanien (|Ui‡gandes) in 1814. Relations between the RMS and the Oorlam proved difficult, and conversion rates remained very slow. The missionaries became an important part of Namibian society, creating mission stations, providing food and shelter to the impoverished, and acting as power brokers between groups. The mission stations, in turn, attracted traders – predominantly Afrikaners – who set up trading posts. The RMS and other missionaries were also instrumental in promoting European and Christian values: rigid

1600s–1700s	1793	1790s	1814
Bantu-speaking peoples, such as the Owambo then the Herero, migrate down from East Africa	The Dutch make the first European land grab, founding Walvis Bay, which the British soon annexes	The cattle-raiding Oorlam arrive from the Cape in increasing numbers	The first Rhenish Missionary Society mission is established in Bethanien

sexual mores, literacy, square houses and Victorian-style clothes – inspiration for the 'traditional' Herero, Damara and Nama dresses today. In the same period, the mining trade in ivory and ostrich feathers, arms and cattle increased, and the frequently cash-strapped missionaries played a pivotal role in this commerce.

Nama-Herero conflicts

The northward migration of the Oorlam caused conflict with the other Nama groupings in southern Namibia, such as the **Bondelswarts**, who were defeated by the Oorlam in 1823 and, in 1830, became the first local grouping to sign a protection treaty with the Cape government. By the 1840s, the greatest of the Nama-Oorlam clan leaders, **Jonker Afrikaner** (grandson of Klaas), had established a de facto state in southern and central Namibia, centred on Windhoek and had two thousand armed men at his disposal. Jonker enriched his followers by raiding cattle and people and trading in them, simultaneously impoverishing the local Herero and San groups.

When Jonker died in 1861, the Herero under **Maharero** (also known as Kamaharero) rebelled, with the encouragement of the local white traders and missionaries, and began the bloodiest conflict so far on Namibian soil, which aimed to break the dominance of the Nama-Oorlam, now under Christian Afrikaner (Jonker's son). At the **Battle of Otjimbingwe** in 1863, Christian Afrikaner died along with two hundred Nama-Oorlam against around sixty Herero. This battle heralded a series of further violent clashes and cattle raids, in which the balance of power began to tip away from the Nama-Oorlam. A period of Herero dominance followed in central Namibia, formally marked by the signing of the **Okahandja peace accords** in 1870, brokered by German missionaries, between Jan Jonker Afrikaner (Christian's brother) and Maharero. The peace accords also permitted the Basters (see page 141) to settle in Rehoboth. The threat of more Boer trekkers migrating from the Transvaal prompted Maharero and other Herero leaders to formally request British protection in 1874. The Cape government was quite interested in extending its control over Namibia and set up the **Palgrave Commission** to canvas opinion in Namibia. Still, the British government was not keen to increase its responsibilities and, in the end, only annexed Walvis Bay and the offshore islands in 1878.

German rule 1884–1915

With the British reluctant to venture further inland from Walvis Bay, the Germans took the initiative. In 1883, the Bremen tobacco merchant **Adolf Lüderitz** bought the anchorage and land around Angra Pequeña for £100 in gold and two hundred rifles, thus founding the first permanent colonial settlement in Namibia. Three months later, he bought another 140km (87 miles) of coastline for £500 and sixty rifles, hoodwinking the local Nama-Oorlam group, the Bethanie people, into including 80km (49.7 miles) inland, too. Thus, **Lüderitzland** was founded, and in 1884 Lüderitz asked Germany for protection (against the British). The German Chancellor, Otto von Bismarck, hesitated until he was sure the British had no colonial ambitions in the area. Then, on 7 August 1884, the crews of two naval vessels raised the German flag at Angra Peqeña, Swakopmund, Cape Cross and Cape Frio, thus laying claim to the entire coast from the Orange to the Kunene rivers and establishing the German protectorate of **Deutsch-Südwestafrika** or German South-West Africa (SWA). Lüderitz then bought up the

1840s	**1862–70**	**1870**	**1884**
Nama-Orlaam Jonker Afrikaner secures control of central and southern Namibia	The Nama-Herero wars are waged; the Herero under Maharero, the Nama-Oorlam under Christian, then Jan Jonker Afrikaner	The Okahandja peace accords are signed between the Nama and Herero	Adolf Lüderitz establishes the first permanent German settlement

rest of the coastline north to Angola, bankrupted himself and in 1885 sold the lot to the Deutsche Kolonial-Gesellschaft für Südwest-Afrika (that he had set up), and then, the following year, drowned in a boating accident in the Orange River.

Raising the flags was the easy bit; asserting German authority over the interior would take over twenty years. The incredibly tiny cadre of German officials started by offering 'protection treaties with African elites in southern and central Namibia in exchange for land and the right to trade and mine. However, the military who would have had to afford such protection did not arrive until 1888, and the German state did not agree to pay for the running of the state until 1892.

The first group to sign a 'Treaty of Friendship and Protection', on 11 October 1884 were the Basters – a group of mostly (and proudly) mixed descent (the word is a corruption of 'bastard') – who had set up the **Free Republic of Rehoboth** in 1872 in southern Namibia, after trekking northwards from the Cape Colony. The first imperial commissioner, **Dr Heinrich Göring** (father of the Nazi air chief), secured the biggest coup, getting Maharero to sign up so that by 1885 most of the people of central and southern Namibia had entered into formal relations with the Germans.

Early resistance to German authority

The first notable resistance to German rule came from the new Nama leader, **Hendrik Witbooi**, a charismatic, religious visionary who refused to negotiate with the colonists. Through armed conflict and persuasion, Witbooi slowly became the dominant leader in the south for the next two decades. It was to protect themselves against Witbooi that many of the clans of central and southern Namibia (including Maharero) had signed treaties with the Germans. Meanwhile, in the north of the country, tensions erupted over the arrival of Boer trekkers from the Transvaal who attempted to settle in Owamboland, buying 50,000 sq km (19,305 sq miles) from the Owambo chief Kambonde. The **Republic of Upingtonia** was declared on 20 October 1885 and named after the leader of the Cape Colony, Thomas Upington (whose protection they hoped but failed to secure). Having withstood more or less daily attacks from other disgruntled groups, including the local San, their leader William Jordan was murdered in 1887, and the republic was dissolved and placed under German protection.

In 1888, Maharero withdrew from the protection treaty with Germany, forcing Dr Göring to retreat from Otjimbingwe to Walvis Bay. The German government sent out **Curt von François** and twenty Schutztruppe (protectorate troops) to try and restore colonial authority; when the force was increased to fifty, Maharero was persuaded to re-sign the protection treaty.

German consolidation

The biggest obstacle to German rule now was the great southern leader, Hendrik Witbooi, whose status was boosted with the death of his great Herero rival, Maharero, in 1890. In April 1893, encouraged by the arrival of extra Schutztruppe, von François launched a surprise attack on Witbooi's headquarters at **Hoornkrans**, killing many of his followers (including women and children). Witbooi escaped with around two hundred fighters, and it took over a year of guerrilla warfare before he finally agreed to sign the Treaty of Gurus in 1894, granting him a degree of independence in return for supplying troops to fight on the side of the Germans. This agreement was just one of a number of

1884	**1884–88**	**1888**	**1894**
Germany claims German South-West Africa as a colony	Local groups are forced into signing treaties of 'friendship and protection' with the Germans	The first Schutztruppe arrive in Namibia to ensure compliance	Nama leader Hendrik Witbooi finally surrenders by signing the Treaty of Gurus

diplomatic (and military) victories ruthlessly achieved by the new head of German colonial administration, **Theodor Leutwein**, whose stated goal was 'colonialism without bloodshed'. The conditions were finally right for German settlers to arrive in SWA in some numbers, and an infrastructure of roads, railways and harbours began to take shape due to the backbreaking work undertaken by African labourers throughout the 1890s. This necessitated the start of large numbers of contract workers being brought down from the north and stricter controls over the movement of the Black populace, including introducing the pass system in certain areas, which anticipated its more widespread institution after the Namibian War. However, with the arrival of **rinderpest** (cattle disease) in 1897, the country was catapulted into a major crisis. The epidemic caused untold suffering among African pastoralists, while settler cattle losses were much lower, as they were given priority (and were more receptive) when vaccinating cattle.

The Namibian war of resistance and genocide 1903–09

Small-scale armed resistance to German rule continued to flare periodically after the rinderpest crisis, as the Germans bought up land for newly arriving German colonists from the devastated farming communities of the **Herero**. By 1904, the Herero had reached breaking point, and in January of that year, taking advantage of an uprising in the south by the Bondelswarts, they staged a full-scale rebellion. Under the leadership of **Samuel Maharero** (son of Maharero), Herero fighters attacked remote German farms across central SWA. They killed as many as 150 Germans, sparing the women, children, and missionaries. The Germans were taken by surprise, and for the next few months, Leutwein struggled to try and defeat the Herero, who now controlled most of central SWA (apart from the garrisons and towns). In June, Leutwein was relieved of his post, and Wilhelm II sent **Lothar von Trotha** out to SWA to put down the uprising 'with rivers of blood and money'. As many as twenty thousand Schutztruppe were sent to the country to ensure it.

The colony thrives and falls.

Following the war, the Germans set about creating a disciplined labour force to supply the country's mines, recruiting from the defeated and displaced African population. They colonised the lands now free of the Herero and Nama, increasing the number of German farms threefold and the German settler population from five thousand to fifteen thousand, with some 21 percent of the country now allocated to commercial farms. For the first time, the Germans began bringing **Owambo Kings** in the north under their control by obtaining declarations of obedience. On the Kaiser's birthday in 1912, on the site of the concentration camp in Windhoek, the victors erected the **Reiterdenkmal**, an equestrian monument of a Schutztruppe, to commemorate the soldiers and settlers who had died in the conflict (see page 86). In the same year, exports exceeded imports for the first time, and SWA became the only German colony ever to make a profit, helped in part by the discovery of diamonds near Lüderitz in 1908 (see page 124) but more by the constant, widespread exploitation and forced labour from the African population.

With the outbreak of **World War I**, the dream came to an abrupt end. The border between German SWA and South Africa became a flash point, with several border skirmishes (and even a Boer uprising supporting Germany). Between September and December 1914, Louis Botha (the South African prime minister at the time) and Jan Smuts – later to become South Africa's prime minister – led over thirty thousand

1897	**1904–09**	**1904**	**1905**
The rinderpest wipes out almost all cattle, causing major suffering among African populations	The Herero and Nama rise up against the German colonists	Over ten thousand Herero die of starvation after being forced into the desert following defeat at the Battle of Omakari	Hendrik Witbooi dies in battle fighting the Germans

THE GENOCIDE

The collective punishment against the Herero and Nama peoples between 1904 and 1907 was one of the first genocides of the twentieth century, in which tens of thousands perished.

German military commander **Lothar von Trotha** spent several months building up supplies and troops to surround the Herero in the Waterberg Plateau. Then, on 11 August 1904, at the **Battle of Omahakari** (also known as the Battle of Waterberg), four thousand heavily armed Schutztruppe attacked around six thousand Herero fighters, defending some forty thousand women and children. Hopelessly outgunned, the Herero managed to retreat into the desert to the east, where ten thousand died of starvation and thirst. The Germans denied the Herero access to the waterholes on the edge of the desert. On 2 October, Trotha issued his infamous **Extermination Order** stating that 'within the German boundaries, every Herero, whether found armed or unarmed, with or without cattle, will be shot' – though this order was belatedly revoked in Berlin. Samuel Maharero and a small number of followers made it to Botswana and were granted asylum by the British; the rest were rounded up in concentration camps, including the so-called 'death camp' on Shark Island off Lüderitz (see page 127), and used as slave labour to build the railways. More than half of those imprisoned died, and altogether, it's estimated around 65,000 Herero (80 percent of the population) perished in the conflict.

Just as the Herero were being exterminated in the east, an alliance of several groups of **Nama** rose up in the south under leaders such as the veteran Hendrik Witbooi, who died in the fighting in October 1905, and **Jacob Morenga**, nicknamed the 'Black Napoleon' by the Germans, who was eventually killed by combined German-British forces in 1907. The struggle against the Nama continued until 1909 because, after every German victory, the Nama dispersed and employed guerrilla tactics to continue the fight. As the war dragged on, Trotha was relieved of his post but sailed back to Germany to a hero's welcome.

Trotha's replacement was the first civilian governor, **Friedrich von Lindequist**, who successfully completed the ethnic cleansing of the Herero, persuaded the Nama to surrender, and then sent them to concentration camps to be used as enslaved labourers. Again, the unspoken policy was to exterminate them as a people. By the war's end, an estimated ten thousand Nama (50 percent of the population) had been killed. Those who survived were forced into 'native territories' in a policy that both anticipated the ghettoes of the Nazi Holocaust and the 'bantustans' of apartheid.

In 2021, the German and Namibian governments reached an agreement that saw Germany officially acknowledge the Herero-Nama genocide and pledge 1.1 billion euros in aid and development for Nama and Herero communities over thirty years to achieve 'genuine reconciliation'. While the Namibian government has accepted the apology and the promised money, the Nama and Herero descendants have been left singularly unimpressed, especially since they were never involved in the negotiations. They also want financial reparations paid directly to them as they fear, with some justification, that they are unlikely to see the benefits. They have taken the matter to Namibia's high court.

troops of the South African Army into Namibia. Heavily outnumbered, the Germans retreated and eventually agreed to an unconditional surrender at **Khorab** on 9 July 1915 – so, without much of a struggle, 31 years of German colonial rule came to an inglorious end.

By 1909	**1908**	**1915**	**1915**
In total, almost 80 percent of the Herero and 50 percent of the Nama populations are killed in battle or die later in concentration camps	Diamonds are discovered in Lüderitz	Following the outbreak of World War I, Jan Smuts leads thirty thousand South African troops into German South-West Africa	The Germans surrender

South African rule 1915–90

The first five years of South African rule were relatively liberal in the **Police Zone** (central and southern SWA) despite being exercised by a military government based in Windhoek. Yet it was ruthless in the north, though much of the work had been done for the regime by the appalling famine of 1914–15, which caused thousands to die of starvation, while those who survived were considerably weakened. Thus, the South Africans could establish a base in Ondonga without bloodshed. However, King Mandume Ya Mandemufayo in neighbouring Oukwanyama resisted South African control and paid for it with his life.

After the war, all of Germany's colonies were forfeited. In 1920, South-West Africa became a **League of Nations Mandate**, a 'trust territory' assigned to South Africa to look after on behalf of the British. The country was never officially annexed but was administered initially as a de facto province of South Africa, its white minority having representation in the whites-only parliament of South Africa, its administrative buildings flying the South African flag. It was granted greater autonomy much later. The South African economic priority in Namibia was to recruit cheap African labour for the region's mines and to subsidise poor Afrikaner settlements in the Police Zone.

Racial segregation and resistance

The interwar South African state also sought to systematically impose racial segregation on Namibia; building on earlier restrictions introduced by the Germans, they created '**native reserves**' (precursors of apartheid's bantustans) in the early 1920s – these reserves were mostly on marginal, arid land, and became places of extreme poverty. At the same time, white settlers were invited in from South Africa and given significant farming concessions and plenty of support to kick-start their enterprises. Over the next twenty years, African populations within the Police Zone, in particular, were further oppressed through greater **restrictions on movement** through the pass system and curfews, unfair **taxes**, and **restricted trading rights**. In the far north, the large population was squeezed into the small strip of land above the newly instituted Red Line, ostensibly a veterinary fence marking the official northern border of the Police Zone. Overpopulation, droughts and food shortages drove larger numbers of men to migrate south as labourers on white farms, in mines or on infrastructural developments.

South African rule met sporadic resistance, with the **Bondelswarts** being the first to take up arms in 1922. The South Africans were taking no chances, however, and the SWA Administrator himself led the attack, with two planes from Pretoria bombing the Bondelswarts into submission, killing one hundred and wounding more than 450 (out of a population of one thousand). The **Rehoboth Basters**' rebellion in 1924 was also put down by the South African armed forces, who marched into the town, backed by warplanes, and arrested six hundred people.

World War II and apartheid

During **World War II**, South Africa extended its control over the country, interning around a thousand German males, incorporating the police into the South African Police, and switching the local currency to the South African Rand. With the League of Nations superseded by the **United Nations (UN)** in 1945, South African Prime Minister Jan Smuts asked permission to officially rule SWA as a fifth province, using the

1920	Early 1920s	1939–45
Under a League of Nations mandate, South-West Africa is officially placed under South African control on behalf of the British	South Africa establishes 'native reserves' for the Black population, dispossessing them of land and violently crushing rebellions	Many Black Namibians fight with the South African army against Nazi Germany

results of a dubious referendum held among Africans in Namibia to support his argument. When the UN refused, South Africa went ahead anyway, formally **annexing** the country in 1947. In 1948, the National Party came to power in South Africa and began to establish **apartheid** or racial segregation, both in South Africa and Namibia.

Early independence movements and the formation of SWAPO

In 1957, migrant Owambo labourers in Cape Town – among them **Andimba Toivo Ya Toivo**, a pivotal figure in the independence movement before being incarcerated on Robben Island – formed the opposition **Owamboland People's Congress (OPC)**. This was followed in 1959 by establishing a group within Namibia, the Ovamboland People's Organisation (OPO), founded in Windhoek by **Sam Nujoma**. At the same time, the Herero-dominated South-West Africa National Union (SWANU) became the first political party to be formed in Namibia, co-founded by **Chief Hosea Komombumbi Kutako**. Throughout the 1950s, the South African authorities had been passing further apartheid legislation but had implemented only a limited number of forced removals. But the protests that followed the attempted relocation of Windhoek's Black population to Katutura – and their violent aftermath (see page 90) – proved to be a watershed moment, prompting Nujoma and other OPO leaders to go into exile and establish a broader nationalist movement. The **South-West Africa People's Organization (SWAPO)**, formed in 1960, became the dominant force in the liberation movement and the only one recognised by the Organization of African Unity (OAU).

Negotiations with the UN

Because of Namibia's history as a League of Nations mandate and the fact that much of the political opposition was now in exile, the **United Nations (UN)** and the **International Court of Justice (ICJ)** became an important focus in the campaign for self-determination for Namibia and remained so until independence. In 1960, Ethiopia and Liberia – free African nations that had been League of Nations members – brought a case against South Africa to the ICJ to try and get their occupation of Namibia ruled illegal. When the ICJ finally made a judgement in 1966, the case was controversially kicked out, so the UN took up the baton and revoked South Africa's mandate.

In 1963, to deflect international criticism, South Africa set up the **Odendaal Commission**, which recommended that the best way forward was an intensification of apartheid and the creation of new bantustans (homelands) for particular non-white ethnic groups, such as Owamboland and Damaraland. These were established in Namibia from 1968 onwards. However, more than half the country was reserved for the white minority on the most agriculturally profitable land and in areas that included most of the territory's mineral wealth.

South Africa's intransigence led directly to the beginning of the armed struggle by SWAPO's military wing, the **People's Liberation Army of Namibia** (**PLAN**), which had been founded in 1962. On 26 August 1966, eight helicopters of the South African Defence Force (SADF) attacked a PLAN guerrilla base in Omugulugwombashe, northern Namibia – an event now commemorated by a public holiday in Namibia known as **Heroes' Day**.

In 1971, the ICJ finally ruled South Africa's occupation of Namibia unlawful, prompting the two foremost Lutheran Church leaders to write an open letter to the South African prime minister supporting Namibian independence. This was followed

1947

South Africa formally annexes South-West Africa, having rejected the UN demand to hand back control of the land

1948

The National Party comes to power in South Africa and begins apartheid policies there, exerting greater control over Namibia

1960

SWAPO is formed by Andimba Toivo Ya Toivo and Sam Nujoma. Nujoma is forced into exile in Angola by a prolonged **general strike** of contract workers and campaigns against the bantustan police by SWAPO's Youth League.

The independence struggle intensifies

The successful campaign for **Angolan independence** from Portugal in 1975 increased pressure on South Africa to withdraw from Namibia – but their response was to step up their military campaign against SWAPO, attacking their bases in southern Angola. Along with the US and Zaire, South Africa became heavily involved in supporting **Jonas Savimbi's UNITA** (National Union for the Total Independence of Angola), whose armed wing was engaged in a civil war against the new Soviet/Cuban-backed MPLA government in Luanda, the capital of Angola. Whenever Namibian independence came up, the Americans would always link it to the withdrawal of Cuban troops from Angola. This 'Linkage', as it became known, was the biggest stumbling block to Namibian independence – the country was effectively at the mercy of the ongoing Cold War between the US and the Soviet Bloc.

The message that the fight was against communism was also a key propaganda strategy in ensuring the continuous enlistment of recruits – both white and non-white – for both the SADF and, later, the **South-West Africa Territorial Force** (SWATF). While white males were automatically conscripted into the army, with stiff jail penalties if they refused, non-whites 'volunteered'. By the late 1970s, the SADF had sixty thousand combat troops engaged in SWA; SWATF had a ten-thousand-strong force, which swelled to 22,000 by 1987. Ironically, Namibia's high-quality road network is due to the SADF's need to facilitate troop movement, just as some of the other infrastructural development in the north came about because of the SADF's presence. Although sometimes portrayed simplistically as a Black liberation struggle against the white colonial oppressors, the war was much more complex. The SADF's successful recruitment of Black Namibians into various battalions – mainly organised according to bantustan – was attributable to several factors: their ability to exploit long-standing ethnic animosity and the widespread fear of communism and their winning of 'hearts and minds' by establishing hospitals, providing school teachers and giving agricultural support. Moreover, the only way for many non-white men to escape crippling poverty and support their families – especially in years of drought – was to sign up for the army. Arguably, the South-West African government's most successful combat force was the notorious **Koevoet**, which consisted predominantly of Owambo members, who eventually led counter-insurgency operations into Angola against SWAPO.

UN Resolution 385

In 1976, the UN passed **Resolution 385**, calling for South Africa to withdraw from Namibia and allow UN-organised elections. Later that year, they also formally adopted the name Namibia to replace SWA and recognised SWAPO as the legitimate representative of the Namibian people. The following year, the UN's **Western Contact Group (WSG)** of five Western powers, dominated by the USA and keen to install a pro-Western government in Namibia, negotiated with South Africa and, in 1978, came up with **Resolution 435**, which didn't require South Africa to withdraw before the elections and let them keep Walvis Bay.

Despite agreeing to Resolution 435, on 4 April 1978, South Africa went ahead with **Operation Reindeer**, attacking a SWAPO base at Cassinga in southern Angola and killing six hundred people – an event commemorated by the national holiday of

1966	1968	1976
The UN formally revokes South Africa's mandate to rule South-West Africa. SWAPO begins military campaign against South African occupation	South Africa begins implementing apartheid 'bantustan' or homeland policies in Namibia	The UN calls for South African withdrawal and UN-run elections, which South Africa rejects

Cassinga Day. South Africa also unilaterally held elections without UN supervision, which were inevitably boycotted by SWAPO and other parties. The elections were won by the multiracial but white-dominated **Democratic Turnhalle Alliance** (DTA), whose support came from a very narrow demographic. However, South Africa was looking to create the broadest possible anti-SWAPO front, so with that in mind, the DTA government was dissolved in 1983, and the Multi-Party Conference was formed. Two years later, a **Transitional Government of National Unity** (TGNU) was put into office, with the South African Administrator-General, Louis Pienaar, given a veto over all legislation. There was no election for the TGNU, but censorship was relaxed a little, and with the release and return of much of its imprisoned leadership, SWAPO began to stage mass rallies and help establish the first Black trade unions.

Independence

By the late 1980s, the financial costs of the Namibian/Angolan conflict were crippling South Africa – in addition, some 2,500 South African soldiers had lost their lives. In 1988, South Africa invaded Angola again to try and destroy SWAPO and PLAN bases but were defeated. They finally signed the **New York Accords** with Angola and Cuba, agreeing to comply with Resolution 435 and to withdraw their troops from southern Angola in exchange for the withdrawal of the Cuban forces. The first-ever UN-supervised elections took place in 1989, with SWAPO winning 57 percent of the vote (and 41 out of 72 seats) and DTA winning just 29 percent. The new assembly unanimously elected **Sam Nujoma**, president of SWAPO since its foundation in 1960, as the **first president of Namibia**.

Namibia's independence officially began on 21 March 1990, with twenty heads of state from around the world (and a recently freed Nelson Mandela) attending celebrations in the National Stadium in Windhoek. Despite fears that far-right elements might try to destabilise the new order, the remarkable feature of Namibia since independence has been its relative **political stability**. South Africa had always insisted that Namibia be a multiparty democracy and a capitalist state, and it held onto Walvis Bay until 1994 when it felt sure SWAPO did not intend to install a one-party state (which had always been their stated aim during apartheid). The same year, Nelson Mandela became president of South Africa and offered to wipe off Namibia's apartheid-era debts.

Nujoma's stated policy of **national reconciliation** assuaged the white minority. Still, there was no Truth and Reconciliation Commission in Namibia, just a de facto amnesty for all pre-independence acts of violence – including SWAPO human rights abuses in Angola and Zambia, attested to by former detainees and greeted with hysterical denials by the SWAPO leadership. However, this failure to allow different populations to air their grievances and attempt a mutual understanding of the historical narratives of the period leading up to independence has resulted in simmering tensions that persist today.

Like much of southern and central Africa, Namibia quickly faced the threat of **HIV and AIDS**, which had infected over 20 percent of the adult population by 2000 – rates have since reduced. However, they are still significant at just under 12 percent in 2021, with women disproportionately affected.

1989	**1990**	**1994**	**1999**
The first Namibian elections are held; SWAPO wins 57 percent of the vote, installing Sam Nujoma as president	Independence formally begins on 21 March	Walvis Bay is finally handed over to Namibia and Sam Nujoma is elected for a second term	The Caprivi secessionist conflict is finally ended by government military intervention and the imprisonment of the rebel leaders

A serious early threat to Namibian stability came from the dispute over the then Caprivi Strip – now the Zambezi Region – where the **Caprivi Liberation Army** (CLA), under their ex-DTA leader Mishake Muyongo, began campaigning for self-rule in 1994. Following the government's discovery of a military training camp in 1998 and a rebel attack on the Caprivi capital, Katima Mulilo, a state of emergency was declared in the eastern Caprivi. The eventual government crackdown a year later silenced the CLA, and development money is being poured into the region to help ensure national unity.

Post-independence

There was (and still is) a widespread feeling among many that President Nujoma's fifteen-year rule – the constitution was changed so he could serve three terms – produced a huge rise in corruption. In 2004, Nujoma's nominee, **Hifikepunye Pohamba**, won the presidential elections, promising to root out corruption, setting up an Anti-Corruption Commission, and restricting the number of foreign trips made by his cabinet. He was also praised for promoting gender equality and increasing spending on housing and education, which won him the prestigious (and lucrative) **Mo Ibrahim Award** for outstanding African leadership.

In 2014, former prime minister **Hage Geingob** led SWAPO to another landslide electoral victory, winning 80 percent of the popular vote (77 out of 96 seats). Yet, his promise of 'shared prosperity for all' sounded distinctly hollow when voting rolled round again in 2019. By then, the country was suffering from a **worsening economic crisis**, exacerbated by successive years of drought, and there was concern that China's increasing penetration into the country's economy was only benefiting the elite at the expense of local businesses. Add to this a constant flow of corruption scandals – including 'Fishrot', in which senior government officials and businessmen have been accused of receiving hefty bribes for awarding lucrative fishing rights to a major Icelandic fishing firm. The scandal broke just before the 2019 elections, resulting in the ruling party losing its two-thirds majority for the first time since independence. The Fishrot trial – Namibia's biggest since independence – was due to start in late 2023.

Land reform has also been high on the political agenda since independence. The initial 'willing buyer-willing seller' approach to redistributing land from white farmers to 'previously disadvantaged' Black citizens has not yielded the desired results, prompting a new ten-year plan in 2023. The intransigence of white farmers, inadequate support for Black farmers to benefit from the land, and elite capture in reallocating land have all contributed to the slow and often unsuccessful process.

As Namibia heads to the polls again in 2024, the public's concern about widening social inequality – including in access to land – unemployment and corruption loom large. Although the deep and lasting scars of colonialism are to blame for many of Namibia's challenges, in addition to global issues that lie outside government control, such as the impact of climate change, the COVID-19 pandemic, and the conflict in Ukraine, many Namibians feel that the country's elite is doing more to help themselves than help ordinary citizens.

2004	2014–2019	2021–2024
Hifikepunje Pohamba becomes Namibia's second president	Hage Geingob is elected Namibia's third president as SWAPO wins 80 percent of the vote, reduced to 65 percent in 2019, following the country's worst drought in 38 years	German-Namibian agreement recognising the Herero-Nama genocide and pledging development aid is rejected. 'Fishrot' corruption trial begins

Peoples

Wading into the political minefield of 'ethnicity' and 'race' is always a tricky affair in Namibia, as in other post-colonial states, since these socially constructed categories have predominantly come into being over the last two centuries, inevitably shaped and manipulated by decades of pernicious racial and ethnic differentiation, segregation and social stratification during successive colonial and apartheid eras. Up until then, social affiliations and lifestyles would seem to have been much more contingent than colonial historical accounts make out. At the same time, the arbitrary carving up of Africa by the colonial powers to demarcate particular nations cut across peoples and, over time, has played its part in eroding or hybridising cultural practices and weakening social ties.

The Namibian government's need to promote a unified national identity for its estimated 2.6 million population has been an understandable post-independence response to all this. Indeed, a favourite metaphor of Namibia's current president, Hage Geingob, is that of 'one Namibian house' in which the 'bricks' of ethnicity and race will gradually be indistinguishable as they are glued together by new legislation, then plastered and painted over. It is also true that intermarriage and co-settlement over many generations, both voluntary and coerced, have also helped to blur racial and ethnic boundaries, as has increasing urbanisation. Moreover, census data no longer collects figures on ethnicity; rather, numbers are imputed from information on first language use in the home. However, many Namibians still identify with one or more ethnicities – historically, culturally, linguistically – at particular times, to differing degrees and for various reasons. For example, the ongoing simmering disputes about land rights are replete with claims of ethnicity and specific cultural identities.

Therefore, terms denoting race and ethnicity should be understood as being looser, more indistinct and more fluid than language permits in the necessarily oversimplified sketch of Namibia's main populations given below. And it's important to acknowledge that race and ethnicity, however constructed, are central to the fault lines of inequality that persist today.

The main social groups

The earliest inhabitants of the land that is now Namibia were those that belong to the **Khoisan** language group (see page 365), who arrived many thousands of years ago: **San** groupings, joined later by **Nama** and then, much later, by **Damara** populations (see page 350). Moving down from East Africa, so colonial history relates, came Bantu-speaking peoples: the **Owambo**, around the fourteenth century, followed a couple of centuries later by **Otjiherero**-speakers, including the **Himba** (see page 352). Other **Bantu**-speaking peoples include the main groups that now primarily reside in the Kavango and Zambezi regions. Speakers of Indo-European languages arrived in the late nineteenth and twentieth centuries: the Germans, ancestors of present-day German Namibians, and various Afrikaans-speaking people (see page 354). Those claiming Afrikaans as a first language include white **Afrikaners**, who came from South Africa and are of Dutch descent, and those with a mixed African-European heritage, including the **Nama-Oorlams** and the **Basters** (see page 141).

WHAT'S IN A NAME

The controversial terms '**San**' and '**Bushmen**' have been both preferred and discarded as **derogatory** by different groups on account of their original meanings: Bushman derives from the Afrikaans *bossiesman*, which probably initially meant 'outlaw' or 'bandit', but was applied to other peoples too; San comes from the Nama word *sa* meaning 'bad person', which also originally had wider application. Most San/Bushman want to be known by their **nations**, such as **Ju|'hoan** or **Khoe**, since a collective term does not exist in their languages. However, some will prefer one collective term over the other.

San (Bushmen)

Renowned for their ancient rock art, tracking and hunting skills, the hunter-gatherer ancestors of the more than thirty thousand **San** or **Bushmen** living in Namibia are considered the original inhabitants of Southern Africa.

Dispersed across various countries in the region, the Namibian populations are currently spread around northern and eastern areas of the country. Members of the **Ju|'hoan**, **Naro**, **‡Aullen** and **!Xoo** who have not become totally Westernised and are living in urban areas predominantly inhabit the Kalahari area of eastern Namibia; the **!Kung** and **Khoe** are found in the Kavango and Zambezi regions, and the **Hai||om** live near the Grootfontein area.

In pre-colonial times, dispersed San groups lived in small family groupings of between fifteen and fifty, congregating in larger groups around a permanent water source during the dry winter months. Rather than owning land, the San believed themselves to be the custodians of **!nores**, their traditional hunting grounds where men would hunt or trap animals while the women would usually forage for roots, nuts and berries, which were the mainstay of the San diet. While different groups' religious beliefs varied, belief in a supreme being among other deities and a focus on healing were common, as well as the importance of ancestral spirits and communication with the spirit world through the shaman. This would often happen during the famous 'trance dances', which persist in some rural communities, though to a minimal extent.

Throughout history, San groups have been denigrated and **persecuted** by both Bantu-speaking and white settlers, being gradually forced off their lands, enslaved and even hunted down. Hai||om communities were famously forced off their land in Etosha National Park (see page 238) during the 1950s. Similarly, the Khoe were displaced in favour of a nature reserve on the Kavango River. During the apartheid era, the demarcation of the Bushman homeland resulted in a 90 percent reduction of the Ju|'hoan's traditional hunting grounds. What's more, unlike in other homelands, the San had no say in its administration. In the 1970s, San lifestyles suffered a further blow when SADF bases were established in or near their areas, and the South Africans recruited San to work as trackers and soldiers in counter-insurgency operations against SWAPO. An estimated quarter of all San became dependent on army wages and services and abandoned any reliance on the land. When the conflict ended and independence beckoned, around half took up the offer to **relocate** to South Africa, afraid of how the Namibian government might treat them for having been on the wrong side of the struggle.

Since independence, San groups continue to be among the most **marginalised**, lacking land, food security and adequate representation, with many suffering from poor health and struggling with social ills such as alcohol abuse and violence both within San groups and against non-San. Though traditional San lifestyles have all but vanished and many communities are disintegrating, there are glimmers of hope: hunting restrictions have been lifted in some areas, and some rural communities, with the help of government and NGOs, are managing to survive with a mixed economy involving foraging, crop cultivation and livestock grazing.

Nama

The **Nama**, who call themselves the **|Awakhoen** (meaning the 'Red Nation'), like the San, are descended from ancient peoples living in southern Africa for several thousand years. Like the San, they also speak a Khoisan click language, **Khoekhoegowab** – more easily referred to as Nama, though many also speak Afrikaans, especially those of **Nama-Orlaam** descent. While the Indigenous Nama were predominantly semi-nomadic pastoralists, herding cattle, goats and sheep, they also lived as hunter-gatherers when the situation demanded. By the 1830s, they were also engaging in long-distance trade, having been influenced heavily by the arrival of Nama-Orlaam with their ox carts, guns and adoption of Christianity.

Although there was initially a lot of **conflict** among and between Nama and Orlaam groups, by the end of the century, their differences had more or less dissolved through co-settlement and intermarriage and the need to come together to confront common threats, such as the Herero, and then later the Germans.

In the nineteenth century, there were fourteen identifiable groups living north of the Orange River – nine Nama, five as Oorlam; these days, the fourteen groups all think of themselves as Nama, generally named after a former Orlaam leader, such as **|Khopesen** (Witboois), or the place where they have settled, such as **!Amain** (Bethanie people). Nearly all live in settled communities in the more arid south of Namibia, around Keetmanshoop, where many Nama work on commercial farms; others struggle with subsistence farming, though communal agricultural projects have been initiated in some places. Exceptions include the **‡Aonin** and **!Gommen** (Topnaars), who live in the Namib's Kuiseb River area (see page 232) and further north in Sesfontein, respectively. These groups also differ from other Nama groups in not owning communal land but inheriting it through particular lineages. Only in the Richtersveld Transfrontier Park, which straddles the border with South Africa (see page 152), do some Nama still practise a semi-nomadic way of life. Like the Herero, the Nama lost much of their land, cattle and people in uprisings against the Germans. Today, they number around sixty thousand, or 5 percent of the Namibian population.

After independence, the **Nama Traditional Leaders Council** was set up to sustain common elements of Nama culture without losing the distinctiveness of individual groups. In particular, Nama are renowned for a strong tradition of praise poetry, music and storytelling.

Damara-speaking peoples

The **Damara** peoples of Namibia share a language with the Nama, now called **Nama-Damara**. They refer to themselves as **‡nūkhoen**, meaning 'Black people', and, along with other Khoisan groups (the San and Nama), are considered some of the country's earliest inhabitants. The Damara migration into present-day Namibia is more of a mystery. However, recent thinking suggests that, like the San, they migrated from the central Kalahari area, though well over a century later. Early European accounts indicate they were the most widespread Indigenous communities with no common group identity, found in pockets all over central and northern Namibia. Colonial historians labelled them hunter-gatherers, but evidence suggests great versatility depending on where they lived. The relatively dispersed populations variously practised livestock farming, agriculture, horticulture, cultivating pumpkins and tobacco, and some were known to be skilled blacksmiths. Their extensive yet dispersed spread of communities led to contact with various other groups, which resulted in different cultural practices and no centralised social structure. Damara tended to live in extended family groups. Only in the second half of the nineteenth century were they forced into a more developed group identity by appointing a chief, or 'king', **Cornelius Goreseb.**

As with the San, the dispersed nature of Damara society also made it easy for them to be squeezed out by the more numerous and better-armed Herero and the Nama in the latter half of the nineteenth century. Some Damara fled to the mountains, gaining them the name 'Berg-Damara'; others were gradually incorporated into a labour economy – sometimes forcibly, working for the Herero, in particular, as servants or herders. From 1879, the Damara were also the first group to be shipped as indentured labourers to the Cape, often under duress.

The first Damara 'reserve' was created in Okombahe in 1906 – after the RMS persuaded the Herero chief to give up some land in exchange for rent. During the apartheid era, Damaraland was extended northwest, as far as Sesfontein, though only around a quarter of the Damara population now live in this area. Many live in Windhoek, where they are variously employed in government – the current president is Damara – and private enterprise; the rest are predominantly in central-northern urbanised areas. However, Okombahe's importance has been revived as the seat of Damara's royal household, where the current 33 Damara groups converge on the first weekend every November for the annual **Damara Cultural Festival**, during which they pay homage to their ancestors, share oral histories, sing and dance. This jamboree only started in the 1970s in an attempt to re-affirm a collective Damara identity.

Oshiwambo-speaking groups

Namibians who might identify as **Owambo** (also Ovambo, previously Aawambo) are a loose association of eight currently recognised social groups collectively forming the country's majority population (around 50 percent). The shared language is **Oshiwambo**, though **Oshindongo** and **Oshikwanyama** are the mutually intelligible standardised dialects taught at school. The Owambo originally migrated down from the Great Lakes area of East Africa, settling on both sides of the Kavango River in what is now southern Angola and northern Namibia around the fourteenth century. Over time, populations grew, spread and separated into the different Owambo groups that exist today in Namibia: the most numerous are the **Kwanyama**, followed by **Ndongo** and much smaller populations of **Kwambi**, **Mbalantu**, **Kwaluudhi**, **Kolonkhadi** and **Ngandjera** and, more recently, the **Owambandja**. Forty-five percent of Owambos currently populate the northern administrative regions of Oshikoto, Oshama, Ohangwena and Omusati – collectively referred to as the Four 'O's – which are Namibia's most densely populated regions outside the Windhoek area (Khomas). They all experience high unemployment.

The Owambo traditionally are crop and stock farmers who also fish when seasonally inundated depressions – **oshanas** – flood. Their primary agricultural produce is *mahangu* (pearl millet), sorghum and beans, with cattle as the primary livestock. Owambos also have a long history of trading. Due to their numerical superiority and the political dominance of SWAPO, Owambos occupy the majority of **senior government positions**. They are involved at senior levels in Namibia's major industries: mining, fishing and tourism.

Pre-colonial Owambo society was organised in kingdoms, with headmen underneath the king. It was polygamous and matrilineal, though the colonial and post-colonial government systems have weakened these structures. These days, only the Ndonga, Ngandjera and Kwaluudhi still recognise their kings, though they are now aided by councillors, as well as headmen. In some groups, females can now occupy senior traditional leadership roles. The spread of Christianity in the north via Finnish missionaries in the late eighteenth century severely eroded traditional belief systems and customs, though they persist, often in hybrid form. In many rural areas, for example, Owambos still recognise **Kalunga** as the supreme being, even as they may also espouse Christianity and indeed use the term to refer to the Christian conception of God; the **onganga** (traditional spiritual healer) is still seen by some as an important medium for communicating with ancestral spirits.

The traditional Owambo **homestead** (*ehumbo*) comprises a distinctive high wooden palisade with rondavels enclosed by yet more fences and labyrinthine passages demarcating activity-specific areas. These are gradually altering; deforestation and pressure on natural resources have led to greater use of mud, cement block and aluminium, while urban migration has led to further housing and lifestyle changes. However, visiting the Uukwaluudhi Royal Homestead at Tsandi (see page 253) or the Nakambale Museum homestead in Olukonda (see page 249) provides fascinating insights into Owambo histories, traditions and changing cultures.

Otjiherero-speaking groups

The **Herero** (or OvaHerero), like the Owambos, are Bantu language speakers who migrated down from East Africa and are estimated to have arrived in the northwest of present-day Namibia in the mid-sixteenth century. Four groups live in Namibia: **Herero**, **Mbanderu**, **Himba** and **Tjimba**. The Himba and Tjimba remained in the northwest, whereas the Herero and Mbanderu migrated in a southerly direction and were well established around central Namibia when the first Europeans landed. The fact that an estimated 80 percent of Herero and Mbanderu lost their lives in attempted genocide by the Germans – by way of reprisal for their failed uprising against the colonists – at the beginning of the twentieth century (see page 342) has left a profound scar on Herero and Mbanderu communities, who are still seeking reparations from the German government. Those who died are commemorated annually on the various **flag days** (see page 72), notably in Okahandja, when the men parade in paramilitary uniforms. The women wear their modern 'traditional' attire. This consists of billowing petticoat-laden dresses culturally appropriated from Rhenish missionaries, topped with an anvil-shaped cloth headpiece turned up at the ends, representing the horns of cattle.

Cattle became central to traditional Herero culture – at least from the latter part of the nineteenth century, since although many arrived in Namibia primarily as semi-nomadic cattle herders, some had no cattle. Besides, they also traded and practised agriculture and horticulture when necessary. Above all, cattle denoted social status and had religious significance, playing a symbolic role in Herero communications with their ancestors. Ancestors, in turn, acted as mediators with the Herero supreme being, **Ndjambi Karunga**, venerated at the **okuruwo** (sacred shrine and hearth) in each **onganda** (homestead). In pre-colonial times, there was no centralised political structure, which was attributed to the Herero's system of dual descent: religious or sacred property, status within the family and place of abode were taken from the father's line (*oruzo*), whereas the inheritance of wealth and secular possessions was passed on matrilineally (*eanda*). However, the spread of Christianity and Western capitalism has caused the matriclans to all but disappear.

These days, Herero-speakers form Namibia's third-largest ethnic group in Namibia. However, having lost many beasts to Nama cattle raiders in the mid-nineteenth century and their traditional grazing lands to the Germans, with further losses occurring through the apartheid homeland system, Herero no longer regards cattle with the same cultural significance. Many Herero now live in urban areas engaged in a range of jobs and professions, though others are employed on commercial cattle farms in central Namibia and some still keep herds on communal lands north of the Red Line.

Himba

The **Himba** (or OvaHimba) share a common ancestry and language with the Herero – **OtjiHimba** being a dialect of Otjiherero. However, different historical trajectories and living in some of the country's most remote, inaccessible mountainous areas have allowed them to maintain many traditions they shared with the Herero and remain more culturally distinct. However, more recent contact with the media, formal schooling, and increased tourism are causing rapid change, particularly among the younger generation. A population of around fifty thousand Himba lives in the northwestern reaches of the Kunene Region and southwestern Angola, on both sides of the Kunene River. As with the Herero in former times, cattle are central to Himba identity, now a marker of social status rather than as a meat provider, though occasionally one is slaughtered for a special occasion. Goats and sheep, supplemented by cows' milk, chicken eggs, as well as cultivated millet and maize, constitute their primary diet. Recent droughts have resulted in huge cattle losses, further threatening their traditional way of life.

Though a few communities still practise a semi-nomadic lifestyle, more and more are becoming settled. Most rural Himba settlements, however, still live in an extended family **homestead** (*onganda*) in a collection of dome-shaped homes constructed with mopane wood covered with goatskin and arranged in a circle surrounding the **sacred fire** (*okuruwo*). This is always kept burning as a means of communicating with the ancestors and through them to the supreme being, **Mukuru**. The kraal for the sacred livestock rarely features these days, as few Himba can now afford to keep cattle purely for ritual purposes.

Polygamy is still widely practised, as are arranged marriages, and the dual heritage structure (now abandoned by the Herero) that allows for differentiated inheritance down both the female and male lines persists.

In recent years, the Himba and related Zemba and Hakaona have made various national and international **protests** against the government of Namibia regarding human rights violations, such as the lack of recognition of their traditional authorities and ongoing plans to build a dam on the Kunene River (see page 259).

Kavango

Named after the region's life source, the **Kavango** peoples are primarily concentrated along the riverbanks and fertile floodplains of the 400km (248.5-mile) stretch of the Kavango (or Okavango) River that forms the northern border between Namibia and Angola. Bantu-speaking riverine people originally came from East Africa and settled in the Upper Zambezi before migrating further south between the sixteenth and eighteenth centuries. Inevitably, fishing was central to their diet and was practised by both women and men, but they also used to hunt water-loving antelope and grow sorghum, *mahangu* and maize on the floodplain terraces. Though the antelope is no more, fishing and crop cultivation continue, and from the latter half of the nineteenth century, cattle farming has become a feature of Kavango life. Equally important was trade with the eastern Owambo groups, especially among the more westerly Kwangali, who arguably interacted more with their Owambo neighbours than with the groups later classified as Kavango. In more recent times, **woodcarving** has also grown as an industry, while many young Kavangans now work as labourers in mines, farms or urban areas.

The two hundred thousand Kavango broadly comprise five Bantu-speaking groups: the **Kwangali**, **Mbunza**, **Shambyu**, **Gciriku** and **Mbukushi**, with the more numerous Kwangali and the Mbunza sharing the same language of **RuKwangali**, which is one of Namibia's national languages, and the other groups speaking other dialects. A king rules each group. Just as crucial to the structure of Kavango societies is clan membership, passed down through the maternal line, though people of the same clan do not necessarily live together. Despite the success of Christian missionaries – both Catholic and Finnish Lutheran – traditional cosmology is still important, such as belief in the supreme being, **Karunga**, and the power of the ancestors to ward off evil spirits and protect the family.

Historically, the biggest threat to the Kavango groups – beyond power struggles and land disputes – initially came from the Tawana in present-day Botswana, supported by the British; the Gciriku, in particular, incurred a significant loss of life and goods; the Shambyu and Mbukushu also suffered. By the end of the nineteenth century, many of the Kavango were impoverished and were reportedly even reduced to selling their kin to slave traders. However, enslaved people were also snatched in raids. German colonial influence was minimal since the lack of mineral wealth made the area unappealing to settlers, and very few Kavango were forced to become migrant labourers. Of greater impact was the arrival in 1909 of the Portuguese, who established forts along the northern bank of the Kavango, where most of the population were living at the time. After failed armed resistance, the Shambyu fled further into Angola, only returning several years later. Once the other polities had been raided regularly, they fled across the river. The South African era, however, was a different matter; following forced removal from the river, Kavangans resisted, resulting in harsh retaliation by the paramilitary Koevoet (see page 345). Following Namibian independence and the end of the civil war in Angola, cross-border trade has increased, and migrating Angolans – many of whom are Kavangans – have caused the population to double in size in recent years.

The Zambezi Region (formerly Caprivi)

The thin 450km (279.6-mile) sliver of land known as the **Zambezi Region** has been a melting pot of cultures for centuries. These days, five main Bantu-speaking groups constitute the ninety thousand-plus population (4 percent of the national total): the **Masubia** and the **Mafwe** are by far the largest groups, with smaller numbers of **Mbalangwe**, **Totela** and **Mayeyi**. Even smaller groups of **Khwe** (San/Bushmen) and **Mbukushu** live in the drier, western part of the region. Unsurprisingly, given that the Zambezi Region shares borders with both Angola and Zambia and is a short hop from Zimbabwe, it has attracted a lot of migrants from these countries in recent years, especially in the regional capital, Katima Mulilo.

Pre-colonial history in the Zambezi Region is particularly hazy about the earliest people; group affiliations, names and identities have shifted substantially over time. Among various small, decentralised groups, including some San, two powerful kingdoms sought variously to impose themselves; both have claimed to be the original settlers. The Masubia, riverine people based around the area of the Linyanti-Chobe confluence in eastern Zambezi (see page 357) who are thought to have arrived around the mid-fifteenth century, named the area Itenge, and the **Lozi**, the dominant kingdom-cum-empire of the time, based in Barotseland (southern Zambia), pushed them out as they expanded their kingdom. The Lozi Kingdom, apart from being overrun by the northward migrating Makololo for twenty years in the mid-nineteenth century, was the dominant force in the area until the Germans instituted direct rule in 1909. Based on the floodplains of the Zambezi, the Lozi Kingdom was highly organised. As well as bringing many disparate groups under its control, it predominantly ruled indirectly, exacting tribute and making the occasional raid to secure enslaved people. Today, **SiLozi** is still the lingua franca of eastern Zambezi and is taught in schools – a legacy of colonialism, which has been reinforced in post-independence language policy even though the actual number of Lozi in the region is very small.

With four perennial rivers in the region and fertile **floodplains**, fishing and agriculture have inevitably been important to the people's predominantly subsistence livelihoods. In addition to mixed livestock farming, *mahangu* and maize are cultivated alongside green vegetables such as spinach and cabbage, supplemented by seasonal fruits. **Commercial fishing** has also become more common, although recent overfishing has led to a depletion of stocks. Craftwork in **basketry** and **pottery** also has a rich history in the region, and the main urban area of Katima Mulilo has long been an important trading centre.

Afrikaans-speaking groups

Just over 10 percent of the population speak **Afrikaans** as a first language. These are a mix of white Afrikaners of predominantly Dutch descent who migrated north from present-day South Africa to escape the British colonisers at the end of the nineteenth century and whose numbers swelled once South Africa took over the custodianship of present-day Namibia in the wake of World War I. The majority of Afrikaans speakers, however, comprise people of mixed heritage, generally African and European, who were labelled 'coloured' during the apartheid years but self-identified in varying ways. These include the **Basters** (see page 141), who consider themselves culturally distinct from other people of mixed heritage, partly because of their particular history, having secured the right to landownership in 1870 and a degree of self-determination for an extended period.

German speakers

German-speaking Namibians are almost exclusively the **descendants of ethnic German colonists** who arrived in the country at the end of the nineteenth century (see page 339), predominantly as traders, troops and government officials, with numbers swelling further during the diamond boom (see page 132) to around 13,000 settlers and fluctuating numbers of Schutztruppe. Immediately after World War I, around half the German settlers were deported, though later, the remainder were granted British citizenship, which was later revoked at the outbreak of World War II. Today, the current German–Namibian population is around thirty thousand, living mainly in the urban areas of Windhoek, Swakopmund, Lüderitz and Otjiwarongo, where they run many of the major businesses and tourism enterprises and hold positions in government. More controversially, some still own large farms acquired during the colonial era, subject to ongoing land disputes.

Many German–Namibians are church-going Lutherans, though over half the Namibian population belong to one of the country's three evangelical Lutheran churches. German food and drink are also important to community identity, the greatest manifestation of which is the annual Windhoek Oktoberfest (W oktoberfestnamibia.com), where traditional activities such as log-sawing, beer-lifting and strongman competitions are held, aided by copious beer and Bavarian specialities such as *obatzda* (a spicy, cheesy concoction) and roast pork knuckle.

Landscapes

Many people imagine Namibia to be wholly desert. Yet, within this overwhelmingly arid and semi-arid country, a surprising variety of landscapes exist, from flat gravel plains to rippling dunes and rocky mountains, which play host to some extraordinary vegetation. Moreover, the curious panhandle that extends eastwards at the far north of the country, along the Kavango and Zambezi rivers, supports a lush sub-tropical environment – in complete contrast to the rest of the country.

The Namib Desert

Although Namibia can arguably be divided into five distinct geographical areas, it is the spectacular dune fields of the **Namib Desert** – now a UNESCO World Heritage Site – that outsiders most readily associate with the country. Probably in existence for about eighty million years, the constantly evolving landscape of the Namib stretches around 1,500km (932 miles) from the Olifants River in the Cape Province of South Africa, along the Skeleton Coast, to San Nicolau in southern Angola, a 200km (124.3-mile-) broad swathe of land bounded on the west by the Atlantic Ocean's Benguela Current, which is pivotal in maintaining the desert environment as its icy waters prevent the formation of rain clouds over the sea. On average, the Namib receives around 15mm (0.59in) of rainfall annually on the coast – though much of the moisture for plant and animal life is gained from fog (see page 211) – and around 100mm (3.9in) on the higher eastern areas inland, though some years it gets no rain at all. In addition to the famous dune seas, the Namib comprises vast tracts of flat gravel plain from which protrude several striking **inselbergs** – isolated hills or mountains that have remained after the surrounding rocks have been eroded – such as the Spitzkoppe and Brandberg.

The Great Escarpment

At the same time as marking the eastern limit of the Namib, these inselbergs constitute part of another of the country's main geographical areas: the **Great Escarpment**. Probably formed around eighty million years ago by the uplifting of the Earth's crust after the break-up of the supercontinent Gondwana, it is not a continuous ridge, as large tracts have been eroded over time, and some areas, such as the Spitzkoppe, Brandberg and the Erongos, have also been shaped by subsequent volcanic activity. The escarpment is at its most dramatic in the Naukluft Mountains. It also includes impressive ranges in the northwest – the Baynes, Stellrand and Hartmanns mountains – and the inaccessible Huns Mountains west of the Fish River Canyon in the south. This imposing geological phenomenon is much easier to appreciate when soaking up the breathtaking views from one of Namibia's loftier highland passes, such as the Gamsberg and the Spreetshoogte. Namibia's mountain ranges are cleft by steep ravines, which run westwards towards the coast and were eroded by flowing rivers in former times. Now, the country's main rivers are mostly dry sandy beds – except in times of exceptional rain – such as the Swakop, Omaruru and Ugab, whose underground water flow nevertheless supports large trees and shrub vegetation, which are vital to the survival of Namibia's desert-dwelling creatures.

The Central Highland Plateau and the Kalahari

The escarpment, in turn, forms the western edge of the undulating **Central Highland Plateau**, which extends roughly from north of Otjiwarongo to close to the border with

South Africa, maintaining an altitude of around 1,000m (3,280.8ft). Here, the climate is less harsh, and the vegetation cover is more pronounced as it receives slightly more rain. The plateau's eastern limit is less defined as it slopes gently downwards, melting into the flat, acacia-studded sand sheet that is the **Kalahari**, which continues across the border into Botswana and northern South Africa. This southern part also contains a burnished, rippling dune scape. For purists, the Kalahari is not a true desert, being classified as semi-arid since much of it receives over 100mm (3.9in) a year. However, few lay people would quibble, given its abundance of sand, extreme temperatures and absence of surface water.

The Zambezi Region

The climate changes dramatically in the far northeast of Namibia and along the panhandle in the Zambezi (formerly Caprivi) Region. Though the area remains flat and often sandy, the **perennial rivers** of the Kavango (Okavango), Zambezi and the Kwando – which morphs into the Linyanti and then the Chobe – plus the higher annual rainfall (roughly 400–600mm/15.7–23.6in and above) nourish relatively luxuriant **subtropical** vegetation and **wetlands**.

Vegetation

Almost three-quarters of Namibia is classified as **savannah** land. In central regions, **thornbush savannah** predominates, comprising prickly, thin-leafed acacia shrubs and grasslands. In the northern areas, which receive greater rainfall, denser, more broad-leafed **woodland savannah** is in evidence. Acacia trees punctuated by giant **baobabs** and clumps of **makalani palms** thrive here, while the even wetter parts of the Kavango and the Zambezi regions support the larger, riverine forests and deciduous broad-leaved trees that characterise **mopane woodlands**. However, the flat land is covered in thick deposits of Kalahari sand.

Trees and grass are scarce along the entire length of the Namib Desert and in the arid southern region. However, ephemeral **stipagrostis grasses** survive by having hardy seeds that can withstand the desert heat and lack of water, lying dormant for decades after the plant has withered; they are ready to germinate in the rare times of favourable rainfall. In such years, Namaqualand, a region just north of the Orange River that spans the |Ai–|Ais/Richtersveld Transfrontier Park and the Tsau ||Khaeb (Sperrgebiet) National Park and stretches over the border into South Africa, is famed for its kaleidoscopic carpet of **spring flowers**, which bloom in August and September.

Succulents, such as the striking **quiver tree**, which adorns many a sunset shot of southern Namibia (see page 147), have various desert survival strategies, notably a waxy coating on their leaves to reduce transpiration and leaves and stems that can swell to store water. Other plant adaptations to the arid environment include slow growth, as epitomised by the scraggly **welwitschia** (see page 218); thin or spiny leaves that reduce water loss and help prevent them being eaten by animals – as exemplified by the **!nara melon** (see page 230); and hollow, large or expandable trunks or stems that can store water, as exhibited by the giant pot-bellied **baobab** and the slightly skinner **moringa** tree, whose silvery bark reflects the sun. **Lithops** – a succulent whose name means 'stone-like' – disguise themselves as beach pebbles to avoid being eaten; their low-lying or absent stems provide another means of preserving moisture.

On the desert gravel plains, **lichens** – ancient organisms that are a mix of algae and fungi – abound, clinging to patches of exposed rock or the gypsum soil crust. Colours and shapes vary, from yellow to green, purple or pink, especially when exposed to moisture, usually in the form of fog. In contrast, some appear like withered, dead plants once the sun beats down on them as they shrivel to avoid losing moisture.

Wildlife

Spotting large mammals in their natural habitat lures many visitors to Africa. Although Namibia can't compete with the vast animal-filled plains of Tanzania and Kenya, numbers are increasing. This is especially true in the north due to the success of the government's conservancy-based conservation strategy (see page 360), the removal of many fences allowing the animals greater freedom to roam, and the higher rainfall in some areas, providing more vegetation for them to eat. Yet, even in the drier desert and semi-desert areas, there is plenty of animal life to engage your attention, especially regarding reptiles and invertebrates. Our Namibia field guide (see page 26) has further detailed information on the main mammals and some birds you'll likely see across the country.

Mammals

There are over 220 identified mammal species in Namibia, 26 of which are endemic (or near-endemic). In the Zambezi Region, where the protected areas have been incorporated into the five-country Kavango–Zambezi Transfrontier Conservation Area, or KAZA (see page 282), numbers of free-roaming **elephants**, **buffalo** and **lions** have shown a significant increase in recent years. It is here, along the perennial rivers, that most of Namibia's **hippo** population resides.

However, the most straightforward and most accessible place for watching large mammals in Namibia is **Etosha National Park**, which harbours four of the 'Big Five' – only buffalo are absent – and a host of other smaller mammals. Namibia possesses the world's largest number of free-roaming cheetahs and black rhinos; again, if you want to improve your chance of a sighting, head for Etosha or one of the private game reserves (see page 243). **Desert-adapted black rhinos** and **elephants** frequent the remote dry riverbed valleys in northwest Namibia, providing a major attraction for visitors to lodges in that area. The endangered **wild dog** is most numerous in Khaudum National Park in the northern Kalahari, although a handful has also been sighted in the Zambezi Region.

Twenty species of **antelope** graze the savannah lands of Namibia, ranging from the large 500kg (78.7st) **eland** to the diminutive **Damara dik-dik**, which weighs a mere 5kg (11lb). Most emblematic is the desert-dwelling **gemsbok** – a large oryx that features on the national coat of arms. Rarer species of antelope in Namibia include the swamp-living **sitatunga**, **puku** and **oribi**, found only in the wetlands in the Zambezi Region, as well as the **black-faced impala**. This near-endemic is only resident in the northwest, but its numbers are swelling, thanks to conservation efforts.

Other safari favourites to look out for in your travels include **giraffes**, **zebra** – Burchell's and Hartmann's mountain zebra – **blue wildebeest**, **spotted** and **brown hyenas**, **black-backed jackals** and **warthogs**, alongside less well-known, smaller nocturnal mammals such as **honey badgers**, **aardvarks** and the **bat-eared foxes**.

Reptiles and amphibians

Even the seemingly lifeless desert areas of western Namibia contain a fascinating array of smaller creatures, including numerous **reptiles** and invertebrates – many unique to the Namib – which have evolved extraordinary ways to survive in the harsh, arid environment (see page 359). With the help of a good guide, you can seek them out in the sand by going on one of the many informative **tours** into the desert from either Sossusvlei or Swakopmund. Observing the swivelling eyes and colour-changing coats of **chameleons** and the seemingly adhesive feet of **geckos** in action can be just as compelling as watching a herd of elephants taking a bath.

Unsurprisingly, given Namibia's arid, rocky landscape, reptiles outnumber mammals in terms of species diversity, with around 250 at the last count, half of which are **lizards**. In fact, the country has more varieties of lizards than anywhere else in Africa. Examples include the highly dapper, multicoloured **Attenborough's flat lizard** (*Platysaurus attenboroughi*) – named after the renowned naturalist and TV wildlife presenter – which is endemic to the Richtersveld area. A more common sight, scarpering across rocky outcrops and boulders in the Erongo and Kunene regions and bobbing its head, is the brilliant blue-and-orange **Namib rock agama** (*Agama planiceps*), another endemic. With its hulking armoured frame, the Nile crocodile is the largest reptile, a spine-chilling fixture along the banks of Namibia's perennial northern rivers, especially in the Zambezi Region. Over a thousand are estimated to be in that region alone, with some adult males weighing in at over 500kg (78.7st) – the equivalent of two quad bikes – and over 4m (13.1ft) long; they are increasingly coming into conflict with the region's growing human population.

Snakes, too, are another feature of Namibian fauna – 11 of the eighty-plus present are potentially deadly, including several spitting cobras and the black mamba, though very few people die of snake bites; moreover, snakes tend to scarper at the slightest detection of human presence.

In contrast to reptiles, Namibia's amphibians are pretty thin on the ground outside the Zambezi Region due to the absence of water. However, there are nevertheless fifty species of **frogs**, seven of which are endemic. Outside the wetland areas, many of these frogs aestivate in the mud round pans and *oshanas* until these briefly fill with water; at this time, the frogs emerge to mate and breed at speed before the water dries up

THE NAMIB'S EXTRAORDINARY ENDEMICS

The Namib Desert – after which Namibia is named – has existed for over 55 million years and harbours an extraordinary selection of resourceful, **desert-adapted creatures**, many of which are **endemic to the region**. These include the **sidewinder snake**, whose lateral shuffle facilitates its movement on the steep dune slope while enabling it to keep most of its body off the hot sand at any one time. The eyes, located on the top of its head rather than the side, allow it to spot its prey while remaining submerged in sand. Another desert inhabitant that uses the dunes' steep slopes is the **cartwheeling spider** (dancing white lady spider), which bundles itself into a ball and rolls downhill at speed to escape predators.

Other Namib curiosities include the various **Tenebrionid beetles** or **tok tokkies**, as they are known locally, on account of the tapping noise made by the males to attract a mate. This acrobatic beetle stands on its head on the tops of dunes facing west to allow the incoming coastal fog to condense and form droplets on its body, which trickle down into its mouth.

The bizarre **Grant's golden mole**, another Namib endemic, is unlike most moles: rather than living in permanent burrows, it 'swims' through sand, covering up to 6km (3.7 miles) a night. This extraordinary-looking creature has eyes long buried under a layer of skin and fur, almost non-existent ears, a leathery snout and fine, dense fur to help it push through the sand.

Another favourite of wildlife documentaries is the **Namib dune gecko**, the world's only fully web-footed gecko, whose feet are adapted to help the reptile walk across the sand at night and burrow into it during the hottest part of the day to escape the extreme temperatures. Its enormous eyes help it spot prey in the dark, while during the early morning fog, the gecko licks the condensation off its eyes and face with its long tongue. The **shovel-snouted lizard** also possesses feet designed to help it bury itself in sand when necessary. However, on the dune surface, it balances on two legs at a time, holding the other two aloft, before switching legs to minimise heat transfer from the sand, earning it the nickname the 'thermal dancing lizard'.

NAMIBIA'S CONSERVANCIES

A landmark policy enacted in 1996 paved the way for rural communities to form **conservancies**; in essence, the government was promoting sustainable natural resource management, including the protection of wildlife, by granting **communities** rights to wildlife management and training. The thinking behind this is that conservation efforts will likely be more successful by involving communities and ensuring they derive greater benefits. While only four conservancies were registered when the programme started in 1998, now 86 are operational. In addition, 43 **community forests** – often overlapping with conservancies – have been established, where villagers manage natural vegetation sustainably, for example, by earning income from harvesting fruits and resin, running plant nurseries, or granting permits for timber extraction (Ⓦ conservationnamibia.com and Ⓦ communityconservationnamibia.com).

THE ACHIEVEMENTS

By and large, the conservancy programme has succeeded in increasing income for communities to spend on **development projects** for education, health care, and so on, as well as providing **extra earnings** for individual households, both in periodic cash handouts and in the employment opportunities generated. Where conservancies are working well, indirect benefits have included greater community cohesion and a sense of ownership, plus skills acquisition through training, while the conservation returns have included improved community awareness and attitudes towards conservation, more sustainable land use, and increases in wildlife.

Most conservancies derive income through **trophy hunting** or tourist-related activities. Controversially, trophy hunting has reaped the greatest financial rewards, providing more immediate returns at the community and household level, including families getting meat handouts after the kill. Moreover, profits from hunting, in many cases, are helping to pay for conservation work. **Eco-tourism initiatives** have had more mixed fortunes. However, 25 community campgrounds are now registered; they receive fewer visitors than commercially run campgrounds, perhaps because nobody knows of their existence or on account of their more basic facilities – they rarely have electricity – or because contact with the community in advance is difficult, especially in remote villages out of mobile phone coverage.

again. If you're in or around Oshakati at the time, you'll find many of the hefty **African bullfrogs** being sold by the roadside or at the market in Oshakati.

Birds

Namibia's diverse **birdlife**, with over seven hundred species, should not be overlooked. Of these, only one – the dune lark – is a true endemic, but fourteen near-endemic species keep twitchers busy, such as the bare-cheeked babbler and the Damara tern. Casual birdwatchers are more likely to be excited by the vast pink carpet of **flamingos** covering Walvis Bay Lagoon – and Etosha Pan during the breeding season – and the many smaller, more colourful birds: dazzling **kingfishers**, iridescent **sunbirds** (distant relatives of hummingbirds) kaleidoscopic **bee-eaters** and **rollers**. Size matters too: elegant **cranes** and stately **ostriches** and **storks** (even the ugly, hairy marabou) are impressive, as are the countless large raptors – the black-and-white **bateleur** with its distinctive red beak, the rare **Cape vulture**, with its bald neck and head, and the splendid **African fish eagle**, which crowns the Namibian coat of arms, and whose evocative call is often dubbed the 'voice of Africa'. The most accessible and the best **birdwatching locations** include the Walvis Bay Lagoon (see page 222), Etosha (see page 238) and the Zambezi Region (see page 266), where two-thirds of the country's species can be found around the perennial rivers and wetlands. The prime birdwatching season is between September/October and April when European migrants arrive, and many birds are sporting their colourful breeding plumage.

THE CHALLENGES

More generally, although some conservancies have succeeded, especially in Kunene, others have struggled. Continuing **challenges** include alleged government interference; social inequalities within communities; tensions between traditional authorities and community-based natural resource management institutions, such as NGOs; and the lack of capacity in some communities to plan and manage resources, in part due to the shortage of capacity and/or resources at the national level to provide adequate support and training. The long-standing Namibian-based NGO Integrated Rural Development and Nature Conservation (Ⓦ irdnc.org.na) has been instrumental in this regard with conservancies in Kunene and, more recently, in the Kavango and Zambezi regions. The National Association of Community-based Natural Resource Management Support Organisations (NACSO) has a helpful website.

Even with support, however, some community ventures struggle to compete with Namibia's well-marketed private lodges and campgrounds. It is no surprise, then, that, increasingly, conservancies are joining forces with **private investors** who have experience in the tourism sector to establish and run a lodge or campground in exchange for a share of the profits, guarantees of employment and training, plus a say in the management. There are now 64 such joint ventures, though the balance of power rarely lies with the community.

More general concerns have also been raised about community-based natural resource management, for example, the fact that relating conservation to tourism might not help address the **loss of biodiversity**, as the focus is likely to be on protecting animals that tourists want to see – or hunt – at the expense of other, less obviously appealing, wildlife. Or indeed, there is pressure from the government to engage in particular wildlife-related land utilisation rather than supporting local communities to decide their priorities. The issue of **human-wildlife conflict** is also an ongoing challenge, especially as predator numbers – due to conservation success – are increasing. Although conservancies often use some of their profits to compensate farmers for losing livestock to predators or help improve livestock protection and repair installations damaged by elephants, there has been an increase in predator killings in some areas.

Marine life

Tourists often neglect Namibia's marine life in the rush to spot large mammals. Yet, the cold-water upwelling of the Benguela Current, which brings abundant nutrients to the surface, provides rich pickings for the many fish that constitute Namibia's buoyant fishing and game fishing industries and may end up on your plate. The current also serves **dolphins** and migrating **whales** (July–Nov, peaking Aug–Oct), most easily spotted on a boat trip from Walvis Bay (see page 222). The small Heaviside's dolphin is the most commonly sighted cetacean, with bottlenose and dusky dolphins much rarer visitors, while humpbacks are more frequently sighted than southern right or Bryde's whales.

Conservation

As the first African country to enshrine the protection of the environment in its constitution, and with around 40 percent of its land protected, Namibia is a world leader in innovative **conservation efforts**. Notably, poaching has decreased in recent years, while numbers of rare or high-value large mammals have increased. Namibia is the only country in the world with an expanding population of free-roaming lions; desert-adapted elephant numbers have more than doubled since 1995; and locally extinct species in the Zambezi Region, such as eland, roan and sable antelope, giraffes and blue wildebeest, have been reintroduced and are thriving. Critical to the successful recovery of wildlife has been the establishment of **conservancies**, a government initiative launched in the late 1990s.

Books

Though Namibia has a strong oral tradition, literature – beyond a few historical and autobiographical accounts – is still in its infancy. This is hardly surprising, given Black Namibians' lack of access to decent formal schooling for many years, compounded by the lengthy independence struggle, during which time energies were focused elsewhere. Thus, contemporary literature written in English by Namibian authors is thin on the ground, though more is available in Indigenous languages and German and Afrikaans. Moreover, the emphasis is often more on content than style. Nor is fiction set in Namibia but penned by non-Namibians exactly plentiful. The little that exists to date has tended to be autobiographical, focusing much on the country's colonial experiences and the fight for independence. What follows is a brief selection of books in English that are mainly still in print but are sometimes only available second-hand or as an e-book. Books marked with a ★ are particularly recommended.

HISTORY

Tessa Cleaver and Marion Wallace (eds) *Namibia: Women in War.* A collection of oral histories mainly collected in 1989 that 'give voice' to women and illustrate the multiple oppressions they faced.

Colin Leys and Susan Brown (eds) *Histories of Namibia: Living Through the Liberation Struggle.* Life histories told to the authors by eleven Namibians who grew up during the 23 years of war give insight into their experiences of anti-colonial resistance and the oppressive, authoritarian structures of the liberation movement.

★ **Henning Melber** *Understanding Namibia: The Trials of Independence.* This important critique of post-independence Namibia chronicles SWAPO's uneasy transition from the liberation movement to the governing party and raises important questions about the country's future. Though a little heavy on detail for the casual reader, the views of this German-born Namibian academic, a member of SWAPO in exile and former Director of the Namibian Economic Policy Research Unit in Windhoek, are well worth digesting.

David Olusoga and Casper Erichsen *The Kaiser's Holocaust: Germany's Forgotten Genocide and the Colonial Roots of Nazism.* This compelling, controversial work argues that the Herero genocide in German South-West Africa by the Kaiser's troops set the pattern for Hitler's Nazism.

★ **Marion Wallace, with John Kinahan** *A History of Namibia: from the Beginning to 1990.* The most comprehensive history of the country to date, scholarly and overly dense in patches, it traces the country's development from the earliest human settlements to independence, drawing on multiple sources and attempting a refreshingly Afro-centric take on Namibian history.

NATURAL HISTORY

Favourite field guides are a matter of personal choice, depending on whether you prefer photos or illustrations or want a weighty, authoritative tome rather than a more selective pocket guide. However, both are usually available in electronic form these days. Several good apps also help with bird and mammal identification: Sasol's *eBirds of Southern Africa* (on iOS and Android) is recommended, and *iTrack Africa* (available on iOS) to help you differentiate one paw print from another.

Vincent Carruthers *Wildlife of Southern Africa: A Field Guide to the Animals and Plants of the Region.* Easy identification of over two thousand plants and animals, written by experts. It is especially handy if you are visiting more than one country, also in a large format.

Alex van den Heever *Tracker Manual.* Newly compiled by the Tracker Academy for its guides in the field. Covers all species, well-illustrated with information about behaviour, droppings, dens, etc.

Louis Liebenberg *First Field Guide to Animal Tracks of Southern Africa.* A pioneering field guide to tracking wildlife. Contains sketches, distribution maps and paw print illustrations to help decipher common tracks found in Namibia and the rest of southern Africa.

Kenneth Newman *Newman's Birds of Southern Africa.* This is probably the most comprehensive field guide to the area, with excellent illustrations. This most recent tenth edition has been updated by the author's daughter, Vanessa. Note that it's a weighty volume – even the paperback version.

Mary Seely *The Namib: Natural History of an Ancient Desert.* Though some years old, this scholarly yet accessible, handy-sized paperback still serves as an excellent introduction to the wonders of the Namib. Written by an expert who has spent countless years living and working in this desert, it is illustrated with drawings and rather faded photos.

★ **Ian Sinclair and Joris Komen** *Pocket Guide: Birds of Namibia.* Light and easy to carry (also available as an e-book). It covers 340 birds, with excellent photos selected to show their most obvious distinguishing features. Ideal for the casual or novice birdwatcher, with distribution maps, timelines indicating when species are present, and behavioural notes to aid identification. The photos are excellent, even if they are harder to use for identification than illustrations.

Chris and Mathilde Stuart *Stuarts' Field Guide to Mammals of Southern Africa.* Covering just over a third of the region's land and marine species, emphasizing the larger, more visible characters, this easily accessible guide is ideal for novice safari-goers or backpackers concerned about weight, though there is an e-book version. Their authoritative tome encompasses almost four hundred mammals, with even their skulls illustrated. Their popular pocket guide covers 120 mammal species.

David Hosking and Martin Withers *Wildlife of Southern Africa.* Nicely photo-illustrated portable guide with a bit of everything – mammals, birds and a few reptiles and smaller critters – which is good for most safari mammals and handy if you want an all-in-one book, but dissatisfying if you're particularly keen on birds or reptiles.

FICTION AND MEMOIRS

Neshani Andreas *The Purple Violet of Oshaantu.* Set in an Owambo village, this first novel is an ambitious and occasionally muddled tale of the friendship between two women with contrasting family situations, which explores issues of culture, patriarchy and women's oppression.

André Brink *The Other Side of Silence.* This is superbly written, but you'll need a strong stomach for this unrelentingly bleak tale of an abused young German girl from an orphanage who is shipped out to service the Schutztruppe in German South-West Africa, where things only get worse.

Margaret Daymond et al (eds) *Women Writing Africa: The Southern Region.* A fascinating, eclectic collection of oral and written narratives by women from all over Southern Africa – including many from Namibia – from the mid-nineteenth century onwards. Entries include praise poems, historical documents, letters, short stories and even legal documents, which aim to make women's voices heard since they are so often absent from historical accounts.

Joseph Diescho *Born of the Sun.* A Namibian classic by the country's best-known Indigenous author, this moving autobiographical tale follows a young man from a northern village under pressure from missionaries and the bullying colonial administration to the harsh realities of South African mines and his resistance to the inhumanity of apartheid.

★ **Damon Galgut** *The Beautiful Screaming of Pigs.* From an award-winning South African author, the novel follows a young white South African who served in the army fighting against SWAPO, the Namibian Independence Party, on his return to Namibia. Issues of race, war and suppression are interwoven with his problems about identity, family relationships and sexual orientation. The main action takes place in Windhoek during the 1989 elections.

★ **Kaleni Hiyalwa** *Meekulu's Children.* This pioneering and thoughtful fictional tale is set in an Owambo village in northern Namibia during the independence struggle – all the more remarkable because the author, who spent years in exile, writes from the perspective of those who stayed.

Sarala Krishnamurphy and Helen Vale (eds) *Writing Namibia: Literature in transition.* An eclectic collection drawing on oral and written traditions since independence, curated by two academics. For serious enthusiasts of literature – in its broadest sense – covering a host of genres in a variety of Namibian languages.

★ **Lauri Kubuitsile** *The Scattering.* Unflinching yet intimate tale of two women caught up in the horrors of war: one a Herero woman whose husband disappears fighting the Germans in South-West Africa, the other a farmer's daughter in the Transvaal, forcibly married to a neighbour who goes off to fight in the second Anglo-Boer War and ends up in a British concentration camp. Both women endure appalling suffering but somehow survive the madness made by men.

Henning Mankell *Daniel.* A bleak exploration of cultural dislocation and colonial attitudes by the author of the Wallander series. An unlovable Swedish entomologist misguidedly rescues an orphan boy in the Kalahari, bringing him to Sweden with tragic results. Set in the 1870s.

★ **Henno Martin** *The Sheltering Desert.* An engaging memoir of Robinson Crusoe-style desert survival as two German geologists and their lovable dog Otto take refuge in the Namib's Kuiseb Canyon for several years to avoid entanglement in World War II.

Ellen Namhila *The Price of Freedom.* An autobiographical account of nineteen years in exile follows the writer's seismic cultural shifts as she travels from SWAPO camps in Angola via the Gambia to Finland and back home. It's a valiant attempt at interweaving how she recalls experiencing events at the time with a more reflective assessment borne of experience and maturity.

Nnedi Okorafor *Binti*. The first book in an award-winning futuristic magical realism trilogy, written by an American-Nigerian author whose title character is a young Himba girl who wins a scholarship to an intergalactic university. The racial discrimination she encounters makes her aware of the importance of her cultural heritage.

Margie Orford *Blood Rose*. The writer, who grew up in Namibia, deftly depicts the seedy underbelly of Walvis Bay, which provides the backdrop for this highly readable thriller featuring serial killer profiler-cum-investigative journalist Clare Hart. Better than it sounds.

Garth Owen-Smith *An Arid Eden: A Personal Account of Conservation in the Kaokoveld*. International award-winning conservationist draws on a lifetime's commitment to the cause in Namibia's northwest, providing a must-read text for all serious conservationists. One of the instigators of community-based natural resource management in southern Africa and co-founder of Conservancy Safaris Namibia (see page 60), leaves the reader with plenty to ponder.

Fran Sandham *Traversa: A Solo Walk Across Africa from the Skeleton Coast to the Indian Ocean*. Although not exclusively about Namibia, this entertaining and witty tale of wanderlust – written by an ex-Rough Guides editor – is a very good read.

Mari Serebrov *Mama Namibia*. A well-researched fictional tale based on true stories told to the author, set in the horrors of the Herero genocide, viewed through the eyes of a young Herero girl and a Jewish doctor in the occupying German army – a compelling read.

PHOTOGRAPHY

★ **Anne-Marie and Michael Detay** *Geological Wonders of Namibia*. Chronological and accessible explanations of the formation of Namibia's varied landscapes (starting 4.567 billion years ago) with stunning photographs. A paperback, but not pocket-book size.

Gerald and Marc Hobermann *Namibia*. The ultimate coffee-table book, brimming with page after page of jaw-dropping photos of the country's incredible scenery, which is matched only by its equally jaw-dropping price tag.

Alistair Lyne *Dunescape*. If you want a tempting view of the spectacular dunes of Namibia before you go, download this e-book and enjoy its artistic approach.

Jim Naughton and Lutz Marten *Conflict and Costume: The Herero Tribe of Namibia*. The stunning photographs of Herero 'traditional' attire take centre stage, but the well-researched text on Herero's appropriation and subversion of German colonists' clothing provides the necessary historical context.

Michael Poliza *Namibia*. Truly spectacular photos, taken from the ground and the air, revealing many aspects of the beautiful and varied landscape of the country; published in hardback in 2021, but it comes with a hefty price tag.

Amy Schoemann *The Skeleton Coast*. Superb photographs accompanied by informed text on the Skeleton Coast from someone whose entire family has been associated with exploring and protecting this inaccessible environment for many years.

Sandra Shields *Where Fire Speaks: A Visit with the Himba*. Award-winning black-and-white photo-narrative interwoven with thought-provoking text as the author, who spent several months among the Himba, looks at changes brought about by modern developments, including tourism, which threatens their traditional way of life.

Language

There are up to thirty languages spoken in Namibia (depending on how you define a language, as opposed to a dialect); fourteen have full orthographies. Thirteen have been recognised as national languages (ten of which are Indigenous); these include eight Bantu languages, predominantly dialects of Oshiwambo, but also Otjiherero, Setswana and SiLozi; two Khoisan click languages, plus the three Indo-European languages of Afrikaans, English and German. After Oshiwambo, which is spoken by around half the population, Nama and Damara are the most widespread, spoken by about 11 percent, followed by Afrikaans (10 percent), Otjiherero (9 percent) and Zambezi Region languages, such as SiLozi (5 percent).

Before independence, Afrikaans and English were **official languages**, though Afrikaans was the dominant means of communication in government, the medium of instruction in schools, and the general lingua franca. German enjoyed 'semi-official' status. At independence, **English** – the first language of less than 1 percent of the population – was chosen to be the sole official language, as it was seen as the language of liberation and national unity and one that would provide economic opportunity and social mobility. The reality, as in many other post-colonial states, is that, despite the government's best efforts, many pupils and teachers in state schools struggle to learn and teach in English, especially in rural areas, and **Afrikaans** persists as the lingua franca, particularly among the older population and in the more rural areas. When you hear English being spoken, it is often **Namlish** – a local variety with many phrases and grammatical usages similar to those used in other southern African countries; phrases such as 'now now', meaning 'right now', or 'I am coming', rather than 'I'll be back', are in common usage.

In lodges, campgrounds and tourist areas, most people are fluent in English, though they will appreciate any effort to manage at least a greeting in their language (see page 367).

THE KHOISAN CLICK LANGUAGES

Khoisan languages such as Khoekhoegowab (Khoekhoe for short) or Nama-Damara, spoken by the Nama and Damara, and Ju|'hoan, spoken by the majority of San communities in Namibia, click **languages**. While you are unlikely to grasp how to pronounce the click consonants correctly unless you spend a long time with communities that speak these languages, you will hear them regularly and come across the written forms on road signs, at the very least. Although Ju|'hoan possesses 48 click consonants – plus four tones to complicate matters further – there are essentially four types of click to get to grips with in any click language, which all only feature at the beginning of a word:

| A dental click that makes a high-pitched 'tut tut!' sound at the back of your teeth.

! An alveolar click that sounds like popping a cork, made by putting your tongue just behind the ridge at the back of your mouth.

|| A lateral click sound is produced by sucking on the molars and is often described as the sound made when urging on a horse, which may not leave you any the wiser.

‡ A palatal click that sounds like a sharper pop or like someone snapping their fingers, made by drawing the tongue down quickly off the roof of the mouth.

There are plenty of online videos on the subject to help you get some practice before you arrive in Namibia.

NAMIBIAN GREETINGS

ENGLISH	OSHIWAMBO	OTJIHERERO
Good morning	(s) Wa lele po? (pl) Mwa lele po?	(s) Wa penduka nawa? (pl) Mwa penduka nawa?
Good afternoon	(s) Wa uhala po (pl) Mwa uhala po	(s) Wa uhara nawa? (pl) Mwa uhara nawa?
How are you?	Ongiini?	Peri vi?
I'm fine	Ondi li nawa	Mbi ri nawa
Thank you	Iyaloo	Okuhepa
You're welcome	Oshi li nawa	Okuhepa
Goodbye	(s) Kala po nawa (pl) Kalei po nawa	Kara nawa *(to someone leaving)* Karee nawa *(to someone staying)*

Glossary

biltong dried cured meat, often chewed as a snack

boerewors long spicy beef sausage comprising 90 percent meat: beef, but with some pork, lamb or a combination of both added

boma originally a word for a protected livestock enclosure; in modern tourism usage, it is an open-sided thatched area, often with a fire pit at the centre, and used for entertainment purposes

bottle store off-licence or liquor store

braai Afrikaans word for barbecue

brötchen German word for bread rolls

circle roundabout

CLA Caprivi Liberation Army

conservancy community registered with the Ministry of the Environment to protect the wildlife and habitats in exchange for rights over tourist operations in the area

cuca shop small, unlicensed bar/shop in northern Namibia that sells alcohol and sometimes other goods, named after a popular Angolan beer

dankie widely used the Afrikaans word for 'thank you'

donkey wood-fired water heater/geyser, commonly used in campgrounds

droëwors dried spicy sausage, often from pork or game meat

guest farm a working farm (usually) that also accommodates a small number of guests and often offers farm-related activities and family-style dining around a single table

inselberg isolated mountain rising out of a flat plain

kopje (or koppie) Afrikaans word denoting a small rocky hill in a generally flat area

kloof Afrikaans word for a ravine

kraal Afrikaans word for a fence or thornbush enclosure for cattle or other livestock, or enclosure for traditional huts in Owambo culture, for example

lapa large, open-sided thatched area supported on poles

location apartheid-era word – still in common usage and synonymous with township – which denoted an underdeveloped urban residential area set aside for non-whites on the periphery of the main town/city

mahangu pearl millet, a staple Owambo crop

mealie-pap South African word for porridge made from ground maize (mealie-meal)

MEFT Ministry of Environment, Forestry and Tourism

mokoro traditional dugout canoe

NWR Namibia Wildlife Resorts

!nara melon a desert fruit

OAU Organization of African Unity

OPO Owamboland Peoples' Organization

Omuramba Otjiherero word for an ancient (dry) riverbed in the Kalahari that only fills occasionally after very heavy rain

oshana shallow seasonally flooded depression in northern Namibia

oshifima Oshiwambo word for porridge made from ground maize

pan a salt and/or clay pan – a large, very slight depression covered in a crust of salt and other minerals where water has collected, then evaporated; theoretically a more degraded vlei, the term is often used interchangeably with vlei (from the Afrikaans)

PLAN People's Liberation Army of Namibia

potjie Afrikaans word for a three-legged cast-iron pot used directly over an open fire to make a slow-cooked stew (potjiekos)

rest camp Simple, inexpensive accommodation – almost always including camping, self-catering and B&B options – where travellers stay overnight, rather than a destination in itself

<table>
<tr><th>NAMA-DAMARA</th><th>RUKWANGALI</th><th>SILOZI</th></tr>
<tr><td>!Gâi||goas</td><td>(s) Moroka
(pl) Morokeni</td><td>Mu zuhile</td></tr>
<tr><td>!Gâi tses</td><td>(s) Muna</td><td>Mu tozi</td></tr>
<tr><td>Matisa?</td><td>Nyove yilye? Or Ngapi?</td><td>U pila cwang?</td></tr>
<tr><td>! !Gâia gangans</td><td>Ame nawa one</td><td>Eni ni iketile hande</td></tr>
<tr><td>Kai-gangans</td><td>Mpandu</td><td>Ni itumezi</td></tr>
<tr><td>Aios</td><td>Name ngocikwawo</td><td>Mwa amuhelwa</td></tr>
<tr><td>!Gâise !gû re
(to someone leaving)</td><td>Tomugendipo nawa</td><td>Mu siale hande</td></tr>
<tr><td>!Gâise hâ re
(to someone staying)</td><td></td><td></td></tr>
</table>

RMS Rhenish Missionary Society
robot traffic light
rock shandy popular soft drink, half lemonade and half soda water, with a dash of Angostura Bitters
rondavel corrupted Afrikaans word for a traditional round African hut with a conical thatched roof, or a Westernised version made of stone, often used as a chalet
SADC Southern African Development Community
SADF South African Defence Force
sangoma IsiZulu, a word in common parlance for traditional African healer
Schutztruppe German colonial troops – literally 'protection troops'
spätzle German soft egg noodles
shebeen formerly an unlicensed bar during the apartheid era but which now often refers to any local, informal bar
sosatie kebab
sundowner alcoholic drink enjoyed at sunset
SWA South-West **A**frica (or Südwestafrika), the name for Namibia when ruled by the German colonists and later South Africa
SWANU South-West Africa National Union – the first political party to be formed in Namibia
SWAPO South-West Africa People's Organization – the former national liberation movement and now the ruling party in Namibia
SWATF South-West Africa Territorial Force – an auxiliary arm of the SADF
township see 'location'
veld from the Afrikaans word for 'field', which usually refers to a wild/uncultivated open expanse of land
vlei the Afrikaans word for shallow marshy depression that fills with water during the rains, often referred to as a pan, though vleis in less arid parts of South Africa, for example, tend to support more vegetation

Small print and index

A ROUGH GUIDE TO ROUGH GUIDES

Published in 1982, the first Rough Guide – to Greece – was a student scheme that became a publishing phenomenon. Mark Ellingham, a recent graduate in English from Bristol University, had been travelling in Greece the previous summer and couldn't find the right guidebook. With a small group of friends he wrote his own guide, combining a contemporary, journalistic style with a thoroughly practical approach to travellers' needs.

The immediate success of the book spawned a series that rapidly covered dozens of destinations. And, in addition to impecunious backpackers, Rough Guides soon acquired a much broader readership that relished the guides' wit and inquisitiveness as much as their enthusiastic, critical approach and value-for-money ethos. These days, Rough Guides include recommendations from budget to luxury and cover more than 120 destinations around the globe, from Amsterdam to Zanzibar, all regularly updated by our team of roaming writers.

Browse all our latest guides, read inspirational features and book your trip at **roughguides.com**.

Rough Guide credits

Editor: Kate Drynan
Cartography: Carte
Picture Editor: Piotr Kala
Picture Manager: Tom Smyth
Layout: Pradeep Thapliyal
Head of DTP and Pre-Press: Rebeka Davies
Head of Publishing: Sarah Clark

Publishing information

Third edition 2024

Distribution
UK, Ireland and Europe
Apa Publications (UK) Ltd; sales@roughguides.com
United States and Canada
Ingram Publisher Services; ips@ingramcontent.com
Australia and New Zealand
Booktopia; retailer@booktopia.com.au
Worldwide
Apa Publications (UK) Ltd; sales@roughguides.com

Special Sales, Content Licensing and CoPublishing
Rough Guides can be purchased in bulk quantities at discounted prices. We can create special editions, personalised jackets and corporate imprints tailored to your needs. sales@roughguides.com.
roughguides.com

Printed in Czech Republic

This book was produced using **Typefi** automated publishing software.

A catalogue record for this book is available from the British Library

Help us update

We've gone to a lot of effort to ensure that this edition of **The Rough Guide to Namibia** is accurate and up-to-date. However, things change – places get "discovered", opening hours are notoriously fickle, restaurants and rooms raise prices or lower standards. If you feel we've got it wrong or left something out, we'd like to know, and if you can remember the address, the price, the hours, the phone number, so much the better.

Please send your comments with the subject line "**Rough Guide Namibia Update**" to mail@uk.roughguides.com. We'll acknowledge all contributions and send a copy of the next edition (or any other Rough Guide if you prefer) for the very best emails.

Acknowledgements

Many thanks to the countless Namibians – as well as Zimbabweans in Vic Falls and Zambians in Livingstone – who helped provide information along the way. Thanks to Val for trawling book lists and Adrian for home support, as ever.

ABOUT THE AUTHOR

Sara Humphreys A freelance researcher, writer and educator, Sara has toiled, travelled and tarried in various countries in sub-Saharan Africa, Latin America and Europe, including a year living in Opuwo, northwest Namibia, helping untangle post-independence curriculum changes. When not travelling, she can be found swinging in a hammock in Barbados.

Photo credits

(Key: T-top; C-centre; B-bottom; L-left; R-right)

All images **Shutterstock** except:
atosan/123RF 22
Dreamstime 14, 29, 39TL, 43BL, 107, 136/137
iStock 2, 4, 13T, 15TL, 15B, 16B, 18B, 19T, 19BR, 21C, 21B, 50, 76/77, 236/237, 239, 294, 336
Namibia Tourism Board 41TL, 264/265
Oleg Znamenskiy/123RF 31TL

Cover: Dune in Namib-Naukluft National Park **Shutterstock**

Index

N

P

R

W

Z

Map symbols

The symbols below are used on maps throughout the book

International boundary	Bus stop	Fortress	Campsite
Region boundary	Parking	Mountain range	Viewpoint/lookout
Chapter boundary	Fuel station	Mountain peak	Mining
Main road	Information centre	Gorge	Immigration post
Minor road	Internet access	Cave	National park
Pedestrianized road	Post office	Cave painting	Gate/park entrance
Path	Hospital	Dune	Dam
Unpaved road	Market	Baobab	Building
4WD	Statue	Forest	Church
Railway	Swimming pool	Sinkhole	Stadium
River	Golf course	Waterfall	Beach
Dry river	Distillery	Spring	Park/forest
Pass	Point of interest	Lighthouse	Swamp
International airport	Grave	Bank	Cemetery
Domestic airport/airfield	Castle	Winery	Pan

Listings key

Accommodation

Eating

Drinking & Nightlife

Shopping

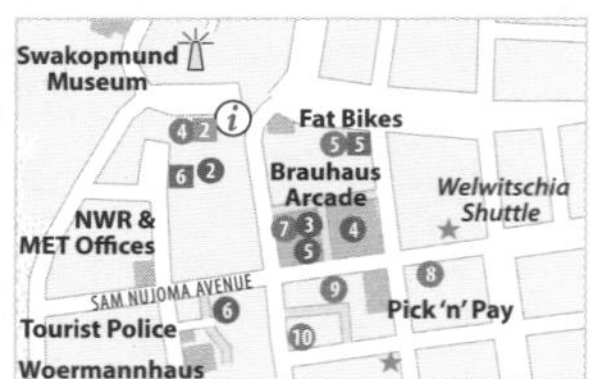